2006

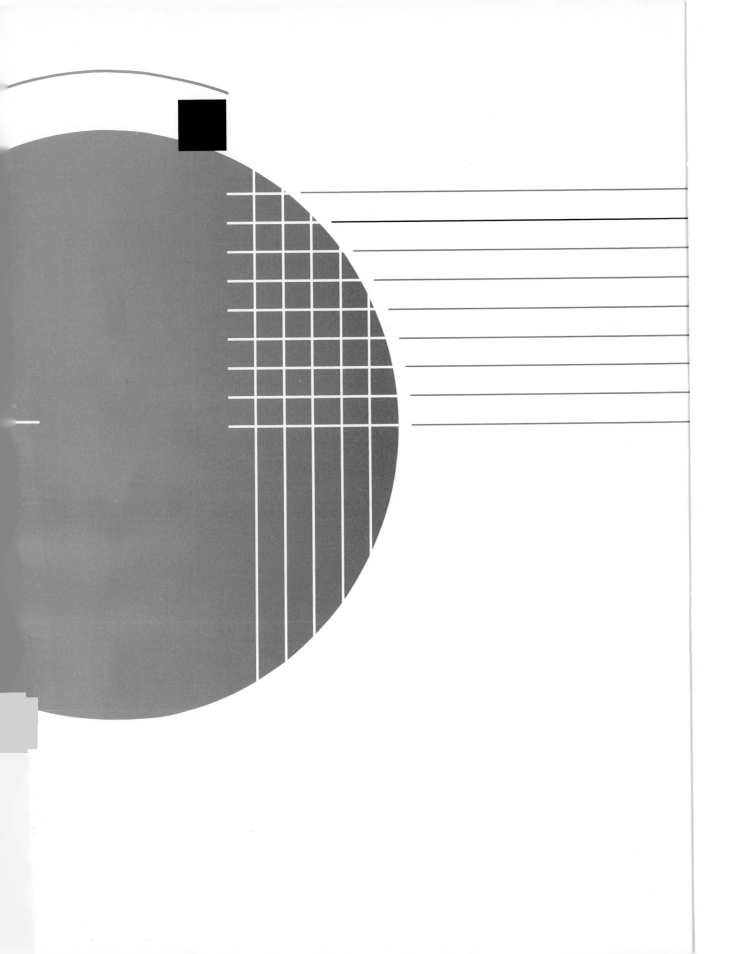

Up to the Challenge?

International Development

From Theory to Practice

International Management

INTERNATIONAL MANAGEMENT

Strategic Opportunities and Cultural Challenges

SECOND EDITION

Dean B. McFarlin
University of Dayton

Paul D. Sweeney
University of Dayton

Houghton Mifflin Company
Boston   New York

Dedication

To Laurie, Andrew, Elizabeth, and Nathaniel . . . no one could ask for a better family (and Amadeus too)!

–DEAN B. MCFARLIN

To the three who support me—Mary, Emma, and Farrell.

–PAUL D. SWEENEY

Editor in Chief: George T. Hoffman
Associate Sponsoring Editor: Susan M. Kahn
Senior Project Editor: Kathryn Dinovo
Senior Manufacturing Coordinator: Marie Barnes
Marketing Manager: Steven W. Mikels

Cover image: *People of the World* by Paul Schulenburg ©The Stock Illustration Source

Printed in the U.S.A.

Library of Congress Control Number: 2001133307

ISBN: 0-618-11333-9

1 2 3 4 5 6 7 8 9 - QUV - 06 05 04 03 02

Brief Contents

Contents

Part III Capitalizing on International Opportunities   229

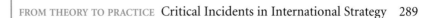

Part V Cases   455

PREFACE

Exploring the Opportunities and Challenges of International Management

The rapid evolution of the field of international management makes writing a book on the subject a challenge. Since the boundaries of the field are under debate, there's no precise set of topics that must be covered in an international management text. Although this state of affairs presents certain difficulties, it also gives us tremendous flexibility. We hope you'll agree with our choices and will conclude that our text offers the most up-to-date and comprehensive coverage of key issues in international management on the market today.

Balancing Strategy and People

In a nutshell, our vision is to bring students inside the real world of international management. The field is rapidly evolving, challenging students, professors, and businesspeople alike. Economies around the world are becoming increasingly integrated, presenting both unprecedented opportunities and tremendous exposure to a sweeping array of risks. We believe that tackling international management in such a volatile environment requires a balanced approach. Some texts emphasize a strategic orientation in grappling with international management. Others emphasize a people-oriented approach, focusing primarily on behavior. But our view is that neither approach should dominate at the expense of the other. Today, perspectives can be fleeting. When you are buffeted by change, you have to adapt. Fast.

Consequently, our approach is one that blends perspectives, is firm enough to offer guidance, but is flexible and pliable enough to accommodate changes as yet unknown. Management needs to think creatively and analytically about potential international opportunities, weighing internal strengths and weaknesses as well as possible competitive threats in the process. Ultimately, that process should culminate in the formation of strategies and methods designed to take advantage of those opportunities. But actually capitalizing on them is another matter entirely. It means executing and implementing. That takes time—and events can overtake a well-laid plan in a heartbeat.

Then there's the human side of the equation. Many plans derail because they fail to anticipate people-related complexities and complications. And when you come down to it, in the international environment those people and culture challenges probably trip up companies just as much as misguided business strategies do—maybe more. So strategy development and cross-cultural management skills are both critically important. Ideally, they should be interrelated. Possible cross-cultural challenges should inform strategy creation. And strategic needs should help shape management approaches and human resource policies around the world. Neither really comes first or is more important than the other.

We present our balanced perspective in a lively fashion. Generally speaking, we take an applications-oriented approach that is solidly grounded in the latest research. Both instructors and students have told us our approach is fresh and engaging. We hope you enjoy it!

Intended Audience

This book will appeal to a wide audience. Students with limited exposure to international issues will appreciate the basic foundations and concepts that are laid out in each chapter. At the same time, students with some international coursework or work experience will be attracted by the book's depth. From a pedagogical perspective, the book will work well as a primary text in a course on international management. It can also be used to cover the management side of an introductory international business course. The strong focus on applications, with a variety of applications-oriented features, appeals to both students and instructors who wish to take a hands-on approach to the study of international management. But before we describe those features in detail, first we'll explain how the book is organized and walk you through our table of contents.

Organizing the Challenge of International Management

The organization of the book reflects our belief that successful international management consists of four basic parts. First, *managers need to understand the broad context of international business.* Specifically, that includes critical trends impacting international management and the legal and political forces driving international business. It also includes grasping the ethical and cultural dilemmas that can pop up in international management and realizing that perspectives about what to do about them can shift when borders are crossed. Second, *managers need to master the essential elements of effective interaction in the international arena.* That means learning how culture affects basic perceptions, developing skills in cross-cultural communication, and figuring out how to negotiate successful cross-border deals. Third, *effective international management means being able to recognize and take advantage of strategic opportunities.* That often means deciding how best to enter foreign markets and then figuring out how to operate successfully once there. Finally, *international managers must motivate and lead people from a variety of cultures and be able to build effective international teams.* It also means taking an international perspective on the hiring, training, and development of employees—if for no other reason than the rules of the game on factors like compensation and labor relations often change when borders are crossed.

Chapter Preview

Our chapters are organized around this four-part scheme. We'll present our chapter preview by walking you through each part of the book.

Part I: On a Global Stage: The Context of International Management   This first part includes Chapters 1–4 and covers the essential foundations for successful international management. *Chapter 1* discusses the basics of international competition, trends impacting international management, and developments in countries and regions around the world. Next, *Chapter 2* focuses on legal and political issues that managers need to take into account in their international operations. We discuss the different legal and political systems that exist around the world and their effects on international business. The chapter also tackles various types of political risk that managers may face in foreign markets and what they can do about them. *Chapter 3* examines ethical values and corporate social responsibility in an international environment. Specific ethical issues, such as bribery, human rights abuses, and social upheavals, are considered in detail. And we offer guidance for responding to various ethical dilemmas (e.g., developing and adhering to corporate codes of conduct). *Chapter 4* concludes the first part of the book by examining culture in more detail. Specifically, we discuss the pervasive impact of culture on international management. We present frameworks that help explain basic cultural dimensions and their implications for managing people around the world.

Part II: Interacting Effectively in an International Environment.   The second part of the book includes Chapters 5–7. The effect of culture on interpersonal interactions is a strong theme throughout this section. In other words, these chapters are natural extensions of the cultural issues raised in Chapter 4. As you'll see, *Chapter 5* examines how culture can affect employees' perceptions of their work environment, their jobs, and the people around them. The chapter also explains how to manage perception problems—such as stereotyping—in a culturally diverse business environment. *Chapter 6* shows how cultural differences can impede communication and offers advice for improving verbal, nonverbal, and written communication in an international environment. *Chapter 7* wraps up this part of the book by examining how to manage international conflicts and conduct successful cross-border business negotiations. Clearly, effective negotiation requires outstanding preparation and an appreciation of the ways that negotiation strategies vary across cultures.

Part III: Capitalizing on International Opportunities.   The third part of the book includes Chapters 8–10 and addresses the broad strategic and operational decisions faced by international managers. *Chapter 8* focuses on defining and developing international business strategy. First, we distinguish among common international strategies and explain when they might be pursued. In doing so, we also present some of the special challenges small firms face in developing an international strategy. Next, we provide detailed coverage of the process involved in developing winning international strategies (e.g., conducting a SWOT analysis). We conclude by discussing how companies need to ensure that their internal systems are aligned to support their international strategy if they want to succeed. *Chapter 9* takes things one step further by considering implementation issues that companies face in executing their international strategies. We present the various options available for entering foreign markets, including the pros and cons of each. In essence, each option can work under the right conditions, whether we're talking about exporting, licensing, or foreign acquisitions, just to name a few possibilities. Consequently, we also make suggestions for weighing and choosing among the options available. *Chapter 10* extends this discussion by examining how managers can make their entry choices work and keep their international operations running smoothly. That includes topics like developing mechanisms to help coordinate international operations, managing business alliances (e.g., international joint ventures) successfully, and maintaining a technological edge abroad.

Part IV: Managing People in the International Arena.   The final part of the book includes Chapters 11–14 and focuses squarely on the people side of the international management equation. And last is by no means least! Mishandling people-related issues can jeopardize even the best strategy, if not the best intentions, of management. Consequently, *Chapter 11* tackles the challenge of how best to motivate and lead employees across cultures. We argue that cultural values can affect how employees behave and that managers should alter their style accordingly. *Chapter 12* explains how managers can build an effective international workforce. That process starts by taking a strategic approach to international human resource management—one that aligns human resource needs with the firm's international business strategy. Next, we discuss the options firms have for staffing foreign operations (e.g., hire locals or send expatriates?) and developing their international management talent. We conclude with a presentation of strategies that firms can use to help expatriates succeed through appropriate selection mechanisms, training practices, and support systems. *Chapter 13* continues this theme by discussing how to ensure the success of an international workforce once it's in place. That means figuring out how to appraise performance and design compensation systems for employees around the world. *Chapter 14* concludes Part IV by examining some of the most vexing "people problems" facing international managers. In particular, we discuss how managers can develop effective international teams, especially in an environment of increasing diversity. We also suggest ways to strategically manage unions and labor relations around the world. These are no small challenges since the scope, purpose, and historical roles of unions vary dramatically across countries.

Part V: Cases.   Given our strong application orientation, this section contains two substantial cases designed to accompany each of the chapters in Parts I–IV. These cases can be used to highlight issues from particular chapters or to provide a capstone experience that integrates material across chapters. They provide an excellent opportunity for students to analyze real international management problems in depth. All cases in Part V are current, of uniformly high quality, and come from the best providers available.

Key Features That Set Us Apart

We hope you'll find our unique array of features hard to resist. Moreover, we've gone to great lengths to support those features and provide additional information in our Instructor's Resource Manual and website.

Up-to-Date and Quality Sources

Our chapters rely on the most recent and most prestigious publications available. They include first-class research journals (e.g., *Academy of Management Journal* and *Journal of International Business Studies*) as well as publications aimed squarely at practicing managers (e.g., *Harvard Business Review* and *The Wall Street Journal*). We believe students must become good consumers of new knowledge and have an appreciation for research about international management. After all, research provides the building blocks for most successful applications in international management.

The Writing: Accessible, Engaging, and Action Oriented

Of course, international management is ultimately about *application* and figuring out what works. Consequently, each chapter is chock full of examples and illustrations from corporations around the world. We've also included concrete guidelines and action recommendations in each chapter. In doing so, we use an accessible and engaging writing style that is also direct, getting quickly to the point. Our job is to pull students in and make them as excited about international management as we are—whether we're describing a piece of research or pitching suggestions for action.

Getting "Real World" with Cases

Each chapter opens with an *International Challenge,* a short case that challenges students with a real problem facing an international manager or company. These problems are directly connected to the content of each chapter. The case concludes by posing questions for students (e.g., Why is this happening and what should be done about it?). As they read through each chapter, students will be exposed to concepts, ideas, and applications that will help them digest the problems and issues raised. A companion case called *Up to the Challenge?* closes each chapter and reveals the steps actually taken to address the problem raised in the chapter-opening case. In making these connections, students are asked to reflect on the steps taken (e.g., Will they ultimately succeed? Is additional action needed?). Additional follow-up information on the opening and closing case for each chapter is presented in the *Instructor's Resource Manual.*

As we noted in our chapter preview, longer, more substantive cases are provided in Part V, *Cases.* These comprehensive cases allow students to integrate what they have learned across several chapters and apply that knowledge to a practical problem.

Special Text Features

Besides cases, two boxed text sections appear in each chapter. The section entitled *International Insights* reports on cutting-edge and creative approaches taken by companies or people grappling with unusual international management issues in particular countries. Of course, these detailed and up-to-date examples dovetail with the topics discussed in each chapter. The boxed section entitled *Reality Check* is a novel feature, one we're really excited about. This feature is designed to provided an "in-the-trenches" snapshot. Using an interview format, this feature asks international managers, trade officials, and others impacted by international business in their jobs for *their* perspectives on issues related to each chapter. Put simply, we let real people doing real work describe, in their own words, the challenges they face and what's important to them. In doing so, they provide some fascinating insights into the nuts and bolts of international management.

Getting "Hands On" with Exercises and Applications

Students will find two special sections at the end of each chapter. The section labeled *International Development* presents students with an exercise or self-assessment designed to build self-insight and promote skill development in chapter-relevant areas. *From Theory to Practice* takes things one step further and gives students a project to pursue. In many cases, these projects involve work that should be completed outside class. Each project is designed to directly apply chapter concepts or assess how international firms are implementing them. If desired, students can present their findings in class.

Other Important Pedagogical Features

To help guide students through the content by pointing out and summarizing key topics, each chapter begins with a set of *Learning Objectives* and concludes with a *Chapter Summary* and *Discussion Questions*. Finally, we've made extensive use of figures and tables throughout the book to make it easier to digest information as well as increase readability and visual appeal. Speaking of visual appeal, we've also included:

● **a full-color insert from the World Bank Atlas** containing maps and charts that help give students a broad snapshot of the world of business.

● **photos in each chapter** to help us underscore key points and issues.

Supplementary Materials

Accompanying this book is an outstanding set of supplements:

● **An excellent *Instructor's Resource Manual with Test Items*** includes chapter outlines, plenty of supplementary lecture materials, comments on special text features, teaching notes for the cases in Part V, and recommended videos.

● **PowerPoint slide shows for each chapter,** available on the instructor website, outline chapter material and present key chapter exhibits as well as supplementary materials.

● ***HMTesting*** is a computerized version of the multiple-choice and essay test items found in the *Instructor's Resource Manual*. This easy-to-use program, available on CD, allows instructors to generate and change tests. The program includes an online testing feature by which instructors can administer tests via their local area network or over the Web. It also has a gradebook feature that lets users set up classes, record and track grades from tests or assignments, analyze grades, and produce class and individual statistics.

● **A comprehensive video package** includes several segments that illustrate chapter concepts using examples of real-world organizations. Teaching notes and suggested uses for the segments appear in the accompanying Video Guide.

● **Student and Instructor websites** are also available. For students, we offer links to related websites, including the sites for those companies highlighted in the text, and self-test questions that are scored for immediate feedback. For instructors, we offer PowerPoint slides, downloadable files from the *Instructor's Resource Manual* that can be edited or used as is to meet specific course needs, and sample syllabi.

Giving Thanks

Behind every successful book is an army of professionals who provide the support, guidance, and advice so vital to making everything click. We are extremely grateful for the outstanding reviewers who contributed their time, energy, and academic expertise toward the development of this project: Lawrence A. Beer, Arizona State University; Charles Byles, Virginia Commonwealth University; John E. Call, New Mexico State University; Lauryn DeGeorge, University of Central Florida; Marios Katsioloudes, West Chester University of Pennsylvania; Norma Carr-Ruffino, San Francisco State University; Selim Ilter, St. John Fisher College; Robert Isaak, Pace University; Dong I. Jung, San Diego State University; Amy McMillan, Louisiana Tech University; Lynn Neeley, Northern Illinois University; John O'Del, Rhode Island College; Roy W. Reeber,

Hawaii Pacific University; Daniel James Rowley, University of Northern Colorado; Deepak Sethi, University of Texas at Dallas; Arnold Sherman, University of Montana; John Stanbury, Frostburg State University; and Richard Steers, University of Oregon.

Likewise, it goes without saying that we owe an enormous debt of gratitude to our wonderful Houghton Mifflin team. First, we want to thank George Hoffman for believing in this project (and us!) from the beginning. His faith—and his willingness to help after we were brought on board—is something that we'll never forget. As our developmental editor, Susan Kahn wore several hats, providing, at various points, enthusiasm, support, cajoling, and suggestions. Her expertise and attention to detail were absolutely second to none. This simply would not have been the same product without her. Our advice to Houghton Mifflin: Hold on to Susan! She's the best in the business! For all her work in keeping the project on schedule and ably coordinating the myriad details and people involved in production, we thank our project editor Kathryn Dinovo. And for helping to spread the word both before and after publication, we thank our marketing team of Steve Mikels and Lisa Boden.

We also owe an enormous debt of gratitude to our dear friend, Amy Anderson. No one could ask for a better author for an *Instructor's Resource Manual,* particularly on international management! Amy's extensive international experience—she's lived and worked in several countries, run an international studies center at a major university, and completed her doctoral thesis on international business education—made her an easy choice. And we'll always be grateful that she signed on.

International Management

Part

I

On a Global Stage: The Context of International Management

International Challenge

Balancing Act for New Balance: Can It Run with Production in the United States?

S O HOW MANY pairs of athletic shoes do you own? Odds are, at least one. Athletic shoes are ubiquitous, as are familiar American brand names Nike and Reebok. What's also interesting is that the industry's biggest players have all of their shoes made in low-wage locations like China, Vietnam, and Indonesia, usually in factories owned and run by foreign subcontractors.

And then there's New Balance Athletic Shoe, Inc. New Balance also has foreign subcontractors. Stroll down the aisle of a subcontractor's plant in China and you'll see young women with precious little in the way of skills and education repeating the same dull sewing tasks on old equipment to produce New Balance shoes. The reward for working like a dog six days a week? A pittance by American standards: 20–40 cents an hour. Of course, by reaping such labor savings, so the theory goes, companies can earn much higher profits. Plus, some experts argue that the U.S. economy is actually better off when low-skill, low-wage jobs can migrate to countries where labor is cheap and plentiful. That allows U.S. firms and employees to concentrate on areas where more capital and higher skills are needed, which helps America's advanced economy sustain its edge and keeps living standards rising.

But New Balance really is different. Unlike its competitors, New Balance also has 1,200 employees making shoes in five U.S. facilities. Over the next few years, company owner Jim Davis wants his $1.1 billion company to make 70 percent of all its shoes in the U.S. Production employees at New Balance earn about $14 an hour, up to seventy times as much as their Chinese counterparts. But what's interesting is that the enormous gap in labor costs notwithstanding, the difference in *total* costs between the Chinese and American plants isn't that great. In China, the total cost of producing a pair of shoes is about $1.30, compared to $4 in New Balance's American plants. The resulting cost differential of $2.70 only represents

4 percent of the $70 price for the average shoe. And that 4 percent is manageable, especially since U.S. production means New Balance can fill orders and change styles more quickly than its competitors in North American markets.

But how does New Balance pull this off? How can it narrow the costs of producing in the United States enough to compete effectively? Clearly, New Balance's U.S. plants are very efficient. The firm's American employees can produce a shoe from scratch in less than 25 minutes. Making the same shoe in Asia takes three hours. Of course, this just prompts more questions. What accounts for the American plants' productivity and efficiency? How can this feat be accomplished with the low-skill jobs and low-tech products that many companies have exported to low-wage locations? And what's the role of management in all of this?

As you read through this introductory chapter, you'll find that when it comes to international business, change is a constant theme. And adapting to change often means challenging old beliefs and coming up with new paradigms, even if they go against what passes for conventional wisdom. After you've read the chapter and digested our thumbnail sketch of international business, take a look at our closing Up to the Challenge? section for an overview of New Balance's approach.[1]

International Business in the Twenty-first Century

A century ago, Dayton, Ohio, natives Orville and Wilbur Wright launched their flimsy craft over the sands of Kitty Hawk. The Wright brothers' persistence and engineering brilliance changed the world forever, revolutionizing transportation and business as we know it. Part of their legacy can be seen at the Dayton airport, where Menlo Worldwide operates its international air freight hub. Dozens of freighters depart daily, shipping

Shoes sold in the U.S. are often made in low-wage locations, like this plant in Mexico. © Danny Lehman/CORBIS

machinery, materials, and parts to factories around the world. It's all part of twin global trends toward increased outsourcing of components and greater reliance on logistics systems that can deliver parts as needed (i.e., on a "just-in-time" basis). In electronics alone, contract manufacturers are expected to produce $160 billion worth of parts for brand name companies in 2003, a 400 percent increase since 1996.[2] Of course, besides flight, astounding innovations in computers and information technologies have made it possible for transportation companies, as well as firms in many industries, to manage inventories, collect customer information, and track shipments around the world twenty-four hours a day, seven days a week.

And that's just the tip of the iceberg. This is a fascinating time to be studying international management. In the twenty-first century, international business continues to experience profound changes that will reshape the challenges and opportunities that managers face. The broad, long-term trend is the continued growth of international business, something that will increasingly weave national economies together. This ongoing connecting process is known as **globalization**.[3] Many experts predict that this process ultimately will increase international cooperation and reinforce overall growth. Over time, tariffs will gradually disappear, worldwide accounting practices will emerge, and business practices that encourage more competition will become widespread.[4]

Of course, concerns and doubts remain. For instance, some worry about the effectiveness of the **World Trade Organization** (WTO). This governing body, made up of over 140 member countries, establishes worldwide rules for trade and commerce. The WTO also monitors trade regulations and has elaborate mechanisms to enforce its rulings on trade disputes between member nations. A key goal for the WTO is to reduce barriers and stimulate trade around the world. But the WTO is also a battleground for national interests as well as a lightning rod for critics who argue that globalization has drawbacks, including lost jobs, painful workforce migrations, social upheavals, and greater threats to the environment.

Clearly, the mission of the WTO and the worldwide trade issues that it wrestles with are complex. Its original principles are outlined in a document that's a mind-numbing 27,000 pages long. A single dispute between the United States and the European Union (EU) over banana **tariffs** (essentially a government-imposed tax on imports) levied against American firms took several years to resolve. Then there's China's 2002 entry into the WTO, the culmination of protracted negotiations spanning fifteen years. In fact, the full effects of China's membership remain to be seen and will take years to fully unfold. On one hand, China hopes WTO membership will help its firms become more competitive and spur additional foreign investment. But China must execute the daunting changes it has promised to make as a condition of membership (e.g., to revamp banking rules, securities regulations, and import-export restrictions, just to name a few). On top of that, China's WTO membership may, at least initially, exacerbate unemployment (e.g., as uncompetitive businesses fold) and increase international pressure about issues such as ongoing product piracy and human rights abuses.[5]

It's also important to note that the WTO isn't the only body that governs international trade. The growth of regional and bilateral trade agreements in recent years is seen as something of a mixed bag. While these agreements have many pluses and are generally positive, they also can make managing broader economic issues more difficult, especially as new powerhouses like Brazil, China, and India start flexing their economic muscles.[6]

The bottom line is that downturns and setbacks will occur along the way, the WTO notwithstanding. And setbacks can occur in the blink of an eye. A horrific example is the terrorist attacks that took place in New York City and Washington on September 11,

2001. In addition to the devastating loss of innocent lives, stock markets around the world lost trillions of dollars worth of value within days and growth prospects in many countries dimmed, at least for the short term.[7]

Overall, grappling with the sheer speed of change and the increasing complexity of international business makes the role of management—and the stakes—more important than ever.[8] And sometimes management is blindsided, even in the best companies, by sudden economic shifts. Just ask networking giant Cisco Systems about the rapid downturn it experienced in early 2001. In announcing layoffs, CEO John Chambers said Cisco "went from over 65 miles an hour down to flat or negative growth in what, two months?" Just eight weeks earlier, Chambers had said Cisco planned to train 100,000 network professionals in India by 2006 to fill expected openings. Whether Cisco will need all that help in the next few years remains to be seen.[9]

But there are many good reasons to be fundamentally optimistic about the long-term prospects for international business. Consequently, the goal of this chapter is to give you a sense of the trends and challenges facing international managers in the twenty-first century. Many of these changes are positive and represent huge opportunities for businesses. In pursuing these opportunities, management must guard against the accompanying risks and dangers, which often rear up suddenly and in unexpected ways. We also want to sketch out how firms approach international competition as well as providing a snapshot of the major players in the global economy. In doing so, we'll be presenting some basic concepts and ideas that will be used throughout the book. But we'll start this chapter by describing the growth of international business and profiling the role countries and regions around the world are playing in that growth.

Globalization and the Growth of International Business

Some experts expect a surge in market-based capitalism to sweep the world in the next few decades. The result may be stronger growth for industrialized countries, if they can take advantage of international opportunities that exist.[10] And therein lies the challenge for international management. Today, the lines between international and domestic operations are gone or continue to blur. Many companies look for ideas, workers, materials, and customers everywhere. Likewise, tough competitors can appear from anywhere. Just ask Motorola about Finland's Nokia! Of course, many industries already operate on a global basis (e.g., computers) or are moving in that direction (e.g., automotive parts). These days, as one European manager put it, "The scope of every manager is the world."

Needless to say, managing that way isn't easy. Among other things, it requires worldwide information networks, a supportive corporate culture, and the ability to take advantage of local needs, strengths, and initiatives when they exist. For instance, Philips, the Dutch electronics giant, deliberately moves unit headquarters to wherever the hottest consumer trends appear for a particular line of business. That meant Hong Kong for audio products and California for digital set-top boxes. But there's no single answer. For some companies, just letting local managers pursue their own ideas is a step forward. Coca-Cola freed its Turkish unit, for instance, to pursue a new pear-flavored drink.[11] For a snapshot of how one company is trying to capitalize on international opportunities, take a look at the accompanying Reality Check box.

The Hottest Growth Areas

So where is all the growth in international business occurring? One way to measure things is by the flow of **foreign direct investment** (FDI) into a particular country over several years. More than just capital, FDI also means that managerial knowledge and technical know-how is flowing into a country from outside its borders. As such, FDI is a good measure of a country's prospects on the international business stage, either as an established market or an emerging one.

The total worldwide flow of FDI hit $1.1 trillion in 2000, and some expect it to exceed $10 trillion by 2005. Exhibit 1.1 lists the top ten projected recipients of FDI through 2005. As you can see, the list is dominated by established players (e.g., the United States) as well as the world's most promising developing markets (e.g., China). Although it's not captured in the exhibit, another encouraging development is that the growth of FDI inflows into poor, developing countries should continue to exceed the growth rates experienced by their industrialized counterparts. By 2005, poor countries should receive nearly 30 percent of global FDI inflows.[12]

In fact, much of the growth in international business is occurring *outside* the traditional economic powerhouses like the United States, the European Union, and Japan (these three regions are often referred to as the **Triad**.[13]) The United States alone did more than $2.3 trillion in two-way trade with other countries in 2001, twice the amount of a decade earlier. But trade *among* Triad nations is becoming less important.[14] For

EXHIBIT 1.1

Foreign Direct Investment Magnets: The Top Ten

Country	Projected yearly FDI inflow, 2001–2005	
	(in U.S. $billions)	Share of worldwide inflows (%)
United States	236.2	26.6
United Kingdom	82.5	9.3
Germany	68.9	7.8
China	57.6	6.5
France	41.8	4.7
Netherlands	36.1	4.1
Belgium	30.2	3.4
Canada	29.6	3.3
Hong Kong	20.5	2.3
Brazil	18.8	2.1

Source: Adapted from——— (2001). The cutting edge. *The Economist*, February 24, 80.

REALITY CHECK

Taking Care of the Planet Makes for a Flourishing International Business

A chat with Robin Harden, export-import manager, Yellow Springs Instruments (YSI) Inc.

Can you tell us a little about YSI?

Gladly. YSI Incorporated (www.ysi.com) provides a full range of measurement solutions in biosensor technology. We have three product lines. YSI Environmental manufactures instrumentation for measuring and monitoring water quality, YSI Temperature makes highly accurate temperature sensing devices, and YSI Life Sciences offers bioanalytical instruments for a broad range of applications.

How is YSI involved in international business?

We've been involved internationally for a long time. Right now we sell in about 80 countries and have over 60 distribution partners. When I say partners, that means everything from dealers to joint ventures. Each of our product lines has its own distribution channel. Although we manufacture the majority of our products in the U.S., we do have some foreign production and are ready to increase that if necessary. We always ask ourselves how we can support our core values—which include ecological sustainability, community, and innovation—through our business practices.

How does your role as export-import manager fit into all of this?

I think of my job as the internal coordinator for all international communications. I field foreign inquiries from everyone, ranging from customers to potential dealers, with everyone in between. My role is to make sure that information is in the hands of the appropriate person, whether that's someone inside the company or a strategic partner overseas. This may sound straightforward, but doing business internationally means taking a lot of things into consideration. Every foreign country where we do business has its own unique location and culture-specific issues. Then there are the specific import and export laws you face in each country, plus the particular organizations and people you're dealing with. Not only that, all of these things have to be considered relative to which YSI product line we're talking about. Switch product lines and many of the overseas variables change, such as the import laws and the folks you're interacting with. It's challenging!

Speaking of which, what are some key challenges facing YSI in the international arena?

Well, change is constant, particularly in international business. So you have to be ready and willing to deal with issues at all levels. That includes local organizational concerns as well as national or even global issues. One of the big challenges for us as an organization is to manage the relationships with each of our strategic partners overseas. Technology is great for sharing information, but you still need to interact with people face-to-face at some point. The key is to develop and maintain excellent relationships with

instance, in 1993, Japan accounted for almost 15 percent of America's trade. By 2000, Japan's share had fallen to less than 11 percent, with **North American Free Trade Agreement** (NAFTA) partners Mexico and Canada making up the difference (see Exhibit 1.2).[15] Moreover, developing markets are increasingly becoming important export targets for the Triad. Mexico, for example, buys 75 percent of its imports from the United States while the Czech Republic and Hungary buy 65 percent of their imports from the European Union.

Part of the reason for this trend is that the total value of economic activity in a country, or **gross domestic product** (GDP), is growing at a faster rate in developing nations than in the Triad. Indeed, developing countries are expected to capture 50 percent of *world* GDP in the near future. The bottom line is that consumer demand in developing markets is rising as they become more affluent.[16] Overall, global GDP is expected to hit $48 trillion by 2010, a figure over 80 percent higher than 1994.[17] Exhibit 1.3 provides some 2010 GDP projections for key regions and countries in the global economy.

Consequently, many American firms consider developing countries as more than just sources of cheap labor. They're also places to build new markets and tap

the foreign individuals with whom you work. We simply must all be on the same page and understanding each other, or we won't keep moving in the same direction. That takes a lot of effort. We invest a lot of time trying to take care of the business relationships with each of our foreign partners. I think sustaining that is a major challenge.

On the other end of the spectrum, companies need to understand the broader context in which they operate. YSI doesn't operate in a vacuum. We need the support of other service sectors such as banking and transportation so we can arrange financing and ship products to foreign customers. In the past decade, there has been a lot of economic integration around the world, much of it through the formation of regional trading blocks such as the EU, NAFTA, and ASEAN. The emergence of these regional trading blocks has some benefits, but it also complicates our lives in other ways. So companies have to develop international skills internally, as well as work to develop those skills locally and nationally.

How does YSI develop the skills needed for success in international business?

Part of it is just realizing that to be successful worldwide, forming strong partnerships abroad is essential. Within the organization, we have consciously made a commitment to our international business and recognize that we need to continue to work at it. Every year for the past three years, YSI has held a global summit at its Yellow Springs, Ohio headquarters. Representatives from each YSI outpost around the world gather for a week of large- and small-group discussions, planning, and presentations—with some recreation thrown in. These interactions help us build the relationships we need to succeed abroad.

At the community level, we get involved with local organizations in order to enhance our own know-how as well as help other local institutions be more active global citizens. For example, we're very involved with the Miami Valley International Trade Association (our local international trade organization) and have served in various leadership positions. We also partner with local institutions of higher education. These relationships not only provide opportunities for us to enhance our skills, but also allow us to help raise the level of understanding about international business in our local environment. In the long run, that helps us and other local firms to be better international competitors.

Sometimes, we even get involved at the national level. Recently, I went to a meeting at the White House to discuss issues surrounding economic integration and the role that governments can play in promoting international trade. You may have heard about the Trade Promotion Authority (TPA; http://www.tpa.gov/). It basically has to do with how much authority Congress gives the executive branch to negotiate international trade agreements. Anyway, women from all over the country, including other African-Americans who are involved in international trade, met with President Bush and other government officials to hear their positions on the issue. We shared our perspectives about how TPA can directly impact American firms that do business abroad.

Any final thoughts?

Just that international companies have to be ready and willing to operate in a complex and changing global business environment. At YSI, we believe that having a global perspective and broadening horizons in our own backyard helps us become a better company.

populations eager for new products and services.[18] That's why Citibank has a huge chunk of the credit card market in Thailand. It's also why customers in just one Chinese province gobble up 100 million bags of Frito-Lay Cheetos a year and why Anheuser-Busch will gladly sell you a locally brewed Budweiser in Shanghai.

But don't forget small companies. They fuel much of the growth in international business. In 1995, for example, firms with less than 500 employees accounted for a bigger share of total manufactured exports than large firms for the first time.[19] And small firms aren't just shipping products abroad. Many are setting up outposts on foreign turf. As our Reality Check profile indicated, Yellow Springs Instruments (YSI) is a case in point. This small Ohio firm, with $50 million in sales, makes, among other things, monitoring equipment that measures water flow and pollution levels. In 2001, YSI opened a sales office in the Chinese city of Qingdao and has plans for several more. With 22 percent of the world's people but less than 10 percent of its fresh water, China has a severe shortage of clean water. As YSI's president put it, "We think we can make a difference there."[20]

EXHIBIT 1.2

Imports and Exports: Regional Partners' Share of U.S. Trade

Region	Percentage Share in	
	1993	2000
European Union	18.9	19.3
Japan	14.7	10.6
NAFTA partners (Canada & Mexico)	28.3	32.8
Rest of the world	38.1	37.3

Source: Adapted from——— (2001). Trade in the Americas: All in the familia. *The Economist*, April 21, 19–22.

EXHIBIT 1.3

2010 GDP Projections, by Country or Region

Country/Region	Gross Domestic Product (GDP)* (in 1993 U.S. $billions)	
	1994	2010
North America	7,812	11,655
Europe	6,790	10,133
China	2,838	8,877
Rest of developing Asia	3,318	7,632
South America	1,660	3,907
Japan	2,540	3,659

*Purchasing power parity.
Source: Adapted from Farrell, C. (1994). The triple revolution. *Business Week*, November 18, 16–25.

A Snapshot of Regional Trends

This section offers brief snapshots of important trends in specific countries and regions. We'll pay special attention to established, dominant countries as well as emerging markets expected to grow rapidly in the years ahead.

The Americas: Searching for the Ties That Bind

A big question mark is whether a proposed continental free trade zone stretching from Alaska to the tip of South America will someday become reality. If enacted by 2006, the **Free Trade Area of the Americas** (FTAA) would create a free trade zone covering 800 million people and accounting for over $11 trillion in GDP. But the trick will be to reach agreement across the region's thirty-four countries by the end of 2005. Some countries worry that their industries will be obliterated if FTAA is implemented and competition becomes unfettered as tariffs and other restrictions fade. Mexico, in contrast, would lose its exclusive access to American markets. Since NAFTA became a reality in 1994, Mexico's exports have surged threefold, with nearly 90 percent headed for the United States.[21]

EXHIBIT 1.4

Commerce in the Americas: Levels of Inter- and Intraregional Trade between Nations

Region	2000 Trade Flows (in U.S. $billions)*				
	AC	CC	CA	MR	NA
Andean Community (AC) (Bolivia, Columbia, Ecuador, Peru, Venezuela)	($5.4)				
Caribbean Community (CC) (e.g., Guyana, Jamaica, Suriname)	$0.5	($1.1)			
Central America (CA) (Costa Rica, El Salvador, Guatemala, Honduras, Nicaragua)	$1.3	$0.2	($2.5)		
Mercosur (MR) (Argentina, Brazil, Paraguay, Uruguay)	$5.9	$0.3	$0.4	($18.3)	
NAFTA (NA) (Canada, Mexico, U.S.)	$43.4	$8.6	$15.6	$42.7	($702.5)

*Trade *within* a region is in parentheses; all other figures reflect *interregional* trade.
Source: Adapted from————. (2001). Trade in the Americas: All in the familia. *The Economist*, April 21, 19–22.

For a summary of recent two-way trade within and between regions in the Americas, take a look at Exhibit 1.4. Merchandise trade levels in four of the six regions within the continent grew faster than the world average over the past ten years. And that's a trend proponents hope will accelerate if FTAA becomes a reality. We'll take a look at NAFTA partners Canada, Mexico, and the United States before turning our attention to key countries in South America. NAFTA has dramatically increased trade and investment among the three countries by gradually eliminating tariffs, import quotas, and barriers to foreign ownership.[22]

Canada   For the most part, the past several years have been good to Canada. The country's growth rates were steady, if unspectacular, and inflation and interest rates remained under control. Nevertheless, Canada's relationship with its southern neighbor, and the world's largest economy, is fraught with awkward comparisons. Canada and the United States are each other's largest trading partner, with two-way trade between the countries topping $400 billion in 2000. But Canada's smaller economy is much more dependent on foreign trade than America's (foreign trade equals 82 percent of GDP in Canada, but only 24 percent in the U.S.). Canada frets about keeping up with its giant neighbor, at least in certain respects. On living standards, for instance, Canada comes up short, with the average Canadian family's after-tax income running about 30 percent lower than their American counterpart's. Put simply, Canadians are taxed more and paid less than their American neighbors.

That said, Canada's situation is enviable, both as a place to live and a place to invest. Traditionally known for its natural resources (e.g., timber, minerals, fish), Canada has received major investments across a range of industries from foreign companies, often to take advantage of lower costs and a skilled workforce. For example, in the auto industry, the major U.S. (Ford and General Motors) and Japanese (Honda and Toyota) giants all operate factories in Canada, along with scores of suppliers. And the reverse is also true. Canadian corporations have invested heavily abroad, especially in the United States. For instance, Canadian Pacific has almost a third of its railroad tracks in the United States and is one of the biggest owners of luxury hotels in America.[23]

Mexico   Predating NAFTA was the *maquiladora* sector. Established by the government, **maquiladoras** are foreign factories that can import parts and materials into Mexico duty free, as long as they are used to make products for export. Most *maquiladoras* are in Mexico's northern states, adjacent to the primary destination for their exports—the United States. NAFTA's implementation was a huge boost to the *maquiladora* sector. Between 1993 and 2001, *maquiladoras* created some 800,000 new jobs as foreign companies, including American household names such as Ford and General Motors, came in to set up shop.[24]

Like Canada, Mexico now seems inextricably tied to its American neighbor. If anything, the connections between Mexico and the United States have increased in recent years. Mexico's exposure to the rest of the world has also grown, thanks to the presence of firms such as Volkswagen and Matsushita. In the process, Mexican firms became more confident as they learned about the practices, standards, and technologies used by foreign firms. Consider Grupo Industrial Bimbo SA (GIB), a Mexican food company and McDonald's exclusive bun supplier in Mexico. GIB recently set up a candy factory in a cheap labor country to serve a rich market next door. The factory is in the Czech Republic and the market is western Europe.[25]

Arguably, Mexico is now healthier for all of this, experiencing fewer dramatic boom-and-bust swings than in the past (e.g., the 1994 debt crisis that caused the collapse of the peso). Yet it's hard to predict when job and wage growth in Mexico would be strong enough to significantly reduce immigration, particularly of the illegal variety, to the United States. Should that occur, any continuing immigration from Mexico may largely consist of people looking for higher-paying jobs as opposed to just having a job at all. But it seems unlikely that American demand for low-wage Mexican labor will evaporate any time soon. And since Mexico still has major problems (e.g., poverty) and economic development is uneven (i.e., concentrated in certain areas and sectors), many of its citizens will undoubtedly continue to look for opportunities elsewhere.[26]

In any case, Mexico is the U.S.'s second largest trading partner, with two-way trade between the countries pushing $250 billion in 2000. Since NAFTA was implemented, foreign direct investment in Mexico rose every year (hitting $14 billion in 2000). Of course, being connected at the hip to the United States could mean being dragged down when the economy up north goes south. That point was underscored in 2001 when DaimlerChrysler said it would shut down three factories in Mexico, a move costing 2,600 jobs. And auto-related exports make up 20 percent of Mexico's total. But for the long haul, both foreign and Mexican-owned suppliers are optimistic. If anything, severe slowdowns may accelerate the pace at which foreign manufacturers seek out lower-wage Mexico when cost cutting becomes critical in higher-wage countries like the United States.[27]

The United States   Although America experienced a recession in 2001, prospects for renewed growth were rising early in 2002.[28] But despite the woes of 2001 (e.g., the dot com debacles, terrorist attacks, and wild stock market swings), productivity continues to be strong. And the United States is still the world's biggest economy at $10 trillion and the biggest magnet for foreign investment. Many foreign companies find the United States an attractive place to set up operations or acquire firms (witness all the plants that BMW, Mercedes, and Nissan have broken ground on in the past few years). The United States also leads in knowledge creation, financial services, and information technology, positions that will be important in the years ahead.[29] For example, the United States has the most creative economic environment in the world, one where it's easy to start new businesses and access sophisticated technologies. Take a look at Exhibit 1.5 for a list of the world's twenty-five most creative nations.[30]

Today, American multinationals operate around the world, with many enjoying dominant positions in their respective industries. Colgate-Palmolive, for instance, operates in some 150 countries, with foreign sales accounting for 75 percent of its revenues. In fact, the four largest companies in the world are American (take a look at Exhibit 1.6 for a list of the world's fifteen largest companies). And American firms were involved in over $1.5 trillion worth of global mergers and acquisitions in 2000, nearly half of the record-breaking $3.3 trillion total.[31]

However, the United States still runs large trade deficits in goods. In 2000, it imported $1.2 trillion worth of goods while exporting only $782.4 billion worth. The result was a $434.3 billion shortfall in goods (offset somewhat by a $79.8 billion surplus in services). Nearly half the deficit in goods resulted from trade imbalances with China, Japan, and Canada. But the United States did have trade surpluses with several countries. Exhibit 1.7 lists the countries producing the top five deficits and top five surpluses with the United States.[32]

Trends in South America   In the 1980s, South American countries were awash in debt, hyperinflation, and fear. They watched as East Asia leapfrogged South America onto the world economic stage. In the 1990s, many South American governments acted to transform the region's 500 million people into a competitive regional trading bloc. How? By privatizing state-owned industries, reducing tariffs, making it easier for

EXHIBIT 1.5

Which Countries Are Most Creative? The Top Twenty

	Rank	Country
More creative	1	United States
	2	Finland
	3	Singapore
	4	Israel
	5	United Kingdom
	6	Hong Kong
	7	Germany
	8	Taiwan
	9	Japan
	10	Hungary
	11	Malaysia
	12	France
	13	Poland
	14	South Africa
	15	South Korea
	16	Turkey
	17	Brazil
	18	Chile
	19	Egypt
Less creative	20	Mexico

Source: Adapted from————. (2000). Creativity. *The Economist*, September 23, 128.

foreigners to invest, and setting up free trade agreements with neighbors and the United States.[33] That said, by early 2002, the region had experienced a variety of economic setbacks, causing optimism to dwindle and some to raise questions about the efficacy of reform.

Nevertheless, many foreign companies are convinced that economic reforms will continue and eventually succeed in South America. Looking back, however, the results

EXHIBIT 1.6

World's Largest Companies by Revenue: The Top Fifteen

Rank/Company	2000 Revenues (US $ billions)	Headquarters	Industry
1. Exxon Mobil	210,392	United States	energy
2. Wal-Mart	193,295	United States	retail
3. General Motors	184,632	United States	automotive
4. Ford	180,598	United States	automotive
5. DaimlerChrysler	150,070	Germany	automotive
6. Royal Dutch/Shell Group	149,146	United Kingdom/Netherlands	energy
7. BP Amoco	148,062	United Kingdom	energy
8. General Electric	129,853	United States	diversified
9. Mitsubishi	126,579	Japan	trading/diversified
10. Toyota	121,416	Japan	automotive
11. Mitsui	118,013	Japan	trading/diversified
12. Citigroup	111,826	United States	financial services
13. Itochu	109,756	Japan	trading/diversified
14. Total Fina ELF	105,869	France	petroleum refining
15. Nippon Telegraph and Telephone	103,234	Japan	telecommunications

Source: Adapted from————. (2001). Global 500: The world's largest corporations. *Fortune,* July 23, F1.

of reforms show that while progress has been made, there's still a considerable way to go. GDP growth in the region averaged 3 percent in the 1990s, a figure that lagged behind that of many Asian economies. Generally speaking, countries enacting the most significant reforms, such as Chile, did better than countries that made fewer changes, such as Ecuador. The region has also been prone to instability because of its dependence on foreign capital. In short, capital can move in or out of the region quickly, depending on the whims of foreign investors and external events. Speaking of instability, political upheavals and guerrilla movements have dogged Colombia, Ecuador, and Peru in recent years, putting a crimp on business.[34]

The region's three economic powerhouses are Argentina, Chile, and Brazil. Chile has the most successful track record in recent years, both in terms of reform and its economic performance as an exporter. At the other end of the spectrum is Argentina. In 2001, Argentina entered the third year of a stubborn recession. Among the reasons cited for Argentina's ongoing problems are high foreign debt ($130 billion), an overvalued

EXHIBIT 1.7

America's Trade Imbalances in 2000: The Top Five Goods Deficits and Surpluses

	Value (US $billions)		
	Imports from the U.S.	**Exports to the U.S.**	**Deficit/surplus**
Top Five Deficits			
1. China	16.3	100.1	−83.8
2. Japan	65.3	146.6	−81.3
3. Canada	178.8	229.2	−50.4
4. Germany	29.2	58.7	−29.5
5. Mexico	111.7	135.9	−24.2
Top Five Surpluses			
1. Netherlands	22.0	9.7	+12.3
2. Australia	12.5	6.4	+6.0
3. Belgium	14.0	9.9	+4.0
4. Hong Kong	14.6	11.5	+3.2
5. Egypt	3.3	0.9	+2.4

Source: Adapted from Thomas, G. S. (2001). Asia, Canada comprise bulk of U.S. trade deficit. *Dayton Business Journal*, April 20, 16.

currency, burdensome regulations, and onerous taxes on investment and production. Indeed, as 2001 came to a close, Argentina's finances collapsed, forcing it to default on its foreign debt. More turmoil ensued in early 2002 as Argentina devalued its currency and unpegged it from the U.S. dollar. How long it will take Argentina to fully recover remains to be seen. But Argentina's experience underscores the challenge of creating stable, open economies in emerging markets—be they in South America or anywhere else.[35]

Of course, Brazil is by far the biggest economy in South America. Brazil's currency sank in 2000–2001, bringing with it renewed fears about inflation and interest rate hikes. Moreover, the spillover from problems in neighboring Argentina helped slow Brazil's economic growth and caused many foreign companies to cut back production, at least for the short term. But the long-term picture seems more positive. Foreign direct investment soared from less than $5 billion in 1995 to over $30 billion in 2000. Brazil's attractiveness is perhaps best illustrated by the moves car companies have made in recent years. U.S., European, and Japanese car firms all have or will have world-class manufacturing facilities in Brazil. Simply put, Brazil and the region has pent up demand for cars. As of 2001, foreign auto companies had sunk billions into Brazil and employed

Shoppers check out a Buenos Aires supermarket after the Argentine peso was devalued by nearly 30 percent in early 2002. ©AFP/CORBIS

nearly 100,000 people. On top of that, companies as diverse as McDonald's, Nokia, and French hotelier Accor Group set future growth targets that require major investment in Brazil.[36]

So there's reason to be cautiously optimistic about the long-term future for South America. Many South American countries are looking beyond the region for trading partners. For instance, among **Mercosur** members (a trading block consisting of Argentina, Brazil, Paraguay, and Uruguay), exports to other South American nations account for less than 30 percent of the total. Over 40 percent of Mercosur exports go to the European Union and the United States. And South America is the fastest growing market for exports from the United States. Some estimate that by 2010 South American countries will buy more U.S. goods than Europe *and* Japan put together.[37]

The Asia-Pacific Mix: Growth, Stagnation, and Economic Dips

The Asia-Pacific region may become the most dominant economic area in the world in the next few years. But along the way there have been plenty of hiccups. In 1996, Asian countries accounted for 40 percent of worldwide commerce.[38] Then in 1997–1998, many nations in the region experienced an economic crisis, only to recover in 2000. Once again, however, 2001 saw a rapid slowdown that left some Asian economies teetering while others were relatively unscathed heading into 2002.

The countries of Asia have some similarities, but also many differences. Countries that have structural problems (e.g., high government debt, weak corporate governance, poor legal protections) and are highly dependent on key overseas markets tend to be most vulnerable to economic shocks. An interesting aspect of business in Asia is that many of the region's most successful companies are part of family-owned empires.

EXHIBIT 1.8

A Profile of Selected Asian Nations*

Nation	Estimated 2001 GDP Growth Rate (percent)	Rank: Corporate Governance Quality	Rank: Transparency	Top Fifteen Family Control (percent)	Rank: Resilience to Global Shocks
China	7.3	8	10	Unavailable	4
Hong Kong	−0.3	2	2	84	3
Indonesia	3.1	9	7	22	8
Japan	−.6	3	3	2	not ranked
Malaysia	0.0	6	4	76	6
Philippines	2.8	4	5	47	9
Singapore	−2.5	1	1	48	1
South Korea	2.5	10	9	13	2
Taiwan	−2.3	5	6	17	5
Thailand	1.7	7	7	39	7

*For ranked items, 1 = best (i.e., best corporate governance, most transparency, most resilience). The numbers under Family Control refer to the percentage of a country's GDP accounted for by the corporate assets under the control of that country's top fifteen families.

Sources: Adapted from————. (2001). Singapore: Death by a thousand cuts. *The Economist*, September 15, 38; ————. (2001). In praise of rules: A survey of Asian business. *The Economist*, April 7, 1–18; ————. (2001). Emerging market indicators. *The Economist*, January 26, 98; ————. (2001). A global game of dominos. *The Economist*, August 25, 22–24; Balfour, F., & Clifford, M.L. (2001). Hong Kong: A city under siege. *Business Week*, July 23, 48–49; Bremner, B., Balfour, F., Shari, M., Ihlwan, M., & Engardio, P. (2001). Asia: The big chill. *Business Week*, April 2, 48–50; Pura, R., & Borsuk, R. (2001). Politics-as-usual hinders Southeast Asia. *The Wall Street Journal*, July 30, A15, A16.

These Asian empires are often formidable competitors that pursue opportunities at home as well as abroad. But the degree of family control varies across the region. In some Asian countries (e.g., Malaysia), a handful of powerful families control vast corporate empires that include 50 percent of all local companies. On the other hand, family control of companies is minuscule in Japan, with the level of family control about the same as it is in Europe (less than 10 percent of all companies). Take a look at Exhibit 1.8 for a profile of estimated economic growth rates and corporate governance issues in selected Asian countries.[39]

In any case, the wild, unbridled optimism that existed about the Asia-Pacific region before 1997 is gone. Instead, opinions for the future range from cautious optimism to fears of long-term stagnation or even protracted recessions. This prevailing mood highlights the fact that companies need to balance the region's potential against the underlying problems that continue to hold back some Asian countries.[40] These include:

- **Infrastructure problems** (e.g., inadequate power and transportation networks, pollution issues, etc.)
- **Rising costs** (e.g., for labor, housing, capital, and materials, especially in certain countries)
- **Excessive manufacturing capacity in certain industries** (e.g., semiconductors).
- **Insufficient innovation** (worker training is weak in some Asian countries)[41]

Next, we'll take a closer look at recent trends in emerging markets in the Asia-Pacific region (e.g., China, India) as well as the more established economic powerhouses (e.g., Japan).

China   Predicted by some to become a $10 trillion economy over the next twenty years, China nevertheless presents some formidable problems to foreign businesses, including a weak legal system and opaque government policies. It's a place where business is often guided by **guanxi** (relationships or connections) rather than by rules and laws. Other challenges for foreign companies include China's incredible ethnic, cultural, and linguistic diversity. Regional differences are huge, and much of the population (70%) lives in rural areas and is quite poor. In 2001, per-person annual income in China was just $950. But income levels in the coastal cities are generally higher than in the less developed interior. Put simply, China is *not* a single, homogenous market of 1.3 billion potential customers.[42]

Then there's China's **competitive intensity**. In other words, China is a tough business environment. Competitors are legion and the pace of business activity is frenetic. Nearly 150,000 foreign companies operate in China, including 40 percent of the world's largest 500 firms, a figure that's steadily rising. No other country has experienced this kind of corporate influx in such a short period. Plus, 6 million privately owned firms offer plenty of formidable competition in China. When we visited China, a manager at a U.S. consumer products firm said that in addition to competing against other world-class multinationals such as Unilever, the company faced thousands of local competitors (mostly small, family-run enterprises) just in Shanghai alone![43]

Clearly, foreign companies often underestimate the difficulties of doing business in China. But even firms that grasp those difficulties are willing to put up with them for the simple reason that China is still the world's largest emerging market, one with tremendous potential for ongoing growth. On top of that, China is a cheap export platform, with a large supply of $2-per-day labor. It's also run by a government that, despite its many failings, is eager to build the country's economic prowess. Over the past twenty-five years, China's slice of total world trade has expanded 400 percent. Through the late 1990s, China's GDP growth rate averaged over 9 percent. And even with the lower growth rates seen in the early 2000s, China remains enormously attractive, especially to Hong Kong, the United States, and Japan, its top three trading partners and sources of investment.[44]

The road ahead for China includes a variety of reforms aimed at creating a more market-driven economy in line with its membership in the World Trade Organization. In 2001, for example, the Chinese government said that it would

- Spend billions to modernize its infrastructure (e.g., new roads, power plants).
- Dismantle state-owned firms in most industries (which still account for 28% of the economy) and encourage those that stay in business to improve their competitiveness (e.g., by setting up joint ventures with foreign companies).
- Eliminate most import barriers and reduce tariffs.

Foreign companies eagerly await the day when they can import products, distribute goods, invest, and own businesses in China without major restrictions. Kodak, for instance, has sunk over $1.2 billion into factories in China in the past few years, buying them from uncompetitive Chinese manufacturers. The firm also opened over 6,000 Kodak outlets there and expects China to knock the United States off as the top market for its film by 2010. As Kodak's Asia president put it, "China is the potential opportunity of a lifetime." For its part, China wants the ability to export goods ranging from computers to shoes without quota restrictions by 2005. If that happens, China may capture 50 percent of the world's export market for certain goods in the apparel, machinery, and electronics sectors in a few years (an increase over 100% in some cases). Such prospects worry many of China's low-wage competitors in places like India, Indonesia, and Mexico.[45]

India   Speaking of India, the country's population is just over 1 billion. But by 2045 or so, India will eclipse China, creating the biggest potential market in the world. And while India is getting ready, it's starting from behind, with a lower literacy rate and higher infant mortality than China. Not surprisingly, a recent survey of international executives found that nearly 60 percent were more likely to invest in China than India, with only 14 percent saying the reverse. Nevertheless, India is improving rapidly, especially in its southern states. GDP growth is expected to average 6–7 percent through 2005. Experts urge the Indian government to speed reform along by

- Accelerating the selloff of state-owned enterprises (such as Air India)
- Reforming India's complex and restrictive labor laws
- Deregulating various industries (e.g., textiles)
- Encouraging private banking and relaxing currency restrictions

And since the government began initiating economic reforms in 1991, foreign companies made direct investments in India approaching $20 billion.[46]

Many of India's biggest foreign investors have been automobile companies, with several forming partnerships with local firms in recent years. Consumer products giants like Coca-Cola and Unilever have also moved into the Indian market. But India's biggest impact on the global economic scene is probably in information technology (IT). In 1991, India's IT was valued at a scant $50 million. In 1999, the figure was $4 billion. And by 2008, India's high-tech exports may hit $50 billion (about a third of its total exports). India is a source of cheap high-tech labor for U.S. firms (e.g., General Electric) and their software code-writing needs. In fact, nearly 40 percent of the world's biggest 500 multinationals outsource some of their IT needs to Indian firms. Today, however, leading Indian software firms like Infosys and Wipro Technologies are aggressively developing new software and technology consulting services. The goal? To compete for worldwide clients in higher margin areas like strategic planning and IT system implementation.[47]

Unfortunately, inferior schooling, poverty, and infrastructure problems still plague many Indian citizens. Some 300 million Indians are poor. How rapidly India grows will also depend on whether infrastructure, energy production, and telecommunications networks can be improved fast enough to meet business demands.[48]

Japan   Still the world's second largest economy, Japan has been in the doldrums for much of the past decade. And the immediate future, despite some long-term reasons for optimism, remains cloudy. In 2001, the Japanese stock market hit a nearly two-decade low amid continued economic contraction and concern about government debt (total debt is around 120 percent of GDP, more than twice the U.S. rate and, at this writing, still rising). Likewise, Japanese unemployment in 2001 stood at levels not seen since the

1950s. In part, Japan's problems reflect the government's efforts to simultaneously protect weak domestic industries (e.g., chemicals, financial services, retailing) and maintain a thriving export machine. In a nutshell, weak industries dragged the economy down, driving up both the cost of living and the cost of doing business in Japan. Consequently, Japanese companies have been voting with their feet for years, leaving the country to pursue lower costs and better markets (e.g., elsewhere in Asia, the Americas, etc.).[49]

That said, Japan has taken some steps to clean up banks riddled with bad debts, encourage foreign investment, reduce import barriers, and increase domestic demand (including the $1.1 trillion in recent years that the government has spent on various domestic projects). But critics say Japan still has a way to go, with deeper and quicker changes needed to reform the banking system, eliminate stifling regulations, and reduce the cost of doing business. Without those reforms, Japanese capital will continue to flow outward in search of better opportunities.[50]

Some say Japanese companies also have to look in the mirror. For instance, many Japanese manufacturers set up operations in cheaper locations without eliminating capacity at home or trimming bloated workforces. While admirable in some respects and consistent with corporate tradition in Japan, these actions have clearly resulted in lower profits for Japanese firms, if not weakened their competitive position worldwide. For example, Japanese car companies' domestic demand has fallen around 25 percent in the past decade. Over the same period, their excess capacity rose to around 25 percent and their collective labor forces have dropped less than 5 percent. But times may be changing, with Nissan, Mazda, and Mitsubishi, arguably the most troubled of the Japanese auto giants, all announcing plans in 2001 to close domestic plants.

Even Japanese **keiretsu**, huge groups of companies with interlocking ownership ties and business interests, are slowly unraveling. The cozy groups of owner relationships behind names such as Sumitomo and Mitsubishi (corporate "families" with dozens of firms, including banks, manufacturers, and trading companies), are becoming too expensive to maintain. The percentage of equities on the Tokyo stock exchange held in these stable relationships has dropped considerably in the past few years, while the percentage of foreign ownership has risen.[51]

Regardless of its problems, it would be a mistake to underestimate Japan. The country has some impressive strengths, including a highly educated workforce, many world-class firms, and excellent capabilities in technology. Japanese firms continue to have enormous success in foreign markets in everything from video games to robotics (e.g., Sony, Nintendo, etc.).[52]

Southeast Asia's other developed and emerging countries Hong Kong, Singapore, South Korea, and Taiwan represent the other developed economies in the region. Of course, Hong Kong has been reunited with China since 1997. And its reputation as a capitalist bastion with low taxes and little government interference remains largely untarnished despite Chinese rule. The uncertainty about Hong Kong's long-term prospects revolve around its liabilities (e.g., it's the sixth most expensive city in the world) and autonomy. China has promised Hong Kong autonomy for fifty years. The worry is that if Hong Kong's freedoms and rule of law erode too much, its status as a great place for multinationals to do business could be jeopardized. On the other hand, much lower costs in other mainland cities like Shanghai for everything from office space to apartments to taxis may do more to lure business away than anything else.[53]

Taiwan also has a tricky relationship with China, especially about its perceived autonomy and its defense relationship with the United States. But the growing trade and business connections between China and its "renegade province" (the label China often applies to Taiwan) paint a more optimistic long-term picture. Two-way trade with

China hit nearly $30 billion in 2000, almost double the rate in 1994. Taiwan's ongoing efforts to liberalize trade restrictions with China should also help smooth out relations. Already, some 40,000 Taiwanese companies operating on the mainland account for over 10 percent of China's exports. For many of Taiwan's increasingly sophisticated firms, China is a welcome source of inexpensive labor. China, in return, gains from the influx of capital ($40 billion in the past several years), jobs, and technological savvy that Taiwanese firms like computer maker Acer bring.[54]

Moving on to Singapore, that city-state has the highest standard of living in the region, with a per-person GDP over $25,000. Well known for its efficient government, openness to foreign investment, and well-trained workforce, Singapore has proved to be stable and resilient in the face of the region's ups and downs. Likewise, surrounding Malaysia has also been relatively stable, although its prosperity falls short of Singapore's. In any case, Singapore needs to do more to cut costs and encourage entrepreneurship if it is to remain competitive, especially given the slump in the electronics that hit hard in 2001.[55]

Finally, South Korea is a key player in the region, with a $500 billion economy and burgeoning information technology industry. But South Korea's challenges continue, especially to reform how its **chaebol** (huge diversified conglomerates such as Samsung that still account for a big slice of the economy) compete. For example, Ssangyong Cement Industrial Co. racked up billions in debt by plowing resources into questionable ventures that had nothing to do with its core business. But instead of letting the firm go under, the government bailed it out in 2001 and planned to spend billions on public works projects that would generate contracts for Ssangyong and other *chaebol*.

Some officials feel that South Korea can't afford to let firms in strategic sectors (e.g., electronics, automobiles) die, especially since they provide jobs and help support thousands of vendors and suppliers. Others counter that South Korea would be better off in the long run if the *chaebol* sold off or shut down losing businesses. In fact, many *chaebol* have disappeared over the past five years, crushed by their mountains of debt. A good example is Daewoo, which made everything from fertilizers to cars around the world. After running up $80 billion in debt, it was split into twelve separate companies. But such corporate collapses stimulate entrepreneurial activity. South Koreans are less enamored with the *chaebol* and are willing to embrace greater risk than ever before. Today, 9 percent of South Korean adults work in firms less than four years old, a percentage far higher than in other industrialized countries (and twice the rate in the U.S.). On top of that, South Koreans are becoming more consumer-oriented, something that may contribute to an increasingly diverse South Korean economy.[56]

Next, let's turn to the region's emerging nations. Indonesia, the Philippines, Thailand, and Vietnam all offer inexpensive labor, large populations, and a variety of assets and resources. Except for Vietnam, these countries all have experienced serious political and social instability in recent years. For example, cries about corruption in government have been heard frequently in the Philippines and Thailand. And flareups of scandals and political instability tend to have a chilling effect on foreign direct investment, as these countries have found out. Take Indonesia. The country has suffered from high government debt and low investor confidence thanks, at least in part, to political uncertainty and a string of government corruption scandals. Ethnic frustrations and local rebellions erupted in 2001, causing security headaches for foreign companies. For instance, Exxon Mobil shut down its Indonesia facilities after secessionist guerrillas shot at airplanes containing its employees.[57]

The issue in Vietnam is how changes in the communist leadership over time may impact business. And despite its low labor costs, Vietnam needs to catch up with its more competitive Asian brethren. Although Vietnam's GDP has doubled in the past decade thanks in large measure to fewer restrictions on entrepreneurship and foreign investment, the pace of growth needs to quicken so that the 1.4 million people who enter the workforce each year can find jobs. Plus, the private sector in Vietnam is still overshadowed by protected and unprofitable state firms, propped up in many cases by a state-run banking system. Vietnam also has some serious corruption problems and large gaps in living standards between the big cities and the poor countryside, where 75 percent of the population lives. Overall, Vietnam and its 80 million people are likely to be only moderately attractive to foreign investors in the near term. [58]

Europe: East Meets West

Over the past fifteen years, staggering political and economic changes have occurred in Europe, especially in Russia and its former satellites. The 600 million people of the region have arguably seen more change in a shorter period than anywhere else in the world. Europe continues to evolve toward greater economic integration. The European Union and its currency, the euro, are established facts of life. And moves to expand the EU, particularly eastward, have considerable momentum. Moreover, Europe has been on a privatization binge, with many western European nations selling off enterprises in sectors ranging from energy to telecommunications. Of course, many eastern and central European countries have taken privatization even further in their efforts to transform themselves from state-dominated to market-oriented economies.

That said, many challenges and obstacles still lie in the path of greater economic integration. For instance, the rate of progress varies considerably across countries. Some, like Poland, have done well by embracing free markets and transforming their management talent to match; while others, such as Albania and Ukraine, still have a long way to go. And the Balkans remain Europe's most unstable and unpredictable region, a potential flashpoint that has chilled business investment in the area. We'll take a quick look at the EU before turning our attention to Russia and the developing nations of central and eastern Europe.[59]

The European Union: Still Growing and Evolving   As of 2002, fifteen western European countries were members of the European Union (Switzerland is an exception), an entity created in 1993 by the signing of the **Maastricht Treaty**. The EU model is unique and clearly reflects European cultures, history, and languages. But like the United States, the EU aims to operate as a single, integrated economic market that uses one currency and is guided by a central bank. EU countries plan to have a unified customs system, no trade barriers, and an umbrella economic strategy for dealing with the rest of the world. And therein lies both the opportunity and challenge for international companies. On one hand, manufacturing in the EU allows firms to move their products to any member country without duties or currency hassles, a highly attractive prospect to say the least. Of course, that's prompted billions in foreign investment in recent years. However, a unified market doesn't mean that Europe's diverse cultures—and the needs and desires that go with them—have disappeared. So companies doing business in Europe often need to be highly responsive to local product preferences if they want to do well, the EU notwithstanding.[60]

But the European Union is already a formidable economic force, with a collective economy larger than that of the United States or Japan. That said, achieving the EU's ultimate integration goals won't be easy. Take the euro. On January 1, 2002, the euro

EXHIBIT 1.9

The European Union: Members Today, Members Tomorrow?

Fifteen Member States	As of 2002, Using the Euro?	Population (millions)	Thirteen Membership Candidates	EU Suitability Ranking*	Population (millions)
Luxembourg	yes	<1	Malta	2	<1
Ireland	yes	3.7	Cyprus	3	<1
Finland	yes	5.2	Estonia	5	1.4
Denmark	no	5.3	Slovenia	1	2.0
Austria	yes	8.1	Latvia	9	2.4
Sweden	no	8.9	Lithuania	10	3.7
Portugal	yes	10.0	Slovakia	8	5.4
Belgium	yes	10.2	Bulgaria	12	8.1
Greece	yes	10.5	Hungary	6	10.0
Netherlands	yes	15.8	Czech Republic	4	10.3
Spain	yes	39.4	Romania	11	22.4
Italy	yes	57.6	Poland	7	38.6
France	yes	59.0	Turkey	13	63.9
United Kingdom	no	59.2			
Germany	yes	82.0			

*Rankings reflect a country's suitability to join the EU based on an index including: current economic integration with Europe, infrastructure quality, productivity, and economic stability. A higher rank suggests greater suitability relative to other candidate countries.
Sources: Adapted from———. (2001). A survey of European enlargement: Europe's magnetic attraction. *The Economist*, May 19, 1–16; ———. (2000). The Nice summit: So that's all agreed, then. *The Economist*, December 16, 25–28; ———. (2000). EU Enlargement. *The Economist*, December 23, 154.

began circulating, replacing national currencies in the twelve EU countries comprising the **Euro-zone** (i.e., members using the euro in cross-border trade since 1999). But three EU members, Denmark, the United Kingdom, and Sweden, have decided, at least for now, to keep their own currencies. Another challenge is how to wrestle with power differences and other disputes (e.g., about movement of labor, corporate tax rates, farm reform, etc.) in the EU's complex governance structure. And then there's the issue of expansion. The EU wants to nearly double its membership by 2006. At this point, it's unclear whether any of the leading membership candidates will join before 2004 (countries must meet certain debt, inflation, and interest rate targets to join). Take a look at Exhibit 1.9 for a list of current EU countries and likely candidates for eventual membership.[61]

In any case, some experts say that EU markets are, generally speaking, less efficient and less flexible than America's for reasons including onerous taxes, red tape, and rigid labor laws. Such factors could limit the EU's GDP growth, at least until additional reforms occur. EU firms also have poured hundreds of billions into the United States in recent years, in effect connecting the EU more tightly to the ups and downs of the U.S. economy. German companies alone have some 800,000 American employees. And the 2001 slowdown in the American economy helped trim near-term estimates for Euro-zone GDP growth. But the European Union may be more economically resilient in the near term than either the United States or Japan. For one thing, Euro-zone trade is pretty diversified. Of the Euro-zone's top ten trading partners, none has even a 20 percent share (the United States's second-ranked share is about 17%). Likewise, telecommunications and other sectors that were hit hard in 2001 represent a smaller share of GDP output in Euro-zone countries than in the United States. Other positives for Euro-zone countries at this point include lower household and corporate debt relative to the United States. EU countries also continue to cut red tape, regulations affecting business, and taxes.[62]

Spain is a good example of a country that's benefitted enormously from EU membership. Once Spain was the poor sister of western Europe. But the EU and the euro, combined with government tax cuts, deregulation, and privatization, have unleashed economic growth in recent years. Now Spanish firms raise capital throughout the EU for expansion and foreign acquisitions. Spain's Repsol did just that to buy Argentina's YPF for $15.4 billion and become the seventh largest oil firm in the world. In Latin America alone, Spanish companies have spent some $60 billion in the past few years. And at home, richer Spaniards are facing some of the problems that accompany success. For example, illegal immigration has soared as people from places like Morocco and Ecuador have sought jobs that Spaniards no longer want.[63]

Central and Eastern Europe: leaders and laggards

Of course, many countries in central and eastern Europe would love to be in Spain's shoes. Among ten central European countries wanting to join the European Union, monthly wages average 85 percent less than those in EU nations. Images of booming capitals like Prague aside, much of central and eastern Europe is rural and poor. And in Belarus, Bulgaria, and Ukraine, the average wage is less than $100 a month.[64]

Actually, eastern Germany's experience offers insights about the challenges of catching up. Since Germany was reunited more than a decade ago, the German government has spent over $640 billion to help the eastern half of the country erase sixty years of communism. And the job's not over yet. Unemployment in the east (17%) is more than double the rate in the western half of Germany. Granted, the east now has excellent roads, superior telecommunications, and many gleaming new factories. But productivity, wages, and GDP growth still lag behind western Germany's.[65]

If we want to mark progress so far in central and eastern Europe, it's clear that Poland, Hungary, and the Czech Republic are the economic leaders. All three nations moved farther and faster than their European counterparts to open up their economies and privatize state-owned industries. They also had the advantage of offering inexpensive, high-quality labor right next door to western Europe. After a slow start, GDP growth in all three nations surged along with foreign investment. Tens of billions have flowed into the three nations in the past decade, with American, Asian, and western European firms all taking part. Sony, for instance, built a new consumer electronics plant in Hungary. Of course, foreign investment means more jobs and rising incomes for local citizens. And that fuels additional investment from companies eager to serve new consumers. That's why GE Capital moved into Poland and bought part of a Hungarian bank—to offer central Europeans credit cards and loans. It's also why Poland, the Czech Republic, and Hungary are expected to attract the lion's share of foreign direct investment in eastern and central Europe through 2005.[66]

These three countries are also among the leaders in terms of positioning themselves for entry into the European Union. (Slovenia and Estonia are other regional candidates that are pushing hard for entry soon). Take Poland, for example. Despite some worries about what will happen to Polish farmers, coal miners, and steel workers, all of Poland's major political parties see gaining EU membership as the country's top goal. But the EU still wants Poland to adopt its laws and standards more quickly as well as modernize its protected farming sector (where, as a result, a box of cereal costs more in Warsaw than in Paris). But Poles know they have the potential for more growth, not just problems. And it's unlikely that the next step toward enlarging the EU will take place without central Europe's biggest economy.[67]

Russia   Of course, an even bigger player lies east of Poland. On the GDP front, Russia's economic output actually shrank during much of the 1990s. However, early into the twenty-first century, the country got back on a growth track, with GDP increasing over 6 percent annually in the past few years. Granted, higher energy prices and a large devaluation of the ruble in 1998 helped the GDP picture improve. But the Russian government deserves credit for moving to privatize and restructure state-owned firms, many of which now make money. Likewise, the government continues to push regulatory, tax, legal, and banking reforms. Some changes, like a new, simplified flat-rate income tax system, have already been put into effect. Other changes have yet to be implemented or need more time before we can judge their success. But the economic environment has stabilized, at least for now. The flight of Russian capital has slowed as business leaders keep more money at home instead of shifting it offshore. And foreign investment has been rising slowly.[68]

Yet another hopeful sign is Russia's growing, affluent middle class. Many are either entrepreneurs or managers in big multinational or local firms. Today, as many as 30 million Russians (some 20% of the population) enjoy middle-class status. To many companies this means a larger pool of potential customers with disposable income. That's why Sweden's IKEA, a home furnishings chain, took the plunge in 2000 and opened its first Russian store in a Moscow suburb. On opening day, 40,000 Russians sat in a two-mile traffic jam just to reach the store.[69]

That said, Russia still faces significant problems and challenges. Inflation is still running in the double digits. Foreign investment is minuscule ($5 billion in 2001) compared to smaller emerging markets like Poland ($7 billion in 2001). Government involvement in the economy is still too high. Poverty and unemployment rates need to come down. And then there's Russia's crumbling infrastructure. It may cost $100 billion to put things right. The list of problems is numbing: bad roads, rampant industrial accidents, toxic waste dumps, decrepit railroads, intermittent electric power, and leaking gas pipelines. The government has plans to sell off utility monopolies to raise money. But finding the money, much less actually repairing and modernizing the infrastructure, will take time.[70] Finally, corruption and organized crime continues to plague Russia and its foreign investors. Take a look at the following International Insights box to see what we mean.

INTERNATIONAL INSIGHTS

Russia: Still the Wild, Wild East

MANY THINK OF Russia as a place where the rule of law is weak. Throw in widespread violence, crime, and corruption aimed at businesses and you have a risky scenario indeed. One western banker said he would "rather eat nuclear waste" than sink money into Russia. Of course, that's a bit harsh. But as countries like Russia dismantled their state-run economies, scam artists, gangsters, and corrupt officials emerged to fill the void. Doing business in Russia has been compared to frontier life in nineteenth-century America. In the old West, American firms often had to rely on themselves for protection against criminals or business shenanigans since there was no strong law enforcement presence to fall back on.

And today, although many changes and improvements have taken place, similar challenges still occur in Russia. For example, many Russian laws are hazy or poorly enforced, creating opportunities for scams and ripoffs. Big Russian firms are routinely accused of hiding assets and cash from stockholders and investors. For instance, questions were raised about why energy giant Gazprom, Russia's largest company (the government owns 38 percent of Gazprom), did $1 billion in business annually with an obscure firm whose majority owners were relatives of Gazprom's senior executives. During a recent crackdown, government officials and several of Russia's well-known business tycoons were accused of tax evasion, embezzlement, and money laundering, among other things. But the end result of such investigations often depends on whether the individuals charged have friends in high places. Critics say that crony capitalism still plays an enormous role in Russia, with connections at the highest levels of government enhancing business prospects and, perhaps, the ability to skirt the law.

And consider this. According to some estimates, 40 percent of the Russian economy and 50 percent of Russian banks are controlled by organized criminal groups. Common are contract killings over disputed business turf as are payoffs and bribes. For instance, many businesses willingly pay 10–20 percent of their monthly profits to criminal elements for *krisha* (the Russian word for "roof"). Having *krisha* means your business will be "protected" against vandals, pesky government officials, and other "large and unpredictable costs." Likewise, if a company wants to build a factory, it may have to pay one official to get it started and another to keep it going. And Swiss food giant Nestle says that it even competes against organized crime at the retail level in Russia. The can of coffee you buy off a Russian shelf may have been put there by criminal gangs that have "arranged" for products to be imported without paying duties.

Perhaps what's most disturbing about all of this is that the criminal figures involved are often part of local firms or even, in many cases, the government itself. But experts say that this kind of pervasive lawlessness is nothing new in Russia. The old communist regime, and the czars before that, basically took what they wanted. Consequently, while some semblance of stability existed, there was also plenty of underlying crime and corruption. The good news is that the Russian government seems to be more serious about reining in corruption than ever. But until corruption is under control, the question remains—why do business in such a difficult environment? Because while the risks are great, so are the potential rewards in Russia's large market of 145 million.[71]

The Middle East and Africa: Uncertain Territory and Untapped Potential

Speaking of regions that come with plenty of risk, uncertainty, and unrealized potential, we turn our attention in this section to the Middle East and Africa.

The shadow on the Middle East　　Despite having some impressive assets, most notably oil, ongoing Arab-Israeli conflicts cast a shadow on economic growth in the Middle East. For instance, as violence increased in 2001, Palestinian incomes plunged along with Israel's GDP growth and trade with its neighbors. Of course, spikes in oil prices can spur export revenues in the region's oil-producing states (e.g., Saudi Arabia, United Arab Emirates), helping to partially offset weakness in other areas, such as textiles.

Tourism is also a potentially huge draw in the Middle East, thanks to its numerous historical and religious sites. However, tourism is stagnant, undeveloped, or held hostage to the vagaries of the area's peace prospects. In recent years, Saudi Arabia, Jordan, and Egypt spent billions to attract foreign tourists (e.g., on hotel construction). Likewise, the Syrian government wants to attract more non-Arab visitors (nearly 80 percent of its tourists are from neighboring Arab states) as well as increase the total number of annual visitors from 2.5 million to 7 million. To do that, it hopes to increase the number of hotel beds available by 500 percent over the next decade or two. But without stability, it's unlikely that those beds will be filled. For example, thanks to ongoing conflict, Israel and Jordan both saw tourism plunge 40–50 percent in 2001.

Overall, long-term prospects for regional GDP growth are uncertain. The Middle East faces major hurdles to becoming an integrated economic power. Countries such as Saudi Arabia and Israel need to spur foreign investment and create more jobs. How? By privatizing state-owned firms, lowering government spending, eliminating barriers to foreign business ownership, and reducing social welfare benefits. Saudi Arabia also hopes that its entry into the World Trade Organization will help open and diversify its economy (oil and gas currently account for over 30 percent of Saudi GDP).[72]

Africa untapped   Untapped potential is the phrase that comes to mind about Africa. In the way are some hard-to-ignore negatives. Sub-Saharan Africa is the poorest region in the world. Of the region's 600 million people, half live on 65 cents a day. On top of that, some African countries are beset with heavy government intervention in their economies, official corruption, tribal conflicts, and weak business infrastructures. AIDS also threatens sub-Saharan Africa's workforce. The region has over 70 percent of the world's HIV/AIDs cases, the vast majority of which involve heterosexual transmission and include up to 30 percent of the population in some countries. All of these factors contribute to the perception that Africa is risky for international companies.[73]

But developed countries have played a role in holding Africa back. Trade barriers in the United States, European Union, and Japan cost sub-Saharan nations about $2.5 billion annually in lost exports. And developed countries spend more to subsidize their own farmers (some $360 billion annually) than the entire African GDP. Speaking with one economic voice would help Africa obtain better access to EU and U.S. markets, especially for its quality textile and agricultural products. But progress on regional, much less continental, integration is slow. Today, more than ten different economic blocs exist in Africa, with some countries having membership in several.[74]

To improve regional cooperation and self-reliance, the presidents of several sub-Saharan countries unveiled the Millennium Action Plan in 2001. Designed to create "sustainable economic development" across the continent, the program includes plans to improve African infrastructure (roads, telecommunications, air service), share resources, eliminate internal trade restrictions, and lobby for easier access to developed markets. Time will tell how effective these efforts will be.[75]

Nevertheless, there are signs of progress throughout the African continent, especially in the sub-Saharan region. For instance, in 2000 the U.S. government removed duties on African textile exports, giving some two dozen sub-Saharan nations a better crack at penetrating the lucrative American market. Indeed, over the next several years, regional GDP growth is predicted to increase, mainly because of changes in a variety of government and economic policies. Over the years, the selling off of state-owned enterprises to private investors has accelerated in many African countries. The fact that

Companies will find an excellent business infrastructure in Cape Town, South Africa. © Charles O'Rear/CORBIS

privatization efforts elsewhere (e.g., eastern Europe) reduced the size of a bloated state sector has grabbed the attention of many African leaders. That said, the overall growth rate in Africa may still lag that of other emerging nations. And big differences will be present among African countries, both in terms of their near- and long-term prospects. As a result, we'll take a closer look at South Africa, a country that continues to show promise and is seen by many as the economic anchor of the sub-Saharan region.[76]

South Africa   South Africa's peaceful transformation from a racist, white minority government to an elected majority-rule democracy led by Nelson Mandela inspired the world. Today, South Africa is both a rich and a poor country, one with extreme income gaps paralleled only by Brazil. But the gap is shrinking slowly, thanks to a growing black middle class.

Still, economic growth needs to quicken if a significant dent is to be made in South Africa's unemployment rate of 25 percent (some say the figure is 40%). Specifically, GDP growth needs to be at least 5–6 percent, something that South Africa has not yet achieved. Of course, foreign investment can help move things along. And South Africa does have a lot to offer, including excellent roads, ports, and telecommunications facilities. It also has abundant natural resources, a growing high-tech industry, open government, a good legal system, and ongoing privatization efforts. In fact, foreign investment has been rising in South Africa since 1994. The world's car companies, including BMW, Fiat, Ford, and Volkswagen, have found the country attractive. Mercedes, for instance, makes all of its C-class cars with righthand drive in South Africa.

Realizing South Africa's potential will not be easy, however. The country has to deal with the legacy of forty years of apartheid, a system that made the black South African majority second-class citizens in everything from housing to education to health care.

And that means spending money to electrify houses and bring clean water to poor areas. Plus, international companies have many emerging markets to choose from for their investments, including places without South Africa's AIDs epidemic, active unions, and tough labor laws. Nevertheless, there are success stories. For example, American firms like Apple Computer, Kodak, and Nike have all returned to South Africa to either manufacture or distribute their products, often with the help of local black partners. [77]

Key Challenges Facing International Business

Our discussion of regional trends underscores the fact that growth and prosperity in the world are not guaranteed. Optimistic projections could be derailed by a variety of factors, including political uncertainty, corruption, disputes over trade issues, tough new competitors, and fiscal mismanagement, just to name a few. Plus, major threats can pop up quickly anytime, anywhere. Indeed, these may be among the most challenging times for global economic development. [78]

Technological Sophistication and International Volatility

And there's little doubt that foreign markets have become increasingly important for American firms. For instance, from 1993 to 1999, the proportion of sales earned abroad leapt 1,400 percent for Wal-Mart, 88 percent for General Electric, and 28 percent for McDonald's. [79] Of course, innovations in transportation, communications, and manufacturing have created new foreign markets and helped firms conduct international business. For example, the growth of computer use and Internet activity in a country may increase international trade flows, a pattern that's most robust in poorer countries. But to obtain a major boost from technology, poor countries must catch up and put the necessary infrastructure in place (e.g., a reliable power supply, high-speed digital connections). As you might expect, that's a tall order in some cases. Nevertheless, computer use in countries like China, India, Russia, and Brazil has jumped over 500 percent in recent years and is expected at least to double again by 2005. [80] Of course, the impact of technology is pervasive and not limited to developing countries. Take a look at the following International Insights box for an example of how technology might be used in a cutting-edge (and risky) effort to help small firms reach international markets.

But technological advances per se do little to eliminate international business problems driven by cultural differences, political upheavals, corruption, and mismanagement. And technology can create new challenges by accelerating how quickly crises hit. And, as the importance of international business grows, the fallout from those crises become more serious. [82]

Currency volatility and implications for management   In 1994, Mexico faced a financial crisis triggered by its inability to pay off foreign bondholders. Alarmed investors fled Mexico in droves, sending the Mexican peso plunging and causing ripple effects worldwide as they pulled money out of emerging markets. The U.S. government helped end the crisis with a $53 billion rescue effort. But in early 2001, the reverse happened when some $10 billion in foreign capital flowed into Mexico in a few months, attracted by a rising peso that was putting the country's export engine at risk. [83]

INTERNATIONAL INSIGHTS

The Challenges of Using Technology to Create a "Cultural Portal" for Small Firms

YOU'RE A SMALL American apparel company that wants to sell tank tops in Japan, where shoppers embrace American fashions in the planet's second-largest economy. But selling in the Japanese market requires resources that you don't have, especially given Japan's expensive retail space. So are you out of luck? Perhaps not if the idea behind Thinkamerican.com ever takes off. The company, backed by Soros Fund Management and American Mall International, wanted to set up 100 interactive kiosks in high-traffic locations in Japan (e.g., train stations, malls). The kiosks would have moving advertisements for American brands as well as keypads for actual ordering. The goal? To build awareness for the "cultural portal" that Thinkamerican hoped to create using the Internet.

Basically, Thinkamerican wanted to bundle the products offered by a variety of small U.S. firms on its website. For a percentage of the sales generated, Thinkamerican would convert each vendor's web page to Japanese, eliminate any cultural *faux pas*, and provide one-stop ordering and shipping across vendors. On its home page, Thinkamerican planned to offer articles on American lifestyles and fashion trends to build interest. In early 2001, Thinkamerican had signed contracts with several small apparel firms, such as Billy Martin's Western Wear, and was hoping to convince bigger players, such as Abercrombie & Fitch, to get on board. Thinkamerican also had agreements with J. Crew and Amazon to let its shoppers link to those sites.

But building a customer base and making money isn't easy in an international virtual environment, as many failed dot coms can attest. In fact, US-style.com, another Internet fashion portal, failed in 2000. Why? The company cited Japanese consumers' ability to find plenty of American fashions in Japan and their reluctance to use credit cards. Along the same lines, a survey of forty American and European firms found that globalizing e-commerce was complicated by cultural differences, internal obstacles (e.g., poor leadership and internal communication), and the difficulties of global logistics, among other things.

Nevertheless, Thinkamerican felt it had some unique advantages. First, it planned to sell products that are tough to find in Japan. Second, customers would be able to order in Japanese while the American merchants received orders in English. Finally, shipping would be consolidated no matter how many vendors a customer bought from. To handle shipping, logistics, and translations on both sides of the Pacific, Thinkamerican formed a joint venture with Bridge to Japan, a Japanese shipping firm. The idea was to put orders in customers' hands quickly at a reasonable cost.

Still, getting off the ground wasn't easy. Handling Japanese characters electronically, much less merging them with English-based software, caused glitches and launch delays for Thinkamerican. Then there were the challenges of how to market in another culture. Of course, some American apparel firms have been successful in Japan. For instance, Sears-owned catalog merchant Lands' End has been selling through its Japanese website and shipping from its Japanese warehouses since 1999. Other big apparel outfits feel that having retail stores in Japan, perhaps augmented by websites, is the best way to go.

But those options are simply out of the question for smaller, resource-poor companies. And that's why Thinkamerican was an idea that appealed. Nevertheless, whether the idea behind Thinkamerican will ever work at all, much less be a big success, remains to be seen. As one manager at Searle Blatt Ltd., a $30 million outerwear firm, put it, "It's a great experiment." And one that many small firms hoped would bring them international sales in the process. That said, the challenges Thinkamerican faced were apparently too great to overcome. By 2002, the firm's website appeared to be deactivated and its domain name was listed for sale.[81]

These volatile currency fluctuations underscore the marriage of technology and sophisticated investors. Virtually anywhere, anytime, an investor can electronically move in or out of international currency markets. Billions of dollars can flow in and out of a country in *minutes*, whether sparked by a real crisis or just a herd mentality. Plus, the sheer size of the currency markets (over $1 trillion is traded *daily*) makes stabilizing currencies difficult.[84]

Sudden currency updrafts can make a firm's exports more expensive overnight, increasing the pressure to reduce costs (e.g., by shopping globally for supplies, moving production to cheaper locations). Likewise, sharp currency downdrafts can make a company's exports cheaper. Some suggest that a weak dollar helps U.S. companies succeed overseas more than any corporate action to improve competitiveness.[85] While that may be overstating the case, currency volatility clearly increases the risks inherent in international business. Not paying close attention to currency issues can be disastrous. Take Xerox. Analysts alleged that poor management oversight cost the firm $1 billion in foreign currency losses in 1999 (much of it in volatile Brazil).[86]

But even with good financial management, currency shocks can impact firms dramatically. For instance, the euro plunged against the dollar in 2000, with the yen following suit in early 2001. The sudden changes played havoc with U.S. manufacturers in both Europe and Japan. In 2000, Goodyear lost $300 million in European sales because of the slumping euro. And in 2001, a $40 radial tire exported to Japan cost around 5,300 yen compared to only 4,500 yen in 1999.

Of course, currency fluctuations don't just impact U.S. companies. For example, the British pound's strength against the euro in 2000 had Toyota, Nissan, and Honda all rethinking the wisdom of manufacturing in the United Kingdom to serve the continental market's euro-wielding customers. In the short term, the Japanese firms cut costs to offset the currency gap. Nevertheless, in 2000 Nissan lost money on certain British-produced models because of the weak euro.[87] But the tables can turn quickly. In 2001, the yen's slump boosted Japanese car makers; cars exported from Japan to the United States helped increase earnings since firms like Toyota paid for production costs in yen but had earnings denominated in a soaring dollar.[88]

So what can international firms do to combat wild currency fluctuations? **Currency hedging** is an option. Companies can buy currency options that fix exchange rates for a period of time. That's how Coca-Cola managed to sidestep the euro's drop in 2000 and any damage to its European earnings. But hedging is basically pricey, complex guesswork. Coke would have lost out had the euro soared. Then there's the expense. Assume a company wants to protect $500 million in earnings against a drop in the euro. If the euro's value slipped from, say, $1 each to 90 cents, that $500 million would be worth only $450 million. But the cost of that protection could run a steep $26 million. Another way to minimize risks associated with exchange rate swings is to use local suppliers and make more products in the places where you sell them. This is referred to as **natural hedging**. Honda, for instance, manufactures three out of every four cars it sells in the United States in American factories. And some companies use both options. Dow Chemical, for example, uses financial hedges and scatters its production facilities around the world.[89]

Actually, some large firms view their facilities as modular. Put simply, when currency gyrations make life difficult in one place, you quickly shift locations. For instance, in 1999 some two dozen major companies operating in Argentina suddenly left to set up shop in neighboring Brazil. Why? A 35 percent plunge in the Brazilian *real* had a lot to do with it. Overnight, it became cheaper to manufacture in Brazil. It also made Argentinian products a lot less attractive to Brazilian consumers. In the process, thousands of jobs were lost in Argentina.[90]

Of course, currency volatility often hits small firms hardest. While currency fluctuations may slice a sizeable chunk off of a multinational corporation's earnings, it's often just a nibble in the overall scheme of things. And such firms typically have more experience with currency problems and more options for dealing with them than their smaller brethren. For a smaller, $150 million firm like Hatteras Yachts, currency swings can be brutal. In 2000, a skittish Italian buyer backed away from a deal on a 65-foot yacht because of the plunging euro. That single lost order was a $2 million blow to Hatteras. And as a Hatteras executive said, "What's the impact in terms of the customers that we're not seeing?" Consequently, more small firms, like Iowa-based Vermeer Manufacturing, are copying bigger firms by shopping for materials from cheaper locations, opening overseas operations in major markets, looking for foreign partners, and dabbling in currency hedging. Nevertheless, many of these steps are beyond the reach of small firms that want to sell abroad.[91]

Overall, while technology helps stitch national economies together, it also makes international business a volatile proposition. As we've seen, one way that firms try to minimize that volatility is by scattering facilities and suppliers across many countries. But those moves lead to another set of challenges, including managing people from diverse cultures. We'll consider some of those workforce challenges next.

International Workforce Challenges

What's also driving the increasing complexity of international management is that companies need innovative and productive employees to compete. And not just in manufacturing. Clearly, America's manufacturing prowess remains formidable. In fact, output has generally risen over the past twenty-five years despite occasional downturns. Of course, one of the reasons why manufacturing's share of United States GDP has been fairly constant over the past two decades is the tremendous growth in the service economy and the jobs that go with it.[92]

Global dispersion   The increasing growth in services has also led firms abroad, where labor costs can be much lower. For example, credit card operations for some American firms are located in low-wage Jamaica, thanks to satellite and telecommunications technologies. Likewise, American companies as diverse as GE Capital Services, Intel, Citigroup, Microsoft, and Analog Devices have flocked to places like India, Ireland, and the Philippines to take advantage of their relatively inexpensive but highly skilled English-speaking labor forces and excellent telecommunications infrastructures. And companies outside the United States are making similar moves. Spanish phone company Telefonica, for instance, has over 2,000 Morocco-based employees handling service calls for French and Spanish customers. Granted, many of these foreign-based jobs are lower level, providing basic customer and service support functions.

But not all. For instance, dozens of American firms such as IBM and Motorola also do much of their software development in India to take advantage of skilled local programmers and lower wages. In fact, General Electric has 10,000 employees in India, many of them scientists and professionals. Skilled professional and service jobs, such as scientific research and pharmaceutical development, are increasingly moving to "centers of excellence" worldwide. And maintaining those jobs abroad is often much less expensive than it would be in the United States or Europe, especially when foreign governments offer help. For example, India's southern state of Tamil Nadu opened an $85 million high-tech complex aimed at attracting skilled work from around the world. On top of that, the state pumps $10 million a year into local schools for computer equipment and computer literacy training. As a result, one Indian official noted that "by 2008, all the citizens in Tamil Nadu will be computer literate." And studies suggest that poor nations, like India, reap double benefits by boosting education and investing in their technological infrastructures. Not only do they increase their ability to use new technologies, they enjoy stronger income growth to boot. Over the long haul, that may reduce the income gap between rich and poor countries.[93]

In the meantime, workforces will continue to become globally dispersed. According to one estimate, by 2015 up to 90 percent of the clerical and white-collar jobs that existed in the United States at the dawn of the third millennium will be outsourced abroad. American skills need to be upgraded to keep up.[94] For instance, despite rising demand, just 13 percent of American college graduates earn degrees in the sciences or engineering annually. And at the moment jobs requiring those degrees are being filled overseas, either as American firms move high-tech positions abroad or bring in foreigners (via immigration or temporary visas) to fill jobs in the United States.[95]

Workforce quality   The bottom line is that international firms need employees who can handle increasingly complex work. Consequently, the number of U.S. manufacturers that train workers in new skills has doubled in the past decade or so. And the best workforce usually wins and keeps their jobs in the process. For instance, Siemens, the German industrial and communications giant, has doubled the skilled jobs in its workforce in recent years while cutting the number of semiskilled positions in half.[96]

All of this raises a question. What makes for a highly qualified workforce? The answer is complex, but education, on-the-job-training, motivation, and computer literacy all matter. Plus, there's little doubt that workforce quality is an important factor for determining how competitive a country is overall. Take a look at Exhibit 1.10. It ranks the world's twenty-five most competitive countries. Although they have many differences, a common thread among the top twenty-five is the general quality of their workforces. But harbor no illusions about what can be done *anywhere* given good worker training and the right infrastructure. After touring several award-winning Mexican plants, one American union official put it this way: "The workers at those

EXHIBIT 1.10

Which Countries Are Most Competitive? The Top 25

	Rank	Country
More competitive	1	United States
	2	Singapore
	3	Finland
	4	Luxembourg
	5	Netherlands
	6	Hong Kong
	7	Ireland
	8	Sweden
	9	Canada
	10	Switzerland

continued...

EXHIBIT 1.10

Which Countries Are Most Competitive? The Top 25 (continued)

	11	Australia
	12	Germany
	13	Iceland
	14	Austria
	15	Denmark
	16	Israel
	17	Belgium
	18	Taiwan
	19	United Kingdom
	20	Norway
	21	New Zealand
	22	Estonia
	23	Spain
	24	Chile
Less Competitive	25	France

Source: Adapted from————. (2001). The International Institute for Management Development's (IMD) *World Competitiveness Scoreboard* (www.imd.ch/wcy/ranking/ranking.html).

plants make a fraction of what American workers make, but there's no drop in quality. Most third-world countries are turning out world-class products."[97]

Increasing workforce diversity   Globalization is also bringing people from diverse cultures and backgrounds together. Many American and European companies recruit foreign immigrants aggressively, especially for jobs requiring specific technical skills.[98] Demographic shifts within nations are having a similar impact. In the United States, for example, people of Hispanic descent will represent 25 percent of the population by 2050, up from 10 percent in 1995. At the same time, the share for non-Hispanic whites will drop to around 50 percent from over 70 percent in 1995.[99] And a diverse workforce can help firms better serve an increasingly diverse customer base. In the United States, African-Americans, Asians, and Hispanics collectively represent about $700 billion in purchasing power. Targeting these and other groups in recruiting brings in employees who can help connect firms with important segments of their customer base.[100]

So if diversity can make the difference between success and failure, companies can't afford to let antiquated attitudes permeate the workforce. For instance, key corporate decisions are increasingly made in cross-functional groups. Such groups automatically bring together people from diverse backgrounds, making their effective interaction critical. In fact, experts recommend introducing cultural diversity into decision-making groups and teams, putting a premium on managers' abilities to overcome the difficulties of making it all work.[101]

But few companies have created an atmosphere where diversity is taken seriously. In one survey, less than 10 percent of firms felt they did a very good job of supporting diversity. Not surprisingly, failure can be costly. Higher turnover rates mean higher recruiting and training expenses. And for some occupations, those costs can exceed $100,000 per job.[102]

Managing in a Volatile and Challenging International Environment

All of this raises a larger question about the impact of today's volatile and challenging international environment on management. Clearly, the goal of international management is to achieve the firm's international objectives by effectively procuring, distributing, and using company resources (e.g., people, capital, know-how, physical assets) across countries.[103]

So what happens if management decides that China (or wherever) is a place to develop, manufacture, or sell a product? What then? How should managers *manage* in the environment they find themselves in? As you will see, this is a tough question to answer. Just imagine all the contextual challenges facing managers in firms that operate in dozens of countries. How do they develop business strategies that take such diversity into account? Or find the best talent worldwide, much less deploy and develop them properly? After all, business practices, laws, languages, cultural values, and market structures may all vary across countries, globalization notwithstanding. These factors can effect every aspect of management, including communication, motivation, compensation, employee development, business strategy, and ethics.[104]

To get a sense of the challenges that international managers are concerned about right now, take a look at Exhibit 1.11. These days, executives are feeling the pressure, especially those charged with running complex global empires. Take Procter & Gamble. Two decades ago, P&G was big, with $7 billion in sales, 50,000 employees, and facilities in twenty-three countries. Today, the firm is downright gargantuan, with over $40 billion in revenues, more than 100,000 employees, and facilities in some seventy nations. As one executive put it, P&G today is "a much more diverse, much more culturally different, much more global company." Senior leaders worry about how to manage their vast operations when information and capital fly around the world in a heartbeat, economies bounce around rapidly, and customer preferences are fickle. Many want to improve communications and somehow knit together company outposts to be more responsive to, if not anticipate, changes in international business.[105]

Overall, this book will provide some guidelines, if not answers, for responding to these challenges. For now, we'll sketch out some principles for international managers who want to succeed in the 21st century. Today, successful international firms will be lead by managers who

● Value ethnic diversity and have multi-cultural experience.
● Embrace teamwork and information sharing.

EXHIBIT 1.11

Try These Questions on for Size: Challenges Facing International Management

Most Critical and Important	Also Very Important
Who are our international competitors and how should we deal with them?	How important is firm reputation in global versus domestic competition?
What global leadership approaches will allow us to perform better as a firm?	What can we do to break the inertia of a domestic orientation?
How do managers in our company become more global?	What factors cause a shift to a more global corporate identity?
What are the requirements of a global organization?	How can management design a global human resource strategy?
How do we integrate competing values in our firm (e.g., across functions and across borders)?	How does firm brand image or reputation cross borders?
How do we best acquire and distribute knowledge throughout the firm?	

Source: Adapted from Zahra, S. A., & O'Neill, H. M. (1998). Charting the landscape of global competition: Reflections on emerging organizational challenges and their implications for senior executives. *Academy of Management Executive, 12,* 13–21.

- Act globally where possible (e.g., selling similar products worldwide) while fine-tuning things for local markets where necessary.
- Look to local managers abroad for ideas and give them a great deal of control.
- Offer employees around the world an implicit contract in which high-quality work will be rewarded with decent wages, continuous learning, and recognition.[106]

But embracing these ideas may require new assumptions about how to run a business. For example, many managers still see their roles in command and control terms, with corporate headquarters making decisions for foreign subsidiaries. Unfortunately, this orientation doesn't take full advantage of local expertise, nor does it permit a quick response to rapidly changing local conditions. In fact, international corporations with a rigid hierarchy and a control mentality are slowly fading from the scene. Wholly owned subsidiaries are giving way to networks of alliances between organizations. Growing a company this way, however, requires flexible managers who are willing to accept the ambiguity inherent in relationships not based on control.[107]

Basic Conceptual Foundations

Some of the points we've made in this chapter rest on several management concepts. Although we'll cover these concepts in detail later, introducing a few of them now will help you approach the rest of the book.

Defining culture   Clearly, culture can play a big role in determining success or failure in international management. As you'll see later, culture can affect how managers lead, hire, and compete in various countries. But what exactly is culture? We agree with Hofstede, who defined *culture* as "the collective programming of the mind which distinguishes one group or category of people from another." This "programming" can't be observed directly. Rather, it can only be *inferred* from behavior. Likewise, people are often unaware of the pervasive impact of culture on their own attitudes, beliefs, and behaviors.[108] Culture is a concept that's only useful if it can accurately predict behavior. And although cultural values can change dramatically when borders are crossed, this isn't always the case. Furthermore, many distinct cultural groups can coexist within individual countries. Despite these complexities, it's important to understand country-specific differences in cultural values that exist and how they impact international management.

International corporations and their evolution   Firms tackle international business in many different ways. Some export products from a home base while others have sales facilities in foreign countries to handle their exported products. Other firms build or buy facilities abroad to manufacture products or deliver services. In fact, a great deal is known about various approaches to international business. We'll cover them in more detail later. But right now, a basic understanding of how firms approach the international business arena might be very helpful.

In particular, you've already been reading about **multinational enterprises** (referred to as *multinationals* throughout the rest of the book). This reflects the fact that *multinationals* are large, well-developed international firms that attract considerable attention. By *well developed*, we mean that multinationals operate facilities that produce products or deliver services in overseas locations and have considerable resources invested abroad. In addition, management in multinationals may make decisions based on a global assessment of business opportunities and threats. This doesn't mean, however, that multinationals all compete in some identical "global" fashion. As you'll see later, some multinationals (like those in the semiconductor industry) compete in global industries where few if any location-specific preferences exist. Other multinationals, however, operate in industries where a high degree of local tailoring has to be done.

Even within industries, multinationals may operate quite differently. This variation results from many factors, including firm values and the moves of competitors. Some multinationals, for instance, have facilities in many countries but try to use the same basic structure, technologies, and human resource practices everywhere. In these multinationals, the "home country" is where the headquarters resides and where decisions about firm culture, policies, and practices are made.

For other multinationals, however, local operations have more freedom to make their own decisions. Such multinationals tend to be more diverse internally in terms of both culture and structure. Business practices, technologies, and cultural values may all vary depending on the needs of particular locations where the firm operates. In short, headquarters may offer suggestions and guidance, but it's up to local managers to make operational choices. This emphasis is often reflected in multinationals that rely on local managers to run foreign operations (as opposed to sending an expatriate from the home country to run operations abroad).

Some multinationals, usually referred to as **transnational firms**, take diversity one step further. Their firm cultures have evolved to the point where organizational diversity is a core value. This value, along with a few other core beliefs, is the glue that both holds the firm together and allows enormous flexibility. Such multinationals tend to be run by teams of managers from several countries. In fact, other than a few practices that are not subject to negotiation, such as indoctrinating employees in the firm's core

EXHIBIT 1.12

The Evolution of Multinationals and Their Approach to Innovation: Three Eras

Era	Time Frame	Description of Multinational Operations
Paternalism	1900–1960s	Firms innovate in the home country, moving products out to the rest of the world from there. As foreign subsidiaries evolved, however, it became clear that the home office did not have a monopoly on good ideas. IBM and Procter & Gamble are prominent examples during this period.
Expansionism	1970s–1980s	Some firms set up R&D or other units abroad in an effort to capture ideas in key markets. But these outposts had difficulty integrating ideas across the company and holding headquarters' attention. Plus, establishing these outposts signaled to other foreign facilities that their ideas weren't needed (e.g., because they weren't in a big enough market or important enough to warrant an R&D operation).
Liberalism	1990s–today	The emerging approach takes a more democratic twist to the pursuit of new ideas. It assumes that great ideas can come from anywhere, especially in parts of the firm that are directly connected to customers or other outside constituencies. It also assumes that the farther a foreign outpost is from the home office, the less constrained it is by corporate traditions and beliefs. So foreign subsidiaries are better viewed as peninsulas than as islands. With that in mind, firms can expect some of their most creative and innovative ideas to come from the edges of the organization instead of the center. How to tap and leverage those ideas are key challenges for management.

Source: Adapted from Birkinshaw, J., & Hood, N. (2001). Unleash innovation in foreign subsidiaries. *Harvard Business Review* (March), *79*, 131–138.

values, these multinationals operate on a diverse basis. Relatively few multinationals have reached this status.[109]

We'll conclude with an evolutionary snapshot of how multinationals have changed in the last one hundred years. As you can see in Exhibit 1.12, multinationals have gradually changed both their geographic scope and their orientation toward foreign subsidiaries. But not all multinationals develop in the same way or at the same rate. That said, multinationals are generally expected to move toward the more liberal model in the years ahead.

Chapter Summary

The purpose of this chapter was to describe the basic landscape of international business and the competitive environment that it represents. We began by describing *globalization* and prospects for increasing international business growth worldwide. Also discussed was the *World Trade Organization*, the body that governs worldwide rules for trade. In any case, the strongest growth will most likely be in emerging markets, although long-term prospects in many developed markets are also good. And as we noted, an important way to assess those prospects is by examining the flows of *foreign direct investment*. Next, we examined trends in specific regions of the world.

In the *Americas*, prospects for greater economic integration are being debated. The *Free Trade Area of the Americas* (FTAA), for instance, holds out the prospect of a continental free trade zone stretching from Alaska to the tip of South America. Clearly, the United States is the region's dominant player, though Canada and Mexico have generally done well since the *North American Free Trade Agreememt* (NAFTA) was implemented. In South America, long-term growth prospects look good. In the short run, however, countries in the region continue to experience significant problems. Argentina's financial collapse in 2001 is a case in point.

The *Asia-Pacific* region may become the world's most dominant economic area in the years ahead. But important differences exist across countries in the region in terms of their current performance, future prospects, and existing problems. Although there may be some setbacks, and major challenges exist in some Asian countries (such as rising costs, political instability, high debt, and weak infrastructures), growth should continue over the long haul. Clearly, China has a large economy and the strongest growth in the region, though it may eventually be eclipsed by India. China is also a challenging place to do business for a variety of reasons, including its *competitive intensity* (i.e., many competitors operate and the pace of business activity is frenetic). Japan, on the other hand, while a major player in the region, continues to struggle economically.

The transformation of *Europe* is continuing, though at an uneven pace. The European Union continues to evolve and may expand in the next few years. Countries nearest to western Europe (Poland, Hungary, and the Czech Republic) have done the best so far. Russia has recently steadied itself economically and resumed a growth track while continuing to combat ongoing problems with regulation, laws, infrastructure, and organized crime. Overall, the prospect of an expanding, integrated European market with a common currency is a tantalizing one that continues to fuel foreign investment.

In the *Middle East and Africa,* major problems, such as political conflicts, poverty, corruption, and weak business infrastructure, still exist. Nevertheless, headway is being made. For example, Saudi Arabia has embarked on major reforms to open its economy and may prove a bellwether for growth prospects in the region. Likewise, if South Africa can build on its accomplishments, it will be an important barometer for the rest of Sub-Saharan Africa.

From there we moved to a discussion of some key challenges in international business. These included sweeping technological changes and the increasing volatility of international business. We examined how rapid currency fluctuations can impact business and what management can do in response (e.g., *currency hedging* and *natural*

hedging). Small firms are particularly vulnerable to such fluctuations, especially since their resources (and consequently, their ability to cope) are often more limited than those of larger firms. Another set of challenges involve the internationalization of the workforce. Companies are willing to look anywhere in the world to find employees with the right skills at the right price for just about any job. So jobs are dispersing throughout the world like never before. And countries are more formidable competitors when they can offer firms a hardworking and skilled pool of employees.

For international executives, maintaining workforce quality and managing diversity are important challenges. And in big global empires, the management challenges are even greater. To meet these challenges, international managers must, among other things, value ethnic diversity, have multicultural experience, embrace teamwork, and be open to ideas from anywhere. Finally, we concluded by discussing the role of *culture* (the collective mental "programming" that sets groups of people apart) in international management and how *multinational enterprises* (large, well-developed international firms) have evolved over the last 100 years.

1. What are the most important trends in international business? Which are the biggest management challenges for international firms? Why? What can firms do in response?
2. Which markets represent the biggest opportunities for international firms? Which markets represent the biggest risks? Why?
3. What is culture? Why is it important for international management?
4. How have multinationals evolved over the years? What are the implications of this for management?

Up to the Challenge?

How New Balance Makes "Made in the U.S.A." Work, at Least for Now

A T THE START of this chapter we said that New Balance was unique among major athletic shoe companies in that it manufactures some of its shoes in the United States. In doing so, New Balance has minimized the cost gap with Asian subcontractors to the point where it can remain competitive. So how did the company pull this off? It started at the top. Owner Jim Davis felt obligated to manufacture in the United States. The son of successful immigrants, Davis

said, "It's part of the company's culture to design and manufacture here." Plus, being close to customers in a major market offers speed advantages in terms of fulfilling orders and changing styles.

But making this philosophy work essentially meant shifting from low tech to high tech, both in terms of equipment and employee skills. Borrowing a page from manufacturing methods in higher-tech industries, New Balance had employees take classes on computerized manufacturing techniques and sophisticated teamwork. Once on the factory floor, employees operate in small, flexible teams of five to six. Employees must master many skills, switch jobs continuously, help each other out, and take responsibility for all production activities. And even on the factory floor, training is constant and ongoing.

New Balance's managers also took a creative approach in adapting high-tech equipment from other industries to their own needs. For instance, the company bought seventy computerized sewing machines that came with a set of templates designed for other stitched products. New Balance factories ripped out the templates and set up facilities to make their own (about thirty templates are needed for the average shoe). Once the right templates were in place, the computerized machines could guide twenty sewing heads at once. The result? A technology-intensive manufacturing operation for athletic shoes. And with a highly skilled workforce to run the equipment, New Balance factories in the United States need only one employee for every six that plants using ordinary sewing machines require.

The New Balance story raises some interesting questions. First, can American firms avoid having to shift production abroad by upgrading the skill levels of work at home? What are the limits to this? After all, one of the reasons low-skilled wages in the United States have been falling for years is that low-skilled jobs have been migrating abroad. What should the role of government be here? Should it encourage the example New Balance has set? If so, how? And what of New Balance itself? What are the costs and risks associated with its approach? What might happen if demand spikes up sharply or drops precipitously? Is New Balance at a disadvantage because it owns and operates some factories, whereas Nike and Reebok don't? Only time will tell if New Balance's approach represents a long-term competitive advantage for the company.[110]

International Development

International Management: Should It Be Life at 35,000 Feet?

Purpose

To give a snapshot of what life is like as an international manager, to discuss the implications of that life, and to present some of the execution challenges companies face in running their international operations.

Instructions

Read the following short case (either before or in class). Then have a class discussion around the questions raised at the end of the case. Alternatively, your instructor will divide the class into groups of three to six and ask each group to consider the discussion questions and develop a list of their three most important reactions or ideas (20 minutes). Time permitting, your group could then make brief presentations about its findings to the class (20 minutes). You may conclude with a general discussion about the rigors of life as an international manager and the implications of those rigors for corporations (15 minutes).

Case: Have Manager, Should Travel?

Accounting powerhouse PricewaterhouseCoopers (PWC) is a bonafide global empire, with some 150,000 employees in over 150 countries. And Ellen Knapp's job is to help keep that empire running well. As PWC's chief knowledge officer and chief information officer, Knapp spends much of her time traveling overseas.

And Knapp's situation isn't unique. Knapp once survived three international red-eye flights crammed into less than a week. In the process, she ran into a colleague in London who was about to endure two

such flights in two days. On another occasion, she ran into an acquaintance from consulting giant McKinsey at the Philadelphia airport. He was bound for New Delhi while Knapp was in transit to London and Frankfurt.

These days, international travel isn't confined to a handful of the most senior executives who hop on corporate jets for two-week business trips spanning a dozen time zones. Increasingly, the growth of international business means that second-tier managers like Knapp slog through airports as they criss-cross the globe on their firm's behalf. But at least Knapp gets to fly business class. A notch below Knapp on the corporate ladder is a pool of employees who must endure nearly as much international travel wedged into economy seats.

Nevertheless, how does Knapp survive? A constellation of skills and abilities clearly help Knapp endure. These include being extremely organized, dedicated, optimistic, and, by a lucky twist, amazingly immune to jet lag. On the home front, Knapp has few complications since her two children are grown. Her two administrative assistants also keep Knapp plugged in at the home office. PWC tries to help by holding meetings near big airports and giving traveling managers like Knapp a phone and a desk when they arrive at a company outpost.

If you're wondering why Knapp has to travel overseas so much, the answer can be summed up in one word: bonding. Most of Knapp's travels are aimed at building relationships and trust between PWC people scattered around the world. The idea, at least in theory, is that over time better relationships will encourage cross-border information sharing and greater collaboration. That said, some question whether direct, face-to-face contact is the best, if not only, way to encourage international sharing and collaboration. Clearly, many believe that relationship building requires plenty of informal face time (e.g., over lunch). Nevertheless, whether Knapp's traveling really pays off or not is debatable. But one thing is certain. Knapp makes airlines happy.

Discussion Questions

1. How does Ellen's work life sound to you? Attractive? Tiring? Why or why not?
2. How would Ellen manage if she had younger children at home? What if she had younger children and a spouse with a demanding career on top of it?

3. Is all this flitting around the world really necessary? How might technology be used to eliminate some of this travel? What are the potential costs and benefits? To whom? The limitations? Can technology really substitute for relationship building, especially in far-flung corporate empires?

———

Adapted from: ———. (1999). On a wing and a hotel room. *The Economist*, January 9, 64.

From Theory To Practice

Hitting Home: Understanding Your Local International Business Environment

Purpose

To do a detailed analysis of export activities in your local environment. The local environment will be defined by your instructor but could be a state, a province, a county, or a city.

Instructions

1. Outside class, break into small groups (ideally 3–6) to do research to answer these basic questions: Which companies are major exporters in the local environment (city, state, etc.)? What industries do they represent? To what regions in the world do these local companies export? What efforts, if any, are being made by local officials to encourage local companies to export or find new foreign markets?
2. If the class is small enough, your instructor may have your groups make brief presentations (10 minutes) about your findings to the class. This may be followed by a discussion about the level of international business participation by local firms. Alternatively, your instructor may make this an individual assignment and have you write a report and ask you to take part in a general class discussion on the issues raised.

Chapter

2

Legal and Political Foundations of International Management

International Challenge

Risky Business: Piracy in the Middle Kingdom

LEARNING OBJECTIVES

After reading this chapter, you should be able to

- Identify at least three major legal systems in place around the globe today.

- Pinpoint important effects that these legal systems have on commerce that is conducted within their jurisdiction.

- Define political risk and understand some of the specific effects it has on international business.

- Understand some of the ways that risk can be managed, reduced, or avoided altogether.

SIMON LICHTENBERG IS A 41-year-old Danish businessman with a stubborn streak. But stubbornness can be a virtue, especially when you need a whole lot of persistence to protect your product and copyright material in China. Mr. Lichtenberg came to Shanghai in 1993 and by 1995 opened a Bo Concepts franchise with his $30,000 dollars and Chinese language skills. Bo Concepts is a high-end furniture company that sells contemporary furniture through department stores and furniture malls. Business was good. The modern Danish designs appealed to the growing young urban professionals who were proliferating in the dynamically growing city of Shanghai. In 1995, the first year of business, sales were $3.6 million and then jumped to $6 million the very next year. By the end of 1997, Lichtenberg had fourteen franchise outlets in Shanghai, Guangzhou, and Beijing. And he was making money. Business was good. But this is when the trouble started.

To take advantage of the expanding home improvement trend fueled by the growing professional set, Bo Concepts was joined in business by some 3,000 furniture companies selling all sorts of interesting products. While Lichtenberg did not mind competition, even of this magnitude, this wasn't the real problem. The real issue was that over twelve companies in the Shanghai area alone started to pump out furniture that "bore an uncanny likeness to Bo Concept's designs."[1]

That was a nice way of saying that Lichtenberg and Bo Concepts were getting ripped off by pirates. Not only was the furniture a drop-dead look alike, some of the stores actually used the Bo Concepts logo as their own in their showrooms. The resemblance was uncanny. Other copycats had the Bo Concept catalog and models in their stores so that customers could peruse the products. Still others went a step further by printing their own catalogs with pictures and marketing concepts taken directly from the Bo Concepts catalog.

Consider the comments of salesman Zheng Yong at the Xujiahui Furniture Company, part of a commodious department store in a shopping district of Shanghai, the kind of place that an up and coming family would go to get a nice couch, bed, or their first computer armoire. "I can make furniture just like Bo Concept's," bragged Mr. Yong. "We can change the length and the width to your specifications. We can stain it whatever tint you want. You don't want to bargain. This is our lowest price," he said, talking right below the company logo on the wall behind him. And Mr. Yong was probably right; the $600 teak bed sold by Bo Concepts was only $96 at his store.

So that was the situation. As is the case in other industries, Chinese companies can create uncanny knockoffs and take a big bite out of a firm's profits. By 1998, the knockoffs in combination with the Asian financial crisis were taking their toll. Bo Concept's revenue declined by 10 percent in 1998 and the outlook was even worse. And as Mr. Lichtenberg put it, "When the company president visits China once a year, he almost has a heart attack when he sees the copies." This is extra pressure that Lichtenberg doesn't need. As you read this chapter, think of options, both legal and political, that Bo Concept's could use to stem the tide of counterfeiting and piracy. Then take a look at our Up to the Challenge at the end of the chapter for an update on Bo Concept's plan of attack.[2]

In this chapter we discuss two related issues—the legal and political frameworks in place in various countries where multinationals do business. Laws are the written codes of conduct that constrain and guide the actions of multinationals. As you might imagine, there are a variety of different legal codes across countries—even among those nations that share a common heritage. Sometimes (perhaps many times), however, a law may be constrained, altered, or ignored altogether because of political concerns. Worse yet, if a new political regime takes power, the legal framework may be changed again. Therefore, in addition to the formal, written legal code, multinationals should closely watch the political activity occurring at home and in the foreign countries where it operates. Additionally, multinationals may wish to engage in political activity to gain an advantage. So although there is a close relation between a country's legal framework and its typical political activity, each should and must be carefully monitored. We will discuss both of these areas in turn.

Legal Issues in International Management

Several systems have been devised for categorizing the types of legal systems within countries. Although no approach covers every legal system in operation, one method that helps familiarize us with cultural variations among laws is presented in Exhibit 2.1.[3]

Types of Legal Systems

The number and types of laws among countries are varied and complex. The types most frequently found are civil and common law.

Civil law   **Civil law** found in over seventy countries, is the most frequently used system in the world.[4] This system, also referred to as *code law*, is based on an elaborate and detailed set of rules. Ideally, a civil law system tries to design a complete set of regulations about what is right and wrong. In Western culture the system was formed in Roman times, and major developments have subsequently included the Napoleonic code and its spread throughout French colonial possessions during the last century as well as the impact of German civil code on that country's colonial possessions. In addition to France and Germany, the Czech Republic, Greece, Indonesia, Japan, Turkey, and

EXHIBIT 2.1

International Legal Systems

Type of Legal System	Characteristics of the System
Civil law	● codified ● based on abstract principles ● predictable because of elaborate code
Common law	● based on precedent ● emphasis on procedures ● flexible
Islamic law	● religious/faith-based code ● codified and predictable ● applicable to daily life
Communist/socialist law	● based on ideology ● based on bureaucracy ● minimal private rights
Sub-Saharan African law	● community oriented ● based on custom ● group-based outcomes
Asian law	● social order/harmony stressed ● low use of legal mechanisms ● bureaucratized

Source: Adapted from Richards, F.L. (1994). *Law for global business.* Boston, MA.: Irwin.

many South American and African countries use the civil law system. Because of the existing code of legal regulations, there is great consistency among countries in the conduct of legal proceedings, especially in contrast to the common law system.

Common law   **Common law** is practiced in about thirty countries, including the United Kingdom and most of its former colonies, the United States, Canada, Australia, and Ireland.[5] Instead of relying mostly on preexisting codes, common law uses the balance of previous cases (common use) or precedent to resolve legal disputes. Often the case under consideration is assessed for similarities to previous cases. Because of the focus on the case at hand and its relation to previous cases—instead of an application of general principles and codes—there is great emphasis on procedural issues in common law. In fact, a judge in a common law system is relatively passive, typically functioning as a neutral referee. The lawyers for the plaintiff and defendant are expected to present evidence and develop the legal case in order to resolve the dispute. In the civil law system, however, a judge takes a much greater part in the proceedings, including the decisions about what evidence will be presented to the court. To those unfamiliar with the common law system, rulings seem widely discrepant, often changing from year to year and even case to case. To a great extent, this is true, and easily traced to reliance on the precedent system. In other words, the effect of previous rulings, court interpretations, and legal modifications lends itself to some inconsistency—especially compared to civil law.

EXHIBIT 2.2

Number of Lawyers and Tort Costs in Various Countries

Country	Number of Lawyers per 100,000 People	Country	Tort Costs (as % of GDP)
Pakistan	508.4	United States	2.40
Singapore	396.0	Switzerland	.70
United States	312.0	France	.55
Belgium	214.0	Canada	.55
Germany	190.1	Austria	.53
Canada	168.5	Belgium	.50
Australia	145.7	Germany	.45
United Kingdom	133.8	United Kingdom	.45
Japan	101.6	Italy	.45
Italy	81.2	Spain	.35
Brazil	69.1	Japan	.35
France	49.1	Denmark	.35
India	34.4	Australia	.30
South Korea	7.7		
China	4.2		

Source: ———. (1994). *The Economist*, March 5, 36; ———. (1992). *The Economist*. July 18, 13.
Reprinted by permission.

Some have said that the common law emphasis on the active role of attorneys pro-motes high numbers of attorneys and litigation.[6] Exhibit 2.2 presents some data that support this claim. The left side of this exhibit shows the percentage of lawyers in a variety of different countries—some with civil and some with common law systems. In general, there is a tendency for civil law countries (e.g., South Korea, Japan, and France) to have relatively few lawyers, whereas common law countries (e.g., the U.S., Canada, Pakistan) have a relatively high number. In fact, the United States alone has nearly 40 percent of the world's lawyers, whereas Japan seems to have only about 12,000 lawyers (see the accompanying International Insights on the role of lawyers and litigation out-side the U.S.). Exhibit 2.2 also provides further data on this point; it shows the tort costs as a portion of GDP in a number of different countries. Roughly, this figure refers to the costs (legal, repayment, and damage awards) associated with lawsuits involving products (e.g., automobiles, cigarettes) and services (e.g., malpractice). The United States (at 2.4%) has about four times the amount of costs as the next closest country (Switzerland, at .7%). Of course, tort costs are not completely the result of the form of legal system, because although the fundamental U.S. legal system has not changed over the past twenty years, the relative growth of tort costs has changed markedly. In fact, from 1970 to 1990, tort costs (relative to GDP) in the United States have tripled.[7]

Islamic law   Islamic law results from religious stipulations in the Quran—the holy book of Islam. **Islamic law** is known as **sharia** (or God's rules) and is basically a moral code. While the Quran is not, strictly speaking, a code of law, it does include requirements to honor agreements and to observe good faith in business transactions. The Islamic system considers that God's law was given to the prophet Mohammed. Many experts claim that by the end of the tenth century religious scholars had determined that divine law had been translated and clarified sufficiently and that no more substantial interpretation (*ijtihad*) was necessary.[10]

Although there are some great differences across the thirty or so countries that embrace Islamic law, the fact that much of the code was developed centuries ago and endures today with relatively few changes can create problems for multinationals. Consider the concept of interest earned on an investment. Islamic law requires that followers obey *riba*, which prohibits the collection of interest on loans in deference and respect to the poor. And many Islamic courts have acted consistent with such principles. In Pakistan, for example, a court recently ruled that over twenty laws dealing with financial and banking issues were in violation of Islamic law. A government commission formed in response to the court's dictates recommended that a banking system without interest be instituted. As you might imagine, several banks have challenged the rulings and recommendations. And the finance minister, Mr. Sardar Asif Ahmed Ali, stated that the ruling would negatively affect foreign investment and the treatment of Pakistan by international agencies such as the World Bank.[11]

To overcome some of the problems this observance presents in international commerce, Muslim businesses have devised some unique approaches. In Iran, for example, banks have charged upfront fees for a loan in lieu of interest payments or have devised leasing arrangements that comply with Islamic law. Likewise, some U.S. banks have developed creative financing arrangements to overcome the Quran's prescription that interest cannot be paid or received. For example, when Dr. Ala-ud-Din, a dentist in San Jose, California wanted to buy a house in this most expensive of U.S. real estate markets, he faced problems. Fortunately, a small Islamic financing company actually bought the house for Dr. Din and leased it to him over a fifteen-year period that eventually made him the owner. And even a few U.S. mutual funds that follow Islamic law have emerged.[12]

Other legal systems   There are other legal systems in operation today, including socialist/communist or bureaucratic law and sub-Saharan African law, among others.[13] In China, for example, the legal system is probably a complex combination of several systems. Like many aspects of Chinese culture, the operation of the legal system is hard for Westerners to understand. Take traffic laws as an example. Many expatriates are not permitted to drive by their firms; instead, even low-level managers are provided cars and drivers. Mostly, this is because in the event of a collision with a cyclist or pedestrian, Chinese law may hold the vehicle operator partially responsible. There is a well-known story of a stationary car (parked by a foreigner) that was hit by a bicyclist. The car's owner was assessed 10 percent of the blame because "if you had not come to China, this would not have happened."[14]

INTERNATIONAL INSIGHTS

Courting Trouble: American Lawyers and Litigation in Japan

FOREIGN LAW FIRMS in Japan must abide by a number of rules that don't apply to their domestic counterparts. For instance, foreign firms must first list the name of their resident partner in Japan, followed by a Japanese phrase meaning "foreign business lawyer," and only then display their trademark firm name by which they're known to the rest of the world. So on their office doors, business cards, stationary, and even in the directory of the American Chamber of Commerce, the Tokyo office of the well-known U.S. firm of Coudert Brothers is called "Stevens *gaikokuho-jimu-bengoshi* Coudert Brothers." The firm of Milbank, Tweed, Hadley & McCloy (already a mouthful) becomes "Dickson, Green, Benson, *gaikokuho-jimu-bengoshi*, Tweed, Hadley & McCloy."

Foreign lawyers, or *gai-ben*, as they are known, say these rules on names are really only a minor irritation compared to other restrictions. For example, foreign lawyers cannot advise on Japanese law, nor can they employ Japanese lawyers who are permitted to give such advice. In fact, for-eigners aren't permitted to join with national firms to get around the restriction. Perhaps most important, *gai-ben* are barred from arbitration proceedings. This is no small matter since arbitration is common and litigation is rare. Partly this results from the Japanese tendency to avoid conflict, but the slowness of courts is also a factor. Cases can take ten years or more to go to trial.

The Japanese bar opposed the opening of the nation's legal market, and they support the current set of restrictions. They still fear foreign competition—even though fewer than fifty *gai-ben* (mostly Americans) have registered there, in comparision to 124,000 registered Japanese legal profes-sionals. Despite fears of opening the market, "the hordes of lawyers the Japanese worried about didn't materialize," says Charles Stevens, the Coudert Brothers *gai-ben*. Those who have come would like to see more freedom to work. This is important, they say, because Japanese lawyers sometimes don't represent foreign clients well; they are seen as overly concerned with preserving social harmony and the existing business relations they have with their countrymen. In one case, a big Japanese brokerage house was tipped off about a company's bankruptcy and thanks to this information they obtained assets that were claimed by a consortium of foreign

China aside, many feel that legal systems around the world share more and more in common as decades pass. It remains to be seen if this is actually the case. For now, how-ever, Exhibit 2.3 shows these legal perspectives can result in varying degrees of legal pro-tection against discrimination across countries.[15] In the United States, the Civil Rights Act of 1964 (and the 1990/91 amendment) forbids U.S. firms from discriminating against employees at home and in foreign countries. Foreign multinationals are also subject to the Civil Rights Act while operating in the United States. The exhibit also shows that gender discrimination is prohibited in Belgium. In the United States, age dis-crimination is also outlawed, whereas it is permitted in France. Interestingly, Greece has a wide degree of protection against discrimination (e.g., gender, race, religion), but no laws dealing with age or national origin. Pakistan also has many forms of legal protec-tion, but an employer could legally use gender as a job qualification variable. Finally, some countries have no specific anti-discrimination laws whatsoever (e.g., Hong Kong, Venezuela). Therefore, it is important to be aware of the legal system that operates where a multinational has a presence.[16] One way that firms can do this is to join forces, as with the recent merger between the U.K. firm Freshfields and Germany's Bruckhaus, Westrick, Heller, & Loeber, creating a legal powerhouse of nearly 2,000 attorneys.[17] Even beyond this, as economies and financial markets outgrow national borders, countries are compelled to blend regulations.[18] For example, when a Saudi broker buys shares of a British company on the Nasdaq exchange, there will be some need to reconcile differences. Interestingly, in many cases there is a tendency toward common law rules and standards (e.g., the system used in the U.S. and U.K.), but this trend is far from

banks. The Japanese lawyers representing the banks never told the bank executives for fear that it would offend the brokerage house.

Despite the problems with the Japanese system, a major benefit is that these very *gai-ben*—particularly the aggressive American type—are limited in their practice. Consider some of the American behavior that Japanese would find offensive. Within 24 hours after a major accident at a Union Carbide plant in India, American lawyers were on the ground soliciting clients, and within four days they were back home and had already filed many lawsuits. The Japanese react very differently to these situations. For example, after a JAL flight crashed near Tokyo not long ago, the airline's president, Yasumoto Takagi, humbly bowed to families of the victims and apologized "from the bottom of our hearts." He vowed to resign once the investigation was complete. Next of kin received condolence payments and negotiated settlements with the airline. Similarly, when another JAL flight crashed into Tokyo Bay, the president also visited families and offered gifts while kneeling before funeral altars. The airline quickly paid families $2,000 each for condolence payments, then reached settlements ranging up to $450,000. Only one lawsuit was filed.

Contrast this behavior with a crash of a Delta Airlines plane at Dallas. After this tragedy, lawyers rushed to set up shop at the airport Marriott. The well-known attorney Melvin Belli said, "I'm not an ambulance chaser—I get there before the ambulance." And one of his associates bragged, "We always file the first suit." Belli told the media that they wanted "to get to the bottom of this and to make ourselves available." Within three days, the first of many lawsuits had been filed against Delta.

The Japanese legal system, as well as many European ones, does not promote this type of activity. For one, since there are relatively few attorneys, they don't descend in droves on an accident because they are too busy. In Japan, only 500 lawyers are admitted to the bar each year, and there are fewer judges per capita now than there were in 1890. Moreover, contingent fee arrangements (where the winning attorney gets one-third of judgment) are not common in Japan; they are illegal and even considered immoral in Europe. European systems require additionally that the losing party pay the winner's legal fees—a strong deterrent to the wanton litigation seen in the United States. Finally, the legal system itself may not allow for litigation on certain topics, such as product liability. Japan has never had any direct laws aimed at protecting the public from defective goods. As a result, there have only been about 100 such cases brought to Japanese courts from 1945 through 1991.[8] It remains to be seen what will happen in Japan if the legal market opens even wider. For now, however, things are likely to stay the same.[9]

universal and there is resistance among countries with different systems. All this means that one additional source of regulation that multinationals need to pay attention to is international law.

International Law

While no single body of law or code applies across borders, some sets of rules or guidelines do exist. Moreover, some important agreements have been reached over the years that can serve as relatively clear guidelines for international law. These agreements have resulted in a number of standing organizations that seek to promote international law.

GATT/WTO   The **General Agreement on Trade and Tariffs** (GATT) is one such agreement that affects commerce on an international level. GATT resulted from a conference in 1948 of fifty-three nations that were concerned with the effect of protectionism and high tariffs on the world economy and political stability. The purpose of the GATT was to extend fair and similar trading and tariff policies to all other GATT members. These members are supposed to be extended the benefits of a "most-favored-nation" status (a set of preferential tariff fees). Currently, over 140 nations are members of GATT (now under the auspices of the World Trade Organization, **WTO**), another 100 are not members but receive special trade considerations, and others are seeking membership and the membershp process can prove contentious. For example, China's

EXHIBIT 2.3

Discrimination Laws of Specific Countries

| Country | | Is Legal Protection Provided for . . . ? | | | | |
Country	Age	Race	Gender	Religion	National Origin	Marital Status
United States	yes	yes	yes	yes	yes	no
Belgium	some	yes	yes	yes	yes	yes
France	some	yes	yes	yes	yes	yes
Greece	no	yes	yes	yes	no	yes
Hong Kong	no	no	no	no	no	no
Italy	yes	yes	yes	yes	some	no
Japan	no	yes	yes	yes	yes	no
Netherlands	no	yes	yes	yes	yes	yes
Spain	no	yes	yes	yes	yes	yes
United Kingdom	no	yes	yes	no	yes	no
Venezuela	no	no	no	no	no	no

Source: Pincus/Belohlav, "Is Legal Protection Protection Provided for . . . ?" *The Academy of Management Executive,* 1996. Copyright © 1996 Academy of Management Executive. Reprinted by permission.

entry into the WTO was delayed by a public fight between the United States and the EU over insurance. The real issue was whether AIG, the largest insurance company in the United States, should continue to receive preferential treatment by China at the expense of its EU competitors.[19]

Once it becomes a member, however, a nation is required to make its tariff and other business laws consistent ("harmonize") with guidelines or it is liable to face rebukes and sanctions from the WTO. (This most-favored-nation status is not automatically extended to nations who are not full members.) In fact, importers currently consult the voluminous (over 100 pages) *Harmonized Tariff Schedule of the U.S.* if they wish to import products to the United States. WTO agreements are reworked every several years during scheduled negotiation periods (or "rounds"). Ostensibly, this multi-country negotiation process is supposed to replace a large number of bilateral trade agreements, although clearly the latter still occur. While the WTO has resulted in several positive outcomes (such as a set of international legal guidelines regarding tariffs), it has also been criticized. For one, the organization is often seen as too slow moving—perhaps because over 100 countries must be heard during the negotiation process, and because it occurs only every few years. Additionally, there are some loopholes in the WTO structure that allow countries to have disparity, not harmony, in their tariffs on a selected few products (like the U.S. has done in the past for textiles, steel, and motorcycles). Finally, despite its reputation as a bit of a bully, the WTO has also been criticized by the *Wall Street Journal* as being indecisive and not powerful enough.[20]

Many other agreements provide some legal regulation of international commerce, including the European Union, NAFTA, and others. Similarly, the United Nations and its many allied organizations (e.g., International Labor Organization, World Bank, International Monetary Fund) provide the legal and regulatory context in which global business operates. The World Bank, for example, was founded in 1944 in large part to deal with wartorn Europe. It is owned by 181 member nations but is dominated by the United States.[21] The World Bank has a loan portfolio of nearly $120 billion, with a focus now on Asia, Africa, eastern Europe, and Latin America. While the bank does not run the projects it finances—that is left to the governments that borrow the money—it does excercise control through a complex set of requirements and regulations. Finally, many feel that the use of international legal principles by the UN after the Iraqi invasion of Kuwait in 1990 signaled a major change in the appreciation and adherence of many countries to international law.[22]

Resolving international disputes   Of course, the presence of an agreement to oversee trade doesn't mean that there won't be conflict between countries. There is considerable trade and legal disagreement among countries. Resolving any disputes across borders can be and is very complex. Partly this is because the trade conflict may be viewed or treated differently by international and domestic laws. The United States, for example, has been castigated by some other countries for trying to restrict U.S. and foreign exports to nations it is in conflict with, such as Cuba or Iraq. They claim the U.S. action violates GATT regulations, whereas U.S. officials point to domestic laws and constraints that force their hand. An important question in situations like this is: Where should the issue be resolved? Which court or country has or should have jurisdiction in situations like this?

Source of jurisdiction   One of the most important recent examples of this issue happened in 1984, when one of the deadliest industrial accidents in history occurred near Bhopal, India. Union Carbide India, Limited (UCIL), an Indian corporation, operated a chemical plant near Bhopal. An accident, allegedly resulting from negligence of the operators, was catastrophic. Winds blew a lethal gas into the densely populated city and the death toll was staggering. Over 2,100 people lost their lives and nearly 200,000 other people suffered injuries—some of which were very debilitating. It is important to note that UCIL was incorporated under Indian laws and its stock was traded publicly on the Bombay Exchange. A majority of its stock (50.9%) was owned by Union Carbide Corporation (UCC), a U.S. company; 22 percent of the stock was owned by the Indian government, and the remaining 27 percent by private Indian investors.

Immediately after the accident, American lawyers traveled to India and signed up many Indian clients (all those affected, including all the plant employees, were Indian). Within four days of the accident, the first of over 100 legal actions was filed in U.S. District Court. To justify the filing of these suits in U.S. courts, the argument was made that the American parent corporation (UCC) controlled the subsidiary (UCIL). Union Carbide countered by claiming that they no longer had operational control over this or the other seven UCIL plants in India. UCC's participation via employees and plant operation was terminated at least a year before the accident. They claimed, therefore, that Indian courts were the correct forum to hear the case. All parties (UCC, the U.S. lawyers, and the victims' families) were of course, aware that any damage awards would be substantially higher in U.S. courts than in India. In addition, the fact that the lawyers would get one-third

REALITY CHECK

Anchors Away: You're in the International Law Field Now

A chat with Peter W. Davis, chief counsel, NCR Caribbean & Latin America

How exactly does someone get to the profession of international law?

It's a long story, but I came to it late. I was born in Dayton, Ohio, and hardly ever left Ohio before going to Columbia Law School. After completing my degree, I joined a firm in New York and worked on domestic antitrust matters mostly. But one Friday afternoon in 1981, a senior partner called me in his office with a request to do some basic legal research over the weekend. It was on an international legal issue, and I have to say that more than anything else I can recall, it generated some overdue reflection about my career and life choices. I concluded that 24 was too young to commit to domestic law for the rest of my life. I needed to get out and learn something about the world. I had no international background/training, so no career options were open to me. I decided one day to put law on hold. After one rewarding year at the firm and a New York bar membership, I traded my Park Avenue office for a shaved head and a Marine drill instructor at the Naval Air Station, Pensacola. I wanted to be

an intelligence officer with the U.S. Navy.

Wow, that's amazing. What was this legal matter that changed your life?

Well, it wasn't so much the event as the whole idea of expanding internationally. But it was an interesting case. The Nicaraguan Sandinista government was seeking the extradition of the surviving members of the Somoza family, then living in the U.S., to face criminal charges. Our firm had been retained to defend the Somozas against extradition, and the partner needed to know our legal position by Monday. The research I performed that weekend was the first I'd ever done that genuinely engaged me. I had to learn some geography (where's Nicaragua really?), some law (how does international extradition work? is a treaty entered into with a government still effective when it is later violently overthrown?), and some politics (has the U.S. ever extradited people with the knowledge that they would not receive due process and might well be summarily executed?). Finally, a legal project that was interesting!

Yes, I see. Can you tell us about your Navy experience also?

of the awards as their fees likely prompted the action in U.S. courts. As it turned out, the U.S. Circuit Court of Appeals ruled in 1987 that India was in fact the appropriate forum to hear the case, provided that UCC submit to the jurisdiction of Indian courts and agree to satisfy any judgment reached against them in those courts. Eventually, Union Carbide (U.S.) reached an agreement with the Indian Supreme Court to pay $480 million to the victims, a relatively small amount by U.S. standards. Although this case raises issues about whether parent companies are responsible for the activity of their foreign subsidiaries, the point here is that it is difficult to decide which country's courts and laws apply in any one situation. Often, this confusion may be the result of political issues surrounding the legal one. We now turn our attention to these political concerns.

Political Issues and Risks in International Management

As we mentioned, it is important to be aware of the prevailing legal system and methods that operate in any one country. Any legal system, however, affects and is affected by the prevailing political situation in the country. That is, the legal system can influence the political events that occur in any one country; this in turn can affect—either positively or negatively—the ability of a multinational to run its business. Many

In five years of active duty, I served with the *U.S.S. Kennedy* battle group throughout the Atlantic and Mediterranean. On duty in D.C., I drafted international agreements with foreign navies and served as a Navy liaison with Washington naval attachés. Without my naval service, and later in the CIA in the Intelligence Law Division, I don't see how I could have even broken into international law. Certainly, I wouldn't have had the insight and perspective that flowed from all this to be an effective international lawyer.

Since 1990, you've been with NCR, steadily moving up the ladder to chief counsel. Via all this experience, can you tell us what you think the three most important international issues are for your firm and what you're doing about them?

I would say that trade barriers, the rule (or lack of rule) of law, and corruption represent the three most important international issues for us. *Destructive tariffs*, duties, and other barriers to free trade persist in many countries. And your readers know all the problems the barriers can create (unfavored nations' products are disadvantaged; local firms are inordinately protected, etc.). The clearest example in my experience is in Brazil, where they continue to impose punitive duties on non-Brazilian IT products. These laws have made it almost impossible for my company, the leading worldwide manufacturer of auto-teller machines, to compete there. To deal with this problem, we—like some other

firms—are working to acquire or form alliances with local companies for manufacturing. And on the macro level management should support those organizations and policy makers that encourage free trade (e.g., President Bush's initiative to create a hemisphere free trade zone).

As for the *rule of law*, it's terribly difficult for a U.S. company to do business in a country where the rule of law is not well established. It's just too risky. When the rule of law isn't established, lawyers and business people have to craft options and possible responses. And frequently, it is necessary to move payments, deliveries, and alternative dispute resolution schemes offshore to avoid exposure to deficient local legal conditions.

Finally, I'd say *corruption* represents the third biggest legal/political challenge in international business. Despite gains in this area, corruption is an established norm in many countries, particularly in Asia, and this puts companies that don't do business this way at a serious disadvantage. While U.S. firms have to obey the Foreign Corrupt Practices Act, (something that I'm sure your students will study), other countries do not. I believe management and government should support organizations and people who work to eliminate corruption in international business. And I believe that the government should aggressively expose corruption by excluding those who engage in this from competition for U.S. contracts. They should also work to support victimized U.S. firms.

multinationals are experienced at evaluating the political environment of their home country. They are less experienced and comfortable, however, with making such judgments about other countries. Nevertheless, such predictions can be important for the firm. Obviously, it is difficult if not impossible for a multinational to run smoothly in times of great political strife, let alone during revolution or war. Less obvious, however, is the fact that there are many other less conspicuous sources of risk for international managers to consider. In this part of the chapter, we will first define political risk, give examples of various forms of risk to a business, discuss predictors of risk that a multinational may wish to use to evaluate a particular subsidiary, and then talk about ways to manage or reduce risk.

What Is Political Risk?

Political risks are the actions by groups of people or governments that have the potential to affect the immediate and/or long-term viability of a firm. This definition encompasses a large number of events—all the way from a revolution that results in confiscation of a firm's operations down to small changes in the tax code. Some of the things we will discuss directly involve legal issues (e.g., a law that does not permit exports to a certain country). We discuss them in this part of the chapter rather than earlier because, although they may be based on legal code, their enforcement or existence itself represents a form of political risk for a multinational.

Many of the factors involved in determining political risk are difficult to predict or anticipate, even for an expert in international politics. For example, many of those experts believed that Iraq would not invade Kuwait in 1990 and therefore did not consider the potential negative effects on international business operations in that country. Although the Middle East is generally viewed by many multinationals as relatively risky, there are forms of risk inherent in most areas and countries of the world. For example, the EU severely restricts Japanese auto imports and the United States has a history of tight control over foreign investment in the banking and airline industries—and there appear to be internal political reasons for such restrictions.

Since even experts have difficulty with political predictions, it would be difficult for those charged with running a business to anticipate all the political risks affecting their many international operations. Nevertheless, because of the potentially catastrophic effects of political events, management needs to do at least two things: (1) investigate political risk before entering a new market, and (2) continually monitor political events that may affect ongoing operations. Some firms, for example, maintain and consult up-to-date descriptions of the political environment in an effort to predict the negative and positive effects on their operations. In general, the extent of concern with political risk is often negatively related to the amount of investment in that country.

Types of Political Risk

What is the nature of the many political risks involved in operating in the international arena? Some feel that there are too many to classify and account for, and this may be true. Nevertheless, there have been some efforts to help companies respond by classifying political risks into manageable categories. One system divides types of threats or risks into three main categories. These include risks resulting from (1) the *political/ economic environment*, (2) prevailing *domestic economic* conditions, and (3) *external economic* relations.[23]

Exhibit 2.4 presents examples of each of these three main categories, and we will talk about each of these in turn. Before we do this, however, please note in Exhibit 2.4 that numbers are assigned to each risk variable. This effort to quantify many (but probably not all) threats to doing business in a particular country has two main purposes. First, if you sum up the total scores for each country, you can get a relatively accurate way to compare the risks of doing business internationally. Second, by quantifying specific types of risk, a company can target and work on specific threats. For example, if there are severe restrictions on money transfers from a country that your firm otherwise finds attractive, this category system can focus your entry efforts on dealing with that threat. Perhaps you can strike a deal with the government that would reduce such restrictions for a reasonable period of time. Let's look more closely at all three types of risk that a company may face.

Political/economic environment risk   First, there are many types of political/ economic variables that could present a risk to conducting business. For example, the stability of a country's government and political system are important sources of uncertainty. In recent years, we have seen the effects of dramatic and sometimes violent changes in political systems, and these changes have had major effects on the multinationals operating in those countries.

Protestors marching on the parliament building in Jakarta underscore the political instability Indonesia has experienced in recent years. © AFP/CORBIS

Perhaps the most important risk faced by firms in such situations is *nationalization.* This occurs when a government forces the transfer of ownership from private to state control. The height of this activity occurred from the 1960s through the 1970s, during which time over 1,500 firms were nationalized by about seventy different countries. Industries that were capital intensive and based on indigenous resources such as crude oil production, mining, and steel were apparently most susceptible to nationalization. The reasons for government takeover of an industry are many. For example, a new government may wish to show that it is tough—tough enough to face up to foreign powers and businesses. A government may also nationalize a company or industry because of its value to national defense or because of the power that industry may wield globally. The crude oil industry is an excellent example of this reason. At the beginning of the century most crude oil operations were foreign owned. Through the decades, especially the 1970s, oil operations were nationalized—so much so that most oil production facilities are now domestically owned.[24]

If a government nationalizes an industry or company and then compensates the multinational that is affected, then that action is called **expropriation**. Many countries (including the U.S.) recognize the right of a country to expropriate assets via a principle called **sovereign immunity**. Basically this principle holds that no nation has the right to judge or challenge the internal actions of another state, provided that state has proceeded justly.[25] Although the concept of just action is complex and open to interpretation, it appears as though a government cannot expropriate property or other assets unless three requirements are met:

- The expropriation must be for a public purpose.
- The action must be performed in a nondiscriminatory way; in particular, foreign investors must be treated the same way as domestic investors.

● Investors must be provided prompt, adequate, and effective compensation for their equity holdings.

Courts have typically ruled that if a sovereign government acts consistently toward domestic and foreign firms, then full compensation may not even be necessary.[26] The mass nationalization of the crude oil industries by many countries in the Middle East and North Africa in the 1970s is an example of expropriation since foreign and domestic firms were typically offered compensation for their losses. Although there may be long-term negative effects for a country that expropriates property (such as future reluctance to invest by foreigners), usually an agreement is reached that both parties find at least acceptable.

When nationalization discriminates against foreign firms by offering little or no compensation for loss of property, however, this action is called **confiscation**. In these circumstances, courts have typically ruled that property owners are entitled to full compensation. Regardless of a court ruling in its favor, confiscation can be devastating to a multinational and there are many recent examples to point to. For instance, in the years following World War II, governments in China and eastern Europe confiscated a great deal of private property with little or no compensation to foreign investors. The same practice was observed in Cuba following the communist takeover in 1959, and more recent examples include Chile, Peru, and Zimbabwe.

Although expropriation and confiscation were rare in the 1990s, multinationals should be aware of the risks of these events, especially because when they do occur their effect is substantial. As shown in Exhibit 2.4, however, many other political/economic events can happen. With the recent wave of nationalism occurring all over the world, civil war represents a greater risk to doing business for a multinational than it has for some time. The recent events in the former Yugoslavia have shown this, and there are many other conflicts that could have the same effects in coming years. Clearly, civil war can result in disruption of production and productivity as well as more important things like threats of injury and possibly even death to employees or their families. Likewise, radical political activity such as terrorism and other forms of violence can and have created great problems. One specific risk that a multinational takes is the threat of kidnapping. The news is full of these crimes, including the recent kidnapping of a Samsung executive in Mexico, a country one does not usually think of when terrorism is mentioned. More detail on this topic and what firms can do about it is provided in the following International Insights.

Exhibit 2.4 presents other forms of political risk. These other forms, although less sensational in their effects, are probably more common. For example, the favorability of the country's labor relations is something to consider in every country where a multinational might do business. As we'll discuss in a later chapter, labor regulations vary dramatically, and some are not favorable to business. It is important to review those relations periodically in the countries where the company already has a presence. Regardless, like the other specific examples of political threats or risks, each can be evaluated and scored by the concerned company.

Domestic economic conditions as risk factors   Exhibit 2.4 also presents a number of domestic economic criteria that could make a foreign investment more or less risky. As you can see there, domestic conditions such as per capita income and growth rate and the presence of roads, airports, and communication systems can add or reduce the amount of risk a company may face. Ordinarily, good infrastructure support reduces risk and thereby facilitates entry and expansion of business. At the same time, however, risk can present opportunity. Take, for example, the telephone

INTERNATIONAL INSIGHTS

In Harm's Way: The Danger in Doing Business Abroad

I F YOU'RE GOING OVERSEAS TO do business, you'd better leave your Rolex watch and your Armani suits at home! And you're better off renting a mid-size Ford rather than a Mercedes. Why? Well, because in addition to the many opportunities offered by the global economy, there also come some very great hazards. One very dangerous possibility is the threat of kidnapping or violence to the employees of a global company.

In fact, U.S. executives were victims of nearly 100 violent attacks in 1995 while doing business in foreign countries. According to the State Department, there were more attacks on business people than on all U.S. diplomatic or military personnel in all worldwide embassies. In fact, *Business Week* reports that the frequency of kidnapping, robberies and other crimes rose throughout the 1990s. One reason may be that Americans are seen as easy targets. Only recently have U.S. multinationals systematically provided security for their executives traveling abroad. However, the elimination of security staff is one of the first things to go when a firm is in a downsizing mode.

Even if you're not an executive, you should have reason to worry about your safety. We know that terrorists often target high-profile executives before they even set foot in a country. Increasingly, the middle- and lower-level employee is also feeling the negative effects of crime, and this is the group that is least likely to be protected by a security service. How can this group—or anyone, for that matter—travel and do business more safely? One way is to follow the advice of Chuck Vance, a former Secret Service agent who worked for three presidents and now has clients in over 1,500 companies in more than fifty countries (www.vancesecurity.com). One of Vance's best pieces of advice is "Learn how to blend in with the scenery." You may become a target simply

because you look very foreign and rich. So don't wear an expensive watch or other jewelry. And fly commercial, not the corporate jet. Criminals monitor the airports and use this as a marker for a good target. Further, rent a car common in the country you are visiting; don't take a big limo or some other luxury car. If you are one of Vance's famous clients and are willing to spend the money—like Henry Kissinger, General Schwarzkopf, or Salman Rushdie—he will make sure there is no trouble ahead of time. Vance Inc. agents will travel to the country in advance of your visit to scout the airport, your proposed routes, and your hotel. If you can't afford these services, Vance recommends that you do your own homework. You can call any or all of these three groups: (1) the regional security officer at the U.S. embassy in the country you're visiting, (2) the State Department's Overseas Security Advisory Council for free tips (http://travel.state.gov/index.html or call 202-663-0533), or (3) the U.S. Commerce Department for more country-specific advice (http://home.doc.gov/; 800-USA-TRAD).

One last piece of advice from Vance: "Think like the terrorist. If I were going to knock me on the head, where would I do it? When would I strike?" This means that once you've landed, stay alert and vary your daily routine. Don't eat every night at the same bistro at 8 p.m. or go jogging every morning at 7 a.m. Of course, not every business trip overseas is terribly dangerous, but you have, potentially, put yourself in harm's way. Countries that make Vance's danger list include Colombia and Peru, where drug cartels and terrorists present problems, as well as Kenya, Nigeria, the Philippines, Russia, South Africa, and increasingly China. History shows that wherever international business goes, bandits are sure to follow![27]

infrastructure in Hungary, where in the early 1990s there were only ninety-six phone lines per 1,000 people (the U.S. rate is 545 per 1,000), and the installation of a new line required a five-year wait. Before they were recently purchased by Qwest, USWest—a regional phone operating company headquartered in Denver—had entered the Hungarian market with their cellular division. Business boomed; they immediately received over 10,000 requests for service.[28] This positive outcome highlights the fact that risk evaluation systems should not be applied thoughtlessly or without creativity.

Other domestic risk factors include the passage of legal regulations on environmental pollution. The enforcement of such laws could restrict how a multinational may operate in a foreign country. In turn, these restrictions almost always increase operation

EXHIBIT 2.4

A Method for Rating Political Risk across Countries

Type of Risk	Examples	Minimum Score	Maximum Score
Political/economic environment	1. Stability of political system	3	14
	2. Possibility of internal conflicts	0	14
	3. External threats to stability	0	12
	4. Degree of economic control	5	9
	5. Dependability as trading partner	4	12
	6. Provides constitutional guarantees	2	12
	7. Effectiveness of public administration	3	12
	8. Quality of labor relations/social peace	3	15
Domestic economic conditions	9. Size of population	4	8
	10. Per capita income	2	10
	11. Economic growth, last 5 years	2	7
	12. Potential growth, next 3 years	3	10
	13. Inflation, last 2 years	2	10
	14. Openness of cap market to foreigners	3	7
	15. Availability of high-quality labor force	2	8
	16. Ability to hire foreign nationals	2	8
	17. Availability of energy resources	2	14
	18. Regulations on environment/pollution	4	8
	19. Degree of infrastructure development	2	14
External economic relations	20. Import restrictions	2	10
	21. Export restrictions	2	10
	22. Foreign investment restrictions	3	9
	23. Ability to enter into partnerships	3	9
	24. Protection for brands, trademarks	3	9
	25. Restrictions on money transfers	2	8
	26. Currency revaluation previous 5 years	2	7
	27. Balance of payments condition	2	9
	28. Amount of oil/energy imports	3	14
	29. International financial standing	3	8
	30. Currency exchange restrictions	2	8

Source: Adapted from Dichtl, E., & Koeglmayr, H.G. (1986). Country Risk Ratings. *Management International Review,* 26, 4–11.

costs to the company. For example, in Germany, companies must abide by rigid packaging laws when selling and shipping their products. This "green dot" law requires businesses to do two things: (1) accept back from consumers all excess packing materials, and (2) encourage recycling of the materials by alerting customers about this option with a green dot on the material and with prominent recycling facilities at the point of purchase.

In Germany, as in the United States, there are also many restrictive environmental laws that affect the production and disposal of industrial wastes. In some countries, however, environmental laws are almost nonexistent. Partially this absence of regulation is because developing countries are struggling to improve economic conditions and often wish to do as little as possible to discourage foreign investment. As a result, these countries may become places for waste-producing countries to dump this material. To deal with this problem, over fifty countries became signatories to the Basel Convention, an agreement on the international transport of hazardous wastes. A key element of the agreement is that informed consent about the movement of the toxic waste must be given and permission received from all countries through which it passes. The exporting country cannot move the waste until they receive written permission, obtain insurance coverage against damage, and enact domestic laws making it a crime to violate the agreement.

The following International Insights reviews the environmental issues that are present in China, a country that is undergoing dramatic industrial growth. As this material illustrates, many countries are increasingly concerned with the effect of industry on their environment. In addition to the direct costs to firms doing business, there are also indirect effects of concern for the environment. Because of several major environmental disasters, such as at Bhopal, the meltdown of the Chernobyl nuclear plant in Ukraine, and the Exxon-Valdez oil spill off Alaska, awareness of these important issues has intensified. Some countries like Germany even have major political parties organized around environmental issues. Thus, there are direct and indirect forms of risk associated with this factor. Clearly, these affect the business decisions of multinationals. A consumer products company may build its plant in Mexico rather than in the United States (their intended market) because U.S. pollution control regulations require expensive equipment. Similarly, a chemical company may manufacture in Indonesia rather than in Germany because of the extensive industry restrictions. These examples raise ethical and other issues, such as whether a multinational should capitalize on weaker restrictions in another country, a topic discussed in the next chapter. For now, we note that the relative presence or absence of legal restrictions in any one country is often considered in an overall risk rating system like that presented in Exhibit 2.4.

External economic relations as risk factors   As also shown in Exhibit 2.4, a large number of factors influence how a country relates economically to another country. Further, whereas some of the earlier factors we considered were quite rare (like civil war), virtually every country restricts its external economic relations in several ways. For example, many countries have restrictions on imports, usually in the form of **tariffs**. A tariff is a fee paid by an exporter to the country of import. A tariff, therefore, would increase the price of a foreign product or service relative to the domestic counterpart. Through the use of import taxes like these, therefore, a country can partially restrict imports and provide protection for domestic industry. This type of restriction presents a risk for the foreign multinational.

Tariffs are not the only way imports can be restricted. One country may wish to **limit imports** in order to force another country to expand its markets to accept more of its goods. The United States, for example, restricts the number of automobiles that Japan may import in order to pressure Japan into purchasing more American-made components. Japan has restricted the latter via subtle, informal measures. Regardless, these limits may also act to increase the price of the product. The EU also limits the import of Japanese autos to a percentage of the total autos sold in the EU. Finally, a country may restrict imports when they are perceived as a threat to the health or safety of its citizens. In 1996 and again in 2001, British (and other European) cattle were affected by "mad cow disease"—an affliction that produces many nervous system symptoms and eventually death. Although the British argued that the disease did not affect the harvesting of the beef, many countries (including EU countries) temporarily

INTERNATIONAL INSIGHTS

The Greening of the River Huai: Environmental Issues in Newly Industrialized China

IT APPEARS THAT MANY NEWLY industrialized countries are facing many of the same environmental problems the United States faced after its rapid period of industrial growth—one of which is environmental pollution. This list of countries would certainly have to include Mexico and the not so newly industrialized, but newly politicized Russia. Topping this list, however, is the People's Republic of China.

Huainan, China, a big city on the Huai River in Anhui Province about 200 miles from Shanghai, has lots of problems. Workers at the Xicheng paper factory arrived one day in June 1996 to find a warning posted on the gates: "Factory closed by order of the Environmental Protection Bureau." Like many formal edicts in China, this one was ignored and workers went in and began their daily shift. Later that afternoon, however, the presses jerked to a halt and all the lights went out. Apparently, this time it was for real, and shortly after that a delegation of officials showed up and told them that this time there was no way out.

Paper mills like this one on the river are responsible for generating much of the toxic sludge that has turned the once beautiful Huai River to the color of coal. When environmentalists won an order to shut down nearly 1,000 plants in China, they had a rare "green" moment. It is rare because so many environmental hazards pile up every day in China. One-fifth of China's river water can no longer be used to irrigate land. Most everyone in urban settings buys and drinks bottled water. Hotels catering to foreigners—even the five-star variety, like the Shangri-La resort hotels in Hangzhou and Shanghai—caution visitors not to use the water or even to brush their teeth with it. In fact, 82 percent of Chinese rivers are polluted, and 20 percent are not even usable for

irrigation. Most coal is burned without emission controls, and the Chinese urban population breathes polluted air that exceeds World Health Organization safety levels by anywhere from four to ten times. Vaclav Smil, a China specialist at the University of Manitoba in Canada, estimates that the problems resulting from environmental pollution (from lost farmland to higher cancer rates) cost China as much as 15 percent of its GNP. This proportion is much larger than in older industrialized economies.

As far as the Huai River is concerned, Chinese environmentalists have made it a priority in order to symbolize their concerns about the country as a whole. For years, many paper mills, printing and dye plants, and other factories sprang up along the river. Their growth was largely unchecked and their toxic discharge flowed untreated into the Huai. Many of the firms were small, but they generated jobs in addition to pollution. So they were tolerated if not encouraged. To Liang Congjie, an environmentalist in Beijing, it is a sign of progress that some of those factories have now been closed—in some cases, with doors chained and windows boarded. Still, Mr. Liang notes that it took years to make this progress and he fears operations may just move to another location or province. Nevertheless, he says, "I consider it the beginning of a turning point. China needs decades before it outgrows the first stage of wealth creation, like the United States one hundred years ago."

The reactions to the closures are mixed. One young farmer said his elder brother lost his job at the mill because of the closures, but he also understands the government's actions. "You can't even take a bath in this water now without smelling bad. It wasn't that way when I was a kid."[29]

banned the import of beef raised in Britain. British farmers incurred great losses as a result of this ban and eventually destroyed nearly half of the cows in Britain. In the United States, foreign producers of food must receive FDA approval regarding their hygiene standards prior to importing their products.

Export controls or restrictions are important concerns for international managers. There are many types of export restrictions. For example, *sanctions, embargoes,* and *boycotts* are examples of limitations that can affect an international business. All three controls can also cover import restrictions, and many times these terms are used interchangeably. All three refer to actions by a country that constrain free trade for political rather than economic reasons, but they differ in their intended magnitude. **Sanctions,**

or sets of specific restraints involving trade, can take many different forms. For example, a country may cancel its preferential tariff fees for another country (most-favored-nation status), restrict access to computers and other high technology, or prohibit the export of certain weapons. Some of these sanctions were used by the United States against China after that government's violence against the pro-democracy movement in 1989, and again in Haiti in 1994 in an effort to restore a democratically elected government; they are still levied against Iraq as of 2002.

An **embargo** is an all-out prohibition of trade with another country—not just commerce in several specific or critical goods and services. Usually these are imposed in order to protect national security or to promote a certain foreign policy, and they have been used by the United States since the Revolutionary War. Often embargoes are instituted during times of war, but they are erected during peacetime as well. The president of the United States has considerable discretion to enact an embargo. The president can direct the Department of Commerce's Bureau of Export Administration to add a country to an embargo list based on the following criteria:

- The extent to which the country's actions affect U.S. national security
- The country's current/future relations with the United States or its allies or enemies
- Whether the country is or is not communist
- The country's nuclear, chemical, and biological weapon policy and degree of compliance with world agreements on these weapons[30]

Based on these criteria, the United States currently has designated Cuba, Iran, Iraq, Libya, North Korea, Sudan, and Syria as countries for which these broad set of controls currently apply.[31] The embargo against Cuba, for example, has been in place since 1961, when the attempted invasion of U.S.-backed forces was crushed by Castro. An extremely strong anti-Castro lobby in the United States has kept this embargo in place despite some efforts to remove the trade ban.

Critics have pointed out that the use of embargoes (and sanctions) are not that effective. For example, an analysis of the nearly fifty different uses of sanctions and embargoes to achieve political goals from 1970 to 1983 showed that few were successful.[32] Partly this lack of success resulted from the diffuse focus of the sanctions, some dealing with improvement of human rights and others as protests against terrorism. But mainly the restrictions were ineffective because other countries filled the void left by the sanctioning country. In fact, this is one of the major complaints from the business community about such restrictions. American businesspeople sometimes object by saying, "Why should we be penalized by our government from doing business in China because their human rights record is not up to our standards?" They maintain that U.S. multinationals are unfairly punished because American sanctions are often not observed by other countries. Thus, South Korea or Japan, while expressing genuine outrage over China's policies, may continue to do business and even take advantage of opportunities created by American sanctions.

The relevant U.S. government agencies (such as the Departments of Commerce, Defense, and State) who are responsible for developing and implementing sanctions and embargoes are familiar with and probably sympathetic to these complaints about controls. The Commerce Department (via its Bureau of Export Administration) is in fact charged with issuing licenses for exports, some of which may override existing sanctions. A business must file an application for an export license, the first step of which is to properly classify for the government the commodity that is proposed for export. This is a complex process that involves classifying the type of product, where the product is going, and the nature of the restrictions that are in place. An application for the export of scuba gear and outboard engines to Iran, for example, would not be permitted because of fears of attacks on oil tankers in the Gulf.[33] After receiving an application, the Department of Commerce then has ninety days to issue or deny a license to export the product(s), although approval recently has averaged only about five days.

The application for license, like a tax return, is a self-report of one's behavior. As such, as with a tax return, there are some applicants who don't tell the truth. One example is those who mislead about the nature of their product or where it is going. An infamous example of this occurred in 1986, when the U.S. Navy determined that Soviet submarines were somehow able to move without any detectable noise. Over the next several months, it was revealed that the Soviets had acquired advanced equipment from Toshiba in violation of Japanese and U.S. export laws. It was discovered that Toshiba received permission to export because they had deceived the Japanese government by changing the description of the exported equipment. Because of this threat to security, the United States reacted strongly. Government contracts totaling over $200 million with Toshiba were canceled, and Congress banned the company from doing business with the government for three years. The Japanese government reacted lightly to the infractions, suspending the sentences given to Toshiba executives and imposing only a $16,000 fine.

More common but much less known, however, is the problem of **diversion**. This term refers to the use of an export license to provide materials to a third party not included on the license. For example, a U.S. oil company may seek a license to export oil field equipment to one country, who would in turn send the equipment to Tripoli—in violation of the U.S. export embargo on Libya. This situation is probably more common than we would like to think, and its relatively high frequency has led courts to rule that the burden is on the exporter in these cases. That is, it is the exporter's responsibility to screen and proceed diligently with foreign buyers regarding their intended uses of the product. There are very extensive civil and criminal penalties in place for those found in violation of export laws.

Even if you proceed with good faith, file a legitimate application for license, and then go to great lengths to investigate your customer, you still may be denied a license. Most likely this will be because of the national importance of the export controls that have been implemented (like weapons technology). Nevertheless, you still have an avenue of appeal. You could request that the Secretary of Commerce determine the foreign availability of your product. If there is a non-U.S. source of the product that is comparable in quality, you may still be granted a license to export despite the controls that are in place. Almost certainly, however, your application and appeal will be denied if your business involves exporting controlled weaponry (such as missile technology or nuclear equipment and materials). Supercomputers are also highly controlled because of their strategic significance. There are many global agreements on the trade in these items, and several important organizations—like COCOM (Coordinating Committee for Multilateral Export Control)—are devoted to the control of such exports. COCOM, in particular, was formed in 1949 to prevent the Soviets from acquiring technology that could lead to a military advantage. The organization grew to seventeen members and many affiliates, but with the breakup of the Soviet Union the perceived need for the group faded and the organization has since been disbanded.

As we have said, export controls—such as sanctions, embargoes and control lists—can often be ineffective because the products can be provided by companies in other countries who are not so constrained. If the issue is important enough, a set of countries may wish to go one step further to restrict trade by enacting a **boycott**. If sanctions and embargoes represent a unilateral unwillingness to engage in trade (such as the U.S. against Cuba), a boycott is a multilateral or collaborative effort to do the same thing. Examples of the collaboration of many countries to try to restrict trade are the COCOM group just mentioned as well as the international coalition formed to confront Iraq's invasion of Kuwait in 1990. This coalition has survived through 2002, although there are signs that it may be breaking up. Boycotts thus have the same purpose as sanctions, embargoes, and other controls; they are simply more extreme in their scope. Because of the collaborative nature of boycotts, they tend to be more effective than export controls established by only one country. This also means that boycotts are very much more difficult to organize and implement. The boycott of Iraq was difficult to organize because it involved putting traditional enemies (Israel and Jordan or Saudi Arabia) on the same side against Iraq, a country with whom some of them have traditionally been friendly.

One other problem with boycotts is that unless the organizing is very complete (like the Gulf War Alliance), they can polarize sides against one another. An example of this situation is the boycott instituted against Israel in December 1954 by the League of Arab States. The League (currently composed of twenty-one nations) agreed that companies that traded with Israel could be blacklisted and not permitted to do business with League members. Because of its close political ties with Israel, the United States enacted **antiboycott laws** that prohibit American firms from complying with or otherwise supporting the boycott, by refusing to do business with Israel or a blacklisted firm. In fact, courts have ruled that just by returning an Arab League questionnaire that sought information about business relations with Israel, Briggs and Stratton Corporation was in violation of the law.[34] Given the volatile situation in the Middle East, it remains to be seen what will happen regarding business risk for firms via the boycott. After the Gulf War, some Arab countries (like Kuwait) resumed doing business with Israel. Although the nearly fifty-year boycott may be crumbling, as of now it still presents a risk to U.S. business that other countries do not face. The following International Insights on Baxter International, a U.S. multinational, shows that the penalties for violating this law still include large fines and prohibition on export licenses.

To summarize, it is important to consider the extent of export controls as risk factors in international business. Exports are significant parts of the economy of every country; they provide a much needed foreign exchange and are the source of many jobs. But they are only one (important) example of external economic risk factors. In Exhibit 2.4, we presented many other types of risk involved, including **restrictions on foreign investment**. For example, one risk factor is the presence of restrictions on the extent of foreign investment present in a particular country. Most EU countries, for example, restrict the ownership of television and radio stations to nationals. Germany gives preference to companies that are majority-owned by its nationals when awarding licenses to broadcast. The United States requires foreign ownership of radio and TV stations to be limited to 25 percent, whereas Greece and Portugal restrict such ownership to 25 and 15 percent, respectively. Typically, restrictions like these are imposed to prevent foreign control of critical industries (e.g., finance, communications, etc.). Clearly, these restrictions increase the risk of doing business since they prevent the foreign multinational from having sole control of the operation of a firm. Interestingly, they have not stopped Australian, British, and Japanese firms from investing in such restricted U.S. industries, although these firms probably weighted the risks against potential rewards.

One of the biggest external risks that companies face is the lack of **legal protection for their products and trademarks** in a foreign country. The most common legal

INTERNATIONAL INSIGHTS

Baxter International and the Arab Boycott of Israel

BAXTER INTERNATIONAL IS A Chicago-based manufacturer of hospital supplies. They do business in many different countries, including Israel. For years, however, they wished to expand their business to the lucrative Middle East market; by all estimates this market seemed destined to produce sales in the billions of dollars in the upcoming years. Over the years, they tried a number of strategies to enter this market, including the acquisition of firms that already had a presence there. For example, Baxter spent $53 million in 1982 to acquire Medcom Inc., a New York-based manufacturer of hospital supplies that had close relations with Saudi Arabia. Their hope was to exploit MedCom's connections with the Saudis to kick-start their Middle East business. After losing money for over a year, Saudi government officials told Baxter executives to "stop wasting their time in the Middle East," according to a company document obtained by the *Wall Street Journal*. After several more years in the red, Baxter sold MedCom in 1986 for just $4 million—or just 7 percent of what it had paid for the company. What was the problem here?

The problem, as it turned out, was Baxter's Israeli business. As a result of this business, Baxter was on the Arab League boycott list and the Saudis wanted nothing to do with Baxter. Being shut out of the Middle East, however, bothered Baxter executives. The recently gained riches from oil sales in the 1970s and 1980s promised rich rewards for the company that gained an early footing there. Baxter executives repeatedly discussed entry strategies with a number of Arab countries, like Syria. They also spoke with prominent Syrian lawyers and specialists on the boycott, some even at their Illinois headquarters. These talks did not result in any concrete agreements. In 1988, Baxter suddenly sold their intravenous fluids plant in Israel, although they claim they had been seeking a buyer for some time. And they almost simultaneously announced plans to build a similar plant in Syria in a joint venture operation with the Syrian army. Within the year, Baxter was dropped from the Arab blacklist.

Although these events were noted by prominent observers, they may have just been seen as a very unusual coincidence by skeptical observers had it not been for some of Baxter's former executives who criticized Baxter's actions. Based on their testimony and other evidence, the Department of Justice filed criminal charges against Baxter. The U.S. grand jury heard evidence about Baxter's sale of discounted hospital supplies to Syria, allegedly as a bribe for being removed from the list. Later, the Department of Commerce also filed civil suits against the company, and shareholders followed with further legal action. In 1993, Baxter plead guilty to the criminal charges, paid a large fine ($6.6 million), and suffered other penalties via their violation of the antiboycott law. For example, the government slapped a two-year ban on exports to Syria and Saudi Arabia, forcing a reduction in purchases by Baxter's U.S. customers. Under intense criticism, the Baxter CEO was even forced to resign his position on the board of trustees at Yale University.[35]

---

protections are the use of patents, trademarks, and copyrights. A number of international agreements are in place to provide protection. The Paris Convention, for example, is a set of international guidelines recognized by nearly eighty countries. Ultimately, however, a multinational must rely on the enforcement of laws within a country to protect its products and intellectual property rights. To comply with WTO requirements, in the year 2005 India will again begin to honor international pharmaceutical patents—something it has not done since the early 1970s. Since that time, market share of foreign drug firms has dropped considerably, but with regulations on the horizon foreign direct investment is again pouring into India.[36] Nevertheless, if the reward is great enough, a firm may wish to take the risk of operating without legal protection altogether or run the risk in a country where the enforcement is lax at best.

Take, for example, the Chinese market. Firms that enter China are often required by the government to reveal the critical design features or recipes of their products.[37] Professor Kenneth DeWoskin, a China expert at the University of Michigan School of

Business, says, "Chinese research and design institutes look for the best technology in the country and spread it around. They also examine plans and specifications of new ventures, so there's bound to be some leakage."[38] Clearly, there is a good deal of "leakage," and the losses extend beyond the entertainment and computer industry. For example, after DuPont introduced its Londax herbicide in China, it decided to build a $25 million plant in Shanghai to produce the chemical. By then, however, a state-owned company jumped into the market with a much cheaper knockoff of Londax. Likewise, shortly after Pilkington opened a plant in China to make glass, a state glass factory sent an order for production equipment to Germany—complete with detailed and obviously pirated plans that were emblazoned with Pilkington's name! And in plain sight of police on main streets in Guangzhou and Shanghai, Chinese music fans can pick up the latest popular music CDs or Microsoft Office for about $1.50. The U.S. Trade Representative's office says, "Anyone can walk into a store in Beijing and buy a pirated copy of Microsoft's Windows. The store simply copies it onto a few blank diskettes while you wait." It's not just products, either—protecting a brand name in the China market is difficult at best. A bogus Chinese breakfast cereal product called Kongalu Cornstrips has a trademark and packaging identical to that of Kellogg's cornflakes. A small Chinese computer manufacturer, called Mr. Sun, has used Sun Microsystem's trademark for all its machines. And mineral water drinkers in China enjoy Pabst Blue Ribbon Water.[39]

Despite the danger of product piracy once its critical features are revealed, many companies move into the Chinese market anyway. Coca-Cola is one firm, however, that steadfastly refuses such revelations and thus has been careful in China. And because of a similar restriction in India, they have left that country all together. Coca-Cola quit India after the government demanded that they reveal their secret recipe and transfer other technical information to local management.[40] Likewise, two years of negotiating for an important minivan venture between Chrysler and the Chinese government fell apart at the last minute when China demanded that Chrysler reveal its manufacturing techniques.

In general, research shows that the presence of laws protecting intellectual property rights has a positive impact on foreign direct investment and that this is especially the case among developing countries.[41] Piracy, the software variety in particular, seems to happen in many places, not just China or other developing nations. For example, the *Wall Street Journal* recently reported on a raid by the Spanish police at a Madrid monastery where Jesuit priests trained their students in computers—relying mostly on pirated software.[42] Exhibit 2.5 shows that while China is a big problem, there are other problem markets (including the U.S. domestic market, where over 35 percent of software is pirated and where the cost is the greatest). Given the importance that knowledge plays in the economy, some analysts have targeted intellectual property as America's main competitive advantage in the next century.[43] Thus, the ability to preserve those property rights may become an even more important risk factor for the U.S. economy in the near future.

Summary of risk factors   As we have demonstrated, there are a large number of legal and political risk factors associated with doing business in a foreign country. One of the pluses of using a category system like the one we presented in Exhibit 2.4 is that this large number can be itemized and evaluated. A firm considering a big investment in a foreign country may wish to systematically weight all these factors themselves or use information provided by companies specializing in risk assessment. Exhibit 2.6 presents the top ten riskiest and least risky countries in which to do business (out of nearly 130 countries). China, for example, had an overall risk ranking of 32 relative to

EXHIBIT 2.5

Losses from Software Piracy for U.S. Firms

Country	Loss (in U.S. $millions)	Piracy Rate
China	527	98
France	771	57
Germany	1,900	50
Japan	2,000	67
South Korea	546	78
Taiwan	620	70
United States	2,900	35

Source: Adapted from Greenberger, R.S. (1996). Software theft extends well beyond China. *Wall Street Journal.* May 20, p. A1.

the other 130 countries. Despite this rating and the large number of risks it represents, many countries are rushing to invest in China. These facts show that a firm must still make a judgment about the overall risk of doing business. If the overall score is indeed too high, a multinational might drop that country from consideration unless the risk can be managed or reduced in some way.

Managing or Dealing with Political Risk

One advantage of quantifying risk is the ability to make better decisions about entering or avoiding a country or whether to scale back existing operations in a particularly risky country. Leaving or scaling back are not, however, your only options. Another advantage of using a rating scheme such as the one discussed earlier is that serious sources of risk can be isolated. It may then be possible for a firm to influence or manage some of the factors that cause the risk. Take, for example, a situation where labor relations are shaky at best. If this is a critical risk factor, then the multinational must recognize the fact that risk is not static. Good management might be able to deal with poor labor relations by making some concessions.

Categorizing risk reduction   There are a large number of ways a multinational could potentially stave off risk. In fact, there are probably as many methods to reduce risk as there are sources of risk. For our purposes, however, we can classify all these techniques into a more manageable set of categories. For example, there are **defensive/reactive strategies** that a multinational could use to deal with risk.[44] These types of methods try to keep company operations or other assets out of the reach of the risk factor—such as a hostile government. There are also **linking/merging strategies**. These usually entail methods by which a firm tries to get closer to the risky country, perhaps

EXHIBIT 2.6

The Ten Least and Most Risky Countries in Which to Do Business

Countries with the Most Business Risk		Countries with the Least Business Risk	
1.	Ecuador	1.	Luxembourg
2.	Iraq	2.	Norway
3.	Cuba	3.	Singapore
4.	Russia	4.	Finland
5.	Myanmar	5.	Switzerland
6.	Sudan	6.	Netherlands
7.	Vietnam	7.	Ireland
8.	Cameroon	8.	Denmark
9.	Pakistan	9.	Brunei
10.	Nigeria	10.	Canada

Source: "The Ten Least and Most Risky Countries in which to Do Business" from www.prsgroup.com/commonhtml/toorank.html. Copyright ©PRS Group. Used with permission.

even making itself indispensable to the local economy. Each of these type of strategies can also be direct, in that it tries to take on the problem in a head-on way, such as by legal action. The strategy could also be indirect, approaching the risk in a roundabout way, with hopes that in the long run risk will be reduced. Exhibit 2.7 presents some examples of each of the four types of risk management.

Examples of risk reduction   Let's look at a few examples of each of these strategies. A type of **direct/defensive risk reduction** is to make operations in the target country dependent on your operations in one or more other countries that are less risky. This dependency allows your firm to preserve control over key supplies, components, and critical technology that are necessary to run the subsidiary, and it can have a number of positive effects on the firm's exposure to risk. For example, operation dependency would make your subsidiary less attractive for expropriation by host government X. This is because the plant could not operate without supplies you provide via a plant in country Y. This strategy would also leave your firm less open to risks of trademark or copyright theft if critical technology was deployed in another country. Thus, a multinational can reap multiple benefits from one action, a characteristic typical of many of the risk management strategies listed in Exhibit 2.7.

A firm can also use several different risk management techniques simultaneously and may also wish to use some **direct/linking strategies**. For example, a multinational

EXHIBIT 2.7

A Classification of Approaches to Managing Risk

	Direct	Indirect
Defensive/Reactive	● Legal action ● Make operations dependent on parent company ● Control makeup of management	● Risk insurance ● Contingency planning methods ● Home country government pressure
Linking/Merging	● Long-term agreements (e.g., NAFTA) ● Joint ventures ● Promoting host goals	● Lobbying of foreign governments ● Becoming good corporate citizen to host country

may wish to enter into long-term agreements with a foreign country that specifies treatment of its subsidiary, and the home country may do the same. The North American Free Trade Agreement that we discussed earlier is one recent example of this method. The option to enter into joint ventures (discussed in Chapters 8 and 9) may be available; in this case, the subsidiary is already jointly owned by either the host government or a firm headquartered in the host country. In situations like this, a multinational has less equity at risk and other national firms share a good deal of the risk.

Concurrently, a multinational may also wish to use a set of indirect methods. It may purchase political risk insurance as an **indirect/defensive strategy**. Political risk insurance is an indirect strategy because it does nothing to deal with or alter the risk; it simply tries to protect the firm if and when the risk materializes. Several private firms provide insurance to cover some risks that may be realized in doing international business. In the United States, a federal agency, the Overseas Private Investment Corporation (OPIC), also provides similar coverage. Started in 1971 in order to promote private American business investment in developing countries, OPIC is self-sustaining, has recorded a positive net income every year of operation, and runs at no net cost to U.S. taxpayers. Currently, the insurance programs are available for new and expanding business in over 140 countries.

Risk insurance covers some, but certainly not all of the risks we discussed earlier. A company can purchase protection against expropriation and confiscation of its foreign enterprise or coverage for property and income losses caused by political violence. For example, the effects of declared or undeclared wars, civil war, revolutions, and many types of civil strife (such as terrorism and sabotage) are covered; OPIC compensates the investor's share of income losses resulting from the political violence and other risk factors. A multinational can even purchase an offsite rider to the policy that compensates for losses resulting from damage outside its facility that affect its business (such as railways, power stations, and suppliers). Finally, OPIC also protects the multinational against currency inconvertibility. This is not insurance against currency devaluation; the company has to assume this risk itself. Instead, investors are compensated if they suffer new currency restrictions that prevent the conversion and transfer of profits from their foreign investment. In general, this insurance is very comprehensive and can help many firms overcome their reluctance to deal with risk factors in a foreign operation or investment.[45] You will learn a lot more about OPIC by completing the exercise at the end of this chapter.

As a precaution, this McDonald's in Karachi, Pakistan covered its name sign in late 2001 after U.S. military action commenced in neighboring Afghanistan. © AFP/CORBIS

Other examples of indirect/defensive strategies are presented in Exhibit 2.7. For example, although many firms clearly recognize the risk of doing business in a certain country is high, they are willing to take on the risk if a set of contingency plans provides a viable way to manage it. Or a firm could gradually increase its investment in a foreign operation while appealing to its government to pressure the other host government. This is now a common practice in Japan, where American automakers (among other industries) perceive that the risks of closed markets and opportunities can be altered by pressuring the U.S. administration to get concessions from the Japanese.

Finally, a multinational can use indirect/linking strategies to remove or reduce some forms of risk. One way it can do this is by making itself a "good corporate citizen." For example, the multinational could contribute to local charities, support public projects, or otherwise promote its good deeds. Clearly, this strategy involves merging with the local community as opposed to pulling away, and it is indirect because it is hoped that the goodwill generated by the donations will eventually spread to the company itself. It has been a traditional strategy for many multinationals, such as IBM. And lately Japanese firms have dramatically increased their philanthropic activity in the United States because of the large amount of capital investment it has in this country. Finally, lobbying is a typical method of possible risk reduction. In the United States, special interest groups in the areas of steel, automobiles, textiles, and computer chips have been adept at gaining import restrictions that reduce the risk in their businesses.[46] Conversely, foreign firms long ago recognized the important role that lobbying plays in the operation of the U.S. federal government. Indeed, the number of registered lobbyists to the federal government has grown from about 7,000 in 1991 to over 15,000 in 1999. Alternatively, a government itself could invest in a venture in another country, as Thailand is now doing with its plans to open over 1,000 Thai restaurants in the United States.[47]

Investing in risky countries These are just a few of the many methods that firms use to reduce their risks in doing international business. Apparently, these methods are enough to convince firms to make what would otherwise be considered unwise investments. As mentioned, the situation in China now is a good example. China is rated by several groups as a relatively risky place to invest, yet foreign capital is rushing into the country. Many of these foreign enterprises have tried to temper their risk by entering into joint ventures and by lobbying their own and the Chinese government.

This situation is equally true in eastern Europe, where companies feel that they face a variety of problems and risks. A recent survey of eighty-seven companies that have invested in eastern Europe suggests that most of the challenges of doing business in these formerly communist countries involve political, economic, and legal uncertainties or risks.[48] Just as with China, however, these risks have apparently failed to deter Western investors. More than half report that they are increasing their stakes in eastern Europe. And even though they report that the former Soviet Union is fraught with risks, 52 percent say they are still considering this area for investment. This trend suggests that for some firms quantitative analysis (as in risk assessment) is helpful, but it does not always and directly lead to a decision. There is not always a clear link between the results of the analysis and the decision to be made. This is even truer when the decision concerns ethical or social responsibility issues. These issues are the subject of our next chapter.

Chapter Summary

We reviewed several of the most important legal systems in operation around the world today, including the *civil law*, *common law*, and *Islamic law* systems. Each system has different implications for commerce that takes place under its jurisdiction. In common law systems, for example, businesses can experience a good deal of litigation because the continual interpretation of statutes is typical in such systems. The other systems have their own characteristics and constraints.

Laws operate (or sometimes fail to operate) within a particular political system, and a new political regime can dramatically change the legal system. So we highlighted the importance of these issues above and beyond the rule of law. We also showed that the amount of *political risk* incurred by a multinational can have major negative effects. Political risk can result from a large number of events or actions taken by governments or groups of people. Examples of political/economic risk faced by a multinational include *nationalization* and *expropriation* of its assets by a foreign government, each of which can have disastrous consequences for a firm. A variety of domestic economic conditions can also affect a multinational's business, including a lack of infrastructure and the enactment of strict environmental laws. Finally, a third set of risk factors include those external economic relations one country has with another. These include *tariffs* and a variety of export controls (e.g., *sanctions, embargoes,* and others). We provided an example of the U.S. export control system and its complexities to illustrate our point. We also discussed other important risks that businesses face and how their impact can be calibrated.

We finished the chapter with a discussion of one of the most important points of all—what a multinational can and should do after it acknowledges the risks it faces. The options include strategies of *direct risk reduction* (e.g., negotiating with the foreign government) and/or *indirect* efforts to stave off potentially catastrophic effects if the risk materializes (e.g., purchasing U.S. government–backed risk insurance). Finally, we recognize that while some multinational actions might be both legally consistent and politically astute or expedient, the action might still be inconsistent with company or society values.

Income per person

GNI per capita, 2000

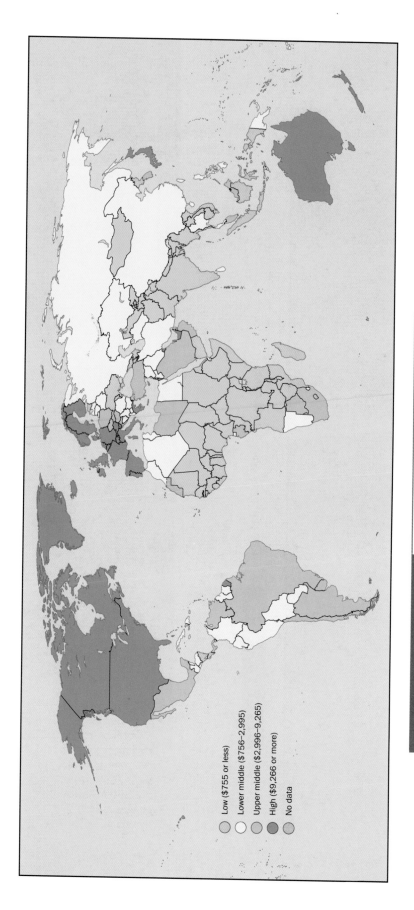

Gross national income (formerly referred to as GNP)—the sum of gross value added by resident producers (plus taxes less subsidies) and net primary income from nonresident sources—divided by midyear population.

Legend (map):
- Low ($755 or less)
- Lower middle ($756–2,995)
- Upper middle ($2,996–9,265)
- High ($9,266 or more)
- No data

GNI per capita, 2000, $

- East Asia & Pacific — 1,060
- Europe & Central Asia — 2,010
- Latin America & Caribbean — 3,670
- Middle East & North Africa — 2,090
- South Asia — 440
- Sub-Saharan Africa — 470
- High income — 27,680

(scale: 0, 10,000, 20,000, 30,000)

Distribution of world population among economies grouped by GNI per capita

- Low ($755 or less)
- Lower middle ($756–2,995)
- Upper middle ($2,996–9,265)
- High ($9,266 or more)

Pie chart values: 41%, 15%, 11%, 34%

GNI per capita, 2000, $

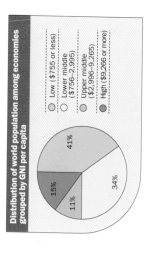

	Number of Economies	GNP $ billions 2000	Population millions 2000	GNP per capita $ 2000
Low ($755 or less)	63	997	2,460	410
Lower middle ($756–2,995)	54	2,324	2,048	1,130
Upper middle ($2,996–9,265)	38	3,001	647	4,640
High ($9,266 or more)	52	24,994	903	27,680
World	207	31,315	6,057	5,170

Source: Adapted from the *2002 World Bank Atlas.* Copyright © The International Bank for Reconstruction and Development/The World Bank. Used by permission.

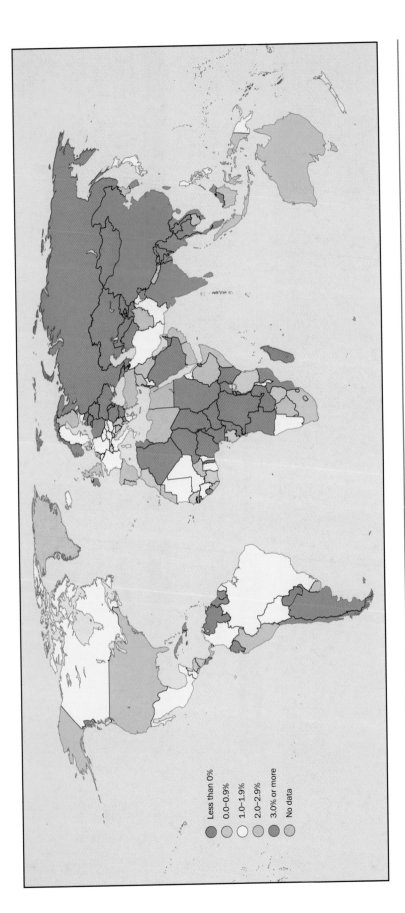

Income growth

GDP per capita growth, 1990–2000

The average annual percentage change in a country's real GDP per capita. To exclude the effects of inflation, constant price GDP is used in calculating the growth rate.

Less than 0%
0.0–0.9%
1.0–1.9%
2.0–2.9%
3.0% or more
No data

GDP per capita annual growth rate, 1990–2000, percent

	Number of Economies	GNP $ billions 2000	Population millions 2000	GNP per capita $ 2000
Less than 0%	53	943	752	1,250
0.0–0.9%	17	496	166	2,980
1.0–1.9%	41	12,578	1,122	11,210
2.0–2.9%	31	13,550	975	13,890
3.0% or more	36	3,618	2,933	1,230
No data	29	129	108	1,190

Index of GDP per capita, 1980–2000, 1980 = 100

East Asia & Pacific
Latin America & Caribbean
Middle East & North Africa
South Asia
Sub-Saharan Africa

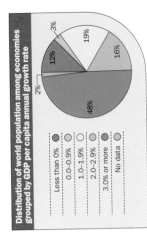

Distribution of world population among economies grouped by GDP per capita annual growth rate

3%
19%
16%
48%
2%
12%

Less than 0%
0.0–0.9%
1.0–1.9%
2.0–2.9%
3.0% or more
No data

Source: Adapted from the *2002 World Bank Atlas*. Copyright © The International Bank for Reconstruction and Development/The World Bank. Used by permission.

Telephones

Telephone lines and mobile phones per 1,000 people, 2000

Telephone lines connecting a customer's equipment to the public switched telephone network and mobile phones, per 1,000 people.

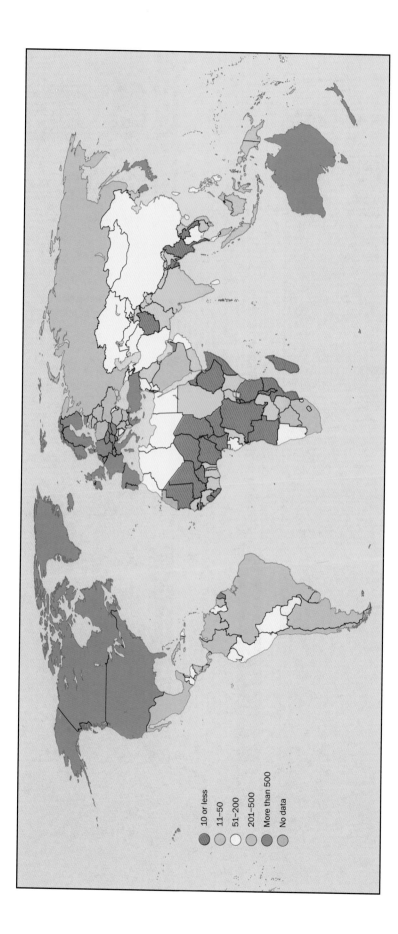

Telephone lines and mobile phones per 1,000 people, 2000

Legend:
- 10 or less
- 11–50
- 51–200
- 201–500
- More than 500
- No data

Distribution of world population among economies grouped by telephones per 1,000 people

- 10 or less
- 11–50
- 51–200
- 201–500
- More than 500
- No data

Pie chart values: 29%, 11%, 17%, 13%, 30%

Fixed lines and mobile telephones per 1,000 people, 2000

East Asia & Pacific	171
Europe & Central Asia	314
Latin America & Caribbean	271
Middle East & North Africa	122
South Asia	31
Sub-Saharan Africa	32
High income	1,136

Scale: 0 400 800 1200

Fixed lines and mobile telephones per 1,000 people, 2000

	Number of Economies	GNP $ billions 2000	Population millions 2000	GNP per capita $ 2000
10 or less	27	162	643	250
11–50	36	810	1,758	460
51–200	42	1,845	1,806	1,020
201–500	42	2,727	803	3,390
More than 500	55	25,763	1,044	24,690
No data	5	9	3	2,640

Source: Adapted from the *2002 World Bank Atlas.* Copyright © The International Bank for Reconstruction and Development/The World Bank. Used by permission.

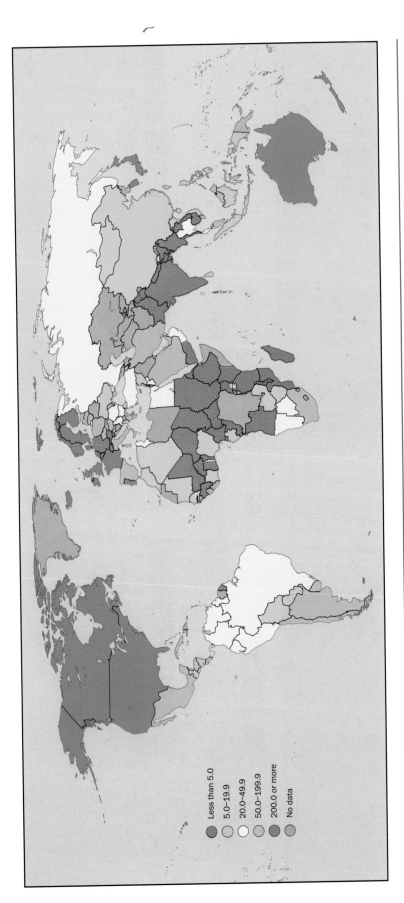

Personal computers

Personal computers per 1,000 people, 2000

The estimated number of self-contained computers designed to be used by a single individual, per 1,000 people.

Personal computers per 1,000 people, 2000

	Number of Economies	GNP $ billions 2000	Population millions 2000	GNP per capita $ 2000
Less than 5.0	30	684	1,729	400
5.0–19.9	32	1,583	2,021	780
20.0–49.9	24	1,660	684	2,430
50.0–199.9	38	3,704	507	7,300
200.0 or more	29	23,430	834	28,090
No data	54	254	282	900

Personal computers per 1,000 people, 2000

East Asia & Pacific	21.7
Europe & Central Asia	45.4
Latin America & Caribbean	43.6
Middle East & North Africa	31.2
South Asia	4.2
Sub-Saharan Africa	9.2
High income	392.7

0 100 200 300 400 500

Distribution of world population among economies grouped by personal computers per 1,000 people

- Less than 5.0 — 33%
- 5.0–19.9 — 11%
- 20.0–49.9 — 8%
- 50.0–199.9 — 14%
- 200.0 or more — 5%
- No data — 29%

Map legend:
- Less than 5.0
- 5.0–19.9
- 20.0–49.9
- 50.0–199.9
- 200.0 or more
- No data

Source: Adapted from the *2002 World Bank Atlas.* Copyright © The International Bank for Reconstruction and Development/The World Bank. Used by permission.

Poverty

Population below the national poverty line, 1984–2000

The percentage of the population living below the national poverty line.

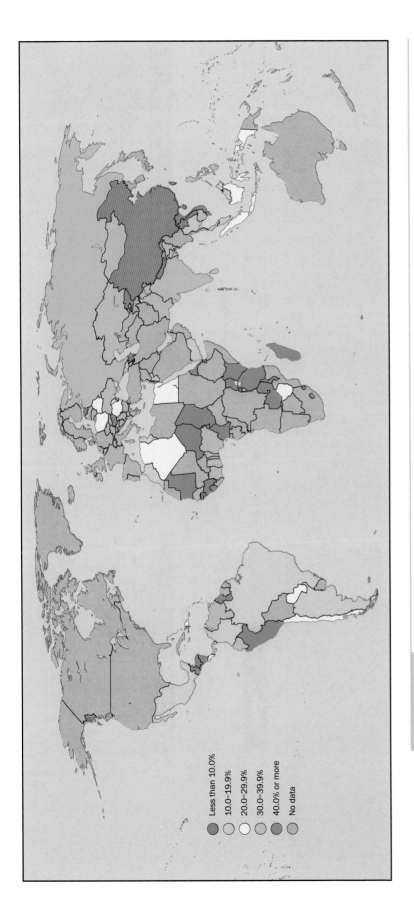

Percentage of the population below the national poverty line in selected developing economies, 1984–2000

Azerbaijan	68.1
Brazil	17.4
China	4.6
Egypt, Arab Rep.	22.9
India	35.0
Vietnam	50.9
Zambia	86.0

0 20 40 60 80 100

Distribution of world population among economies grouped by population below the national poverty line

- Less than 10.0%
- 10.0–19.9%
- 20.0–29.9%
- 30.0–39.9%
- 40.0% or more
- No data

27% 21% 8% 7% 30% 6%

Percentage of the population below the national poverty line, 1984–2000

	Number of Economies	GNP $ billions 2000	Population millions 2000	GNP per capita $ 2000
Less than 10.0%	3	1,115	1,274	880
10.0–19.9%	12	1,745	499	3,500
20.0–29.9%	13	615	427	1,440
30.0–39.9%	21	1,151	1,836	630
40.0% or more	31	200	373	540
No data	127	26,489	1,649	16,060

Source: Adapted from the *2002 World Bank Atlas.* Copyright © The International Bank for Reconstruction and Development/The World Bank. Used by permission.

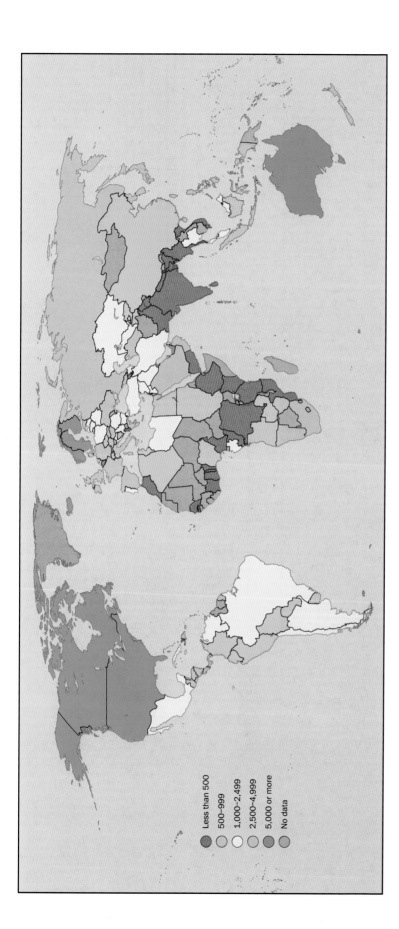

Energy use

Energy use per capita, 1999

Annual consumption of commercial energy divided by the population, expressed in kilograms of oil equivalent.

Less than 500
500–999
1,000–2,499
2,500–4,999
5,000 or more
No data

Energy use per capita, 1999, kilograms of oil equivalent

	Number of Economies	GNP $ billions 2000	Population millions 2000	GNP per capita $ 2000
Less than 500	24	750	1,785	420
500–999	30	1,767	2,014	880
1,000–2,499	29	2,621	785	3,340
2,500–4,999	33	14,373	883	16,280
5,000 or more	15	11,651	372	31,280
No data	76	152	218	700

Energy use per capita, 1999, kilograms of oil equivalent

Region	kilograms of oil equivalent
East Asia & Pacific	920
Europe & Central Asia	2,628
Latin America & Caribbean	1,171
Middle East & North Africa	1,279
South Asia	441
Sub-Saharan Africa	671
High income	5,448

0   2,000   4,000   6,000

Distribution of world population among economies grouped by energy use per capita

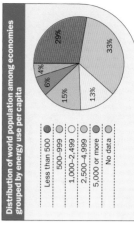

- Less than 500 — 29%
- 500–999 — 4%
- 1,000–2,499 — 6%
- 2,500–4,999 — 15%
- 5,000 or more — 13%
- No data — 33%

Source: Adapted from the *2002 World Bank Atlas.* Copyright © The International Bank for Reconstruction and Development/The World Bank. Used by permission.

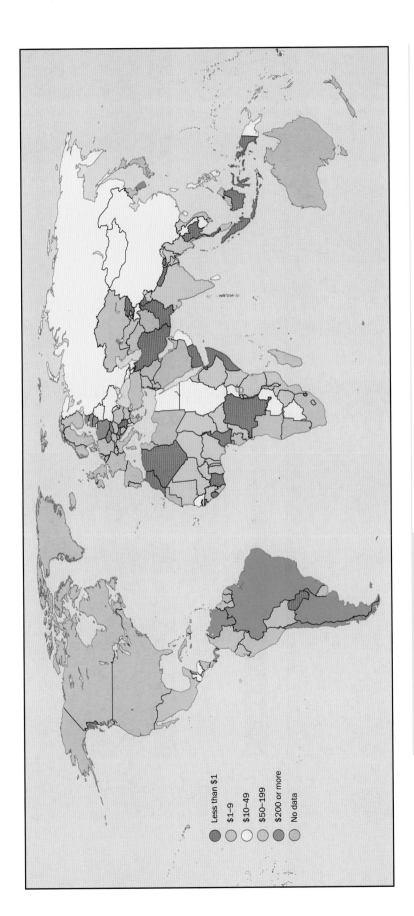

Private capital flows

Net private capital flows per capita, 2000

Net private debt and nondebt flows to developing economies, including commercial bank lending, bonds, other private credits, foreign direct investment, and portfolio equity investment, divided by population.

Map legend:

- Less than $1
- $1–9
- $10–49
- $50–199
- $200 or more
- No data

Distribution of world population among economies grouped by net private capital flows per capita

- Less than $1
- $1–9
- $10–49
- $50–199
- $200 or more
- No data

Pie chart values: 11%, 17%, 6%, 7%, 29%, 29%

Net private capital flows per capita, 2000 and 2001, $ billions

- 2000
- 2001

Region	2000	2001
East Asia & Pacific	65.7	45.0
Europe & Central Asia	45.4	22.5
Latin America & Caribbean	69.4	97.3
Middle East & North Africa	1.1	4.3
South Asia	9.3	4.3
Sub-Saharan Africa	7.1	14.5

Net private capital flows per capita, 2000, $

	Number of Economies	GNP $ billions 2000	Population millions 2000	GNP per capita $ 2000
Less than $1	25	560	696	810
$1–9	32	684	1,747	390
$10–49	28	1,655	1,779	930
$50–199	29	1,299	440	2,950
$200 or more	23	1,803	373	4,840
No data	70	25,314	1,022	24,770

Source: Adapted from the *2002 World Bank Atlas.* Copyright © The International Bank for Reconstruction and Development/The World Bank. Used by permission.

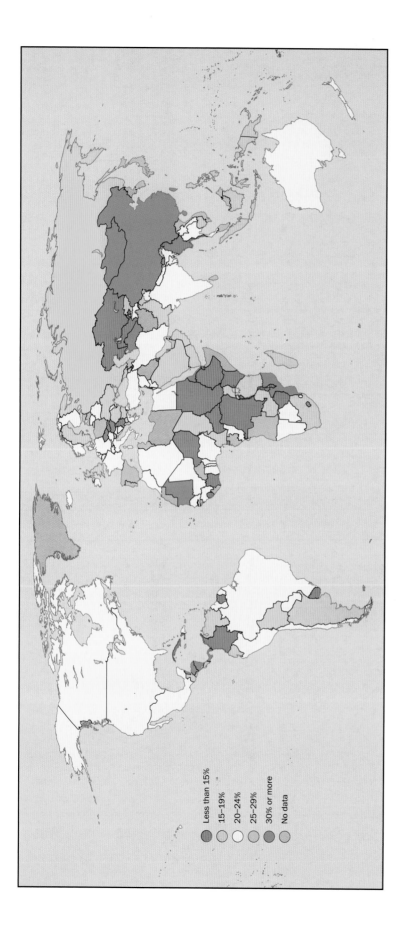

Investment

Gross capital formation as a share of GDP, 2000

Outlays on additions to the fixed assets of an economy plus net changes in the level of inventories, as a percentage of gross domestic product.

Legend:
- Less than 15%
- 15–19%
- 20–24%
- 25–29%
- 30% or more
- No data

Gross capital formation as a share of GDP, 2000, percent

	Number of Economies	GNP $ billions 2000	Population millions 2000	GNP per capita $ 2000
Less than 15%	25	277	409	680
15–19%	43	3,239	1,071	3,020
20–24%	55	20,083	2,687	7,470
25–29%	26	6,246	447	13,970
30% or more	24	1,328	1,346	990
No data	34	142	97	1,470

Gross capital formation as a share of GDP in selected developing economies, 2000, percent

Economy	Percent
Argentina	16
Brazil	21
China	37
India	24
Korea, Rep.	29
Mexico	23
Russian Federation	17

Distribution of world population among economies grouped by gross capital formation as a share of GDP

- Less than 15%: 7%
- 15–19%: 18%
- 20–24%: 44%
- 25–29%: 7%
- 30% or more: 22%
- No data: 2%

Source: Adapted from the *2002 World Bank Atlas.* Copyright © The International Bank for Reconstruction and Development/The World Bank. Used by permission.

Discussion Questions

1. What are the major differences among the three main legal systems that exist? How might each affect commerce that is conducted within its purview?
2. How might a Japanese and American lawyer react in each other's country? What behaviors might you see,

and which ones could you tie to their respective legal systems?
3. What are some of the forms of political risk? Why might Nigeria, Peru, or Indonesia be considered relatively risky places to do business? What steps would you recommend to deal with this risk?
4. What steps would you recommend to deal with other forms of risk in the above and other countries?

Up to the Challenge?

Bo Concepts: How Do You Knock Out the Knockoffs?

IN THE OPENING box we presented a tough situation for Bo Concepts. Their thriving business in China was being dramatically threatened by Chinese copycats; revenues were dropping dramatically and the number of copycat competitors was growing exponentially. Worse yet, copying is common in China because it's easy to get away with. Laws are sketchy and ambiguous and enforcement is suspect, to say the least. With all this in mind as well as the issues raised in the chapter, what is Bo Concepts and its franchise owner Simon Lichtenberg to do?

In his home country and some others, Lichtenberg would begin by asking a judge to order a preliminary injunction to stop the firms from copying. But China does not have a set of detailed procedures for such injunctions, and as a result their judges rarely invoke them. Undeterred, Lichtenberg hired private investigators from Pinkerton to collect evidence and present it to the Chinese agency responsible for such trangressions (the State Administration for Industry and Commerce, SAIC). This was also a dead end; nothing resulted from the investigation.

With sales continuing to drop, Lichtenberg didn't let the matter sit for long. Six months later, he was back at the SAIC's doorstep. But who was he to talk with about this? While he could speak Mandarin, who would he speak it with? The agency has literally hundreds of departments, and only one officer in each with the authority to take action. "The system is not made for foreign investors to find these guys," said Lichtenberg. So instead of the rule of law, he used good old-fashioned connections—called *guanxi* in China. A friend of Lichtenberg's knew the head of Shanghai's SAIC and informed him of the situation. This person in turn called a district director, who assembled a committee of twenty-five experts to review the matter. As input into this deliberation, Lichtenberg was keen to convince the committee that using the company's name and catalog was unfair. Unbelievably,

these items are not specifically covered in Chinese law and thus officials are loathe to rule on them for fear it would upset a superior who more properly should decide.

It was even worse among some Chinese officials. "Their attitude was, if your furniture sells well, why wouldn't others copy it?" Lichtenberg reported. It took nearly four months to do the convincing, but once done, the board moved quickly. By early 1999, a set of committee-ordered raids resulted in confiscations and some changes. These and related efforts reduced the pirating of Bo Concept's product and catalog. Part of the stoppage came from the intimidation of facing the SAIC board. But not all were so persuaded. No arrests were made, nor were any fines handed out. And the committee did not perceive jurisdiction over design infringement, only the brand issue and some unfair competition. To deal with the infringement issue, the persistent Lichtenberg turned to the Chinese patent bureau, which he found was located on the third floor of an old building in a seedy part of Shanghai. The toilets were backed up and stank and the place was in very poor shape, but the old men who sat at their desks drinking green tea got to work looking at the problem.

This group was also helpful to Bo Concepts. The bureau began a series of meetings with an intimidated group of copycatters. Some claimed they weren't copying and others said they didn't know it was illegal; regardless, the board was convincing and required the firms to cease and desist or to combine forces with Bo Concepts in a joint venture. On a final front, Bo Concepts brought suit against one of the larger firms they thought responsible for a majority of the copying, asking for $180,000. The case is currently stuck in the Intermediate Court, and it's not clear that Bo Concepts will win this one. The defendant claims that Bo Concepts did not apply for patents in China during the six-month period since it filed the original patents in Denmark, a Chinese requirement and a mistake often made by foreigners. The Counterfeiting Coalition actually recommends to foreign businesses that they automatically apply for such patents, even if they don't plan to do business in China in the foreseeable future, to protect themselves.

Whatever happens with this case, Bo Concepts feels it has made significant progress. Even though some new and smaller copycats pop up now and then, they no longer represent that much of a threat to the company. And many of the high-end outlets that sell Bo Concepts products are also refusing to stock the knockoffs because of the legal action and the effect on their image. For Lichtenberg, persistence paid off. While it required considerable time and money to protect their product, along with some significant help from the Danish embassy, it does seem possible to stem the knockoff tide in China.[49]

International Development
Culture Knowledge Quiz

Purpose

Few, if any, traditions and values are universally held. Many business dealings have succeeded or failed because of a manager's awareness or lack of understanding of the traditions and values of his or her foreign counterparts. With the world business community so closely intertwined and interdependent, it is critical that managers today become increasingly aware of the differences that exist. Toward that end, the purpose of this exercise is the following:

● To stimulate awareness of cultural differences
● To promote consideration of the impact of cultural differences in a global economy
● To stimulate dialogue between domestic and international students
● To explore issues raised by culturally diverse workforces

Instructions

Working alone or with a small group, complete the sentences. If you are taking the quiz with students from countries other than your own, explore what the answer might be in your country and theirs. Your instructor will lead a discussion of the correct answers in class.

1. In Japan, loudly slurping your soup is considered to be
   a. rude and obnoxious.
   b. a sign that you like the soup.
   c. okay at home but not in public.
   d. something only foreigners do.

2. In Korea, business leaders tend to
   a. encourage strong commitment to teamwork and cooperation.
   b. encourage competition among subordinates.
   c. discourage subordinates from reporting directly, preferring information to come through well-defined channels.
   d. encourage close relationships with their subordinates.

3. In Japan, virtually every kind of drink is sold in public vending machines except for
   a. beer.
   b. diet drinks with saccharin.
   c. already sweetened coffee.
   d. soft drinks from U.S. companies.

4. In Latin America, managers
   a. are most likely to hire members of their own families.
   b. consider hiring members of their own families to be inappropriate.
   c. stress the importance of hiring members of minority groups.
   d. usually hire more people than are actually needed to do a job.

5. In Ethiopia, when a woman opens the front door of her home, it means
   a. she is ready to receive guests for a meal.
   b. only family members may enter.
   c. religious spirits may move freely in and out of the home.
   d. she has agreed to have sex with any man who enters.

6. In Latin America, businesspeople
   a. consider it impolite to make eye contact while talking to one another.
   b. always wait until the other person is finished speaking before starting to speak.
   c. touch each other more than North Americans do under similar circumstances.
   d. avoid touching one another as it is considered an invasion of privacy.

7. The principal religion in Malaysia is
   a. Buddhism.
   b. Judaism.
   c. Christianity.
   d. Islam.

8. In Thailand
   a. it is common to see men walking along holding hands.
   b. it is common to see a man and a woman holding hands in public.
   c. it is rude for men and women to walk together.
   d. men and women traditionally kiss each other on meeting in the street.

9. When eating in India, it is appropriate to
   a. take food with your right hand and eat with your left.
   b. take food with your left hand and eat with your right.
   c. take food and eat it with your left hand.
   d. take food and eat it with your right hand.

10. Pointing your toes at someone in Thailand is
    a. a symbol of respect, much like the Japanese bow.
    b. considered rude even if it is done by accident.
    c. an invitation to dance.
    d. the standard public greeting.

11. American managers tend to base the performance appraisals of their subordinates on performance, while in Iran, managers are more likely to base their performance appraisals on
    a. religion.
    b. seniority.
    c. friendship.
    d. ability.

12. In China, the status of every business negotiation is
    a. reported daily in the press.
    b. private, and details are not discussed publicly.
    c. subjected to scrutiny by a public tribunal on a regular basis.
    d. directed by the elders of every commune.

13. When rewarding an Hispanic worker for a job well done, it is best not to
    a. praise him or her publicly.
    b. say "thank you."
    c. offer a raise.
    d. offer a promotion.

14. In some South American countries, it is considered normal and acceptable to show up for a social appointment
    a. ten to fifteen minutes early.
    b. ten to fifteen minutes late.
    c. fifteen minutes to an hour late.
    d. one to two hours late.

15. In France, when friends talk to one another
    a. they generally stand about three feet apart.
    b. it is typical to shout.
    c. they stand closer to one another than Americans do.
    d. it is always with a third party present.

16. When giving flowers as gifts in Western Europe, be careful not to give
    a. tulips and jonquils.
    b. daisies and lilacs.
    c. chrysanthemums and calla lilies.
    d. lilacs and apple blossoms.

17. The appropriate gift-giving protocol for a male executive doing business in Saudi Arabia is to
    a. give a man a gift from you to his wife.
    b. present gifts to the wife or wives in person.
    c. give gifts only to the eldest wife.
    d. not give a gift to the wife at all.

18. If you want to give a necktie or a scarf to a Latin American, it is best to avoid the color
    a. red.
    b. purple.
    c. green.
    d. black.

19. The doors in German offices and homes are generally kept
    a. wide open to symbolize an acceptance and welcome of friends and strangers.
    b. slightly ajar to suggest that people should knock before entering.
    c. half-opened suggesting that some people are welcome and others are not.
    d. tightly shut to preserve privacy and personal space.

20. In the area that was formerly West Germany, leaders who display charisma are
    a. not among the most desired.
    b. the ones most respected and sought after.
    c. invited frequently to serve on boards of cultural organizations.
    d. pushed to get involved in political activities.

21. American managers running businesses in Mexico have found that by increasing the salaries of Mexican workers, they
    a. increased the numbers of hours the workers were willing to work.
    b. enticed more workers to work night shifts.
    c. decreased the number of hours workers would agree to work.
    d. decreased production rates.

22. Chinese culture teaches people
    a. to seek psychiatric help for personal problems.
    b. to avoid conflict and internalize personal problems.
    c. to deal with conflict with immediate confrontation.
    d. to seek help from authorities whenever conflict arises.

23. One wedding gift that should not be given to a Chinese couple would be
    a. a jade bowl.
    b. a clock.
    c. a basket of oranges.
    d. shirts embroidered with dragon patterns.

24. In Venezuela, New Year's Eve is generally spent
    a. in quiet family gatherings.
    b. at wild neighborhood street parties.
    c. in restaurants with horns, hats, and live music and dancing.
    d. at pig roasts on the beach.

25. If you order "bubble and squeak" in a London pub, you will get
    a. two goldfish fried in olive oil.
    b. a very cold beer in a chilled glass, rather than the usual warm beer.
    c. Alka Seltzer® and a glass of water.
    d. chopped cabbage and mashed potatoes fried together.

26. When a stranger in India wants to know what you do for a living and how much you earn, he will
    a. ask your guide.
    b. invite you to his home and, after getting to know you, will ask.
    c. come over and ask you directly, without introduction.
    d. respect your privacy above all.

27. When you feel you are being taken advantage of in a business exchange in Vietnam, it is important to
    a. let the anger show in your face but not in your words.
    b. say that you are angry, but keep your facial expression neutral.
    c. not show any anger in any way.
    d. end the business dealings immediately, and walk away.

28. When a taxi driver in India shakes his head from side to side, it probably means
    a. he thinks your price is too high.
    b. he isn't going in your direction.
    c. he will take you where you want to go.
    d. he doesn't understand what you're asking.

29. In England, holding your index and middle fingers up in a vee with the back of your hand facing another person is seen as
    a. a gesture of peace.
    b. a gesture of victory.
    c. a signal that you want two of something.
    d. a vulgar gesture.

From Theory to Practice
Calibrating International Business Risk

Purpose
To provide some hands-on understanding of risk in an international environment and to apply that to one or more specific countries.

Instructions
In this chapter we talked a good bit about managing risk. The Overseas Private Investment Corporation (OPIC) is a U.S. federal agency whose purpose is to provide services, including insurance, to companies that invest overseas. One of the services they offer is political risk insurance to protect firms against the risks of expropriation, war, revolution, and some negative economic events (e.g., inconvertibility of local currency). The OPIC is particularly well-organized and service oriented. Their website is excellent and they also have an automated information line that allows customers to request many documents explaining OPIC programs. For this exercise, we want you to choose one or two countries in conjunction with your instructor. Once you target your countries, either check out the OPIC web page (www.opic.gov) or call their information line (202-336-8400) to request information. Alternatively, you can call OPIC's automated fax service (202-336-8700), if you'd prefer.

Either way, please request document 1001 (*Directory of Program Related Documents*). If you use the fax line option, you will begin to receive a fax immediately after you complete your call requesting the documents.

This service is easy to use; you are prompted for information to enter one by one via any contact method you employ. After you receive the document, look through it and see what information you would find useful for investigating the countries you have chosen. Call or visit the OPIC webpage again and request the additional documents.

After you receive your documents, prepare a brief (one page or less) report on your country/countries. Some of the questions you may wish to address in this report are:

● In general, what is the OPIC and what is its purpose?
● Are your countries eligible for OPIC support?
● In particular, what kind of support is available?
● How would you or an interested company request support?
● What exactly is insured by your participation in the program?
● What is the approximate cost to your company of such insurance?

To complete this report, you may wish to provide the political risk rating of your chosen countries. To get this number and an interpretation, you will need to refer to one of three sources: (1) Euromoney's

Annual Survey of Country Risk, (2) a more widely available source, such as the annual risk ratings that appear in the *Wall Street Journal*, or (3) the *Planning Review*'s annual issue on political and economic risk for 101 countries. If the countries you choose are not on this list, select others that you think are similar in political risk and briefly mention in your report why you think the risk is similar. Finally, you may wish to contact the Department of Commerce Trade Information Center (http://www.trade.gov/td/tic/ or 1-800-USA-TRADE) and/or the Export-Import Bank Export Financing Hotline (http://www.exim.gov/ or 1-800-424-5201) for further information about the countries you have chosen for your report.

Doing Things Right: International Ethics and Social Responsibility

International Challenge

Competitive Intelligence: Dumpster Diving for That Extra Edge

"I DON'T EVER want to be in a fair fight. I want an edge every-place I go." — Herbert M. Baum, CEO of Quaker State Corp.

Mr. Baum's comment gives you a sense of the high stakes in the competitive fight facing many U.S. multinationals. The "edge" that he refers to, however, is **competitive intelligence** (CI). While it isn't supposed to involve blatantly illegal acts like stealing another firm's proprietary documents, CI is often a fuzzy business that skates close to (and sometimes over) the line when it comes to ethics and legal-ity. Thus, in many ways, CI is a gentle term for what we know to be spying! When Oracle went dumpster diving in Microsoft's trashcans for documents and hints of that company's moves, the whole notion of CI received much attention. But most companies have more panache than Oracle. Indeed, that trash operation "was the sort of thing that gives legitimate business intelligence a bad name," say Alden Taylor of Kroll Associates, a large CI firm in New York.

But what exactly is CI? Part strategic planning, CI is designed to anticipate competitors' moves and includes a range of data collec-tion techniques. CI often involves sifting through vast amounts of information for emerging trends and what competitors might be doing about them. Who does CI? Analysts range from librarians to ex-spies, from in-house experts to outside consulting firms. They prowl web pages and trade shows, tramp through the patent office, and keep their eyes and ears open in airports. Companies like Real World Intelligence, for instance, offer customized versions of soft-ware created for the CIA. The software scans through voluminous Internet data, such as new product information on firms' web pages. It also turns out that European and Asian multinationals have been at CI (and industrial espionage, too) longer than their American counterparts. Partly this disparity is cultural. Americans seem more likely to find the whole CI process morally questionable.

How well does CI work? Pretty well, according to insiders. Former bosses of Monsanto's CI unit estimated it was worth $50 million annually to the company. Motorola's chair, Robert Galvin, hired former intelligence officers to set up a CI unit for the firm back in the 1970s. Since then, Motorola has never been blindsided in the way Xerox was in the 1980s, when Japanese firms cut into the firm's copier market share. Indeed, their unit is now directed by its third ex-CIA operative in a row!

The real issue for ethicists isn't whether CI helps the bottom line, but whether it is morally defensible. Consider this sequence of events carried out by a food company that wanted to win market share from a competitor with a surprise price cut. First, CI agents interviewed ex-employees of the competitor. The idea was to find out when the competitor's sales reps had to get approval from senior management before giving retailers a discount (like after a rival had cut prices). Next, the *neighbors* of the competitors' senior executives were telephoned under various pretexts in an effort to learn about their schedules. That's when it was discovered that the competitor's executives were on a European plant tour. A cooperative travel agent even handed over their entire itinerary! As a result, the food company's price cuts were launched immediately. Because their approval was needed and they were several time zones away, the competitor's executives couldn't respond quickly. The competitor lost business as a result.

Such activity is on the rise. Indeed, the number of countries spying on U.S. industry has actually increased since the end of the Cold War. Some of it is relatively blatant, as when a few years ago Russian President Boris Yeltsin chided domestic business leaders for not effectively using stolen technological secrets! Being an ally is no assurance you'll be free from CI. The former head of French intelligence publicly admitted that he organized a unit to spy on U.S. firms. He also revealed that Air France flight attendants eavesdropped and taped conversations of American businesspeople flying on that airline.

So here's your challenge. Is any part of the sequence just described unethical? Illegal in any way? Why? Answer the same questions for these information-gathering activities:

- Digging through a company's trash on public property.
- Deliberately eavesdropping on private company conversations.
- Sending phony job seekers in response to a competitor's want ads.
- Hiring a competitor's former employees.
- Sending phony visitors to tour a competitor's facilities.
- Attending trade shows where a competitor's wares are displayed.

Finally, what recommendations might you have for multinationals interested in protecting their secrets from competitors' prying? Take a look at the Up to the Challenge box at end of this chapter for some surprising answers to these questions.[1]

Ethics and Social Responsibility in International Management

In this chapter we discuss international issues related to ethics and corporate social responsibility. This topic goes beyond the discussion of politics and laws presented in Chapter 2. Although certain business activities may not violate any legal codes or political norms, they are often seen as simply the wrong thing to do. Of course, many firms have already dealt with ethical issues in the domestic arena. However, with falling trade barriers and rising international commerce, it seems likely that firms must increasingly confront ethical issues on a global level in the years ahead.

As we showed, international managers must understand the legal and political framework of the countries in which they do business. However, the fact that some business steps are legal or politically expedient doesn't mean that action should be taken. There are many cases where an action might impact on some larger personal, organizational, or societal concerns.[2] As a result, firms might be better served in the long run by acting within a broad set of value-based guidelines. Although those rules are often difficult to develop and implement, following such guidelines may increase customer goodwill, help avoid future litigation, and even benefit society in various ways.[3] These issues bring us into the realm of ethics and the effects that they have (or should have) on the way business is done.

We'll start by discussing **ethical values**, with the focus on individuals' moral judgments about what is right or wrong. Then we will move beyond the personal guidelines within which managers conduct international business and consider how multinationals can serve the communities and nations in which they do business. Many experts have called on multinationals to build such corporate social responsibility explicitly into their international business strategies.[4] In fact, several frameworks have been proposed to help multinationals move in this direction by distinguishing between various types of ethical and socially responsible corporate behavior.[5] In general, however, the topic of ethics traditionally focuses on more narrow personal issues, while corporate social responsibility is broader and more general since it is driven by the ethical posture of the multinational.

Even with the great strides made in international business over the last twenty-five years, many still feel that the concept of international business ethics is murky at best and impossible to use in practice at worst. Part of the problem is that ethics turns out to be an intricate and complex issue when we move from country to country. The political and economic systems we discussed have direct and indirect effects on the moral values held by people doing international business. In turn, such values affect what people in different cultures perceive as ethical behavior.[6] Finally, these perceptions can drive behavior, such as questionable payments, human rights at work, and standards for treating employees. We will talk about each of these in this chapter.

Philosophies and Perspectives on Ethics

How should we act and what are our feelings about how others should act? These are major and enduring philosophical questions that have been debated for many years. This ongoing debate has made it clear that there are a variety of ways these questions could be answered and many different justifications on which the answers could be based. Since these philosophies are not our direct concern here, we'll boil them all down to two main positions, universalism and relativism. These two perspectives suggest sharply different behavior for international managers.[7]

Universalism   Universalism, as the label implies, holds that there are widespread and objective sets of guidelines that cut across countries and cultures. Advocates of this position agree that there are moral rules that everyone should follow. These universalists point to the fact that there are many behaviors that most every culture considers wrong (e.g., harming others or their property).

They also point out that there is wide acceptance of some basic principles for doing business. For example, it has been observed that virtually every country in the world has some sort of law that prohibits bribery, lying, and stealing in a business context.[8] Of course, as we'll show later, not every country enforces such laws and many choose to "look the other way." Nevertheless, our point is that many believe that there are widely applicable "rules" for doing business that everyone should obey. Universalists typically are not content to sit back passively and hope that people will discover these basic principles and then act accordingly. Instead, a common strategy has been to develop actively a set of behaviors that constitute universal guidelines. In fact, efforts have been made to develop "transnational" or "global" codes of ethics that managers in multinationals should follow.[9] For example, universalists have developed a set of minimal rights for international workers. Among other things, these include the right to physical security, free speech, subsistence, and nondiscriminatory treatment.[10]

Exhibit 3.1 lists some of the guidelines that have been developed to transcend the specific person and corporation.[11] These codes deal with topics as diverse as basic human rights, product safety, environmental concerns, and illegal payments. To give you a more in-depth look, we present one such code in detail in Exhibit 3.2. This code consists of seven ethical principles that multinationals should follow. Of course, these principles aren't intended to exhaust a firm's ethical responsibilities but rather exemplify the things multinationals should take into account to operate with integrity.

In practice, however, at least two problems emerge with the implementation of universal principles such as these. First, because the codes try to be broad and universal, there is plenty of ambiguity about how they should be interpreted. In turn, this has led to inconsistency in the way that different multinationals view and use principles such as "favorable working conditions" and "cooperation with local government."

A second issue is that many countries and companies have not officially adopted all (or even some) of these ethical obligations. For example, although the United States is often seen as being highly concerned with ethical issues, it has not signed on to several sets of these global principles.[12] Partly this is because the United States seems to disagree

EXHIBIT 3.1

Sets of Ethical Obligations for Firms Conducting International Business

1. UN Universal Declaration of Human Rights

2. Organization for Economic Cooperation and Development Guidelines for Multinational Enterprises

3. European Convention on Human Rights

4. Helsinki Final Act

5. International Labor Organization's Declaration of Principles Concerning Multinational Enterprises and Social Policy

6. International Covenant on Economic, Social, and Cultural Rights

7. International Covenant on Civil and Political Rights

8. UN Code of Conduct on Transnational Corporations

9. European Economic Community Code of Conduct for Companies with Interests in South Africa

10. Sullivan Principles: A set of seven rules, set forth by Rev. Leon Sullivan of the United States, for companies doing business in South Africa during the apartheid-era regimes (pre-1994). They include issues of equal treatment for all races in terms of pay, advancement, and other employment practices.

EXHIBIT 3.2

DeGeorge's (1993) Seven Basic Ethical Principles for Multinationals

1. Multinationals should do no intentional direct harm.

2. Multinationals should produce more good than harm for the host country.

3. Multinationals should contribute by their activity to the host country's development.

4. Multinationals should respect the human rights of their employees.

5. To the extent that local culture does not violate ethical norms, multinationals should respect the local culture and work with and not against it.

6. Multinationals should pay their fair share of taxes.

7. Multinationals should cooperate with the local government in developing and enforcing just-background institutions.

with certain aspects of the guidelines. Internal political pressures also play a role in the U.S. position. On the other hand, sometimes the United States has endorsed various international agreements dealing with ethical issues but has had trouble getting other countries to cooperate. Even when many countries have signed on in principle, things don't always go the way the United States wants them to. In fact, the United States has doubts about some of its own efforts to put such agreements into place, even though they were partially designed to ensure ethical behavior in international business. In the last chapter, for example, we discussed the battles that the United States has been losing—and may continue to lose—in the World Trade Organization. In 1996, for example, the United States lost the first case it brought before the WTO court in Geneva. The United States wanted foreign oil suppliers to follow pollution standards outlined in the U.S. Clean Air Act, taking the position that those foreign refineries need to be socially responsible and make sure they could minimize the effect of production on air pollution. Unfortunately, from the American perspective, the WTO ruled that U.S. law discriminated against foreign suppliers in this case. These and other defeats have made the United States distance itself from the WTO. Indeed, in 1998 the United States backed away from slapping Japan with sanctions about some of their trade practices out of fear of losing at the WTO.[13]

Relativism   For these reasons and more, **cultural relativism** has become a popular alternative to universalism.[14] Proponents of relativism believe that ethical behavior in any one country is determined by its own unique culture, laws, and business practices. Therefore, if it is common to provide a public official with a nominal payment to process paperwork for your imports, this may be the thing to do even though it is illegal in your own country. This perspective of "when in Rome, do as the Romans do" is often justified on several counts. Perhaps the most important argument is that to do otherwise is to disrespect the culture into which you come as a guest. The obvious implication of this argument is that international managers should follow the practices of the country in which they are doing business.

An example of this situation occurred some time ago when American actress Michelle Pfeiffer was in Moscow filming the movie *The Russia House*. She left the set after a few weeks of filming to protest the fact that Russian extras were not allowed to eat the lavishly catered food provided to foreign actors. She was embarrassed by this since the movie was being made at a time and in a place where it was often difficult or very expensive to get quality food, soap and other necessities. There was a law, however, forbidding Western film companies from feeding the Russian extras they employed. Local officials were called in to beg Ms. Pfeiffer to return to the set; they explained that this was just the way things were done in Russia. Pfieffer was eventually convinced, stating, "I didn't sleep that night. Then I realized, this is so typically American of you. Whether I was right or wrong wasn't the issue. The issue was, do I have the right as an outsider to come in and force my sensibilities on this culture?"[15] Ms. Pfeiffer's reaction clearly exemplifies the cultural relativism position.

Nevertheless, behaving as a relativist could cause big problems for international managers. Just because a country has different customs than a manager is used to doesn't make it immune to analysis or judgment. Clearly, most people would not agree that the suppression of political freedom, the use of slave or prison labor, and other violations of human rights seen in China and Myanmar are morally acceptable because it is "Rome" rather than Paris, Zurich, or New York.[16] Most people are in fact universalists as far as these extreme behaviors are concerned.

This does not imply that everyone believes something should be done about such situations. Indeed, there are a variety of possible responses and justifications for continuing a firm's business activity in countries where immoral actions are taking place. In apartheid-era South Africa, for example, many foreign multinationals pointed out that if they divested their interests in South Africa, it would probably result in greater harm to those who it was intended to help, at least temporarily. Multinationals argued that divestiture would cause many black employees to lose their jobs. Some multinationals also argued that they would be better able to push for government reforms by remaining a player in the South African economy.[17] These are basically the same arguments that PepsiCo made to justify its business in Myanmar (known previously as Burma), a country run by a repressive regime.[18] However, under increasing pressure from the U.S. government and human rights organizations, PepsiCo decided in 1997 to end its presence in Myanmar.[19] Similar arguments continue to be made by the many U.S. multinationals that currently do business in China.[20] For another look at some of the ethical pressures multinationals are under—and how they're responding—take a look at the accompanying International Insights.

Cross-National Differences in Ethical Perspectives

The debate between universalism and relativism raises the question of whether countries diverge in terms of how they view and act upon ethical principles in business. As it turns out, many studies have examined cross-national business ethics. It also should come as no surprise by now that these studies generally confirm that there are widely different ways to approach ethical issues across countries.

For instance, one study found that American managers were more likely to view certain personnel issues (such as employee theft and misuse of company information) in ethical terms than their counterparts from Austria and Germany. On the other hand, Austrian and German managers were more likely to view involvement in local politics in ethical terms. These differences may reflect cultural values. Americans tend to be highly individualistic and, as a result, may feel that the individual is the main source of ethical values. Germans and Austrians, however, tend to be more community oriented. In fact, business ethics in these countries has been described in terms of the relationship between businesses and their local environments.[23]

INTERNATIONAL INSIGHTS

Changing Hearts and Minds: Multinationals Try to Balance Ethical Behavior and the Bottom Line

MULTINATIONALS ARE BEING pressured to take a more ethical view of their business decisions around the globe. Protesters and critics have been making themselves heard and as a result, multinationals are feeling the heat. Consider these recent examples:

- Protestors showed up at Unocal gas stations in the United States and claimed the firm helped support an authoritarian regime in Myanmar through its participation in a gas-field development project. Bowing to similar pressures, Carlsberg and Heineken recently terminated their investments in Myanmar.
- Environmentalists have attacked the mining operations run by RTZ-CRA (a British firm) and Freeport-McMoRan (a U.S. firm) in Indonesia. At a recent RTZ-CRA meeting in London, Indonesian tribespeople showed up to protest and an environmentalist tried to take over the podium.[21]
- The environmental group Greenpeace opposed Royal Dutch/Shell's efforts to dispose of an old oil platform by sinking it at sea. International human rights groups also criticized the firm because of its relations with the despotic military regime that runs oil-rich Nigeria.
- ABB Asea Brown Boveri's efforts to build a dam in Malaysia have been criticized by environmental groups worried about the destruction of the rainforest in the process. Likewise, several large Asian multinationals have been pressured by various groups to cut back their aggressive logging operations on some 30 million acres of Amazonian timber.

Multinationals are taking such protests more seriously than before because ethical lapses—real or perceived—can cause consumer boycotts, poor employee morale, strained relations with foreign governments, and legal sanctions. In other words, the bottom line suffers. Ironically, many multi-nationals helped raise the stakes associated with ethical behavior in recent years by signing international agreements, adopting codes of conduct, and generally using their "ethical standards" as a public relations vehicle for winning over customers and foreign governments.

What's also happening is that critics of multinationals, such as environmental groups, have become more sophisticated and organized. Greenpeace, for instance, is a professional and international organization with offices in thirty-three nations. In fact, Greenpeace intends to expand right along with multinationals into Asia and other Third World locales. The tactics groups like Greenpeace use are also more hard hitting than they've been in the past. Filing lawsuits in developed nations like the United States in an effort to hold multinationals accountable for ethical missteps in developing countries is just one example of some of the new pressure tactics.

Some multinationals are responding by listening up front to environmentalists and other groups representing local concerns. U.S. oil firm Chevron recently gave money to protect forests in New Guinea. Barama Co., a joint venture between Malaysian and South Korean firms, has funded a local hospital near its Guyana logging facility and allowed independent experts to monitor its timber-cutting operations. Eager to avoid the trouble it got into over Nigeria, Royal Dutch/Shell now meets with Amnesty International. Shell also met with local people and sixty interested international groups before signing off on a gas field deal in Peru. After riots near its Indonesian mining operations, Freeport-McMoRan promised to give 1 percent of annual revenues to the local population, with much of it to be spent on education and health care. It appears as if continuing pressure is beginning to change the mind, if not the hearts, of many multinationals.[22]

Another interesting study compared the reactions of managers in the United States, France, and Germany to several important ethical concerns, including illegal payments, coercion, conflict of interest, and environmental issues. These issues were presented to the managers in the form of short stories that provided background. Here is an example of one of the stories that managers read:

Rollfast Bicycle Company has been barred from entering the market in a large Asian country by collusive efforts of the local bicycle manufacturers. Rollfast could expect to net

5 million dollars per year from sales if it could penetrate the market. Last week a businessman from the country contacted the management of Rollfast and stated that he could smooth the way for the company to sell in his country for a price of $500,000.

The managers were then asked whether they would pay the bribe. In most cases, U.S. managers were less likely to pay the bribe than either of the European managers, who in turn did not really differ all that much from one another. Managers were also asked about the reasons for their behavioral reactions. Not surprisingly, the reasons varied across countries. For example, nearly 50 percent of the U.S. managers said they would not pay a bribe because they thought it was unethical, illegal, or against company policy. Only 15 percent of the French and 9 percent of the Germans mentioned these reasons. Instead, the Europeans were much more likely to say that it was competition that forced them to act that way ("It is the price to be paid to do business in that country" or "Competition forces us to take the offer"). Overall, the U.S. managers were more concerned about ethical issues, while the Europeans were more concerned about maintaining a competitive business presence.[24]

By the way, if you're wondering how ethical differences between U.S. multinationals and their European competitors actually play out in reality, take a look at the following International Insights on bribery.

Other researchers working independently and with different countries and research methods have reached similar conclusions.[26] Interestingly, studies have also shown that even when attitudes about ethical issues are similar across countries, they may be the result of different moral reasoning processes.[27] These different perspectives may result from the legal frameworks of each country, their economic environments, or their unique cultural values. Nevertheless, cross-national differences in ethics may also be fairly resistant to change in the short term, even if the political, social, and economic conditions in a country are shifting dramatically. For instance, despite the incredible changes that have occurred in South Africa over the past few years, attitudes towards ethical business practices in the country have remained remarkably stable.[28]

In any case, people from other nations often think Americans go too far with their ethical principles. Some also accuse the United States of being pious and hypocritical since Americans have had their share of scandals and ethical problems. Europeans, for instance, think the United States needs to "lighten up a little"[29] and be less naive about separating business and personal ethics. Speaking of perceptions, an interesting survey was conducted by Transparency International, a nonprofit organization that tracks corruption worldwide. The survey ranked ninety nations based on the overall level of corruption as perceived by various international institutions. **Corruption** was defined as the amount of bribery, embezzlement, and behind-the-scenes activity typically involved in doing business. Exhibit 3.3 presents a set of the ten most corrupt and the ten least corrupt nations obtained from the survey, organized by their rank (from most to least corrupt) and by a total corruption score. Interestingly, the United States ranked 77th (out of 90) in the survey with a score of 7.8.[30]

Codes of ethics Another example of the different emphasis nations place on ethics can be found by looking at the presence (or absence) of corporate codes of conduct across countries.[31] One interesting study looked at this issue by comparing 600 European firms (British, French, and German) with a similar sample of American companies. The results? First, U.S. firms were more likely even to have ethical codes in the first place. Only about 30 percent of French firms had codes of ethics in place, and in German and British firms the corresponding percentages were 51 percent and 41 percent. These numbers don't even come close to the 75 percent of American companies that said they had a written code of ethics in place.[32]

INTERNATIONAL INSIGHTS

In the International Bribery Game, U.S. Multinationals Lag Behind

A RECENT U.S. government report revealed how far American multinationals lag behind their French, German, and Japanese competitors in the use of bribery to secure international business deals. In addition to outright payoffs, some of America's competitors offer inducements to their international customers or attach "conditions" to foreign aid (like signing business deals). Consider these alleged improprieties:

- France offered aid to Vietnam in exchange for 20 percent of the Vietnamese telecom market. Likewise, France said it would pull loan guarantees to an African nation unless a French firm won a $20 million telecom contract there.
- A European aerospace firm said it would lobby against European Union membership for Malta and Turkey unless those countries bought its airplanes.
- A German high-tech firm used bribes to help win eleven contracts from 1987 to 1997.
- Japan offered to cancel $30 million of Brazil's debt to Tokyo if it purchased a supercomputer from a Japanese multinational. The computer's price tag was $30 million.
- Several high-ranking Indian government officials, including an ousted prime minister, were indicted on corruption and extortion charges—some of which involved U.S. firms such as the now infamous Enron Corporation.

So what do such "greased palm" approaches cost U.S. multinationals? According to one 1994 estimate, foreign multinationals used bribery in efforts to secure 100 business deals worth $45 billion. Although it wasn't clear that corrupt practices were responsible, 80 percent of those deals were actually won by foreign multinationals. Plus, with nearly $1 trillion in foreign infrastructure projects available through 2006, there is a lot at stake for U.S. multinationals.

Foreign officials have long complained about a U.S. double standard on these issues. They point out that diplomats in America's 162 foreign embassies often help U.S. multinationals land contracts and push products. In fact, U.S. multinationals have been caught in their own bribery tangles. In 1995 a former executive at Lockheed Martin was sentenced to prison for using bribery to secure a cargo plane deal from an Egyptian government official, a clear violation of the U.S. law that forbids American firms from using bribery to get business. Other U.S. multinationals, however, have tried more unique methods to nail down international deals, including flying foreign officials to the United States where they can be wined and dined and given "spending money" for shopping.

Nevertheless, U.S. multinationals are clearly also-rans when it comes to bribery and other forms of corruption. In fact, bribery is culturally and legally permissible in many countries. In France, paying off foreigners can be written off as a tax deduction. Germany's tax laws contain similar allowances. Many U.S. business and government leaders say the answer lies in a more aggressive effort to push foreign multinationals to play the international business game by American ethical rules. In all likelihood, however, such an effort will be a tough uphill battle. [25]

Also, most European firms that did have codes of conduct had instituted them after 1984. The Zeiss company of Germany introduced a code for its employees as early as 1896, but this is the exception rather than the rule. What is more, European firms with corporate codes are much more likely to have a strong U.S. connection than those without codes. For example, 25 percent of the European firms with codes are actually subsidiaries of U.S. multinationals, whereas only 2 percent without such codes are U.S. subsidiaries.[33]

In addition to looking at whether a company had a code in place, research has also looked at differences in the content of the codes.[34] Although there are some differences among European companies, when considered as a whole they differ sharply from the codes of U.S. firms. For example, 100 percent of European firms mentioned employee conduct somewhere in their corporate codes; only 55 percent of U.S. firms dealt with this issue. In keeping with the traditional American focus on marketing, however, U.S. firms (80%) were more likely to mention customers than European companies (67%).

EXHIBIT 3.3

Rankings of the Most Corrupt and Least Corrupt Nations

Rank/Nation	CPI Rating	Rank/Nation	CPI Rating
1. Nigeria	1.2	81. United Kingdom	8.8
2. Yugoslavia	1.3	82. The Netherlands	8.9
3. Ukraine	1.5	83. Singapore	9.1
4. Azerbaijan	1.5	84. Norway	9.1
5. Indonesia	1.7	85. Iceland	9.1
6. Angola	1.7	86. Canada	9.2
7. Cameroon	2.0	87. Sweden	9.4
8. Russia	2.1	88. New Zealand	9.4
9. Kenya	2.1	89. Denmark	9.8
10. Mozambique	2.2	90. Finland	10.0

Source: Adapted from Transparency International (2000; www.transparency.de). The higher the rank and the CPI score, the lower the corruption.

Likewise, U.S. firms (86%) referred to government relations much more frequently than their European counterparts (20%).

The statements of U.S. firms about political issues also reveal important things about their outlook. Many U.S. firms state their commitment to abiding by the law but appear to mistrust the role of government in business. The corporate code of Dow Chemical, for example, states, "We pay our taxes *gladly,* yes, but we do not pay them *blindly.* We have the right to question the wisdom of regulatory zeal" (Dow's emphasis, not ours). In contrast, the few times when European firms mention political issues, they do so in general, positive ways. For example, Bertelsmann (Germany) states that it "supports a free, democratic and socially responsible society" and Wella Corp. (Germany) says that it "welcomes political, social, and cultural activities of employees."

Ethical Behavior and Human Rights

As we said earlier, almost everyone agrees certain behavior is wrong. The question that many multinationals face, however, is how should they react when they are doing business in countries run by governments that commit these wrong acts against their citizens. The reactions of firms run the gamut of possibilities. A few (such as Levi Strauss), have steadfastly refused to do business in such circumstances, whereas others (such as Mobil and Ford) continue to do business, arguing that more good can be accomplished by staying in a country.

Human rights issues in South Africa A well-known example of this range of reactions was seen in apartheid-era South Africa. Practiced by the white South African government for several decades, **apartheid** prohibited blacks from voting and from living in white areas, permitted job and pay discrimination against blacks, and required blacks get special permission to enter certain areas. For many years, it was clear that most of the world found these practices reprehensible and morally wrong. Nevertheless, South Africa remained an economic power in Africa during apartheid, accounting for 25 percent of the GNP of the whole continent. In fact, much of the world continued to do business with South Africa while apartheid was in force.

In the 1970s and 1980s, however, the issue of apartheid became more acute for multinationals doing business in South Africa. Multinationals began to feel pressure from civil rights activists and stockholders to curtail their business with South Africa. In 1977, Rev. Leon Sullivan, a Baptist minister and member of the board of directors of General Motors, developed guidelines for firms doing business in South Africa. The essence of his seven principles was that U.S. multinationals should not obey apartheid laws. To their credit, many U.S. multinationals did not—with General Motors taking the lead.[35] Ten years later, Rev. Sullivan concluded that the principles failed to result in any government changes. As a result, he changed his position and advocated a divestment strategy as well as a trade embargo rather than "constructive engagement."

Many shareholders of U.S. corporations, including large pension funds, eventually adopted the same perspective. Likewise, about 25 percent of the U.S. multinationals doing business with South Africa pulled out of the country. By 1991, there were only about 110 U.S. multinationals operating in South Africa compared to 267 in 1986. However, these figures do not include joint ventures or forms of indirect investment (e.g., Ford sold parts to a South African firm, even though it no longer made cars there).[36] In any case, it wasn't exactly clear how important the corporate boycotts were in leading to the 1994 election of President Nelson Mandela.

Interestingly, U.S. multinationals like Honeywell found that the route back into South Africa was as wrenching as their original decision to leave.[37] While the concern now is the potential for making money, multinationals returning to South Africa have also been urged to help redress the inequities that still remain from the apartheid era.[38] For example, multinationals that contribute money to build homes and schools in the squalid townships where many of the black majority still live are helping to create a more stable and ultimately more prosperous South African society.[39] Overall, the trends suggest a steady return of U.S. multinationals to South Africa. By the time President Mandela was elected in 1994, some 150 U.S. multinationals were operating in South Africa, a 40 percent increase over the previous three years. This activity leveled off at the end of the 1990s. In any case, multinationals' behavior in South Africa illustrates that even when most of the international community finds a nation's behavior morally reprehensible, a clear and consistent reaction from corporations does not necessarily follow.[40]

Human rights issues in China This last statement can also apply to China. This country has seen an enormous influx of foreign investment in recent years, and as we have documented in earlier chapters, is booming in many ways. The trouble, however, is that by many accounts China is responsible for a wide variety of human rights violations. According to groups like Amnesty International and Human Rights Watch, the Chinese government is responsible for suppressing individual freedoms that many countries take as a given and for other serious abuses.

These include the operation of some 1,200 prison labor camps (where the majority of prisoners are political criminals), capricious arrests, the use of child labor, and unsafe working conditions (outside prison camps). In fact, a recent U.S. State Department report on human rights in China referred to a variety of human rights abuses that included arbitrary detention and forced confessions.[41] The following International Insights documents what happened to one Chinese man who was employed by Chrysler at its joint venture operation in China.

Nevertheless, most U.S. multinationals—as well as the U.S. government—continue to press a familiar argument. They say that a business presence in China must be maintained in order to be able to influence the human rights situation there, the same argument used decades earlier in South Africa. It may be the right one. In fact, experts say that by improving working conditions in China, multinationals can help change attitudes towards human rights in general and workers in particular. This goes beyond having a multinational set a positive example by providing good pay and a safe working environment. For instance, multinationals can give local employees opportunities for

INTERNATIONAL INSIGHTS

Human Rights Issues for U.S. Multinationals in China: The Case of Gao Feng

GAO FENG was an employee at Beijing Jeep, a joint venture between Chrysler Corporation and the Chinese government. We say "was an employee" because he was suspended and told to either resign or be fired by the company. His offense? A serious level of absenteeism by the standards of almost any company—he was a no-show for over a month! However, there is much more to the story than this.

When he returned to the factory after his month-long absence, Gao told his boss that he had been arrested by the police. During a Christian memorial service that commemorated the victims of the government crackdown and violence in 1989, police raided the location and arrested the participants, among them Gao, and held them for over four weeks. Because the police failed to provide proof of his whereabouts during this period of time, Beijing Jeep suspended Gao and gave him the resign-or-else ultimatum.

This may have just been another of many sad cases had the Associated Press not picked up the story. A few months later, the media also linked Chrysler's Chinese partner with a sweatshop that used forced prison labor for production. Chrysler has denied the reports, reiterating its pledge not to use components that are produced by prison labor. All this had occurred in the context of a failed negotiation with the Chinese government to produce minivans and reports that Chinese factories were manufacturing low-cost, knockoff versions of the Chrysler Jeep. Therefore, even if the prison

labor claims were not true, they were bad publicity for Chrysler. That publicity—in combination with the acknowledged troubles that Chrysler was having—made doing business in China all that more difficult. So Gao's case was something of an embarrassment.

Gao told reporters that he refused to quit. Eventually he was reinstated by Beijing Jeep. He attributes his success to a sense of moral obligation from the company, to public pressure from the media, and to Human Rights Watch (the organization that championed his case). Chrysler's side of the story was that Gao was never suspended or dismissed. He simply overreacted when he returned to see his job posted and jumped to the wrong conclusions. Chrysler said jobs were routinely posted after two weeks of absence. Plus, no one told Beijing Jeep of Gao's whereabouts and the police denied holding him more than one day. Chrysler also said that it could not check into the incident further because doing so would be inconsistent with the way business is done in China. In effect, Chrysler worried that it would be unable to push Chinese authorities to the extent that it would in the United States. The concern was that if Chrysler criticized the actions of the police, it might offend Chinese authorities to the point where they would tell the firm to leave. By maintaining a low-key approach, Chrysler felt it was helping China become a better place for all employees at Beijing Jeep.

This worker naps on a pile of hoses in downtown Beijing, providing a backdrop for the debate about how employees are treated in China.
© AFP/CORBIS

personal growth and development, including training designed to increase respect for individuals and tolerance of differences. This kind of training could increase upward mobility within the multinational and also create opportunities for employment else-where if necessary. Over time, these steps may help contribute to the development of a more sophisticated and enlightened workforce in China.[42]

Others, however, feel that doing business with countries like China only condones their poor human rights records. In fact, this is the position of the **Laogai Research Foundation**, headed by Harry Wu of Stanford University. The institute claims that despite the increasing presence of foreign multinationals, conditions are actually getting worse in China as the authorities become more edgy about what will happen when a new generation takes the lead. Mr. Wu himself spent nineteen years in Chinese prison labor camps for his public criticism of Chinese support for the 1956 Soviet invasion of Hungary. Since then he has been a thorn in China's side by revealing evidence of many human rights violations. A few years ago, Mr. Wu entered China illegally (he is a U.S. citizen) and videotaped several prison labor camps like the Hangzhou Hardware & Tool Works, where nearly 1,600 political prisoners march to work every day. Tools from the factory are exported all over the world, including to the United States. The institute estimates that nearly 10 million people are being held in such camps, most of whom were sent there for speaking out against the government. These people are forced to work against their will in dangerous conditions for many hours a day; they are often beaten, tortured, and poorly fed.[43]

Despite these revelations—that few deny outside China—almost no multinationals have taken stands similar to those that were seen in South Africa. There are a few prominent exceptions. Reebok International, while continuing their presence in China, has at the same time made their position clear to the government. The company sent an unambiguous notice to the Chinese government after the Tiananmen Square massacre in 1989 by creating a human rights award. The award was given to the four main leaders of the Chinese democracy movement. To further ensure that its Chinese partners don't use prison labor, Reebok asks them to sign affidavits. So far, the response has been good. Reebok, along with rock star Peter Gabriel and the Lawyer's Committee for Human Rights, also provides financial support for the group Witness. This group provides video cameras and fax machines to local human rights groups all over the world, including those in China.

Other firms, like the Timberland Company, a shoe and apparel manufacturer, pulled out of China in 1993 because the government did not support the firm's beliefs about the value of employees. Levi Strauss, the San Francisco–based firm that is the world's largest apparel maker, also pulled out of China. Levi Strauss is internationally known for their products. What is not so well known is the clear and strong stand the firm takes on ethical guidelines for conducting international business. The company is one of the few American multinationals that has gone against the grain with their business practices around the globe in general, and in China in particular.

Levi Strauss's interests in China were not large, amounting to about $50 million per year. But in May 1993 the firm announced that it would phase out operations in China. The decision to leave China was based on an application of a clear set of corporate values that had been developed a few years earlier. In fact, since the mid-1980s, the firm has embraced a management style that emphasizes values and ethical practices.[44] During this time, a company task force worked for three years on developing a set of guidelines for doing business overseas. The result was a two-part set of guidelines (see Exhibit 3.4) that Levi Strauss uses with foreign contractors and business partners. The first part, called **Business Partner Terms of Engagement**, deals with issues that its business partners can control. As you can see, these include issues such as workplace health and safety, employment practices, and general ethics. For example, Levi Strauss clearly states that it will not do business with partners who use prison or child labor.

According to Levi Strauss, most of its foreign partners wanted to treat their employees well, and even those not in compliance were often interested in working toward adherence to company principles. Nevertheless, Levi's did find that a portion (about 5%) were not meeting the guidelines and there was no indication that they ever would. As a result, Levi Strauss terminated these business relationships. This was true in China, where Levi Strauss had great concern about worker safety, prison labor, and China's one-child policy. Arriving at this decision was difficult and took weeks of meetings and debates among Levi Strauss's China policy group.[45]

Eventually, the firm chose to drop China. Levi Strauss continues to review such decisions (such as leaving Myanmar) via their terms of engagement (Exhibit 3.4) and other country selection criteria. As far as China is concerned, however, critics of Levi-Strauss have suggested that leaving was nothing more than a public relations move. They noted that the company had little direct investment in China and would have no trouble finding contractors to operate in other low-cost countries. Levi Strauss admitted that its decision could be an image boost but still claimed that it sacrificed great economic potential by leaving China.[46] In 1998, the company lifted its self-imposed restrictions on doing business in China after one of its periodic reviews. With a changing competetive landscape, and more experience in working with contractors to assure they work within the terms of engagement, Levi's felt the change of policy as warranted.

EXHIBIT 3.4

Levi Strauss's Business Partner Terms of Engagement

1. **Ethical Standards:**
   We will seek to identify and utilize business partners who aspire as individuals and in the conduct of all their businesses to a set of ethical standards not incompatible with our own.

2. **Legal Requirements:**
   We expect our business partners to be law abiding as individuals and to comply with legal requirements relevant to the conduct of all their businesses.

3. **Environmental Requirements:**
   We will only do business with partners who share our commitment to the environment and who conduct their business in a way that is consistent with Levi Strauss & Co.'s Environmental Philosophy and Guiding Principles.

4. **Community Involvement:**
   We will favor business partners who share our commitment to improving community conditions.

5. **Employment Standards:**
   We will only do business with partners who adhere to the following guidelines:

   ● **Child Labor:** Use of child labor is not permissible. Workers can be no less than 15 years of age and not younger than the compulsory age to be in school. We will not utilize partners who use child labor in any of their facilities. We support the development of legitimate workplace apprenticeship programs for the educational benefit of younger people.

   ● **Prison Labor/Forced Labor:** We will not utilize prison or forced labor in contracting relationships in the manufacture and finishing of our products. We will not utilize or purchase materials from a business partner utilizing prison or forced labor.

   ● **Disciplinary Practices:** We will not utilize business partners who use corporal punishment or other forms of mental or physical coercion.

   ● **Working Hours:** While permitting flexibility in scheduling, we will identify prevailing local work hours and seek business partners who do not exceed them except for appropriately compensated overtime. While we favor partners who utilize less than 60-hour workweeks, we will not use contractors who, on a regularly scheduled basis, require in excess of a 60-hour week. Employees should be allowed at least one day off in seven.

   ● **Wages and Benefits:** We will only do business with partners who provide wages and benefits that comply with any applicable law and match the prevailing local manufacturing or finishing industry practices.

   ● **Freedom of Association:** We respect workers' rights to form and join organizations of their choice and to bargain collectively. We expect our suppliers to respect the right to free association and the right to organize and bargain collectively without unlawful interference. Business partners should ensure that workers who make such decisions or participate in such organizations are not the objects of discrimination or punitive disciplinary actions and that the representatives of such organizations have access to their members under conditions established either by local laws or mutual agreement between the employer and the worker organizations.

   ● **Discrimination:** While we recognize and respect cultural differences, we believe that workers should be employed on the basis of their ability to do the job, rather than on the basis of personal characteristics or beliefs. We will favor business partners who share this value.

   ● **Health & Safety:** We will only utilize business partners who provide workers with a safe and healthy work environment. Business partners who provide residential facilities for their workers must provide safe and healthy facilities.

Source: These Terms of Engagement are copyrighted by Levi Strauss & Co. and presented here by permission. An original copy of the Terms and the corresponding "Guidelines for Country Selection" can be obtained by visiting their web site at http://www.levistrauss.com/about/ (by permission). Business Partner Terms of Engagement: Copyright © 2001 Levi Strauss & Co.

Overall, however, Levi Strauss clearly considers many ethical issues to be universal in nature and that these principles should guide corporate behavior. To ensure this, Levi Strauss believes the best answer is to develop and enforce a specific set of conduct codes that foreign business partners must follow. At the same time, however, Levi's became aware a few years ago that two of the company's contractors in Bangladesh were employing children under 14 years of age. Although acceptable under Bangladesh law, it violated international labor standards and Levi's code. After studying the situation further, however, the company discovered that the underage children were often the sole source of support for their families. Levi's asked the contractor to have the children quit work and go back to school at their expense (including books, tuition, uniforms) until they came of age.[47] Take a look at our Reality Check Box, where similar issues are touched on in our interview with a global manager.

Enforcement issues with codes of conduct   In fact, the use of such conduct codes have been increasing lately, at least among U.S. multinationals. Unlike Levi Strauss, however, many multinationals take a more relativistic view in their codes for foreign business partners. For instance, Nike at one point relied on language that suggested it would be sufficient if its foreign contractors adhered to local labor laws. Nike toughened its code after critics said that requiring contractors to comply with local laws did little to protect workers in places like China and Indonesia because the laws were so weak to begin with.[48]

But tougher codes aren't always enough. The real issue may be enforcement. For instance, Levi Strauss conducts periodic audits of all their partners to see if they are in compliance with their conduct code. In 1992, an audit of over 700 partners in more than fifty countries showed relatively high compliance rates, with nearly 70 percent found to be observing company standards.[49]

Despite its industry-leading systematic enforcement efforts, Levi-Strauss has admitted that it doesn't catch everything. Part of the reason is that when code inspectors probe the operations set up by foreign contractors, there may be a tendency to refrain from going so deep as to cause offense. Other companies, however, rely on contractors to police themselves. For instance, J.C. Penney Co. has foreign suppliers sign a conduct code that prohibits violations of local labor laws. But Penney's own Guatemalan contractors say that the company is only concerned with product quality and that it doesn't check on working conditions in their operations. In fact, these contractors sometimes use child labor, pay less than the legal minimum wage, and require unpaid overtime when producing apparel for Penney's. The response of Penney's and other U.S. retailers such as Target is that enforcing conduct codes is virtually impossible because they are supplied by thousands of factories in dozens of countries. But even limited enforcement may help. Wal-Mart, for example, conducts occasional inspections at its Guatemalan plants, and this practice resulted in fewer labor violations than did comparable factories doing work for Penney's.

Overall, critics charge that without enforcement, conduct codes are nothing more than public relations efforts designed to assuage customers about poor working conditions in developing countries.[50] Even with such legal protection, however, there can be serious problems. Indeed, a cover story in a recent *Business Week*, titled "Workers in Bondage," has documented many of these same effects in many European countries.[51] Western Europeans have long prided themselves on the high standards they impose on employers. And workers have many more legal protections than in the United States. Yet despite this, the hundreds of thousands of economic refugees who are pouring into Europe from China, India, the old Soviet bloc, and elsewhere are sometimes facing horrific conditions in countries such as England, France, Italy, and Spain.

REALITY CHECK

Ethics Is No Carnival in Brazil

A chat with John Williams (a pseudonym), global purchasing manager for a medium-sized multinational

Can you tell us a little about yourself? What is your background in international business?

I have been with this firm for my whole career. I'm over 50 now, and I've been with this company for twenty-six years. During this time, I've had a variety of assignments, but probably none more interesting than that in Brazil.

What was especially noteworthy about your expat experience in Brazil?

Well, there I encountered a very thorny ethical issue, one that frankly bothers me still today.

Could you tell us a little bit about your firm as background for understanding this issue?

Sure. We're an American firm and we've got operations in a number of different countries, including Brazil. In fact, when this issue occurred, we had just purchased an operation from a large Brazilian company. We then moved the equipment to a new building and started back up in record time—actually in about three months. We hired new line employees, but we

used the existing staff line in Brazil as well as some divisional support from the United States.

Can you give us some details about this issue you faced?

It all started when I as the country manager exhorted various groups such as quality and purchasing to (big surprise) cut costs and improve quality. The managers of these groups began to tour factories of our suppliers in some small rural towns to address these issues. In one factory, they noticed that about a half dozen of the workers were very young, maybe 13 at most. Recalling the company's ethical code that had been drummed into them, they were deeply concerned. One of the managers raised this child labor issue and this made the supplier very embarrassed; they began a frantic discussion in Portuguese to the firm's Brazilians who were in the visiting party. After several minutes of emotional discussion, an explanation was offered by the suppliers (in English) to us. And our Brazilians supported the explanation; indicating it was normal, acceptable, and legal—generally not a problem.

What exactly was this explanation? Our readers would definitely want to know.

Ethics Associated with Questionable Payments and Bribery

Concerns about whether multinationals are responsible for protecting workers—even when they work for foreign contractors—are big ethical questions, to be sure. However, there are many other issues around which the universalism versus relativism debate swirls. In Saudi Arabia, for example, it is illegal to hire female managers for many jobs.[52] For an American, however, there is legal protection for gender discrimination in employment. So is it unethical to do business in Saudi Arabia? Likewise, is it unethical to avoid strict environmental laws by locating facilities offshore? Finally, is it right for a U.S. multinational to market a drug in Malaysia that failed to receive U.S. government approval because there are questions about a possible link to cancer?

U.S. multinationals in many of these cases have cogently argued that their ethically questionable actions are justified and even morally correct. Indeed, as we mentioned earlier, the relativistic position enjoys a great deal of credence and is apparently attractive to some multinationals, even though some prominent observers have rejected it.

One common practice in international business that intersects with ethical relativism is the use of **questionable payments**. This refers to practices like bribery, extortion, and "grease" payments to bureaucrats and business leaders, both foreign and

It was that even in this small town, children are left homeless and parentless. The only alternative for these kids is to live off the street, and they end up begging and stealing. If they do, the townfolks pressure the police to "run the delinquents off." Strangers may victimize the children or recruit them for criminal activities in the big cities. So the courts have required local large businesses to provide room, board, and other services (medical care, education, an allowance) to these homeless kids. In return, the businesses can have them do some tasks similar to household chores (run errands, wash cars, etc.). They said that this was a successful program to not abandon children, unlike what they had heard is done in the United States. Interestingly, every one of our Brazilian managers thought it was okay. They also pointed out that the firm's headquarters in Brazil has office boys that run errands and the like, and that Brazilian law lets 12-year-olds work in some jobs.

So was it okay from your perspective? What did you do?

My response was one of suspicion. I asked for copies of documents that sanctioned the relationship between the courts and the children/company. Our Brazilians told me that it would be insulting to ask for this and "a sign we didn't trust them," and that "besides it would be in Portuguese and you don't read the language." I said that I understood this cultural issue, but that I needed my American cultural values met, too—which meant some form of proof. I went back to my office without a resolution.

How did it get resolved? Or is it resolved?

In followup visits in smaller, informal groups I asked a Brazilian with lots of U.S. experience to make the request again, in private, to the supplier's management. The result of this was that we got a promise that we'd get some documentation. Feeling pretty satisfied with my cleverness, I returned to the office. But the documentation never came. Over time, the issue was always in the background and never quite resolved. We never got any paperwork! We ended up not giving them any new business and as the "legacy" business was completed, we dropped them from our bidder's list.

What's your take on this now, after all this time?

We never really documented that we quit doing business with them because of child labor/ethical issues. But I have often wondered if we lacked the courage of our convictions in not formally criticizing the supplier and disassociating ourselves earlier. Or whether we were protecting the flow of material for our company, or if by not creating documents that could later be used to prove our knowledge of this situation in a news story or lawsuit? I really don't know. I also don't know that the children were exploited by the company any more than they would been by an orphanage, foster parents, or by begging on Sao Paulo streets. I do know, though, that I still have a very uncomfortable feeling about the whole affair.

domestic. Bribery and related activity has a long and venerable history in international business.[53] In addition to direct monetary payments, this activity also includes things, such as giving expensive gifts (jewelry, art, and other collectibles), providing lavish entertainment, and offering free trips to foreign or domestic dignitaries.

In fact, the use of illegal or questionable payments has been common practice in many societies throughout recorded history—whether it is Africa, Asia, the Middle East, Europe, or the Americas.[54] Records of many early civilizations show that bribery was common. Indeed, bribery is so much a part of nearly every culture that most languages have a word for it.[55] While we're certainly not suggesting you use these words in business dealings, Exhibit 3.5 does show examples of words from around the world that reflect such questionable payments.

For example, the payment of *baksheesh* in some Arab and Turkish-speaking countries reflects the questionable or illegal payoffs to which we are referring. The presence and frequency of political payments in such countries may reflect centuries of rule by an all-powerful state (like the Ottoman Empire). Here, *baksheesh* could provide the protection for businesses that an imperfect and abusive legal system could not. Likewise, in Mexico the term *la mordida* (literally, "the bite") might reflect a similar history and sense of powerlessness with the government bureaucracy.[56] The terms in

EXHIBIT 3.5

Words That Mean Bribery in a Variety of Different Countries

Country	Word	Country	Word
Brazil	*jeitinho*	Japan	*wairo*
Egypt	*baksheesh*	Malaysia	*makan siap*
France	*pot au vin*	Mexico	*mordida*
Germany	*Trink Gelt/Schmiergeld*	Nigeria	*dash*
Greece	*baksissi*	Pakistan	*roshvat*
Honduras	*pajada*	Peru	*coima*
Hong Kong	*hatchien*	Philippines	*lagay*
India	*speed money/baksheesh*	Russia	*vzyatha*
Indonesia	*uong sogok*	Thailand	*sin bone*
Iran	*roshveh*	United States	*grease money/payola*
Italy	*bustarella*	Zaire	*tarif de verre*

Source: Adapted from Jacoby, N. H., Nehemkis, P., & Eells, R. (1977). *Bribery and extortion in world business: A study of corporate political payments abroad.* New York: McMillan.

other languages—like the Italian *bustarella* ("little envelope") and the French *pot au vin* ("jug of wine")—carry vivid and evocative images. In Nigeria, the foreign firm that doesn't "dash" local bureaucrats may not be able to function in that country.

Of course, the United States is hardly the perfect bastion of proper business practices. The history of American business is replete with examples of such corruption. In fact, some experts feel that certain U.S. industries, such as food, retail, and construction, are still fertile areas for corruption.

Interestingly, almost every country in the world explicitly outlaws bribery of its own officials.[57] So if someone representing a multinational makes such an illegal payment to a foreign official, they technically risk prosecution in that country. In some countries there is actually little or no risk involved since bribery is commonplace if not expected. In some cases, however, the magnitude of the bribery and other forms of corruption (like embezzlement of company or government funds) may be just too great to ignore, even if bribery is an accepted and common practice. When this occurs, the corrupt official or business leader may be hauled into court and prosecuted.

Bribery across countries   This seems to be what is happening in France. A crackdown has been underway, led by French magistrates who are fed up with an elitist system of cozy relationships between business and government. The widespread corruption (bribery, kickbacks, embezzlement) that is a side effect of this system (known in France as *dirigisme*) is what the magistrates have zeroed in on. Part of their motivation is a concern that pervasive corruption has contributed to France's anemic economy, high unemployment rate, and inward-looking, uncompetitive companies. What's stunning about the French crackdown is its scope. Since 1995, *dozens* of top executives and politicians have been targeted for investigation, if not already convicted and jailed, and these include leaders of some of France's most well-known companies.[58]

Clearly, France is not the only country where concern about bribery and other corrupt practices, especially those linked to cozy relations between government and business, has prompted local crackdowns.[59] Consider this roster of incidents that have either resulted in criminal convictions or that have prompted various investigations:

- A $350 billion bad loan scandal in Japan exposed the close cooperation that often exists between Ministry of Finance bureaucrats, political leaders, bankers, and organized criminal gangs (collectively known as the **yakuza**). Questionable loans were allegedly made to yakuza front companies even as yakuza members were attending fundraisers for Japanese politicians. Criminal prosecutions are expected.[60]
- Top executives of eight South Korean firms (including Samsung and Daewoo) were given prison terms in 1996 for bribing a former South Korean president. All of this resulted from the discovery of the former president's $650 million slush fund, apparently built in large part by bribes from South Korean companies.[61]
- In Tanzania, an anticorruption commission is uncovering evidence of widespread bribe taking among high-level officials of the Chama Cha Mapinduzi (CCM), the current ruling majority party. Who's behind the bribes? Businesses that want to avoid Tanzania's heavy tax burden. A bribe can get a company a tax exemption.[62]
- In the United States, the Justice Department scrutinized donations made to the Democratic Party by Indonesia's Lippo Group, a $12 billion real estate firm. The donations may have violated U.S. law prohibiting foreign money from being used in American elections. Critics also alleged that Indonesian money helped secure favorable treatment from the Clinton administration on foreign policy positions affecting Indonesian business. The issue crosses party lines since Republicans have also received Indonesian money in the past.[63]
- Opposition party leaders in Moscow are threatening investigations and legislative changes to curb emerging Russian conglomerates that seem to have "uncles" (*dyadyas*) within the government to watch out for them. They provide the conglomerates with breaks on taxes, import duties, and legislation involving foreign competitors, allegedly in return for payoffs. Some thirty-two of these Russian industrial giants run 500 factories, 72 banks, and have 2.5 million employees.[64]

The examples that we've been talking about so far involve investigations of internal forms of possible bribery and corruption, where a country's political or business leaders may somehow be "on the take." Very few countries, however, outlaw bribes by their citizens to public officials of a *foreign* country. Most countries take the "when in Rome" perspective, maintaining that common practice should be followed by its citizens in that foreign nation. In fact, some countries like Switzerland go further than that by allowing their businesses to take tax writeoffs for bribes paid to foreign governments.[65] This is at minimum a tacit endorsement of such practices.

Until a few decades ago, payoffs by U.S. firms to foreign representatives were also common. In the mid-1970s, however, several high-level cases of corporate corruption became widely publicized. At the time, the United States was very sensitive to corruption because of the Watergate scandal that eventually caused President Richard Nixon to resign. For instance, Carl Kotchian, president of Lockheed, made payments to Japanese government officials and agents in order to secure a large contract from Nippon Air to buy Lockheed airliners. Mr. Kotchian was contacted by Japanese officials and told that if Lockheed wanted the contract, they would have to make some payments to close the sale. He was approached several additional times for further payments, which ended up totaling $12.5 million.[66] When the press uncovered the Lockheed payments, the firm was charged with many tax code violations as well as with falsifying records. Interestingly, experts point out that although such illicit payments were supposed to be a common business practice in Japan, the public disclosure of the Lockheed payments created quite a furor in that country as well.[67] Government officials involved in this incident were criminally charged and one even committed suicide.[68]

In any case, the Lockheed incident received wide attention and explanation, including an article detailing the events by Mr. Kotchian himself.[69] More detailed analysis shows that this represented only one facet of Lockheed's foreign bribery payments.[70] Lockheed, however, was hardly alone. Apparently, nearly 450 U.S. corporations made inappropriate payments to foreign officials or companies during the period of 1974 to 1976 when the Lockheed situation occurred. The reaction of the already outraged American public pushed Congress to pass the *Foreign Corrupt Practices Act* (FCPA), which became law in 1977 and was later amended to clarify some ambiguous provisions.

The Foreign Corrupt Practices Act   The FCPA made it illegal to pay or offer to pay officials of foreign governments to gain or increase business. Penalties for violators include fines up to $1,000,000 for companies, as well as fines and up to five years' imprisonment for the individuals involved. Interestingly, the current version of the FCPA *does not* prohibit all "questionable" payments to foreign officials or governments. Actually, a distinction is made between bribes and facilitating payments. The latter are often called **grease payments** because they are made to "grease the wheels" of business. It is not illegal to make payments to low- and middle-level officials so that they will perform functions that they are ordinarily obliged to do as part of their job.

For example, in many countries, it is absolutely necessary to provide small payments to customs officials in order to get them to do what they legally should do, such as inspect and pass the imports of a U.S. multinational. Sometimes foreign customs officials will impede or backlog a shipment until they receive the grease payments. Other examples of grease payments that are not illegal under the FCPA include: (1) providing "gifts" that help overcome bureaucratic technicalities that impede business; (2) "gifts" given to supplement an environment of low wages, with the gifts acting as gratuities for services performed; and (3) the facilitation of permits and equipment that are allotted via the extra payments. Essentially, the difference between a bribe and a grease payment usually is that grease payments are relatively small and they are not offered to get anything more than a business is entitled to anyway (such as an import license). To some ethicists, however, this is a distinction without a difference.

Effects of the FCPA   Although the FCPA was signed by then President Jimmy Carter with some fanfare, a number of U.S. multinationals complained about it. The complaints largely centered around the effect of the law on the competitiveness of American business. Several prominent business leaders pointed out that they had lost contracts with foreign governments in the past because they refused to pay requested bribes. In fact, they noted that companies with inferior products and services—who in a fair environment would not receive the contract—often ended up getting the business.

These business leaders argued that the FCPA would dramatically exaggerate this effect. In order to compete effectively, U.S. businesses must also be allowed to use methods of competition—including bribery—that foreign multinationals are able to use.[71] Furthermore, as we pointed out earlier, some executives noted that other governments not only do not outlaw bribes, they sometimes sanction them by allowing bribes to be tax deductible (e.g., Germany and Switzerland). How, then, can U.S. business compete in world markets with such restrictions?[72]

Actually, research has been done to answer the question of whether or not the FCPA had a negative effect on the competitiveness of U.S. business. One study looked at the market share of U.S. business since the passage of the FCPA in two different types of countries. This involved surveying U.S. embassy and Department of Commerce officials about business practices in over fifty different countries. The goal of this part of the study was to identify countries where the prevalence of improper payments was very high and countries where this practice was rare. Having done this, the study then examined whether the passage of the FCPA was more likely to be an export disincentive in countries where illegal payments are common. It also looked at change in market share before the passage of the FCPA (1971–1976) and after passage (1977–1980). Interestingly, the FCPA did not decrease the overall competitiveness of American multinationals overseas. In fact, there were no differences in market shares between the two types of countries either before or after the passage of the FCPA.[73]

However, this study does have some limitations. For one, the researchers studied the effects over a relatively short time interval, after passage of the FCPA. Competitiveness could decline slowly over time as a result of the act. Second, the market share data themselves are quite variable. For example, in the airline industry it was common to observe market share changes of nearly 100 percent over a year. Although this was not consistently associated with countries where bribery is common, it does show that the data can jump around dramatically. Boeing, for example, may sign a contract with Saudi Arabia one year and be shut out entirely next year when Airbus Industrie gets the next Saudi contract.[74]

Nevertheless, although the data are far from perfect, an initial conclusion would be that the FCPA does not significantly affect American international competitiveness overall. This doesn't mean, however, that U.S. multinationals don't lose out on specific business ventures because they won't provide a cut to a foreign partner. For example, American telecom firms complained about being shut out of contracts awarded by Ecuador as it privatized the state-run phone company. Some 90 percent of the nearly 200 contracts awarded went to non-U.S. firms, allegedly because American firms wouldn't pay 10 percent of a contract's value to government officials.[75] Likewise, Ford Motor Co. felt it lost out on a car venture in Indonesia because rival Hyundai cut a sweetheart deal with one of President Suharto's sons. In fact, some multinationals at the time felt that without an ally in the Suharto family, business deals simply didn't get done in Indonesia. Plus, having one of President Suharto's six children as a joint venture partner wasn't illegal per se under American law.[76] However, such a situation serves to illustrate once again the many ethical gray areas that exist in international business.

Summing up questionable payments   At this point, we can only speculate about the level of corrupt activities currently being carried out by American multinationals. Certainly, some questionable behavior is still going on. With few exceptions, however, American multinationals have done quite a bit to eliminate corruption in their international dealings. Nevertheless, in 1988, one of the largest ad agencies in the world, Young & Rubicam (Y&R)—and three of its executives—were indicted under the FCPA. The U.S. Justice Department claimed that the firm had violated the act by using one of its Jamaican agents to indirectly bribe the Jamaican Minister of Tourism in an illegal effort to obtain business. Y&R agreed to pay a $500,000 fine to settle the case.[77]

One response of many U.S. firms—like Y&R—is to develop clear corporate guidelines about illegal payments and to communicate them directly to their managers. In fact, it is estimated that almost 80 percent of U.S. multinationals have incorporated

Enforcement of India's child labor laws is lax, as this six-year-old, who works at a construction site to help support his widowed mother, demonstrates. © AFP/CORBIS

such guidelines into their operations. As we pointed out earlier, the percentage for U.S. multinationals with such guidelines is much larger than for multinationals of several other nations. Some of these codes, like Caterpillar's, provide detailed guidelines about what payments are and are not permitted. In fact, some corporate codes, like IBM's (and now Y&R's), take a very strong ethical position. IBM, for instance, does not allow its managers to even use grease payments that are legally permitted under the FCPA. In general, however, these codes are not very precise, and they usually tell managers what they shouldn't do as opposed to what they should.[78]

As a result, some experts actually recommend that multinationals set up ethics hotlines that employees can call anonymously.[79] Although there are many hurdles to overcome, including how to deal with false allegations, at least some firms are starting such hotlines. Another proactive step that some U.S. multinationals are taking is to make efforts to convince foreign multinationals and their governments—mostly through U.S. government channels—to implement stronger laws against bribery and other corrupt practices.[80] In general, however, such efforts have not been very successful. The following International Insights provides more details on these and other obstructions that U.S. managers face in conducting international business.

Ethical Issues Emerging from Countries Converting to Capitalism

In this final section, we examine the social problems that multinationals may help create in countries moving toward more competitive market economies. For instance,

INTERNATIONAL INSIGHTS

Making Friends and Influencing People: How U.S. Firms Compete Where Bribes Flourish

U.S. MULTINATIONALS are often constrained by their own corporate codes of conduct as well as by the Foreign Corrupt Practices Act (FCPA). The bottom line is that U.S. businesspeople can't engage in many of the practices that other countries permit their firms to do. So how do U.S. firms compete in this environment? Well, consider Percy Chubb III. He's spending a million dollars trying to make friends and presumably influence people. Mr. Chubb, the vice chairman of Chubb Insurance, wants a license from Chinese officials in order to tap that country's potentially large insurance market. So the company has set up a $1 million program to teach insurance at Shanghai University. It has also named as board members some of the officials who eventually will decide if Chubb gets its license. "You try to show them this is a two-way street," explains Mr. Chubb, who says his company has spent "millions" on similar projects to improve its prospects overseas.

Such behavior exemplifies the strategy used by many U.S. firms, an approach that contrasts sharply with the blatant bribery that is still common in much of the world. Aggressive European and Asian companies commonly use payoffs to gain access to big, fast-developing markets. Of course, some U.S. firms are doing the same thing. Unlike their European and Asian counterparts, however, they are subject to the big teeth of the FCPA if they get caught. For instance, Lockheed-Martin Corp. was convicted in 1995 of paying $1.5 million to an Egyptian official who helped the firm get an aircraft contract. The company paid $24 million in fines, which was more than twice the profits from the contract itself. Likewise, Goodyear Tire & Rubber Co. recently pleaded guilty to offering bribes to an Iraqi company and paid fines of $250,000. Also, U.S.-based Napco International recently paid a $1 million fine after admitting it paid bribes to government officials in Niger to obtain an aircraft contract.

A much more common strategy, however, is the Chubb approach of using donations and other "philanthropic" activity to exert influence, actions that are permitted under the FCPA. When IBM chairman Louis Gerstner visited Beijing in 1995, for instance, the company donated $25 million in hardware and software to twenty Chinese universities. Another common example of this strategy is to offer foreign officials trips to the United States. "Those trips provide an excellent opportunity to build relations with customers," said William Warwick, chairman of the China operations for AT&T Corp. For instance, when Union Texas Petroleum formed a joint venture with Pakistan's government, the company said it would spend more than $200,000 a year training those government officials in the United States and Europe.

Once in the United States, foreign officials often spend at least part of their time visiting factories and the like. But side trips to places such as Disney World, Las Vegas, and Atlantic City appear to be very common. For example, Dow Jones & Co. arranged an Atlantic City trip for one delegation from China. In fact, Atlantic City casinos often give such foreign visitors $25 to play at the slot machines. Although this may seen like small change, for some Chinese officials it is the equivalent of a week's salary. In addition, the daily allowances given to the Chinese by their U.S. hosts, even just over a two-week period, can equal a year's pay. One U.S. electronics company operating in China pays allowances of $125 a day for visitors to its California headquarters.

None of these payments is illegal under the FCPA. "But is it corruption?" an executive asks. "I mean, if someone came up to me and offered me something worth eighteen months' salary, it would certainly get my attention." Even the U.S. government lends a hand. A U.S. diplomat in eastern Europe says that sometimes the government will pay for a ministry head to visit America before a U.S. company bids on a big contract. The U.S. Department of Commerce employs this strategy with many countries around the world.

All this activity and more is likely to continue in the future. One reason is that U.S. government efforts to get foreign countries to ban bribery have faced great resistance. In fact, France, Germany and Britain have all been quick to cite reasons why they can't adopt their own versions of the FCPA. That's why many U.S. firms will continue to use "creative" strategies to help win business.[81]

privatization is a trend sweeping the globe. This is especially true in China, Latin America, the former Soviet Union, and eastern Europe. Africa is likely to follow in a big way.[82] Multinationals often view this trend as an opportunity to buy up state-owned firms, thereby providing a foothold in what are becoming important emerging markets. Likewise, low wage rates in developing nations have become an irresistible lure for many multinationals.

However, multinationals also need to be aware of the social problems that they may contribute to as a result of increased economic activity. For instance, because of weak regulations in many emerging countries, as their economic growth rates have shot up, so has the pollution of their water and air. In fact, the deteriorating environment in these countries threatens to be an expensive social headache and major source of conflict. Just creating the infrastructure to provide an adequate water supply for developing Asian nations will cost an estimated $100 billion in 2002. Another $50 billion or more will be needed to combat serious air pollution problems in many Asian cities. Recently, officials in India's Delhi state say court-ordered shutdown of small polluting industrial units will eliminate the jobs of 2 million people.[83]

Ironically, the transition to market economies can also create poverty. A recent United Nations report suggests that the economic growth of many countries that are transitioning to market-based systems masks the fact that millions of people are becoming impoverished as a result of the transition.[84] For example, millions of workers lost their jobs in state-owned firms in eastern Europe in recent years. In places such as the Czech Republic, Hungary, and Poland, multinationals have purchased many former state enterprises and promptly proceeded to slash workforces. Granted, many communist-era state businesses were overstaffed, backward, and inefficient. Nevertheless, wholesale terminations have raised unemployment rates, hurt worker morale, and caused resentment.[85] In some places, the numbers are staggering. The unemployment rate in eastern Germany is about 17 percent, roughly three times the rate in the western half of the country. Almost 200,000 jobs in this former communist country were lost in 1996.[86]

A similar trend exists in many Latin American countries like Argentina. There, privatizations are resulting in massive layoffs that are driving up unemployment and poverty.[87] Likewise, many African countries have bloated and inefficient state-owned businesses, but privatizing them will mean job losses and increased social costs. Africa also faces some unique difficulties because of its already high level of poverty. For instance, in Kenya, Del Monte grows pineapples on former state farms. As a result, Kenya earns critical foreign exchange through exports of the fruit. However, the huge plots of land controlled by Del Monte means that less land is available for subsistence farming, making the Kenyans in the area among the poorest people in the country.[88]

In China, tens of millions of workers are idled as state-owned enterprises crumble before the onslaught of foreign multinationals or strive to be "leaner and meaner" in partnership with Western firms. According to some experts, if this trend continues it could lead to a variety of devastating social problems, if not outright rebellion. Why? Little or no social safety net exists for Chinese workers—there is no significant equivalent of unemployment compensation or social security.[89] Plus, because most of the available jobs are in cities and coastal areas, millions of Chinese are flocking in from the provinces looking for work, some as young as 10 or 11. In the process, families are being split up and crime in the cities is on the rise.[90]

This desperation can also result in what some would call the exploitation of workers, often by multinationals or their foreign partners. Because of low wages and high levels of poverty in many developing countries, adults are often unemployed or underemployed. The result? Children are going to work to help feed the family. In 1999, a staggering 250 million children under 15 were estimated to be working in developing nations. Many of these children end up working for foreign contractors that supply multinationals. Exhibit 3.6 lists the percentage of children under 15 who work in certain developing countries. For another look at what might be considered exploitation, read about what Hong Xiaohui went through in landing a job for U.S.-based toymaker Mattel in the following International Insights.

As you might suspect, there are no easy answers here. Clearly, multinationals offer many benefits to emerging economies. However, they can also contribute to the social problems that accompany the transition to market-based economies. So what should multinationals do as a result? At a minimum, we suggest that multinationals learn to be sensitive to the fact that some of their actions may have negative effects on local populations, unintended or not. There also seems to be an assumption among some multinationals that any suffering (from layoffs, pollution, etc.) is a "necessary" or "inevitable" part of a "temporary" transition process. While it is too soon to tell in many cases, multinationals may be underestimating how long it will take to halt the "temporary" suffering.

All of this argues for a greater emphasis on ethical behavior and social responsibility by multinationals. Experts suggest, for example, that multinationals adopt strict codes of conduct for their own behavior on environmental issues. In fact, multinationals have also been encouraged to raise environmental awareness in the nations where they do business and to make investments in local efforts to clean up and protect the environment.[92]

EXHIBIT 3.6

Estimated Percentages of Children Who Work in Specific Countries

Country	Estimated percentage of Children Who Work	Country	Estimated percentage of Children Who Work
Kenya	42	India	14
Bangladesh	30	China	11
Haiti	25	Egypt	11
Turkey	24	Indonesia	10
Pakistan	17	Vietnam	9
Brazil	16	Philippines	8
Guatemala	16	Mexico	7
Thailand	16	Malaysia	3

Source: Adapted from Zachary. ———. (1994). Levis tries to make sure contract plants in Asia treat workers well. *Wall Street Journal,* July 28, A1, A6.

INTERNATIONAL INSIGHTS

A Job Seeker's Odyssey

ONE OF THE greatest migrations in history is under way now. Some estimate that as many as 100 million Chinese are on the move. Millions of peasants are fleeing their villages for the lure of economic prosperity in big cities such as Shanghai and Guangzhou. One of these stories is about Hong Xiaohui, who traveled 1,200 miles from her remote village in China to Mattel's Barbie doll plant in Guangdong province. This 18-year-old's journey says a lot about what it's like to be in the middle of the economic upheaval reshaping China. Unfortunately, it isn't a very pretty story. In fact, it's one that raises a variety of ethical concerns about the responsibilities that multinationals have in recruiting their Chinese workforces. But one thing is clear. Hong Xiaohui's odyssey is one that 100 million Chinese from the interior provinces are making in the quest for work.

To reach the Mattel factory, Ms. Hong spent several days (and sleepless nights) on a bouncing, rickety bus. There was no food or water provided except what Ms. Hong brought herself or was willing to pay for. After a while, the bus reeked from sweat, vomit, and rotting food. Bathroom breaks often meant finding a spot on the side of the road or waiting in line with the 100 other women traveling on the bus to use a country outhouse. Believe it or not, the women on the bus

had to *pay* 415 yuan (about $50) for this trip. But they did so willingly. When local labor officials showed up at their villages to recruit workers for Mattel, many leapt at the chance to escape China's grim rural poverty.

However, when Ms. Hong reached the Mattel plant, there were some unpleasant surprises. Mattel offered a pay level of 200 yuan per month (about $25), despite the fact that the labor officials recruiting for Mattel had promised her 350 yuan. The factory is also run strictly, with three absences resulting in termination. Off the job, Ms. Hong is housed (crammed, actually) in a small room with eleven other employees. The amenities? A concrete floor, single lightbulb, and a tiny bathroom with no hot water.

Nevertheless, Ms. Hong signed a contract to work at Mattel for three years. Doing what? Putting the hair on Barbie doll heads—a sometimes painful job that requires punching holes in the heads and weaving in the hair. When asked about working conditions and the other things that Hong Xiaohui had to suffer through, Mattel refused to comment. In spite of everything, though, Ms. Hong says she'd make the same choice again. To do otherwise would leave her "like a flower in a greenhouse. It can't feel the wind blow and it can't grow stronger."[91]

Similarly, investments in the community (to schools, hospitals, retraining programs, land grants to farmers, etc.) may help lessen the social impact of economic change. Multinationals may also want to help governments in emerging nations develop and implement policies similar to those that already exist in many Western industrialized countries (such as programs designed to provide unemployment benefits, assist budding entrepreneurs, and provide loans to existing local businesses). One such program is being established by Hewlett-Packard.[93] Even with HP stock in the doldrums, CEO Carly Fiorina is thinking long-term. She recently unveiled an impressive program to sell products to the poor of the world. The program is called World e-Inclusion and is on the leading edge of a trend some call B2-4B, or "business to four billion." In the next two years, HP will sell, lease, or donate $1 billion of its products to governments and agencies in countries such as Bangladesh and Senegal. Fiorina feels this will eventually position HP to be in on the ground floor of a huge market and to tackle some issues immediately. To support this giveaway, HP will also set up funds for potential entrepreneurs, low-power devices for the equipment and more. There are critics to be sure, but Fiorina is no wide-eyed philanthropist. "There's a big difference between creating a sustainable business model around products and services that raise the standard of living and . . . . just pouring in money on an ongoing basis." Time will tell. Nevertheless, such steps might smooth out some of the bumps in the road that emerging nations must endure on the way to becoming market-based economies.

Chapter Summary

In this chapter we dealt with *ethical values* and *corporate social responsibility*. We reviewed two major perspectives on ethics. On one hand, *universalism* argues that there are sets of ethical values that should apply everywhere, and many international and corporate codes of conduct have been developed based on this perspective. On the other hand, *relativism* is a perspective that embraces the idea that countries often have different sets of ethical values that are shaped by their own unique laws and practices. The implication for business in this case is "When in Rome, do as the Romans do."

Next, we considered cross-national differences in ethical perspectives. Most research suggests that Americans tend to be more concerned with ethical issues than their counterparts in Europe, Asia, and other parts of the world. U.S. multinationals are also more likely to have written codes of conduct in place that spell out what is considered unethical behavior than are European multinationals.

We then moved on to consider specific unethical practices by foreign governments and what firms are willing to do about them. With respect to human rights, we noted that there is general agreement that certain types of behavior is unacceptable. What is less clear, however, is what multinationals should do as a result. In apartheid-era South Africa, for instance, some multinationals believed that they could have more influence by remaining engaged in that country's economy, whereas others decided to withdraw to protest racist policies. Despite well-documented human rights abuses now in China, few multinationals have pulled out; one exception was Levi Strauss.

Likewise, multinationals need to confront the issue of *bribery* in international business. In many countries, such payoffs are common if not expected. Most nations, however, have laws that prohibit the bribery of officials. Few, however, actually outlaw bribes that their citizens may pay to foreigners. Many nations, in fact, view bribery as just part of the cost of doing international business.

Bribing foreigners to get business also was sometimes practiced among U.S. multinationals, although the high-profile cases that came to light in the 1970s eventually led to the passage of the *Foreign Corrupt Practices Act* (FCPA). While this law made it illegal to pay foreigners bribes in an effort to win business, the FCPA does allow for *facilitating payments* that will ensure foreign officials do what they are supposed to do (e.g., clear a shipment through customs). Research done on the FCPA's impact suggests that there is no systematic disadvantage suffered by U.S. multinationals because of the act's prohibitions.

We concluded this chapter by discussing some of the social costs that are associated with many nations' ongoing transition to more competitive, market-based economies. In doing so, we looked at how multinationals may sometimes contribute to the suffering of the people living through such transitions (such as by exploiting local workers or increasing pollution, unemployment, and poverty) as well as how multinationals might be able to improve the situation.

Discussion Questions

1. What are the relative merits of universalism and relativism for international management?
2. How should multinationals deal with human rights abuses by foreign governments? Bribery attempts? Other questionable practices? Should they involve themselves in the issues at all? Why?
3. What is your assessment of the Foreign Corrupt Practices Act? Is it likely to be a major hindrance for U.S. multinationals? What position should the U.S. government take regarding the tactics used by foreign multinationals in international competition?
4. What are some of the social costs associated with emerging nations' ongoing transition to market-based economies? How do multinationals contribute to these problems? What should they do about them, if anything? Why?

Up to the Challenge?

Competitive Intelligence: Lots of Gray Areas, No Easy Answers

WE CHALLENGED YOU AT THE beginning of this chapter to make some judgments about the ethics and legality of some specific behaviors associated with the increasingly popular practice of competitive intelligence gathering. The following exhibit summarizes the behavioral incidents we mentioned and whether, according to experts, they are legal, illegal, or in an ethically gray area. In essence, deliberate theft of company materials or secrets from company property is illegal, at least in the United States. However, several of the examples of competitive intelligence we've cited would be considered unethical by many Americans.

Behavioral Example	U.S. Legal/ Ethical Status
1. Calling neighbors under false pretenses to assess managers' whereabouts	ethically gray area

2. Securing a copy of a competitor's travel itinerary from a travel agent	ethically gray area
3. Digging through a company's trash on public property	legal
4. Deliberately eavesdropping on private company conversations	illegal
5. Sending phony job seekers in response to competitor's want ads	ethically gray area
6. Hiring competitor's former employees	legal
7. Sending phony visitors to tour competitor's facilities	ethically gray area
8. Attending trade shows where competitor's wares are displayed	legal

Many of these situations have involved U.S. companies. For example, a crayon company employee posed as a potential customer and easily gained access to the firm's production processes. While this is unethical, what about standing outside a plant to count employees who leave various shifts? What about the Japanese firm that sent employees to measure the thickness of rust on train tracks leaving a U.S. plant and then using that data to estimate plant output?[94] Of course, U.S. firms aren't immune to this activity. Just last year Raytheon Co., the defense contractor, agreed to pay a multimillion settlement to resolve charges that it hired private detectives to eavesdrop in a failed attempt to outrun Ages Group's bid for a U.S. Airforce service contract. Even universities are getting into the act. At the University of Missouri classes are taught in how to do "pipeline" analysis in the drug industry. This involves using public sources to ferret out what products are in the competition's research pipeline.[95]

Finally, we asked about recommendations that you might give multinationals interested in protecting their secrets from competitors' prying. Here are some tips:

- Have all joint venture partners and consultants the multinational works with sign nondisclosure agreements.
- Make sure the multinational tightly controls access to all facilities and electronic mail systems.
- Use written policies to make all employees more aware of the risks of security lapses.
- Test areas within the firm itself that might be vulnerable to information leaks.
- Establish a centralized electronic reporting system that will allow employees to report any suspicious incidents.

International Development
Bribery in International Business

Purpose

To discuss ethical issues associated with bribery and corrupt practices that may be encountered in international business dealings. To accomplish this, twelve short minicases are presented that are designed to get you thinking about ethical issues associated with bribery. Your instructor may review the Foreign Corrupt Practices Act and Kohlberg's stages of moral reasoning as background before getting started. These brief minicases deal with issues including bribes versus grease payments, whistleblowing, the black market, and governmental interaction.

Instructions

Your instructor will divide the class into groups of four to six members. Depending on the time available and number of groups, your group may be assigned to all twelve or some subset (like four, six) of the minicases. Discuss each minicase with your group and decide what course of action should be taken (20–30 minutes, depending on the number of cases your group must tackle).

Your instructor will then lead a discussion about the ethical issues raised by the minicases (20–30 minutes, depending on whether your group will be asked to present its recommended courses of action).

Minicases

1. You are driving to a nearby country from your job as a manager of a foreign subsidiary. In your car are a number of rather expensive gifts for family and friends in the country you are visiting. When you cross the border, the custom official tells you the duty will be equivalent to $200. Then he smiles, hands back your passport, and quietly suggests you put a smaller sum, say $20, in the passport and hand it back to him. What do you do?

2. You have been hired as an independent consultant on a U.S. development grant. Part of your job involves working with the Ministry of Health in a developing country. Your assignment

is to help standardize some procedures to test for various diseases in the population. After two weeks on the job, a higher-level manager complains to you that money donated by the World Health Organization to the ministry for purchasing vaccines has actually been used to buy expensive computers for top-ranking officials.
What do you do?

3. You have been trying for several months to privatize what was formerly a state-owned business. The company has been doing well and will likely do better in private hands. Unfortunately, the paperwork is slow and it may take many more months to finish. An official who can help suggests that if you pay expenses for him and his family to visit the parent company in the United States (plus a two-week vacation at Disney World and in New York), the paperwork can be complete within one week.
What do you do?

4. One of your top managers in a Middle Eastern country has been kidnapped by a terrorist group that has demanded a ransom of $2 million, plus food assistance for refugees in a specified camp. If the ransom is not paid, they threaten to kill him.
What do you do?

5. On a business trip to a developing country, you see a leather briefcase (which you badly need) for a reasonable price in the local currency (the equivalent of $200 at the standard exchange rate). In this country, however, it is difficult for the locals to get U.S. dollars or other hard currency. The shop clerk offers you the briefcase for $100 if you pay in U.S. dollars.
What do you do?

6. You are the manager of a foreign subsidiary and have brought your car with you from the U.S. Because it is a foreign-purchased car, you must go through a complicated web of lines and bureaucracy (and you yourself must do it—no one can do it for you), which takes anywhere from 20 to 40 hours during business hours. One official tells you, however, that he can "help" if you "loan" him $100 and buy him some good U.S. bourbon.
What do you do?

7. Your company has been trying to get foreign contracts in this developing country for several months. Yesterday, the brother-in-law of the Finance Minister offered to work as a consultant to help you secure contracts. He charges one and one-half times more than anyone else in a similar situation.
What do you do?

8. You have been working as the director of the foreign subsidiary for several months. This week, you learned several valued employees have part-time businesses that they run while on the job. One of them exchanges foreign currency for employees and visitors. Another rents a few cars to visitors. And so on. You are told this has been acceptable behavior for years.
What do you do?

9. As manager of a foreign subsidiary, you recently discovered your chief of operations has authorized a very convoluted accounting system, most likely to hide many costs that go to his pocket. Right now, you have no real proof, but rumors are circulating to the effect as well. This chief, however, has close ties to officials in the government who can make or break your company in this country.
What do you do?

10. You have been hired to do some management training in a developing country. The costs of the program are almost entirely covered by a U.S. government agency. The people responsible for setting up one of the programs in a large company tells you they want the program to be held in a resort hotel (which is not much more expensive than any other) in a beautiful part of the country. Further, because they are so busy with all the changes in their country, they cannot come to a five-day program, which is what has been funded. Could you please make it a little longer each day and shorten it to three days? You would get paid the same.
What do you do?

11. You have been hired by an investment firm funded by U.S. dollars. Your job is to finance companies in several former communist countries. If you do not meet your quota for each of three months, you will lose your job, or at least have your salary severely cut back. One of the countries is still run by communists, though they have changed the name of their political party. They want you to finance three companies that would still be tightly controlled by the state. You know they would hire their relatives to run those companies. Yet if you don't support them, no other opportunities will exist for you in this country.
What do you do?

12. Your new job is to secure contracts with foreign governments in several developing countries. One of your colleagues takes you aside one day to give you "tips" on how to make sure you get the contracts you are after. He tells you what each nationality likes to hear, to soothe their egos or other psychological needs. For example, people in one country like to be told they will

have a better image with the U.S. government if they contract with your company (of course, this is not true). If you tell them these things, he says, they will most definitely give you the contracts. If not, someone in another company will tell them similar things and they will get the contracts.

What do you do?

From Theory to Practice
Analyzing Corporate Codes

Purpose

To understand important elements of corporate codes and the complexities involved in constructing such guidelines for behavior.

Instructions

In this chapter, we talked a good deal about corporate codes of ethics and the ways they are both similar and different. For this exercise, do some research to find codes of conduct for three multinational corporations. Using websites or library information, compare the codes and evaluate them. After getting this information, please do the following:

1. Answer these questions about the codes you've chosen and those of others discussed in class. What topics are covered in the codes? Which topics are not covered? How are these issues communicated in the codes? The instructor may wish to keep a tally of the common themes across the various companies. Compile a list by industry and jot down what you think the reasons are for possible differences across those industries.

2. Put together *your* version of a generic corporate code of ethics. Many international accords exist that provide a good base for your work (and for corporations), and a variety of websites are useful for this purpose and for answering the questions raised above:

   ● www.arq.co.uk/ethicalbusiness/ This site provides convenient access to other sites and organizations concerned with international business ethics.
   ● www.ethics.ubc.ca/resources/business This site includes a discussion of many business ethics issues and links and discussion of corporate codes of ethics.
   ● www.bnet.bentley.edu/dept/cbe/ The site of Bentley College's Center for Business Ethics and the source of a good deal of information on this topic.
   ● www.depaul.edu/ethics/newspaper.html The site of DePaul University's business ethics center.
   ● www.transparency.de The site on international corruption mentioned earlier in this chapter.

Cultural Dimensions: Implications for International Management

International Challenge

Two Sides of the Japanese-American Cultural Divide

LEARNING OBJECTIVES

After reading this chapter, you should be able to

● Understand how countries can be clustered according to their cultural values.

● Describe how cultural values can affect employee attitudes about work.

● Understand the implications of cultural values and dimensions for international management.

● Understand how employees and corporations can go about making better sense of culture.

MAKING GENERALIZATIONS about culture is always a risky proposition. But it's safe to say that the culture gap between American and Japanese society is sizeable. And to the extent that such a gap filters down to individual employees, it can make working together difficult. Take a look at Exhibit 4.1, which summarizes the value differences that may exist between American and Japanese employees.

Now imagine that you're an American, working in the United States for a Japanese-owned subsidiary, and your immediate supervisor is Japanese. What issues might that present for you in terms of performance appraisals and promotions? Or how about the reverse? What kinds of challenges and difficulties do you think a Japanese supervisor would run into with American subordinates? Think about these issues as you read this chapter. You'll be learning a great deal about cultural values and some of their managerial implications. Then take a look at the Up to the Challenge? box at the end of this chapter for some insights into the difficulties that can come up when Americans and Japanese work together and how to bridge them.[1]

EXHIBIT 4.1

Summary of Contrasting Japanese and American Values and Behavior

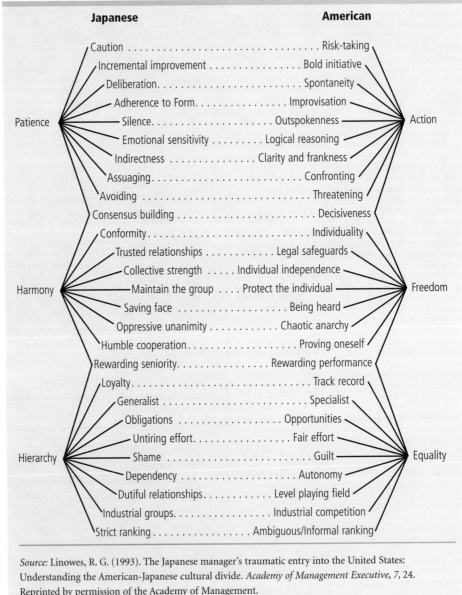

Japanese		American
	Caution . . . . Risk-taking	
	Incremental improvement . . . . Bold initiative	
	Deliberation. . . . . Spontaneity	
	Adherence to Form. . . . . Improvisation	
Patience	Silence. Outspokenness	Action
	Emotional sensitivity . . . . Logical reasoning	
	Indirectness . . . . Clarity and frankness	
	Assuaging. . . . . Confronting	
	Avoiding . . . . Threatening	
	Consensus building . . . . Decisiveness	
	Conformity. . . . . Individuality	
	Trusted relationships . . . . Legal safeguards	
	Collective strength . . . . . Individual independence	
Harmony	Maintain the group . . . . Protect the individual	Freedom
	Saving face . . . . Being heard	
	Oppressive unanimity . . . . Chaotic anarchy	
	Humble cooperation. . . . . Proving oneself	
	Rewarding seniority. . . . . Rewarding performance	
	Loyalty. . . . . Track record	
	Generalist . . . . Specialist	
	Obligations . . . . Opportunities	
	Untiring effort. . . . . Fair effort	
Hierarchy	Shame . . . . Guilt	Equality
	Dependency . . . . Autonomy	
	Dutiful relationships. . . . . Level playing field	
	Industrial groups. . . . . Industrial competition	
	Strict ranking . . . . Ambiguous/Informal ranking	

Source: Linowes, R. G. (1993). The Japanese manager's traumatic entry into the United States:
Understanding the American-Japanese cultural divide. *Academy of Management Executive, 7,* 24.
Reprinted by permission of the Academy of Management.

Revisiting Culture

In Chapter 1 we defined culture as "the collective programming of the mind which distinguishes one group or category of people from another." We also pointed out that people are unlikely to be fully aware of the pervasive impact of culture on their own attitudes, beliefs, and behaviors.[2] But there's plenty of evidence that culture has a major impact on the management of international business, often in some surprising ways. In fact, cultural differences can impact everything from how expatriates adjust to foreign

Japanese vending machines sell beer: What might Americans make of this? ©John Dakers; Eye Ubiquitous/CORBIS

assignments to how and where firms invest overseas. And the impact itself may cut both ways. In other words, cultural differences have the potential to produce friction and disruption as well as enormous benefits (e.g., better international performance if firms are able to put the best of what various cultures offer to good use).[3] Consequently, throughout the rest of this book we'll explore how culture plays a role in just about every facet of international business.

Of course, the stakes, at least for management, have never been higher. The ongoing growth of international business brings with it the increasing demands associated with managing culturally diverse workforces. And cultural values (such as a belief in the importance of hard work and thrift) may affect employee motivation in ways that can help explain different economic growth rates among nations.[4] So managers need to know which motivation strategies are applicable across cultures and which are culture specific. But that's just the beginning. Human resource practices, organization structure, strategy formation and implementation, conflict management approaches, negotiation tactics, and leadership styles can also vary dramatically across cultures.[5] Even the reasons entrepreneurs start companies to begin with can be driven, at least in part, by culture. For instance, in East Asian countries (e.g., Indonesia, Korea, Thailand), the level of interest in entrepreneurship may be more strongly connected to social status concerns (e.g., gaining face from success or losing it from failure) than it is in Anglo countries (e.g., Australia, the United States).[6]

In any case, the management challenge is not only to be aware of the role that culture can play, but to turn that awareness into an advantage where possible. For example, research shows that foreign subsidiaries perform better financially (e.g., have a higher return on assets and return on sales) when they use management practices that are consistent with the local culture.[7] Not surprisingly, however, managing "smart" from a cultural perspective isn't easy. Part of the problem is the complexity of culture itself. The "collective programing of the mind" that characterizes a particular culture can have roots in historical events, geography, shared traditions, economic developments, language, and religion. Moreover, cultural values, while relatively stable in the short run, are constantly evolving. And that means culture is something of a moving target for managers. On top of that, individuals don't always embrace the ostensible values of their cultural group. In other words, you don't have to look very hard to find, for example, Americans who are group oriented as opposed to individualistic and Japanese who are the reverse.[8]

The point is that managers need to be careful not to oversimplify culture and its effects. Indeed, applying blanket cultural labels to people, nations, and business situations, while tempting, can create new problems. Part of the issue here is that research and theory on culture has been unable, at least so far, to both capture all of the

---

EXHIBIT 4.2

Comparing High- and Low-Context Cultures

Culture Example	Context
Chinese Korean Japanese French Arab Greek Spanish Italian	HIGH ● What is unsaid but understood carries more weight than written/verbal comments. ● Relies on trust for agreement. ● Personal relations add to business.
English American Scandinavian German Swiss	LOW ● Focus on specifics of what was said or written. ● Handshake is insufficient. ● Trust secured with legal agreement; personal relations detract from business.

Source: Adapted from Hall, E.T. (1976). *Beyond culture.* (Garden City, NY: Anchor Press.)

cultural complexities that exist and develop specific, tangible advice for managing them.[9] Consequently, the theories and approaches that do exist tend to reduce culture to sets of bipolar adjectives (e.g., individualism–collectivism), which are then used to categorize and classify people and nations. In fact, we will review several prominent perspectives on culture that do just that.

But managers need to be mindful that these perspectives, while useful, can result in a kind of "sophisticated stereotyping" that doesn't fully capture the complexities and nuances of specific cultures. A good way to illustrate the dangers of this approach is by looking at cultural paradoxes. For instance, if Americans are the most individualistic people in the world, then why are Americans so willing to drop everything to help when community emergencies and disasters strike (e.g., tornados, floods, etc.)? Likewise, why do individualistic Americans have the highest rate of charitable gift giving in the world? Here's another example. Many Latin American cultures are well known for the positive regard and warm personal displays shown in interpersonal interactions. Then why do service employees in many Latin American countries express so much indifference to their customers? One survey done in Costa Rica found that many bank customers would rather deal with ATMs (because they were programmed to be polite) than human tellers.[10]

The Dimensions of Culture

In this section, we'll examine the major perspectives on culture that have influenced our thinking about international management. In doing so, we'll acknowledge both the benefits and limitations of these perspectives. We'll conclude this chapter by suggesting ways that both individual managers and international corporations can better understand cultural differences and the dilemmas that may come with them.

Culture and Context

According to Edward Hall, cultures vary in terms of how contextual information is typically viewed and interpreted. In short, Hall argues that our perceptions of the world all occur within some kind of context. For instance, an identical statement could mean dramatically different things, depending, of course, on the context. Many of us know this intuitively, but others have had firsthand experience with this phenomenon (e.g., those who have been quoted inaccurately in the news media). So you could say that the need for context is relatively universal. Nevertheless, Hall also claims that some cultures are more or less reliant on context in their perceptions and interactions with others.

Exhibit 4.2 shows how some countries might line up in terms of their general reliance on context. In **low-context** cultures, like in the United States or Germany, the interpretation of people and behavior often depends on what is actually said or written. That is, the message is often explicit, with the words themselves carrying most of the real message. In such cultures the meaning of a business interaction would have to be explicitly stated, discussed, and probably written down and mutually agreed upon before any deal could go forward.

However, people in a **high-context** culture might approach a business event very differently. In high-context cultures, the context itself often provides information that can be used to interpret what might otherwise be an ambiguous event. Put simply, people may not require or expect much detailed, explicit information about an event. In such cultures, verbal or written information may take a back seat to the meaning that

EXHIBIT 4.3

Ronen and Shenkar's Synthesized Country Clusters

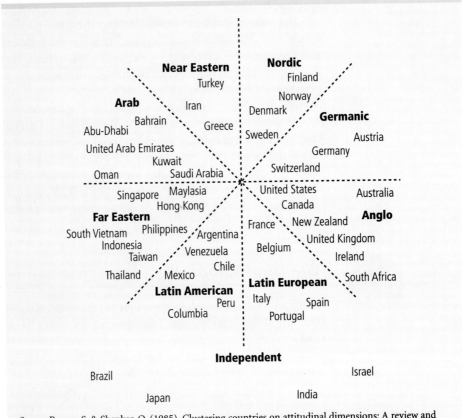

Source: Ronen, S, & Shenkar, O. (1985). Clustering countries on attitudinal dimensions: A review and synthesis. *Academy of Management Review*, 10, 449. Reprinted by permission of the Academy of Management.

the context provides. Consequently, high-context cultures tend to be concerned with long-term relationships, a person's word or reputation, and establishing trust over time. In contrast, people from low-context cultures tend to be concerned with getting all the context up front. And that means that they would tend to be concerned about the details of an arrangement and want to be clear about the "rules" for conducting business. Consequently, people from low-context cultures are likely to prefer exhaustive legal documents to establish clarity about business deals as opposed to relying on trust or relationships.

For instance, Japanese tend to be high context and Americans tend to be low context in their orientation. This may explain some of the complaints we've heard from Americans about their dealings with the Japanese, and vice versa. Specifically, some Americans claim that it's hard to "get straight answers" from the Japanese, so everything should be explicitly written down. Consider an American who makes a suggestion regarding a possible business deal with a Japanese firm. A Japanese person might reply, "That is interesting and worthy of future study." If the American possessed the high level of context offered by the Japanese culture, he or she would probably understand that this statement may actually mean: "This idea is unacceptable to us."

The Japanese tend to worry that spelling everything out would be a condescending putdown. Of course, the flip side is that Japanese sometimes say that Americans don't want to spend the time to understand their business environment and are overly oriented to the short term. If the Japanese understood the low-context culture embraced by many Americans, they would know that Americans' insistence on detailed contracts is a business necessity rather than an indicator of a lack of trust.

Hall argues that differences in how context is viewed may explain many cross-cultural problems that arise in international business. In fact, we'll examine some of these problems in more detail in the next chapter. But for now, the basic lesson is that it's important to know when and how to use context to your advantage. Obviously, you need to keep in mind who you are dealing with and how much context might be necessary. Consider the following example. A German manager working for a French company was terminated within a year because his performance fell short. The German was shocked, especially since "nobody told me what they wanted me to do." A French employee who resigned from a German company had the opposite experience. The French employee became fed up with being constantly told what to do by his German boss. He felt both his pride and intelligence were threatened.

What we have here is different perspectives involving context. The French tend to be high context and typically would expect the German employee to pick up on the message. The low-context German employee, in contrast, would usually expect intervention and direction by the French manager. Unfortunately, that intervention came way too late.[11] For another look at how culture can impact international business on a day-to-day basis, even in a small company, take a look at the accompanying Reality Check box.

Ronen and Shenkar's Country Clusters

Trying to make sense of cross-cultural differences when hundreds of countries and cultures are involved is an extremely difficult task. One way to make things easier is to try to identify a core set of values that are shared by specific **country clusters**. Such clusters could help companies modify their management tactics to better reflect the values they expect to encounter in different groups of countries.[12]

In 1985, Ronen and Shenkar created clusters based on their exhaustive and comprehensive review of previous research. This included an assessment of how thousands of employees in nearly 50 countries responded to questions about:

- **The importance of various work goals** (i.e., what employees want from work, such as interesting work, job security, or promotion opportunities)
- **The extent to which work satisfies certain needs** (e.g., for various rewards, personal accomplishment, job satisfaction)
- **Various organizational factors and management issues** (e.g., preferences for autocratic versus democratic leadership)
- **The nature of work roles and interpersonal relationships** (e.g., how well managers relate to subordinates)

In a nutshell, Ronen and Shenkar clustered countries on what they felt were patterns of similarity in employees' attitudes toward work and how well it met their needs.

The clusters Ronen and Shenkar came up with are presented in Exhibit 4.3. Notice that eight country clusters were identified along with four countries that were viewed as separate and independent. Countries within a particular cluster are said to share some basic cultural values. But the exhibit also positions the richer, more developed countries within each cluster closest to the center. For example, the Nordic cluster

REALITY CHECK

Life in a Small Firm Can Mean Big Cultural Challenges

A chat with Glenn Coarson, product marketing representative, Isotec, Inc.

Can you tell us a little about your company?

Isotec is a small specialty chemical company. We synthesize unique chemicals labeled with stable (that means nonradioactive) isotopes. Those isotopes are used for nutrition and metabolic studies, drug development, medical imaging, and medical research. It's pretty complex stuff and the company does business around the world.

How about your role in the firm? What's your exposure to international business?

I'm on the marketing side of things. Since we sell worldwide, my work has a constant international component to it. Basically, I analyze the competition and our current pricing of products for both domestic and foreign markets. I use that information to develop or adjust pricing schedules, marketing promotions, and customer service for new or existing products. There's also a marketing communication piece to my job. I write the technical copy for brochures and information sheets for new product launches. Those materials are used by both our overseas and U.S. sales representatives.

Before that, I handled all pricing and product inquiries for our overseas agents in Taiwan, Italy, Switzerland, Germany, Britain, Belgium, and the Netherlands. These agents are exclusive distributors for the countries in which they reside. They sell our specialty chemicals through their distribution channels under the Isotec product name. I also managed five product lines for Isotec that required frequent interaction with our Japanese representative.

How do cultural differences impact your job responsibilities on a day-to-day basis?

I think culture impacts just about everything I do internationally. But there are really three areas where cultural differences come into play most clearly. The first is in relationship building. I rely on our overseas agents to retrieve market information. That information helps us give our agents better support and is necessary for the growth of Isotec as a company. But I need to be sensitive to differences in how our foreign representatives see relationships. For instance, for our Taiwanese agents, I had to develop a trusting relationship before they would provide me with the market information I needed. Taiwanese culture is very collective and serious minded. There's also a strong emphasis on loyalty. Once I spent the time to demonstrate my loyalty and seriousness in working with our Taiwanese agent as a team member, I was able to retrieve useful market information. In my experience, the relationship-building process is just more important in

suggests Sweden is the most highly developed, whereas in the Latin European cluster France is most highly developed.

The level of development and technological progress in a country is one of the factors driving the clustering of countries, according to Ronen and Shenkar. As development proceeds, cultural values may change. You'll also notice that the clusters generally include countries that are close to each other geographically. This organization reflects the idea that cultural values should develop first in those areas nearest to a particular culture's point of origin. The fact that great geographic distances exist between countries in the Anglo-American cluster may reflect immigration patterns from the British Isles that took Anglo cultural values to many different parts of the globe.

Another similarity within clusters is language. For example, the Latin American cluster contains Spanish-speaking countries and the Anglo cluster English-speaking countries. While the countries in the Latin European cluster have different languages, they are all considered Romance, or Latin-derived, languages. Many work values, goals, and attitudes are shaped by linguistic meanings and interpretations.

Work values and goals may also reflect religious attitudes and beliefs. Catholicism is the major religion in both of the Latin clusters; Buddhist and Confucian values tie the countries together in the Far Eastern cluster. These values emphasize the obligations

Taiwan than it is in other places like Britain or Germany.

I also think cultural differences affect the best way to deliver customer service. Because of the nature of our products, customers frequently want answers to highly complex questions or need additional technical details. But how you provide that information can vary quite a bit because of cultural preferences.

For instance, British customers tend to want speedy, precise answers. They also think that passing technical details through our representative in Britain risks losing information and is slower anyway. So British customers will often call Isotec directly and want to speak to a technical expert. I support this because it's comfortable for British customers and meets their need for speed.

However, I wouldn't dream of doing the same thing with Japanese customers. They prefer to work through their Japanese representative, even though doing so takes more time and information can be lost or mistranslated in the communication process. Japanese customers place great value on showing respect. Bypassing our Japanese agent to get answers would be seen as a shameful and disrespectful violation of the established hierarchy.

The third area where cultural differences show up routinely is in international correspondence and communication. When I write foreign customers or representatives, I'm generally very formal and emphasize courtesies, especially when the person is Japanese, Taiwanese, or German. Titles (Dr., President of firm X, Herr Director) and last names are expected to be used in these places. Not doing so would cause offense in many cases and make you look ignorant. If I'm dealing with someone in the United States, letters and communication would be much less formal or even casual. In many cases, I use first names when speaking with American customers. But even after a good rapport is built up, I never use first names in Japan, Germany, or Taiwan.

What's your advice for handling ongoing cultural challenges? What skills do you need?

I think adaptability is really important. You must be ready to adapt your techniques to match what's appropriate from the perspective of the foreign customer, vendor, or employee you're dealing with. It helps to keep an open mind and to always remember that there's more than one way to manage a situation. A typically American style—by that I mean aggressive, with a strong emphasis on achievement—just doesn't work in every culture. As a matter of fact, it can be detrimental to your success with overseas contacts.

My advice is to learn about how different cultures have evolved. Try to understand what values are most important in any cultures that you have to interact with. I think living and working in a foreign culture is an excellent way to figure out how culture is woven into business and management practices. If that isn't practical, then go for as long a visit as you can. Or enroll in courses that provide exposure to not only the culture, but also to foreign managers and professors who can demonstrate the different management techniques and explain why they are implemented. The broader your exposure to cultural differences and management styles, the more you'll understand why being able to think and work in diverse ways helps you succeed in international markets.

people have to their families and the shame that is associated with failing to live up to those obligations. Finally, the countries labeled as independent (Brazil, Japan, India, and Israel) have unique religions, languages, and histories. In the case of Japan, this also includes a level of geographic isolation that further contributed to a unique culture.[13]

Overall, Ronen and Shenkar's clusters provide a useful snapshot for international managers interested in knowing where broad similarities and differences may exist between countries in terms of values and attitudes. This is important since such similarities and differences are often reflected in the business practices and approaches used in various countries. Consequently, international managers armed with such knowledge are more likely to operate effectively in foreign environments, everything else being equal. Today, efforts are underway to refine the concept of country clusters, including the methods used to measure the differences in values between them. As you might suspect, the issues involved are quite complex. For instance, cultures are constantly changing, presenting researchers and managers alike with "moving targets." Likewise, the impact of specific cultural differences can vary dramatically, with some differences having very little impact on the performance of international firms and others mattering a great deal. We need to better understand which differences matter most and why.[14]

EXHIBIT 4.4

Defining "Harmony" Differently in Japan, China, and Korea

Relevant Harmony Term	Japan *Wa*	China *Guanxi*	Korea *Inhwa*
Definition	Stress on group harmony, mutual cooperation to reach group goals	Stress on friendly relationships that are based on the exchange of favors	Stress on harmony between unequals; workers are loyal, bosses are obligated
Employees' commitment	To company	To boss, family	To boss, family
Role of the individual	Effective group member	Maintain favorable exchange relations	Be loyal to boss
Decision making	Participative, consensus-based, illusion of agreement key	Based on personal loyalties and favors owed	Based on family ties, hierarchy
Performance feedback	Indirect, often done via third parties to preserve group harmony	Indirect, often done via third parties to maintain equity in relationships	Indirect, often done via third parties to preserve harmony among unequals
Management style	Group facilitation	Benevolent paternalism	Clan management

Source: Adapted from Alston, J. P. (1989). Wa, guanxi, and inhwa: Managerial principles in Japan, China, and Korea. *Business Horizons*, March–April, 26–31.

Limitations of Ronen and Shenkar's approach Of course, these complexities also underscore some of the inherent limitations associated with Ronen and Shenkar's approach. For instance, their clusters are missing many countries (e.g., none of the countries in the former Soviet Union are included). In particular, few developing countries (e.g., China) are represented. Where would these countries fit today? Obviously, we don't know for sure, but the answer might be more complex than you would expect. For example, it's easy to imagine a new Asian cluster consisting of Japan, China, and South Korea. All three countries are well-known for emphasizing harmony in interpersonal relations, an emphasis traceable to some common Confucian values. However, "harmony" takes on a different meaning in each country. In Japan, harmony is often defined in terms of group activities and membership, whereas in China and Korea harmony is often defined in terms of relationships between individuals (Exhibit 4.4 presents a summary of these differences).

As a consequence, Japanese may value *wa* (i.e., group cohesion and group loyalty) above individual needs. Japanese often work for the group's benefit and identify strongly with their company. Since harmonious group relations are so important, interpersonal conflict tends to be minimized. For example, achieving consensus in decision making is critical, even if it requires maintaining an illusion of agreement among everyone during the decision-making process. Open disagreements tend to be avoided. While American managers often disagree in frank terms, some Japanese managers avoid conflicting views at all costs. For Americans, the word *sincerity* means telling the truth. The closest Japanese equivalent, *makoto*, means promoting harmony and showing support for colleagues.[15]

INTERNATIONAL INSIGHTS

Looking for Rugged Individualists . . . in Japan?

JAPAN SPENT MUCH of the 1990s in a protracted domestic slump. Now into the third millennium, angst continues in the wake of failed banks, takeovers, and layoffs, all shocking inconsistencies relative to Japan's traditional "contract" with employees. That social contract between companies and employees traded job security and generous benefits for an emphasis on tranquility, consensus, and the greater good.

The result? Doubts about the viability of the old social contract are leading many Japanese to conclude that building their lives around a relationship with one company is a huge mistake. Consequently, some Japanese are embracing individualism and personal responsibility like never before. One Japanese manager, who saw his forty-year career at a securities firm come to a screeching halt, put it this way: "I have to stand firmly on my own and think for myself. I wish I had realized this earlier in life." And if you don't, according to the same manager, "In this age of cutthroat competition, you'll just end up drowning." Some Japanese corporations also are picking up on this theme, pushing personal responsibility as a way to grow the economy.

Of course, there's always the possibility that the luster of individualism in Japan is merely a passing fad. When the United States experienced economic doldrums in the 1980s, for instance, some Americans faddishly embraced the Japanese emphasis on harmony and consensus. Nevertheless, meaningful signs of real change are also present in Japan. Consider:

- The number of personal injury lawsuits is rising.
- Whistleblowing activity is increasing.
- Entrepreneurship is becoming more attractive as an alternative to corporate careers (e.g., parents can enroll their 4-year-olds in "Sun Kids," a privately run course designed to teach basic entrepreneurial principles and counteract Japan's traditional educational focus on rote learning and group consensus).
- More Japanese companies, like trading giant Itochu, are using merit-based pay and promotion systems.
- Death from overwork (*karoshi*) and workplace bullying by managers (*ijime*) are now important social issues.

But don't equate Japan and America just yet, especially when it comes to individualism and entrepreneurship. World-class entrepreneurs from Japan are still relatively infrequent. And while the feelings of intense gratitude and obligation toward employers have weakened, they still persist. Eliminating these aspects of Japanese culture will take a lot more time. And perhaps a lot more layoffs.[16]

Of course, as we mentioned earlier, cultural values are always evolving. Although that process may be slow and incremental, it's often observable. That may, indeed, be the case with Japan, a society that's faced tough economic times in recent years. Take a look at the accompanying International Insights box to see what we mean.

In China, however, harmony is expressed by ***gaunxi***, the special relationship that two Chinese have when they are mutually obligated to each other. This obligation includes the fair exchange of favors and can take precedence over laws, firm procedures, and company goals. A failure to return favors results in a loss of face and may lead to the end of the relationship. Employees tend to be loyal to their individual *guanxi* relationships, rather than to the company. *Guanxi* can exist between two people of unequal status, like a manager and a subordinate. In this case, the subordinate will be loyal in exchange for being taken care of by the manager. This unequal exchange honors the more powerful member of the relationship and is linked to Confucian expectations that powerful family members help weaker members.

The result in China is a benevolent paternalism where managers may act as kindly father figures who provide for their "children" (subordinates). These complex but informal relationships affect how business gets done; laws, procedures, and regulations are routinely circumvented because of *guanxi*. In fact, developing *guanxi*-based "connections" can help foreign companies succeed in China.[17]

Like China, the South Korean version of harmony (***inhwa***) is defined by relationships between individuals. In South Korea, however, the relationship is explicitly between people of unequal status and power. The guiding principle is the Confucian norm that individuals be loyal to parents and authority figures. So harmony is a function of observing hierarchical rankings. At work, managers often expect the same loyalty and obedience a person would give to a parent. In fact, in many large Korean firms *real* parent-child relationships exist in executive ranks. Traditionally, a company's founder brings members of his family or clan into top positions. Nevertheless, all parties are expected to be emotionally supportive of each other, regardless of their rank or family status. One consequence is a strong reluctance to engage in direct criticism or provide negative performance feedback.[18]

Overall, these differences among Japan, China, and Korea illustrate the limitations of clustering countries that appear to have very similar cultural values. In fact, significant differences also exist among countries within the other clusters identified by Ronen and Shenkar. For example, in the Anglo cluster, British managers tend to be more formal, more class conscious, and more autocratic than their American counterparts.[19]

Moreover, *within-country* differences cannot be ignored. For instance, in the United States new immigrant populations have put managers in the position of having to motivate employees from diverse cultural backgrounds. Doing a better job of managing this diversity can enhance the competitiveness of American companies.[20] Another example of a country with big *internal* differences is South Africa. Approximately 10 percent of South Africa's 45 million people are white descendants of Dutch and British settlers. South Africa's black citizens come from several ethnic groups (e.g., Zulus, Xhosas).[21] Given this diversity, it isn't surprising that cultural differences affect work in South Africa in complex ways.[22]

In summary, Ronen and Shenkar's approach to clustering countries has important limitations. Indeed, these limitations are shared by *all* cluster frameworks to an extent. Hofstede's efforts to cluster countries is no exception.

Hofstede: Clustering Countries on Work-Related Value Dimensions

Geert Hofstede's work represents the largest and most influential effort to cluster countries by cultural values. And the impact of his work continues to rise.[23] Hofstede's conclusions are based on a survey that asked over 116,000 employees in more than seventy countries about their values and beliefs. From these data, Hofstede extracted four basic cultural dimensions that are now well known and established: Individualism–Collectivism, Masculinity–Femininity, Power Distance, and Uncertainty Avoidance. To help integrate his results, Hofstede also created cultural "maps" that position each country in terms of pairs of culture dimensions. Since countries also tend to cluster, similarities and differences between groups of countries can be assessed. Overall, Hofstede's work has important implications for managing employees around the world. We'll begin our discussion by defining Hofstede's four basic cultural dimensions.[24]

Individualism–collectivism   This dimension describes whether people in a culture tend to view themselves primarily as individuals or as members of a group. In individualistic cultures, people are expected to take care of themselves and a high value is placed on autonomy, individual achievement, and privacy. In collectivist cultures, however, people are more likely to view themselves as part of a group that protects and takes care of them in exchange for loyalty and devotion. The group may be the family, a clan or tribe, or an organization.

Individualism–Collectivism is the most widely studied of Hofstede's cultural dimensions, and it also may be among the most complex. Recent research suggests that collectivism and individualism are multifaceted values. In short, people may view collectivism and individualism in terms of a variety of components. For instance, individualism may include both economic (e.g., "I achieve things by competing") and expressive (e.g., "I want to be seen as a unique person") elements. Likewise, collectivism may also contain economic (e.g., "members of the group should share their resources") as well as expressive (e.g., "group members should be emotionally involved with each other") components. On top of that, cultures may vary considerably when it comes to how they view a particular component of individualism or collectivism. For example, while cultures that share Confucian and Latin roots tend toward collectivism, at least compared to the United States, they may view expressiveness quite differently. In many Latin American countries, open displays of emotion and warmth are expected and encouraged. On the other hand, such displays are much less likely to be found in Japan. In short, what constitutes "collectivism" (or "individualism," for that matter) may vary from place to place.[25]

Masculinity–femininity   This dimension describes whether success and the assertive acquisition of money and power (at the expense of others, if necessary) is highly valued, or whether people, the quality of life, and good relationships with coworkers should take precedence. Hofstede noted that in most cultures men were more likely to endorse the assertive (or "masculine") view of things. Masculine cultures are strongly achievement oriented, tend to view the ambitious pursuit of high performance as the ideal, and feel that men are better suited for positions of power. School systems in such cultures tend to identify and develop "high performers." Likewise, an important social value is having a "successful career." Workplaces tend to be competitive, stressful, and prone to conflict.

Feminine cultures, on the other hand, emphasize the equality of men and women, place a high value on taking care of the disadvantaged, and desire harmony in the workplace. Consequently, there is a stronger emphasis on job security and creating stress-free work environments. Career pressures also tend to be lower and labor-management discord less likely.

Power distance   This dimension reflects the extent to which people in a culture can accept large differences in power between individuals or groups in an organization. Put another way, how acceptable is it to have power distributed in an unequal manner? In high power distance cultures, people are more likely to accept their station in life and follow whatever commands those with greater authority are likely to issue. Put simply, the view is that some people are destined to be in command and others are not. So a company hierarchy that spreads powers unequally is acceptable because managers and subordinates are seen as different types of people. And, as you might suspect, managerial authority tends to be more concentrated and centralized in high-power-distance cultures.

People in low power distance cultures, in contrast, are more likely to fear concentration of authority. Consequently, power is more likely to be used in a decentralized way, with companies having fewer layers of management. In such cultures, managers tend to develop close, trusting relationships with their subordinates and use their power with care. The use of power in such cultures is often subject to a variety of laws, procedures, and standards, which, if violated, can create a backlash as well as other problems for managers.

Uncertainty avoidance   How people react to uncertain or ambiguous events defines Hofstede's uncertainty avoidance dimension. People in cultures that are low in uncertainty avoidance embrace the idea that life is unpredictable by definition. As a result, there is less concern with or adherence to rules, procedures, or organizational hierarchies. Risk taking, especially in the pursuit of individual achievement, is desirable. Competition and conflict are both viewed as inevitable parts of life in an organization.

People in cultures where uncertainty avoidance is high, however, tend to feel threatened by ambiguity and will go to great lengths to create stable and predictable work environments. In such cultures, there is an emphasis on absolute truths and unusual behavior or ideas tend to be rejected. As a result, rules and procedures designed to keep uncertainty at bay proliferate. Likewise, there tends to be less risk taking and personal initiative (e.g., in decision making or your own career moves) in high-uncertainty-avoidance cultures.

Hofstede's cultural maps   Hofstede created three cultural maps by crossing pairs of cultural dimensions and plotting the corresponding scores for each country. Each map is divided into quadrants representing different combinations of the dimensions

EXHIBIT 4.5

Abbreviations for Countries and Regions Used in Hofstede's Culture Maps

ARA	Arab countries (Egypt, Lebanon, Libya,Kuwait, Iraq, Saudi Arabia, UAE)	JPN	Japan
ARG	Argentina	KOR	South Korea
AUL	Australia	MAL	Malaysia
AUT	Austria	MEX	Mexico
BEL	Belgium	NET	Netherlands
BRA	Brazil	NOR	Norway
CAN	Canada	NZL	New Zealand
CHL	Chile	PAK	Pakistan
COL	Colombia	PAN	Panama
COS	Costa Rica	PER	Peru
DEN	Denmark	PHI	Philippines
EAF	East Africa (Kenya, Ethiopia, Zambia)	POR	Portugal
EQA	Equador	SAF	South Africa
FIN	Finland	SAL	Salvador

continued...

EXHIBIT 4.5

Abbreviations for Countries and Regions Used in Hofstede's Culture Maps (Continued)

FRA	France		SIN	Singapore
GBR	Great Britain		SPA	Spain
GER	Germany		SWE	Sweden
GRE	Greece		SWI	Switzerland
GUA	Guatemala		TAI	Taiwan
HOK	Hong Kong		THA	Thailand
IDO	Indonesia		TUR	Turkey
IND	India		URU	Uruguay
IRA	Iran		USA	United States
IRE	Ireland		VEN	Venezuela
ISR	Israel		WAF	West Africa (Nigeria, Ghana, Sierra Leone)
ITA	Italy		YUG	Former Yugoslavia
JAM	Jamaica			

Source: Hofstede, G. (1991). *Cultures and organizations: Software of the mind.* London: McGraw-Hill U.K., 55. Used with permission.

plotted. Countries whose pairs of scores tend to cluster together are also identified. The basic idea is that countries may possess certain combinations of cultural values that have unique managerial implications. We'll address these implications in more detail later. For now, we'll focus on understanding Hofstede's culture maps. Exhibit 4.5 shows the abbreviations for the countries used in Hofstede's research.

We'll start with the positions of countries on the individualism–collectivism and power distance dimensions. As Exhibit 4.6 shows, only Costa Rica combines collectivism and small power distance. Instead, large power distance and collectivism go together, with most countries in this quadrant being either Asian or Latin American. Similarly, small power distance and individualism go together, with northern European and Anglo countries such as Sweden and Great Britain dominating this quadrant.

Exhibit 4.7 displays the map crossing the uncertainty avoidance and masculinity–femininity dimensions. Hofstede suggested that cultures with weak uncertainty avoidance and masculine values will be **achievement oriented.** These tend to be Anglo countries or their former colonies (such as India, Hong Kong, and the Philippines). The second quadrant, combining high uncertainty avoidance and masculinity, produces **security motivation.** For countries in this quadrant, both performance and job security are valued. In contrast, the combination of feminine values and high uncertainty avoidance produces **social motivation**. Here job security, positive relationships, and a

EXHIBIT 4.6

Culture Map for Power Distance and Individualism

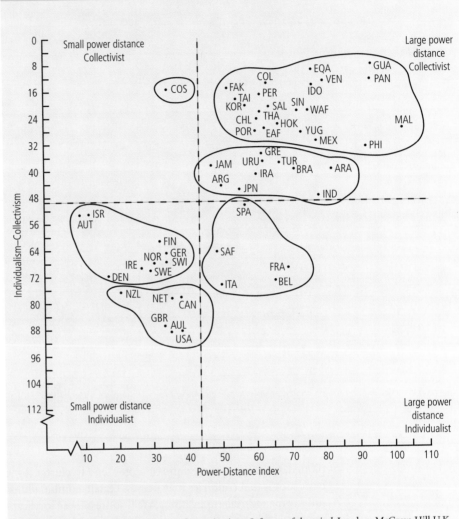

Source: Hofstede, G. (1991). *Cultures and organizations: Software of the mind.* London: McGraw-Hill U.K., 54. Used with permission.

good quality of life are prized. Scandinavian countries dominate the fourth quadrant, which combines feminine values and low uncertainty avoidance. In these countries, risk and performance are acceptable, but social relationships and a high **quality of work life** are valued more than individual achievement.

Exhibit 4.8 displays the final map crossing uncertainty avoidance and power distance. Asian countries dominate the **family quadrant** (large power distance and weak uncertainty avoidance). In these countries, there's often less concern about laws and procedures than on being loyal to strong, paternalistic leaders. In contrast, the **pyramid of people quadrant** (large power distance and strong uncertainty avoidance) produces cultures accepting of powerful leaders, but in a context that is fairly

EXHIBIT 4.7

Culture Map for Uncertainty Avoidance and Masculinity–Femininity

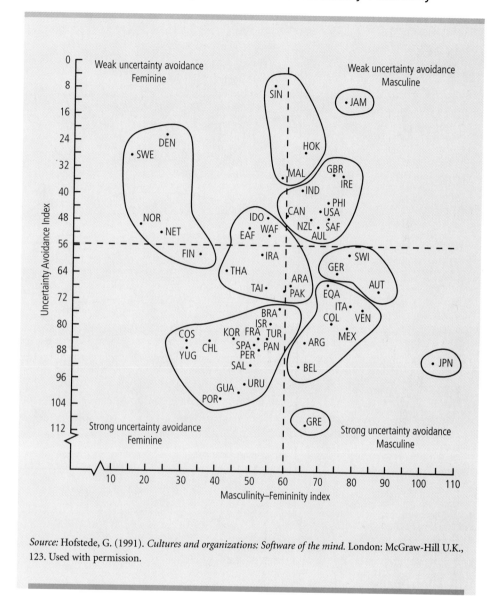

Source: Hofstede, G. (1991). *Cultures and organizations: Software of the mind.* London: McGraw-Hill U.K., 123. Used with permission.

hierarchical and rule bound. This diverse quadrant contains Mediterranean, Latin, and some Asian countries.

Germanic countries dominate the **well-oiled machine quadrant** (small power distance and strong uncertainty avoidance). In this environment, leaders are less important than having clear rules and procedures that promote efficiency. Finally, the **village market quadrant** contains Anglo and Scandinavian countries. Here the combination of small power distance and low uncertainty avoidance allows for a great deal of experimentation and risk taking that's not automatically limited by powerful leaders. In such cultures, good negotiation and conflict management skills may be critical for getting things done since elaborate procedures or dominant leaders are often absent.

EXHIBIT 4.8

Culture Map for Power Distance and Uncertainty Orientation

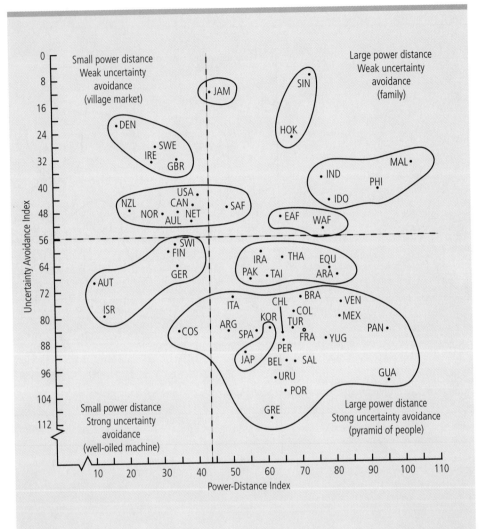

Source: Hofstede, G. (1991). *Cultures and organizations: Software of the mind.* London: McGraw-Hill U.K., 141. Used with permission.

Limitations of Hofstede's cultural dimensions   Like Ronen and Shenkar, Hofstede misses some key countries in his clustering effort. For example, countries in eastern Europe are basically missing, as are developing Asian nations like Vietnam. To help rectify this, Hofstede has made cultural value estimates for emerging economic powers like China and Russia. He views China as a country that is high on power distance, low on individualism, and moderate on uncertainty avoidance and masculinity. Russia, on the other hand, is seen as high on power distance, strong on uncertainty avoidance, moderate on individualism, and low on masculinity. Nevertheless, certain regions of the world remain underrepresented even in the most recent efforts to cluster countries by culture.[26]

Another limitation of Hofstede's work is that it ignores differences that exist between countries within a specific cluster or quadrant. Research suggests, for example, that cultural differences exist between the United States and Australia despite their similar scores on Hofstede's cultural dimensions. Specifically, Americans tend to be more interested in intrinsic rewards like responsibility and recognition, while Australians tend to be more interested in having job security and a good income.[27] Hofstede's framework has a hard time explaining these results. Despite its limitations, however, Hofstede's work continues to have a tremendous impact on the field of international management and remains a valuable guide for interpreting the effects of culture. In fact, take a look at the following International Insights and think about how you might apply Hofstede's framework if you were managing this American firm's foreign subsidiaries.

INTERNATIONAL INSIGHTS

One American Firm's European Subsidiaries: A Cultural Mosaic

AMERICAN COMPANIES ARE often well-known for emphasizing values such as freedom and individualism. But sometimes those American values may not completely survive a move abroad. Indeed, when an American company sets up shop overseas, its operations there may take on hues from the local cultural environment. That seems to be the case in the European subsidiaries of one well-known icon of corporate America. This particular company sells about 25 percent of its annual production abroad, with Europe being a major overseas market.

On top of its regional offices and distributors, the company operates five subsidiaries in Europe that cover specific territories. Recently, the firm profiled these European subsidiaries in a company publication, including how employees in each subsidiary described themselves and their work culture. The result is a glimpse into how local cultures can shape work environments, even in the midst of what is one of America's strongest corporate cultures and most identifiable brands. How do the self-descriptions of each subsidiary relate to the cultural dimensions presented in this chapter? Then think about what it might be like to work in each subsidiary. Which would you choose to work in? And what does that tell you about yourself and your values?

Subsidiary Location	Territory Covered	Employees	Self-Description
1. Brackley, England	U.K. and Ireland	British	Creative, inventive, reserved, multicultural, resourceful
2. Paris, France	France	French	Generally dislike authority; we always complain but we enjoy life (good food, wine)
3. Frankfurt, Germany	Austria, Czech Republic, Hungary, Poland, Slovenia	German, French, American	Hardworking, punctual, accurate, tidy-minded, thirst for knowledge, open to new technology, enjoy food/wine
4. Milan, Italy	Italy	Italian	Chic, passionate, and stylish
5. Amsterdam, Netherlands	Benelux countries	Dutch, Belgian	Dutch are direct and tolerant; Belgians are more modest, and always friendly.[28]

Trompenaars's Alternative: Another Look at Cultural Dimensions

Fons Trompenaars's recent work represents perhaps the most ambitious attempt to identify cultural dimensions since Hofstede's earlier effort. Focusing on values and relationships, Trompenaars surveyed more than 15,000 managers over a ten-year span. These managers represented twenty-eight countries, and Trompenaars was able to identify a variety of bipolar cultural dimensions as a result.[29]

For example, people may differ in terms of how they view their environment. **Outer-directed** employees tend to accommodate their behavior to their situation in life. Why? Because they feel that life's outcomes aren't under their control. Such employees may desire stability as well as have a strong need for harmonious relationships. In contrast, **inner-directed** employees tend to believe they control their own destinies. Consequently, they're likely to be more willing to change their environment and pursue their own goals. According to Trompenaars, Americans tend to be inner-directed, while at the other extreme Chinese tend to be outer-directed. Along the same lines, research comparing managers from the United States and four Arab countries found that inner-directed values

EXHIBIT 4.9

Trompenaars's Key Cultural Dimensions and Representative Countries

↑ Universalism	↑ Neutral	↑ Specific	↑ Achievement	↑ Individualism
United States	Japan	Austria	Austria	United States
Austria	United Kingdom	United Kingdom	United States	Czech Republic
Germany	Singapore	United States	Switzerland	Argentina
Switzerland	Austria	Switzerland	United Kingdom	former Soviet Union
Sweden	Indonesia	France	Sweden	Mexico
Hong Kong	Brazil	Singapore	Singapore	France
China	China	Hong Kong	former Soviet Union	Indonesia
Indonesia	Switzerland	Spain	China	Japan
former Soviet Union	Netherlands	China	Indonesia	Thailand
Venezuela	Mexico	Venezuela	Venezuela	Singapore
↓ **Particularism**	↓ **Emotional**	↓ **Diffuse**	↓ **Ascription**	↓ **Communitarianism**

Sources: Adapted from Trompenaars, F. (1993). *Riding the waves of culture.* London: Brealey; Trompenaars, F., & Hampden-Turner, C. (1998). *Riding the waves of culture: Understanding cultural diversity in global business* (2nd Ed.). New York: McGraw-Hill.

were endorsed most by the Americans, while outer-directed values were more dominant on the Arab side. Because of outer-directed concerns, business in Arab countries often functions on a more relationship-oriented basis than it does in Western nations.[30]

Speaking of relationships, several of the most important cultural dimensions identified by Trompenaars are explicitly relationship oriented. Exhibit 4.9 presents five of these dimensions along with rankings for countries most representative of each polar extreme. We'll turn our attention to these dimensions next.

Universalism–particularism   This distinction refers to the extent to which people usually believe that one set of rules and practices should apply to everyone (universalism) or whether the rules should be adjusted depending on the person or situation (particularism). Many countries stress good relations with family and friends (particularism) rather than focusing just on the performance-based considerations (universalism) that dominate in countries like the United States. However, countries as diverse as Venezuela, Indonesia, and China tend toward particularism. Overall, managers from cultures that embrace particularism are more likely to take an employee's personal family troubles and job demands into account when deciding on rewards than are managers from cultures that embrace universalism.

Neutral–emotional   Cultures in which emotions are suppressed and stoicism is important are said to be on the neutral end of this dimension. For example, the Japanese are well known for their reserve and composure. The flip side, of course, is an emotional culture, where feelings are expressed with gusto. Mexico is a good example of an emotional culture. You can imagine some of the challenges that might occur if employees from neutral cultures find themselves in an emotional culture or vice versa. In either case, adapting to the rules of the game that you're in is probably the best bet (e.g., by being more expressive in an emotional culture or more reserved in a neutral culture).

Specific–diffuse   In specific cultures such as the United States, life tends to be compartmentalized. Work and family roles, for instance, are kept relatively separate. Consequently, the behavior you see, the titles used, and the level of formality displayed will all vary depending on what role people happen to be in (e.g., boss, friend, colleague). And that means that having a relationship with someone carries little risk, at least initially. Why? Because the relationship can be limited to a specific role (e.g., you can be very friendly with people on the job but never see them outside of the workplace). But in diffuse cultures like China, the lines between roles are fuzzy. For instance, a person's job title might affect the way that person is treated and viewed in many other spheres of life. Consequently, people in such cultures tend to be somewhat cautious in dealing with others for the first time, especially since access to one area of life may mean access to all.

Achievement–ascription   In achievement cultures, your status depends on how you've performed and the goals you've been able to reach. That might mean obtaining a degree from a top university or landing a prestigious promotion. "Being the best" at whatever it is that you do carries a great deal of weight. In ascription cultures, in contrast, status depends on things like age, connections, class, or gender. For instance, connections probably will have a larger impact on hiring and other business decisions in ascription cultures like China, Indonesia, or Venezuela than in achievement cultures like the United States.

Individualism–communitarianism   This dimension is similar to the distinction Hofstede draws between individualism and collectivism. Basically, individualism means that you think of yourself as an individual first, while communitarianism means that you think of yourself as part of a group first. A comparison of the two frameworks, however, reveals some differences. For instance, Argentina and Mexico are described as relatively group oriented by Hofstede but as individualistic by Trompenaars. Why this is the case isn't completely clear. One possibility is that each researcher defines his terms somewhat differently. Another possibility is that Trompenaars's newer data may be revealing shifts in cultural values that have occurred over the years. As we said earlier, cultures are constantly evolving and changing. And Trompenaars's work may help underscore that point.

The Implications of Culture for International Management

Up to now, we've provided some brief commentary about the implications of culture for management. We've also noted that culture can potentially impact just about everything, from how international business strategy is formed to specific human resource management practices. In fact, we'll explore some of these issues in later chapters. For now, however, we'll examine how culture may affect what people want from their jobs and how they view leadership. We'll conclude the chapter by offering some practical suggestions for moving beyond the kind of "sophisticated stereotyping" that comes with the limitations of current culture frameworks.

Culture and What People Want from Work

How central is work in the lives of employees? What goals do employees seek to accomplish by working? Do they work primarily for relationships, money, or for the job itself? The answers have important implications for how managers should approach employees in various cultures. Research suggests that what we want from work may be culture dependent to an extent. For instance, a survey of 14,000 employees in eight countries (Belgium, Britain, Germany, Israel, Japan, Netherlands, the U.S., and the former Yugoslavia) found that **work centrality** (how important work is in the lives of employees) varies across countries. Americans fell in the middle of the pack, while the British had the lowest work centrality scores and the Japanese the highest. In fact, the Japanese not only had the highest centrality score, they were also significantly ahead of the other seven countries as a group.[31]

Of course, it's likely that work centrality in Japan has eroded in recent years (see our earlier International Insights box). That said, the tendency to feel that work is a critical part of life will undoubtedly persist at some level in Japanese culture, at least for now. Why? One reason is that it's hard to imagine long-standing Japanese traditions being completely undercut in just a decade or two. For centuries Japan was a feudal society made up of small, isolated farming communities. Such isolation required hard work and cooperation among all the farmers in the community to ensure its survival. This agrarian system began changing significantly only within the last one hundred years. The legacy of this system in modern industrial Japan is the value placed on hard work and group solidarity.[32]

This belief in work, combined with a still-strong emphasis on the group, may help explain the high degree of commitment many Japanese still feel toward their firms. It may also explain the Japanese willingness to put up with things that workers in other countries find intolerable. How many Americans, for example, would trade places with the average Japanese white-collar worker (known as a "salaryman"), someone who routinely puts in 60+ hour work weeks, endures two-hour commutes, rarely takes vacations, and feels obligated to spend several nights a week socializing with coworkers?[33]

But Japanese concern about these working conditions is rising. According to a recent survey of employees in industrialized countries, Japanese respondents came in last in terms of morale. Only 44 percent of the Japanese workers surveyed said they were satisfied with their employers. In contrast, 65 percent of the Americans surveyed were satisfied. The percentages were even higher for German (66%), Canadian (73%) and Swiss (82%) workers. In addition, less than 40 percent of the Japanese surveyed thought they were fairly paid. Finally, only 33 percent of Japanese said their firms were well managed, compared to 45 percent in an earlier survey. These numbers appear to reflect a growing feeling among Japanese that big employers are less likely to provide benefits, such as lifetime employment, that made enduring difficult working conditions tolerable.[34]

But what about other aspects of work? Exhibit 4.10 summarizes the importance of eleven different work goals across eight countries. You'll notice that employees in most countries ranked interesting work first or second in importance. Good pay also was an important goal for most employees, although Dutch and Japanese employees both ranked it lower. Substantial differences across countries were found for most of the

EXHIBIT 4.10

Rankings of the Importance of Work Goals by Country

Work Goal	Belgium	Germany	Israel	Japan	Netherlands	U.S.	Former Yugoslavia	U.K.
Interesting work	1	3	1	2	2	1	2	1
Good pay	2	1	3	5	5	2	3	2
Good interpersonal relations	5	4	2	6	3	7	1	4
Good job security	3	2	10	4	7	3	9	3
Good match between you and your job	8	5	6	1	6	4	5	6
A lot of autonomy	4	8	4	3	1	8	8	10
Opportunity to learn	7	9	5	7	9	5	4	8
Work variety	6	6	11	9	4	6	7	7
Convenient hours	9	6	7	8	8	9	10	5
Good physical working conditions	11	11	9	10	10	11	6	9
Good opportunity for promotion	10	10	8	11	11	10	11	11

Source: Adapted from MOW International Research Team (1987). *The meaning of working.* London: Academic Press, 123.

Seeing Bill Gates as a corporate hero is consistent with how many Americans view leadership. © Reuters NewMedia Inc./CORBIS

remaining work goals. For example, job security was very important to Germans, but not very important to Israelis. The Japanese felt that achieving a good match between their job demands and their talents was the most important work goal, while most countries rated it fifth or lower. Finally, while having autonomy was the most important work goal for Dutch employees, British employees rated it near the bottom.[35]

Nevertheless, these results suggest that providing interesting work will have a positive effect on workers in all eight countries. If these findings generalize to other nations and cultures, managers could view "interesting work" as something that employees universally want from their jobs. The results also suggest that managers need to adjust their approach to match the values of specific cultures. Of course, this adjustment must be made cautiously. Cultures change and individual values, needs, and goals may diverge from existing cultural norms in any case.

Other studies have produced similar findings and implications. One survey, for example, found that both American and Asian executives valued hard work. But Americans tended to value things like personal achievement much more than the Asians, while the reverse was true for respect for learning. Also interesting was the fact that there was considerable divergence in values among Asians managers. Executives from Japan, for instance, were more concerned with harmony than their counterparts from Singapore and Hong Kong.[36]

Culture and Views about Leadership

Speaking of executives, the culture we're imbedded in inevitably colors our views about leadership.[37] As a result, the definition of leadership can vary because of cultural factors like history and shared experience. Americans, for instance, tend to see leadership as an influence process in which the leader is somehow able to affect the attitudes and behaviors of employees in ways that allow company goals to be achieved.[38] They also see a leader as a person whose job is to motivate others to produce. The leader is a "hero" who is responsible for making the organization work. In contrast, the engineer, not the manager, is held in high esteem in Germany. The German tradition of craftsmanship and emphasis on apprenticeships, which dates back to the Middle Ages, means that for many Germans the purpose of management is to attack technical problems and to distribute tasks, not to "motivate" employees.[39]

Research on management philosophies in Europe, Asia, and the United States supports the idea that culture impacts how the role of leadership is perceived. In one survey, less than 20 percent of American, Dutch, and Swedish managers thought it was important to have exact answers ready in response to questions that subordinates might have. In these countries, managers felt that they should help subordinates to find their own answers and solve their own problems. On the other hand, almost half the German managers (46%) and more than half of French (53%), Italian (66%), Indonesian (73%), and Japanese (78%) managers wanted to have precise answers ready for subordinates. In these countries, projecting an image of expertise that provides comfort and stability to subordinates is often viewed as an important part of a leader's job.[40]

Where leaders come from can also vary across countries because of cultural factors. Japan, for instance, is a classless country in which merit largely determines who ends up in positions of leadership. "Merit" is defined here in terms of successful performance in highly selective schools designed to funnel students into specific roles. Anyone who demonstrates the necessary capabilities can succeed in this context, regardless of his or her particular background. In other countries, however, business leaders tend to come from certain classes of society. For instance, Turkish leaders usually come from the upper classes. Likewise, in certain Arab countries, prominent leaders usually emerge from powerful tribal families.[41]

Culture may also affect assumptions about the characteristics that business leaders need to be effective. For example, Americans tend to think that a leader's success depends on personal traits such as intelligence, self-confidence, and decisiveness. Most of these characteristics have been associated with cultures that value individual performance. But should we expect countries with different cultural values to use the same criteria to judge managerial effectiveness? In many cases, the answer is clearly "no." That said, there's also evidence that attitudes about what makes for effective leadership have been changing.[42]

In one study, senior managers working in eight different countries for large multinationals were given a list of leader characteristics and asked to select the five that were most important. A few characteristics (e.g., the ability to articulate a vision) were ranked in the top five by managers in most countries. This suggests that senior executives everywhere share certain challenges, especially in large international firms. However, there were no countries that had identical sets of rankings. And for certain pairs of countries, there was little or no overlap between the characteristics ranked in the top five. Cultural values may explain these differences. For instance, Japan was the only country that ranked empowering others in the top three. The focus on group-oriented work in Japanese culture lends itself toward seeing effective leaders as people who share power and encourage a harmonious work environment. Likewise, the American, Australian, and British emphasis on "getting results" is consistent with the tendency to value individual performance in Anglo cultures. In such cultures, leadership and heroic levels of performance are often equated.[43]

Finally, there's been considerable interest in discovering whether cultural perspectives on leadership are converging. One clever investigation compared the relationship between personal characteristics and evaluations of managerial effectiveness in Canada, Hong Kong, and China. The characteristics examined tend to be valued in Anglo countries, such as achievement motivation, interest in self-actualization (i.e., realizing your highest potential), and intellectual ability. The idea was that if cultural values affect the importance of managerial characteristics, then executives in Canada, Hong Kong, and China should differ in terms of how they rate the effectiveness of the managers that work for them. In fact, Chinese executives might not see any relationship between "Western" criteria and managerial effectiveness. On the other hand, if attitudes toward leadership are converging as industrialization proceeds worldwide and countries like China become more "modern," then the criteria for effective management should be similar in all three countries.[44]

The results painted a mixed picture. Canadian executives felt that being interested in self-actualization was most important for managerial effectiveness. However, Chinese executives felt that a manager's intellectual ability was most important. These results support the idea that culture continues to affect which characteristics are seen as critical for effective management. On the other hand, although the rankings were different, most characteristics were viewed as indicators of effectiveness by all executives. This supports the convergence idea since only "Western" characteristics were included. In fact, the Chinese executives in the study all worked for large, modern firms in urban areas and had been exposed to North American management techniques. So the results may reflect the ongoing evolution of Chinese management, with traditional values being slowly eroded by Western management philosophies. Indeed, a similar evolution has been observed in many former communist countries such as Poland and eastern Germany.[45]

How Individuals and Corporations Can Make Better Sense of Culture

This discussion underscores the complexities associated with culture, a point we've been making throughout the chapter. So far we've presented a series of cultural frameworks and dimensions. We've also discussed their limitations, including the broad-brush portraits they often paint of cultures around the world. And even if we view these "sophisticated stereotypes" as helpful and useful, they may, at least to some extent, already be outdated. After all, cultures may be stable most of the time, but they're certainly not static.

So how can managers working in a new country—or international corporations, for that matter—do a better job of figuring out the cultures they have to operate in? Let's start with some suggestions for international managers:

- **Approach other cultures with the idea of testing your "sophisticated stereotypes."** In other words, be aware of any cultural stereotypes that you might possess and treat them not as "truths," but as hypotheses to be tested. The most effective international managers change their stereotypes about people from other cultures and countries during the course of interacting with them.
- **Find cultural informants and mentors to help.** Look for someone who: (1) can really make sense of a culture's nuances, paradoxes, and internal logic; and (2) is willing to share his or her insights and information. After all, the more you understand a culture, the more tolerant and effective you'll become.
- **Carefully assess information that seems inconsistent with cultural stereotypes.** Sometimes managers can "plateau" in their learning about another culture without realizing it. This may occur when managers have done pretty well, at least initially, in other cultures and, as a result, become less open to deeper learning. In doing so, managers may be more likely to make bad decisions based on faulty assumptions or a superficial understanding of the culture. This trap can be avoided if managers seek

deeper meaning by looking for and analyzing behavior that seems paradoxical to a culture's basic values (e.g., why are many U.S. executives autocratic if Americans pride themselves on equality and egalitarianism?).

● **Learn mental maps that will increase effectiveness in different cultures.** This doesn't mean trying to uncover all the rules of a different culture. What it does mean is that understanding the core values behind the mental maps used in a culture will help you behave more appropriately in that context. And being able to do that will increase both your effectiveness and self-confidence.

But what about suggestions at a broader level? Here are some ideas for international corporations to consider when trying to make better sense of culture:

● **Put people who have cognitive complexity in international positions.** In short, the last thing companies should want are black-and-white thinkers running around as expatriates or serving in other international roles. Instead, select people based on their ability to handle alternative viewpoints as well as plenty of ambiguity. Employees with such skills are best equipped to make sense of the complexities and paradoxes inherent in all cultures.

● **Emphasize in-country training for people going overseas.** Too often, cultural training: (1) takes place in a classroom environment back home and (2) emphasizes concepts and facts instead of hands-on experience. So if at all possible, put people on the ground in the culture where they're going to work and challenge them to figure out answers to actual cultural problems. That's likely to produce more motivation to figure out what's going on.

● **Assess the level of cultural expertise among expatriates or other personnel posted in a particular country.** The idea here is that not everyone will be on the same page from a cultural learning perspective. There will be different levels of understanding. Part of this variation may result from individual differences in skills as well as the amount of time spent in the country. In fact, a good reason to assess cultural expertise is to help the company figure out how long personnel should stay in a country to achieve the cultural understanding needed to function well.

● **Become a learning organization when it comes to cultural understanding.** In short, put mechanisms into place that will help share and disseminate knowledge about different cultures. For example, have expatriates report their insights and understanding about a culture once they return home. This type of sharing can both increase the firm's collective know-how about different cultures and help expatriates make sense of their cross-cultural experiences.[46]

Chapter Summary

We began this chapter by saying that culture has a pervasive impact on the management of international business. Human resource practices, organization structure, strategy formation and implementation, conflict management approaches, negotiation tactics, and leadership styles can also vary dramatically across cultures. And the importance of understanding culture, at least for management, has never been higher because of the ongoing growth of international business.

But *culture* is a complex concept. The "collective programing of the mind" that characterizes a particular culture can have roots in historical events, geography, shared traditions, economic developments, language, and religion, among other things. Plus, cultures are constantly evolving, presenting something of a moving target for managers. So managers need to be careful not to oversimplify culture.

We reviewed prominent efforts to cluster countries by shared cultural values. For instance, Hall argues that some cultures are more or less reliant on context in their perceptions and interactions with others. In low-context cultures, the interpretation of people and behavior often lies in what is actually said or written. People in a high-context culture might approach a business event very differently. In high-context cultures, the context itself often provides information that can be used to interpret what might otherwise be an ambiguous event. Put simply, verbal or written information may take a back seat to the meaning the context provides.

Ronen and Shenkar found eight major *country clusters* based on shared cultural values. Geography, language, and religion are all factors that contribute to shared cultural values across specific groups of countries. However, one limitation of Ronen and Shenkar's effort is that many developing countries were not included. In addition, clustering countries together runs the risk of ignoring real cultural differences that exist between countries as well as the cultural diversity that may exist within a single country.

These limitations are also shared by Hofstede's effort to cluster countries on work-related cultural dimensions. Nevertheless, Hofstede's work continues to be a valuable guide for international managers. Hofstede argued that all cultures could be described in terms of four basic dimensions. *Individualism–collectivism* reflects the extent to which people in a particular culture see themselves as individuals or as members of a group. *Masculinity–femininity* describes whether people in a culture place a higher priority on the acquisition of money and power or on things like good relationships with coworkers. *Power distance* reflects the extent to which people in a culture can accept large power differences across ranks in an organization. Finally, *uncertainty avoidance* reflects the level of tolerance people in a particular culture have for ambiguity and uncertainty.

By crossing pairs of these dimensions, Hofstede produced some valuable *cultural maps* that allow international managers to identify countries in terms of various combinations of cultural dimensions and how they cluster together. Hofstede's findings have implications for motivating employees in different countries. For example, countries with low uncertainty avoidance and masculine values tend to be achievement oriented. The combination of high uncertainty avoidance and masculine values tends to produce security motivation. Social motivation may result from the combination of femininity and high uncertainty avoidance. More recent efforts to cluster countries by shared cultural values have tended to support Hofstede's views and have added to our knowledge about many developing countries.

In particular, Trompenaars identified several cultural dimensions based on his research. For example, employees in *outer-directed cultures* feel that life's outcomes aren't within their control, whereas in employees *inner-directed cultures* believe they control their own destinies. *Universalism–particularism* refers to the extent to which people usually believe that one set of rules and practices should apply to everyone (universalism) or whether the rules should be adjusted depending on the subordinate or situation (particularism). Cultures in which emotions are suppressed and stoicism is important are said to be *neutral*. The flip side is an *emotional culture*, in which feelings are openly expressed. In *specific* cultures, life tends to be compartmentalized. But in *diffuse* cultures, the lines between

roles are fuzzy. In *achievement cultures*, your status depends on how you've performed and the goals you've been able to reach. That might mean obtaining a degree from a top university or landing a prestigious promotion; "being the best" at whatever it is that you do carries a great deal of weight. On the other hand, in *ascription cultures*, status depends on things like age, connections, class, or gender. Finally, *individualism* means that you think of yourself as an individual first, while *communitarianism* means that you think of yourself as part of a group first.

Next, we explored how culture may affect what people want from their jobs as well as their perspectives about leadership. Even the origins of leaders can be driven by culture, at least in part. We concluded with practical suggestions for moving beyond the kind of "sophisticated stereotyping" that comes with the limitations of current culture frameworks. Specifically, for managers and employees, that involved (1) approaching other cultures with the idea of testing your "sophisticated stereotypes"; (2) finding cultural informants and mentors to help; (3) carefully assessing information that seems inconsistent with cultural stereotypes, and (4) learning mental maps that will allow you to be more effective in different cultures. For corporations, suggestions included: (1) putting people who have "cognitive complexity" in international positions, (2) emphasizing in-country training for people going overseas, (3) assessing the level of cultural expertise among expatriates or other personnel posted in a particular country, and (4) becoming a learning organization when it comes to cultural understanding.

Discussion Questions

1. Describe the basic cultural dimensions proposed by Hofstede and Trompenaars. What are their similarities, differences, and limitations? How do these dimensions relate to Ronen and Shenkar's country clusters?
2. How might international managers use information about cultural dimensions? Why is understanding culture such an important part of success in international business?
3. Are there any work-related goals that appear to be universal? Which work-related goals vary significantly across countries? How might cultural values impact these work-related goals?
4. How can companies and international managers go beyond the "sophisticated stereotyping" that a superficial understanding of cultures might produce? What are some of the challenges or difficulties associated with doing so?

Up to the Challenge?

Working Together in the U.S.: Implications for Managing the Japanese-American Cultural Divide

AT THE BEGINNING OF THE chapter, we asked you to think about what it might be like for Americans and Japanese to work together. We were especially interested in how potential gaps in cultural values might complicate life for American subordinates and Japanese managers. Here are a few examples of the problems those gaps can create.

Performance appraisal   Most Americans expect positive reinforcement for their efforts and see performance feedback as providing motivation for higher achievement. Criticism is fine, too, as long as it's constructive and delivered in private. Many Japanese managers, however, find touting personal achievements unacceptable and expect great modesty from subordinates. Japanese managers may criticize subordinates in front of other coworkers. To Japanese subordinates, this can mean that their boss sees them as having potential. Plus, on-the-job criticisms are usually offset by the "stroking" that Japanese managers informally give subordinates during after-hours socializing. In fact, much criticism is only symbolic since in many Japanese firms the human resources department, rather than the manager, controls personnel decisions. Japanese managers are often surprised that their American subordinates expect them to regularly provide detailed performance appraisals.

As a result, Americans may be puzzled when their Japanese managers provide less performance feedback and career guidance than they expect. When Japanese managers do give formal feedback, it's often delivered in a vague, impersonal fashion (e.g., a brief letter thanking employees for their service). Since Americans are less likely to participate in the Japanese tendency to socialize regularly after work, they may miss opportunities to receive more informal and positive feedback. Americans often see such socializing as cutting into their leisure and family time, while Japanese often see it as an essential part of maintaining work group harmony.

Promotions   Many Americans working for Japanese companies complain about slow promotions and their inability to penetrate upper management ranks, a phenomenon referred to as the *Gaijin ceiling* (*Gaijin* is the Japanese word for "foreigner"). Many Americans see themselves as individualists out to fulfill their career goals. In contrast, many Japanese think such self-focused behavior creates too much conflict. Americans sometimes fail to appreciate the strong collective orientation of many Japanese managers and the fact that seniority may count for a great deal when it comes to promotions in Japanese firms.

Small wonder that Japanese managers sometimes have trouble "reaching" their American employees. For example, one Japanese manager gave a speech to motivate his American subordinates. It had the opposite effect. The Japanese manager said the company was doing poorly and urged the Americans to work harder to turn things around. Many Japanese subordinates would accept the blame for the situation and redouble their efforts to rectify it. Instead, the Americans polished their résumés and mailed them out in droves. Soon most of the Japanese manager's best American employees had left for jobs elsewhere.

Japanese executives are sometimes reluctant to put Americans in top management jobs because of the language barrier. Few Americans speak Japanese well, forcing Japanese managers to use English. And that creates problems since Japanese managers may be embarrassed to put their English language weaknesses on display for American subordinates. On the other hand, even Americans who speak Japanese can commit linguistic gaffes that threaten their careers in Japanese firms. In Japan, the context is very important for interpreting the meaning of a phrase. It took one American manager at Matsushita five years before she finally understood that when told by her Japanese superiors that a proposal "needs more study," several interpretations were possible. In some contexts, it meant, "The proposal needs some fine-tuning," while in others it meant, "The proposal is dead."

Bridging the cultural gap   Resolving these cultural differences takes time and effort. Americans must learn to respect the idea that many Japanese place a higher value on things such as group harmony. Likewise, Japanese must learn to appreciate the fact that many Americans are quite comfortable being assertive and individualistic. Both sides must learn to be more accommodating while retaining their own unique cultural values. That said, how can this be done? How can greater understanding and a "meeting of the minds" translate into different management practices?[47]

International Development
Understanding Your Orientation toward Individualism-Collectivism

Purpose

To develop a greater understanding of your own attitudes toward individualism and collectivism.

Instructions

Assume that you are in the United States or Canada and want to have a good career in an American or Canadian corporation. Please answer the following questions about your behavior in the workplace. Please use the following scale, placing the appropriate number in the blank before each question.

5	4	3	2	1
strongly agree	agree	not sure	disagree	strongly disagree

1. _____ I would offer my seat in a bus to my supervisor.
2. _____ I prefer to be direct and forthright when dealing with people.
3. _____ I enjoy developing long-term relationships among the people with whom I work.
4. _____ I am very modest when talking about my own accomplishments.
5. _____ When I give gifts to people whose cooperation I need in my work, I feel I am indulging in questionable behavior.
6. _____ If I want my subordinate to perform a task, I tell the person that my superiors want me to get that task done.
7. _____ I prefer to give opinions that will help people save face rather than give a statement of the truth.
8. _____ I say "No" directly when I have to.
9. _____ To increase sales, I would announce that the individual salesperson with the highest sales would be given the "Distinguished Salesperson" award.
10. _____ I enjoy being emotionally close to the people with whom I work.
11. _____ It is important to develop a network of people in my community who can help me when I have tasks to accomplish.
12. _____ I enjoy feeling that I am looked upon as equal in worth to my superiors.
13. _____ I have respect for the authority figures with whom I interact.
14. _____ If I want a person to perform a certain task, I try to show how the task will benefit others in the person's group.

Now, imagine yourself working in one of the following countries. Choose the one about which you have the most knowledge because of actual overseas experience, reading, having friends from that country, classes that you have taken, and so forth.

Japan	Mexico	Brazil
Philippines	Hong Kong	Thailand
Taiwan	Peru	Venezuela
India	Argentina	Greece

If you do not have enough knowledge about any of these countries, imagine yourself working on a class project with three foreign students from any of these countries.

The next part of the exercise is to answer the same fourteen questions, but to answer them while imagining that you are working in one of the countries listed above or working on a class project with three students from that country. Imagine that you will be living in that country for a long period of time and want to have a good career in a corporation there. Use the same scale and place the appropriate number (5 for strongly agree, 4 for agree, 3 for not sure, 2 for disagree, and 1 for strongly disagree) in the blank.

1. _____	8. _____
2. _____	9. _____
3. _____	10. _____
4. _____	11. _____
5. _____	12. _____
6. _____	13. _____
7. _____	14. _____

Scoring

The scoring of this exercise is different from most in that it involves comparison of the two sets of numbers, the one for imagining a career in the United States or Canada and the one for imagining a career in one of the other listed countries.

Let's call the first time you answered the questions the "first pass" and the other time the "second pass." In scoring, give yourself 1 point according to the following guidelines.

Question 1:   Give yourself a point if your number in the second pass is higher than in the first pass.

Question 2:   Give yourself a point if your number in the first pass is higher than in the second pass.

Question 3:   A point if number is higher in the second pass.

Question 4:   A point if number is higher in the second pass.

Question 5:   A point if number is higher in the first pass.

Question 6:   A point if number is higher in the second pass.

Question 7:   A point if number is higher in the second pass.

Question 8:   A point if number is higher in the first pass.

Question 9:   A point if number is higher in the first pass.

Question 10: A point if number is higher in the second pass.

Question 11: A point if number is higher in the first pass.

Question 12: A point if number is higher in the first pass.

Question 13: A point if number is higher in the second pass.

Question 14: A point if number is higher in the second pass.

If you scored 6 or more points, this means that you are sensitive to the cultural differences summarized by the concepts of individualism and collectivism. You are sensitive to the fact that different behaviors are likely to lead to the accomplishment of goals and to success in one's career depending on the emphasis on individualism or collectivism in the culture.

———

Source: From Brislin, R. W., & Yoshida, T. (Eds.), *Improving intercultural interactions: Modules for cross-cultural training programs.* Copyright © 1994 by Sage Publications. Reprinted by permission of Sage Publications, Inc.

From Theory to Practice
The Cultural Minefield of International Gift Giving

Purpose

To explore cultural differences in the gift-giving process. In doing so, you have the opportunity to learn something about the complex historical, religious, and linguistic factors that have shaped gift giving in particular countries.

Instructions

Read the background material below outside class (unless your instructor tells you otherwise). Your instructor will assign you to small groups of three to six and give each group a specific country to research outside class. Your group should be prepared to present your findings in a subsequent class (10–15 minutes per group) and/or prepare a group report. Alternatively, your instructor may make this an individual assignment and have you write a report. Be prepared to take part in a general class discussion on the specific countries assigned. In any case, you should focus on answering these gift-giving questions for the country assigned:

● What gifts might be appropriate for the country in a business context or relationship?
● When should gifts be given, generally speaking? What about gift giving if you're visiting the country in question on business?
● How should gifts be wrapped? What colors are appropriate or inappropriate? What presentation issues come into play (e.g., when should a gift be presented during a visit)? What other delivery issues might come into play?
● What gifts should be avoided?

Some Background on Gift Giving in an International Context

Differences in cultural values around the world can make managing an international business a tricky proposition. Even behavior that has the best of intentions—like gift giving—can be complex and have great potential to give offense. In many countries, it is appropriate to give foreign clients, contacts, customers, and employees a gift as a sign of appreciation. However, what constitutes an acceptable gift can vary widely. The failure to be aware of local rules can create misunderstandings or even lead to the loss of overseas business.

This begs the question of what you should give as gifts in other countries. Many experts recommend giving something that is unique to your own country or that would otherwise be difficult for the recipient to obtain. For an American manager, this might mean giving Native American handicrafts or books about the United States. But in other cases, it might be best to research the cultural, religious, and holiday traditions of a particular country to figure out what might make an appropriate gift. Better still, get to know your foreign contacts well enough so that you begin to understand their individual hobbies, tastes, and so on.

Giving gifts overseas, however, means more than just finding an appropriate item. In many countries, there are fairly elaborate rules regarding how gifts should be wrapped and presented. For instance, yellow and red have positive connotations in India. Likewise, white is a bad choice for many Asian countries (it's associated with death) while gold or red would be better selections. Then there is the presentation of the gift itself. In many Asian countries, using both hands to give and receive gifts is a sign of courtesy. However, if you find yourself in an Islamic country you would want to present a gift with just the right hand since the left hand is viewed as unsanitary.

Timing gift giving is also important. The Christmas season is generally pretty safe because most countries celebrate a major holiday around this time period. Usually, giving gifts in private is the best bet. However, Japanese typically engage in gift giving after business is concluded, while the Chinese usually present gifts at the beginning of a visit. In any case, don't necessarily expect Asians to praise aspects of the gifts you give; it is considered impolite to open gifts in front of the giver. Finally, it should be obvious that we're just scratching the surface here on gift giving overseas. If you have a foreign trip coming up and you're looking for specific gift-giving advice, do your homework and call the embassy of the country that you'll be traveling to.

For a brief snapshot of what we've been talking about, take a look at some recommendations of what to give, when to give, and what to avoid giving for the four countries listed here.[48]

Country	Good Gifts	When to Give Gifts	Gifts to Avoid (with explanation)
China	Ties, pens, modest items	Chinese New Year (January or February)	Clocks (the Mandarin word for clock is similar to "final resting place")
India	Sweets, nuts, fruit	Hindu Diwali Festival (October or November)	Leather goods (cows are sacred to Hindus)
Japan	Americana, liquor	Oseibo (January 1)	Four of anything (associated with death)
Saudi Arabia	Compasses, cashmere	Id al-Fitr (December or January)	Liquor (Muslims don't drink alcohol)

Part

II

Interacting Effectively in an International Environment

5

Perception, Interpretations, and Attitudes across Cultures

International Challenge

Doing Business in Vietnam

LEARNING OBJECTIVES

After reading this chapter, you should be able to

- Recognize the influence of culture on our perceptions, interpretations, and resulting attitudes.

- Identify some of the important ways that perceptual effects can be manifested in our interactions with those from different cultures.

- Be able to classify and distinguish cultures along several perceptual dimensions.

- Understand some of the ways—both verbal and nonverbal—that people from other cultures will see you, evaluate you, and act toward you.

DIPLOMATIC TIES BETWEEN THE United States and Vietnam have recently been restored.[1] If we can use past experience to predict what will happen in Vietnam, then we probably will see U.S. firms moving in to take advantage of business opportunities. Some experts seem to predict that Vietnam eventually will become Asia's newest tiger because of its many assets. For one, its people are young—80 percent of the population (73 million) are under 40 years old. Additionally, the Vietnamese are well educated: the literacy rate is nearly 90 percent. The Vietnamese people are also said to have a natural sense of entrepreneurship, despite several decades of a communist government. Add all this to the low cost of labor, and it is easy to see why capital should flow into the country[2].

Just as in China, however, the going will not be easy. There are many potential impediments to economic growth, including an underdeveloped infrastructure, a large bureaucratic government, corruption, and a rudimentary legal system. Nevertheless, perhaps the biggest challenge for U.S. businesspeople might be a very familiar one—recognizing and understanding cultural differences. This chapter discusses the ways that perceptions of others are formed and maintained and the problems that occur in this process. Likewise, attitudes toward one's own group and other groups are also discussed. As you read this chapter, please try to think of some of the ways that perception, interpretation, and attitudes might differ between the United States and Vietnam. At the end of the chapter, we'll review some of the actual differences that have been observed between these two countries.[3]

Perceptions

The subtlest way that culture can affect us is through our perceptions. Perception involves the selective mental processes that enable us to interpret and understand our surroundings. These include attending or selecting the events in the first place, organizing/processing the information that is selected, and finally interpreting the meaning of what was attended to and processed. The key word in this definition is *selective.* We do not perceive all that is going on around us at any one instant. Take right now as an example. You are reading (perceiving) the words on this page, but many other things are also occurring around you. Your radio may be on, someone may be walking and talking in the hall, noises can be heard outside, and so on. But we do not attend to all these random events. Instead, we selectively attend to stimuli that are important to us or help us make decisions. We certainly do not perceive things at random, but instead we impose order on all the environmental stimuli we are exposed to. (In fact, the defining symptom of schizophrenia is the inability to organize and selectively process one's perceptions!)

If we are imposing order on an inherently disorganized environment, how does this happen, and what role does culture play? It appears that members of a culture teach us what is important to perceive in our interactions with others. Experts say that what people in one culture need to perceive may be different from what those in other cultures need to perceive. In other words, culture may subtly sensitize people to information and behavior that is important in that culture.[4]

Differences in Perceptions of People and Events across Cultures

Does research support this conjecture about perceptual differences across cultures? And even if differences in perception exist, are there also some similarities in what people look for in, say, forming an impression of another person?

Perceptions of people   One group of researchers provided a partial answer to our question about culture and perception.[5] They asked groups of Chinese and Australians to read various descriptions of a fictitious person. The descriptions of the people were very detailed, including how conscientious, outgoing, and sensitive they were. Care was taken to see that the Chinese and English versions of the descriptions were similar and thus could not muddy up any conclusions. The participants were then asked to predict how these people might behave. The goal was find out which specific pieces of information would be selected and emphasized by the two groups.

First, however, it's important to note that the two groups were chosen deliberately—the Chinese because their culture is oriented to the group and the Australians because their culture is oriented to the individual. For this reason, it was expected that the Chinese would selectively pick out characteristics that involve consideration of others, whereas the Australians might emphasize more person-oriented traits when forming impressions. The researchers found exactly that—the Chinese were more influenced by a person's conscientiousness toward others in forming impressions, whereas the Australians focused on outgoingness (a person-focused characteristic) in forming their impressions. Of all the information presented, the Chinese and Australians selected culturally sensitive traits to form impressions of others. One implication of these findings is that it would benefit us to understand how other cultures may form opinions of people with whom they negotiate, communicate and otherwise do business.[6]

Coca-Cola is one of the U.S. firms that has set up shop in Vietnam—this plant is in Ha Tay, a northern province. © AFP/CORBIS

In other research these same researchers provided even more evidence for the cultural effects on perception of other people.[7] They argued that some cultures are more naturally conscious and respectful of power differences among people, whereas other cultures give less weight to authority. Again, participants were chosen from cultures in which the importance of status varied dramatically. Americans were chosen because they accord relatively little importance to status, whereas Chinese were chosen because they value status highly. The researchers predicted that the Chinese would give more leeway to higher-status persons in their treatment of others than would the Americans—so much so that a high-status Chinese could go as far as to insult another person at a business meeting with little recrimination.

Since it is difficult to observe a personal insult firsthand, researchers instead had people read a story about a business meeting during which a manager publicly insults an employee. But there were two different versions of the story: In one version the insulter was a high-status manager, in the other he was low-status. Participants were asked to read one version of the story and then to offer their perceptions of the insulter. Interestingly, Americans made no distinctions between high- and low-status managers who insulted others; their perceptions of this person were generally negative. The Chinese, however, were less critical of the insulter when he was a high-status manager. These results tell us that culture allows or directs one to be more or less critical about another depending on that person's status. The results also suggest that different leadership styles (the topic of a later chapter) may be more or less effective in different cultures.

Perception of events   A follow-up study looked at cultural differences in the perception of everyday events, not people.[8] This study also used Chinese and Australian subjects because of their contrasting group and individual orientations. Everyone read a list of common everyday social events (a conversation with a friend, arriving late to class, going out with friends) and then rated the events on nearly thirty different scales (e.g., boring–interesting, pleasant–unpleasant, etc).

A complicated statistical technique was then used to reduce the responses to a few underlying dimensions, and different dimensions were found for the two groups. The Chinese organized their perceptions of these events mainly along an individual versus group dimension. In other words, the Chinese seemed sensitive to events involving several other people; they were more perceptively attentive to these events and thought they were more involving than events that included few or no other persons. The Australians, however, rated the same events as more enjoyable than the Chinese. Apparently, group events imply more fun to Australians whereas to the Chinese such events conjure up perceptions of social obligation.

Implications of research on perceptions of people and events   All in all, these studies show that culture affects perceptions about life events and the people involved in those events. The insidious thing about perceptions is that most of the time they are automatic. In fact, these studies actually show that the perception process is far from a neutral or unbiased processing of information that we encounter. Instead, we use filters and organizing tools (i.e., how group oriented is another person?) that exemplify an important part of our culture. We may rarely, if ever, reflect on the source of our perceptions because of their automatic nature. As a result, we may rapidly form impressions of business partners that are based on our own cultural filters, and we may equally not appreciate the filter of another culture. This kind of perception can create problems. For example, in many Western cultures individual reward and recognition are accepted (and largely unquestioned) motivational methods. The only debate seems to be about which one—reward or recognition—is more motivating. Yet the use of similar motivation techniques by an American expatriate manager in China, for example, may fail because of cultural differences in personal and group orientations. Another area where there seems to be little conscious decision making about our perceptions is in the area of nonverbal behavior.

Perception of Nonverbal Behavior

The studies just cited show that people in different cultures look for and see different things in the behavior of others. But we must recognize that people use all kinds of cues and information to figure out what others are like, some of which are very subtle and indirect. Some writers, for example, claim that the nonverbal behavior of others offers clues about what they are really like.[9] Nonverbal behavior includes features like people's appearance, facial expressions, and body movements, and these can be important signals that affect our perceptions.[10] In fact, sometimes, even the way we present our business card becomes an important nonverbal behavior (see the following International Management Insights).

One example of this effect comes from research on personal space conducted by Hall and his colleagues. By *personal space*, Hall meant the distance we have between ourselves and others when we talk and interact. This seems like an odd thing to study, but in fact interpersonal space varies dramatically depending on what you are doing and whom you are interacting with. As it turns out, we probably make very subtle decisions about how much space to have between ourselves and another person.[11] To illustrate, look at pairs and groups of people talking to one another, just after or before a class break. How did they decide to have a foot or two between them and the person with whom they are talking? And please note differences among people. Hall finds that

INTERNATIONAL INSIGHTS

Perception and the Meishi: Business Card Rituals in Japan

BUSINESS CARDS IN the United States show little variation. Most people have them ordered and constructed by assistants or by printing companies; they generally pay little thought to the style of their card, nor to the actual exchange of cards with colleagues or prospective clients. The routine is well known to all—you introduce yourself, talk a little bit, and then give the other person your card. You may even toss it across a table as you take the other person's card and shove it in your pocket.

This is all so familiar that you're probably wondering why we even waste time describing it here. The reason we do so is because other cultures exchange business cards quite differently. In fact, if you are not aware of their rituals and the resulting perceptions, you may be committing a terrible *faux pax*. In Japan, the *meishi* (business card) carries much greater importance than in the United States, starting with the construction of the card itself, which is typically printed on the finest paper. The layout subtly accentuates the importance of the group to which one belongs rather than that of the less important individual. A typical American card will list one's name first, with one's title underneath in smaller print, and the firm's name and address below or in a corner. The Japanese *meishi* always presents the company name first and most prominently, then the employee's rank, and next his or her name—reflecting this decreasing order of importance![12] But there's more. The *meishi* is usually bilingual, with English on one side and Japanese on the other. If you can read the Japanese side, you may pick up additional information. The firm name is often more detailed (and sometimes even different), than on the English side, and the logo usually appears only on this side. Likewise, if the card is printed vertically rather than horizontally, this can mean the firm is more conservative and traditional.

And we haven't even talked about the actual mechanics of exchanging cards yet. This is a much more elaborate and meaningful act in Japan than it is in the United States. First, have plenty of cards with you. Not having a card is equivalent to refusing a handshake. The cards should be presented, not passed, with both hands. You should be sure to have your name facing the receiver. And you must bow. The angle of bowing when presenting a card is a fine art; a quick, small bow, however, will do the trick. While Westerners are generally not expected to know the fine points of bowing, Japanese employees must practice the "house style" during the training they'll get right after joining the firm. Finally, you must be able to receive the card properly as well. Again, you should take it with both hands and spend some time studying it. Examine the Japanese side even if you don't know the language and you'll be given credits by your host or partner. Don't shove the card in your pocket, and don't write on the card for the same reason: the *meishi* represents the other person's identity and it's therefore considered rude to treat this symbol disrespectfully. If you're about to have a meeting, place the card (or several cards) down in front of your partner during the meeting and leave it there until the meeting is over. At that time, pick up their cards. But put them in a special place; they are never to be taken and placed in your pocket casually. Instead it is *de rigueur* to carry a relatively elaborate card holder for this purpose. Take the holder out of a coat pocket, place the new card in the holder, and then place the holder back in your pocket—as though you really value the card. And, they apparently do value the cards.

The authors recently made a trip to Japan and read in advance about these and other rituals. So, we thought we were prepared for the correct ritual of card exchange. While we were relieved that we had practiced the card exchange, we made a mistake in a later trip, not realizing how far this ritual extended as a sign of respect. After a long plane flight and several delays (about 25 hours total), we arrived exhausted at our hotel outside Tokyo, ready to check in and get some needed sleep. Instinctively, McFarlin took out his credit card to pay the room deposit and he tossed it out on the counter (as we all may have done in the U.S.). Unfortunately, this act offended the clerk who perceived it as a sign of disrespect. We should have presented the card as we would have a business card. The clerk glared at us thereafter when we strolled through the hotel lobby.[13]

American men like to keep 2 to 4 feet between themselves and another man when conversing. Women talking together, however, prefer a smaller amount of space. Hall notes several other interesting facts about personal space, but the most germane here has to do with cross-cultural differences in personal space. Hall noted that Americans and northern Europeans prefer about 2 feet of personal space when conducting business, whereas Asians prefer about 3 feet and Arabs like even closer personal space. You can imagine the effect of these differences in a cross-national business interaction. If an American likes about 2 feet and an Arab businessperson likes about a foot, what is likely to occur? The Arab might perceive the American as stuffy and standoffish, whereas the American businessperson might see the Arab as pushy. Obviously, Hall believes that a knowledge of cultural space differences can avert a negative perception that could otherwise interfere with a business transaction. We will return to this topic in our chapter on communication.

Context as nonverbal behavior   While we discussed context in Chapter 4, it's also relevant here because perception occurs within a context and because some cultures rely more on context than others do in their perceptions. In low-context cultures, such as the United States or Germany, perceptions often result from what is literally said or written between two people. In high-context cultures, the culture itself often provides the background that can be used to interpret what might otherwise be an ambiguous event. In such cultures, verbal or written information may take a back seat to what is generally understood via the context. Thus, as we noted earlier, high-context communication relies on social relationships to bring meaning, whereas low-context communication eschews relations in favor of a focus on the explicit agenda or deal at hand.

The Japanese are high context and Americans are low context, and this difference may explain some of their interaction problems. Some Americans claim that you can't trust what the Japanese say and therefore everything should be explicitly written out. For example, in response to an American's suggestion for a new business arrangement, a Japanese might reply, "That is interesting and worthy of future study." If the American had the high level of context offered by the Japanese culture, he or she would probably perceive that this statement actually means: "It is unlikely that such an idea would be acceptable to us." Conversely, Americans sometimes complain that the Japanese are too circuitous; they never get down to the real issue. The Japanese, however, wouldn't dream of spelling everything out; they feel that this would be a condescending putdown.[14] If the Japanese understood the low-context culture of Americans, they would know that Americans' insistence on contractual agreements is a business requirement, not necessarily an indicant of lack of trust.[15]

Differences in the Perception of Time

If you are still not convinced that the study of perception in general and cultural differences in particular are important, you are not alone. Many people feel that perception—like beauty—lies in the eye of the beholder. That is, some feel that the study of perception is too subjective to be of great value. To answer this criticism (and for other reasons), several researchers in international management decided to study perceptions of time. They chose to study time because of its objective quality. In fact, one could hardly think of a more objective quantity than time, since everybody has a watch, waits for a plane according to schedule, plans a travel itinerary, and arranges for a meeting—all on an understood time schedule. Ten minutes is 10 minutes, time is time—right?

The answer to this question is no! Even though the whole world is ostensibly on the same time system, there appears to be wide differences in perceptions of this most objective of things—time. At an anecdotal level, one can see this difference in simply how some Eastern and Western cultures describe and value time. In Western cultures, time is apparently perceived as a commodity ("time is money," "you're losing/saving time here," "time is running out," etc.). In many Eastern cultures, however, time is seen as more flexible and fluid. Beyond this anecdotal level, however, Robert Levine and his associates have systematically studied this topic.

Research on time perception across cultures   Levine became interested in culture and time when he took a teaching position in Brazil for a year.[16] On the way to his first class meeting he began to worry about his watch since many of the clocks he glanced at (on public buildings, other people's watches) showed a different time. He did, however, arrive to his classroom a few minutes before the start of his 10–12 class. But no one was there! Instead, many of his students came late, several after 10:30, a few right around 11 o'clock, and even two others later than that! Interestingly, no one seemed to be particularly bothered by being late—all wore smiles and gave friendly hellos as they entered class. Since he had taught at California State University for several years, Levine was very surprised by these things; students are definitely expected to arrive on time in the United States. Even more interestingly, however, students in his Brazilian class did not get up and leave when class was over at 12 o'clock. In California, he was used to being told when class was over (the ubiquitous shifting of books, moving of backpacks, hungry looks, etc.). In Brazil, however, few people left on time. In fact, many lingered to ask questions and interact—many actually staying beyond 12:30.

These observations led Levine to conduct a study of American and Brazilian students' perceptions of time in several situations. He found a number of interesting differences between countries, for example, in what might be considered "late" for a lunch appointment with a friend. The average American defined late as 19 minutes or more, whereas the Brazilians were more forgiving, defining lateness as about 34 minutes or more. Interestingly, he also asked the students about their impressions of people who were late. Brazilians were less likely to blame others for being late than were Americans. The Brazilians typically felt that unforeseen circumstances were important causes of lateness. Americans were more likely to blame the tardy person and to attribute the lateness to a lack of caring. Even more interesting, Brazilians believed that people who were consistently late were more successful than those who were on time. (They are late because they have more friends to talk to, more partners with whom to do business; therefore lack of punctuality "equals" success!). Although there is some disagreement among Americans in time perceptions, punctuality is relatively critical and lateness is definitely to be avoided.

Levine was not completely satisfied with this first study of time. He wanted to show that the effects were not the result of language/translation problems, and he wanted to study several different countries. The problem clearly facing Levine, however, was exactly how to study time without relying on language and/or self-reports, and he dealt with this problem in a very clever way. He devised several objective indicants of time in six different countries.[17] First, he checked the accuracy of bank clocks by taking a sample of fifteen city banks in each country and comparing their times with the time provided by the telephone company (Greenwich Mean Time). Banks were of special interest because of their relative formality and because they are tied closely with activity in other countries (via monetary exchange and interaction). Banking, therefore, is an industry where time is monitored very closely. The researchers reasoned that if cross-country differences exist in this critical area, then there are probably lots of other perceptual differences in less important areas of life. Their results showed that bank clocks in Japan were the most accurate—averaging only about 30 seconds off—with U.S. clocks not far behind in accuracy. Clocks in Indonesia were the least accurate, averaging over 3 minutes late (see Exhibit 5.1).

EXHIBIT 5.1

Measures of the Pace of Time*

Country	Bank Clock Accuracy	Walking Speed	Post Office Speed
Japan	1	1	1
United States	2	3	2
United Kingdom	4	2	3
Italy	5	4	6
Taiwan	3	5	4
Indonesia	6	6	5

*Numbers are the ranking of each country on the measures of pace of time (1 = top ranking).
Source: Adapted from Levine, R. V., & Bartlett, K. (1984). Pace of life, punctuality, and coronary heart disease in six countries. *Journal of Cross-Cultural Psychology, 15,* 233–255.

The data presented in Exhibit 5.1 also show some additional findings from Levine and colleagues' study. Walking speed was another way that time perceptions were measured: Levine and his colleagues clocked how long it took people to walk a 100-foot stretch of downtown that they had premeasured. They were careful to choose randomly people who were walking alone in order to avoid those who would talk, socialize, and probably slow down. As you can see from the exhibit, once again the Japanese were at the top of the list—they took about 21 seconds to walk the distance (a pretty good clip, if you want to try it!), with the British and Americans tied as very close seconds (about 22 seconds each). The Indonesians took about 27 seconds on average. The difference among countries doesn't seem that long, but if you try counting out six seconds to yourself and consider that the whole "trip" only took about 20–25 seconds, then you'll probably agree that the difference is significant (6 seconds represents a 30 percent difference).

Finally, these researchers measured how long it took a postal clerk in these countries to serve a customer. In each country, including the United States, the researchers presented a clerk with a handwritten note in his or her native language requesting a common letter stamp and gave each clerk an equivalent of a $5 bill. Once again, there was wide variance in the service times, which ranged from a low of 25 seconds in Japan to a high of 45 seconds in Italy.

So what does all this mean? We think it shows that very subtle processes operate within cultures that affect our perceptions of the world, even about one of the most objective and indisputable things around—time. In turn, a person who perceives time differently than a business partner from another culture can encounter problems. If we can understand these differences, there is less potential for conflict. One way to better understand these differences is to classify cultures on this time dimension.

Classifying countries by their emphasis on time   The studies above illustrate how far culture extends into the perceptual domain. The effects are not, however,

How fast these Japanese are walking may be a function of their orientation toward time. © Robert Holmes/CORBIS

restricted to topics like accuracy of clocks and walking speed. Some people think that we can actually classify whole groups of countries around this concept of time perception. Edward Hall, in particular, believes that there are at least two different ways that time is perceived and experienced across cultures: *monochronic* time and *polychronic* time.[18] Roughly, this distinction refers to paying attention to and doing one thing at a time versus doing many things at once. Like most concepts we will discuss in this book, there is considerable variation within cultures and countries in how people view time. Nevertheless, let us focus on cross-national differences.

In a mostly monochronic culture, time is divided up precisely, with certain slots reserved for certain activities. For monochronic people, a schedule is sacred and to violate it is to face considerable irritation. As mentioned earlier, monochronic people view time as a commodity; they often say that "time is money" or that they are "spending" or "saving" or "borrowing" time. Hall claims that the choice of such economic language to describe time is no accident—it reflects their monochronic view of time. Clearly, monochronic views of time are predominant in most business conducted in the United States, and it is probably true of many northern European countries as well. Anyone who has ever traveled on trains throughout Europe knows, however, that there are dramatic differences in how countries view their train schedules. Many a tourist has arrived less than a minute late for a German train only to find it already gone. It is likewise no surprise that the Germans and the Swiss are known for their quality time pieces.

Polychronic cultures, in contrast, take a more flexible view of time. Polychronic cultures seem very foreign and even hard for Americans to understand. Hall points out, for example, that some Latins (typically polychronic) would much rather finish an impromptu conversation on the street rather than abruptly (and rudely) terminate it in order to get to an appointment. Polychronic cultures certainly do not have an economic view of time, and translations of phrases such as "time is money" often don't make a good deal of sense. In Spanish, for example, the closest saying might be the phrase "to pass time."

Time bounces around in a polychronic culture, and interruptions are often not seen as such. The word *interruption* implies an unscheduled and unwanted derailing of an activity. To a polychronic person, however, the unscheduled and ad hoc tends to be the expected and so naturally fits in with the way life flows. Two or more activities can be engaged in concurrently or intermittently over a period of time. A U.S. businessperson in Spain, for example, may resent sitting in a waiting room beyond her appointment time while her polychronic contact entertains several other people at once. Since time is so valuable in a monochronic culture, to be kept waiting is a sign of rudeness or irresponsibility. The monochronic American would want an apology. In turn, the polychronic Spaniard may feel that the American has an overly demanding and self-important attitude. Hall contends that this lack of understanding of time perception across cultures has been very costly for business and relates the following example to illustrate:

> A French salesman working for a French company that had recently been bought by Americans found himself with a new American manager who expected instant results and higher profits immediately. Because of the emphasis on personal relationships, it frequently takes years to develop customers in polychronic France, and, in family-owned firms, relationships with customers may span generations. The American manager did not understand this, and ordered the salesman to develop new customers within three months. The salesman knew this was impossible and had to resign, asserting his legal right to take with him all the loyal customers he had developed over the years. Neither side understood what had happened.[19]

Exhibit 5.2 presents some characteristics of people in monochronic and polychronic cultures. Some of these differences have been documented with empirical research. Interestingly, one study found that developing countries (e.g., China, Brazil, Morocco) tend to favor the monochronic interaction style in their business negotiations.[20] Yet their actual behavior is more exemplary of the polychronic style. Regardless, we might interpret extreme monochronic behavior as pushy and overly demanding, and extreme polychronic behavior as a lack of concern or as reflecting a tightly knit group with whom it's difficult to interact. Finally, it is worth noting that Americans' penchant toward monochronic time is well known around the world and some use our vulnerability to long waits to their advantage. In fact, Hall quotes a Japanese

EXHIBIT 5.2

Differences between People Who Use Monochronic and Polychronic Time

Monochronic Time	Polychronic Time
● Does one thing at a time	● Does many things at once
● Task oriented	● People oriented
● Comfortable with short-term relations	● Needs longer-term relations
● Sticks to plans	● Often changes plans
● More internally focused	● More externally focused

businessperson as saying "You Americans have one terrible weakness. If we make you wait long enough, you will agree to anything."[21] To help identify this difference in time orientation, we include a scale that measures time orientation at the end of this chapter.[22]

Interpretation of Perceptions

All of our discussion shows that a culture predisposes us to selectively focus on some things like use of time and to ignore others. We do not mean to imply, however, that all we see is fraught with perceptual bias. Sometimes—perhaps many times—what we see in others is what is really there. That is, two people or groups may accurately perceive the same behavior occurring in the environment. But even though we may "see" the same thing, we must still interpret what we see. In the case of other people, for example, we must make sense of what caused their behavior and what it means. Consider a person who completes a project successfully and is presenting the results in a business meeting. It is quite possible that nearly everyone at the meeting perceives that the project is a success. An important issue, however, is our interpretation of why the person succeeded. Our answer to this "why" question will have an important effect on our impression of that person and on our future planning. If we see this success as resulting from a lucky break, it will have different implications for the future than if we think the performance came from hard work. The consideration of how we assign causes like these to someone's behavior is the purview of **attribution theory**.

Attribution theory   This theory has been tested extensively in the United States and more recently in many other countries. It predicts that we as humans have a driving need to figure out what makes other people tick. We can never really know the answer to this question since we can't get inside someone's head to read his or her motives or personality. So our next best method for figuring a person out is to examine behavior. Accordingly, we spend a lot of time scanning and evaluating behavior to figure others out. In other words, because we can't ever really know what other people are like, our best guess is to use their behavior to infer or attribute characteristics they may have. (One thing we've argued throughout this book is that culture is a big determinant of behavior. So it can often be a mistake to look at a person's behavior and then make a personal attribution when this behavior could be the result of cultural norms!)

REALITY CHECK

Perception as a Key to Intercultural Understanding

A chat with Amy Anderson, former business advisor to DICARCO, Ltd. and U.S. AID

Can you tell us a little about yourself and what you do?

Sure, I have an MBA, and I'm currently working on a Ph.D, both of which specialize in international business. I was fortunate to have had the opportunity to work overseas, mostly with small businesses, first in West Africa as a Peace Corps volunteer, and then in South America through a U.S. AID program. Currently I work in higher education in the international student area.

Can you tell us a bit about your work in South America?

One of the most interesting jobs I had was as a business advisor for a small company in southern Chile. DICARCO processed and sold seeds as well as a variety of farm implements. They faced a number of organizational issues as they expanded their business. The company expected that their North American business advisor could make significant improvements to the firm. As a result, they pretty much set me loose to use my contemporary MBA knowledge to work with their people to see what we could accomplish.

Can you think of examples of cultural differences in perception that you faced in Chile?

They came up all the time and were real learning experiences for me. For example, I spent lots of time my first two months in Chile interviewing employees and observing what went on. It became clear there were the chronic problems with getting new products and prices into the sales system. Given my U.S. training, I immediately set out to systematize the process, and develop forms that would track the new products. The *cajera* (company cashier), I'll call her Elena, was responsible for inputting the information from the new form into the computer. Elena and I sat down together for several hours and reviewed the new process. She followed the procedure with no problems and assured me that this was doable.

I was very pleased with our progress and, over the next few weeks, checked with Elena to see if all was well. She repeatedly assured me that things were great. But another employee—who happened to be French and never had a problem letting me know what he thought—told me that the "new system was a mess." Frustrated, I confronted Elena about the problem. The look of horror on her face said it all. The last thing she wanted was to not live up to the expectations of the visiting *gringa* (this term is commonly used and

Self-attribution effects One of the most reliable findings in the hundreds of studies done on this topic is known as the *self-serving bias*. This refers to our tendency, when making attributions about our own behavior, to take credit for success (*internal attribution*) and to blame failure on other causes (*external attribution*). This finding may not seem very surprising to you, but it certainly underscores our recognition of the importance of perception in management. The main reason is that the self-serving bias is essentially saying that what happens *after* you performed a behavior affects why you did it in the first place (an internal or external cause). This "back to the future" logic may also underscore the extent to which self-serving biases reflect Western cultural norms about work behavior.

A study illustrates what we mean. Researchers interviewed nearly 700 people from five countries—the United States, India, Japan, South Africa, and the former Yugoslavia.[23] These people completed a form that measured their attributions about a variety of life events that could be considered successes or failures (e.g., performing well at a job). The researchers did a very careful job of translating the questionnaires and of checking the accuracy of the translations. As we might expect from existing research, Americans showed the typical self-serving bias. In fact, to an extent the tendency to take more credit for success than failure was observed in all the countries in this study. In comparing across countries, however, the researchers noted several interesting

doesn't have the negative connotation in Chile that it may have in other Latin American countries). In reality, Elena hadn't wanted to tell me that my Spanish stunk and that she hadn't completely understood the new procedure. Instead, during our training, it was more important to make me—the new foreign visitor—feel comfortable than to express her own concerns. I took a large part of the blame by explaining to her that it was my fault. We eventually got the system in place, but it taught me a valuable lesson about saving face.

Are there any other examples?

Yes! . . . how much time do you have? During initial interviews with employees, many expressed a desire to have more voice in decision making. Coming from a U.S. MBA perspective, I was all gung ho on participative management. I started to talk to management about this when an issue of work uniforms arose. In Chile, it's common for firms to provide uniforms to women employees, and typically they are quite fashionable, locally tailored business suits. Many women like this since it saves money and, much like school uniforms, it reduces competition. So I was allowed to use this issue as a way to get employees involved. We formed a group of people from throughout the company, very diverse and including men and women, management and employees. We met every week for a few months, and the dialogue impressed me. A lot of people spoke openly about a range of issues and ideas. There was discussion about the inequity of only providing clothes for women, that even for women pants were preferred

since it got cold in the winter, and that the informality of pants would make their customers (mostly farmers) feel more comfortable also. The owner, while not an official group member, often sat in, but his presence didn't seem to inhibit discussion. The time came to vote on the plan, which management already agreed in advance to accept. Given our wide-ranging discussion, I expected a entirely new concept in uniforms, one that would include men. But, on the day of the vote, the group unanimously decided to retain the traditional business dress just for women. At first, I was stunned, but again I learned a lesson. People can talk apparently openly, but other subtle cultural factors often come into play. I'm sure your students will study concepts such as power distance and high/low context, but these are hard to see in practice. It takes a lot of careful and constant attention to perceive and remain aware of their operation.

That's a good recommendation. Can you leave us with any more practical advice?

Good communication is essential in any setting, but especially an international one. And perception skills are a big input into that. Learning the language, if only even a few words, can sometimes give you a leg up on perceptual skills. But the biggest thing to remember is that true cross-cultural understanding is a long-term, if not lifetime, endeavor. After thirteen years of working internationally, I'm still learning something new every day. It's fun.

differences. First, the causal attributions of the Japanese were more internal for failure than were the attributions of people from any of the other countries. In other words, the Japanese were more likely to take responsibility for a failure than anyone. If these results were accurate, then the stereotype of the American as the take-charge, buck-stops-here manager is not supported by these data.

The Japanese were also the least likely to take credit for success! In fact, this latter effect was dramatic: While the Indians' and Americans' scores were over eight (8.0) on this 10-point scale and the remaining country scores were over 6.0, the Japanese average score was only 3.9. The results of this research were at least partially supported by another more recent study.[24]

In summary, this study showed two important things. First, the self-serving bias has some cross-national applicability. People from countries as diverse as India, South Africa, and the United States have showed this tendency to take credit for success and to externalize failure. Second, the effect is not universal (probably far from it). In particular, the Japanese showed a strong tendency toward responsibility for failure and modesty regarding success. Clearly, the Japanese are strongly concerned with themselves as members of a group, more so than as individuals per se. Accordingly, self-effacing behavior as well as a strong sense of duty toward the work group is common. So in group-oriented cultures, modesty appears to be valued, whereas in individually oriented cultures (such as the U.S.) a bolder assertion of competence and credit is valued.

Attributions about others   A subsequent set of studies looked at the attributions or causes we assign to others' behavior.[25] In the first study, Japanese university students read a story about a man who had worked nearly two years for an organization. There were, however, several different versions of the story. Even though most details about the story were the same for everyone, about half were then told that the man was demoted to a lower position after these two years (the "failure" condition). The other half were told that he was promoted to a higher position ("success"). In addition to this factor, the nationality of the man was also varied in the stories. About equal numbers of subjects were told that the man was either (1) a Japanese citizen working in Japan, (2) a U.S. native working in the United States, or (3) a citizen of a developing country who also worked in that country.

After reading the materials, the Japanese students made attributions about the cause of the success (promotion) or failure (demotion) of the other person. It was predicted that the Japanese students would make self-serving attributions for people from all three countries. However, the researchers also predicted an even stronger effect when people were asked to interpret the cause of behavior for someone within—as opposed to outside of—their own group. This in-group bias is similar in form to the self-serving effect. An in-group bias occurs when one is more self-serving for members of one's own cultural group. Interestingly, however, the predictions were not supported—the Japanese students did not show the in-group bias when interpreting the behavior of someone from Japan. In fact, if anything, there appeared to be a pattern that showed a more generous pattern of attributions for people from the other countries (the man who was described as from the United States or a developing country). These findings dovetail with the earlier study that showed that Japanese were less self-serving than those of several other countries. These findings show that Japanese tended to be modest; they were more likely to assign responsibility to themselves for failure and deemphasize credit for success.

Recall that in this study only the Japanese made attributions about others. It would have been nice to include people from those other countries as well and to ask them to read the same description of the promotion and demotion. This is exactly what the researchers did in their second study.[26] Americans and people from a variety of developing countries also read and reacted to the same description of the man just discussed. They found that Americans were more likely to give the man credit for success (internal attribution) than were subjects from developing countries. Since this group included people from many different countries, it is difficult to pinpoint a specific cultural mechanism in operation. Taking both studies into account, however, we can say that Americans are more likely to attribute success to the person—especially compared to the modest Japanese.

In fact, researchers have found similar effects in other group-oriented cultures. This idea was first tested with a group of Chinese.[27] They were asked to rate another person who was either self-effacing in their attributions (did not take personal credit for success) or was self-serving (took credit for success). The self-effacing person was much better liked by the Chinese. Finally, this cultural effect is so robust that it apparently even affects our attributions about very bad events. One study found that English-language newspapers were more personal and that Chinese-language newspapers were more situational in their explanations of the same crime.[28] The story, which attracted press attention in both the United States and China, dealt with a Chinese graduate student in the United States who murdered his Ph.D. advisor and several others after losing an award competition. The researchers painstakingly collected all the articles that were written on the topic in the United States and China and then coded the "attributions" about the student's crime into internal (personal) or external (situational) categories. American newspaper reporters were more likely to emphasize internal attributions about the student (quotes included: "very bad temper," "sinister edge to his character well before the shooting," "darkly disturbed man," and "whatever went wrong was internal"). The Chinese reporters, however, were more likely to emphasize situational causes of the murder, including relationships ("did not get along with his advisor," "isolated from the Chinese community") pressures in Chinese society ("Lu was a victim of the Chinese educational policy") and aspects of American society ("murder can be traced to the availability of guns").

Implications of cross-cultural attribution   These attribution effects emphasize our original point: Perception is not limited to selectively seeing or missing a certain event. Even when many people agree about what they saw, culture can affect the interpretation or assignment of causes as to why something happened. In fact, each study we reviewed made it clear that someone succeeded or failed; there was no ambiguity about these events in this set of studies. Yet perception still had an effect on the interpretation of outcomes that occur to the self and others (see the following International Insights). This is the insidious thing about perception across cultures—it gets you coming (whether you even see the event itself) and going (even if the outcome is clear, the cause can be attributed away).

Attitudes

Perceptions often start out as isolated events—mostly determined by our environment (loud noise grabs your attention, etc.). Gradually, however, when perceptions occur over and over again, you might form an attitude about them. An **attitude** is a learned tendency to react emotionally toward some object or person. According to social psychologists, we can have attitudes about nearly everything, including ourselves. Attitudes toward the self, toward others/groups, and toward work have all been studied cross-culturally.

Attitudes toward the Self

We have feelings and attitudes toward many aspects of our lives. Individuals differ in how much control they feel they have over their life and in how much they like and respect themselves. In this section we will focus on attitudes toward the self that are work related or have direct implications for management.

Interdependent and independent selves   One of the broadest differences in attitudes toward the self deals with the degree of autonomy or uniqueness of the self. The Western view of the self as independent and individualistic is exemplified in cultures that emphasize uniqueness, self-reliance, and individual achievement.[30] American culture is a good example because it emphasizes independence in so many different ways: Parents encourage their children very early on to be independent, school is by and large structured to foster independent activity, and performance on the job is typically evaluated at the individual level.

In contrast, many non-Western views of the self are different. These cultures often make it difficult to separate the self from others and from situations. Such cultures may

INTERNATIONAL INSIGHTS

Attributions on TV

AN INTERESTING STORY highlights the significance of the attribution process perhaps even better than the research we reviewed.[29] Barbara Walters, of course, is famous for her interviews of notable people from many walks of life. Several years ago, she interviewed Muammar Abu Minyar al-Qadhafi, the leader of Libya. Tensions between the United States and Libya were quite high at the time and much of the discussion centered around this topic. Interestingly, after the interview the media had little to say about the content of the interview itself. Instead, there was considerable comment about Mr. Qadhafi's behavior. During much of the interview, Mr. Qadhafi shifted his eyes away from Ms. Walters and appeared to be very reluctant to look her in the eyes at all. Ms. Walters herself remarked, "he wouldn't look me in the eye. I found it disconcerting that he kept looking all over the room but rarely at me." The wide and general interpretation of this was that Mr. Qadhafi was shifty and evasive and that the behavior was indicative of someone who was, at best, not telling the whole truth.

Now, whether or not Mr. Qadhafi was telling the truth is not our point here. Our point is instead similar to that made by the attribution researchers. Here we have a case where many people probably saw the same thing (eyes shifting, unwillingness to look someone in the face). Indeed, we could systematically go through the video of the Walters interview and unassailably document this behavior. But the interpretation of the same event—the attribution—could vary dramatically across cultures. Had we asked an Arab, for example, to explain Mr. Qadhafi's behavior, it probably would be at variance with the negative opinion of Americans. To an Arab, Mr. Qadhafi would have been perceived as showing proper respect to another person, especially a woman. To stare at another person—especially a woman—is considered very rude in Arab culture. Thus, instead of attributing the unwillingness to look at Ms. Walters eye to eye as shifty and untrustworthy, the very same behavior is interpreted as the height of politeness by another culture. This story demonstrates that attributions are important—especially across nations and cultures.

often emphasize qualities like paternalism, interdependence of people, solidarity, and group cohesion. Viewed from this perspective, the self is not a standalone thing but instead is changeable and deeply affected by others.

Let's take a look at this attitude in some Asian cultures. In many of these countries, people view themselves as intertwined in complex ways with others, as we noted in our earlier discussions of the collective nature of their societies. In Japan and China, independence among children is not necessarily emphasized, school activity that joins people with groups is often fostered, and work performance is often defined as group performance. Some U.S. companies use work groups or teams as a defining structure. The rationale for adopting them is that it is important to let everyone know that "we're all in this thing together" or even to "have people recognize that we're a family here." These statements reflect a non-Western view of the self, one in which individuals are part of—and very much obligated to—the group. It remains to be seen whether these efforts will be successful in the long run. One major obstacle in the way, however, is the lifetime of experience many Westerners have in viewing the self as apart from others, as individuals. In fact, perhaps one reason for the success of such efforts in, say, Japan is that work teams are compatible with cultural norms about the self. A Japanese saying has it that "the nail that sticks out gets hammered down." This proverb refers, in part, to the need for people to fit in well with others.[31] In contrast, a common Western saying is, "The squeaky wheel gets the grease." Exhibit 5.3 provides a summary of these differing attitudes about the self.[32]

EXHIBIT 5.3

_____

Two Views of the Self

Interdependent Self (non-Western)	Independent Self (Western)
● Defines self as part of the group	● Defines self apart from group
● Focuses on similarity to others	● Focuses on uniqueness of self
● Encourages efforts to sublimate self	● Encourages "finding oneself"
● Teaches children dependence on/to others	● Stresses independent children
● Fears exclusion from others/group	● Fears inability to separate from group/stand up
● Can "read the mind"/intentions/ feelings of others	● Believes in importance of "saying what's on your mind"

Sources: Adapted from Markus, H. R., & Kitayama, S. (1998). Culture and the self: Implications for cognition, emotion, and maturation. *Psychological Review, 98,* 224–253; Triandis, H. C. (1989). The self and social behavior in differing cultural contexts. *Psychological Review, 96,* 506–520.

Self-descriptions   How do people describe themselves in other cultures? If the preceding distinction is accurate, we should see widely varying self-descriptions between Western and non-Western cultures. This assumption was the starting point of an interesting study.[33] Researchers conducted a study whose method was very straightforward and simple—they simply asked U.S. and Japanese students to describe themselves in a very open-ended and unstructured way. They were asked to respond, in any way they wished, to the question "Who am I?" The students were allowed up to twenty responses to this question.

Then the researchers had some hard work to do—they had to take all the responses and place them in categories. Although a number of categories were coded, of special interest to us was how often the students mentioned *abstract* versus *concrete* self-descriptions. Abstract self-descriptions would include general responses like "I am extroverted" or "I am sensitive," whereas concrete descriptions would include statements like "I am happy when I work with my friend" or "In social situations, I tend to hold back." This dimension reflects Western and non-Western views of self. If it is true that Westerners have more independent views of the self, then their self-descriptions should be more abstract and devoid of special or concrete qualifications.[34] Likewise, non-Westerners should describe themselves in ways that are specific and embedded in the concrete as opposed to abstract. This is exactly what was found: Americans were more likely to use general trait descriptions of themselves and less likely to use situational descriptions than were the Japanese.[35]

Studies using people from different countries have produced similar results. In one study, people in India and the United States were asked to describe several close friends.[36] These researchers found that 46 percent of the descriptions by Americans were the abstract, context-free variety (e.g., "He is a tightwad"; "He is selfish"). Only 20 percent of Indians, however, made general statements like these. The Indians were much more likely to make situation-specific descriptions ("He is hesitant to give money away to his family"). Other studies found similar results: Americans (40%) were more likely than

INTERNATIONAL INSIGHTS

Face: How to Give It, Get It, and Keep It

SELF-PRIDE AND THE respect of others are probably important in all cultures. However, experts say that this need for pride and dignity—face—may be *the* single most important concept to be aware of when doing business with many Asian cultures.[38] In fact, one authority claims that "to speak or act in a way that causes an Asian to lose face is tantamount to physical assault in the West." Since many Asian cultures are interdependent, they also try to save face for others. It is easy to see why Asians go to great lengths to "save face." In fact, in a study of about one hundred Chinese managers, all of them said that face was mutual—that it should be returned when given.[39] For example, if you were to ask an Asian for directions to the post office, he or she may actually take you there, even if it's out of the way. If they don't know where it is, they still may point and say, "That way." To not know is to lose face. Likewise, if you ask Asians to build a product, they will do so even if they know it will fail immediately because of poor design. They would not tell you that your design is flawed up front because doing so may cause you to lose face.

The notion of face can explain why some Americans may perceive Asians as indirect.[40] Americans pride themselves on their frankness and honesty and expect similar behavior in others. Asians are also very honest people, but the social demands of face can present problems in interactions with foreigners. The solution to this problem for Americans is complex. Sometimes they might simply use a more indirect approach than they are used to, like asking for any suggestions or advice regarding the design of a product that an Asian may be asked to build.

In general, the moral is: Don't mistake smiles as a solid connection with your business contact. In fact, it's quite possible for an American to create resentment and even not pick up on it. If you did offend, it isn't likely that you will be told, since no one wants you to lose face. Alternatively, you might be told in such a subtle fashion that you would miss the message. For example, you'll find that things will slowly become more difficult, no one will seem very cooperative, and not much will be accomplished.

There are some general notions to keep in mind about giving, getting, and keeping face that are useful for all concerned:[41]

- Frankness in Asia is almost always rudeness; more subtle, high-context communication is the norm.
- An inviolate rule in Asia is: Compliment but never criticize, even if asked for criticism. You may be tested on small things. Your host may say, "People here are poor workers, aren't they?" If you say yes, you will not pass the test—in fact, you should start packing. One authority goes as far to say that if you can't think of the correct answer to that question—one that saves face for everybody—you shouldn't even be trying to do business in Asia.
- Asians are likely to laugh if you say something that causes loss of face or that demeans their culture or country. Don't mistake the laugh for anything other than as defensive—as a way to save face.
- If you ask a question in Asia and don't get an answer, don't push it. It probably has something to do with face. Save it for a later time and setting, preferably a private one.
- Never show anger, even if you feel it. The public display of such a strong emotion will do you no good and you will be labeled a "peasant."
- Do not be in a rush—it is an attack on the face of others. To Asians, your sense of hurry says they are not important enough to spend time with—that you have better places to be.

Some Americans claim that obeying these social rules is akin to capitulating to the business demands of the Asian partner (e.g., asking questions and not getting answers). But experts point out that acknowledging this difference does not mean you have to be a pushover. In fact, they suggest you should sometimes use face to your advantage. Sometimes simply saying, "I would lose face at home if I were to agree to this deal" will carry more weight than a rational, numbers-based argument. Nevertheless, you should be persistently firm, with some flexibility and willingness to explore options. One expert advises business people, "Be firm, but avoid obstinacy and rudeness. A calm and relaxed stubbornness is advised. Be persuasive in a gentle way." That same expert provides this advice above all else: "Go slow, be calm, never loud. Listen more than you talk." This is probably good advice for doing business anywhere—but especially in Asia.

Indians (17%) to attribute the behavior of others to abstract dispositions ("He is dishonest") than to situational circumstances ("It is not right, but in this situation, he needed the money").[37] One important way that this differing view about the self is illustrated is via the concept of **face**, the subject of the accompanying International Insights.

Effects of having different self-views   If some cultures emphasize fitting in rather than standing out, we should also see differences in self-ratings of performance between interdependent and independent cultures. In the United States, self-ratings of job performance are typically higher than corresponding ratings by supervisors or outside raters. This "leniency bias" had led some experts to express misgivings about the use of self-ratings in performance evaluations.[42] Given the nature of the self across cultures, we'd expect that this leniency bias in the United States might not be observed in more interdependent cultures.

This was the premise for a study of nearly 1,000 employees of various organizations in Taiwan.[43] Researchers asked both supervisors and employees to make a variety of ratings of the employees' performance. The ratings for each employee-supervisor pair were then compared. As predicted, the Taiwanese did not show a leniency bias—they were more modest in their self-ratings. Given that there is pressure not to stick out from the group in this interdependent culture, this tendency to be more modest in self-ratings might be expected. It is important to note that people in this study made their ratings anonymously, so the modest tendency probably does reflect some kind of important internalized attitude.

In a subsequent study, workers and supervisors from several Asian (e.g., Korea, Japan) and Western countries (e.g., the U.S., Mexico) were compared and similar results were found.[44] This study included nearly 1,000 employees and an elaborate set of controls (e.g, gender, age, religion) yet still found the same pattern of effects—a more modest self-rating by Asians. A final study suggested that it is important to consider the nature of the specific culture and not to lump all Asian countries together.[45] It may be a specific set of attitudes in a culture that produces the modesty effect (such as those stressing order and respect for social hierarchy). It is this aspect of culture, not East or West, that drives this effect. As a result, some Western countries may be even more likely to show modesty effects than selected Asian countries. If this is correct, we should be examining differences among countries and cultures and specific self-attitudes of interest. The section to follow will discuss some important work attitudes that may directly affect performance on the job.

Specific self-attitudes   One self-attitude that falls into this category is the so-called **Protestant work ethic** (PWE). The term refers to the desire to maximize one's material prosperity and is tied closely to strong beliefs in capitalism. The term *Protestant*, however, has been questioned by some since high beliefs in the value and ethic of work have been observed among non-Protestants, let alone those not adhering to the Christian faith.[46] Nevertheless, to examine the effect of this self-attitude, researchers have developed scales to measure PWE and a good deal of research has been completed using these scales. For example, one study compared the PWE scores of nearly 2,000 college students from thirteen different countries. They found that PWE scores are related to the degree to which a country values prestige, wealth, and power, and they found that countries that had great inequality of wealth and status were more likely to endorse PWE beliefs.[47] Also, in a large study of developing nations, it was found that PWE was also correlated with per capita income.[48] These data suggest that self-attitudes such as PWE may affect economic behavior and growth. For this reason alone, the self-attitude of PWE across cultures is very important to study.

Another important self-attitude is the belief in a **just world**. This dimension gets at differences among people and countries in the need to believe that we live in a world where people generally get what they deserve. Varying beliefs across countries could also be of importance to those studying international management. Using a well-known scale that measures just-world beliefs, it was found that the higher the gross domestic product of a country, the higher the general beliefs in a just world.[49] This suggests that the belief that the world is just can motivate people to acquire more wealth. Alternatively, the just-world belief may simply be a rationalization. In other words, it could indicate that those who are wealthy maintain beliefs that they deserve those rewards because the world is just. Regardless of the interpretation, the correlation between just-world beliefs and economic behavior is intriguing.

Attitudes about Others and Groups

Attitudes about the self are one thing, but we also hold attitudes towards other groups and cultures. Large numbers of managers are now interacting with their colleagues from different cultural groups and countries. Many even work and reside as expatriates in foreign countries. So it may be more important now than ever to understand other groups.

What are our attitudes toward other countries and people? Most of us have **stereotypes** about people from other countries. Stereotypes are inferences about what other people must be like based on group membership (e.g, racial, religious, cultural groups). A notable percentage of Americans may think the French are romantic, the Germans technical, and the Japanese good at details. Of course, we even have stereotypes about people from other regions, provinces, or states, so cross-country stereotypes are hardly a surprise.

Attitudes toward Americans   Some people have clear views about Americans that they most certainly act upon. Americans are often said by other cultures to be self-focused. This is part of what is implied by the term *ugly American*, which refers to an ethnocentric person who believes that the American way is the right and only way. This person is not concerned with other cultures and makes little or no effort to understand the behavior of others. As a result, the ugly American can easily offend a person from a different country or culture.

There may be some larger reasons for why Americans are self-focused and myopic in their attention to other countries (assuming that they are!).[50] For example, the United States is relatively isolated geographically and has a high level of natural resources. Thus, there is little inherent pressure to look abroad. At the same time, however, the U.S. has always had large levels of foreign investment and those investments are on the rise. In addition, competition from other countries is fierce. So perhaps more than ever it is necessary to examine our attitudes toward other countries and how these affect our behavior.

Exhibit 5.4 presents some data collected a few years ago by *Newsweek* magazine on views that six different countries have about Americans. Two questions were asked of the large representative samples in each country. Respondents were asked to go through a large list of trait descriptors (e.g., industriousness, honest, etc.) and then choose the traits that were most and least often associated with Americans. As you can see in the exhibit, Americans are stereotypically seen as industrious and energetic by others. In

EXHIBIT 5.4

Oh, to Know How Others See Us*

Country	Traits Most Often Associated with Americans	Traits Least Often Associated with Americans
Brazil	intelligent inventive energetic industrious greedy	lazy self-Indulgent sexy sophisticated
France	industrious energetic inventive decisive friendly	lazy rude honest sophisticated
Germany	energetic inventive friendly sophisticated intelligent	lazy sexy greedy rude
Japan	nationalistic friendly decisive rude self-indulgent	industrious lazy honest sexy
Mexico	industrious intelligent inventive decisive greedy	lazy honest rude sexy
United Kingdom	friendly self-indulgent energetic industrious nationalistic	lazy sophisticated sexy decisive

*Traits are listed in the order mentioned by respondents from different countries. Respondents were allowed only four responses to the "least often" question.
Source: Newsweek, July 11, 1983. Reprinted by permission.

general, attitudes about Americans by people in other countries are fairly positive. The Japanese are the only group to use more than two negative characteristics in their description of Americans.[51] If you scan the list of characteristics least often associated with Americans, there is also some agreement. For example, Americans are rarely seen as lazy. On the other hand, Americans apparently aren't seen as either sexy or sophisticated.

But what if you had contact with these other nationalities? Would their stereotypes fade away? To address this question, researchers studied managers from different cultural backgrounds who worked together.[52] Four different groups of managers—British, Japanese, Singaporeans, and American—were asked to rate themselves and the other groups on two main dimensions. One dimension measured expectations about typical performance levels (high or low), and the other rating dealt with management style (open vs. closed). Some of the results of the study were interesting. For example, the U.S. and Japanese managers saw themselves as better performers than they are seen by any of the other groups. Another interesting finding was that expatriates rated their host nationals very highly, whereas this was not true if there was no employment relationship. The results on the management style measure were also provocative. The U.S. managers perceived themselves as being much more open (e.g., extroverted, frank, decisive) than the other groups. And this opinion was shared by the other managers since the U.S. group was actually rated higher in this area by all other groups. The Japanese managers saw themselves as slightly closed (e.g., introverted, cautious, secretive), but actually are regarded as considerably more closed by all the other managerial groups. These results suggest that firms need to be aware of these perceptions and the effect they may have on relations among various managerial groups (e.g., nationals and expatriates). This may be particularly true for American managers, who seem to engender relatively consistent perceptions by other groups.

The following International Insights takes this survey one step further by presenting some quotes from non-Americans about what they think Americans do best. Some of these quotes are consistent with the traits presented in Exhibit 5.4, but they provide a much richer source of feedback about Americans.

Formation of stereotypes   How do others get these attitudes or stereotypes about Americans and, conversely, how do Americans form attitudes about others? Given that so few people interact cross-culturally, we have to assume that media portrayals must contribute to stereotypes across countries. For instance, one expert points out that beyond the fact that religious and ideological differences play a role in affecting attitudes toward Arabs, the American media has done more than its share of perpetuating stereotypes.[54] An analysis of TV programs, for example, showed that the Arab was TV's most popular villain.[55] An analysis of movies made from the 1920s to the present also shows Arabs as consistently greedy, blood thirsty and sexcrazed. U.S. newspapers foster this same impression with their portrayals of Arabs. For example, it was not uncommon in the 1980s to see an editorial cartoon that depicted an Arab with loads of money buying up American investments. (Despite this popular belief, Arabs account for less than 3 percent of all foreign investment in the United States.[56]) Likewise, books and textbooks have a long history of being equally unkind to Arabs. The reaction of an Arab to Jack Kerouac's book about the Beat generation of the 1950s called *On the Road* underscores this point. The reader was bewildered to read passages like the following: "We were like a band of Arabs coming to blow up New York," and "Paul drove into a gas station. . . noticed that the attendant was fast asleep. . . quietly filled the gas tank and rolled off like an Arab."[57]

It is tempting to explain these statements as an attitude of the 1950s since Kerouac wrote during that time. However, a cursory examination of contemporary TV will show the same bias toward other countries. In a *Frasier* episode rerun not long ago, Frasier's brother Miles is lamenting the fact that his wife was spending lots of money ($25,000!) on plastic surgery. In response, Frasier's dad said, "For that, you could get a whole new wife from the Philippines." Of course, this anecdote does not prove the point. What it does show, however, is that 2002 did not leave us as sophisticated as we might think. In

INTERNATIONAL INSIGHTS

What Do People from Other Countries Say about Americans?[53]

What the U.S. does best is to understand itself. What it does worst is understand others.

—CARLOS FUENTES, *MEXICAN WRITER*

The American people possess a spontaneous kindness and freshness of spirit that is genuine. If Americans think you've done something creative, they will respond with tremendous enthusiasm. Your nationality doesn't count. We in Europe tend to create idols and then destroy them, whereas Americans go on supporting you. I'm struck by the way American actors and actresses continue working into their 80s and being showered with love and affection by their fans, even though they are no longer glamorous. Americans are the first to believe in you and the last to drop you.

—VALENTINO, *ITALIAN FASHION DESIGNER*

One thinks first of the Americans' generosity. That trait distinguishes them from almost every other society on earth. Few other nations have remained so eager to continue to admit and accept people from other lands within their midst. In recent years, the Americans have been pained and hurt in some of their experiences with the outside world and may have hardened somewhat. But still, after 200 or 300 years, they remain astonishingly young, occasionally naively so, but still sympathetically, truly young.

—HELMUT KOHL, *FORMER CHANCELLOR OF GERMANY*

If you're going to make a million of something, do it in the U.S. If you're going to make only one, do it here.

—GIORGETTO GUIGIARO, *ITALIAN AUTOMOTIVE DESIGNER*

What I like about Americans is their frankness, their openness. In America, I feel I can openly express whatever opinion I have, and it is welcomed, even if it conflicts with other opinions. In Japan, even among friends we can't have a difference of opinion—disagreement destroys friendships. But in America, a difference of opinion can make friends, bring people closer together. That open-mindedness and frontier spirit is why I am so comfortable in the U.S.

—AKIO MORITA, *COFOUNDER AND FORMER CHAIR OF SONY CORP.*

America is the place where raw ideals of faith, hope and charity are mobilized into real, effective human organization.

It is some kind of wild and beautiful experiment.

—LEONARD COHEN, *CANADIAN WRITER AND COMPOSER*

From my first days in the U.S., I have been a regular student and admirer of America. But today the U.S. faces a crisis in education. The level of primary and secondary education is well below the worldwide average. Young Americans entering college can hardly write a decent one-page text. They take little time and no pleasure in reading. They also ignore that there is a world of human beings outside the borders of the U.S. and they are confident that the U.S. remains No. 1 and unchallengeable.

—JEAN-JACQUES SERVAN-SCHREIBER, *FRENCH TECHNOLOGY EXPERT AND WRITER*

The outstanding achievement of the U.S. has been to build a nation from the most widely disparate human resources. This is summed up for me in such names as [filmmaker] Steven Spielberg, [soprano] Jessye Norman, [Chrysler chair] Lee Iacocca and [computer manufacturer] An Wang.

—BOB HAWKE, *FORMER PRIME MINISTER OF AUSTRALIA*

America has promoted and spread all over the world the simple ideal of individual happiness. Various religions, civilizations and ideologies throughout history regarded happiness as a collective rather than an individual experience. Almost all of them are losing ground to that triumphant American vision of private happiness. Hundreds of millions of people, from Tokyo to Leningrad, from Cairo to Buenos Aires, dream of being happy in the American way. Sometimes they dream of being happily American. But is the new global America, this international happiness-oriented village, a happy place? I'm afraid I can only propose an un-American answer to this highly American question. The popular American dream of living happily ever after, while dazzling the world, reminds me of the American landscape itself: plentiful, elusive, and forlorn.

—AMOS OZ, *ISRAELI WRITER*

I think Americans are best at making ice cream.

—JANET MORGAN, *SPECIAL ADVISER TO THE DIRECTOR GENERAL, BBC*

EXHIBIT 5.5

Attitudes toward Four Countries Held by Americans, 1982 and 1993*

Response Chosen	France 1982	France 1993	United Kingdom 1982	United Kingdom 1993	Israel 1982	Israel 1993	Russia 1983	Russia 1993
Close ally	29	25	57	61	27	26	1	10
Friendly but not a close ally	51	49	34	28	34	43	4	56
Not friendly but not an enemy	13	16	3	3	18	17	30	20
Unfriendly and an enemy	1	3	2	1	5	5	63	7
Not sure	6	7	4	7	16	9	2	7

*Entries in the exhibit are percentages of a national sample who responded to the question "Do you feel that (country) is a close ally of the U.S., is friendly but not an enemy, is not friendly but not an enemy, or is unfriendly and is an enemy of the U.S.?"
Source: Adapted from Hastings, E. H., & Hastings, P. K. (1993). *Index to international public opinion, 1992–1993*, Westport, CT: Greenwood Press.

fact, perhaps, it shows that as the media continues to be a powerful influence, the choice of targets has changed from older ones (e.g., Russians, Arabs) to newer ones (e.g., Chinese, Filipinos). Interestingly, however, analyses of Arab portrayals in the media post–September 11 reveal a relatively evenhanded treatment. Ironically, the wide call to avoid blaming all Arabs or Muslims for the September 11, 2001 murders may have improved the treatment of these groups in the U.S. media. It remains to be seen whether more long-term analyses of media and U.S. public opinion will show the same effects.

In fact, an analysis of U.S. public opinion about other countries supports these points. Exhibit 5.5 shows how such public opinion/stereotypes can change, given some time and a lot of information.[58] It shows, for example, how attitudes toward Russia as an enemy have atrophied over the 1983–1993 decade, whereas attitudes toward some other countries (e.g., China and Japan) have been relatively stable or have declined.[59]

The in-group as a cause of stereotypes   Besides these media influences, it appears that we simply have a tendency to rate our in-group higher than an out-group. Members of a group tend to emphasize their own positive characteristics and accentuate the negative traits of other groups. This pattern has been noted, for example, in the studies of perceptions between Americans and Russians, Arabs and Israelis, and Catholics and Protestants, among others.[60] In some cases, these stereotypes can manifest themselves in a pattern called **mirror imaging**. This is a case where each group perceives similar positive traits in itself and similar negative traits in the out-group. This pattern is especially likely to occur between groups under conflict (e.g., Arabs and Israelis; Indonesians and Chinese-Indonesians).[61]

Even when mirror imaging is not found, there does appear to be a natural tendency for us to see in-group members as more varied and complex (heterogenous) and out-group members as less varied and more homogenous. Americans, for example, may recognize and perceive wide differences among themselves while perceiving Russians to be relatively similar. Some point out that this contrast is only natural since we have lots of experience with our in-group and are relatively inexperienced with the out-group.

If this is true, then increased contact and interaction with people from different cultures (out-groups) should result in a more articulated view of people in that culture. This prediction was tested with a sample of Americans and Chinese.[62] Researchers assessed the actual amount of contact that each group had with each other; both primary contact (actual experience in China/U.S.) and secondary contact (number of Chinese/U.S. friends, how often they read about China/U.S., etc.) were assessed. They also measured the perceived similarity of the other cultural group with questions like "The more I know Chinese, the more similar they are to each other" and "In China, all people tend to behave alike." Results showed that increased contact with the out-group did result in greater heterogeneity. For example, the more contact the Chinese had with Americans, the more likely they were to see variety in Americans' attitudes, behavior, and dress (among other things).

It has also been shown that the familiarity gained through intergroup contact not only resulted in a more varied set of perceptions, it also increased the *accuracy* of group stereotypes.[63] For instance, perceptions of Japanese and U.S. managers working together for a Japanese-owned commercial bank were compared.[64] These managers were asked to rate themselves and the other group on a variety of trait dimensions. If accuracy is defined as ratings by others that are similar to one's own group rating, then a good deal of accuracy was found in this situation. For example, both the Japanese and U.S. managers perceived U.S. employees to be more extroverted, outspoken, assertive and less patient than the Japanese. Similar effects were also found among Chinese and U.S. exchange students who had a good deal of interaction with one another.[65]

Although stereotypes often represent biased perceptions of other group members, not all stereotypes are wholly inaccurate. Indeed, research shows that some stereotypes may reflect a partially accurate assessment of some objective group characteristics. In one study, Chinese perceived Americans as more heterogenous than another group of Chinese, in contrast to the usual in-group/out-group effect noted earlier.[66] The authors claim that this result reflects the greater variety in Americans than the Chinese and that the ratings were rightfully influenced by this reality. We might expect similar results in Japan where the non-Japanese born population is only about 2 percent. Such a position reflects the "kernel-of-truth" hypothesis: that stereotypes of another group are at least partially based on some objective characteristics of that group.[67]

The effects of attitudes and stereotypes   One reason to understand these attitude and stereotype differences across countries is that they may impact whether and how business might be conducted. An interesting case in point occurred in India, where color TV transmission was first broadcast in 1982.[68] Because there were no Indian color TV manufacturers, the government allowed the domestic firms that already produced black-and-white TVs to import "knocked-down" sets (kits with all the parts, but unassembled) to be assembled and sold in India. Identical kits from German, Japanese, and Korean suppliers were imported and put together with Indian brand names.

Interestingly, the German and Japanese TV sets commanded much higher prices than did the Korean sets. In fact, it apparently was common for Indian consumers to bring along a screwdriver to a store in order to open the back of the set to determine the country of origin. Thus, despite identical parts, the Japanese and German companies had an advantage in the marketplace thanks to a *country-of-origin stereotype* among

Indians. Those in marketing have long known about country-of-origin stereotypes and of course still make manufacturing decisions based on these stereotypes. For example, the Panasonic line of stereo and related equipment is actually manufactured by Matsushita Electric Company of Japan, although the brand name may not directly bring this country to mind. Likewise, brand names such as Häagen Daz are often chosen to avoid penalties associated with, or to take advantage of, country-of-origin stereotypes. This is an important concept in marketing, one that some advertisers have capitalized on (e.g., the "Made in the U.S.A." television campaign). In fact, a consumer ethnocentrism scale had been developed that measures the tendency to prefer to purchase U.S.-made goods.[69] Research has shown that those who score high on this scale accentuate positive aspects of domestic products while overlooking or deemphasizing the negative aspects. However, the real trouble may be simply in distinguishing a domestic product from a foreign-made one, as the following International Insights shows.

Of course, the insidious thing about stereotypes is that some will forget that even at their best stereotypes often reflect a "kernel of truth" about the other person. Worse yet, the perceiver may have a brief personal encounter or experience with a member of that group and use this incident as further evidence that all group members are very similar (homogenous). A reasonable perspective on this problem is to recognize that our personal knowledge is very limited, perhaps to a handful or even only one or two persons. Therefore, to categorize a whole group of people (e.g., Arabs, Americans) as having a single trait is a huge and specious leap of inference. One frequent objection, of course, is that the field of international management itself engages in just this stereotyping. After all, in this chapter thus far, we have tried to distinguish Japanese from Americans, Brazilians from Germans, and so on. Although this is generally true, please note that we have usually emphasized relative differences. We certainly are not saying that all Japanese are dissatisfied with their jobs or that all Brazilians don't care about punctuality. We instead refer to observed statistical differences between groups. As you probably know, most statistical tests involve a difference (American vs. Japanese job satisfaction scores, for example) over a pooled variance. The fact that there *is* variance or differences within groups proves our point. In this book, moreover, we have taken an empirical approach—one based on much data not just opinions of a few people.

Attitudes about Work

Many people spend a good deal of time at work and getting ready to go to work. There are, however, great differences among countries in the number of hours worked. Americans, for example, work about 1,900 hours a year per person. This number appears to be on the high side of the international averages, although the Japanese lead the world by a fair amount. Regardless, we certainly must conclude that work is one of the most important (or at least time-consuming) activities for most Americans and for many other nationalities as well. Accordingly, it should be no surprise that attitudes toward work and related topics is one of the most studied issues around.

Job satisfaction   In fact, the single most studied topic is job satisfaction. Literally thousands of studies have been conducted, mainly with American employees. The prevailing opinion in the popular literature is that Americans rank woefully low in job satisfaction. We are also told that compared to other countries, U.S. workers are particularly dissatisfied with their lot at work. Furthermore, Americans are portrayed as fickle

INTERNATIONAL INSIGHTS

Made in the U.S.A.?
Caveat Emptor!

A LETTER SENT TO THE editorial offices of the *Arizona Republic* newspaper a few years ago criticized the alleged superior quality and fuel efficiency of foreign-made cars.[70] The writer claimed that the United States makes cars that are on par with anything made in Germany, Japan, or Korea. In fact, to prove his point, the writer pointed to the Geo—a series of General Motors products—that were the most fuel-efficient cars on the road of their day.

The author was right in one sense—the Sentra, the Celica, and the Passeo are gas guzzlers in comparison to the Geo. But this superiority is hardly a testimony to American ingenuity. Depending on the model, the Geo is produced in several places and by several different manufacturers—all of them Japanese. The Geo Metro was built by Suzuki in Japan; the Prism by Toyota in Fremont, California; the Storm by Isuzu in Japan; and the Tracker by Suzuki in Canada.

The same is apparently true for many other "American" cars. The Ford Crown Victoria is made with American, Japanese, Mexican, Spanish, and German parts and is assembled by Canadians. The Honda Accord, on the other hand, is made by American workers in Maryville, Ohio, using 75 percent U.S.-made parts, and the Toyota Camry is made in Kentucky. Which one of these is an "American" car? Of course, it depends on how you define "American-made." Some define it as a company in which Americans have a 50 percent controlling interest, whereas others define an American company as one where no profits are sent overseas.

Unfortunately, labels and brand names are all but useless ways to determine the origin of a product. Although the Ford Escort was assembled in Wayne, Michigan, it was also assembled in Hermosillo, Mexico. The Pontiac LeMans had a Continental-sounding name, but it's certainly not French. It was designed in Germany, reengineered in Michigan, and manufactured in Korea. Worse yet, how do we account for the fact that some American firms have large equity positions in other firms? Sticking with the auto industry as an example, many people do not know that GM owns 50 percent of Saab, 100 percent of Lotus, 40 percent of Isuzu, and over 40 percent of Daewoo Motors. Likewise, Ford has a 40 percent position in Mazda, owns Jaguar outright, and has interests in many other firms.

A trip to the corner grocery is no less confusing. Hungry Jack Pancake Mix and Pillsbury Flour come from foreign-owned companies. Baby Ruth is made by Nestle, a Swiss firm, whereas Ghiradelli Chocolate is made in the United States. Backyard cookouts may be an all-American tradition, but Cattleman's Barbeque sauce is made in Britain. Bon Appetit and Grey Poupon are American-owned products, as is Swiss Miss cocoa. However, the Baltimore Spice line comes from Germany and the Jolly Green Giant is English. *Bon Appetite* and *Connoisseur* are American-owned magazines, whereas *American Baby* and *Western Sportsman* are not. That cowboy cologne Chaps is made in France, while Aramis is as American as mom, baseball, and apple pie. But, we should also point out that Mother's Cakes and Cookies is a French-owned firm, that major league baseball already has three foreign-owned teams, and that a lot of fruit—including apples—is grown in South America. Apparently, buying American is a lot easier said than done!

and fidgety as a consequence of this low level of satisfaction. As a result, they are said to have extremely low commitment to their jobs and companies, willing to move or change companies at the drop of a hat.

Have you ever asked yourself, however, why we widely believe this to be the case? On what basis do so many of us have these beliefs about the relatively low level of job satisfaction and commitment of American workers? Many scholars feel that the source of these beliefs is often specious at best. Perhaps a reporter or professor briefly visited Japan or Europe for several weeks or months and then wrote an article or book about his or her experience. Although we must and should respect the opinions of others, we also have a responsibility to examine critically the source of the evidence. Whom was spoken to? How many people were observed and, more important, how were they selected for observation? Quite often, such observations tend to be nonrepresentative. A foreign observer may be invited to tour or study a factory precisely because it is special or different (nonrepresentative) from the majority. Likewise, we must suspect that companies having great trouble or difficulty would be unlikely to invite in any observers, let alone foreign ones.

To continue our line of thought here, we ask you to guess what percentage of Japanese workers have what is called "lifetime employment." People in our classes often guess that about 75 percent or more of Japanese workers have lifetime employment. In reality, the figure is closer to 20 percent. Furthermore, this policy is not a longstanding one that emanates from Japanese culture. Rather, it appears to be a post–World War II phenomenon that resulted from deals cut by labor unions with some large companies to end the terrible labor strife that continued into the 1950s. Finally, some companies that have traditionally had lifetime employment policies are now laying off workers (e.g., Matsushita, Nissan, and others). The reason we and most other Americans think that the percentage of Japanese workers covered by lifetime employment policies is higher is not completely clear. Perhaps it is because of the popularized version of Japan we see in well-circulated magazines or in brief TV reports. Regardless of the reason, this example suggests that we should examine the source of our international attitudes and then possibly reevaluate them.

Accordingly, we should put more confidence in research studies that systematically examine such issues—especially those conducted on representative samples from two or more countries. Of course, larger-scale and systematic sources of information are in relatively short supply because of their difficulty and expense. Nevertheless, some studies do exist. One such project was conducted by researchers at Indiana University in conjunction with colleagues in Japan.[71] These researchers selected companies randomly so that the sample represented a wide range of industries. This was a first very good step since even some of the better earlier studies only selected and surveyed worker attitudes in, say, the auto or electronic industry. Next, a representative sample of employees from organizations representing these industries was chosen. This second step was all the better since most earlier research also included nonrepresentative samples of workers. This study ended up surveying over 8,000 employees that included workers from over 100 randomly selected factories in central Japan (51 factories) and in Indiana (55 factories).

Some results of this study contradict what many believe about Japanese and American workers and underscore the value of such elaborate and complete studies. For one, it was found that U.S. workers were much *more satisfied* with their jobs than were the Japanese. The researchers went to great lengths to deal with cultural and language differences that might have affected the results. One important potential problem they examined was a tendency for Americans to be typically (and overly) positive and for the Japanese to express even very positive attitudes as neutral, if not bleak. Several patterns in the data, however, eliminate this as a problem. For one, the pattern of responses by both groups to different types of job satisfaction questions jumped around. When asked to respond to the question, "All in all, how satisfied would you say you are with your job (1 = not at all to 5 = very much)?" Americans were much more satisfied than the Japanese. By itself, this result could be explained by the Japanese tendency to be modest. But responses to the question "If a good friend of yours told you that he or she was interested in working at a job like yours at this company, what would you say (0 = advise against it, 1 = would have second thoughts, 2 = would recommend it)?" also showed the same pattern. This question is behavioral and focused on others and would therefore be less subject to the modesty explanation. Yet an even stronger pattern of effects was found: Nearly 70 percent of Americans said they would take their job again compared to only about 24 percent of the Japanese.

A closer look at other relevant studies suggests that these findings are accurate. When you look at research that uses different measures and methodologies, nearly every existing study that compares job satisfaction of Japanese and Americans finds the same results.[72] Evidence in support of the position that this is a true difference in job satisfaction between Japanese and Americans comes from yet another study.[73] These researchers asked managers from Canada, France, Japan and the United Kingdom (about 100 from each country) about their overall level of satisfaction. They also asked, however, about satisfaction with specific components of the job and their work.

Two findings emerged from this study. First, as in previous studies, Japanese were less satisfied than any of the other groups. Second, when they looked at the specific pattern of responses (such as to pay level, working conditions, evaluations of coworkers, etc.), Japanese responses were quite varied. In some cases, they indicated low satisfaction, but in other cases they were among the most satisfied. Thus, the tendency for Japanese to be either systematically bleak or modest in their self-evaluations is less of an issue than may have been thought. If this bleakness is the driving force, why does it come into play for some aspects of job satisfaction, but not for others? In support of these effects was another survey of about 2,500 Japanese workers. Results similar to those just described were found, but some additional findings are worth mentioning. There was much variation among Japanese workers in their level of satisfaction, which rose strongly with age, seniority, and rank, among other things. These findings suggest that many Japanese are willing to state their level of satisfaction, and some are more willing to do so than others. In fact, older, more senior workers—the very people most likely to hold traditional Japanese values of modesty/self-deprecation—are the ones most likely to say they are happy with their jobs!

We have been focusing on Japanese-American differences in job satisfaction, but obviously there are more countries of interest in the equation.[74] The fact is, however, that most of the research in cross-national job satisfaction focuses on U.S.-Japan differences. Japan was and is one of the major economic powers in the world and a major competitor for the United States, so the high volume of research should be no real surprise. Actually, in other areas of work attitudes the same observation could be made. Let us now turn our attention to some of those other important work attitudes.

Organizational commitment   Another important and commonly measured work attitude is commitment to one's organization. Like our discussion of job satisfaction, the popular belief is that Americans are not as committed to their organizations as workers in other countries. Interestingly, however, few people have actually systematically studied organizational commitment across country and culture. As for job satisfaction, most studies of commitment have been conducted in the United States or in Canada.[75] One exception to this trend is a survey of over 1,600 employees from a wide variety of firms in the United States, Japan, and Korea.[76] Workers in those countries were asked to read and complete a standard and widely used measure of organizational commitment (e.g., "I am willing to work harder than I have to help this company," and "I would turn down another job for more pay in order to stay with this company").

U.S. workers showed significantly higher levels of commitment than either Japanese or Korean employees. The commitment levels of the latter two groups were not different from one another. This finding itself is interesting because, like the findings for job satisfaction, they contradict the popular belief that people from some Asian cultures have higher commitment to their firms.

Other studies that employ even more controls have found similar effects.[77] On questions such as "I'm willing to work harder to help the company succeed" and "I'm proud to work for this company" (among others), U.S. employees scored higher than the Japanese. This was not true of all the commitment questions, however. For example, in response to the question "I would turn down a higher-paying job to stay with this company," there was little difference between U.S. (mean = 2.71) and Japanese (mean = 2.68) employees (on a 5-point scale where 1 = disagree and 5 = agree). In fact, this item showed the least amount of agreement of any of the commitment items in general; apparently, both Japanese and Americans are willing to entertain higher-paying job offers! Nevertheless, Americans seem to report more commitment to their organizations than do the Japanese. These findings, in combination with the initial belief that Japanese would report higher allegiance to their firms, is an interesting topic that we will return to in later chapters.

Earlier research was careful to distinguish **organizational commitment** from **work commitment**. The former refers to the degree to which one identifies and holds allegiance to one's company and is motivated to act on its behalf. Work commitment, on the other hand, refers to the importance of work in one's life—the extent to which it is an important value or motivator relative to other general life activities (e.g., money, family, leisure time, etc.). We will discuss values and the relative emphasis that cultures place on these topics in the next chapter on motivation.

In summary, then, we have an interesting pattern of effects. In contrast to what is commonly believed, American workers are as or more committed to their organizations than are Koreans or Japanese. In terms of work commitment, however, Japanese appear to be more committed.[78] The Japanese, for example, are more likely to subjugate family issues and problems to those that occur at work. (This finding itself is interesting since the Japanese are also popularly thought to place high value on family compared to other cultures.)

Before we leave this topic, however, a discussion of one more study may clear up the issue we raised about work (not organizational) commitment across culture. This study investigated the job or work involvement of over 5,000 employees of a large multinational firm from twenty different countries from five continents.[79] The results showed that culture (country) had very little predictive value for work commitment or involvement. Instead, a far more important predictor was a person's occupational level. In fact, the author noted that the pattern of work commitment by occupational level was "remarkably similar" across the twenty countries. In particular, as an employee rises in an organization—whether that firm is in Korea, the United States, South Africa, or Israel—so did his or her work commitment.[80] Another way of stating these results is that sometimes situational or personal variables—like occupational level—can be more important predictors than culture or nationality. In this case, there was more commonality among people in the same occupation across country than among people in different occupations within a country. One lesson we can learn here is that we should try to eliminate situational variables before we leap to the conclusion that country or cultural differences are driving the findings. This will be a special challenge faced in Chapter 11, which examines motivation.

Chapter Summary

In this chapter, we highlighted the importance of perceptions. While it might be tempting to pass over the study of perceptions as too low level and idiosyncratic, we showed that not only can they be analyzed in detail but they also can play an important role in cross-cultural interaction. In particular, we saw that there are systematic differences in the way that various cultures process information about people and events. The perceptions in turn can be modified by reliable differences in nonverbal behavior and in the importance placed in *context* by a given culture. Some cultures are *high context* and provide lots of background information that helps tailor one's perceptions; other cultures are *low context* and place heavy emphasis on what is explicitly said or written. Interestingly, these perceptual differences even extend to cultural views about time—ostensibly one of the most objective factors in our lives. Yet we saw that *monochronic cultures* perceive time as an economic commodity that should be carefully monitored and measured, in contrast to *polychronic cultures,* which view time as fluid and flexible.

Perception is one thing, but we also have to make sense of our perceptions. This topic of interpretation—or *attribution*—was discussed next in this chapter. Attribution theorists say that humans are obsessed with asking why something happened. Just because an event catches our attention and we perceive it, however, doesn't mean that we will all interpret it the same way. For example, we showed that some cultures make typically more modest attributions about their successes—they tend to attribute the cause not only to themselves but to the larger group to which they belong. Other cultures, however, seem to encourage a *self-serving attribution*, in which people take credit for success and externalize blame for failures.

If a perception tends to occur over and over again, we may form an attitude about that topic. Accordingly, we next discussed the topic of *attitudes*—both about the self and about others. Again, there seem to be some cultural

determinants of how we view ourselves as well as a tendency to view out-groups (e.g., those from different cultures) in common ways. We concluded the chapter with a discussion of these stereotypic attitudes toward Americans as well as the attitudes of Americans and others toward their job and their work.

Discussion Questions

1. Compare the effect of verbal and nonverbal influences on our perceptions. When do nonverbal signs play a bigger role than what is actually said (verbal behavior)?
2. Think of the ways that the idea of context could affect perceptions in cross-cultural interactions. In addition to the role it could play in communication itself, what might be the effect in negotiations, in meetings in general, and for a firm's human resource practices as a whole?
3. Reflect on the differences—if any—between the stereotyping process within and across cultures and the process of classifying and distinguishing cultures that we have been engaged in throughout this book.

Up to the Challenge?

Doing Business in Vietnam

WHAT ARE SOME OF THE things you may have picked up throughout this chapter that could be of help in doing business in Vietnam? Maybe the most important thing about this chapter is the point that culture sometimes has a very subtle effect—one that at times is not recognized or appreciated when we interact with others. One of those subtle things is context. Like many Asian countries, Vietnam is a high-context culture. This means that the culture or context itself provides people with a great deal of cues that are used to interpret what might otherwise be an ambiguous event. In such cultures, people do not require or expect much detailed, explicit information about events—the context often provides this for the Vietnamese. Americans, as you know, are relatively low context—we base our perceptions and interpretations a good deal on what is explicitly said or written.

This basic difference can create some misunderstanding but is easily adjusted to when the difference is recognized. For one, Vietnamese businesspeople will probably want to get to know you personally before getting down to business. Thus, you probably should expect little if anything to be accomplished during

initial meetings with Vietnamese, at least from a U.S. cultural perspective, anyway. In fact, what the Vietnamese hope to accomplish is to get some context. During initial meetings, they will want to use that time to understand your background, your temperament, and your interests; all this will help them better able to interpret your verbal and nonverbal behavior. From the U.S. low-context perspective, the amount of time spent discussing "nonproductive" topics could be frustrating. Patience in the form of understanding this basic difference, however, could pay off later.

The question of context brings up a second important issue that was discussed in this chapter—time orientation. As you may also have guessed, the Vietnamese have a more polychronic view of time, viewing it as more flexible and extended than do most monochronic Americans. In part, this orientation results from the agricultural nature of traditional Vietnamese society and its concomitant focus on seasons. At the same time, however, the Confucian virtue of patience emphasizes time flexibility even more. The Vietnamese generally react negatively to a need for urgency in a business deal, whereas the American typically believes that "time is money."

The Vietnamese view of self is *inter*dependent, whereas the American is more likely to have an *independent* self. This difference can have many implications for conducting business. For example, because the Vietnamese are more likely to see themselves as interconnected with others, singling out a person (even for praise) is very likely to be embarrassing and may have a backfire effect. These contrasting views of self can be manifested in a number of different attitudes but perhaps none more diverse than those concerned with the concept of "face." In Vietnam, face is all important. Open criticism in Vietnam is very rare because it can cause irreparable harm to a business relationship. Likewise, a loss of temper and overt expression of anger is considered very rude and causes the person who expresses anger to lose face. Criticism and praise are best handled privately when dealing with Vietnamese; the same is probably true, in fact,

for criticism for U.S. employees. Finally, other ways to show respect and provide face to a Vietnamese business partner include (1) remaining on the formal side in your interactions, (2) showing great respect for age (the oldest member of a Vietnamese team is usually the most powerful) and (3) giving more interpersonal space to a Vietnamese than you may be used to with U.S. businesspeople. To be effective in doing business with one another, you will need to establish trust. Recognizing and accommodating for differences may provide the foundation for beneficial business relations for Americans and Vietnamese alike.

International Development
Measuring Your Perceptual Orientation to Time

Purpose
To get a feel for your views about time in order to better understand different views across cultures.

Instructions
In this chapter we documented the importance of studying perceptions. One area on which we focused our discussion was the perception of time. We pointed out, for example, that some cultures may be relatively monochronic in their perception of time, whereas other cultures may be more polychronic. A scale has been developed to measure monochronic and polychronic perceptions of time. We present the 4-item scale here so that you can fill it out. Read each item and then choose a number from 1 to 5 that reflects your feeling about the item.

1	2	3	4	5
Strongly Agree		**Neutral**		**Strongly Disagree**

_____ 1. I do not like to juggle several activities at the same time.

_____ 2. People should not try to do many things at once.

_____ 3. When I sit down at my desk, I work on one project at a time.

_____ 4. I am comfortable doing several things at the same time.

Now take the score you assigned to each item and add all four up to create a total. As you probably guessed, the lower your score (below 12), the more monochronic your orientation; the higher your score (above 12), the more polychronic you probably are. How does your score compare to the average for U.S. students (3.03) and for students in Brazil (4.15).

We also encourage you to think about the experience you might have interacting in a business setting with someone who is very mono- or polychronic in orientation. As Hall suggests, we might interpret extreme monochronic behavior as pushy and overly demanding and extreme polychronic behavior as unconcerned or reflecting a tightly knit group that is difficult to join or enter. Furthermore, people with a monochronic orientation have a number of common characteristics. For one, they are very task oriented and they tend to stick with their plans—sometimes at all costs. The task orientation also tends to make them more oriented toward the short term in their relations with others. The polychronic person, in contrast, tends to emphasize relations over tasks and thus is more open to changing plans and schedules. When these two types of people meet in a business setting—either within or across cultures—there is great potential for frustration and conflict.

Source: Bluedorn, A. C., Kaufman, C. F., & Lane, P. M., (1992). How many things do you like to do at once? An introduction to monochronic and polychronic time. *Academy of Management Review,* 6, 17–26. Copyright © 1992 by The Academy of Management. Reprinted by permission.

From Theory To Practice
Cultural Stereotypes

Purpose
To understand the presence, frequency, and deleterious effects of various stereotypes.

Instructions
Complete the following questionnaire before class. Your instructor will divide the class into diverse groups of three to six members. Your group will discuss each other's responses to the questionnaire and try to come to a consensus about the stereotypes of the various ethnic groups (20 minutes).

After you have done this, the instructor will lead the whole class in a discussion of the common stereotypes, including similarities and differences between the groups. Finally, you can consider how stereotypes can hinder and block productive business relationships.

Questionnaire

Use one word to describe each of the following groups:

1. English
2. French
3. Norwegians
4. Latins
5. Japanese
6. Middle Easterners
7. Chinese
8. Africans
9. Italians
10. Americans

Answer the following questions about Canadians (please answer these questions from memory rather than researching the answers):

1. One word to describe the people.
2. Who is the current prime minister?
3. Name three Canadian historical figures.
4. List four Canadian provinces.
5. What is the main language?
6. What type of government does it have?
7. What is its relationship to England?
8. Name of currency and relationship to U.S. dollar.
9. Main exports to U.S.

Answer the following questions about Mexicans:

1. One word to describe the people.
2. Who is the current president?
3. Name three Mexican historical figures.
4. List three states of Mexico.
5. What is the main language?
6. Type of government.
7. Relationship to Latin America.
8. Name of currency and relationship to U.S. dollar.
9. Main exports to U.S.

Source: Marcic, D., & Puffer, S. (1994). *Management international.* St. Paul, MN.: West Publishing. Marcic and Puffer adapted this exercise from Axtell, R. E. (1990). *Do's and taboos around the world.* New York: Wiley and Sons. Reprinted by permission.

Communicating Successfully across Cultures

International Challenge

Lost in Translation: Bridgestone's Communication Effort Goes Flat

IN 2000, JAPAN-BASED Bridgestone Corporation had a major problem. In a nutshell, the company's American subsidiary, Firestone, Inc., was under assault by consumers, lawyers, and even the U.S. government. The reason? Millions of allegedly defective tires that supposedly caused rollover accidents that injured more than 700 people and claimed over 170 lives. Many of the accidents occurred in Ford SUVs, and Firestone alleged that Ford's design was a contributing factor while Ford claimed Firestone's tires were to blame. To make a long story short, Bridgestone eventually recalled millions of tires and provided free replacements.

Put simply, this series of events has been prohibitively expensive for Firestone and disastrous for its brand. Some experts predicted the Firestone name would eventually disappear as a result. But our purpose here isn't to discuss problems with tires. What we're focusing on are the communication tactics used by Firestone's Japanese parent Bridgestone to manage the situation. These tactics, at least from an American audience's perspective, may have made a bad situation worse.

First, let's set the stage. Firestone's communication strategy was essentially controlled by Bridgestone executives in Japan. This is hardly a new phenomenon. Many Japanese multinationals centralize power and decision making, with all roads from foreign subsidiaries leading back to Japan. And when they are faced with problems, many Japanese executives will say nothing in the belief that silence and stoicism communicates that things are being handled calmly and deliberately. Moreover, Japanese executives tend to avoid directly confronting external criticism, preferring instead to stay disengaged from any conflicts.

Up to Bridgestone's announcement in August 2000 that it would recall millions of Firestone tires, then-President Yoichiro Kaizaki had little to say about the controversy swirling around his company. And despite rising outrage in the United States after the announcement, Bridgestone's Japanese leadership maintained its low profile. Then in September 2000, Firestone CEO Masatoshi Ono went before a U.S. Senate subcommittee to answer questions. Mr. Ono said he took "full and personal responsibility" for some of the accidents involving Firestone's tires. But one senator stated that if Firestone had knowingly put out bad tires, it would be tantamount to "second-degree murder." Mr. Ono's response to this harsh assessment was silence. One American press report described Mr. Ono's appearance as "deferential but fumbling" while another said he "came across as tentative and unforthcoming."

Critics argued that Bridgestone made the mistake of using Mr. Ono, an executive with weak English language skills, to press its case. Indeed, Mr. Ono, as well as many of the other Japanese executives on the Bridgestone crisis management team had trouble following the line of questions coming from the U.S. senators. The result, many felt, was that Mr. Ono, as well as Bridgestone in general, was not effectively communicating the message they wanted the wider American audience to hear.

A few days later, President Kaizaki finally stepped into the spotlight during a Tokyo news conference, expressing regret but deflecting blame and strenuously denying a company coverup. And he continued to refuse requests for one-on-one media interviews. A few months later, however, Mr. Kaizaki adopted more of an open stance and was willing to share important financial information about Firestone's situation. Nevertheless, it all seemed too late. In early 2001, Mr. Kaizaki stepped down. An American manager who once worked for Bridgestone described the communication tactics Bridgestone's Japanese executives used this way: "They just don't have a clue how to handle this."

As you read through this chapter, you'll learn a great deal about the myriad communication challenges facing international managers. In doing so, consider these questions. What communication errors did Bridgestone executives make, in your opinion? How would their efforts be interpreted by an American audience? Why? What cultural factors are relevant? And given the damage already done to Firestone's reputation, how should Bridgestone communicate now? Then take a look at the Up to the Challenge box at the end of this chapter for some insights into the communication adjustments that Bridgestone made.[1]

The Value of Communications Savvy in International Business

In the previous chapter we discussed many of the important cross-cultural problems and challenges presented by perception issues. Here we pick up right where we left off. That is, once you perceive and interpret the behavior of another person, you need to communicate your feelings or reactions. And that's where your prowess and insight into others' way of thinking is critical, especially in an international business environment.

Although it may strike you as obvious that communication comes in many different forms, managers sometimes get themselves into trouble by assuming that communication is the same everywhere. To an American, for instance, a gap in conversation usually is seen as an opportunity to respond or interject. And long gaps tend to provoke discomfort and a desire to fill in the silence. But in Finland and Japan, longer periods of silence in conversation are normal, even expected. Pauses suggest that someone is carefully contemplating what has been said. In fact, responding too fast can give offense.[2]

So in negotiation situations with the Japanese, unprepared Americans may be very uncomfortable when they encounter silence and may interpret it as dissatisfaction with any offers on the table. Japanese representatives, however, are likely to feel that it is important to consider offers seriously and communicate that by pondering matters in silence. Of course, many astute Japanese negotiators know that Americans are uncomfortable with silence and try to use this cultural trait to their advantage. This underscores the importance of understanding the strategic use of communication in international business, especially in negotiations.[3] And we'll consider international negotiation in more detail in the next chapter.[4]

In any case, even speaking the "same" language carries pitfalls. Decisions are often a function of culture, background, and experiences, a shared language notwithstanding. Take what often happens when Americans are posted to places such as Australia or the United Kingdom. Not only is the "English" used not identical, but the communication style is different too (e.g., the use of irony, sarcasm, understatement). Those differences can cause huge problems if not properly understood. Of course, nonverbal communication matters, too. For example, putting your feet up may be acceptable in the United States, especially if you want to convey a relaxed and familiar atmosphere, but in most other countries it would be viewed as crude and offensive. The bottom line, as one expert put it, is that in international business "what blows deals is a failure to understand communication styles."[5]

Consequently, this chapter will review various forms of personal communication, both verbal and nonverbal. We'll also look at the ways that multinationals communicate, something that our opening box suggests is important. We'll also review some of the barriers to effective communication across cultures and suggest ways to overcome them.

Spoken and Written Communication

The single most important way that we communicate is through language, both spoken and written. Let's look at the role language plays in international communication.

Languages of the World

There are over 2,500 distinct languages currently spoken along with another 7,000–8,000 dialects. However, only about 100 of these languages have more than 1 million speakers. In fact, about ten languages account for most of us on the planet (see Exhibit 6.1). A few languages are mostly limited to only one nation (e.g., Polish, Japanese, and Greek). Others, however, are spoken across many borders (e.g., English, French). Nevertheless, the dominant language in any one country or region has a great effect on and can even define a particular culture. An interesting case in point is the Chinese government's efforts to promote Mandarin as the official national language in a country that arguably has the most linguistic diversity on earth. Take a look at the following International Insights to see what we mean.

Speaking (and Not Speaking) Other Languages

The large number of spoken and written languages presents several challenges to international managers. First and foremost, to be effective you need to communicate in the language of the country where you want to do business (or be willing to place enormous trust in a translator!). Few Americans, however, speak second or third languages (see Exhibit 6.2 for this and other interesting language tidbits). There are many reasons for Americans' general lack of interest in other languages. The most

EXHIBIT 6.1

The Ten Most Widely Used Native Languages in the World*

Language	Native Speakers in the World (%)
1. Chinese (Mandarin)	20.0
2. English	6.0
3. Hindustani	4.5
4. Russian	3.5
5. Spanish	3.0
6. Japanese	2.0
7. German	2.0
8. Indonesian	2.0
9. Portuguese	2.0
10. French (tie)	1.5
10. Arabic (tie)	1.5

*These figures reflect only the number of native speakers and do not include those who speak second languages.
Source: Adapted from———. (1991). *The economist atlas,* 116. London: The Economist Books.

INTERNATIONAL INSIGHTS

The Languages of China

EXHIBIT 6.1 SHOWS that Mandarin Chinese is the world's most frequently spoken first language. But that doesn't mean that Mandarin is the language of China. Far from it. The Chinese government's efforts to unify the country with *Putonghua* (a common language) notwithstanding, there really is no such thing as "standard" Chinese. In effect, China has eight distinct regional languages, not counting the many dialects within each. For instance, Mandarin (and its offshoots) is the language of Beijing and the surrounding northern plains. Used by over 50 percent of China's population, Mandarin is the most common language group in the country. But Mandarin is hard to comprehend to people from Shanghai and its surrounding provinces, who speak various dialects of Wu. In fact, the eight languages of China are very different from each other, as different as Spanish would be from French.

Where this language diversity will lead China remains to be seen. Interestingly, local languages and dialects have experienced a revival recently, especially in major cities and other areas of China that have strong connections to the rest of the world. This trend may make the government's ongoing goal of promoting nationalism via a common language more of an uphill struggle than ever.[6]

China is perhaps the most linguistically diverse country in the world. © Macduff Everton/CORBIS

popular explanation is that the United States is relatively isolated geographically and, as a result, has had no great need for additional languages. This explanation, however, doesn't hold up well in the face of the large numbers of immigrants and ethnic minorities in this country. Plus, technology has made the rapid transmission of information a given, rendering geographic isolation more illusory than real.

But part of the reason for Americans' relatively poor language proficiency may be ethnocentricism. Perhaps you've heard the story (fictional or not) of the American tourist in Germany who sneezed on a public bus. A German turned and said *"Gesundheit."* The tourist then said to a friend, "How nice—he speaks English." Likewise, as shown in Exhibit 6.2, it's possible to graduate from college in the United States

---

EXHIBIT 6.2

Americans on Foreign Languages and Foreigners on English

- Only about 15% of American high school students now study a foreign language, compared to nearly 25% in the 1960s.

- The United States continues to be one of the few places in the world where it is possible to graduate from college without taking even one year of a foreign language.

- While the United States is one of the most ethnically rich nations in the world, the languages accompanying immigrant populations have not spread very widely.

- English is the most popular second language in Europe, the Middle East, Africa, Japan, and China.

- Many foreign companies routinely translate their memos into English.

- The average European knows two languages; many know three or more.

- Chinese children are required to take foreign languages in grade school and to demonstrate mastery prior to college graduation.

without taking a single foreign language course. This lack of acknowledgment of the importance of other languages reflects the low value that Americans attach to this skill.[7]

One factor that has made it easy for Americans to be complacent about being monolingual is that the rest of the world increasingly uses English in business interactions. For example, English is the language for international air traffic, regardless of city of departure or arrival. And that's not all. Peruse French job adds and you'll find that most management and professional positions require *anglais courant.* English is the official language of oil firm Totalfina, the second biggest company in France—this in a country that ferociously protects its language. In fact, France has created a government ministry of culture to foster the French language and culture. But why is English becoming more pervasive in international business circles, even in France? First, much of the business on the Internet is dominated by American firms. And in the process, the Internet is exposing people everywhere to English more than ever. Then there's the sheer size of the American economy and the global reach of U.S. multinationals, which effectively makes using English "good business sense," at least in the minds of some. Moreover, English is fairly simple, grammatically speaking, and consequently makes for a relatively easy "common tongue" to use in international business. So when French pharmaceutical firm Rhone-Poulenc merged with German competitor Hoechst a few years ago, English was made the common language of the merged companies.[8]

There are many different languages spoken in EU countries. Yet today more than half the people in the European Union claim to be reasonably conversant in English. In fact, a survey of 16,000 people living in EU countries found that almost 70 percent agreed with the statement "Everyone should speak English." And the Dutch are closest to already being there, with more than 80 percent indicating that they speak English as a second language. English has also been weaving its way into local languages around the world, with Europe no exception. German has become so littered with English phrases that some now refer to it as *Denglisch.* German executives these days may conduct media interviews in a *Pressebriefingraum* and then go work off their stress at a *Businesssportcenter.* But like the French before them, some German officials worry about the intrusion of English into their culture. One member of the German parliament decried the trend, calling it a "flood of Anglicisms descending on us from the media, advertising, product description and technology." Nevertheless, the trend of creeping Anglicism seems likely to continue. And if you add all the people who speak English with some competence as a second language to native English speakers, English speakers become the most numerous in the world (at around 1.3 billion, compared to about 900 million for Mandarin Chinese).[9]

Overall, English is the most popular second language in Europe, Africa, Japan, and China, among other places. Consequently, it's probably no exaggeration to consider English as the language of international business. In fact, speaking English can pay off in career terms. In China, for instance, speaking English means better jobs, better pay (often double), and foreign travel opportunities. No wonder teaching English is big business, with up to $3 billion annually being spent on English language training in Asia alone.[10]

That said, other languages really aren't going away, in business or otherwise. For instance the World Trade Organization's costs related to language have soared over 120 percent since it was founded in 1995. Language service to the WTO's more than 140 members eats up 22 percent of its budget. It seems that along with global organizations come global-sized bills for translators.[11]

And what does "competence" in English, or any other second language that you might speak, really mean? There's little doubt that many people overestimate their language skills. And as we mentioned at the beginning of the chapter, perception and decision making may be linked to cultural values regardless of what language is spoken. So communication in international business is likely to have plenty of rough edges to it, even when a "common" language is used. Those rough edges can often create real problems and even great danger, as we illustrate in the following International Insights.

Nevertheless, competence in another language can definitely pay dividends in international business. And that's why the American reliance on English represents a distinct disadvantage, one that will continue to cause problems as the ferocity of foreign competition from places like China escalates. That said, many American firms continue to ignore or underplay the value of having managers fluent in other languages. In one survey, managers in American multinationals felt that while cross-cultural understanding was valuable, foreign language skills were not as important. The perception was that language problems could be easily overcome by using translators or by hiring foreign nationals.[13] Not surprisingly, studies show that American businesspeople have the lowest foreign language proficiency of any major trading nation in the world.[14] And as you can see in Exhibit 6.3, the United States receives poor ratings for knowledge of foreign cultures and languages relative to other countries. In particular, this exhibit, which is based on a survey of over 10,000 business people from around the world, shows that the United States has the lowest rating of any country.

Communicating in Foreign Languages: Plenty of Room for Error

Clearly, not having foreign language skills puts you at a disadvantage in international business. But assuming that you speak Mandarin, French, or Russian, your problems are far from over. Even with great proficiency, you will find that many problems can arise in verbal communication. First, there can be many dialects within a particular language group. Moreover, distinct languages can be found in many countries, as we suggested in our earlier International Insights box on China's linguistic diversity. Beyond regional differences in languages, however, there are also accent and usage variations as well as many other subtle differences in language use.

For these reasons, international managers must be sensitive to the possibility that what they intended to communicate was not understood. This is even true with interactions between British and American managers, people who ostensibly share the

INTERNATIONAL INSIGHTS

Cross-Cultural Miscommunication in the Air Can Be Dangerous

SECONDS BEFORE KAL flight 2300 landed in a storm in Cheju, South Korea, First Officer Chung Chan Kyu tried to abort the landing by grabbing control of the plane from Captain Barry Woods. The aircraft's black box recorded what happened when the plane was only 30 feet above the ground and about to land. Captain Woods shouts: "Get your hand . . . get off. Get off! Tell me what it is . . ." Seconds later a terrible crunch is heard over the grunts of Mr. Chung and an alarm bell. The plane crashed and exploded in flames. Astonishingly, all 157 people aboard escaped with their lives.

Many observers felt that the crash at Cheju reflects a rising occupational hazard—the language obstacle. As fast-growing Asian airlines scoured the world for pilots, cockpit crews have become more culturally and linguistically diverse. The problem in Korea, say foreign pilots, is acute. "It's like an air show up there, and it's hard to tell where everything is because the Koreans are all speaking Korean," said an American who flew for Asiana Airlines for several years before taking a job with a U.S. firm. "There are a lot of opportunities to get hurt."

Under Korean law, foreign pilots must be matched with a Korean first officer so that communication with the control tower is effective. Unfortunately, as was probably the case in the Cheju accident, Korean first officers receive only a rough familiarity with English as they go through flight school. Worse yet, communication may be further hindered by the hierarchical Korean culture that discourages copilots from asking questions or volunteering information. In fact, one foreign pilot who trained many Korean pilots said that in the hundreds of preflight briefings he gave, the trainees did not ask a single question.

These and other factors make flying in Korea more risky than should otherwise be the case. Korea's airlines have higher fatal accident rates than their North American and Latin American counterparts. And investigators acknowledge that miscommunication contributed to the Cheju accident. In fact, as the plane was on its final approach, Captain Woods asked First Officer Chung to turn on the windshield wipers. Because he didn't respond, Mr. Woods repeated the request. A few seconds later, Mr. Chung replied: "yeah . . . wind shears." Apparently, Mr. Wood's order to "get off the controls" also caused confusion. Experts say that a clearer command would have been "Don't touch the controls." Both pilots were charged with criminal neglect.

Clearly, this is a case where culture affected communication. The Confucian tradition in Korea produces a high power distance. This can make it difficult for Korean flight officers to be proactive enough in providing information to superiors. Likewise, asking questions is often regarded as disrespectful. Showing lack of experience or knowledge, even in an airline cockpit, may be considered a loss of face. Fortunately, no lives were lost at Cheju.[12]

"same" language. Consider, for instance, how each side interprets the phrase "table the proposal." To Americans, it means that the proposal will be put aside or delayed indefinitely. To the British, however, it means the opposite (i.e., to act immediately on the proposal). And Exhibit 6.4 lists examples of how different words are used to capture similar meanings in Britain and the United States. Of course, misunderstandings between British and Americans are likely to be cleared up fairly quickly given that the core language is the same. But in more complex transactions involving distinct languages, resolving communication problems will be much more difficult, especially if managers are not fluent in the languages involved and cannot completely check any translations provided.

Even if managers are proficient enough to avoid these problems, they can still make major errors that can harm their international business. For instance, Swedish manufacturer Electrolux once used the phrase "nothing sucks like an Electrolux" to promote their vacuum cleaners. Besides being racy or vaguely obscene, this phrasing could be interpreted as something less than rousing evaluation of the product! Exhibit 6.5 presents additional communication blunders committed by companies as they

EXHIBIT 6.3

The Relative Ranking of Developed and Developing Countries on Knowledge of Foreign Languages and Cultures

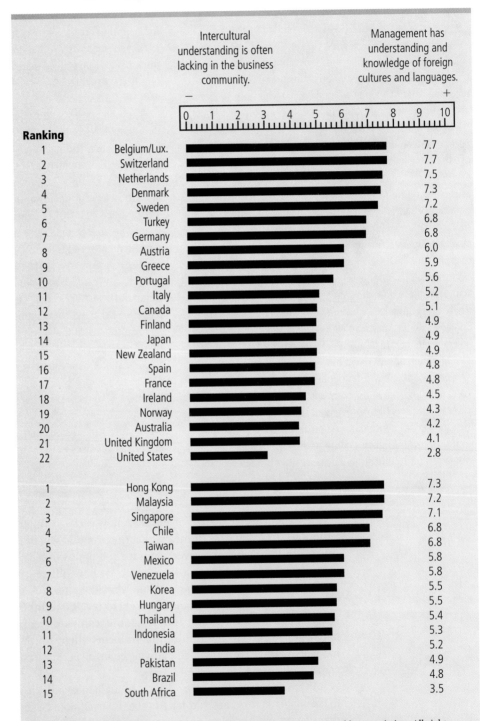

		Intercultural understanding is often lacking in the business community. (−)	Management has understanding and knowledge of foreign cultures and languages. (+)
Ranking			
1	Belgium/Lux.		7.7
2	Switzerland		7.7
3	Netherlands		7.5
4	Denmark		7.3
5	Sweden		7.2
6	Turkey		6.8
7	Germany		6.8
8	Austria		6.0
9	Greece		5.9
10	Portugal		5.6
11	Italy		5.2
12	Canada		5.1
13	Finland		4.9
14	Japan		4.9
15	New Zealand		4.9
16	Spain		4.8
17	France		4.8
18	Ireland		4.5
19	Norway		4.3
20	Australia		4.2
21	United Kingdom		4.1
22	United States		2.8
1	Hong Kong		7.3
2	Malaysia		7.2
3	Singapore		7.1
4	Chile		6.8
5	Taiwan		6.8
6	Mexico		5.8
7	Venezuela		5.8
8	Korea		5.5
9	Hungary		5.5
10	Thailand		5.4
11	Indonesia		5.3
12	India		5.2
13	Pakistan		4.9
14	Brazil		4.8
15	South Africa		3.5

EXHIBIT 6.4

British and American Phrases:
A People Separated by a Common Language

American Version	British Version
candy	sweets
cookie	biscuit
dessert	pudding
chips	crisps
french fries	chips
doctor's office	surgery
apartment	flat
elevator	lift
flashlight	torch
gasoline	petrol
diapers	nappies
to phone	to ring up
Band-Aids	plasters
raincoat	mac
subway	tube
toilet	loo
trunk of car	boot
hood of car	bonnet
soccer	football

tried to do business internationally. The exhibit shows two main types of blunders—errors in translation and errors due to a lack of understanding of local norms and culture.[15] If you think such errors are a thing of the distant past, please read the following International Insights about the problems that Microsoft experienced with the translation of its word processing program. And consider the fact that Microsoft, as well as the companies discussed in Exhibit 6.5, hired professionals to work on and translate their ads or products but still had problems. So real-time communications in international business are likely to produce as many problems, if not more.

EXHIBIT 6.5

Language Blunders Abroad

Examples of translation errors

● A foreign airline operating in Brazil advertised plush "rendezvous lounges" despite the fact that in Portuguese "rendezvous" implies a room for making love.

● One German translation of the phrase "Come alive with Pepsi" literally meant "Come alive out of the grave with Pepsi."

● A memo from an African subsidiary of Dutch electronics giant Philips referred to "throat-cutting competition" instead of "cut-throat competition."

● A sign on the elevator in a Romanian hotel read: "The lift is being fixed. For the next two days we regret that you will be unbearable."

● A sign in the window of a Paris dress shop said: "Come inside and have a fit."

Examples of failing to appreciate local norms and cultural values when communicating

● One U.S. firm operating in Europe handed out fake coins with "$1 billion" emblazoned on them. Instead of spreading goodwill, this was largely seen as a reflection of American pomposity and feelings of superiority. And the Europeans wondered why the dollar sign was used instead of local currency.

● In Britain, General Mills used a breakfast cereal package that showed a clean-cut child saying "See kids, it's great!" Although this was a prototypical American ad, the product received a poor reception. General Mills failed to appreciate that English families are less child centered when making food purchases than their American counterparts.

● A foreign appliance company used an ad in Middle Eastern markets that showed a refrigerator full of food, including a large ham. The ad was insensitive if not offensive since Muslims are forbidden to eat pork.

● Listerine was introduced in Thailand with an ad that showed a boy and a girl, obviously enthralled with one another. After learning that the public depiction of romantic relationships was objectionable, the ad was adjusted to show two girls discussing bad breath. The revised ad was much more effective.

Source: Adapted from Ricks, D. A. (1983). *Big business blunders: Mistakes in multinational marketing.* Homewood, IL: Dow Jones Irwin.

For example, imagine a meeting between American and Japanese managers. Despite accuracy in the literal translation of words, the actual meaning can vary considerably. In Japan, it is generally considered inappropriate to say no in a blunt or direct fashion. The Japanese tend to avoid explicitly saying no to the other party so that both sides retain face. Instead, the Japanese rely on a variety of very indirect ways to say no. A person not savvy about such cultural norms may not understand that "I will consider your proposal" could actually mean no. It is so common for the Japanese to avoid direct negatives that the Japan Export Trade Organization provides a pamphlet to foreigners to help them understand the difference between a yes and a no.[17] Exhibit 6.6 presents some common phrases that actually mean "no" but allow for the bad news to be cushioned. Apparently, even the structure of the language itself seems to be designed in part to preserve this harmony. The verb in Japanese comes at the end of a sentence. A

INTERNATIONAL INSIGHTS

Habla Usted Español? Microsoft Has to Brush Up

THE LAST THING YOU want to do is offend your customers. And you certainly wouldn't refer to valued clients as vulgar, abrasive, or ridiculous. Apparently, however, this is exactly what Microsoft did to many of its Spanish-speaking customers with one of its products a few years ago. In fact, to some this incident made many of the infamous gaffes of the past look tame.

The problem centered on a Spanish-language version of Microsoft's popular Word program and its thesaurus feature in particular. Unfortunately, the thesaurus function offered a number of offensive synonyms for various ethnic groups, creating a massive public relations headache for the company. The program, for example, suggested that "man-eater," "cannibal" and "barbarian" could be substituted for the Spanish term for black people. The program also likened Indians to man-eating savages and provided the Spanish word for "bastard" as a substitute for people of mixed race. *Lesbian* was equated with "vicious" and "perverse," while *Occidental* was matched with "white," "civilized," and "cultured."

The insulting language was first uncovered in Spain but was later widely discussed in the Mexican press. Microsoft issued a public apology, claimed that the translation errors were "unintentional mistakes," and promised to quickly fix the software. But by then criticism had reverberated in prominent Mexican newspapers and radio stations. In denouncing the program, a local historian told the *La Jornada* (a major newspaper in Mexico City) that "those who made this dictionary of synonyms are imbeciles and cretins."

How did a major company like Microsoft get things so wrong? A company representative said that the firm contracted out the thesaurus code to an unnamed American supplier. In turn, Microsoft failed to detect many of the outdated terms and incorrect translations. The representative said, "If you went and bought a printed dictionary in Mexico today, you would find some of these mistakes." Some experts, however, were incredulous and skeptical. "It's unbelievable," said the chair of the Spanish department at the University of California at Berkeley.[16]

communicator can present the subject and object first, then alter the verb after gauging the reaction. Further, the speaker can easily add a negative at the end of a sentence that entirely changes the meaning in order to preserve harmony.[18]

Of course, in all cultures it can be difficult to confront someone directly. So it's probably universal to try to cushion bad news to some degree. But Americans in particular are often irritated when they feel they are being "strung along" or not given a "straight answer" when the news is bad.[19] Going back to our Japanese example, the problem is that Americans *should* be hearing a no but they are not. In other words, it's not that the Japanese are insincere, it's just that they are probably working very hard to maintain harmony and show consideration for the feelings of others when communicating a no. A flat-out refusal would certainly be the worst option to take for many Japanese. And conversely, many Japanese perceive the communications of Americans as "blunt," "too insensitive," "overly critical," or just plain "prying." Of course, it would behoove both sides to gain a better understanding of the other.[20]

Embarrassment and Apology as Communication

But what happens once offense is given or a loss of face occurs? Are there cross-cultural differences in how people experience that and respond to it from a communications standpoint? The answer appears to be yes. In one study, Japanese and Americans were asked to describe recent embarrassing situations that they had experienced. The Japanese

EXHIBIT 6.6 _____

Ten Ways to Avoid Saying No in Japanese

Phrase That Really Means No	A Common but Incorrect American Interpretation
"That would be very hard to do."	Some adjustments are needed, but the deal is still possible.
"It is very difficult."	The matter is difficult but not impossible.
"I will consider it."	The issue is under consideration for future use.
"I shall give it careful consideration."	Even more attention will be given to the proposal.
"We shall make efforts."	Energy will be put into exploring options.
Silence/delay in response	The other party is thinking about the topic or they are offended by our message; time is being wasted.
A change of subject	The new topic is more important now.
"I'll think about it."	The issue is still alive and under consideration.
"I'll do my best, but I'm in a delicate position."	It will be extremely tricky, but he or she will give it a shot.
"Yes, but . . . ."	Conditional agreement

Sources: Adapted from Imai, M. (1975). _Never take yes for an answer._ Tokyo: Simul Press; Ueda, K. (1978). Sixteen ways to avoid saying "no" in Japan. In J. C. Condon & M. Saito (Eds.), _Intercultural encounters with Japan. Communication—contact and conflict,_ 185–195. Tokyo, Japan: Simul Press.

tended to mention predicaments involving in-group relations (e.g., interactions with family, spouse, friends, and coworkers). American respondents, however, were more likely to mention relations with out-group members (e.g., acquaintances, friends of friends, strangers, and the like). Also interesting were the differences in reactions to these social predicaments. Most of the Americans (65%) felt embarrassment, but only a small portion of the Japanese had this reaction (5%). On the other hand, the Japanese were much more likely to feel shame (42%) in response to the loss of face than were the Americans (4%). These findings are supportive of the perspective that Japanese and Americans are generally on opposite ends of the individual–collective dimensions of culture. Our point here is that one major effect of these orientations is a difference in communication styles.[21]

An interesting follow-up issue is how people resolve their embarrassments and other interaction predicaments? In other words, are there cross-cultural differences in how people respond? Again, the answer seems to be yes. Of course, one option is to apologize for creating the problem itself, or at least for our part in the social mess. And as it turns out, Japanese and Americans (among others) tend to react differently in situations where one person harms—physically or psychologically—another person. For example, as we discussed although rare, fatal airplane accidents do happen. When such accidents occur, there's always a major effort made to determine the cause. Some years ago, a Japan Airlines flight crashed into Tokyo Bay near Norita International Airport. Twenty-four people died and many others were hurt. After the accident, the president of JAL publicly apologized, personally visited each family affected by the tragedy, and offered his resignation. It is difficult to imagine the management of an American airline engaging in the same course of action.

Researchers have also examined how apologies are communicated across cultures. In one study, Japanese and Americans were asked to describe a recent incident in which they had apologized to someone else. The results showed that the Japanese preferred to apologize directly and extensively (as in the airline example), without offering explanations and reasons for their actions. Interestingly, Americans, while not quite as direct as the Japanese, also generally preferred to apologize directly. However, the American apologies were not as extreme, and they offered many more justifications and attributions to explain their behavior. The Japanese were highly sensitive to lapses in their social obligations and went to great lengths to try to make amends. The American tendency to provide many explanations of "social failure" may reflect the higher value placed on the self in an individualistic culture, which may make the admission of failure or guilt much more difficult. Alternatively, the concern for the collective or group may make it easier to express such feelings for the Japanese.[22]

In fact, experts suggest that international companies should help their employees understand that the type of apologies, face management, and accounts and explanations provided for various situations may be driven by culture-specific values and attitudes. Managers who fail to adjust their communication and account-giving strategies accordingly risk provoking conflict and creating misunderstandings in cross-cultural contexts (e.g., in international negotiations, cross-cultural team operations, and international performance appraisals, to name just a few).[23]

Compliments as Communication

Of course, sometimes we communicate not to deal with interaction problems, but to smooth such interaction in the first place. For example, research shows that Americans praise each other much more frequently than do the Japanese. Americans are also much more likely to commend personal traits and physical appearance than are Japanese. Why these differences? The value placed on the self in U.S. culture—so much so that there is great difficulty in accepting a mistake—may lead many Americans to be especially solicitous of compliments that make the self feel better or otherwise stand out.[25]

Actually, there appear to be wide differences across cultures in terms of how often praise is given, what is praised, and how people respond. For instance, Egyptians tend to have a "complimenting" culture. While they may not compliment as much as Americans, their salutations tend to be longer and have more depth. Here's an example. On one occasion, a host complimented an Egyptian dinner guest on his necktie. The Egyptian promptly took off the tie and gave it to the person who offered the praise. The host politely refused the gift but found it neatly folded on the couch after the party was over.[26]

And consider this. For years American children have been told that "sticks and stones may break my bones, but names will never hurt me." Interestingly, Egyptians have a nearly opposite saying: "A sharp tongue cuts deeper than the sword." Clearly, there are differences in compliments (and insults) across cultures. Some are very stingy with their praise, while others may be willing to give you the ties off their shirts. And this behavior, like other communication, is often linked to underlying cultural norms.[27]

INTERNATIONAL INSIGHTS

Japanese Dairy "Pours" on the Apologies

YUMI ITO WAS standing in front of two representatives of Snow Brand, Japan's largest milk company, and they literally "floored" her. Both men were bowing so deeply in apology that their heads touched the floor. In fact, they bowed over and over again to express regret that a batch of their milk had caused Ms. Ito's young daughter to become sick. As their heads literally touched the floor, Ms. Ito said to herself, "This is too painful to watch."

This show of humility was dramatic, even in a country that has made apologies an art form. And Ms. Ito wasn't the only person receiving such attention. In fact, Snow asked 2,000 of its employees to personally visit the more than 14,000 people made sick by their milk to bow, apologize and offer cash compensation. Other Japanese firms have asked their employees to pitch in with apologies, but no one has approached the scope of Snow's efforts. To understand this unprecedented campaign, you have to also appreciate what happened and what was at stake for this $12.1 billion food company giant. About two weeks before the apologies such as that received by Ms. Ito, Snow's milk was blamed for causing diarrhea and vomiting in thousands of people. It took several days for the company to isolate a dirty valve at its Osaka plant and then they ordered a recall. Shortly after this event came revelations about contamination in other products, more sick people, and additional recalls.

Worse yet, a few days later the government accused Snow of recycling and reselling milk products that had been returned by retail stores. Snow promised a full investigation and closed all twenty-one of its plants temporarily for safety reasons.

In an attempt to regain its reputation, Snow Brand engaged in this mass humility effort. On the weekend after the last allegation, about 700 Snow Brand employees gathered early in the morning for a briefing and instructions on the apology campaign. The basic instructions were to apologize first and then to inquire about the victim's health. Then they were to broach the compensation issue. If there were health-related expenses, the employees were to get a receipt. If none was available or if the victim got mad, employees were instructed to pay them anyway. "How much?" asked one employee. "If the amount is within 30,000 yen [$280], that should be okay," said the supervisor. "And don't talk back, no matter how angry the customer gets." This brings us back to Ms. Ito, who was also presented a white envelope with calligraphy on it that's often used when giving cash to ill people. It included cash and related gift certificates. For Ms. Ito, an apology would have been enough. She refused it first, but the Snow Brand employees implored her to accept the envelope. "We won't be able to go back to our company if you don't take it," they said.[24]

Criticism as Communication

Of course, the opposite of compliments are *criticisms*. Once again, differences across cultures are apparent. One study found that Americans and Japanese tend to use distinctly different styles when criticizing others. The Japanese are more likely to use "passive" forms of criticism, like references to a third party and humorous or ambiguous comments. Americans are much more apt to criticize directly, sometimes with overt anger that might also be accompanied by constructive suggestions. It appears that the need for group harmony in collectivist cultures impacts how people deliver critical comments. Causing someone to lose face, such as through publicly expressed hostility, is something to avoid.

And as we implied earlier, this could help explain why it is difficult to directly say no in some cultures. For instance, many foreigners have experienced irritation by the apparent unwillingness of many Chinese to say no directly to an impossible request. Instead, the response is that the request is said to be "complicated" or that "the responsible person is busy at the moment." Likewise, some feel that many Spaniards would sooner take a business loss than openly admit that they made a mistake. These are common observations in more group-oriented cultures.[28]

Monitoring Others as a Communication Tool

If we assume that styles of communication are often taught and learned early in life, then it's probably the case that people in some cultures tend to be more sensitive to other people in the first place. After all, if you're able to communicate consistently in a way that doesn't offend others, then you must have a keen ability to "read" people and related interpersonal clues. In other words, you have to be sensitive enough to know when there is potential for offense or if you have already given offense to those around you.

We've all heard about Americans traveling overseas who have no idea how they are coming across. Americans are often characterized as blundering loudly through shops and museums, pompously wondering why foreigners don't speak English and why they can't get ice cubes in their drinks. We hope that this thumbnail sketch of the "ugly American," one that says more about the odd tourist than any business managers, is fading. Nevertheless, it raises the question of how attuned Americans are, compared to people of other cultures, to receiving and interpreting communication cues from others. Researchers who have studied this "self-monitoring" issue found that American and Australians (individualists) are more self-focused than Koreans, Taiwanese, or Japanese (collectivists), who focused more on situational cues (e.g., context, status) than on the self. This finding suggests that how to act on situational cues is something that Koreans, Taiwanese, and Japanese would generally score higher on than Americans and Australians.[29] Speaking of self-monitoring, take a look at the following Reality Check for one international manager's insights about cross-cultural communications.

Written Communication

Perhaps one way to avoid all these potential problems is to communicate via letter or e-mail. If you don't speak the language well, you can at least hire someone with writing expertise or carefully craft the message yourself before sending it. But neither possibility is as simple as it seems. Hiring writing help is impractical much of the time, given the volume of written communication businesspeople have to deal with.

And according to one estimate, the average corporate e-mail user can expect thirty to forty-five new messages to appear each day. For international managers, the e-mail volume is likely to be much higher. In fact, the growth of international business may account for a good chunk of the rising use of e-mail. Believe it or not, some managers may routinely spend 50 percent of their office time on e-mail. After all, the convenience of e-mail is seductively attractive—a manager in Dayton, Ohio, can quickly fire off a memo to a counterpart in New Delhi without having to think about what time it is on the other side of the world. Of course, we wonder if all the time spent on e-mail is a function of sheer volume of messages or the hours that some international managers spend to painstakingly craft e-mails to colleagues in another language (something that may be more common when foreign executives want to send their American colleagues e-mails in what for them is a second language—English). It may be a little of both![30]

In any case, how could you construct a letter or e-mail to get your point across, make your supply order clear, or request some key information? If you're an American, you probably would: (1) use English, (2) keep the letter short and to the point, (3) stress the use of the personal tone (personal pronoun) and (4) avoid flowery or exaggerated language.[31] If you were French, however, you would probably be less concise (maybe the letter would spill onto a second page), and your openings and endings would be much more formal and polite. In fact, Americans might perceive these parts of the letter to be

REALITY CHECK

Working in the International Communication Business

A chat with Elias Jimenez, marketing manager, Latin America, Nortel Networks

Can you tell us a little about yourself and what you do?

I grew up in the suburbs of New York City and am a first-generation Latin American. I earned an MBA in International Business with an emphasis in the Latin American region. Prior to my current employment, I lived and worked in Peru and Chile. I'm now a marketing manager for Nortel Networks and my job is to support our business partners in the Caribbean and Latin American region. My job involves a lot of training all over the region to keep our partners up to speed on new products and services. Nortel is a global internet and communications leader for service providers and enterprises with capabilities spanning optical long haul networks, wireless networks, and metro networks. I've had several roles in Nortel, beginning with a sales job supporting distributors in South America. Later, I moved into product marketing, commercial marketing, and now business partner marketing.

Since you are working in a multicultural environment (Canadian company, U.S. base, Latin American markets), what unique communication challenges and/or opportunities does this present?

Obviously, since we're in the telecom business, communication is very important to us. And the rapid change that's characteristic of our business affects what we do, including how we communicate. As a global organization, the firm typically pitches an overall goal and expects us to formulate a "local" best way to get there; this also applies to our communication strategies. Because telecom is a rapidly changing, high-tech industry, we probably have a lot less structure in terms of the way things are done than other industries. Interestingly, I think this allows us to customize or make culturally appropriate communication occur. At the same time, employees from all over the world learn to communicate via the "corporate culture" that emanates from headquarters. So reports, updates, presentations, announcements and the like tend to follow a general model. However, this does not mean that we are free from cross-cultural challenges.

"old fashioned" or "too formal."[32] Japanese writers often prefer to hint at something, partly because their language itself is ambiguous and partly because, as we've noted, being overly direct could be seen as condescending or an affront to one's face. Exhibit 6.7 shows a sample letter you might receive from a Japanese business partner. Note that it is typical to begin with set phrases about the season or weather and to close with comments that are similar in form. Clearly, the second paragraph is the real message and the remaining text (comments about seasons, humble attitude) illustrates the cultural norms about communication. Even bad news would be presented very indirectly.[33]

An interesting and comprehensive study of business letter writing involved asking 100 major U.S. corporations for sample letters sent to foreign companies as well as samples of letters received from those foreign firms. Letters were collected from over twenty countries (e.g., Brazil, Mexico, Italy, Thailand, India, Caribbean countries). The results are summarized in Exhibit 6.8. As you can see, Americans sending letters tend to use an informal, casual tone, especially in contrast to the more formal third-person letters they receive from other countries. Likewise, Americans appear to avoid "exaggerated" courtesy and compliments that other cultures are likely to consider important. Perhaps one lesson to be learned is that if you want to impress someone from another culture, do your best to imitate that person's written communication style.[34]

That said, keep in mind our earlier warnings about the pitfalls inherent in what you might be saying when sending written communications abroad. You may be successful at being more flowery and more subtle than you normally would, but you could still create communication problems in other areas. For example, suppose you send an e-mail

Can you give us some examples?

Sure. In the United States, we are more informal when giving presentations, even at the highest levels. In Latin America, though, it is important to be aware of the appropriate level of formality. If one is too informal, it can be seen as unprofessional. But this varies among countries. On a recent trip to South America, I conducted training sessions in both Chile and Argentina. In Argentina, the trainees were from the beginning very open and participative in the training—they were very comfortable and asked a lot of questions throughout. I expected the same in Chile, but it was quite different. I've found Chileans to be much more reserved and more reluctant to ask questions. They preferred a formal presentation on my part.

Another difference is that Latin Americans are very cognizant of the position you hold. It is important to have people who are on the same level do the communicating in meetings. Sending a junior person to meet with an executive would probably be perceived as a lack of respect. My job is to mediate these and other differences and find a better way to communicate with our partners.

Are there cross-cultural communication pluses and minuses to having a bicultural background such as yours?

Yes to both, although I would say there are more advantages than downsides. In fact, the company expects me to use these very skills and abilities to do my job. One big advantage is that I have a broader understanding of cultural norms and idiosyncrasies. I am comfortable in both contexts and don't often think about the fact that I'm communicating across cultures. The automatic nature of these skills comes from my bicultural background. On the other hand, one disadvantage is that I'm given less leeway by customers in terms of misreading the other culture. I'm expected to fully understand and represent both cultures and this can be quite a challenge because of all the regional differences I spoke of earlier.

What advice would you give others working with international partners to enhance communication?

My advice is very simple. Do away with arrogance and show respect. Keep an open mind and listen to what others have to say. I also try to keep in mind the individual, as there are significant differences among people within the same country. And, importantly, it is imperative to spend time developing relationships and trust in order to facilitate good communication. We always have some type of social event, for example, during a training session to allow informal contacts and relations to develop. This goes a long way in international business. The stronger the relationship, the better the communication.

to a Japanese business partner about projected profits. Even if you've done everything else right, just the use of the word *profit* may imply something about long-term, collective growth to your Japanese counterpart. To Americans, however, the meaning of the word tends to be multifaceted, with a core theme of personal gain.[35] If your letter had been sent to a Russian, it's possible that the word *profit (prybl)* would suggest exploitation.[36] The phenomenon we're describing here is called *bypassing*. It occurs when people define the same words quite differently. The insidious thing about bypassing is you may not even know it is happening until well after the communication process is over.

In fact, you may wonder if it's possible to come to grips with this and related communication problems on a systematic basis. Ford Motor Company thinks it has, at least when it comes to internal communications across it's facilities around the world. The following International Insights describes Ford's approach. As you'll see, it included both verbal and written communications. It also provides pictures to go with the words. And nonverbal communication is the subject of our next section.

Nonverbal Communication

Besides the challenges associated with verbal and written communication, it's also important to consider nonverbal communication. **Nonverbal communication** is the transmission of messages without the use of words or writing. That is, above and beyond what is being said, often *how* it's being said carries plenty of information value.

EXHIBIT 6.7

An Example of a Japanese Business Letter

August 21, 2002

Mr. Kaneyuki Taeshiro
International A & M Corp.
Yokohama, Japan

The summer heat is still lingering, but we hope that you are as prosperous as ever and we thank you very much for your constant patronage.

Concerning your request that the inquiry report be sent you not by sea mail but by air mail and that two voucher copies be sent you immediately upon publication, we have asked Hitchcock to meet your request as you see in the enclosed copy. We shall be happy if you find it satisfactory.

It has not yet been long since I took over my duties from my predecessor and I may not be up to your expectations in many respects. But I am determined to do my very best, so please give me your further patronage and guidance.

It will be some time before autumn cool. I pray that you take good care of yourself.

Sincerely,

Kazunobu Marusugi

Source: Adapted from Haneda, S., & Shima, H. (1982). Japanese communication behavior as reflected in letter writing. *Journal of Business Communication, 19,* 19–32. Reprinted by permission.

Interpersonal space preferences can vary widely across cultures. © Yang Liu/ CORBIS

EXHIBIT 6.8

An Analysis of Letters Written to and Received from Foreign Countries

Writing Element	Foreign Letters Received Using a Writing Element (%)	U.S. Letters Sent Using a Writing Element (%)
Use of personal tone (personal pronouns, informal language, etc.)	25	37
Impersonal tone (formal, passive voice)	25	6
Exaggerated courtesy	44	19
Obvious compliments	16	6
Words omitted from sentences	38	6

Source: Adapted from Kilpatrick, R. H. (1984). International business communication practices. *Journal of Business Communication, 21,* 33–44.

How you stand and what you wear, for example, can add credibility (or not) to your presentation. Other examples of nonverbal behavior include facial expressions, body posture and alignment, eye contact (or lack of it), movements, and gestures. We'll discuss how nonverbal communication can vary across countries and cultures.

Interpersonal Space

One major nonverbal behavior has to do with the amount of **interpersonal space** we prefer to have between us and others in social interaction. As noted in Chapter 5, we actually "choose" to have a certain amount of space between us and another person when we interact with that person. For instance, women tend to have a closer interpersonal space than men do and friends are physically closer than strangers. And, in the earlier chapter we noted that a message can be communicated by space differences and violations of norms across cultures.

Touch

Closely related to the concept of space is the use of touch, or **haptics,** with other people. In general, Americans tend not to use touch all that much, except with people whom they are very familiar or intimate with. Touching in some cultures, however, is a natural and expected part of social interaction. One study addressed this issue by observing people as they sat in outdoor cafés in four different countries. During a 1 hour timed period, there were 180 touches in San Juan, Puerto Rico, 110 in Paris, 1 in Gainesville, Florida, and none in London.[38] Likewise, Americans show two to three times greater

INTERNATIONAL INSIGHTS

Ford Builds Global Bridges with Communications . . . to a Point

FORD IS VIEWED BY some as a model for internal cross-cultural communications. How to share know-how and information, especially across borders and cultures, is both critical and an enormous challenge in Ford's farflung global empire. Ford's answer to this challenge is its Best Practices Replication Process.

Employees all over the world are constantly coming up with great ideas in Ford plants. The trick, however, is to somehow share those ideas so that everyone benefits. After all, a great idea that pops up in, say, Mexico, might be able to help the folks in Kansas City, too. In the past five years, some 3,000 superior ideas have migrated across all of Ford's manufacturing facilities. Ford estimates the company has saved over $1.25 billion in the process.

Of course, that begs the question of how Ford actually accomplishes this savings. The answer lies in a 42-step replication process that involves a clear set of communication strategies and support mechanisms. Basically, it works like this:

● "Community practice" managers look for outstanding new ideas with proven impact wherever they occur worldwide, visiting plants and speaking with local employees to understand how the ideas work.

● Digital photos are taken of the idea in action (e.g., new manufacturing process, new tools, etc.). Accompanying the string of photos is a verbal description. Each idea is "translated" into the appropriate jargon used by the manufacturing groups involved and only then converted to other languages for sharing (e.g., a innovation developed in auto painting by French employees would be described in paint-related terminology first, then translated into Spanish so Mexican employees could understand and use it). These words serve as picture captions.

● The pictures and verbiage are then loaded into an existing Internet template and electronically sent to a "community practice administrator" who assesses the idea and, if things look good, forwards it to every plant manager worldwide who might be able to use it.

● Local managers, after receiving an idea, must then officially report a response (adopt, adapt, or reject and provide justification).

But here's an irony to think about. If Ford's so good at communication, why did things with Bridgestone/Firestone get so out of hand (see our chapter opener)? Some say that if information had been shared about the apparent problems associated with pairing Firestone tires and Ford SUVs, the situation would have been brought under control much more quickly. Both companies apparently had information about the mismatch floating around internally.

Part of the issue may be the difference between internal and external communications. Ford's internal information sharing involved like-minded employees with common goals. Firestone, on the other hand, was an external supplier. Neither company had an external communication network that could share the information necessary to discover the tire problems early on. In addition, when information is widely dispersed, mechanisms have to be put into place to support sharing. Managers have to be judged on how well they communicate and processes and procedures have to be in place to support them. Ford's Best Practices Replication Process is a good illustration of that point. But apparently neither Ford nor Bridgestone/Firestone had parallel processes in place to support interfirm communications.[37]

physical contact with their parents and about two times the amount of contact with friends than do the Japanese.[39]

Arabs tend to use a lot of touching, eye contact, and other nonverbal behavior. The British, however, tend toward the opposite in their nonverbal style, generally avoiding touch and prolonged eye contact. After interacting with each other, many Arabs might feel that the British are aloof and distant, while many British might wonder why Arabs are so interpersonally aggressive and invasive. Actually, this was the starting point for a study that examined the effect of nonverbal training on impressions of people from other cultures. A group of Britons were trained to perform nonverbal behaviors that were appropriate to Arab culture (such as extensive touching, etc.). Next, this group, and a control group that did not receive training, interacted with Arabs. Later, it was found that the Arabs expressed more liking for the Britons who had received the training.[40] This study underscores that nonverbal communications do differ across cultures and can have an impact on relationships. It also tells us that people can be trained in nonverbal communication styles that will have positive effects on international business partners.

Vocal Qualities as Nonverbal Communication

Vocal qualities such as speed and the loudness of your voice can also project an image and add credibility to your explicit message. These vocal characteristics have been the subject of a considerable amount of cross-cultural research. One study compared the impression conveyed by a message that was delivered either quickly or slowly, even though the message itself was the same. This was done by having Koreans and Americans watch a videotaped speech about the perils of smoking. Although the content of the information presented was always identical, the presentation was varied so that the message was delivered at either a slow, normal, or fast rate while retaining its natural sound.[41]

After listening to the message, the Koreans and Americans rated the speaker and the speech on a number of characteristics. Consistent with previous studies, Americans thought that a relatively fast voice conveyed power and competence. For the Korean subjects, however, a slow delivery was more effective in increasing the credibility of the speaker. One explanation of this difference is that Koreans live in a more collective culture and, as a result, are more concerned with measuring their words carefully so as not to offend.[42] Likewise, Egyptians and many Middle Eastern/Arabic countries use phrases that reflect a more colorful and emotional stance toward others (e.g., "my most esteemed colleague," or "my honored guest"). These emotional and complimentary communication patterns are reflective of a cultural value to create a sense of warm friendship and more personal relations among business partners and guests. In the Muslim faith, readings aloud of the Quran in mosques reflect great oratory skill and are considered a profound occasion. Likewise, the public "cry" for prayer in this faith, not seen in some other faiths, is another example of emotionally charged communication.[43]

Context Revisited

What we've discussed so far should remind us that how something is communicated carries importance above and beyond what is being said. In Chapter 4, for example, we introduced the concept of high- and low-context cultures. Low-context cultures are those that require explicit statement of facts and conclusions in order for a message to be communicated. High-context cultures, in contrast, are those where the setting, surroundings, or cultural mores provide input into the communication process. In Chapter 4 we concluded that culture may often provide for the ability to properly interpret an otherwise ambiguous message. So "context" itself may be the ultimate example of nonverbal communication. In fact, your particular context level should provide clues about communication in your culture.

For example, the degree to which you rely on written or verbal communication may be a function of context.[44] In low-context cultures such as Germany and the United States, people tend to rely on written communication because such a medium allows for a permanent and explicit record of a message. In high-context cultures such as Japan, however, people may prefer verbal and face-to-face communications because they are more dynamic and allow for greater subtlety than written messages. Indeed, experts warn that international managers need to understand that many Japanese are reluctant to communicate via letters.[45]

But whether we are writing or not, context seems to affect our communication style. Indeed, one study found that Japanese business communications were indirect and relied on an intuitive style. In contrast, Americans and Canadians were much more direct and relied on a rational, fact-based approach to communication.[46] This is consistent

EXHIBIT 6.9

Characteristics of Communication in Low- and High-Context Cultures

Communication Feature	Low Context	High Context
General approach	direct/explicit	indirect/complex
Degree of precision	literal/exact	approximate/relative
Dependence on words	high	low
Nonverbal dependence	low	high
View of silence	negative; poor/no communication	positive; good communication
Attention to details	high	low
Value placed on intentions	low	high

Source: Adapted from Victor, D. A. (1992). *International business communication,* 153. New York: Harper Collins.

EXHIBIT 6.10

Improving Your Cross-Cultural Communication Skills: Four Basic Suggestions

1. Assume that people are different, not similar.

2. Delay judgment; emphasize description of events, not evaluation or interpretation.

3. Practice putting yourself in other people's shoes. If they were visiting the United States, how might you react to them?

4. Treat your interpretations as temporary and subject to further analysis.

Source: Adapted from Adler, N. J. (1997). *International dimensions of organizational behavior* (3rd Ed.). Cincinnati, OH: South-Western.

INTERNATIONAL INSIGHTS

Is the Grass Greener in German, English, or French? Putting Communication into Context

IN LOW-CONTEXT cultures, communication has pretty much the same meaning regardless of the situation. As a result, messages should be direct and to the point. For this reason people from low-context cultures often strike those from high-context cultures as rude. Letters, meetings, and other forms of communication in high-context cultures must be approached with nuance and subtlety. In turn, this explains the frustration experienced by low context communicators.

It's rare to see a message that simultaneously communicates well to both types of cultures. One writer, however, told a story about a sign he saw in Switzerland that was translated into three languages—German, English, and French. Equally important, the words were also modified to reflect

the different levels of context exemplified by these three cultures. In German, the sign read "Walking on the grass is forbidden." This direct, unambiguous message is typical of a low-context culture like Germany. The English portion of the sign read "Please do not walk on the grass." Clearly, the same message was conveyed, but the change reflected the higher level of context among the English. Finally, the French version read "Those who respect their environment will avoid walking on the grass." This is the highest context message, reflecting that trait among the French. Although the intent of the message is still the same, it is much more indirect and conjures up related issues that may compel the French to comply with it.[49]

with our argument that high or low context can serve as an important nonverbal backdrop to communication.

Along the same lines, another study found that people who were more verbal were perceived as more attractive by Americans (low context), but those who were less verbal were seen as more attractive in Korea (high context).[47] So if you need to communicate in a high-context culture, face-to-face communication is probably a better bet than written communication.[48] In a low-context culture, however, it's usually wise not to "beat around the bush." Here communication will be more effective if concrete, specific, and logical statements are made. Exhibit 6.9 presents some communication characteristics of high- and low-context cultures. And the International Insights illustrates how communication can be tailored to cultures that differ in context. In general, however, it might be best to follow the advice presented in Exhibit 6.10 when communicating across borders and cultures is required.

Chapter Summary

In this chapter, we discussed the important topic of communication across cultures. Communication comes in many different forms, yet managers sometimes mistakenly assume that communication is the same everywhere.

The single most important way we communicate with others is through the spoken word. Unfortunately, some countries, like the United States, are largely monolingual. Indeed, American businesspeople's foreign language skills rank among the weakest in the world. Popular explana-

tions for this situation include geographic isolation and American ethnocentrism. Some U.S. firms feel that Americans' foreign language deficits aren't a big problem since English seems to be the de facto language of world business. But native English speakers still run the risk of major communication problems across borders and cultures, many of which were reviewed in this chapter. Part of the reason for these ongoing problems is that communication is filtered by local cultural values and experiences as well as taking place through a variety of different verbal, written, and nonverbal channels.

International managers also need to be aware of the

complex ways that cross-cultural differences can manifest themselves in communication. For instance, cultures differ in terms of how they communicate as well as their responses to embarrassment, apology, compliments, and criticism.

Cross-cultural differences are also apparent in written communication styles. Americans, for instance, tend to keep their letters and memos informal, short, and to the point, generally avoiding flowery or exaggerated language in the process. Other cultures, however, have written communication norms that are inconsistent with these customs. But even if you correctly capture the communication style of your international business colleagues, you could still experience the problem called *bypassing,* the miscommunication that occurs when people define the same words differently.

Nonverbal communication is the transmission of messages without the use of words or writing. We discussed cross-cultural differences in *interpersonal space,*

touch or *haptics, vocal qualities,* and *context interpretation* as well as how these nonverbal channels can create problems for international managers.

1. Explain why both spoken and written cross-cultural communication presents many challenges to non-native communicators.
2. How do the cultural dimensions of collectivism, power distance, and uncertainty avoidance affect communication across cultures?
3. How would a country's standing on the context dimension affect its communication patterns? Would high-context cultures prefer written or spoken language as a communication medium? What about the preferences of those from low-context cultures?

Up to the Challenge?

Bridgestone Turns the Americans Loose

AT THE BEGINNING of this chapter we described what many American critics saw as a communications debacle in Bridgestone's handling of its "Firestone problem." Allegations that Firestone's tires were defective cost the firm's Japanese parent hundreds of millions of dollars and put its executives' communication skills to the test. And as we suggested, those skills seemed to leave something to be desired, at least from a cross-cultural communication standpoint.

But after succeeding Yoichiro Kaizaki in 2001, Bridgestone's new president, Shigeo Watanabe, took a different tack in the face of a controversy that wasn't going away. Mr. Watanabe adopted a more aggressive communication effort, one in which Americans did the heavy hitting on Firestone's behalf. Mr. Watanabe put the new American CEO of Firestone, John Lampe, in charge of the effort rather than sending Japanese managers to lead things. He also gave Mr. Lampe the authority to act without always having to solicit Tokyo's approval first, an unusual step for most Japanese multinationals, especially when such critical decisions are involved.

And Mr. Lampe went on the offensive. In May 2001, he announced that Firestone would end its century-long status as a Ford supplier. Why? Because the car giant supposedly kept blaming Firestone tires for accidents in Ford Explorers without owning up to

alleged safety problems with its SUVs. Bridgestone supported Lampe's decision and his more aggressive approach out of concern that the communication battle was being lost in the United States. Something needed to be done to push back effectively against Ford's public accusations, and the dramatic announcement about cutting ties with Ford was designed, at least in part, to do just that.

And that was just the beginning. CEO Lampe became very active in speaking out publicly on Firestone's behalf. That contrasted sharply with the practice of his predecessor, Masatoshi Ono, perhaps best known for his awkward exchanges with U.S. senators at an earlier hearing. Speaking of which, Mr. Lampe put a well-known lobbyist in a Washington office to give Firestone a more prominent voice with the U.S. government. Of course, where things will eventually end up with Firestone, its tire problems, and its reputation remains to be seen. But from a communications standpoint, the critics seemed to like Bridgestone's new moves. As one auto analyst put it, "It's a credit to the management of Bridgestone in Tokyo that they did replace the linguistically challenged [Mr. Ono] with an American who is prepared to trade punches with [then-Ford CEO] Jacques Nasser."

But what's your assessment of this latest communication effort by Bridgestone? Is it a better match culturally for an American audience? And even if it is, will it be enough to salvage Firestone's damaged brand name? If not, what other steps would you recommend? Finally, how should Bridgestone have communicated about this problem from the beginning?[50]

International Development
Experiencing Language Barriers:
An Exercise

Purpose

● To examine language barriers that contribute to breakdowns in communication.
● To demonstrate the anxieties and frustrations that may be felt when communicating under difficult circumstances.
● To illustrate the impact of nonverbal communication when verbal communication is ineffective and/or restricted.

Instructions

1. Your instructor will divide the class into subgroups of four, five, or six and ask your groups to create a language of its own. This language must be significantly different from English and must include the following:

   ● a greeting
   ● description of some object, person, or event
   ● an evaluative statement about an object or a person
   ● a farewell.

   Group members must be able to "speak" their group's language at the end of this step (45 minutes).

2. Within each language group, members number themselves sequentially, i.e., 1,2,3,4, etc. The instructor announces the location of a new group to be composed of all participants numbered 1. The instructor likewise forms new groups of participants numbered 2, 3, 4, and so on.
3. The instructor directs members to pair off in the new groups. Each member must teach his new language to his partner without using English or any other recognized language. (Twenty minutes).
4. The instructor distributes a blindfold to each group. A blindfolded volunteer from each group teaches his language to the group. A second volunteer repeats this task. (Twenty minutes.)
5. The instructor distributes blindfolds to all remaining participants. Participants are told to stand in their second groups, and all chairs are moved aside. Participants blindfold themselves and are instructed to find their original groups without the use of any conventional language or people's names.
6. When the original groups have been re-formed, the instructor instructs them to discuss the activity and to answer the following questions:

   a. What did this experience illustrate about communication?
   b. How did you feel during the experience?
   c. What did you learn about yourself from it?

7. The instructor leads a general discussion on the problems faced by people who do not understand a language and on the difficulties that blind people may have in communicating.

   Alternatively, your instructor may ask you to try one of these variations:

   ● The requirements for the new vocabulary can be changed to make the task more difficult or less difficult.
   ● All participants can be blindfolded for step four.
   ● Real language can be used. The phrases can be preset.

   ───────
   Source: Ericson, P. M. (1975). Babel: Interpersonal communications. In: *A handbook of structured experiences for human relations training*, vol. 5, 16–17. Published by Pfeiffer, a Jossey-Bass imprint. Reprinted by permission.

From Theory to Practice
Moshi, Moshi: Overcoming Cultural Barriers to Communication

Purpose

To understand how culture can impact verbal communication in a telephone conversation and to suggest alternative ways to conduct telephone conversations effectively in a given cross-cultural context.

Instructions

Read the following telephone transcript, either inside or outside class. John Smith, an American marketing manager from Weyerhaeuser, is trying to speak with his Japanese counterpart at Rising Run Company, a Mr. Yamamoto, about a possible business deal.

The conversation:
The phone rings and a woman answers.

Woman: *Moshi, moshi* ["Hello, Hello"].
Smith: Hello, this is John Smith. May I please speak with Mr. Yamamoto?
Woman: Oh, I'm sorry. Who is calling, please?
Smith: This is John Smith calling for Mr. Yamamoto.

Woman:	I'm sorry, what is the name of your company?
Smith:	I'm calling from Weyerhaeuser.
Woman:	I'm sorry, could you spell that please?
Smith:	W-E . . .
Woman:	I'm sorry, "W-Z"?
Smith:	No, W-E-Y-E-R-H-A-E-U-S-E-R. Is Mr. Yamamoto there?
Woman:	Oh, Weyerhaeuser. Thank you very much. Your name please?
Smith:	John Smith.
Woman:	And who do you wish to speak to?
Smith:	As I said, Mr. Yamamoto.
Woman:	I'm sorry, which department? We have many Yamamotos.
Smith:	Uh . . . of course. Mr. Yamamoto in the international marketing department.
Woman:	Thank you very much, wait just a minute please. (*Smith is put on hold. Music plays in the background. Meanwhile, a phone rings in a big room where many employees are working at their desks. Someone passing by picks up the phone.*)
Man:	*Moshi, moshi.*
Smith:	Hello, Mr. Yamamoto?
Man:	Oh no, this is Suzuki. Who is calling please?
Smith:	This is John Smith calling for Mr. Yamamoto.
Man:	I'm sorry, what is the name of your company?
Smith:	Weyerhaeuser.

Man:	Could you spell that please?
Smith:	W-E-Y-E-R-H-A-E-U-S-E-R.
Man:	Thank you very much. Just a minute please. (*On hold again. Music plays*).
Man:	I'm very sorry, but Mr. Yamamoto is in a meeting. Could you call again later?

Intensely frustrated, Smith hangs up the phone after "wasting" an international call.

Your instructor will divide the class into small groups of three to six to answer the following questions (15–20 minutes). Your group can present its answers, followed by a general class discussion about international communication and its implications (30 minutes). Alternatively, your instructor may lead a general class discussion about the following questions:

- Why is Smith so frustrated? Would you be in this situation? What cultural factors explain Smith's reaction (and perhaps yours)?
- What mistakes did Smith make, in your opinion? Why? How do Japanese culture and business practices fit in here?
- How would you recommend that Smith approach the call if he had to do it all over again? What specific advice would you offer? Why?
- What if the cultural context was different? For instance, what if Mr. Smith was trying to reach a counterpart in Cairo? How might that shape Mr. Smith's approach to the conversation?

Source: Elashmawi, F., & Harris, P. H. (1993). *Multicultural management: New skills for global success,* 108–111. Houston: Gulf. Reprinted by permission.

Conducting Negotiations and Managing Conflicts

International Challenge

Two Sides of a Common Border

LEARNING OBJECTIVES

After reading this chapter, you should be able to

● Appreciate that cross-cultural miscommunication can create conflict among people and groups.

● Identify the causes of cross-cultural conflict.

● Understand some of the ways that cross-cultural conflicts can be managed, especially in international negotiations.

● Explain the four main stages of negotiation and understand how cultural values can impact the way those stages unfold.

YOU'VE PROBABLY READ about negotiations between American companies and their foreign counterparts over various deals. Likewise, there are plenty of stories out there about conflicted negotiations between national governments and foreign companies, again over a wide variety of issues. And in these cases, much is often made of how the lens of culture shapes each side's perspectives and tactics, often to the point where the parties are, in effect, looking past each other. But you may not have to look beyond your own company for examples of what we're talking about. The increasing internationalization of business has also internationalized workforces in many companies. And therein lies the potential for conflict. As many of you know, negotiations are a fact of life within as well as between companies, especially in bigger firms.

So here's the scene. You're in a room observing negotiations between two departments in the same international company. The issue at hand is who will control the process of buying computers for the firm. On one side of the table are two American managers, who represent the operations area. Operations wants to be able to buy its own equipment and is focused on predictable installation, equipment quality, and outstanding maintenance. On the other side sit two Mexican managers, who represent purchasing. They believe it is their responsibility to do the buying, and their top priority is price, getting the best equipment for the money. Both departments have about the same amount of power, status, and authority within the company. Finally, time is pretty short, especially since major computer needs are on the horizon and actual purchases have to be made.

But as negotiations unfold, it quickly becomes apparent that a clash of cultures is also occurring that goes beyond any differences of opinions about computers. Consider this exchange between one of the Mexican purchasing managers and his American counterpart from operations:

MEXICAN: I think it will better for the total organization, and [smiling] don't forget that we all work for the same company. It will be viewed as better from all points in the corporation if we, the purchasing department, are the ones that take charge of negotiating with the vendor. Although I fully understand that we have to get all the information from you who are going to be using the equipment . . . from a quality of process and strength of position it really is a better and more natural position to have us talking to them and consulting with you on whether or not the prices seems reasonable. [Is about to continue but the American interrupts . . . a recurring pattern through the negotiations.]

AMERICAN: It's unacceptable to us that operations be totally left out of the negotiation process . . . you people have short term goals regarding price . . . we've got to live with this product month to month . . . so you people zip in there, do your thing, save your 20 percent, look great to the company, and we've got to live with a shoddy product because you've pissed off the vendor, low-balled the price, and then the vendor comes in with a shoddy installation.

MEXICAN: Are you aware that I allowed you to talk? Well, be aware and consider it next time.

AMERICAN: [Ignoring the previous comment] Since the computers are being bought for our department, we've got the bottom line say . . . we understand the technical aspects better than you. Now I want to get this done in a short amount of time so I want to cut to the quick of the matter. I don't want to deal with someone who looks like they are just a messenger.

MEXICAN: I feel, as we say, the shoemaker to his shoes. We are in the purchasing position, that is precisely our function. When one needs a blender at home, the one who decides what kind to get is the one who will use it. But the one who decides to buy it or not is the one who brings home the money. Excuse me for being so stubborn in this respect, but you could buy a pen, but what do you know about buying a ship? You don't know about ships.

As you read through this chapter, you'll learn about how culture can impact international conflicts and the negotiation process. As you'll see, tactics and strategies may be culturally driven, at least to an extent. Of course, we'll also discuss ways that international managers can overcome the challenges that these issues represent. In the meantime, what are the specific negotiation tactics, styles, and strategies being used by the Mexican and American in this example? How might they illustrate the cultural values and perspectives of the two managers?

After you've pondered these questions, take a look at the Up to the Challenge box at the end of this chapter for some insights into this exchange as well as some new things to think about.[1]

A World of Conflict

As Chapter 6 vividly illustrated, communicating effectively in an international business environment can be quite a challenge. There are many ways that a message can get distorted, confused, or missed altogether across cultures, leaving the door wide open for potential differences and disagreements. In other words, miscommunication can lead to conflict. Conflict occurs when disagreements and friction arise in the course of social interaction because of opposing interests, cultural differences in communication styles, and the like. Compounding the communication challenge is that today international managers are more like diplomats than ever, with an increasingly burdensome set of "missions" to carry out that often involve serious disagreements of substance. For example, international managers may have to handle foreign labor strife, negotiate with overseas vendors, clients, partners, and suppliers, lobby governments, soothe relations with outside pressure groups (e.g., over environmental issues), and somehow convince employees with conflicting interests to work together.[2] Additionally, a major reason that firms send expatriates abroad, at least for the short or medium term, is to fix a problem and resolve a conflict.

Of course, not all conflict is bad. In fact, sometimes conflict helps focus people's attention to get things done. In any case, conflict is incredibly common. American managers spend about 20 percent of their time at work dealing with conflict situations.[3] And given all the cross-cultural communication problems we reviewed in the previous chapter, it wouldn't surprise us to learn that conflict occupies an even greater portion of time for managers with international responsibilities.

Consequently, this chapter will review some of the causes of conflict and how to manage it effectively in an international context. And we'll devote a considerable amount of space to the subject of negotiation in international business. As you'll see, how the negotiation process is viewed, as well as the tactics that are used, are the result of many factors. One of the most prominent factors is culture. Failing to understand the role of culture in negotiations will cause conflict and, in the end, undoubtedly cost you business.

Cultural Causes of Conflict in International Management

Given the stakes, international managers need a good understanding of the basic causes of conflict. Some of these causes we've already addressed, at least indirectly. For instance, *language* difficulties represent one. As we pointed out, a misinterpretation because of a poor translation can cause two sides to be very angry at each other. We also know that differing *cultural norms* may give rise to conflict, especially when each side lacks an appreciation or understanding of the other's cultural frame of reference. More than one American manager has been greatly offended to be kept waiting well beyond a scheduled appointment time in a foreign country, with some even storming out at this "offense."[4] Of course, in this example, the resulting conflict could have been avoided had the American been aware that he was bringing his monochronic perspective about time into a polychronic culture. Along the same lines, had the meeting actually taken place, different norms about how direct (low context) or indirect (high context) communication should be have might have created conflict and, very possibly, a loss of business.

The way a company makes decisions can also be a potential source of conflict, especially if there's a mismatch with employee values. Some international firms are structured to be highly centralized, with power and decision-making control concentrated in a few people at the top. Some international companies, however, operate in a more dispersed fashion, with decision-making control decentralized and pushed down into lower ranks. But employees in high-power-distance cultures may have a preference for centralized and hierarchical decision making. They see it as perfectly acceptable for those higher up in the firm to make important decisions without any of their input. In fact, in such cultures, attempting to decentralize decision making by implementing participative management strategies (e.g., involving employees in setting goals) can backfire, as

EXHIBIT 7.1

The Road to Conflict: A Conversation between a Greek and an American

Words Spoken	Perception/Interpretation by Each Party
AMERICAN: How long will it take you to finish the report?	AMERICAN: I asked him to participate. GREEK: His behavior makes no sense. He is the boss. Why doesn't he tell me?
GREEK: I don't know. How long should it take?	AMERICAN: He has refused to take responsibility. GREEK: I asked him for an order.
AMERICAN: You are in the best position to analyze the time requirements.	AMERICAN: I press him to take responsibility for his actions. GREEK: What nonsense—I'd better give him an answer.
GREEK: Ten days.	AMERICAN: He lacks the ability to estimate his time; this estimate is totally inadequate.
AMERICAN: Take 15. Is it agreed? You will do it in 15 days?	AMERICAN: I offer a contract. Greek: These are my orders: 15 days.

Source: Triandis, H. C. (1977). *Interpersonal behavior.* Pacific Grove, CA: Brooks/Cole Publishing Company, a division of International Thomson Publishing, Inc. Reprinted by permission.

Exhibit 7.1 suggests. Clearly, conflict could have been avoided here if the American manager had understood the Greek preference for centralization.

A final cause of conflict in international business is the *propensity* for people in a given culture to be involved with conflict in the first place. That is, some cultures go to great lengths to avoid friction between individuals and groups. Indeed, in collectivist cultures, people often erect many different social mechanisms to make conflict less likely to occur. For example, we've mentioned the Japanese tendency to use indirect ways to say no as a way to smooth interpersonal relations. Yet paradoxically this tendency can be extremely frustrating and conflict-provoking when it is used across cultures. Again, the risk of damaging conflict may be highest when a cultural mismatch occurs with another party—say, an American who thinks that conflict should be addressed openly and aggressively. Although a tendency to be open and blunt may be seen as honest and good within American culture, few traits may be more offputting to a Japanese.

Managing Conflict Effectively

So if conflict is nearly inevitable in international business, how can you manage it effectively to minimize the damage, if not prevent it from happening? To begin with, international managers need to understand that there are different styles for resolving conflict once it occurs.[5] Exhibit 7.1 shows a typology of these styles. Basically, this approach balances concern for your own outcomes against concern for outcomes of others with whom you are interacting. The result is the five relatively distinct styles portrayed in the exhibit. There's plenty of research on these styles, although most studies focus on American employees. Of course, even within a culture there are individual differences in style preferences. You can probably think of people who like to confront conflict headon (**competition**), while other acquaintances with a similar cultural heritage prefer to try to ignore it altogether (**avoidance**). And once people learn or choose a style, they tend to stick with that approach—it becomes part of their personality. But research does show that some general, culture-based tendencies exist that can distinguish how people tend to handle conflict.

For instance, it appears that many Americans like a good argument. One study compared Japanese and Americans on a scale that measured the tendency to either embrace or avoid arguments. The results showed that the Japanese were less inclined to argue in the first place, but once they were involved, their degree of argumentativeness was less than Americans'.[6] Based on this and other studies, some experts have gone so far as to say that Americans feel stimulated by an argument and enjoy the intellectual challenge it provides.[7] The Japanese, on the other hand, may feel mortified that open conflict has occurred and worry that it may disturb group harmony. Based on these findings, it is reasonable to conclude that Americans tend toward the competitive conflict management style while Japanese tend to fall in the avoidance area shown in Exhibit 7.2. That said, we would remind you that these generalizations may not apply to individual Americans or Japanese.

Nevertheless, other studies have compared Americans with people from a variety of other countries on their conflict styles. Basically, these studies show that people from collectivist cultures tend to prefer a conflict avoidance style while people from individualistic cultures tend to prefer a direct, competitive style of dealing with conflict. Examples of countries with a collectivist orientation include China, Japan, Korea, and

EXHIBIT 7.2

A Typology of Conflict Styles

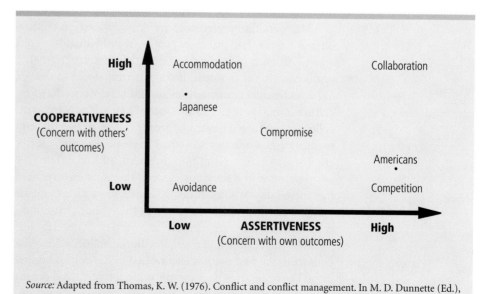

Source: Adapted from Thomas, K. W. (1976). Conflict and conflict management. In M. D. Dunnette (Ed.), *Handbook of Industrial and Organizational Behavior.* Chicago: Rand McNally (p. 889–935).

A culturally appropriate account can soften the blow of a negative outcome, such as U.S. computer maker Gateway's decision to close its Asian facilities in 2001. © Reuters NewMedia Inc./CORBIS

Mexico, while the United States has been the primary individualistic culture studied.[8] So as we implied in our earlier discussion, Americans often prefer more active, confrontational approaches, while Koreans, Chinese, and Mexicans tend to use more passive or avoidance approaches when handling conflict.[9]

Experts also point out that conflict preferences may vary depending on who is party to the conflict. Managers from Turkey and Jordan, for example, tend to use an overall conflict handling style that isn't all that different from their American counterparts. But when peers are involved, Turkish and Jordanian managers tend to avoid conflict even as they take a much more forceful approach when conflict erupts with subordinates.[10]

Many conflict preferences are deeply rooted in culture and extend to a variety of different areas. For instance, people in individualistic cultures often prefer an *equity norm* ("to each according to what they deserve") when dividing up organizational resources.[11] In other words, if you're sitting down to determine pay raises for subordinates, individual contributions should be closely related to the eventual raise. In such cultures (such as the U.S.) this is the "natural" way to figure out who deserves what. In collective cultures, however, people often prefer an **equality norm** (every group member gets a more or less equal share of rewards). Our point here is that these preferences may in part result from inherent cultural differences in dealing with conflict. As we mentioned in a previous chapter, the Japanese say that "the nail that sticks up gets hammered down." Consequently, displaying a direct, out-in-the-open conflict style is a "nail" that sticks out in Japan and other collectivist cultures. In the United States, of course, there are many myths and stories that celebrate rugged individualists (the "nails") who oppose and conflict with the majority. Likewise, the tendency to engage in conflict in the first place is also related to the cultural dimension of uncertainty avoidance. Those cultures high on this value tend to avoid conflict.

Clearly, then, there are cultural prescriptions about how to deal with conflict. There is perhaps no better place to look for those prescriptions than at Disney, the icon of American culture. The U.S. pavilion at Disney's Epcot Center used to display twelve statues that symbolize national virtues. The statues are said to represented the most important American attributes or values. Four of the statues represented "individualism," "self-reliance," "independence," and "freedom." It's unlikely that these four would stand out in any dramatic way to most Americans. Yet people from other cultures often focus on these attributes because they are so different from their own values. As we've noted, while individualism is a virtue for Americans, it can have negative connotations (e.g., selfishness) in other cultures.[12]

But to this point we haven't really explored how people *respond* when conflict rears its head in the form of anger, frustration, disappointment, and loss of face. In other words, what happens in a international business interaction, say, when an American manager gives a Chinese employee a poor performance rating? Such a circumstance arguably violates social norms in China and could easily cause the employee to feel an enormous loss of face. The resulting dissatisfaction could destroy the employee's commitment and ultimately lead to poorer performance or even a resignation. Or how about a situation where the Mexican hosts are visibly upset after a visiting American manager says they need to do much more to modernize their "inefficient" plant. In both cases, the reactions to the conflict that's been provoked constitute an indirect request to "repair the damage," often to a loss of face or reputation. An astute manager would be sensitive to these messages and respond with an appropriate **account** (basically an explanation for a negative action that is, at least in part, designed to soothe the pain). Better still, the astute manager might be wise to offer an account even before taking what may be seen as a negative or conflict-provoking step by someone from another culture.

The whole issue of managing account giving across cultures is an emerging area of research in international management. Current thinking is that culture can impact both how various actions are perceived (i.e., actions that initially create conflict because of loss of face, etc.) and what kinds of accounts might serve to mollify any perceived slights. So managers need to understand how the values of the people they are interacting with might shape both the perceptions of the actions they take in the first place and the accounts they use to explain them later. Take a look at Exhibit 7.3. It provides an overview of the account-giving process we're describing here.

From an international conflict management perspective, it's the last two steps in the account sequence that arguably matter most. After all, some negative actions may be unavoidable in any case. But how managers respond with accounts if offense is taken may go a long way toward determining whether the situation is ultimately salvaged or not.

On one end of the spectrum are **mitigating accounts,** which generally are designed to lower tensions caused by the original action or conflict. For instance, a **concession** is a type of mitigating account where the person acknowledges the conflict, takes responsibility for it, and offers regrets or even some form of compensation (e.g., "It was my poor choice of words that gave offense. For that I am very sorry."). A **justification** is an account that often provides a less extreme form of mitigation. Here the person admits that the action or conflict has occurred but claims that it wasn't intentional or couldn't be helped under the circumstances (e.g., "I was late for our meeting because an accident on the road caused a major delay."). An **ideological account** may be less satisfying to another party. Here the person owns up to actions taken or the conflict provoked but makes the argument that this was legitimate under the circumstances (e.g., "The poor performance rating I gave you will help make you a better employee in the long run"). Finally, a **refusal** is an account where the person either denies the existence of any negative actions or declines to share the reason for taking them (e.g., "Yes, I'm going to refuse to go along with your request and let's let it go at that—it would take me half the day to explain why"). As you might suspect, this type of account may aggravate rather than reduce tensions.[13]

EXHIBIT 7.3

International Conflict Management: Linking Culture and Face to the Account-Giving Process

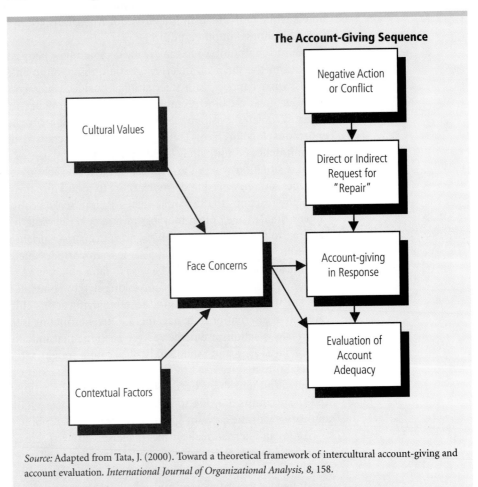

The Account-Giving Sequence

Cultural Values

Face Concerns

Contextual Factors

Negative Action or Conflict

Direct or Indirect Request for "Repair"

Account-giving in Response

Evaluation of Account Adequacy

Source: Adapted from Tata, J. (2000). Toward a theoretical framework of intercultural account-giving and account evaluation. *International Journal of Organizational Analysis, 8,* 158.

Of course, what would be helpful at this point is a conflict management road map that could explain how specific cultural values are linked to perceived conflicts (e.g., about losing face), the accounts that will be used, and how accounts will be evaluated. It would be very useful to know, for example, which accounts would play best in certain cultural circumstances.

Unfortunately, such a map would be pretty complex to construct. For instance, there's evidence that when Americans or other foreigners make a significant effort to adapt to the interaction rules of collective cultures (e.g., Japanese), it may be viewed quite positively (i.e., as a sign of respect). But let's say we reverse this scenario. If foreigners try to fit in with the interaction and conflict management patterns found in the United States or other individualistic cultures, it may buy them precious little. Why? Because individualists may view such adaptation efforts as failing to present yourself honestly as you really are. In any case, the road map is incomplete at this point and more research needs to be done to flesh out all the issues. And another interesting issue that's starting to receive attention is the nature of work-family conflict. It turns out that cultural factors may impact how work-family overload occurs and the problems it creates. Take a look at the following International Insights to see what we mean.

Nevertheless, we present Exhibit 7.4 as a partial effort to connect the dots when it comes to account giving in conflict management. As you can see, it illustrates how combining two of Hofstede's cultural value dimensions (individualism–collectivism and masculinity–femininity) relate to concerns about face and the account-giving and account-receiving process. You might remember from Chapter 4 that masculine cultures tend to stress values like autonomy, achievement, and assertiveness, while feminine cultures tend to place more emphasis on relationships and cooperation.[15]

Of course, knowing how to manage accounts effectively in a cross-cultural negotiation context would be extremely valuable. Negotiations that often reach impasses and concerns about face, either real or perceived, are also part of the process. Speaking of negotiation, there's been quite a bit of research about how that process unfolds and the factors, including culture, that impact it. We'll turn our attention to negotiation next.

INTERNATIONAL INSIGHTS

Work-Family Conflict: Is It the Same in the U.S. and China?

MANY PEOPLE THINK OF *work-family conflict* as largely an American phenomenon. But globalization may be changing all that, even in developing nations such as China. That said, attitudes toward work, family, and the relationship between them are inextricably linked to cultural values. So it might, for instance, be reasonable to expect that while employees in the United States and China will both experience it, the nature of work-family conflict may be quite different in the two countries. In fact, that's a prediction that researchers are starting to explore. And the answers may have implications for how a company should respond to and deal with work-family conflict in their international workforces.

One recent study addressed how time impacted the work-family equation in the United States and China. We're sure most of you can relate to this: time spent on work can make it impossible to spend any "quality time" with family. Likewise, you may start finding it harder to do as much at work if you're cutting out early to engage in family activities. Interestingly, scholars have suggested that individualistic cultures like the United States may place a higher value on personal family time than do more collectivistic societies, especially in Asia. This hypothesis seems to run counter to our images of Americans as career obsessed and our perception of Chinese as intensely family oriented.

But the basic idea is that when push comes to shove, individualistic Americans will put self-interest (time with family) above collective interest (work). The more collectivistic Chinese may do just the opposite. Another perspective on this issue is that in the United States careers are viewed as vehicles for personal achievement. The stated ethic at least is that "a good family person" won't let personal ambitions harm the family. And having a solid family environment is ostensibly part of the high "American quality of life." In contrast, Chinese employees often seek work as a vehicle for bringing prosperity and honor to their families. So working 120 hours a week and not seeing much of your family would be considered a personal sacrifice you are making for the family rather than a selfish statement about your career objectives that hurts your family in the process.

In short, family demands may cause more work-family conflicts in the United States than in China, while the reverse may be true for work demands. And that's exactly what the study found. Of course, more research needs to be done to tease out the exact role of culture and other factors such as economic development. Nevertheless, managers in China, or anywhere else for that matter, should first try to identify the source of work-family conflict before trying to design "balanced" workplaces that reduce employee strain and stress. Like so many other issues in international management, one size may not fit all when it comes to work-family conflict.[14]

EXHIBIT 7.4

The Use of and Reactions to Accounts in International Conflict: The Impact of Culture and Face

Cultural Value Combination	Concern with Face	Accounts Most Likely to Be Used	Likelihood of Aggravating Accounts Being Viewed Negatively
Collectivistic-feminine (e.g., Thailand)	High	**Mitigating**	High
	↑	(concessions)	↑
Collectivistic-masculine (e.g., Mexico)		(justifications)	
Individualistic-feminine (e.g., Sweden)		(ideological)	
Individualistic-masculine (e.g., U.S.)	Low ↓	(refusals/denials) **Aggravating**	Low ↓

Source: Adapted from Tata, J. (2000). Toward a theoretical framework of intercultural account-giving and account evaluation. *International Journal of Organizational Analysis, 8,* 169.

Understanding International Negotiation

In fact, negotiation is perhaps the best way to avoid conflict or at least keep it to a minimum. **Negotiation** is the process of communicating back and forth with another person or group with the explicit purpose of making a joint decision or reaching agreement about a particular issue or dispute. Consequently, all negotiations have four key elements:

● Multiple parties (two or more)
● Mixed motives (i.e., areas of disagreement or conflict, but also some interests in common)
● Movement of the parties (e.g., shifting or changing positions over time)
● A goal of reaching an agreement[16]

Basic Approaches to International Negotiation

As we've said, because of the ubiquitous nature of negotiation in many aspects of international business, it's been studied heavily. Indeed, there are two well-established approaches to studying international negotiations

The **macrostrategic** approach focuses on how the relative bargaining power of the parties in an international negotiation impacts outcomes. For instance, consider a

EXHIBIT 7.5

Setting Up Shop in Developing Countries: How Negotiating Strength May Shift over Time

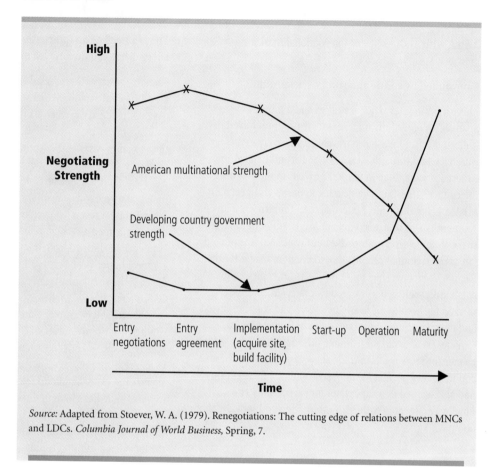

Source: Adapted from Stoever, W. A. (1979). Renegotiations: The cutting edge of relations between MNCs and LDCs. *Columbia Journal of World Business*, Spring, 7.

situation where an American multinational wants to set up operations in a developing country—say, Tanzania. To pursue that, the American firm may end up in a series of negotiations with the Tanzanian government (along with other local constituencies). As the negotiation issues shift from initial entry to site acquisition to ongoing operations, the relative power of the parties may also shift, as illustrated in Exhibit 7.5. Basically, a multinational's leverage tends to decrease once it has made its initial investment, while the local government's power tends to increase. Of course, we'll address the strategic issues associated with international market entry in the next section of the book (Chapters 8–10).[17]

For now, however, we'll mainly focus on the **comparative** approach to international negotiations. The primary emphasis of this approach is on what happens between negotiators during face-to-face interactions and how those interactions shape the outcomes that result. Consequently, a considerable amount of attention is paid to how cultural factors may affect the way the negotiation process unfolds between individual negotiators.[18] For a practical perspective on the role of culture from someone who has witnessed and been party to plenty of international negotiations, take a look at the following Reality Check.

REALITY CHECK

Fending Off Conflict in International Business at MeadWestvaco Corporation

A chat with Andrew Keelor, international marketing manager, MeadWestvaco Corp.

Can you tell us a little about your background?

I have a BA in international studies and a minor in Spanish. As part of my undergraduate program I lived in Chile and Costa Rica. I also traveled extensively in these countries, and throughout a lot of South and Central America. I went there to immerse myself in the language and the culture. After this, I came back to the states to earn my MBA. During this time, I interned for a Chilean company for six months and continued my Spanish studies. In total, I spent about two years abroad. After my MBA, I was offered a job as international product development manager for the Evenflo Company. They make products for babies and small kids, such as bottles, feeding materials, and the like. I worked for Evenflo for nearly two years and communicated and negotiated on a daily basis with people in Mexico, Canada, France, and Asia, among others. In this job I got a chance for more travel to trade shows and plants in these countries. I've been at MeadWestvaco for about a year now. I had also worked as a supervisor for seven years with UPS. Finally, I'm fluent in Spanish, both written and spoken. That's about it.

That's a heck of an international background. Can you tell us what you do now for MeadWestvaco?

Sure. My position was created about eight months ago to fill a void. The international marketing manager focused on developing MeadWestvaco's big push in Mexico and had his hands completely full. So he was unable to give adequate time to other parts of the world; this is my role. It is a real challenge since so many different cultures are involved. But it's also a challenge because business is very seasonal and bunched up a good deal around the back-to-back school season (bts). I recently developed and led a project that offered our media storage projects directly in Asian markets (rather than shipped from the U.S.). This allowed us to compete better (a 40% reduction over our domestic prices) while at the same time we're projecting an additional $1.5 GM as a result.

Shortly, I'll be traveling around the world to visit nine countries in twenty days. Our intent is to see where MeadWestvaco stands in various markets and what we can do to increase our presence. On the trip, I'll also check on an advertising campaign that I'm coordinating for the bts season in the Middle East. I am in direct contact with our retailer, distributor, and advertising companies with whom we've negotiated deals, and I'm making sure we work through all the logistics, costs, and timing to minimize problems and possible conflict.

Frameworks for Understanding the Process of International Negotiations

Several frameworks have been developed that can help managers understand the international negotiation process from a comparative perspective. We'll consider two of these frameworks here. The first framework is the broadest. It describes twelve sets of factors where cultural issues may be relevant in international negotiations, including the frame of reference of the negotiators. This framework is displayed in Exhibit 7.6. However, the exact relationships between the factors listed have yet to be fully researched. Nevertheless, the framework presents a valuable guide for helping managers grasp the cultural forces that may impact international negotiation outcomes.

The second framework focuses more narrowly on four specific stages that the negotiation process goes through once the people begin interacting face to face. Once again, the emphasis is on how cultural differences may impact interactions as well as the final outcomes. We'll consider this framework in some depth next. Actually, it's probably best to expand the process here to include all the planning and preparation that should go into a negotiation prior to any interactions between the parties. We'll start by providing

Speaking of these topics, can you give some examples of how you dealt with problems/conflict?

Let me first say that these are both excellent companies. But of course, even excellent companies do have problems from time to time. In fact, in both of these organizations, the culture and general lack of understanding on how to conduct international business has by far been the biggest obstacle to overcome. We (the U.S.) have a tendency to believe that the way we conduct business is the only way—we are somewhat ethnocentric in our views of what should and should not be. As a result, international departments sometimes lack autonomy and find themselves having to justify projects and ideas to those who have little idea of all the local implementation problems. Sometimes, therefore, projects get mired in red tape and conflict.

Evenflo, for example, holds the admirable position of selling the highest-quality, safest juvenile products. But the cost of maintaining this position has priced them out of many international markets. You can't expect a typical Mexican family to buy a $200 stroller when they can get one for as little as $10. Granted, the quality of the $10 one is pitiful, but it's plentiful and affordable so they buy. I was able to find much cheaper Asian sources for our stroller that would far exceed the quality of the $10 strollers, but senior management was convinced we needed to sell the same products throughout the world. After some conflict and convincing, I led a group of the managers to Mexico City to do a store survey. While this was a reality check for some, it still took another year of convincing on my part before I got

the go ahead to use the cheaper sources. It was a smashing success, by the way.

Are there other examples?

As mentioned, I was in direct contact with the director and marketing manager of Evenflo, Mexico while at the firm. They are both fluent in English and I in Spanish, so you'd think there would be few difficulties in communication. This just wasn't the case. Understanding the business culture is almost as important as speaking the language. Although I championed the needs of Evenflo Mexico, I also had to maintain a realistic understanding of what could and could not be done. This often led to conflict and a battle of wills, and was generally a waste of time on both sides. We're actually not the only ethnocentric-minded business people in the world. These managers could not understand that there were procedures that needed to be followed; they appeared only to be red tape from their perspective. My guess is that if left to run free, they would have introduced a myriad of products that simply were not safe by U.S. standards. So I had to deem them unsafe for Mexico. From their point of view, I wasn't cooperating or collaborating with them, when in reality I was, but I also had to maintain the Evenflo brand name. If there is anything I can leave your students with here, it's the importance of continuing to talk and meet, and travel if necessary. There has to be a lot of give and take, and I'm guessing that most U.S. students and aspiring managers see this as an annoyance instead of an important part of their jobs.

advice about this part of the process, something that we think should be the first stage in international negotiation.

Preparing for negotiations   American participants have long been accused of failing to adequately prepare for international negotiations. And concerns about the consequences of inadequate preparation have been around for a long time. Over thirty years ago, one expert cautioned American executives to pay close attention to the negotiating style often used in Japan. He reasoned that if Americans did a good job of studying Japanese customs and negotiation tactics, the United States would be much better off. In particular, he thought that this kind of homework would help prevent the U.S. trade deficit with Japan from rising to the then "impossible level of $4 billion" (you may recall from Chapter 1 that the U.S. goods deficit with Japan exceeded $80 billion in 2000).[19]

Much of the advice that's been around for decades about how to prepare for international negotiations is still sound. After all, since the same advice continues to be echoed today, imitation may indeed be the sincerest form of flattery. Moreover, that advice is often supported by research on international negotiation success and failures.[20]

EXHIBIT 7.6

Where Culture Comes In: A Framework for Understanding International Negotiations

General Category	Elements to Consider
Basic model used by negotiators	How the negotiation process might be conceived: ● a bargaining effort ● joint problem solving or exploration ● a debate What the most significant issues might be: ● concerns of substance ● relationships ● procedures/rules ● internal or personal goals
Perspectives on individuals	How negotiators are chosen: ● knowledge/experience ● personal characteristics/status Aspirations of individuals (individual vs. community goals) Group decision making (authoritarian vs. consensual)
Dispositions affecting interactions	Time orientation (monochronic vs. polychronic) Risk-taking orientation (high vs. low) How trust is determined: ● intuition ● common experiences ● reputation ● threat of sanctions
Views about the interaction process	Importance of protocol (formal vs. informal) Complexity of communication (low vs. high) Tactics for persuasion: ● logic/facts/experience ● dogma/tradition ● emotion/intuition
Outcomes	Agreement preferences (contractual vs. implicit)

Source: Adapted from Weiss, S. E. (1994). Negotiating with "Romans"—Part I. *Sloan Management Review,* Winter, 53.

So consider the following general suggestions before undertaking an international negotiation:

● International negotiation is notoriously complex and replete with opportunities to fail; never underestimate it.
● Take whatever steps are necessary to gain an in-depth understanding of the other side—not just on issues of substance, but how their negotiating styles, view of the process, and cultural values may come into play (Exhibit 7.6 should prove very helpful here in terms of laying out the various issues that need to be considered).

- Seek outside help if the necessary expertise or knowledge is missing inside the company (plenty of consultants and cultural trainers are available for international negotiations).
- If negotiators' language skills are insufficient, use interpreters that are hired by your company (don't rely on interpreters provided by the other side).
- Consider the use of an international negotiating team (more on this later).
- Be prepared to spend significant time and effort on the preparation process. This task is not something to be impatient about.

As you might suspect, the last point is one that many Americans have trouble with. For example, an American manager leaving the United States for a negotiation in Asia generally should be prepared for a long stay. Many Americans still assume that they can spend a few days on the ground in a place like Japan or China and quickly wrap up a negotiation. In fact, when we were in Shanghai a few years ago, we ran into an executive from an American automotive company. He groused that he had already "wasted" a week in the country without getting anything done other than "eating and drinking" with officials. And he was angry about having to choose between spending an unknown and indefinite period of time in the country or simply calling the effort a failure and going home. Unfortunately, many people from Asian countries expect a good bit of time to be spent on establishing a rapport, whereas Americans want to "get down to business." Worse yet, some foreign negotiators are savvy to Americans' time sensitivities and will end up using this against them.

As we mentioned, using a negotiating team is often advisable in an international context. Once again, however, some Americans believe teams are cumbersome and feel that they're better off going it alone. Sometimes American negotiating teams are small because of the costs associated with larger groups. In other cases, the team is small because of the negotiators' inflated views of their own abilities. Either way, Americans may find themselves outnumbered in international negotiations. And the sheer number of details, let alone the language and cultural issues, often greatly reduce the odds of a good outcome for an understaffed negotiation team.[21]

Of course, even if the team is solid, its members may not be properly prepared or understand how best to work with the team's translator. Experts will often recommend plenty of advance meetings with your interpreter and, ideally, making them a team member from the start. Apparently, companies that follow this advice have more success in negotiations. For example, a survey of over one hundred multinationals revealed that nearly 90 percent felt the presence of a bilingual team member improved the quality of the negotiation process with Japanese companies. Likewise, about the same number of firms thought that such a team member also helped speed up the process. And among those firms without a bilingual team member, most indicated that they would include one in future negotiations. Taking this point a step further, other studies suggest that international negotiating teams should be multicultural in any event. In other words, a company's negotiating team would ideally consist of employees from both the home country as well as the country represented by the other side in the negotiations. This idea goes beyond language issues. A multicultural team could make bargaining perspectives, traditions, and tactics clearer for all sides and help resolve any culturally driven impasses.[22]

But regardless of the size and composition of the negotiating team, we want to repeat the point that familiarity with the prominent features of the host country's culture and customs usually pays big dividends for everyone. For example, when asked about it, Japanese managers said that the most important factor for ensuring success in negotiations with U.S. firms was the willingness of Americans to devote time, effort, and patience to building relationships. Not far behind was "cultural awareness." This included things such as a familiarity with Japanese business norms, customs, and practices. It's likely that these two factors are important in most or even all international negotiations, not just those involving the Japanese. Fortunately, these two factors, among the others we discussed, can be worked on and fine-tuned well before the actual negotiation process begins.[23]

That said, we don't want to create the impression that preparation will automatically lead to successful negotiations. The complexities of international negotiation are such that while preparation should improve the odds, there are no guarantees. Even if you are well prepared and display behaviors and tactics that are comfortable for your counterparts, research suggests that your efforts to "adapt" will be viewed more positively in some cultures than in others. In addition, training may not always have the intended effects in any case. Even after they went through identical training in negotiation tactics, Danish and Spanish negotiators in one study still used distinct bargaining styles. The Spaniards tended to connect relationships to the issues at hand and were willing to attack the other side, while the Danes preferred to focus on the issues and avoid direct conflicts. Consequently, Spaniards were likely to view the Danes as being too focused on the business issues and emotionally distant, while the Danes were likely to view the Spaniards as uncooperative and confrontational. All of this suggests that training alone is unlikely to completely suppress the styles that people have become comfortable with over the years, whether it results from cultural influences, direct experiences, or both.[24]

Finally, consider this. Whatever its drawbacks and limitations, more training is usually going to be more desirable than less. And that's where big firms have an advantage over small ones. In fact, research shows that larger firms tend to do better in international negotiations than their smaller counterparts. And it's not size per se that counts. Rather, it's the resources that often come with size. Big firms are more likely to have the money for consultants, trainers, and interpreters. In short, big firms often have the luxury of taking more time to prepare and spending more money in doing so.[25]

International Negotiation: A Four Stage Process

Regardless of the amount (or lack) of preparation, eventually you must begin face-to-face interaction and negotiation. Experts suggest that the complete negotiation process can be divided up into four main stages.[26] The first stage is called **nontask sounding.** This is often a relatively long stage, especially outside the United States. The basic purpose of this stage is to establish a rapport or to get to know the other party. In other words, interaction in this stage is not directly related to the task of negotiating but instead involves "sounding out" the other party. The next stage involves the **task-related exchange of information.** This process basically involves an exchange of the two parties' needs and preferences as well as an explanation of background issues. After this stage comes a **persuasion** stage of negotiations, in which, as the label implies, there are overt attempts to modify each other's positions. All three of these stages lead to the final **agreement** stage, in which bargains are agreed upon and perhaps contracts signed (see Exhibit 7.7). There is a good deal of research comparing cultures across these four stages, and we'll present some of that work next.

Stage 1: nontask sounding First, let's consider nontask sounding. This is probably a normal stage in most conversations, especially among those meeting for the first time. That is, the effort to establish rapport or to get to know someone is not only typical across cultures, it is common within cultures. But that doesn't mean that

EXHIBIT 7.7

Stages in the International Negotiation Process

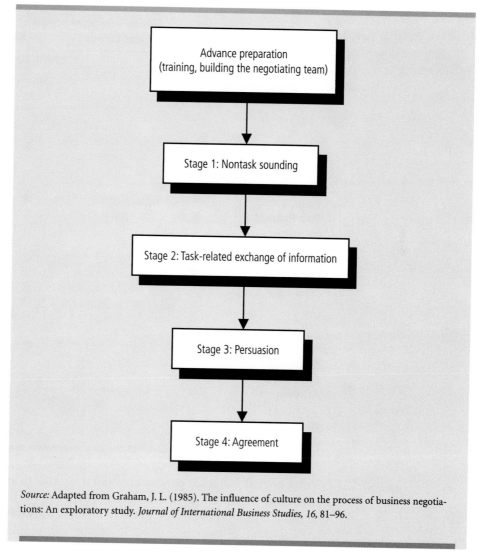

Source: Adapted from Graham, J. L. (1985). The influence of culture on the process of business negotiations: An exploratory study. *Journal of International Business Studies, 16*, 81–96.

nontask sounding unfolds the same way everywhere. In fact, there often are great differences between Americans and many other cultures about how this stage is approached.

One important variable in the nontask-sounding stage is the amount of time spent on entertaining one's guests in an effort to feel them out and establish personal relationships. You may, for example, encounter people who want to know about you and the company you represent in great detail. In fact, they may even identify themselves when first introduced as belonging to that company. For instance, in many Asian cultures we would introduce ourselves by saying, "We are the University of Dayton's Paul Sweeney and Dean McFarlin." Obviously, in the United States we would almost certainly introduce ourselves by saying, "Hi, I'm Paul Sweeney and this is Dean McFarlin; we're with the University of Dayton." This is a subtle difference, but substantial in its underlying meaning. It reflects what we have already discussed—that people in individualistic cultures like the United States tend to give primary emphasis to the person, while people in collectivistic cultures give primacy to the group (the organization, in this case).

EXHIBIT 7.8

Behavior in the Stages of Negotiation: Differences across Low- and High-Context Cultures

Stage of Negotiation	Low-Context Culture	High-Context Culture
Stage 1: Nontask Sounding	● Briefly exchange social niceties ● Will get to the point (i.e., stage 3) quickly ● Not especially concerned with status of other group	● Will want to know all about you and your company ● Long presentations and meetings in order to get to know you ● Give careful attention to age, rank, status of other negotiators
Stage 2: Task-Related Exchange of Information	● Relatively brief stage ● Young, ambitious, likely to do well	● Among the longer stages ● Advantage given to older, higher-status team member
Stage 3: Persuasion	● Argumentative ● The most important stage ● "To the point" negotiating style ● Cost-benefit approach; face saving not very important	● Declarative ● The least important stage ● More guarded style ● Face saving very important
Stage 4: Concession/ Agreement	● Favor or require detailed written contract ● Decision/agreement is impersonal ● Profit motive determines agreement	● Less emphasis on long contracts ● Deal is sealed on the basis of the contextual variables ● Good setting necessary for final agreements

But nontask sounding goes well beyond this. What to an American might seem to be discussions about irrelevant personal details or tangential issues often means a great deal to, say, a Chinese negotiator. In fact, it might be vital from their perspective to have such "irrelevant" discussions early on. Remember that people from low-context cultures like the United States often don't want a lot of personal "background" before undertaking negotiations. Their perspective often is that since a "contextless" contract (one that's explicit and in writing) should be the result of the negotiation process, spending enormous amounts of time to get to know the other part is not only unimportant, but a waste of time. The perspective of people from high-context cultures such as China, Japan, and Mexico, is often precisely the opposite, making it extremely important to spend a significant amount of time on nontask sounding. The personal and organizational information that they seek provides the context that is critical for understanding messages in their culture. Exhibit 7.8 summarizes this and other differences that might be observed between high- and low-context cultures in the nontask sounding stage.

So the amount of time spent on what Americans might consider "meaningless" interaction can vary dramatically across cultures. And in high-context cultures, it really does matter in ways that impact final outcomes. For example, one study showed that for Brazilian and Japanese negotiators, interpersonal comfort was much more likely to lead to outcomes that satisfied the negotiating partner than it was for American negotiators.

This finding underscores the role of nontask sounding as an important mechanism for building the personal relationships that are so essential for successful negotiations in high context cultures.[27]

Another sign of a culture's emphasis on the "getting to know you" stage is the importance negotiators place on status. The status of the participants involved in the negotiation, while not directly relevant to the issues being discussed, is relevant in some cultures during the nontask-sounding stage. Once again, the distinction between high- and low-context cultures is useful for making this point. Negotiations among equals is much more common in low-context cultures such as the United States. American negotiators often downplay status in any number of ways (e.g., by using first names, dressing casually, and soliciting input from all team members). But in many high-context cultures, title and status are very important and, as a result, interactions are more formal.[28] It would be rare, for example, for a high-context negotiator to address the other party by his or her first name. The Chinese, for instance, are very aware of status differences among people on negotiation teams and prefer to negotiate with the head of the foreign company.[29] This is also an apparent preference among Japanese and French negotiators.[30]

Status or position acts to provide background to impending negotiations for high-context negotiators, but it is relatively unimportant in low-context cultures. To illustrate this point, one study had groups of English, French, Germans, and Americans participate in a simulated negotiation. The study found that the French (i.e., the highest context of the four groups) were most interested in and affected by the status of other negotiation team members. Another study involved observations from more than 700 business people from eleven different cultures. The cultures ranged from very low context (e.g., the U.S., Germany) to very high context (e.g., Korea, China, Taiwan). This study also found that high status and personal relations mattered more to people from high-context cultures. In Japan, for example, status distinctions can be based on age, gender, and relative position in the firm. So if you're older, male, and higher up in the firm, the odds are it will impress a Japanese bargainer. In the low-context United States, however, Americans often want to establish equality between people, even where it clearly does not exist.[31]

Stage 2: task-related exchange of information   This second stage involves the exchange of both parties' needs and preferences. For some cultures this is the most important step in the negotiating process. In high-context cultures such as Japan, long and in-depth explanations of initial bargaining positions are expected. This exchange and the meetings that go along with it will probably be long and drawn out and will involve receiving many questions from the other negotiating party. The long-term approach taken by high-context cultures also means you're likely to see an initial offer that is not very good (too low or much too high). The belief is that a poor initial offer will leave plenty of room to maneuver in later stages of the negotiation process. For example, one study had groups of businessmen from the United States, Japan, and Brazil participate in simulated negotiations. The Japanese asked for higher profit outcomes in their initial offer than their American and Brazilian counterparts. The American negotiators, however, were more likely to offer a price that was closer to the eventual terms agreed upon by both parties. And, the Americans and Brazilians were irritated at the Japanese for their "greedy" initial offers. A second study with the same three cultural groups found that American bargainers could reduce this irritation and improve their outcomes by stretching out this second stage of negotiations. In particular, the more Americans encouraged information exchange from their bargaining partners, the better their financial outcomes in the negotiation.[32]

Stage 3: persuasion   Still, Americans are often skimpy in the attention they pay to task-related information exchange. Sure, Americans may spend some time talking about sports or their families, but dramatically little time compared to other cultures. Instead, a slight glance at the wristwatch is enough to move an American onto the next stage of negotiations. This third stage—persuasion—involves attempts to modify each others' positions. To Americans, this is the most important step in the negotiating process. And it's the stage where they expect to spend most of their time. But how the persuasion stage unfolds in other cultures may end up surprising many Americans.

Consider the amount of time spent at this stage. As we've said, Americans usually spend relatively little time and effort in the earlier two stages in order to spend greater amounts of time here. Other cultures, such as the Japanese, take the time to sound each other out earlier and therefore they spend relatively little time engaging in the kind of overt persuasion many Americans are used to.

Then there are the actual tactics used to persuade. As you might expect, most Americans believe that this stage is where the "real" negotiating takes place. So Americans typically pay very close attention to the interactions that occur in this stage. For example, throughout this part of the process, Americans will often continuously compromise and make modifications to their initial bargaining position. Concessions are common throughout all stages of negotiations for most Americans. However, unlike American bargainers, Japanese negotiators tend to wait until the end of negotiations before making any concessions.[33] Consequently, Americans engaged in international negotiations may go too far and give too much away in the persuasion stage.[34] On top of that, the meaning of compromise can differ dramatically across cultures, as shown in the following International Insights.

INTERNATIONAL INSIGHTS

The Devil is in the Details:
The Meaning of Compromise across Cultures

IF YOU'RE WONDERING ABOUT how important language is in international business, consider the language of negotiation. Take the word *compromise,* which generally has very positive connotations for Americans. The United States was founded on compromise and many famous compromises have dotted its history. Americans may be the world's best compromisers. It follows, of course, that compromise has been an essential part of American business dealings as well. It fact, to many Americans a compromise or concession is a very strong sign of good faith and fair play between negotiators.

Interestingly, however, the word *compromise* has some very different meanings in other cultures. And many of those meanings are far more negative than those conjured up by Americans. In the Middle East, for example, *compromise* carries with it many negative associations, as in the phrase "his virtue was compromised." The Persian word for *mediator* translates to "meddler." In many Latin American cultures, compromise presents an issue of personal honor; here, compromise would mean giving in. Since giving in raises many issues of face and personal integrity for Mexicans, it can prove problematic in negotiations. Russians typically see compromise as a sign of weakness. To concede even a minor point can suggest a loss of control or the influence of another's will. As a result, negotiations with Russians can be confrontational.

Likewise, many other terms that relate to the negotiation process are open to different interpretation. The word *aggressive* may be an insult to the British or Japanese, while to Americans such a characterization may indicate a tough, respected bargainer. So it clearly pays to become aware of national sensitivities, especially as far as communication about negotiation goes.[35]

Another reflection of the American belief that this is where the real negotiation takes place is that they now are ready to "lay their cards on the table." Basically, this means that Americans give, and expect to receive in return, "honest" information at this stage of negotiations. For example, in one study examining the appropriateness of various bargaining tactics, Americans were less likely to endorse tactics such as bluffing, feigning threats, or misrepresenting information than were Brazilians.[36]

Fundamentally, Americans believe that the ideal position for both parties should be put on the table, at which time progress can be made—often on an issue-by-issue

The buyers and sellers in this Hangzhou market may approach
negotiation differently than their Western counterparts.
© Macduff Everton/CORBIS

basis—toward some kind of compromise. But "honesty" issues aside, this style often does not mesh well with the bargaining approaches used in other countries and cultures. The Chinese, for example, often make sudden demands that are presented as nonnegotiable. Such demands often place Westerners at a disadvantage if they're not well prepared.[37] With sufficient patience, however, Americans might find that concessions will appear from the Chinese side at the last minute.[38]

Exhibit 7.9 presents ten elements of what might be considered the American negotiating style. Most of these elements play a role here in the persuasion stage of negotiations. Put simply, some argue that the quintessential American style is that of the frontiersman or cowboy in the old West. This "John Wayne" style of interaction may work well within the United States, but the characteristics that define American individualism often go over poorly on a foreign stage. After all, negotiation is by definition interdependent in nature. And interdependence, in most shapes or forms, arguably has not been a major emphasis in American culture.[39]

So what can happen when the John Wayne negotiator meets another culture—say, an Asian one? Americans would, in all likelihood, quickly present a complex set of arguments. They may conclude their presentation with an offer that is not too far from what they eventually expect. A Japanese or Chinese businessperson may be surprised by the abruptness of the offer but will probably consider it. They may know that Americans like to get to the point. What they may not know, however, that the

EXHIBIT 7.9

Ten Elements of the American Negotiating Style (The John Wayne Style)

American Style	Prescriptions for Use in Other Countries
1. **I can go it alone:** We're often convinced that we can handle complex negotiations by ourselves.	1. **Use team assistance wisely:** Don't hesitate to include extra team members with expertise in technical areas or language.
2. **Just call me John:** Americans downplay status and titles, as well as other formalities like lengthy introductions.	2. **Follow local customs:** Our informality is simply out of place in most other cultures; foreign clients are more comfortable when we follow their customs.
3. **Pardon my French:** We're not much good at speaking other languages—and often we don't make any apologies, either!	3. **Speak the (a) language:** Even a rudimentary knowledge of foreign terms can be useful.
4. **Get to the point:** Americans, like no others, want to dispense with the small talk and get down to business.	4. **Getting down to business:** This is defined differently across culture; getting to know the other party is important in many countries.
5. **Lay your cards on the table:** We expect honest information at the bargaining table ("You tell me what you want and I'll tell you what I want").	5. **Hold something back:** Foreign executives seldom lay everything on the table; the negotiating process is expected to take time with concessions made along the way.

continued...

American offer is pretty close to their best offer possible. In fact, almost everywhere else in the world but the United States, bargainers leave themselves plenty of room to maneuver. Accordingly, the Chinese or Japanese may counter by asking for a lot, which makes perfect sense, given their cultural perspective. But Americans may react angrily in many cases. This is exactly what happened in a study based on a simulated negotiation session. American negotiators initially asked for a "fair" price—one closer to their final offer—while Japanese negotiators initially asked for much higher profit options, a position that upset the Americans.[40]

Despite these feelings, Americans would probably press on. They may try dealing with one issue at a time. Here they may experience more frustration and anger, for several reasons. For example, the Japanese typically do not like dealing piecemeal with issues—which explains why their concessions are bunched toward the end of the negotiation process. Second, even if Americans are very persuasive, they may get a silent response—which the Americans may interpret as stonewalling. A cultural analysis shows the source of frustration here. The Americans may have used their on-the-spot latitude to grant a concession. But Japanese rarely have the same amount of discretion

EXHIBIT 7.9

Ten Elements of the American Negotiating Style (The John Wayne Style) (Continued)

American Style	Prescriptions for Use in Other Countries
6. **Don't just sit there, speak up:** Americans don't deal well with silence: we get into trouble by feeling pressured to fill in silence with possible concessions.	6. **Silence can be a powerful negotiating tool:** Consider its use, but also be aware of its use against you.
7. **Don't take no for an answer:** We are taught to be persistent and not to give up; negotiation is mostly persuasion.	7. **Minds are often changed behind the scenes:** If an impasse is reached, ask more questions; take a recess; try a more subtle approach.
8. **One thing at a time:** Americans approach a negotiating task sequentially ("Let's settle the quantity issue first, and then discuss price").	8. **Postpone concessions:** Until you've had a chance to get all issues on the table; don't measure progress by the number of issues that have been settled.
9. **A deal is a deal:** When we make an agreement, we give our word. We expect to honor the agreement no matter the circumstances.	9. **What we take as a commitment:** Means different things in Tokyo, Rio, or Riyadh; deals, particularly new ones, are more uncertain than we're used to.
10. **I am what I am:** Few Americans take pride in changing their minds, even in difficult circumstances	10. **Flexibility:** Is very important in cross-national negotiations; we must adapt to changing economic circumstances and interdependence.

Source: Adapted from Graham, J. L., & Herberger, R. A. (1982). Negotiators abroad—don't shoot from the hip. *Harvard Business Review,* July–August, 160–168.

at their disposal. Instead, the Japanese decision-making style is to take time after hearing an offer to discuss it as a group and, ideally, reach a consensus. Consequently, the Japanese negotiators are not likely to react immediately to an offer.[41]

If they are frustrated enough at this point, Americans counter with a very aggressive tactic. They might tell the Japanese, "If you can't lower your price, we'll just go with another supplier." This may be the worst thing the Americans could do. Just the mere directness of this approach, let alone the aggressiveness, will probably turn off the Japanese. It would be much more appropriate if this option were presented through a third party or, if it must be done directly, then in a completely different way. For example, the American might say, "Lower prices on your part would go a long way toward our not having to consider other options." Additionally, other tactics, like repeating the reexplanation of your position in more detail, asking questions, playing dumb, or even silence can go a long way.[42]

Stage 4: agreement Of course, eventually many negotiations do come to a conclusion where an agreement is reached. Agreements are the culmination of all the concessions and persuasion used in stage 3 and earlier stages. That said, an agreement is only as good as the followthrough. In other words, all the considerable time and effort you invested in the previous three stages (sounding out other party, trying to understand their culture, traveling, persuading, etc.) could be wasted if both parties don't behave in ways that are consistent with the agreement. Recognizing this fact, many American companies will insist that elaborate formal contracts be signed that bind each party to the agreement. Not unexpectedly, this demand is sometimes viewed as a negative or even something to resist outright. In some parts of the world, negotiators are loath to seal the deal with a final, written contract. Instead, they hope that the ties that they spent so much time building and strengthening in the earlier stages of the process will now pay off. They hope that the general trust established via an extended nontask-sounding phase will allow a much more general agreement to be drafted and acknowledged by each party.[43] Clearly, however, most foreign firms nowadays expect a lengthy formal contract to be requested if they are negotiating with U.S. companies.

The Chinese have similar views about the form of a good agreement. Instead of a specific contract, they prefer broad agreement about general principles. Some say the Chinese want broad agreements because they believe that if all parties agree to the principles, the details can be worked out later by people of good intention and trust.[44] Of course, Americans and other Westerners often take the position that if trust exists, then the Chinese should be willing to make clear commitments. Who is right probably depends on the specific case. One thing, however, is certain: Americans tend to slight the process of establishing broad principles. To Americans, these principles are similar to the corporate philosophies that are all the rage these days—they are nice words, but in practice, they are unimportant, if not meaningless. (Ironically, however, you will recall from Chapter 2 that U.S. firms are more likely to have such codes than their foreign competition.)

What many Americans fail to realize, however, is that these principles are the standards the Chinese use to evaluate future agreements. As result, Americans often agree to them with little input. Ultimately, this may be the right thing to do anyway, since general items can be interpreted to support your position. Nevertheless, experts recommend that Western firms provide input into this process, thereby articulating important business concepts (such as quality products, profit, shareholder return, etc.) instead of just going through the motions.

Whether it is broad or narrow, however, even the very notion of a contract can have different implications across countries. For example, in Russia a party to a contract can only do what is expressly allowed. Generally, in the United States you can do anything that is not prohibited by contract (provided it is legal). Accordingly, foreigners doing business in Russia may want to include a "no competition" clause in contracts to prevent Russian partners from becoming competitors.[45]

Once again, however, an agreement is only good if it is kept. Whether other parties live up to their end of the agreement is determined, at least in part, by the potential long-term impact. This impact, in turn, is determined by the trust we have in the other parties and our satisfaction with the agreement. So it probably pays in the long run to make sure the other parties feel they also got a good deal out of the negotiation process.[46] Global competition is so fierce today that general principles are probably worth abiding by in order to communicate effectively and negotiate a good international business agreement.

Chapter Summary

Conflict is a common occurrence in international communication and negotiation, and important causes include differing cultural norms, decision-making styles, and the characteristic cultural tendency to engage in or avoid conflict. We discussed a number of different styles that cultures use to deal with conflict issues once they arise. These balance concern for your own outcomes against concern for the outcomes of others. For instance, Americans tend to use a competitive style. There are also cultural differences in the accounts or explanations that people provide once an action has occurred that produces conflict between parties. Cultures that are more collectivist and focused on harmony tend to use mitigating accounts (e.g., concessions) while more individualistic cultures often use aggravating accounts (e.g., denials). Likewise, culture can shape how people respond to these accounts. For example, aggravating *accounts* are likely to be viewed negatively in collective cultures.

Perhaps the most important way to avoid or minimize conflict is through negotiation. We presented two negotiation frameworks. The broader of the two is intended to be used as a general guide to how culture can impact negotiations. It covers twelve basic factors and includes everything from how people conceptualize issues in negotiations to how the process of negotiation should unfold. The second framework focused on the stages of the negotiation process itself, but it also highlights the importance of preparation. Preparation should include things like learning about the other side in-depth (about their culture and how that impacts negotiation), seeking outside experts when necessary, using translators and a multicultural negotiating team, and generally being willing to spend significant time getting ready.

Once preparation is complete, the actual negotiations typically proceed through four main stages and we showed how different cultures put more or less weight on each stage. For example, Americans tend to undervalue the first stage of negotiating—nontask sounding—relative to other cultures. This "getting to know one another" phase is viewed by Americans as best kept brief and perfunctory, whereas it is a relatively long and important stage for other cultures. The next stage, task-related exchange of information, is also typically more important for countries other than the United States (e.g., Japan). In a high context culture such as Japan, long and in-depth exchange of bargaining positions is expected. Persuasion is the third stage, and one that is typically seen as the "heart" of negotiation for most Americans. This is the stage where modification and persuasion of others' positions unfolds. Yet, for, some high context cultures, it can be less important, and relatively little time is spent in the kind of overt persuasion that Americans are used to. Agreement is the final stage and again some big differences are commonly observed. Americans prefer elaborate contracts that bind parties to the agreement. Others, mostly high context cultures, rely a great deal on the trust established in earlier stages to truly seal a deal. Finally, we examined some of the mistakes than can be made in an international negotiation process as well as some techniques that may result in more beneficial outcomes.

Discussion Questions

1. In this chapter we have elaborated on the negative sides of intercultural conflict. Can you think of any positives that might result from such a conflict experience?
2. What interpersonal assets might Asians, Latins, and Americans (U.S.) be able to bring to bear on dealing with conflict? How might these characteristic ways of managing conflict create a sense of frustration when dealing with the other groups?
3. Reflect on how an American and a Saudi might move through the four stages of negotiation. How might each stage be approached and what areas might each nationality emphasize?

Up to the Challenge?

*Understanding the Mexican
and American Negotiation Gap*

AT THE BEGINNING OF the chapter, we presented a scenario and part of an exchange between Mexican and American managers in the same company who were charged with negotiating which department would buy some computer equipment. Just in case you were wondering, this was an exchange between real managers, part of a training program that the managers were going through on negotiations. So while the stakes involved were simulated, it nevertheless prompted some amazing cross-cultural differences, along with plenty of anger, frustration, and misunderstanding.

In a nutshell, the Mexicans displayed more concern for relationships than their American counterparts during negotiations. The Mexicans tended to use stories and allegories to help support their points, attempted to find collaborative outcomes that were mutually beneficial, and acknowledged the arguments of the other side in the negotiations. Likewise, the Mexicans also tended to be more effusive, though they would respond by rejecting the Americans' arguments and making demands on their own if they felt pushed too far. Americans, in contrast, used interruptions and attacking arguments more than their Mexican colleagues. In short, they were more competitive in their approach. The Americans also tended to focus more on moving things along by making allusions to time and requesting additional information. That said, Americans were often willing to accommodate Mexican negotiators in the end, preferring to present specific alternatives and work through them, conceding or compromising as necessary. The Mexicans, however, were more concerned with establishing a positive working relationship first and then preferred to explore options jointly rather than consider specific arrangements.

Overall, many Mexicans felt the Americans were too aggressive and confrontational. The Americans, on the other hand, tended, to view the Mexicans as indecisive, weak, and tangential. All of this, from the tactics used to the reactions of each side, may be influenced by cultural differences. In particular, Mexicans tend toward collectivism while Americans tend toward individualism. Americans tend to worry less about relationships and be focused more about "winning" in a negotiation. They may also view conflict and arguing as positives (they "help clear the air"). But to many Mexicans, being respectful, harmonious, smoothing, and empathetic in interactions (***simpatía***), especially with friends and family, is an important aspect of their cultural values (i.e., part of "Mexican collectivism"). In addition, Mexicans tend to be polychronic (high context) while their American counterparts tend to be more monochronic (hence the American emphasis on time, feeling rushed, being exacting with language, etc.).

As we presented it here, this was arguably a negotiation between in-groups of a sort, since everyone was part of the same firm. How might the two sides be impacted as a consequence? Why? In this circumstance, do you have any suggestions about how each side might better respond and adapt to the other, or have been better prepared to do just that? And what if the situation were different? What if each side had to interact with an out-group? For instance, how might negotiation tactics have played out differently for each side had this been a negotiation between companies? Say, with an outside supplier? Why?

As we noted in this chapter, perhaps the biggest mistake a manager can make is to be unfamiliar with the norms and typical behaviors of another culture. If both sides had been better prepared about the potential for "cultural disconnects" during the negotiations, things might have indeed gone more smoothly. And international negotiations these days don't always require a passport. Sometimes it's no farther than a walk across the hall.[47]

International Development

*An International Negotiation
Scenario*

Purpose

To diagnose and assess an international negotiation that has gone wrong, to learn how better to approach this and other cross-cultural negotiations, and to gain self-insight into your own negotiating tendencies and styles.

Instructions

Read the following scenario independently, either inside or outside class. Next, divide into groups of four to six. Discuss the questions posed at the end of the scenario with your group and develop consensus answers if possible (allow 20–25 minutes). Then report your group's answers, followed by a class discussion and wrap-up (20 minutes).

The Scenario

Econ, a rapidly growing electronics retailer located in

the Southwest, is currently attempting to negotiate a number of agreements with manufacturers located in Japan and elsewhere in the Far East. Econ has a reputation for selling the newest products at discounted prices and, at the same time, having the largest inventory possible. Its slogan is, "Never be undersold or out of stock." To demonstrate their desire to develop close ties with the new suppliers, management has decided to send Peter Nelson, one of the firm's top purchasing agents, to the Far East. He has been given the responsibility to negotiate a set of contracts that will improve Econ's market share in the Southwest and, at the same time, enhance its reputation as an up-and-coming electronics firm. Accompanying Peter is Reid MacLeod, a technical expert in computer hardware and software.

One organization of particular interest to Econ is Nagaoka, Inc., a Japanese firm that has established itself as a leader in writable disk drives and wireless hardware. Before leaving for Japan, Peter set up a number of meetings with Mr. Washsami, Nagaoka's vice president of sales. These meetings represent the first-time encounter with a Japanese firm for both Peter and Reid. Peter and Reid arrive at the Nagaoka plant as scheduled and are escorted to a well-appointed meeting room. Besides Mr. Washsami, there are three other individuals present. They are Mr. Asakawa, Director of Production, Mr. Matsuata, Mr. Asakawa's assistant, and Mr. Konatshima, the company's interpreter (Mr. Konatshima was asked to attend because only Mr. Washsami speaks English). After several minutes of formal introductions, the two sides sit down to begin discussions. To break the ice, Peter indicates to the interpreter that, since the group will be working together for several days, it would be desirable to use first names. He then repeats his and his colleague's first name. The Japanese nod their heads but continue to use last names. Peter tries a second time but the response is the same. He decides not to push the issue further, but wonders why the Japanese are being so formal.

Peter again takes charge by explaining what he and Reid hope to accomplish and Econ's business philosophy. Peter directs his comments to Mr. Washsami because he is the most senior person on the Japanese team. The interpreter repeats his comments for the benefit of the others. They respond by nodding followed by long periods of silence. Feeling uncomfortable with the silence, Peter begins to explain the specific needs that Econ has to Mr. Washsami. Of particular importance to Econ are discounts for large volumes and a multi-year contract. In response to Peter's comments, Mr. Washsami indicates that it would be difficult to make decisions so soon. He receives accepting glances from his colleagues. Not accepting Mr. Washsami's statements, Reid presses the issue of price. However,

the more Peter and Reid press, the more adamant and withdrawn Mr. Washsami becomes and the longer the periods of silence. Finally, Peter and Reid accept Mr. Washsami's unwillingness to discuss price at this time.

Peter turns his attention to important technical specifications for the drives Nagaoka manufactures. In this case, Peter directs his comments to Mr. Asakawa, director of production. Peter assumes that because Mr. Asakawa is the director, he is the person with the technical understanding to answer questions. In response to the questioning, Mr. Asakawa hesitates and, before responding, talks to his assistant. It soon becomes clear to Peter that the person with all the answers is not Mr. Asakawa, but his assistant. Peter, however, is confused because he does not want to offend the director or place Mr. Matsuata in an awkward position with his boss. Peter attempts to overcome his dilemma by directing his comments to the interpreter without specific reference to either Mr. Asakawa or Mr. Matsuata. Unfortunately, such a strategy only confuses the interpreter and makes the situation worse.

The group has been meeting now for two hours and Peter is becoming anxious about the amount of progress being made. As far as he can see, there has been very little progress. Even worse, the Japanese negotiators' casual and relaxed style, coupled with their reluctance to talk, has given Peter the impression that they are not very interested in doing business with Econ. In a final attempt to salvage something from the meeting, Peter turns his attention to the issues of delivery dates and how long it would take to receive an order once it had been placed. Here again, the Japanese are reluctant to make a commitment on quantities and delivery times. However, sensing some movement by Mr. Washsami, Peter presses on. After about 30 minutes of interpreter-assisted conversation, Mr. Washsami finally says yes to the specific delivery date requested by Reid. Mr. Washsami's yes, however, is followed by a long explanation about why such a date would be difficult to meet and how it would put considerable strain on Nagaoka's production facility.

Believing that he has finally obtained a commitment from Mr. Washsami, Peter decided that this would be a great opportunity to begin writing down points of agreement. Peter continues by suggesting that, since there is agreement on a delivery date, they can begin to write up a tentative agreement between Econ and Nagaoka. At first the interpreter is reluctant to repeat Peter's comments, but finally translates the message. To Peter's surprise, the Japanese look shocked and indicate that there is still not agreement on a delivery date. Peter is totally confused and suggests that they take a luncheon break to reconsider their position. The two sides agree to meet at 2:00 p.m. and leave for lunch together.

1. What do you believe went wrong with the negotiations between Econ and Nagaoka?
2. Who is at fault?
3. What would you have done differently?

Source: Mealiea, L. W. & Latham, G. P. (1996). *Skills for managerial success: Theory, experience, and practice.* Chicago: Irwin, 166–167, 170–172. Reprinted with permission.

From Theory to Practice
International Negotiation Exercise

Purpose
To explore the difficulties that can occur when negotiating with people from other cultures.

Instructions
Divide into groups. Your instructor will assign each group one culture to study. Outside class, do research to find three dominant cultural values and their corresponding behaviors for its assigned culture. Your group should

● meet to discuss each value and some of the behavior it produces.
● next, make some predictions about how negotiators from that culture act as a result.
● finally, come up with a strategic negotiating response for each of the predicted negotiating behaviors.

In class, your group will have 10 minutes to present its research findings and suggested negotiating strategy. The instructor will wrap things up with a discussion of cultural differences and their relationship to international business negotiations.

Source: Adapted from Whatley, A. (1979). *Training for the cross-cultural mind.* Washington, DC: SIETAR. As appeared in *Management international: Cases, exercises, and readings* by Dorothy Marcic and Sheila Puffer. Copyright © 1994 by West Publishing Company, Minneapolis/St. Paul, Minn., a division of International Thomson Publishing Inc.

Part

III

Capitalizing on International Opportunities

International Challenge

Developing a Strategic Menu for Beating McDonald's

JOLLIBEE FOODS IS a fast-food chain based in the Philippines that began as a family-run ice cream parlor in 1975. Today, Jollibee's major "local" competitor is global giant McDonald's Corporation, a company with some 29,000 restaurants that serve about 45 million people *daily* in 120 countries. Of course, McDonald's is one of the best-known companies in the world, with products, like the Big Mac, that look and taste just about the same wherever they are ordered. This, combined with its reputation for high quality, cleanliness, and fast service, makes McDonald's a very tough competitor indeed. Moreover, McDonald's has a track record of picking excellent, high-traffic locations for its stores and successfully pulling in kids—with jungle gyms, signature characters, and licensed toys and novelties.

But Jollibee wasn't intimidated. In fact, Jollibee has thrived in the face of the McDonald's challenge in its home market. Over the past few years, McDonald's has grown in the Philippines, but Jollibee has grown faster. In 1996, Jollibee had some 200 outlets and commanded 46 percent of the Philippine market, compared to ninety outlets and 16 percent of the market for McDonald's. By 2001, however, Jollibee had expanded to over 760 outlets in the Philippines, with McDonald's trailing at 236. Over the previous year, Jollibee opened sixty-seven new outlets in the Philippines while McDonald's opened only fourteen. Between 1996 and 2001, Jollibee also embarked on a foreign expansion plan of its own. By 2002, Jollibee had some thirty restaurants in foreign locations, including Hong Kong, Vietnam, and the United Arab Emirates. And Jollibee even invaded McDonald's home turf, opening several outlets in California, with more planned for the east coast.

The bottom line is that Jollibee has developed a successful strategy for competing against McDonald's, arguably the world's most formidable fast-food retailer, since the 1980s. So here's *your* challenge. What strategic recipe did Jollibee come up with to beat back McDonald's in the Philippines? How should McDonald's

LEARNING OBJECTIVES

After reading this chapter, you should be able to

- Describe basic international strategic concepts and the theory of national competitive advantage.

- Identify the major types of international strategies and the firm and industry factors that affect them.

- Describe the steps involved in the process of creating international strategy.

- Identify the organizational features that companies need to develop and implement their international strategies successfully.

respond to win back some of its Philippines market from Jollibee? As you read through this chapter, you'll come to understand the process of developing international strategy and some of the factors that make for successful forays into foreign markets. If you can, do a little research on the Philippines as part of your evaluation and assessment of both companies. The Philippines has cycled through bouts of political instability and economic weakness over the years, factors that gave foreign companies pause about investing there. While Jollibee took advantage of some of these factors, they don't fully explain its success. Come up with your own strategic analysis for Jollibee. Then take a look at the Up to the Challenge box at the end of the chapter to see what steps Jollibee took to take a bite out of the Big Mac.[1]

International Strategy: Deciding How to Compete

As we've seen in previous chapters, operating internationally means facing a diverse quilt of cultures, values, and practices. That complicates life for companies trying to figure out the best way to operate across countries. And one key challenge is to develop an overall plan for managing business needs and differences across countries that will allow the company to compete effectively. Of course, firms must first decide what businesses they want to be in before tackling the thorny questions of how they should compete.[2] That said, deciding how a company should compete abroad is a critical part of **international strategic management**. Consequently, this chapter will focus on that piece of the strategic equation for international firms. Generally speaking, the process of formulating international strategy involves developing international goals and then implementing whatever approach to international business the company has adopted. And the stakes are high, particularly because of the volatility of the global

Lunch patrons line up at a Jollibee restaurant in the Philippines. © Reuters NewMedia Inc./CORBIS

economy and the intensity of international competition. Today, companies must be able to anticipate and react quickly to changes in markets and technology or lose their ability to compete effectively.

Clearly, advances in communication and transportation have made it easier for all companies to source the best parts, materials, and labor from anywhere in the world. So you might think that the importance of location as a competitive weapon isn't what it used to be. After all, if everyone can source globally (e.g., manufacture products in China because labor is cheap), then there's no unique advantage to doing so. But that assessment overlooks how important it is to figure out where the best places are to manufacture, to innovate, to buy supplies, to sell products, and so on in the first place. And there's plenty of compelling evidence to suggest that when it comes to innovation and long-term success, location still matters a great deal.[3] For instance, the world's best consumer electronics firms are based in Japan, the best entertainment firms are located in Hollywood, and the best in leather fashions comes from Italy. Understanding how and why these clusters of excellence exist around the world is a key piece of the international strategy puzzle and a reason why strategic planning may be the most important task facing international managers.[4]

Despite the potential value of having a coherent international strategy, a surprising number of companies enter overseas markets without a clear, well-designed approach. This failure to plan can lead to a variety of problems:

- *Inability to predict accurately the direction of foreign markets* (making it impossible to adapt accordingly)
- *Poor use of resources abroad* (e.g., because of improperly selected investments or bad decisions about how or where to enter foreign markets)
- *Underestimating the resources needed to compete effectively abroad*
- *Failing to anticipate operational problems in foreign environments* (e.g., overlooking the need to stockpile raw materials that can't be reliably obtained from local suppliers)[5]

So what does having international strategy do for a company? Regardless of the industry in which companies compete or their level of overseas sophistication, all international strategies should provide answers to the same basic questions, including:

- *What products or services will be sold abroad?*
- *Where and how will services be delivered or products made?*
- *What resources are necessary for international competition and how will they be acquired?*
- *How competitors will be outperformed?*[6]

Traditionally, developing international strategy was the exclusive purview of top executives. Although many large firms still have planning staffs to assist executives, this formal, top-down approach to strategy development is slowly fading, at least in the United States. Today, many American firms involve teams of people who are close to the marketplace in the creation of international strategy. The idea is to react more quickly to specific changes in an evolving international environment. For instance, line managers are often in a better position to spot trends (good or bad) and test new ideas than senior management. If the goal of strategy development is to stay nimble and quickly take advantage of international opportunities, then involving people who understand the marketplace best should help this process.[7]

In fact, some companies like Hewlett-Packard even involve suppliers and customers in strategic planning to help identify new business opportunities. Overall, research suggests that the best strategic planning process is one that combines formal and specific elements with plenty of built-in flexibility and openness to change. Particularly in rapidly changing environments, companies may have to modify, amend, and tweak their international strategies as they go, or even dump them altogether if conditions warrant.[8]

As we've suggested, the goal of this chapter is to introduce you to the competitive issues surrounding the development of international strategy. In doing so, we'll look at some basic concepts about strategy and competitiveness. Next, we'll discuss some strategic options for multinationals and outline the process of strategy development. Along the way, we'll examine some of the special challenges facing small firms when it comes to developing international strategy. Finally, we'll review some of the organizational features that companies should possess to successfully develop and implement their international strategies.

Basic Strategic Concepts for International Competition

Back in Chapter 1 we provided snapshots of the economic powers that are emerging to challenge the dominance of the European Union, Japan, and the United States. The past several years have seen dramatic increases in the growth of international business, much of it fueled by developing countries such as China.[9] And on the corporate side of the ledger, international business is no longer just the purview of big firms. Small and medium-sized companies have contributed greatly to the growth in international business in recent years. In fact, they actually account for a bigger slice of international trade than large firms. For instance, the fifty biggest American exporters (e.g., Boeing) account for only about a third of exported merchandise, with small and medium-sized firms accounting for most of the rest.[10]

Nevertheless, international strategy experts tend to focus most on large firms, perhaps because their influence and global reach is still enormous. Take Mitsubishi Corporation. This Japanese giant actually represents a family of some thirty companies with interrelated ownership. This ownership structure, called *keiretsu*, is slowly fading but is still relatively common in Japan. One of the family members is usually a trading company (called a *sogo shosa*) that helps market products from the rest of the corporate family to the outside world. In this role, Mitsubishi at one point sold as many as 100,000 products to some 45,000 customers worldwide.[11]

Of course, this discussion begs the question of how international companies actually compete. All companies make money through *value creation*, offering products or services that customers want. There are three general strategies for pursuing this end, either alone or in combination.

One way companies can meet customer demands is by **differentiating** their products or services from those of competitors. In other words, they provide unique or superior products that customers are willing to pay for. That's the route Mercedes-Benz takes in offering what it believes are the world's best production cars. But a Mercedes isn't cheap. So another tack on providing value is to pursue a **cost leadership approach**, offering cheaper products or more efficient services than competitors. For example, southeast Asian computer firms and component manufacturers have done well by combining efficient manufacturing operations and inexpensive labor, allowing them to undercut their Japanese competitors on price (e.g., Taiwan-based Acer). Finally, a **niche strategy** involves focusing on a specific line of products or services relative to competitors who operate more broadly. By serving a specific market segment, firms hope to do a better job of responding to customers and meeting their needs (e.g., on price or differentiation) than their competitors. Porsche might be a good example of a firm that pursues a niche strategy (the company focuses exclusively on upscale sports cars), one based on providing superior performance compared to competitors (i.e., differentiation).[12]

Regardless of the basic approach used to attract customers, companies can add value by changing any of their **primary activities** (e.g., manufacturing products, marketing products) or **supporting activities** (e.g., procuring raw materials, designing products), either alone or in combination. In fact, as Exhibit 8.1 suggests, the firm itself can be thought of as a linked set of these primary and supporting activities, referred to as a **value chain**. Consequently, a company's international strategy is really about the choices it makes in terms of how value chain activities are **configured** (e.g., where do value chain activities actually happen?) and **coordinated** (e.g., are dispersed activities tightly controlled from headquarters, or do they remain under local control?).

Often companies change these activities to improve their **core competencies**, skills that are hard for competitors to imitate. Core competencies can be located anywhere in the firm's value chain and provide the basis for international competitiveness. For instance, one company's prowess might be in logistical execution (e.g., Wal-Mart), while another's might be in product innovation (e.g., 3M), and a third's in manufacturing quality (e.g., Toyota). If firms actually possess a core competency that helps them outperform competitors (e.g., they attract more customers because they have the best logistics, are the most innovative, or have the highest quality), then they have developed a **distinctive competency**.

EXHIBIT 8.1

Understanding the Value Chain

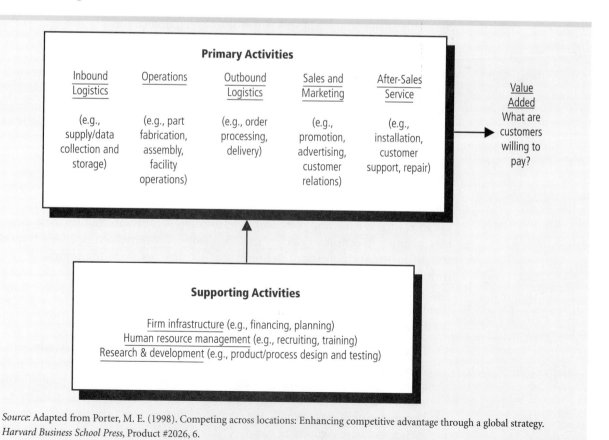

Source: Adapted from Porter, M. E. (1998). Competing across locations: Enhancing competitive advantage through a global strategy. *Harvard Business School Press*, Product #2026, 6.

Since international business should continue to grow and barriers to trade fall over the long term, one popular view is that firms compete best by moving different value chain activities to wherever **location economies** exist. For instance, if the cheapest and most productive labor for product assembly can be found in Vietnam, then that's where a company should locate production operations. If the best product designers are found in the United States, then that's where R&D activities should be located.[13] Scattering certain value chain activities to locations that offer such benefits can provide companies with a source of **competitive advantage** compared to firms that fail to do so. For instance, companies that need software development and maintenance may gain an edge over rivals by locating those activities in India, a source of inexpensive and well-trained programmers. Of course, the advantages associated with dispersing value chain activities to various locations can sometimes be offset by coordination problems, among other things. So the idea is to capitalize on the advantages that certain locations present while still managing to coordinate and integrate operations effectively across those locations. Clearly, that's easier said than done.[14]

On top of that, features of location economies such as low labor costs or plentiful raw materials only offer companies a **sustainable competitive advantage** if other firms find it hard to follow suit. In other words, there's nothing terribly unique about moving plants to low-wage locations or sourcing materials from certain overseas locations. You may be at a disadvantage if your competitors operate in a low-wage environment and you don't, everything else being equal. But joining them in a low-wage location won't set you apart. Instead, locations that somehow help companies continually improve their productivity, processes, marketing savvy, or capacity for innovation may do more to provide a long-term competitive advantage. Put simply, it's the ability to constantly change and adapt that allows many international firms to outperform their competitors.[15]

Locations and competitiveness   All of this suggests that competitiveness is a complex concept involving both companies and the places where they do business. Of course, companies compete. But in a sense, nations also compete economically. According to one definition, nations are competitive if they: (1) produce goods and services that international markets demand; and (2) provide their citizens with a rising standard of living that can be maintained over time.[16] In doing so, nations may also offer certain strengths and competitive advantages to companies operating there.

This raises the question of how nations become competitive and why certain nations seem to produce firms that are very successful in specific industries. For instance, why do American companies lead in computer software, but Japanese companies dominate in consumer electronics? The **theory of national competitive advantage** tries to answer such questions. It argues that four factors shape the context in which nations, and the firms based there, compete. These factors are presented in Exhibit 8.2 and represent a combination of national and firm-specific characteristics. Understanding how they interact can help explain why industries and companies succeed or fail in particular locations:

1. **Factor conditions.** Does a nation offer the components needed for competitive production in a particular industry, such as abundant raw materials and skilled labor (e.g., the prime grape-growing land in California and a large pool of expert winemakers are key reasons why the United States is a leader in this industry)?
2. **Demand conditions.** What's the nature of the market in a particular country for an industry's goods or services? Large, sophisticated home markets often force firms to become more innovative, which may foreshadow where worldwide

EXHIBIT 8.2

Locations Factors That May Offer an International Competitive Advantage

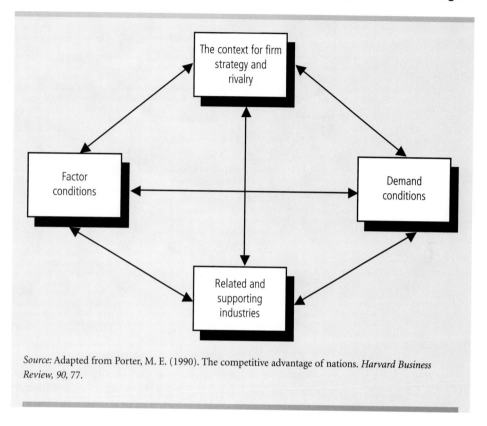

Source: Adapted from Porter, M. E. (1990). The competitive advantage of nations. *Harvard Business Review, 90,* 77.

markets are ultimately headed. This early awareness can help firms stay ahead of competitors from other countries. For instance, Americans' desire for convenience and speed has spawned efficient fast-food companies, many of which have done well overseas where similar desires have emerged (e.g., McDonald's).

3. **Related and supporting industries.** Does a cluster of suppliers or related industries that are internationally competitive exist in a country? If so, their presence can provide superior and mutually beneficial access to components, technology, and innovation (often thanks to shorter lines of communication and established working relationships). For instance, Italian shoe companies owe much of their overseas success to the close relationships they have developed with local leather suppliers, shoe component manufacturers, and specialized equipment firms.

4. **Firm strategy, structure, and rivalry.** How does the domestic competitive environment, as well as local laws, culture, and business practices, affect the ways that firms organize and operate in a particular country? Tough domestic competition forces firms to be more innovative, productive, and cost conscious, all characteristics that may serve them well in international markets. For instance, Honda's excellent performance in the American auto market is partially a consequence of the intensive competitive struggles it endured with formidable homegrown rivals in Japan (e.g., Toyota and Nissan). Likewise, management practices can also make it easier or harder for firms in certain countries to compete in specific industries.[17]

The unique products in this Japanese grocery store illustrate the pressure food companies face to tailor products to local tastes. © Reuters NewMedia Inc./CORBIS

As we've suggested, the four factors driving national competitive advantage can combine to affect how successful firms are in international markets. These interactive relationships are depicted in Exhibit 8.2. For example, just having demanding domestic customers may not be enough to give a firm in a particular country a competitive advantage. But if that firm is forced to respond to tough domestic competition and positive factor conditions support its efforts to develop more innovative products (e.g., the technology infrastructure is excellent), then a competitive advantage may result when the company tries to compete in other countries.

Overall, the theory of national competitive advantage is useful for thinking about how country-specific factors can affect international competitiveness. That said, critics have argued that the theory's key concepts are ambiguous or need to be defined more precisely. Others contend that the theory either underestimates or overestimates the impact of certain country-specific factors on competitiveness (e.g., government regulation).[18] Moreover, having a positive environment doesn't necessarily mean that a particular industry or company will thrive in a particular location. Conversely, companies have emerged from locations without some of the positive factors specified by the theory and still become formidable international competitors.[19] Nevertheless, the factors described in the model do seem to impact the international strategies used by firms in certain countries.[20]

Strategic Approaches Used by Multinationals

We'll now turn our attention to firm and industry factors that impact the competitive strategies multinationals often use in executing their fundamental approach to business (i.e., to add value based on differentiation or low cost). Clearly, firms may evolve through several levels of internationalization and be successful competitors in each. Many small companies begin by exporting and later establish overseas facilities. Some firms eventually build subsidiaries in dozens of countries and form alliances with other companies. Foreign market entry strategies are typically driven by a variety of factors, including the nature of (1) the industry the firm is in, (2) the particular market being entered, (3) the firm's strengths and weaknesses, and (4) the firm's stage of international development. We'll address some of these evolutionary issues in the next chapter when we consider various options for entering foreign markets. For now, however, we'll examine four common strategic options used by multinationals to compete—large companies that already have an extensive international footprint.[21]

Actually, many multinationals have multiple strategies that reflect the diverse needs of their various business units or product lines. For example, General Electric offers an incredible array of products and services that cut across several industry categories. These include appliances, communication and media services, electrical equipment, financial services, jet engines, lighting, medical diagnostic systems, and plastics (and this isn't a complete list!). Consequently, the degree to which GE has to tailor its products and services to local customers' needs (versus being able to sell the same thing everywhere in the same way at the same price) to compete effectively can vary considerably across business units. And that has implications for the international strategies those units need to pursue.

So it may be appropriate to think of large, diverse multinationals like GE as networks of relationships that exist among many dispersed organizations, each with somewhat different goals and perspectives. Understanding "strategy" in this context involves figuring out the internal movements of information, people, resources, and products through the multinational's entire web of linkages.[22] In fact, some experts suggest that multinationals can use network concepts to effectively develop and implement their strategies.[23]

The Multidomestic Strategy

Nevertheless, we'll simplify things by treating multinationals as if they used a single strategy to guide all of their international operations. With this in mind, let's examine the relationship between strategy and industry character. A multinational's international strategy may reflect the type of industry in which it competes. In certain industries like commercial banking and beverages, multinationals often face tremendous pressure to respond to a diverse set of local preferences and needs. Put simply, in certain industries, what will satisfy customers varies from country to country, sometimes dramatically. Responding to these customer needs could involve modifying product features, marketing/packaging approaches, service delivery methods, and pricing, either alone or in combination.

And in some industries requiring local responsiveness, there's little pressure for integrating or centralizing operations on a global basis. In fact, differences in local needs may obliterate any advantages that might otherwise be obtained by taking a more centralized or integrated approach to operations. For instance, centralizing production of certain food products makes little sense for companies like Nestle and Unilever (both of which operate hundreds of manufacturing facilities worldwide). Transportation costs would offset any savings from economies of scale and centralization would make it more difficult to offer an extensive array of tailored products for specific locations (e.g., by size, price, packaging, taste, etc.) in the first place.

As a result, foreign subsidiaries of multinationals in multidomestic industries are often given a high degree of operational independence. In a sense, they operate more or less as intact companies so as to provide tailored products and services for the local markets that they serve. In short, multinationals taking such an approach are using a **multidomestic strategy,** where goals are developed and implemented independently for specific countries.[24]

The Global Strategy

At the other end of the spectrum are industries in which country-specific tastes are basically nonexistent. In this case, the same standardized products or services can be sold everywhere with few, if any, adjustments. Boeing is a good example of a company competing in a global industry. It sells commercial aircraft worldwide with no real differences across countries and pretty much approaches the selling process the same way everywhere.

As a result, multinationals in such industries may pursue a **global strategy**, where goals and directions are set on a worldwide basis. Companies pursuing global strategies often eschew scattering value chain activities around the world. Instead, they often prefer to concentrate important value chain activities such as manufacturing and product development in a few key places. And that's basically the approach that Boeing takes in competing against Airbus, its European rival. Boeing is essentially an exporter, sending the same planes around the world from its U.S. base (where all product development and assembly occurs).

The Transnational Strategy

Other companies compete in industries where tailoring products or services to local market preferences and the ability to operate on an integrated basis worldwide are both important. Consequently, these firms are more likely to move their value chain activities to wherever they can be done "best" (e.g., cheapest, most efficiently, with the highest value added, etc.), while still adapting to local product or service preferences where appropriate.[25] This is the essence of a **transnational strategy**. To some extent, this approach represents a "best of both worlds" blend of global and multidomestic approaches, one in which firms seek economies of scale and location advantages worldwide while still "acting locally" with their products or services out of competitive necessity.[26]

Not surprisingly, some companies that pursue a transnational strategy want to tilt the balance toward the global side when it comes to product standardization. For instance, Procter & Gamble has simplified its personal care product lines and formulas worldwide. The firm's Vidal Sassoon hair care products now use a single fragrance everywhere in the world. However, to satisfy local tastes, less of that fragrance is used in places where customers prefer subtlety (e.g., Japan) and more is used where customers like intense scents (e.g., some European countries). Although moving toward similar products or services worldwide simplifies things for companies, taking things too far risks alienating customers to the extent that significant preference differences exist across markets.[27] Consequently, firms pursuing a transnational strategy must tweak and juggle the sometimes competing demands for local responsiveness and global integration. Balancing these demands well requires effective managerial coordination of operations around the world.[28] In fact, multinationals using a transnational strategy must quickly transfer their core competencies throughout their worldwide organization and be prepared to take advantage of new or improved core competencies wherever they are developed.[29]

Another Alternative: The Regional Strategy

Despite the hype sometimes associated with them, global and transnational strategies aren't always good fits for a multinational.[30] Indeed, multinationals often have great difficulty figuring out just how responsive they need to be to local preferences. Some products may fall into an area where lifestyles and tastes are converging worldwide (favoring global strategies), while others are in an area where customers in specific countries still hold on to their own unique preferences (favoring multidomestic strategies).

Take a look at Exhibit 8.3 for a summary of factors that tend to favor global versus multidomestic strategies. You'll notice that the formation of regional trading blocks (e.g., NAFTA) is listed as a positive factor under the multidomestic column. Consequently, even some multinationals that compete in supposedly "global" industries might be better off considering a **regional strategy**. A regional strategy involves giving managers in a particular geographic area like South America the freedom to make decisions, set goals, and respond to customers' needs. Part of this strategy also involves achieving efficiencies and economies by leveraging any location advantages that may exist within the region (e.g., to minimize production costs).

EXHIBIT 8.3

Some Factors Favoring Global versus Multidomestic Strategies

Factors Favoring a Global Approach	Factors Favoring a Multidomestic Approach
● Converging income across industrialized nations	● Industry standards remain diverse across nations
● Increasing similarity of consumer lifestyles and tastes worldwide	● Customers continue to demand products/services tailored to local needs
● Rapid advances in technology, communications, transportation; globalized financial markets	● Being seen as a "local" company is often a competitive asset
● Increasing worldwide trade, formation of global alliances	● Global organizations are hard to manage and control
● Reduced trade barriers, more open markets, and privatization of state-dominated economies	● Globalization can undercut unique competencies of foreign subsidiaries
● Emergence of nations with productive, low-cost labor (such as Thailand and Indonesia)	● Formation of regional trading blocks and agreements (e.g. NAFTA, the European Union)

Sources: Adapted from Morrison, A.J., Ricks, D. A., & Roth, K (1991). Globalization versus regionalization: Which way for the multinational? *Organizational Dynamics, 19* (1991); 17–29; Yip, G.S. (1995). *Total global strategy.* Englewood Cliffs, NJ: Prentice-Hall.

EXHIBIT 8.4

Mapping International Strategy: Responding to Pressures for Local Responsiveness and Global Integration

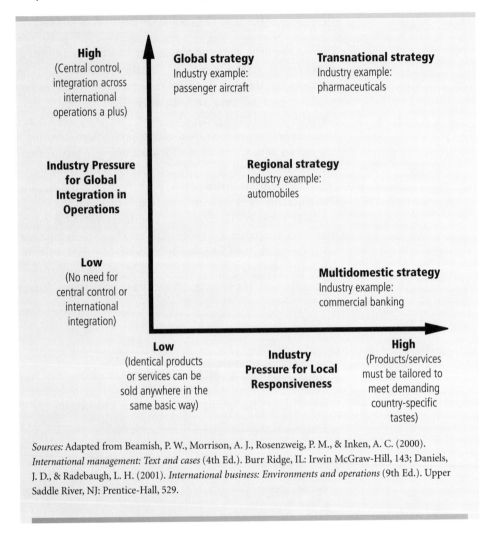

Sources: Adapted from Beamish, P. W., Morrison, A. J., Rosenzweig, P. M., & Inken, A. C. (2000). *International management: Text and cases* (4th Ed.). Burr Ridge, IL: Irwin McGraw-Hill, 143; Daniels, J. D., & Radebaugh, L. H. (2001). *International business: Environments and operations* (9th Ed.). Upper Saddle River, NJ: Prentice-Hall, 529.

For instance, French multinational Thomson Consumer Electronics uses a regional strategy for its television lines. Plants in Britain, Spain, Germany, and France each make specific types of televisions for the European market. Thomson's North American operations are run independently and focus on producing televisions with the RCA and GE labels just for that market, largely using regional suppliers of components. This regional approach lacks the worldwide integration found in a transnational strategy but offers more local product customization than a global strategy would. That said, a regional strategy allows for more geographic coordination than a multidomestic strategy, in which multinationals set up mostly independent subsidiaries to serve specific national markets. As such, a regional strategy often represents a good compromise for companies in certain industries.[31] Before we leave this section, look at Exhibit 8.4. It summarizes how industry pressures match up to the four international strategies that multinationals often employ.

When Strategy Provides a Competitive Advantage

At this point, you may be wondering when a firm's international strategy matters most. Of course, being able to execute a strategy well is important. But the strategy itself can provide an important competitive edge, depending, in part, on the alignment between the nature of an industry and the strategies typically used by competitors. For example, a multinational's global strategy may offer a competitive advantage when: (1) competitors tend to take a multidomestic approach, and (2) the underlying character of the industry actually favors globalization (e.g., where customer preferences are becoming the same everywhere and global economies of scale are possible). In other words, a multinational that uses a global strategy in an underglobalized industry will have an advantage because competing firms are using strategies that don't fit the industry's character as well. In fact, research supports the idea that the match or mismatch between the actual level of international competition in an industry and its underlying potential for globalization affects the relationship between multinational strategy and performance. See Exhibit 8.5 for a summary of the points we're making here.[32]

The Cultural Backdrop to International Strategy

Overall, it's clear that multinationals should carefully analyze their competitive context before moving ahead. Of course, that doesn't happen in a vacuum. For instance, relative to American and Japanese multinationals, why are European multinationals more likely to give foreign subsidiaries more autonomy? Likewise, why do foreign sales tend to account for a larger percentage of total sales in European multinationals? In part, these differences may reflect the small home markets of many European multinationals. On the other hand, the huge American home market may be one reason U.S. multinationals have been slower to internationalize than their European and Japanese counterparts.[33]

But these patterns may also reflect cultural differences in values, perspectives, and attitudes. As we've seen, managers from different countries often bring divergent views about time frames, risk taking, and goal setting into the strategic planning process. In short, culture impacts how managers interpret the "rules of the game" in international business.[34] For example, many Japanese multinationals have a strong tradition of centralized management and control, with all roads leading back to Japan. This tradition has been linked to Confucian values, the importance of in-group networks, and a desire to avoid uncertainty, to name a few possibilities. Cultural values may also impact the methods companies use to develop their international strategies in the first place. For example, companies based in countries with high individualism (e.g., the U.S.) tend to rely more on subjective information than on quantitative data or forecasting methods in formulating strategy.[35]

Even perceptions about cultural differences matter. For example, the wider the perceived cultural gap between headquarters and foreign subsidiaries, the tighter the management control from the parent company will be.[36] Likewise, perceived similarity can impact strategy. Firms often make their first international moves in countries viewed as having similar culture, language, business practices, laws, and so on. The rationale, of course, is that it's "safer" to start off in foreign contexts similar to your home market. But what happens if your perceptions about similarity are inaccurate or overstated? This may explain the high failure rate of Canadian retail firms entering the American market, many of which assumed that the United States was merely a bigger version of Canada. Perceptions notwithstanding, real differences in consumer tastes, cultural values, and business practices exist between the two countries.[37]

EXHIBIT 8.5

When Multidomestic and Global Strategies Matter Most: Taking Advantage of Mismatches between Industry Character and Competitors' Strategies

Underlying Industry Character	Strategy Generally Used in Industry	Resulting Level of Industry Globalization (and Example)	Implications for Multinational Strategy and Performance
Most Global	Domestic	Under-globalized (Credit card industry)	Global strategies may offer real competitive advantages and higher performance relative to multidomestic strategies.
	Global	Optimum (Ship-building industry)	Global strategies may result in good perfomance but may not necessarily offer a competitive advantage relative to other firms.
Most Domestic	Domestic	Optimum (Funeral industry)	Multidomestic strategies may result in good performance but may not necessarily offer a competitive advantage relative to other firms.
	Global	Over-globalized (Tire industry)	Multidomestic strategies may offer real competitive advantages and higher performance relative to global strategies.

Source: Adapted from Birkinshaw, J., Morrison, A. & Hulland, J. (1995). Structural and competitive determinants of a global integration strategy. *Strategic Management Journal, 16:* 637–655.

Finally, culture can impact the extent to which firms take an ownership position in their foreign operations. For instance, multinationals based in high power distance, high uncertainty avoidance countries (e.g., France) are more likely to maintain majority ownership over foreign subsidiaries than multinationals based in low power distance, low uncertainty avoidance countries (e.g., the U.S.). And managers with a low power distance perspective are more likely to be comfortable establishing overseas operations where control is shared with a partner (e.g., as in a joint venture).[38] Consequently, our view is that international managers should consider how their values, perspectives, and viewpoints may shape their approach to strategy development and implementation.

Winning Big: Small Firms and International Strategy

Of course, thinking about cultural issues may seem like a luxury you can't afford if you're a small firm (i.e., a company with less than 500 employees). Put simply, developing and executing an international strategy is often a struggle for small firms.

The Strategy Struggle

Compared to large multinationals, small firms have fewer managerial and financial resources. Certain market entry strategies (such as building new plants overseas) may simply be beyond the reach of small firms' resources. On top of that, the strategic planning process in many small firms is reactive and informal instead of proactive and systematic as is often the case in large multinationals. In fact, some small firms may not even see the need for developing a specific international strategy to begin with.

Often small firms are preoccupied with their domestic business. And when they do make international contacts or otherwise attract attention from potential overseas customers, they may not respond well, as loads of unanswered e-mails and clogged fax machines will attest! Take the case of New York–based MMO Music, a small family-run business that makes the CDs used in karaoke machines. For years MMO lost overseas sales because the firm's president was so busy handling domestic growth that he couldn't respond quickly to foreign clients, much less develop an export strategy.

Many small firms also underestimate how much expertise, money, and time is needed to develop and execute an international strategy. For example, doing business in China usually means hammering out contracts in person. So a small firm's top management (often all the management there is!) might spend weeks in Beijing, usually after spending months trying to figure out China's business practices and trade laws. Not surprisingly, small firms sometimes let such opportunities pass or have trouble capitalizing on them.

Getting Help

Help is available for small firms, however. Even simple export deals can prove challenging for small firms because they lack overseas contacts or relevant expertise (e.g., on how to handle transportation issues or legal matters). Overcoming these challenges often means spending money and giving up some control, usually the hardest things for small firms to make themselves do. But after MMO finally hired an international sales director, its overseas sales tripled. Other small firms turn to consultants to learn exporting skills (e.g., how to pursue trade show leads). For instance, if you have a product to sell overseas, California-based Meridian Group can develop an export strategy and even implement it for you, managing sales, distribution, and shipping in the process.[39]

Government agencies are also there to help. For instance, small firms can visit the U.S. Department of Commerce's website (www.doc.gov) for help and advice. Actually, small companies may have to look no farther than their own city or state governments for assistance. In fact, local governmental agencies charged with supporting and promoting international trade often do an outstanding job. Many have grown and evolved their services to keep up with the number of small firms moving into the

REALITY CHECK

The Buckeye State Steps Up to Help Smaller Firms Succeed in International Business

A chat with Randy Hochstetter, Senior Commercial Officer, International Trade Division, State of Ohio (www.exportohio. state.oh.us)

Can you tell us what the International Trade Division is about?

We're about promoting international trade for the state of Ohio. Our customers are Ohio companies and we try to help them overcome the challenges they face in doing international business.

How has your mission evolved over the years?

Initially, we had a small office in Columbus and two overseas offices in Tokyo and Brussels. The overseas offices primarily focused on promoting foreign investment in Ohio, while the Columbus office focused on promoting overseas trade for Ohio firms. At the time, large American multinationals accounted for the bulk of U.S. exports.

Then in the mid-1980s, American exports grew rapidly and our emphasis shifted as small to medium-sized U.S. firms increased their participation in international business.

Exports from Ohio alone grew from $8.6 billion in 1986 to over $26 billion in 2000. This rapid growth increased the demand for trade promotion services in the state. Small to medium-sized firms are our core customers and we looked at their needs and where their overseas markets were located to better serve them. We ended up shifting the focus of the Tokyo and Brussels offices to trade promotion, something that would more directly serve Ohio companies. We also opened new trade offices throughout the 1990s, including in Hong Kong, Toronto, Mexico City, Tel Aviv, Sao Paolo, Johannesburg, Buenos Aires, and Santiago. Today we can pretty much deliver export promotion services to all our customers in all the regions of the world where they do business.

You referred to the challenges facing firms abroad. Can you elaborate?

Let me mention three challenges that are based on our experiences dealing with Ohio companies over the years. The first challenge is gaining market access. Protectionist policies in foreign countries still make it hard for some

international business arena. For an overview of how things have changed in one state agency, as well as some interesting perspectives on international business challenges, take a look at the accompanying Reality Check.

When Small Firms Succeed Overseas: Finding and Exploiting a Specialized Niche

Interestingly, small firms that have a specific international strategy tend to be manufacturers. For many of these companies, their international strategy is built around exporting a product with unique features or capabilities.[40] In fact, small, highly specialized firms are the most common type of company found in the international economy. Many are tiny start-ups that offer unique products for very narrow market segments. Ironically, these specialized firms seem to be most commonly found in global industries. Because they can focus on a specific product, have low overhead, accessible management, and make quick decisions, small specialists may be able to outperform large multinationals in global industries. For instance, offshore oil drilling equipment is basically a global industry, with a number of large multinationals competing. However, small firms in this industry have done well by providing very specific types of equipment for underwater drilling, with some equipment used only in certain water or seabed conditions.[41]

American firms to gain market share abroad. For example, it's very difficult for an American company to sell machinery in Brazil because of high duties and local taxes. This creates a protected market for local Brazilian machinery manufacturers.

A second and related challenge facing American firms is that the United States has been comparatively slow to make use of free trade agreements to reduce foreign trade barriers. The European Union has free trade agreements with over two dozen countries, while at the moment the United States has agreements with only three (Canada, Mexico, and Israel). This relative lack of free trade agreements puts American firms at a disadvantage. For example, Chile has a Canada-Chile free trade agreement which gives Canadian exports to Chile an additional 10 percent price advantage over potential U.S. exports. Some American companies will actually ship product from their Canadian operations to Chile to take advantage of the cost savings.

The third and perhaps biggest challenge really has to do with American companies themselves. Many small to medium-sized Ohio companies just don't have the resources to properly assess a foreign market and what's needed to penetrate it. Another complaint we hear is that companies lack the connections needed to meet the right people abroad and get business going. Companies must have the commit-ment of top management along with the budget and personnel to really go after international business. Without it, they fail.

I've talked with people who couldn't follow up after participating in an international trade mission or trade show because the boss said it would cost too much money. They had made the contacts and developed leads, in many cases with our help, but any potential business died because support from top management wasn't there. Many Ohio companies also need assistance in identifying possible agents and distributors because they don't have the time, resources, or even a full-time person assigned to international business activities. Even in some larger companies we've found no full-time international salesperson. Instead, you may see a V.P. of Sales who handles international leads when he or she has the time. So you can imagine follow-up often doesn't get done or falls short.

Any final thoughts?

Just that I can't emphasize enough that it takes so much time and effort to develop international business. We tend to underestimate that. I heard one presenter at a trade seminar who does a lot of business in China say it takes three Ps to do business there: Patience, patience, and patience.

The Process of Developing International Strategy

Up to this point, we've been saying that firms ought to develop an international strategy that best fits their competitive context. This raises the question of how international strategy is developed in the first place. According to one well-known approach, the process of developing international strategy consists of five steps. These steps are outlined in Exhibit 8.6 and we'll consider them next.

Step 1: The Mission Statement

Many firms start the process of developing an international strategy by creating a mission statement that summarizes key values and an overall purpose. Ideally, such a statement should express common goals in a way that succinctly captures management's vision for what the firm can accomplish.[42] For example, in its mission statement, motorcycle maker Harley-Davidson describes itself as "an action-oriented, international company—a leader in its commitment to continuously improve the quality of mutually beneficial relationships with stakeholders." Other firms eschew formal mission statements or produce them after much of the strategic planning process is complete. For instance, General Electric's mission statement was the result of a strategic planning process that involved the input of some 5,000 employees.[43]

EXHIBIT 8.6

The Process of Developing International Strategy

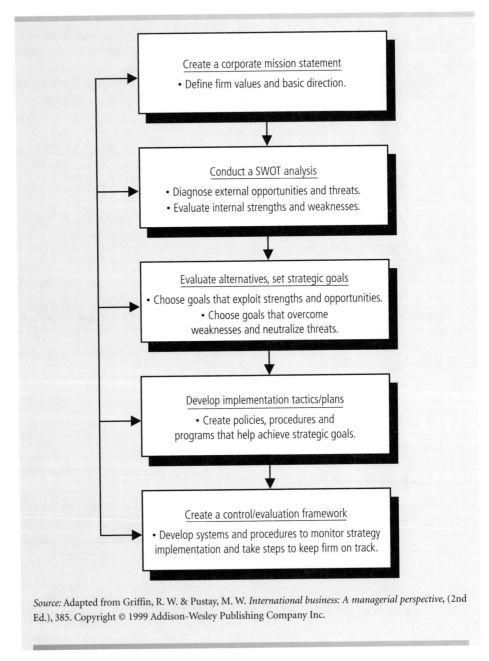

Source: Adapted from Griffin, R. W. & Pustay, M. W. *International business: A managerial perspective,* (2nd Ed.), 385. Copyright © 1999 Addison-Wesley Publishing Company Inc.

Step 2: Conducting a SWOT Analysis

Assuming a mission statement is developed first, the second step in creating international strategy is to perform a **SWOT analysis**. SWOT stands for **strengths**, **weaknesses**, **opportunities**, and **threats**. It involves an assessment of the company's internal circumstances and external environment. That assessment usually involves

INTERNATIONAL INSIGHTS

Krafting an International Strategy

KRAFT IS AN AMERICAN icon when it comes to food. Its more than five dozen brands are household names like Velveeta, Oscar Meyer, Triscuit, Planters, Lifesavers, and Maxwell House. The largest food corporation in the United States, Kraft is a giant. And thanks to its $19 billion acquisition of cracker and cookie maker Nabisco, Kraft's 2001 sales were around $35 billion. Interestingly, Kraft's majority shareholder is another giant. Philip Morris bought Kraft in 1988 and then sold about 16 percent of the company to the public in June of 2001.

But it may surprise you to know that Kraft, which has dominated American store shelves for decades, is something of an also-ran overseas. Less than 30 percent of Kraft's sales come from foreign markets. By comparison, Heinz earns 44 percent of its sales abroad, McDonald's comes in at over 50 percent, and Coca-Cola exceeds 80 percent. Walk through supermarkets in Australia, for instance, and you'll be hard pressed to find Kraft products. One Australian supermarket owner said that Kraft wasn't a major supplier and noted, "They would be classified as a slow-moving line." And in Great Britain, one of Kraft's strongest foreign markets, the company only ranks eighth in size among food companies.

And therein lies Kraft's growth challenge. The company badly wants to grow. But that's hard to do when your dominant market, the United States, is saturated and slow growing. If anything, the food business in the United States is nothing short of cutthroat. Brand loyalty is undercut by supermarkets' own brands and intense competition on price. Take salad dressing. Shoppers often just buy what's on sale— one week they buy Kraft, while the next it's Wish-Bone or Hellmann's.

So Kraft is turning to overseas markets for growth. And it's playing catch-up in a game in which the outcome is by no means assured. The global competition is formidable and includes the likes of Anglo-Dutch Unilever, Switzerland's Nestle, and France's Groupe Danone. All three moved rapidly into fast-growth emerging markets in Latin America, eastern Europe, and Asia. Nestle and Unilever both realize over 30 percent of their sales from developing countries alone. The contrast with Kraft couldn't be greater. As one expert said about Kraft, "A truly global organization would have a quarter to one-third of their business in North America, not three-quarters."

Part of the difficulty is that Kraft's forte, convenience foods, often has a tough time in foreign markets where basic foodstuffs are largely what people can afford. For instance, Unilever has done well in India by pushing basics like rice and salt. In contrast, Kraft's visibility in India is minuscule.

But Kraft has a two-pronged plan for boosting revenues in emerging markets. First, it plans to build its presence in countries where it already operates by expanding the range of products and brands it sells. Second, the company also wants to acquire local competitors, particularly in beverages and snacks, as a way to quickly enter emerging markets where it currently lacks a presence. Whether and to what extent these moves will help expand Kraft's international reach remains to be seen. That said, people around the world may be seeing more Kraft products on store shelves in the years ahead.[46]

environmental scanning, a process in which information about the internal and external situation facing the firm is collected and evaluated.

The external side of this equation is referred to as an **environmental analysis**. Here the company assesses both (1) **opportunities** that make international business more promising for its products or services (e.g., weak competition in certain markets); and (2) **threats** in foreign markets that could prevent those opportunities from being realized (e.g., increasing competition, political instability).[44]

Firms also can examine opportunities and threats at a multinational, regional, or country-specific level. Ideally, all three levels should be examined. From a multinational perspective, companies look at how worldwide trends might impact their businesses. For instance, many consumer products companies are optimistic about their long-term prospects for international sales growth because the number of people with disposable income is rising in developing countries.[45] As you might suspect, however, assessing external opportunities and threats is easier said than done, particularly for companies that have been largely domestic in their orientation. Such firms may lack the staff or expertise to conduct an environmental analysis, especially when it comes to international markets. Consequently, these firms may fail to perceive international opportunities or significant foreign threats to their business.

In any case, it's often difficult for companies to take advantage of international opportunities that do exist because of their internal weaknesses or pressure from competitors. Take a look at the International Insights about Kraft Food's international growth challenges to see what we mean.

Analyzing from a regional perspective involves looking at emerging trends in a particular geographic area. For example, some South American governments loosened regulations and improved their business infrastructures in recent years. And that created huge opportunities for multinationals specializing in construction, energy, and communications.[47]

Speaking of opportunities, Chinese companies have moved into Africa in a big way over the past decade. Of course, many multinationals are put off by what they feel are the region's negatives (e.g., poverty, political instability, poor infrastructure, etc.). But many Chinese mining, energy, and construction companies see these negatives as opportunities that they are uniquely qualified to take advantage of. In short, Chinese firms think they can fill needs in Africa that once were concerns in China. As the director of a Chinese well-digging firm doing business in Africa put it, "China doesn't need many new water wells. But Africans struggle to find drinking water every day." And Chinese investment isn't limited to infrastructure projects. Chinese consumer-products firms view Africa as a region where they can avoid tough competition from Japanese, European, and American multinationals. That perception led office-supply company Shanghai Hero Co. to build an $11 million facility in South Africa, giving it convenient access to the wider African market.[48]

Finally, environmental analysis can also take a country-specific perspective. This involves an analysis of the cultural, legal, economic, and political circumstances in a particular country as well as the opportunities or threats that they represent. For example, some years ago, multinationals wanting to do business in Saudi Arabia had to consider the fact that electricity was in short supply. The Saudi economy had been growing twice as fast as its electricity-generating capacity. Some multinationals canceled or delayed plans to build new facilities. Others installed diesel generators to keep things running during power blackouts.[49]

Before we move on, it's important to note that managers' "scanning abilities" may be slanted by their own cultural values or prior experiences in particular environments. Put another way, managers from different countries may pay attention to different things in the environmental scanning process. For instance, one study found that Nigerian managers paid more attention to governmental and political issues than their American counterparts. Conversely, American managers paid more attention to technology issues. In many developing countries like Nigeria, the political environment is unstable and can drastically affect business. The United States has a stable political system, but a rapidly changing technological environment. In short, managers coming from these contexts may have to adjust their "environmental scanning weights" when considering business opportunities in other countries.[50]

At this point, take a look at Exhibit 8.7. It presents the environmental scanning process that a marketing-based multinational might use (e.g., a packaged goods firm

EXHIBIT 8.7

The Environmental Scanning Process in a Marketing-Based Multinational

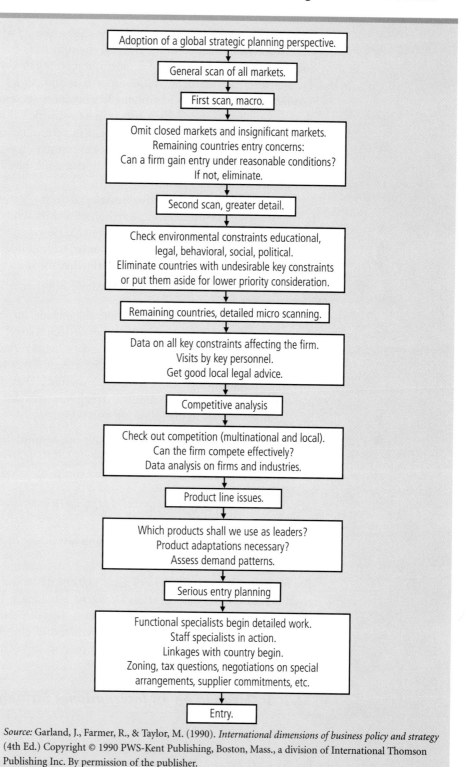

Source: Garland, J., Farmer, R., & Taylor, M. (1990). *International dimensions of business policy and strategy* (4th Ed.) Copyright © 1990 PWS-Kent Publishing, Boston, Mass., a division of International Thomson Publishing Inc. By permission of the publisher.

such as Procter & Gamble). The process often starts broadly before narrowing to the point where the multinational collects specific information in preparation for entry into a particular country. It's also important to note that what multinationals pay attention to in this process is usually driven by their own internal needs. For instance, a multinational that needs hard-to-obtain materials or highly skilled labor to produce its products will make these issues a priority when assessing where to put a new plant.[51] So multinationals' evaluation of the external environment often goes hand in hand with an assessment of their internal environment, something that we'll consider next.

The internal side of a SWOT analysis is sometimes referred to as an **internal resource audit**. It involves identifying **key business success factors**, things that a firm must accomplish to effectively compete in its industry. Exhibit 8.8 presents examples of key business success factors for companies in three different industries. These factors can vary over time as well as from country to country. In essence, firms want to see how their internal resources stack up against the demands they'll face in the countries where they do (or want to do) business.[52]

For instance, an effective distribution system is a key success factor for Wal-Mart. In fact, Wal-Mart's computerized warehouses and its ability to influence suppliers with large orders helps it keep prices low in the U.S. However, when it first opened stores in Mexico, Wal-Mart's Mexican suppliers wanted to ship smaller orders directly to stores, not warehouses. Wal-Mart had underestimated the difficulties of creating a Mexican version of its American distribution system and experienced lower initial sales in Mexico as a result.[53]

So the internal resource audit should include an evaluation of both internal strengths (e.g., a skilled workforce, superior technology) and weaknesses (e.g., high debt, poor name recognition, lack of international experience) relative to competitors. Firms typically want to build on distinctive strengths that would be tough for competitors to duplicate in the short term (i.e., strengths that might provide a sustainable competitive advantage).[54] To identify a strength as truly distinctive, management should be able to answer yes to the following questions:

- Does the strength help the firm exploit opportunities or avoid threats in international markets?
- Is the strength rare or unique, or do competitors possess similar "value-added" capabilities?
- Is the strength too difficult or expensive for competitors to duplicate or find substitutes for?
- Is the firm organized to take maximum advantage of the competitive potential of a strength?[55]

For instance, Japanese electronics giant Matsushita built a network of 150 plants scattered across dozens of countries. Doing so provided a buffer against currency and economic fluctuations in particular locations. This dispersed manufacturing capability, combined with cutting-edge technology and world-class brands like Panasonic, gives Matsushita a global presence that few competitors can match.[56]

Step 3: Deciding on an International Strategy and Setting Goals

After the SWOT analysis, the firm's next step is to adopt an international strategy. Ultimately, strategic goals should be set that exploit firm strengths and opportunities while neutralizing competitive threats and internal weaknesses. And that includes

EXHIBIT 8.8

Key Business Success Factors for Companies in Specific Industries

Industry	Key Success Factors
Processed Foods	● Taste ● Sales promotion ● Price ● Distribution channels ● Brand identification
Pharmaceuticals	● Product efficacy ● Product innovation ● Patents held/filed ● Company image
Automobiles	● Styling ● Service ● Quality ● Price ● Fuel efficiency ● Distribution system

Source: Phatak, A. V. (1995). *International dimensions of management,* (4th Ed.) 106. Copyright © 1995 South-Western College Publishing, Cincinnati, Ohio, a division of International Thomson Publishing Inc. By permission of the publisher.

deciding how broad or narrow the breadth and depth of the firm's international operations will be. For instance, will the firm

● Compete in specific countries or wherever opportunities exist?
● Offer all its products/services abroad or just a subset?
● Own its overseas operations or use other entry options (e.g., licensing)?

Once these general goals are set, more specific objectives can be developed.[57] These goals should be achievable and have a specific time frame for accomplishment.[58] Here are some areas where international goals might be set:

● **Profitability** (e.g., increase international profit growth 20%)
● **Production** (e.g., increase the ratio of foreign to domestic production)
● **Marketing** (e.g., integrate marketing efforts across European countries)
● **Finance** (e.g., minimize foreign exchange losses)
● **Technology** (e.g., successfully transfer technology to foreign subsidiaries)
● **Research and development** (e.g., disperse R&D capability world-wide)

Consider how Mercedes-Benz defined some of it strategic goals. Mercedes is a luxury brand that embodies German craftsmanship and quality. But high German labor costs, among other things, made it very difficult for Mercedes to export cars to North America at a profit. So Mercedes's strategic goal was to move a substantial amount of manufacturing capacity out of Germany and into the United States. Mercedes built an assembly plant in Alabama, allowing the firm to manufacture at lower cost in a key

Although it manufactures many of its cars abroad, Mercedes remains a symbol of German craftsmanship. © AFP/CORBIS

market. Likewise, Mercedes bought more components from non-German suppliers. On one hand, achieving these and related strategic goals may dilute Mercedes' image as the embodiment of German craftsmanship, something that could ultimately hurt sales. On the other hand, Mercedes's strong sales suggest that the risk of being seen as "less German" was worth taking, at least so far.[59]

Step 4: Developing Implementation Tactics and Plans

After strategic goals have been set, companies must develop specific plans and tactics that will deploy corporate resources (material, money, people, etc.) to achieve them. It may also mean developing new procedures or processes that help achieve firm goals, including taking specific steps to neutralize competitors. Basically, a support system must be in place to actually move the firm from where it is to where it wants to be internationally.[60]

That said, firms often underestimate what's needed to effectively compete abroad. PepsiCo Inc. may be a case in point. In the 1990s, the company decided that it wanted to increase international revenues some 300 percent. Consequently, the firm quickly expanded its global presence in foreign markets. Unfortunately, this expansion didn't result in higher profits or growth. In fact, by the late 1990s Pepsi was actually losing money overseas and pulled out of some important international markets. Experts suggest that to secure a competitive advantage in foreign markets, multinationals must carefully design and execute actions that support their international strategies and improve key value chain activities. For example, multinationals can neutralize a common advantage of local competitors—greater understanding of the local market—by developing products tailored to local preferences. Consider Japanese soft drink maker Suntory Ltd. It was one of the first local firms to introduce "Asian tea" drinks in response to local tastes. But multinational Coca-Cola countered by developing and offering "Sokenbicha," an Asian tea aimed only at the Japanese market. Of course, such tactics carry a number of risks. Adapting products for specific markets can increase costs. It can also prove wrongheaded, as restaurant chain TGI Fridays discovered when it set up shop in South Korea. Customers turned up their noses at its adapted menu, which included a variety of local specialities. The reason? Customers wanted and expected an "American" dining experience. This example underscores the difficulty of teasing out exactly when and how adapting products or services to local preferences makes good competitive sense.[61]

Companies in other industries face equally daunting challenges. For instance, Texas Instruments' (TI) semiconductor group wanted to establish a manufacturing and technology presence quickly to better absorb market growth wherever it occurred. That meant getting capital-intensive facilities and plants up and running in record time to preempt competitors. To achieve this, TI had to develop new tactics and practices. One of TI's unique moves was to create a ten-person team to facilitate the building of new plants worldwide. The team developed processes and procedures to set up world-class chip manufacturing plants some eight months faster than competing firms. For example, the team developed speedy ways to cut through red tape and find the quality local suppliers needed to build and help operate TI plants.[62]

Step 5: Putting Control and Evaluation Procedures in Place

This final step involves the control and evaluation procedures companies must put in place to make sure all the work done to this point isn't wasted and the firms' strategy implementation efforts stay on track. This "last" step is also about making sure companies can adjust, if not reinvent, their strategies as business circumstances change. Put simply, the development and implementation of international strategy is a dynamic and ongoing process.[63]

For example, in the 1980s and 1990s, Japanese car companies such as Nissan, Honda, and Toyota all built car plants in the United States to meet the needs of the American market. And by 2002, all three were building truck plants in the United States, assaulting a bastion of profitability for both Ford and GM. But when growing export demands needed to be met around the world, Japanese plants in the U.S. ramped up production in response. As a result, in 1995 Japanese firms actually shipped more cars abroad from their American plants than did GM, Ford, and Chrysler combined! This shift in strategy allowed Japanese automakers to take advantage of lower U.S. production costs relative to Japan. Moreover, the type of cars that emerging markets were clamoring for happened to be the ones the Japanese firms were already making in the U.S. For instance, Toyota met Chinese demand by shipping its Kentucky-built Avalons to China. Finally, their American plants helped Japanese firms sidestep import restrictions in Taiwan and South Korea on cars built in Japan. This strategic flexibility is one reason why Japanese car companies have proven to be such formidable international competitors.[64]

We conclude this section with an example of how one unique multinational develops its international strategy. Take a look at the following International Insights on Nokia.

INTERNATIONAL INSIGHTS

Nokia: Creating International Strategy from the Ground Up

HELSINKI-BASED NOKIA has grown spectacularly in recent years. In 1996, Nokia had 21 percent of the world's mobile phone market. By 2002, Nokia's market-leading share was almost one-third, more than second-place Motorola and third-place Ericsson combined. But 2001 was a tough year for Nokia, with mobile phone markets, save for emerging economies such as China, reaching the saturation point. Consequently, Nokia's growth and earnings sagged.

That said, optimists point to Nokia's industry-leading track record in design, marketing, and technology as reasons not to worry about the long term. One analyst criticized rival firms' heavy emphasis on outsourcing and cost cutting, noting the futility of making "ugly phones that no one wants." Much of Nokia's success results from a strategy development process that has proven adroit at predicting customer preferences. And that process can be traced back to CEO Jorma Ollila. A few months after he became CEO in 1992, Mr. Ollila felt that Nokia should become a global heavyweight in telecommunications. This basic mission has guided Nokia's strategy to this day. And given the industry's volatility, Mr. Ollila's operating strategy is to react quickly to changes in international markets. For instance, when Nokia overestimated how quickly digital phones would penetrate the United States, Ollila quickly turned loose independent "commando teams" of managers to fix the problem. Within months, they did (e.g., by refocusing marketing efforts).

Such involvement is also central to Nokia's efforts to anticipate future trends and adapt its strategy to match them. Nokia routinely brings together hundreds of managers from the dozens of countries where it operates. In small groups, they conduct brainstorming sessions to identify lifestyle and technological trends that represent opportunities for Nokia in various markets. The company also drills this captive audience on the need to understand local customers. For instance, Nokia responded to American football fanatics by making Dallas Cowboy phones. The company feels that involving line managers in this way generates ideas that would never come up otherwise. Nokia then uses a "strategy panel" of top managers that sifts through the ideas generated from these brainstorming sessions on a monthly basis.

But Nokia is also aware of internal weaknesses that it must struggle with in business downturns. When asked what the firm's biggest internal threat was, CEO Ollilia had a quick, one-word response: "complacency." Such self-awareness helps Nokia's managers stay focused on uncovering new opportunities. In the years ahead, Nokia will need all the help it can get. The company's newest high-stakes gamble centers around creating a mobile Internet network. So far, daunting technological and financial challenges have slowed progress. But Ollilia and Nokia have overcome challenges before. And we wouldn't bet against them.[65]

Organizational Requirements for Successful International Strategy

In this last section, we'll briefly discuss organizational features that can help companies develop and implement their international strategies. Consider a situation where a multinational competes in a global industry (or one that is evolving in that direction). There are many cases where multinationals in such circumstances fail to develop or implement a global strategy. That failure may reflect a lack of resources or the company's inability to grasp what's needed to execute a global strategy.

Supporting Organizational Features

Generally speaking, four organizational features have important implications for multinationals' ability to successfully develop and implement their international strategy:

- **Corporate structure** (the way reporting relationships in the multinational are put together and business units are organized)
- **Management processes** (the planning, budgeting, coordination, and performance appraisal activities and systems used to run the multinational)
- **Human resources** (the people who staff the multinational worldwide)
- **Corporate culture** (the expectations, values, beliefs, and unwritten rules that guide behavior and actions in the multinational)[66]

Multinationals must build characteristics into these organizational features that will support strategy development and implementation. When firm characteristics and strategic demands are aligned, better performance results.[67]

For example, a global strategy requires a corporate structure with some centralized global authority to assist global product development and make global decisions. This doesn't necessarily mean that "headquarters" makes all decisions. But some structure must exist to coordinate worldwide operations and make decisions, often with input from local operations. Having all units in a particular business line worldwide report to a global business manager is one way to accomplish this. GE Canada's lighting business is a case in point. In the past, this unit had to compete at GE corporate headquarters with all other GE business units in Canada to get its share of resources. Now the unit goes directly to the global head of lighting at GE for funding. We'll consider this and other structural options for international firms in more detail in Chapter 10.[68]

Management processes that facilitate global coordination and strategic decision making are also critical if companies are to respond quickly to the competitive environments they face. For example, companies may have more success developing and implementing global strategies if they use teams of key employees from different countries to make decisions with worldwide implications. Such teams can bridge cultural and geographic barriers to develop and execute complex global strategies effectively.[69]

Likewise, management processes may include specific capabilities that help the firm outperform competitors in areas that are important to customers. For instance, in the semiconductor industry this might involve developing cutting-edge chips more quickly than competitors. Identifying and developing capabilities that are complex and diffused through the company (they cut across functions) and that rely on well-developed interfaces (e.g., often sophisticated networks of informal communications) are best because they are tough for competitors to imitate.[70]

The structures and processes designed to support an international strategy are themselves supported by a firm's culture and human resources. For example, cultural values that emphasize global flexibility and responsiveness help give the firm a global identity and foster the development of global strategy. Exhibit 8.9 illustrates how corporate structure, culture, human resources, and management processes should be aligned to support a multinational with a global strategy. Of course, for other strategies, these organizational features will undoubtedly look different. For example, a corporate structure in which decision authority for products, marketing, and so on is delegated to foreign subsidiaries in specific countries makes sense for firms using a multidomestic strategy.

Designing a Fair Strategy Development Process

Finally, companies should pay attention to how strategy is created if they expect managers at subsidiaries around the world to behave accordingly. It turns out that if the

EXHIBIT 8.9

Corporate Features That Support a Global Strategy

General Area	Specific Corporate Feature Necessary
Corporate Structure	● Centralized global authority ● No international division ● Strong business dimension
Management Processes	● Global strategy information system ● Global strategic planning ● Cross-country coordination ● Global budgeting
Human Resources	● Global performance review and compensation ● Use of foreign nationals ● Frequent travel ● Statements and actions of leaders
Corporate Culture	● Global identity ● Commitment to worldwide employment ● Interdependence of businesses

Source: Adapted from Yip, G. S. (1995). *Total global strategy.* Englewood Cliffs, NJ: Prentice-Hall.

processes used to create strategies are perceived to be fair, then local managers are more likely to implement them. "Due process" in this case means that:

- headquarters makes a serious effort to familiarize itself with local operations.
- real two-way communication occurs when strategy is being developed.
- headquarters is consistent across subsidiaries in making decisions.
- local employees can challenge headquarters' strategic perspectives and decisions.
- local employees are given an explanation for the strategic decisions ultimately made.[71]

Chapter Summary

Figuring out how a company should compete abroad is part of international strategic management. Unfortunately, a surprising number of companies enter overseas markets without a clear, well-designed approach. This can lead to problems, such as (1) the inability to accurately predict the direction of foreign markets, (2) the poor use of resources abroad, (3) underestimating the resources needed to effectively compete, and (4) failing to anticipate operational problems in foreign environments. All international strategies should help firms decide (1) what products/services will be sold abroad, (2) where and how services will be delivered or products made, (3) what resources are necessary and how will they be acquired,

and (4) how competitors will be outperformed.

Firms make money through *value creation*, offering products or services that customers want. One way to do that is by *differentiating* products from competitors. Another tack is the *low-cost approach*. Finally, a *niche strategy* involves focusing on a specific line of products or services relative to competitors who operate more broadly. A company can also add value by changing any of the *primary* or *supporting activities* in its *value chain*. International strategy is ultimately about how value chain activities are *configured* and *coordinated*. *Core competencies* can be located anywhere in the value chain and are the basis for international competitiveness. Firms often compete by moving value chain activities to wherever *location economies* exist.

The *theory of national competitive advantage* explains how specific countries can help companies obtain a competitive edge. *Factor conditions* describe whether a nation has the components for competitive production in an industry. *Demand conditions* describe the markets in a country for certain goods and services. *Related and supporting industries* describe whether competitive suppliers or related industries exist in a country. *Firm strategy*, *structure*, and *rivalry* describes how the local environment affects firms in a particular country.

Four strategies used by multinationals were discussed. *Multidomestic strategies* may be best when local product or service preferences vary considerably and integration pressures in an industry are low. *Global strategies*, in contrast, work best in industries where the same products can be sold everywhere and integration pressures are high. A *transnational strategy* may be appropriate when firms need to move value chain activities to wherever they can be done best but still must adapt products to local preferences. A *regional strategy* represents a compromise between global and multidomestic approaches. After presenting these strategies, we discussed how the match or mismatch between international competition in an industry and the industry's underlying character can impact the effectiveness of a firm's strategy. We also discussed how differences in cultural values and perspectives can influence the strategies that managers pursue. Finally, we considered some of the limitations that small firms face in developing international strategies, particularly in terms of their limited financial and managerial resources. Overcoming these limitations often means seeking help (e.g., from consulting firms and government agencies), which is readily available.

Next, we outlined the process of creating international strategy, which consists of five key steps. First, firms often develop a mission statement. Second, companies conduct a *SWOT analysis*. The internal side of a SWOT analysis is called an *internal resources audit* and involves an assess-

ment of both internal strengths and weaknesses. The external side of the equation is an *environmental analysis* that involves the assessment of external opportunities as well as external threats. Next comes the actual selection of a strategy and goals, followed by the development of implementation tactics and plans. Finally, steps have to be taken to monitor strategy implementation on an ongoing basis.

We concluded by pointing out that organizational features such as corporate structure, management processes, human resources, and corporate culture all need to be aligned with a firm's international strategy to maximize performance. Likewise, companies need to realize that if the processes used to develop strategy are perceived to be fair, managers worldwide are more likely to act accordingly. To create fairness, company managers should, among other things, make a serious effort to familiarize themselves with local operations and ensure two-way communication with local employees when developing international strategy.

Discussion Questions

1. What is the value of having a coherent international business strategy?
2. What factors determine national competitive advantage?
3. Explain the differences between global, transnational, and multidomestic strategies. What roles do industry and firm characteristics play in the choice of strategy?
4. What is a SWOT analysis? What do you do with the results?
5. What organizational features are needed to successfully develop and implement a global strategy?

Up to the Challenge?

Jollibee's Strategy for Chewing Up McDonald's

A T THE BEGINNING of the chapter, we asked you to think about how Jollibee could outperform global giant McDonald's in the Philippines. Now's your chance to see how close you came to matching Jollibee's competitive moves. Jollibee decided that it had to copy certain aspects of McDonald's own approach that clearly work across borders. Specifically, Jollibee felt it had to offer the same type of clean and speedy service that McDonald's offers worldwide. Jollibee strictly adheres to what it calls its "FSC"

standards for excellence ("food, service, cleanliness") in all outlets. Employee training is comprehensive, and pay and benefits lead the fast-food industry in the Philippines. Jollibee also makes much of its own food products in two centrally located "commissaries" in the Philippines (one ships almost 70 tons of Jollibee products daily). In setting up new outlets, Jollibee goes after prime locations. In fact, it often surrounds McDonald's outlets in the Philippines with restaurants of its own. Finally, Jollibee aggressively markets itself to kids with in-store novelties, activities, and signature characters—just like McDonald's.

That said, Jollibee felt that it had to outperform McDonald's in certain areas to gain a competitive advantage. The best way to do that was to be more local than the Big Mac. First, the company incorporated unique aspects of Philippine culture in developing its service delivery model. Anytime a customer approaches a Jollibee counter, employees say, "*Magandang umaga po*, welcome to Jollibee." The first part of this phrase is a traditional Filipino greeting and is designed to underscore the company's local heritage as well as create an atmosphere of humble Filipino hospitality, something that its customers relate to. On top of that, Jollibee prices its food lower than comparable items at McDonald's, taking advantage of weak local economic conditions. The firm's "value meals," for instance, cost only $1–2.

Perhaps most important, Jollibee offers a broader menu than McDonald's, one that strongly plays to Filipinos' sweet-and-spicy tastes. These flavors are incorporated across Jollibee's entire menu, from chicken to noodles to hamburgers. For example, the Aloha Burger is a Jollibee concoction that includes a layer of pineapple, while Palabok Fiesta is a noodle and meat sauce dish topped with smoked fish, deep fried pork skin, bean curd, and onions. Along with the spicy flavors, Jollibee serves rice with its meals, another local preference (or you can opt for french fries).

Of course, whether Jollibee can maintain its edge over McDonald's indefinitely remains to be seen. McDonald's, well known for its flexibility, responded to Jollibee's success by spicing up the food it sells in the Philippines. And as legal restrictions about foreign ownership fell away in the Philippines, McDonald's was in a better position to open more company-owned outlets and use its financial clout to regain ground lost to Jollibee.

Ironically, Jollibee's own foreign expansion brought it face-to-face with some of the same difficulties McDonald's encountered in the Philippines and other international locations. Jollibee brought only a portion of its menu to the American market in order to test reactions and build a reliable supplier base. Nevertheless, Jollibee found that it still had to make adjustments, including offering larger portions in the United States than it did in the Philippines. Other surprises were more pleasant. Jollibee's foreign outlets tend to be located in areas with large populations of Filipino expatriates. But in California, only 50 percent of Jollibee's customers had connections to the Philippines. In fact, one Jollibee manager said that Americans were acquiring some Filipino tastes. He noted that his non-Filipino customers in California "love the Aloha Burger and they return to the store and order it again and again."

That said, what kinds of challenges is Jollibee likely to face if it continues to expand in foreign markets? How should it respond? Do you worry about Jollibee's ability to stay on top in its home market? If so, what can Jollibee do to maintain its dominance in the Philippines (see www.jollibee.com)?[72]

 ## International Development
Is It Global or Local?

Purpose

To develop your thinking about why some products and services might be more global in nature while others are more local.

Instructions

Your instructor will divide the class into small groups of three to six and ask you to consider the following list of products and services (your instructor may add to the list). Specifically, each group should place each item into one of four categories and come up with a rationale for their choices (this will take about 20 minutes).

● **Pure Global** (Product/service can be sold everywhere without variation)
● **Leaning Global** (Product/service can be sold everywhere with minor variations)
● **Leaning Local** (Product/service has some features that must be tailored for local markets)
● **Pure Local** (Extensive changes must be made across local markets to sell the product/service)

Product/Service List: Global or Local?

Life insurance	Industrial solvents
Household floor cleaners	Shaving cream
Construction equipment	Coffee
Digital cameras	Cardboard containers
Washing machines	

Next, each group will make a brief report to the class and explain their reasoning (this should take about 15 minutes). Your instructor will record the responses for each item. After that, your instructor will lead a general discussion and ask you to consider the following questions (this should take about 10 minutes). If class time is insufficient, your instructor may make this a written assignment that is researched outside of class. Another alternative that your instructor may select to save time is to ask you to meet in groups outside class but then share your findings during class time.

Discussion Questions

1. What are the features that make certain products or services more global? More local?
2. Could certain products or services be sold or presented identically within a region but not across regions? Why or why not?

3. Are certain products or services likely to move more toward the global side of the ledger in the years ahead? Why or why not? What about the reverse?

From Theory To Practice
Conducting a Company Situation Analysis

Purpose

To find out more about a company's international business situation relative to competitors and to experience part of the analytical process involved in developing international strategy.

Instructions

Your instructor will divide the class into groups of three to six people. Each group should interview a senior manager (preferably one with responsibility for a major line of business) at a local company that has some international activity. Ideally, the interview should focus on a specific line of business. For instance, if you interview managers at diversified companies like Procter & Gamble, you should focus on specific product lines sold abroad, such as diapers and toothpaste, since strategies are often different across business lines.

The interview should cover the issues listed here. Ideally, the manager should answer questions for the business line he or she is responsible for in the company and also should answer the same questions for two or three major competitors.

1. *The nature of management*

   - Is the company's vision global or basically domestic?
   - Are there foreigners in senior management positions?
   - How extensive is the cross-cultural training for managers?

2. *Company strategy*

   - Is there a global plan governing all countries or regions?
   - How willing is the firm to embrace alliances with foreign firms?
   - Do units in different foreign locations operate independently or as a single global company?
   - How important is global enviromental scanning in the company?
   - To what extent does the home country control key decisions?

3. *Operational issues*

   - Where are the company's major facilities located (in the home country or abroad)?
   - Are product design decisions centralized or decentralized?
   - Are manufacturing decisions centralized or decentralized?

After the interview is completed, each group should make an assessment about the extent to which the company (and its major competitors) operates as a global firm. Each group should then develop recommendations about what the company can do to either (1) close the gap with competitors in terms of international practices or (2) maintain the advantages the company already enjoys.

Depending on the class and time available, your instructor may ask you to conduct additional research about the company interviewed and its industry before you come up with group recommendations. These recommendations could be part of your group presentations or even be written up and given to the companies interviewed.

Assuming a more basic assignment, each group should make a 15-minute class presentation about their findings (allow 20 minutes if presentations are to include the group's own recommendations). Your instructor will then lead a class discussion (another 15–20 minutes), focusing on these issues:

- How "globalized" were the companies interviewed? Did they generally tend to be ahead or behind their competition in this regard? Why or why not?
- What industry, firm, or competitive factors might account for the differences or similarities observed across firm practices?

An Alternative Approach

If the class size is too large or other contraints (e.g., time, availability of senior executives) make an interview approach impractical, your instructor may convert this activity into a library research assignment. You may be asked to do an in-depth analysis of the strategic approach taken by a particular international company or even an industry group. If so, you may also be asked to use the interview questions listed to predict the responses that senior managers in the company or industry might make.

Jumping In: Foreign Market Entry and Ownership Options

International Challenge

GM, Ford, and Toyota:
Driving in Different Directions Internationally?

LEARNING OBJECTIVES

After reading this chapter, you should be able to

● Describe the various stages of international development that firms sometimes pass through and how this transitioning relates to foreign market entry.

● Describe the strengths and weaknesses of various foreign market entry options that do not require ownership.

● Describe the strengths and weaknesses of various foreign market entry options that require some ownership responsibilities.

● Understand the different types of strategic alliances between international companies and why they are used.

THERE'S BEEN A TREND TOWARD consolidation in the automotive industry in recent years. Today, about 75 percent of the cars sold worldwide come from just six groups of car companies. They include GM, Ford, DaimlerChrysler, Toyota, Volkswagen, and Renault-Nissan. A big chunk of that consolidation came in 1998 with the massive takeover that created DaimlerChrysler. But companies with big global footprints still have to deal with the fact that the world's consumers often have wildly different preferences when it comes to cars. For instance, Asian customers tend to want small cars that can dart in and out of narrow, crowded city streets. Take China, where most customers want high-quality but low-cost subcompacts. In response, Ford in 2002 moved to sell a $12,000 version of its Ikon subcompact in China, a vehicle originally made for the Indian market. In the United States, however, Ford must play to the American love affair with large trucks and lumbering SUVs through offerings like its Explorer and Expedition.

America's two car giants, GM and Ford, have done business overseas for years, but the two competitors have taken somewhat different strategic routes. Yes, both have tried to become more flexible and get out of the parts manufacturing business to a good degree, with each firm spinning off parts operations into separate companies (e.g., GM established Delphi and Ford set up Visteon). Both auto giants want to buy from whatever supplier provides the best parts at the best price.

But GM has also decided to pursue alliances big time, often involving partial stock swaps in the process. In 2000, GM grabbed a 20 percent stake in Fiat, while Fiat picked up 6 percent of GM. The alliance with Fiat is GM's largest to date. Nevertheless, GM's focus is to coordinate its alliances by management control rather than by ownership control. That explains why the firm tends to take minority instead of majority stakes in its alliance partners.

GM's goal is to evolve into a true global automobile company, not just continue to be a U.S. giant with large subsidiaries scattered around the world. In addition to Fiat, GM also has effective control over Sweden's Saab and Japanese car firms Isuzu and Suzuki. Nevertheless, some analysts are skeptical, particularly since the benefits associated with these alliances have, at least as of 2002, yet to fully materialize. According to one razor-tongued critic, GM is "a redneck company that wants to be global but does not know how."

Of course, GM begs to differ. The company says that its approach is to meet local tastes by partnering with foreign automobile firms with relevant expertise. The result, at least in theory, is a network of alliances that will allow GM to grow more quickly at a lower cost. There are no expensive mergers, both partners benefit, and the political problems associated with foreign takeovers are sidestepped. According to some, for instance, the DaimlerChrysler "merger" is a poster child for just about everything that can go wrong when firms from different countries combine. Billed as something of a merger of equals, critics argue that DaimlerChrysler is really the product of a takeover of Chrysler (U.S.) by Daimler (Germany). And that's the kind of experience GM says it's trying to avoid (i.e., misjudged "synergies," hefty acquisition premiums, and clashing cultures and management styles).

That said, alliances come with their own challenges, not the least of which is that partners often compete, rather than cooperate, in certain areas. And that can make things awkward when it comes to the areas where the partners do want to play ball together. For instance, in the next decade, the bulk of the growth in the auto industry is predicted to come from the Asia-Pacific region, an area where Japanese automakers have been dominant. But Western firms like Ford, GM, and BMW have been rushing into places like Thailand and building manufacturing capacity. So at one point, "partners" GM and Fiat were actually bidding against each other for Daewoo, the defunct South Korean car company. GM won the bidding war in 2001, paying what seemed like a paltry sum of $400 million (building one new plant usually costs GM more). But Daewoo, with its ongoing union troubles and lackluster reputation overseas, is no bed of roses for GM. Nevertheless, GM hopes that Daewoo will give it access to faster growing Asian markets and even help it fine-tune its small car lineup in the United States.

Daewoo aside, GM's constellation of alliances accounts for about a quarter of all the cars sold on the planet. Clearly, GM is the world's biggest car producer. Lurking in the background, however, are Ford and Toyota. Both want to become the world's strongest automotive company and use alliances to an extent. Likewise, both have developed a global network that ostensibly reflects their "global" strategies. So here's your challenge. What approach do you think Ford and Toyota have come up with to battle GM on a worldwide basis? Is there a strategy that is superior to GM's alliance-heavy approach? Think about these questions as you read through this chapter, especially our sections on modes of entry in foreign markets and their associated pros and cons. If you can, do a little research on the international auto industry and on Toyota, Ford, and GM in particular. Then take a look at the Up to the Challenge box at the end of the chapter for a glimpse of Ford's and Toyota's strategy as well as some of the difficulties that all the major automakers face.[1]

Taking the Plunge

This chapter examines the options companies have for entering foreign markets. Choosing an option is often the first concrete step companies take to execute their international strategies. Of course, how companies choose to proceed is often a direct reflection of that strategy in the first place. But a host of other factors also drive firms' choices, including the pros and cons of the various entry options, the nature of the foreign market, and the firm's level of international development (and how successful it is). We'll consider some of these factors in this chapter.

Stages of International Development

Let's start that process by considering the impact of companies' level of international development. A small company might first dip into foreign markets by exporting. As we'll see later, exporting is a common option for small firms since it doesn't require large capital outlays (e.g., to set up foreign plants, etc.). But as companies grow and evolve, they may, for instance, move from relying on exports to building manufacturing facilities overseas. That said, the international developmental process we'll describe is anything but exact. In other words, many firms will not develop in a clear sequence of steps or move in a linear fashion through the general stages we outline here. For instance, companies can jump from exporting to establishing an international division without establishing an overseas sales subsidiary first. Likewise, overseas acquisitions may allow firms to leapfrog some steps.[2]

And consider the basic dichotomy between service and manufacturing firms. A manufacturing firm is more likely to go through a gradual series of stages as it expands internationally. In contrast, service companies, like banks or insurance providers, essentially have to jump in with both feet when they decide to become international, often through an acquisition. Unlike manufacturing firms, service companies don't have the luxury of starting out slowly and gaining experience (e.g., by exporting a product overseas) before setting up operations abroad.

For instance, GE Capital, the financial services arm of parent GE, lends money and offers insurance worldwide. Accounting for a big slice of GE's corporate profits, GE Capital has arguably become a master at setting up foreign operations quickly, either building them from scratch or rapidly integrating foreign acquisitions. A few years ago, GE Capital bought troubled Toho Mutual, a Japanese insurance firm. In short order, GE Capital installed its own procedures and accounting methods while scrapping Toho Mutual's seniority-based personnel system.[3]

Nevertheless, many firms evolve through relatively distinct stages as they become more sophisticated in their international operations. Not surprisingly, there are different perspectives about how to define those stages.[4] But most experts assume that companies can be successful in any stage and that the time it takes companies to progress through internationalization stages varies. Take a look at Exhibit 9.1. It presents a six-stage framework for understanding the process of internationalization.

Stage 1: exporting   In stage 1, a domestic company begins internationalizing by exporting its products or services to foreign customers. This may include marketing of products or services abroad, perhaps through an export department run by a manager and small supporting staff. Such departments typically rely on and are considered ancillary to the firm's domestic sales and marketing activities. In other cases, domestic firms that are new to international business may turn to banks or export management firms to handle most export-related activities and provide the necessary expertise (e.g., dealing with documents, currency issues, shipping, and letters of credit). Mail-order company L. L. Bean is an example of a stage 1 firm. The company largely serves the U.S. market but also exports to a variety of countries.[5]

EXHIBIT 9.1

Common Stages in the Process of Corporate Internationalization

Stage 1: Export
Stage 2: Sales subsidiary
Stage 3: International division
Stage 4: Multinational
Stage 5: Global or transnational
Stage 6: Alliances, partners, and consortia

Source: Adapted from Briscoe, D. R. (1995). *International human resource management.* Englewood Cliffs, NJ: Prentice-Hall.

As overseas sales continue to grow, some firms may feel the need to contract with distributors to represent their products abroad (e.g., to promote products, answer questions, provide follow-up service, etc.). For an example of how a small company uses overseas distributors to support its export efforts, take a look at the following Reality Check on Systran Corporation.

Stage 2: Sales subsidiary   As you can see in our Reality Check, Systran is content to rely on distributors to represent its products. However, if Systran decides to open overseas sales offices in the future, the firm would essentially move to stage 2. That point is reached when a firm establishes sales offices or sales subsidiaries in a foreign country. Up until recently, U.S. motorcycle-maker Harley-Davidson was the quintessential example of a stage 2 firm. Strong growth in foreign markets prompted Milwaukee-based Harley-Davidson, which exports around 25 percent of its motorcycles, to set up overseas offices to provide marketing and sales support.

Stage 3: International division   As you might expect, this stage usually involves the assembly and production of a significant amount of product overseas. Sometimes this stage represents a natural progression from the creation of overseas sales subsidiaries. In other cases, companies move from exporting to setting up an international division in one fell swoop. Regardless, establishing an international division means that a more sophisticated organizational structure has been developed to oversee all forms of foreign market activity and to support future expansion in international operations. Usually, an international division also means that the company has decided to invest more heavily in staff who are knowledgeable about international business.

For instance, a few years ago Harley-Davidson established its first foreign assembly operation. The company began shipping motorcycle kits to Brazil for final assembly and subsequent sale. So while the overwhelming majority of Harley-Davidson motorcycles continue to be manufactured and assembled in the United States, Harley-Davidson is arguably evolving toward stage 3. In many cases, the move to overseas production is

REALITY CHECK

Systran Corporation Makes International Business Compute

A chat with Susan Chicoine, chief operating officer, Systran Corporation

Can you tell us a little about your company and its products?

Systran (www.systran.com) is a privately held company with 100 employees. We design and manufacture seven different product lines. Each product line is specialized for various high-speed computer data communications. Our products are used in a variety of applications, including simulation, data acquisition and control, avionics, mass storage, virtual reality, industrial process control, and imaging systems, to name some examples. We have different competitors depending on which product line we're talking about. Most of them operate outside the United States using distributors, but some have opened their own field offices internationally.

What about Systran? How have you decided to sell your products internationally?

We've chosen to use agents and distributors to resell our products overseas. Today, we have nineteen distributors that cover forty countries for us. And we have no plans to open offices outside the United States at the moment. Our first entry into international business was back in 1990. The

strategy was to find a single master distributor that could effectively sell our products into as many western European countries as possible. About two years later, a company in Japan contacted us about reselling our products. The company liked our cutting-edge technology. We were thrilled and felt lucky because entry into Japan is so difficult. Today we have three distributors in Japan and they all cover different markets with only a tiny overlap. Since the mid-1990s we've transitioned to using individual distributors in most European countries. And we've also expanded into eastern Europe, India, China, Australia, the Middle East, Turkey, Russia, Argentina, Brazil, and South Africa. A very important point is that excellent customer service is critical to success, especially outside the United States. So early on, we actually turned down overseas opportunities until we learned to provide excellent international customer service.

How do you find overseas distributors or assess the distributors who approach you?

In many cases, distributors have approached us because they'd heard about our products. Some of it is following up on people that I know or have worked with before. Our intent with distributors is to find someone who understands our products technically, has a good reputation and a presence in

---

accompanied by a decision to create a separate international division that is responsible for monitoring and controlling all overseas operations from the home office.

Stage 4: Multinational The remaining stages describe more complex multinational operations that may evolve over time. In stage 4, companies recognize that while headquarters may need to play a key role in making important strategic decisions, local operations often do best when staffed by local employees who have a keen understanding of the environment. In fact, the role of the foreign subsidiary in stage 4 is to serve the needs of the national or regional market where it is located. But achieving the right balance between headquarters control and local fine-tuning usually doesn't come easy.

J. C. Penney's foray into the Brazilian market is a good case in point. To enter the market, J. C. Penney bought Lojas Renner, a family-run regional department store chain. But rather than turning Lojas Renner into just another J. C. Penney outpost, the company kept things local. After running into trouble in other countries, J. C. Penney realized that successful retailing can often be a very localized phenomenon. So J. C. Penney didn't want to lose the local skills that were the backbone of Lojas Renner's outstanding reputation for service and value. Consequently, J. C. Penney kept the Lojas Renner name on storefronts in Brazil and kept the local management team in place to

their own country, speaks the local language, and understands the local culture. That formula has worked for us over the past twelve years. We've also sold directly into some countries where we didn't feel there was enough business to seek out a distributor or where we are exploring a new market or application for our products.

But if we want to find distributors in a country and no one has contacted us, there are several things that we can do. One is to talk to the companies that use our products and ask for recommendations. Another is to talk with people we know or have worked with before. Many of them are high-tech firms like ourselves that pursue markets that are similar to ours (and in many cases we now share the same distributors). We also work closely with the U.S. Department of Commerce. They make connections for us at embassies and help set up interviews with distributors and customers. We also search the web to identify potential distributors.

How do you see things at Systran evolving in the future?

We are constantly reviewing our distribution approach and making changes to fine tune things and make sure we have the right distributor for the right product in the right place in the right market. Sometimes changes in our market strategy for a particular product will prompt changes in the distributors we use.

Do I see us opening international offices staffed by our own people in the future? Maybe in five or ten years but not now. Opening such sales or support offices creates an entirely new set of issues that we don't need to tackle right now. We are fortunate to have two very competent, full-time people in our home office who are dedicated to the international portion of our business. The way we've chosen to approach international business works very well for us.

What do think are your key competitive weapons for international business?

First, we receive excellent support from the CEO on down the management chain. Second, international distribution takes patience and persistence. For example, it took us three years to make our first sale into China. Third, we are very big on cultural aspects. We do business in other countries as they do business, not as we do business in America. It's important to have distributors who understand the language and culture and not force them to do things "the American way". And fourth, we believe in building relationships with our overseas distributors. That's especially important in the Asia-Pacific area. We focus on getting to know distributors and their families. In many countries, a personal touch and outstanding customer support are more important than they are in the U.S. We're proud to say that the feedback we get tells us we're doing a better job of customer support than many of our competitors. I believe people buy from people, not from businesses. If we don't take care of our customers and the people who are selling and servicing our products around the world, then someone else will.

run things. Those steps, along with J. C. Penney's financial help, allowed Lojas Renner to grow more than 100 percent in two years.[6] Wal-Mart, the world's biggest retailer, arguably hasn't gone quite as far as J. C. Penney in its willingness to project a local image and rely on local expertise. For some, that reluctance suggests that Wal-Mart doesn't fully embrace a multinational perspective just yet. Indeed, some critics suggest that Wal-Mart struggles with a "headquarters knows best" mentality and lacks sufficient international business experience in its top management ranks. They claim that Wal-Mart largely relies on its "American approach" overseas and needs to introduce more local products to its foreign stores. In contrast, France's Carrefour, which operates in over thirty countries, says that over 90 percent of the products in its stores are local in origin. As one Carrefour executive explained, "In China, we are Chinese; in Spain, we are Spanish." Dutch competitor Ahold goes even farther, operating under different store names and emphasizing local brands in the more than two dozen countries where it operates. As Ahold's CEO put it, "Everything the customer sees we localize. Everything they don't see we globalize."

Despite its belief that overseas growth will be a profit engine in the future, Wal-Mart lags behind some of its overseas competitors, operating in just nine countries at the beginning of 2002. Moreover, some of Wal-Mart's recent forays abroad (e.g., in Germany, Indonesia, and Argentina) suffered big losses, at least initially. In Germany,

Wal-Mart initially experienced difficulties when it entered the German market. © AFP/CORBIS

for instance, Wal-Mart didn't fully understand German shoppers, government regulations, and the pervasive role of German unions, much less the competitive landscape. And according to Wal-Mart's CEO, "incompetent management" didn't help, either. Wal-Mart now aims to have all its overseas retail teams led by locals rather than American expatriates. The company also is taking steps to be more culturally savvy and to look for outstanding ideas overseas that can help its domestic operations back in the United States (e.g., by soliciting more input and reaction from local employees as well as shoppers in foreign markets). That said, it would be wise not to underestimate Wal-Mart over the long haul, as its rising overseas sales figures will attest. Already Wal-Mart is the number one retailer in both Canada and Mexico. The rest of the world may be next.[7]

Stage 5: Global or transnational   Speaking of the rest of the world, it's a more global or transnational orientation that marks companies in stage 5. Of course, some companies never reach this point, perhaps because their industries don't require operational integration worldwide. As we discussed back in Chapter 8, companies that operate on a global or transnational basis try to ignore geographical boundaries in terms of their ongoing operations. In short, they will build product, source materials, or perform services anywhere in the world if doing so somehow minimizes costs and maximizes returns. Doing this requires flexibility, interdependence across all units, and a global management perspective, among other things. However, a transnational orientation also will allow for location-specific tailoring of products or services, often to a surprising degree. And for large, diverse companies like General Electric, assessing whether the firm operates "globally" or "transnationally" really makes little sense. Instead, it's up to each business unit (e.g., plastics, medical imaging, etc.) to decide how local it needs to be to succeed against the competition.[8]

Stage 6: Alliances, partners, and consortia   Stage 6 highlights the fact that firms are increasingly linking up, often to leverage their combined resources (such as people, equipment, technology, and research). For many multinationals, various partnerships and alliances are a way to access resources that they believe are either too expensive or otherwise impossible to secure alone.[9] So multinationals are rushing to form joint ventures and other types of cooperative alliances. Telecommunications giant MCI/WorldCom subcontracts out much of its own research and development to other companies. In doing so, it gains access to the intellectual horsepower of thousands of scientists and engineers who are not company employees. Likewise, DaimlerChrysler, Mistubishi Motors, and Hyundai are partnering to jointly develop a new engine that might enter production as early as 2004. By sharing key technologies and minimizing development costs, the three companies hope to use the engine, in a variety of configurations, in cars sold in Europe, Asia, and the United States. As one auto executive put it, "You collaborate or die. You must achieve economies of scale."[10]

Despite the increasing popularity of such linkages, building trust between partners can be quite difficult, especially when the firms involved are separated by cultural differences. However, even these gaps can be bridged. For instance, one study found that American automotive suppliers developed greater trust with Japanese automakers operating in the U.S. than with American automakers. One factor that seemed to make a difference was the greater tendency for the Japanese firms to be helpful (e.g., by sending consultants to help American partners for months on end without charge). In short, to build trust in partnerships, you may have to give it first.[11] We'll address these and related human resource management issues in future chapters.

Foreign Market Entry Options

Our discussion so far suggests several options for firms when it comes to entering foreign markets. But what we haven't done yet is to present all of the entry options in detail, along with their respective pros and cons. That's the purpose of this section. It may surprise you to learn that there's quite a variety of entry possibilities. And one theme that will emerge from our presentation is that the choice of entry mode reflects both the entry barriers that exist in certain foreign markets as well as the resources that firms have to overcome those barriers.[12] Of course, how much time a firm has, its strategic goals, and the opportunities present in foreign markets also help drive entry choices. That said, Chapter 10 will explore in more detail some of the factors driving the entry choices companies ultimately make.

Entry without Ownership

In this section we consider entry options that don't involve ownership of overseas facilities or plants. The next section will focus on entry options that involve at least partial ownership of overseas assets. In both sections, we'll evaluate the pluses and minuses of various options and the circumstances that might make them most attractive.

Exporting Exporting involves sending goods or services to other countries where they can be sold. And as we've said, many companies' first exposure to international business is through exporting. Part of the reason for this is that there is no foreign ownership required and, as a consequence, the costs of exporting are low, at least compared to other options. Likewise, exporting allows companies to shift gears relatively painlessly since export agreements can generally be terminated fairly quickly and inexpensively. Another plus is that as companies start exporting to foreign markets, they can use initial feedback from customers to further tailor their products and increase their overseas business. In fact, quick profits may not be the primary motivation for many small firms' forays into exporting. Instead, learning about new markets, new technologies, and new ways of doing things also are key motivations.[13]

But cost containment isn't only an issue for small firms. Manufacturing products in one place and then exporting them abroad can help bigger companies, like Boeing, take advantage of economies of scale. On the other hand, by not moving manufacturing overseas, firms may miss out on foreign location economies that represent long-term advantages, such as cheaper labor.[14]

There are also costs associated with exporting that shouldn't be overlooked. For instance, shipping the product, setting up a distribution system, and buying foreign advertising can carry hefty price tags. Some large firms feel they must make substantial direct investments overseas to support their exporting activities. To help sell the cars it exported to Japan, Chrysler at one point spent $100 million to buy Japanese car dealerships, sank another $10 million on a parts distribution center outside Tokyo, and dropped $180 million more to modify its cars for the Japanese market. So much for exporting always being "cheap."[15]

In fact, exporters must grapple with a variety of barriers and challenges. For instance, substantial tariffs are still in place in many countries for certain imported products. And that presented Boeing with a major headache in its effort to sell planes to Russia's Aeroflot. Faced with slumping air travel in the wake of the tragic events of September 11, 2001, Boeing had to scramble to land new orders wherever it could get them. Aeroflot's aging fleet represented a tempting target, with Boeing offering dozens of planes in a deal worth billions. But standing in the way was a steep 40 percent tariff on imported planes, making Boeing products expensive for the cash-strapped Russian carrier. By the end of 2001, no agreement for a sale had been reached and none appeared likely without Russian government intervention (e.g., to roll back tariffs or subsidize the purchase). Of course, U.S. exporters aren't the only ones facing tariff challenges. For example, steel companies in Europe and Asia fretted about their exports to the United States when, in 2002, the American government imposed tariffs as high as 30 percent on a variety of foreign steel products.[16]

Besides tariffs and other import/export regulatory barriers that boost costs, exporters also face two sets of logistical challenges that can prove tough to overcome: (1) Communications can be difficult because of the distance from customers (e-mail and other communication technology notwithstanding); and (2) certain modes of transportation are too slow, unreliable, or expensive for particular types of exported goods. In many situations, the key to overcoming these drawbacks is to do what Systran Corporation has done: find a foreign distributor who has both the knowledge and resources to market imported products successfully.[17] In any case, for another look at how export rules can blindside U.S. firms, read the following International Insights.

So what type of firms concentrate on exporting? Clearly, small firms (those with less than 500 employees) are well represented. However, small firms run by managers who embrace risk taking and innovation tend to be the most successful exporters. Small firms led by managers who have such "entrepreneurial" attitudes tend to export a

INTERNATIONAL INSIGHTS

Trouble Can Start at Home for U.S. Exporters

Optical Associates, a small company that makes components for semiconductor firms, was rolling along well in the exporting game. That is, until the company shipped equipment to an Indian nuclear research facility without obtaining an export license. Federal authorities told the firm that doing so had violated U.S. export restrictions on selling to "forbidden entities." As a result, Optical Associates faced a $500,000 fine. And that's hardly the worst that a firm could face. IBM paid a whopping $8.5 million fine for shipping computers to a Russian nuclear lab. Other penalties can include the loss of export rights and jail time for company officials. For instance, Texas-based Macosia International lost its export privileges for seven years after being found guilty of shipping leg irons and handcuffs to Mexico without the required license.

Of course, some might say that Optical Associates and IBM should have known better. Nevertheless, the number of companies accused of violating U.S. export laws has grown steadily in recent years, with the list of the accused including plenty of household names. And estimates are that American companies are losing billions annually because of export control laws.

So what's going on here? A general rise in international trade, combined with ongoing threats from terrorism and weapons development, has led the U.S. government to step up enforcement of export laws and expand export restrictions to some fifty countries (e.g., India and Pakistan were added to the list in 1998 after performing nuclear tests). Even allies, such as Israel, are subject to restrictions on products like high-speed computers and encryption software. Critics charge that export laws have become too complex and difficult to fathom, costing firms a bundle in lost business and late shipments, not to mention various government-imposed penalties. Plus, the complexity of international business has made it harder for companies to follow the law in the first place. As one manufacturing association executive put it, "When you're sourcing from ten to fifteen countries for a product, or you're part of a supply chain, knowing who your customers are is much more difficult than you think."

Naturally, big companies, particularly those in chemicals, aerospace, or other sensitive industries, tend to have the best resources for coping with the daunting array of export restrictions (e.g., export managers, software to help track and comply with export regulations). But for smaller firms, the complex and cumbersome nature of existing regulations can be intimidating. Most American companies have taken the position, at least in public, that while export restrictions are needed and should be kept in place in many cases, the regulations governing them should be simplified (e.g., less paperwork, short approval times for export licenses, etc.). In the meantime, companies that "put their heads in the sand" when it comes to U.S. export laws do so at their own peril.[18]

higher percentage of their total sales and have higher export growth rates than competitors run by more conservative bosses.19

Of course, big firms also export, such as corporate giant Boeing. And Boeing helps us illustrate that there are different types of exporting. When it sells a plane to a foreign airline, Boeing is engaged in **direct exporting**, where sales of a firm's products or services directly involve foreign customers. However, the many U.S. companies that supply Boeing with parts or components are involved in **indirect exporting**. This type of exporting occurs when a domestic firm sells a product to another domestic firm, which then exports the product, often after changing it in some fashion. The final major type of exporting is an **intracorporate transfer**. In this case, a firm located in one country sells a product to an affiliated company in another country. For instance, Ford plants in Mexico produce a variety of products (e.g., fuel tanks) that are then exported to Ford car assembly plants in the United States.[20] It might surprise you to learn such intracorporate transfers account for about a third of international trade world wide. Take a look at Exhibit 9.2 for a snapshot of the role that intracorporate transfers play in U.S. imports and exports.

EXHIBIT 9.2

The Role of Intracorporate Transfers in U.S. Imports and Exports

U. S. Trade Flow	Percentage of Total U.S. Trade Accounted for by Intracorporate Transfers from:	
	American Mutlinationals	**Foreign Multinationals**
Imported goods	18 (overseas subsidiaries to U.S. parent)	25 (foreign parent to U.S. subsidiary)
Exported goods	26 (U.S. parent to overseas subsidiary)	10 (U.S. subsidiary to foreign parent)

Source: Adapted from Koretz, G. (1997). A new twist in trade numbers, *Business Week*, May 12, 24.

Before we move on, we want to conclude by pointing out that exporting and importing are deeply woven into the fabric of international business. In other words, exporting isn't just an initial entry option for companies that want to get their feet wet in international business. For firms like Boeing, exporting is a way of life. Moreover, even firms that don't view themselves primarily as exporters often export extensively in conjunction with other market entry options. For instance, a U.S. manufacturer might build an assembly plant abroad, import the needed parts and components from all over the world, and then export finished products to other foreign markets.

Indeed, Honda is a good example of a company that uses exporting and importing extensively, often in very creative ways. You probably know that Honda operates a variety of facilities in the United States, including a major auto assembly plant in Marysville, Ohio. But you might be surprised to learn about how Honda cleverly uses its $1 billion trading arm, Honda Trading America Corporation (HTAC). To help supply its American assembly operations, Honda ships parts and components from Japan to the United States. The challenge, however, was to make use of the empty transport ships heading back to Japan. Thanks to HTAC, those ships return to Japan fully loaded with everything from scrap metal to frozen salmon to soybeans. And believe it or not, adjacent to Honda's Marysville auto plant sits a huge warehouse that sorts and packages soybeans grown under contract by over 100 American farmers. Operated by a HTAC subsidiary, soybeans are loaded onto rail cars and sent to California, then put on ships bound for Japan. In 2002, HTAC expected to export 800,000 bushels of American soybeans to Japan, accounting for about 14 percent of the high-end foreign soybeans sold in Japan. Profits from this soybean venture not only help buffer Honda from downturns in the auto market but have introduced many American farmers to exporting and international business. Sounds like a win-win to us.[21]

Licensing   Besides exporting, another relatively inexpensive foreign entry option is licensing. This option is often used when firms have limited resources and want to reduce their financial exposure in risky or unfamiliar foreign markets. Licensing also makes sense when high tariffs make importing goods too expensive or when a high level of product customization is needed that can best be done locally. Likewise, when a company in a competitive industry wants to sell a product abroad that's a bit long in the tooth (e.g., an older product or one with dated technology), margins may be slim. In that case, heavy investments in overseas markets make little sense. So licensing often represents a low-cost entry alternative that will allow the firm to still make good money on the product.

In essence, licensing involves selling the right to a company's brand names, patents, manufacturing technology or any other intellectual property to a foreign firm (the **licensee**). In many cases, the license granted comes with specific restrictions (e.g., licensed products can only be sold in a particular location or set of locations for a fixed amount of time, usually several years). The firm providing the license (the **licensor**) obtains quick access to foreign markets and an immediate benefit in the form of royalties or other fees that are paid by the foreign licensee, all without having to set up costly overseas plants. Royalties can be paid up front in the form of a flat fee. They can also be paid as a percentage of sales value or as a flat fee paid per sale.[22] But licensing also has drawbacks. For example, firms wishing to license their intellectual property to foreign companies should carefully craft the licensing contract. The contract needs to spell out clearly the obligations of both the licensor and the licensee. The licensor typically wants the licensee to make limited use of its intellectual property and not to pass on trade secrets to competitors. Negotiating such terms is rarely easy since the two sides involved typically have conflicting motivations. For instance, the licensor often wants a fairly short-term agreement, especially if it's using licensing as a way to test a market before jumping in with major investments. On the other hand, the foreign licensee often wants a longer agreement, one that will allow it to recoup costs associated with producing and distributing the licensed product.[23]

Even when an equitable licensing deal is struck, there are still major risks. For instance, the licensor gives up considerable control by definition and can be hurt if the licensee produces shoddy goods or behaves in other ways that damage the licensor's reputation. The lack of control also makes it more difficult for licensors to take advantage of location economies. Finally, firms that end up licensing their technology and production processes to foreign companies may be "educating" a potential competitor. Firms often overestimate their ability to control technologies once licensed.[24]

This is a troubling prospect since the management of technology may be the biggest contributor to international firms' success or failure in many industries.[25] Nevertheless, multinational firms often find themselves on the horns of a dilemma. Consider Mitsubishi Motor's experience with Hyundai of South Korea back in the mid-1990s. To gain access to fast-growing Asian car markets, Mitsubishi felt it needed to license some of its proprietary technology to help Hyundai build a better car on its behalf. This strategy did help Mitsubishi increase its Asian presence. At the same time, however, Hyundai became a potential rival to Mitsubishi in Asia. Thanks in part to its licensing agreements with Mitsubishi, Hyundai felt it became self-sufficient in most critical technological areas.[26]

Licensing technology is especially risky where the protection of intellectual property rights is weak. So why did Microsoft license parts of its proprietary computer codes to Chinese firms at bargain-basement rates? Microsoft felt that close ties with Chinese organizations, including those with government connections, would give it more leverage in the fight against software piracy. Roughly 80 percent of the PCs in China use bootlegged copies of Microsoft products. By licensing its technology, Microsoft hoped to develop Chinese versions of its products that could then be sold as upgrades to customers' bootlegged products.[27]

In fact, MNCs often find themselves pressured into licensing agreements by nations eager to acquire new technology. At one point, for instance, Chrysler refused to license

This Pizza Hut outlet in Thailand underscores the success American fast food companies have enjoyed abroad. © AFP/CORBIS

production of components and related technology to Chinese firms. China wanted to export Chinese-made minivans and parts without having to pay Chrysler a licensing fee and wouldn't include intellectual property protections in any contracts. General Motors, in contrast, signed 9 production deals after agreeing to Chinese demands to license its technology, betting that the potential was worth the risks.[28]

Franchising   Imagine having the contractual right to operate a business using the methods, procedures, products, trademarks, and marketing strategies created by another company. And compared to licensing, signing that contract may involve longer commitments and require tight controls as well as strict adherence to specific operating rules. That's the essence of franchising. The company offering the methods, trademarks, products, and so on is the **franchisor**, while the firm that agrees to run the business using those methods and products is the **franchisee**. Service firms, in particularly in the food and lodging industries, are most likely to enter foreign markets as franchisors. McDonald's is a good example. The company looks for foreign firms or investors who are willing to run McDonald's restaurants in a particular country. In exchange for use of company trademarks, operating procedures, products, and various support services (like training and logistics help), the foreign franchisee pays McDonald's a fee. Sometimes the franchisee also has to fork over a portion of their revenues to the franchisor. Perhaps the most important aspect about franchising, however, is that franchisees must adhere to strict guidelines about how the business has to be run. That's one key reason why McDonald's restaurants look and operate just about the same worldwide.[29]

The greater control franchising offers is a key advantage compared to licensing. Like licensing, franchising also allows the franchisor to shift costs (and risks) to the franchisee. So when a foreign firm signs a deal to run a McDonald's restaurant, it often has to come up with the money to start up the business. This requirement allows franchisors, especially established ones like McDonald's, to expand quickly worldwide.[30]

And McDonald's success has led smaller fast-food companies to dip into international markets, including A&W, Au Bon Pain, Big Boy, Schlotzky's Delicatessen, and Shakey's Pizza, just to name a few. As you might suspect, however, smaller franchisors can't support franchisees to the same extent that bigger firms like McDonald's and Burger King can (e.g., with global supply networks, extensive employee training programs, etc.). Consequently, franchisees may have to scramble to find suppliers on their own or make innovative menu changes to stay in business. One Big Boy franchisee in Thailand ended up with a menu loaded with food aimed at Thai locals and passing European tourists, selling few of the chain's trademark "American" hamburgers in the process. As the franchisee put it, "We thought we were bringing American food to the masses. But now we're bringing Thai and European food to the tourists."[31]

That said, franchising also has other challenges that even the biggest firms have to grapple with. For instance, control issues are still a concern. Service firms often have very high standards that their franchisees are not always motivated to duplicate, at least to the same extent. In fact, a brand name and the expectations that go with it are often precious commodities that the franchisor must protect. Customers come to McDonald's, for example, with high expectations of speed, cleanliness, and food quality. The foreign franchisee who does not live up to these expectations can hurt McDonald's reputation. Sometimes the franchisor will reassert control by replacing poorly performing franchisees or by setting up company-owned outlets in foreign countries if local firms can't meet the franchisor's standards. Take a look at the following International Insights on some of the franchise conflicts McDonald's has experienced in Brazil.

Of course, company-owned outlets are expensive and undercut a major advantage of franchising: that someone else puts up the resources needed to run the business.[33] In fact, because of the high costs of owning foreign facilities, some multinationals have shifted to a greater reliance on franchising. This was the route PepsiCo Inc. took with its international operations. For instance, after spending billions to battle Coca-Cola globally with new bottling plants and joint ventures, PepsiCo decided to use more franchisees to bottle beverages in overseas markets as a way to reduce costs.[34]

Management contracts   With an international management contract, one company provides a foreign organization with specific services, technical help, or managerial expertise for either a flat fee or a percentage of sales or profits. Usually such a **management contract** is for a specific period of time. Like the other entry modes we've considered so far, this is a relatively low-risk way for a company to increase international revenues since no ownership costs are involved.[35]

For instance, some years ago Argentinean oil producer Yacimientos Petroliferos Fiscales SA (YPF) used management contracts at its main refinery in La Plata. Thanks to some government leadership and technical help from managers at U.S.-based Hughes Tool Co., YPF was able to modernize the plant and cut the cost of oil production in half. Later, Chevron Corp. supplied executives under a management contract with YPF to help run the ongoing operation.[36] Likewise, U.S. Steel's consulting group provided managers and engineers to help Slovakia's Vychodoslovenske zelziarne AS (or VSZ) modernize and refine its automated steelmaking equipment and capabilities. U.S. Steel later bought VSZ (see our discussion later).[37]

Turnkey projects   Sometimes management contracts are a consequence of international **turnkey projects**. These projects typically involve a contract to design and build a facility in a foreign country. When the project is complete, the facility may be

INTERNATIONAL INSIGHTS

McDonald's Moves in Brazil Fry Local Franchisees

McDONALD'S HAS BEEN on a tear in Brazil over the past few years. In 2000, McDonald's passed the 500-restaurant mark, a figure it expects to double by 2003. Over 34,000 people work at the American icon in Brazil, making it the nation's third-biggest corporate employer. And Brazil is a huge market for McDonald's, coming in at eighth place worldwide.

But some Brazilian franchisees have complaints. They grouse that the rapid expansion of McDonald's, which can put new restaurants in the vicinity of old ones, has cut into their sales. Plus, given Brazil's roller-coaster currency, the price of imported material, like ketchup packets, can shoot up unpredictably, further complicating franchisees' profit picture. Then there are franchisees who claim that McDonald's is ripping them off, taking about a 17 percent cut of sales as a rental fee (almost twice what U.S. franchisees supposedly pay). In fact, a group of franchisees sued McDonald's in Brazilian court over the disputed fees.

Predictably, McDonald's rejects the franchisees' complaints, arguing that they were "spoiled" by the easy profits they made earlier in Brazil. On the rental fee controversy, the company points out that the rental fee helps it recoup the cost of designing and building restaurants in Brazil as well as providing technical help to local franchisees. In short, McDonald's doesn't believe the courts should intervene to limit rental fees. So far the Brazilian courts have agreed. But McDonald's Brazilian experience is a reminder that what's under the arches abroad isn't always golden.[32]

run for a short time by the contractor to ensure smooth operations. In many cases, however, an operational facility will eventually be turned over to the company or government issuing the contract. Most international turnkey projects involve building things like power plants, dams, airports, oil refineries, and so on. Some countries lack the local expertise to construct such complex facilities and turn to foreign firms for help. Often this is a way for local firms to learn about the technology and processes associated with building these facilities. Turnkey projects are especially attractive when more direct forms of foreign investment (like ownership) are impossible or when political or economic instability makes such investments a risky proposition. On the other hand, turnkey projects are often limited, one-shot deals that can transfer know-how to potential competitors.[38]

Then there's the risk that a foreign government will scuttle approved projects or take steps that dramatically increase costs. Some countries have a reputation for putting bureaucratic obstacles in the way of foreign companies. India is just one of many examples. Although free market reforms have been made in the last several years and hundreds of U.S. firms do business in India, a shifting morass of bureaucracies and convoluted regulations remain major sources of frustration for multinationals. Foreign companies may have to deal with the central government as well as one or more of thirty-five state governments. That said, many foreign companies are attracted to opportunities in India. Among other things, India's power grid, telecommunication system, and transportation network (e.g., rail, roads) leave something to be desired. And therein lies plenty of potential business for foreign companies.

But capitalizing on those opportunities isn't easy or cheap. Take electricity. Several agreements to build power plants were signed between Indian governments and foreign firms in the early 1990s. By 2001, however, financing troubles were still being worked out with some projects and foreign companies from the United States, France, and South Korea had given up and pulled out of others.[39]

Some of the big risks often associated with turnkey projects are underscored by Houston-based Enron Corp.'s contract to build a $3 billion power plant in Maharashtra, India. This expensive venture evolved from a deal that was originally inked in 1992. Designed to bring power to the Indian heartland, the gas-fired plant was to be Enron's signature project in Asia and a portent of more power plants to come. But it didn't work out that way. Local officials, concerned about high prices and exploitation, nullified the initial contract in 1995 to force Enron to trim costs. Then national elections forced Enron to again seek project approvals from the central government. Construction finally resumed in late 1996 after sixteen months of negotiations. The plant eventually opened in 2000, but Enron decided not to build more power plants in India. At the time, Enron said it would engage in power trading once the deregulation planned for India's power market allowed it. That dream, however, appears dead. In December of 2001, Enron declared bankruptcy. Some suggested that Enron's involvement in enormous and expensive overseas projects (e.g., its Indian power plant and Wessex Water project in the U.K.) provided little in the way of returns and helped put the firm on the road to collapse.[40]

Entry Options Involving Ownership

As we suggested earlier, many firms progress from nonownership strategies like exporting to those involving ownership of overseas facilities as they become larger and more sophisticated. Moving to ownership may also reflect a desire to make more money abroad, something made easier with the control that ownership affords. Ownership also allows a firm to more closely coordinate worldwide operations, something that many multinationals find increasingly attractive. That said, ownership typically entails greater expense and risk.[41]

Wholly owned foreign subsidiaries: the greenfield approach   A straightforward ownership option for firms, known as the **greenfield approach**, is to enter a foreign market by establishing a wholly owned subsidiary there. Doing that from scratch means scouting for a piece of property on foreign soil that can accommodate subsidiary operations and then buying it. Once this site is acquired, construction can begin on the facility. Later, workers can be hired to staff the new operation.

This approach gives companies maximum control. A firm can pick a site that maximizes location economies (e.g., being close to target markets or being able to access low-cost local labor) and then put a modern facility on it. Location economies explain why Asian companies have spent billions in recent years to build new plants in Mexico near the American border. Such *maquiladora* facilities allow the parent company to pay duty only on the value that local Mexican labor adds to exported products. This arrangement, combined with low Mexican wage rates, proximity to the American market, and access to the U.S. transportation system, lowers overall production costs. For instance, Japanese multinational Sanyo trims up to $20 off every $250 TV set it produces in Tijuana, a major savings. Another advantage with the greenfield option is that proprietary technology can be easily protected. And workers can be hired in an environment where there is no prior history of labor troubles.

But the negatives about the greenfield option are clear. Building a greenfield facility takes time and is very expensive. And while facilities are under construction, companies may be particularly vulnerable to the whims of the host government (e.g., taxes may be raised, onerous environmental requirements may be imposed, etc.). Nor does recruiting and training a new workforce happen overnight, especially in a new culture. Unfortunately, firms sometimes ignore these realities and push too fast to set up new foreign subsidiaries. For instance, U.S.-based Lincoln Electric Co. lost money for the first time after the firm built sixteen new plants in eleven countries within a four-year period. The company ended up closing plants in four countries and switched to exporting and alliances as its main international entry modes.[42] Tyco Toys had a similar experience before being purchased by rival Mattel. The firm lost over $100 million in the 1990s after trying to ramp up subsidiary operations in Europe too quickly.[43]

Wholly owned foreign subsidiaries: the acquisition approach

Multinationals can also establish wholly owned foreign subsidiaries by acquiring foreign companies. This **acquisition approach** usually involves complicated negotiations and financial transactions. There may also be legal or political hurdles to surmount, especially if the multinational is acquiring a foreign company with a strong local reputation or one that is state owned.

In fact, many countries that want to develop more market-based economies have engaged in **privatization efforts** on a large scale (i.e., governments selling off state-owned enterprises or assets, either in whole or in part, to private companies or individuals). China is a good case in point. With the full implications of its 2002 entry into the World Trade Organization bearing down on it, many of China's state-owned business are poorly equipped to survive, particularly when matched against foreign firms. China views privatization as one way to convert state-owned businesses into more effective competitors. Often that means having foreign companies purchase or otherwise invest in state-owned enterprises. But turning around moribund state-owned enterprises is rarely simple or cheap.[44]

And that fact underscores some of the major risks associated with the acquisition approach. When it acquires another firm, either a private company or one owned by the state, the multinational also is buying all the problems the acquired firm had, such as poor labor-management relations, debt, and inferior product quality.[45] On top of that, cultural and managerial differences between the multinational and the foreign firm being acquired can prove difficult to overcome.[46] In fact, national culture can affect the way multinationals manage their international acquisitions.[47]

For instance, U.S. Steel acquired steelmaker Vychodoslovenske zelziarne AS (VSZ) for $1.2 billion in 2000. U.S. Steel's goal in buying VSZ, a former state-owned enterprise in Slovakia, was to position itself to supply steel to the developing countries of eastern Europe, a region where demand should grow over time. However, along with the acquisition came antiquated equipment, management corruption, lousy customer service, a bloated workforce of 17,000, and resistance to the "American business culture." But U.S. Steel is in for the long term. The company expects to spend hundreds of millions over the next several years to make VSZ a world-class supplier.[48] And U.S. Steel's experience is hardly unique. Take a look at the following International Insights on the challenges steelmaker Ispat International inherited when it bought a steel plant in Kazakhstan.

Nevertheless, one advantage that acquisitions have over a greenfield approach is that they allow multinationals to move into international markets faster. The multinational is, in most cases, buying an operational foreign facility that comes complete with workforce, equipment, product, distribution system, brand names, and reputation. That explains Nestlé's acquisition of Polish chocolate maker Goplana. The Swiss giant felt that building a new plant would delay its entry into Poland by two years. Waiting that long would prevent Nestlé from seizing a large share of one of eastern Europe's largest markets.[50]

Multinationals also target foreign companies for acquisition precisely because they have assets, such as successful brands or unique technologies, that represent valuable

INTERNATIONAL INSIGHTS

Want a Piece of the Old Soviet Empire? The Spies Are Included

PRIVATIZATION IS TAKING the world by storm. In fact, over $700 billion in assets was privatized in the past decade. The most common form of privatization occurs when governments sell off state-owned firms to private companies. Privatization raises money, makes organizations more efficient, and reduces reliance on governments. For countries that were once part of the Soviet bloc, another motivation is to complete the conversion from a socialist to a market-based economy. In Russia alone, tens of thousands of state-owned firms have been sold to private companies in recent years. Many of these newly privatized firms have restructured themselves and become better competitors as a result.

Western multinationals looking for good acquisition deals in developing markets often turn to the former Soviet bloc. Many feel that the risks of investing there have diminished and that local managers are able to adapt to Western business practices. Ispat International is one Western firm that has taken the plunge. The London-based steelmaker is the world's fourth largest. Ispat built its reputation by buying up state-owned steel mills from Indonesia to Mexico at very low prices and then turning them around by putting in new technology and cutting costs. That said, Ispat's $1 billion purchase of Kazakhstan's huge Karmet steelmaking complex in 1996 produced some interesting problems.

Like what, you ask? How about twelve former KGB agents who refused to leave their gadget-filled spy suite in the complex? After all, a KGB unit had been assigned to the complex since Stalin built it as a labor camp in the 1940s! It took Ispat two months to convince the spies to leave. Or how about the Chechen fighters who hung around the complex and demanded payoffs from suppliers? Or the hundreds of workers who showed up drunk every day?

Actually, Ispat faced even bigger problems. Most of Karmet's former customers had disappeared. And exporting Karmet steel was complicated by Kazakhstan's abysmal rail system (it took weeks to ship steel to the nearest port). Moreover, while Ispat felt that some 40 percent of Karmet's 38,000 employees were unnecessary, the local union saw the company as a rich target and asked for a 75 percent wage hike.

Consequently, Ispat expected to spend more than $550 million over several years to repair the complex and introduce new technology. By 2002, most of the renovations and restructuring were complete. Ispat now describes Karmet as a modern facility that will produce over four million tons of high quality finished steel annually by 2005. But only time will tell if Ispat's investment was a good one.[49]

---

competitive advantages. When added to the multinational's "portfolio," these advantages have the potential to quickly add to international revenues. For instance, in 1996 Coca-Cola acquired Parle Exports, India's number one soft drink supplier. Doing so allowed Coke to scoop up all of India's local soft-drink brands, plus fifty-odd bottling plants. As a result, Coke owned brands accounting for some 60 percent of the Indian soft-drink market.[51]

In fact, the ability to enter foreign markets quickly, especially in response to competitors' moves, has become an increasingly attractive option as international competition intensifies and demands for worldwide efficiency rise. This may explain why 48 percent of U.S. manufacturers in one survey said that the best international entry strategy was to acquire existing foreign plants. Only 31 percent said the best bet was to build greenfield facilities.[52]

This acquisition trend is not unique to American firms. European multinationals, for instance, spent $250 billion to buy U.S. firms in 2000 for similar reasons (i.e., tending to prefer acquisitions over the greenfield option). This figure represents 80 percent of all foreign direct investment in the United States during 2000. This buying

EXHIBIT 9.3

Will Foreign Acquisitions Pay Off?
A Decision Matrix

		Is your industry really becoming more concentrated globally?	
		Yes	**No**
Is your company pursuing foreign acquisitions as part of an effort to consolidate globally?	**Yes**	Foreign acquisitions are most likely to pay off.	Overexpansion is the likely outcome of foreign acquisition.
	No	Failing to pursue foreign acquisition risks putting the firm at a disadvantage.	Not pursuing a foreign acquisition is appropriate.

Source: Adapted from Ghemawat, P., & Ghadar, F. (2000). The dubious logic of global megamergers. *Harvard Business Review, 78,* 71.

pattern is unlikely to disappear anytime soon since European firms continue to want quick access to the large and cohesive American market. Indeed, French media giant Vivendi Universal plunked down $2.2 billion in 2001 to buy Boston-based Houghton Mifflin, the publisher of this book, for just that reason.[53]

Nevertheless, a global economic slowdown became more apparent in late 2001, punctuated by the tragic events of September 11. Consequently, multinationals, particularly those based in the United States, began to back away from direct foreign investments, including acquisitions. Heading into 2002, a diverse array of household names, including Ford, Gateway Computer, and Merrill Lynch had either reduced overseas operations or pulled out of some foreign markets altogether. Experts warned U.S. firms against withdrawing too much or for too long, arguing that ignoring foreign opportunities, especially in developing markets, could leave the door open for new competitors. As former General Electric CEO Jack Welch put it, "The biggest competitive threats on the horizon are those companies whose names we can't spell or pronounce."[54]

But big cross-border acquisitions aren't always the best way to go in any case. One of the often-stated reasons for doing such deals is that consolidation and size in "global" industries results in greater efficiencies. Nevertheless, the savings that acquisitions are supposed to produce are often overestimated, undercut in many cases by the complexities inherent in cross-border deals. Managers also need to ask themselves whether their industry is really becoming more concentrated on a global basis or if they're just jumping on the proverbial bandwagon. Only then can a decision be made about whether a strategy that includes foreign acquisitions makes sense. Take a look at Exhibit 9.3. It presents a basic decision matrix for figuring out whether a foreign acquisition is the right move. Of course, as simple as it looks, deciding how global an industry is becoming is hardly child's play. Nevertheless, managers routinely succumb to various types of traps in thinking about these issues (e.g., getting caught up in the hype, wanting to match the "big deals" made by competitors, etc.).[55]

Joint ventures   Of course, one cheaper alternative to acquisitions is to pursue various types of alliances and partnerships with other firms. Some alliances, like joint ventures, involve shared ownership between companies. But ownership of a foreign operation need not be complete. A joint venture is a specific type of strategic alliance between two companies that is set up as a separate legal entity. Joint venture ownership can be split 50/50 between the parent companies or one firm can have a more dominant stake. Partners that hold more than a 50 percent share usually do so in order to have tighter control over the joint venture. Some countries, however, limit foreign partners to no more than a 49 percent ownership stake in the joint venture.[56]

In fact, multinationals with sophisticated technology often want a controlling stake in joint ventures, especially if the partner is a local firm whose role is largely to supply expertise about local markets.[57] This is the approach that U.S.-based Whirlpool took to quickly position itself in key Asian markets. In the mid-1990s, Whirlpool parted with $265 million to start joint ventures with four Chinese and two Indian firms. In each case, Whirlpool bought a controlling stake in an effort to balance costs with maximum control. Nevertheless, the expensive nature of this rapid expansion and effective local competitors eventually caused Whirlpool to pursue cheaper alternatives.[58]

Not all international joint ventures involve manufacturing a final product. Sometimes they're designed to procure raw materials, produce components, or deliver services. Creating a joint venture may also involve construction of greenfield facilities, the acquisition of existing firms, or both. Finally, joint ventures may have more than two partners. Clearly, the form and purpose of joint ventures can vary considerably.[59]

That said, a common goal for many international joint ventures is to market, produce, and distribute a product in a particular foreign country or region. Often the partners are a large multinational and a smaller local company, as is the case with Whirlpool and its Asian counterparts. In these circumstances, it's easy to see why both parties would be attracted to a joint venture. For example, the multinational might provide product design and technological expertise (something the local company might desire), while the local partner might provide marketing know-how and knowledge of local culture, laws, and business practices (something the multinational might desire). In short, both sides benefit.[60]

Cost and risk sharing are also major reasons for creating joint ventures. This can be especially important for firms that want to be the first to position themselves in risky emerging markets. For instance, United Technologies' (UT) Pratt & Whitney unit signed a joint venture agreement with Russia's Aviadvigatel in 1995 to put engines on Russian-built jets, even though big profits were unlikely in the near future. Likewise, UT's Otis Elevator unit was among the first U.S. firms to enter China in the early 1980s. In fact, Otis started negotiating with eastern European partners just hours after the Berlin Wall fell.[61]

However, joint ventures are not limited to partnerships between large multinationals and small local firms. Increasingly, the costs and risks of entering a particular international market or coming up with a saleable product are driving even the biggest multinationals into joint ventures with each other. For instance, several years ago Chrysler and BMW formed a 50/50 joint venture to build a $500 million engine plant. The facility was designed to crank out small engines (under 2.0 liters) for a variety of markets. Building the plant was important to both sides since over 50 percent of the cars sold outside the United States have engine displacements of 1.6 liters or less and neither firm had small engines available. The joint venture setup was attractive because the economies of scale required to recoup the costs of investing in new engine design and production meant selling 400,000 engines. Neither company thought it could sell that many small engines alone. The joint venture was meant to solve that problem.[62]

Joint ventures can provide access to markets that otherwise would be difficult to penetrate because of foreign ownership restrictions (e.g., China, where joint ventures can be either equity based or contractual in nature). Having a local firm as a partner in such markets can also be a useful buffer against pressures from foreign governments and changes in local regulations.[63] A local partner can also allay some of the mistrust that certain countries feel toward foreign multinationals because of fears of exploitation or a history of colonialism. Many developing countries, for instance, are concerned that foreign multinationals will overwhelm local firms. Joint ventures can help allay these fears and teach local firms to be more competitive.[64]

Of course, that could also prove to be a disadvantage to a multinational if key technologies or know-how is transferred to a local partner. Like licensing, the joint venture may turn the local firm into a formidable competitor later on. One way to handle this is to have the joint venture agreement expressly forbid the transfer of key technologies. But getting this agreement in the first place can be tough, especially in places like China where technology transfer is encouraged.

In addition, a variety of cultural and managerial conflicts can plague joint ventures. And decisions about selecting a partner, managing the venture, and developing performance appraisal strategies are incredibly thorny in themselves.[65] Nevertheless, resolving such issues is critical if the joint venture is to perform well.[66] One mechanism for minimizing conflict between partners is to manage the joint venture using a **delegated arrangement**. In other words, the partners agree to step back from the management of ongoing operations and instead either hire new executives or reassign executives already working for the partners. As you might suspect, however, this is only a partial solution. Many conflicts can erupt over who will be hired or transferred.[67]

Other disadvantages of joint ventures revolve around control issues. Decisive decision making may be hampered because of the need to consult with the joint venture partner, especially if the partners do not see eye to eye on matters. Joint ventures also may fail to provide the level of control a multinational needs to take full advantage of location economies or coordinate worldwide operations. A common way to minimize these disadvantages is for the multinational to have majority control over the joint venture. Of course, foreign companies don't want to play second fiddle in many cases. So finding a partner willing to accept a minority position can be difficult. And while taking a majority position means greater control, it also means more financial risk.[68]

Nevertheless, the additional financial commitment may be worth it. For example, having a dominant position in a joint venture in China can pay big dividends. And U.S. multinationals are finding it easier to acquire larger shares of Chinese joint ventures. This may allow American managers involved in Chinese joint ventures to gain more leverage over

● Key business decisions
● How an effective local sales force is developed
● The strategies used to retain key Chinese personnel
● How aggressively the local partner lobbies government officials on the joint venture's behalf

Not surprisingly, American managers tend to feel that Chinese joint ventures are more efficient and profitable when dominant control is maintained.[69]

If this sounds like multinationals' ideal joint venture is one where they can run things as usual despite having a local partner, you may be right. Multinationals often seem most satisfied with joint ventures where they can ignore the local partner, at least on certain issues, and run operations in their own way. But acting that way may mean that the partner's perspective, and the opportunities for learning that go along with it, will be lost. When this happens, it undercuts one of the major benefits of establishing a joint venture in the first place.[70]

We want to mention two things before we move on to the next section. First, take a look at Exhibit 9.4. It summarizes some of the key pluses and minuses of the market entry options that we've presented. Second, Chapter 10 will explore the challenges associated with joint ventures and other types of strategic alliances in more detail.

EXHIBIT 9.4

Pluses and Minuses of Foreign Market Entry Options

Entry Mode	Pluses	Minuses
Exporting	● fairly inexpensive ● easy foreign access ● no ownership risks	● missed location economies ● logistical difficulties (transportation/communication)
Licensing	● fairly inexpensive ● useful where trade barriers/ tariffs preclude exporting ● leverages location economies without ownership concerns	● risky where intellectual property protection is weak ● control ceded to licensee may inhibit coordination ● may help create new competitors
Franchising	● low cost, low risk ● offers more control than licensing ● builds presence fast	● control still an issue ● franchisee may not be motivated to adhere to franchisor's standards
Management contracts	● very inexpensive ● low-risk revenue	● no long-term presence ● may create competitors
Turnkey projects	● an option if direct investment is out ● lowers risk if long term instability exists	● no long-term presence ● may create competitors ● vulnerable to political and legislative changes
Greenfield subsidiaries	● allows high control ● offers location economies ● can pick own site, workers, technology	● very expensive to set up ● time-consuming to set up ● requires considerable international expertise ● risky due to ownership
Acquired subsidiaries	● allows high control ● rapid market entry ● offers location economies	● risky due to ownership ● cultural differences may be formidable ● may be buying problems
Joint ventures	● less financial risk than subsidiaries ● leverages partner's resources, know-how	● risks giving some control or technology to partner ● still some ownership risk

Sources: Adapted from Griffin, R. W. & Pustav, M. W. (1996). *International business: A managerial perspective* (Reading, MA: Addison-Wesley); Hill, C. W. L. (1994) *International business: Competing in the global marketplace* (Burr Ridge, IL: Irwin).

Other Types of Strategic Alliances

Speaking of which, joint ventures are just one of many possibilities for developing some form of strategic alliance. That said, making alliances work well requires trust between the parties, a clear set of shared objectives, and a diplomatic management style, among other things. A good example of a success story, at least so far, is the Renault-Nissan partnership. In 1999, France's Renault took a 37 percent equity stake in struggling Nissan. Making this partnership work and moving from losses to profits in the process is arguably thanks in no small measure to Renault's charismatic leader, Carlos Ghosn. His goal is clear. Ghosn wants all Renaults and Nissans to share platforms and basic components by 2010. While the cars produced will look and be marketed differently, Ghosn hopes the savings from sharing will be impressive. Interestingly, part of the alliance's success has been Ghosn's sensitive and effective management of, as he puts it, "the contradiction between synergy and identity." According to Ghosn, each corporate partner must maintain its unique identity ("because it is the basis of motivation") while still embracing common goals.[71]

In any case, other types of alliances are typically narrower in scope, less stable, and shorter in duration than most joint ventures or Renault-Nissan's particularly deep relationship. These alliances may also lack the formal structure and independent legal status found in joint ventures. As such, they are formed when multinationals believe that a cooperative arrangement is the best way to advance their own self-interest in specific areas. For a variety of reasons, including ease of market entry, the sharing of risk, and the ability to realize competitive advantages quickly, the use of strategic alliances has grown dramatically in recent years. Specifically, the number of cross-border connections between firms has been rising at double-digit rates annually over the past decade. And the advantages associated with alliances are especially critical in less developed countries—where deregulation has created more demanding and more competitive markets.[72]

Of course, other entry options provide similar advantages. However, strategic alliances are often a better way for a multinational to learn invisible skills from a foreign partner. These skills are usually informal forms of expertise or know-how that can only be learned through the kind of close observation possible in cooperative relationships. Often, they are quite complex and evolve from a specific cultural context, such as Honda's expertise in developing and producing engines. This expertise has been applied to diverse products (Honda cars, motorcycles, lawn mowers) and reflects a complex blending of know-how in disciplines like flexible manufacturing, customer service, quality control, product development, and just-in-time materials management.[73]

Acquiring such expertise is often part of the motivation behind **production alliances**. Such alliances involve firms that agree to manufacture products or deliver services in a shared facility that is either built from scratch or owned by one of the partners. For instance, prior to its acquisition by Boeing, McDonnell-Douglas and Shanghai Aviation Industrial Corp. had a production alliance to assemble jetliners in China using kits shipped over from the United States. The alliance was seen by the Chinese side as a way to learn how to develop and build commercial aircraft.[74] Costs can also be part of the equation. H. J. Heinz, for instance, asked food business competitors Unilever and Nestle to consider sharing production facilities as a way to reduce manufacturing overhead.[75]

Research and development alliances are another way for multinationals to stay ahead of rapidly changing technology. These alliances involve joint research aimed at the development of new services, products, or technologies. Often partners agree to cross-license any new developments that result from joint research so that all participating firms can equally share in any applications. Hewlett-Packard's cooperative arrangement with Japan's Canon Corp. to develop new printer technology is an example of this type of alliance.

Strategic alliances are popular in other areas as well. **Financial alliances** are formed by partners whose primary goal is to reduce the monetary risks of doing a particular project. Such was the case when IBM and Toshiba entered into an alliance to share the $1 billion cost of developing new computer chip manufacturing facilities.[76]

Finally, **marketing alliances** are designed to share marketing-related expertise or services. Such alliances are often formed by firms that want access to the other partner's markets and are willing to pool resources to get it. For instance, a code-sharing agreement with KLM Royal Dutch Airlines allows Northwest Airlines to sell U.S. customers "seamless" tickets for flights from American cities to various European and African destinations. For example, to fly from Detroit to Johannesburg, a Northwest flight will move customers from the United States to KLM's Amsterdam hub, with a KLM flight picking up the leg from Amsterdam to South Africa. KLM does the reverse by tapping into Northwest's extensive route structure inside the United States. Exhibit 9.5 summarizes the different types of strategic alliances we've considered in this section.

EXHIBIT 9.5

Beyond Joint Ventures:
Other Types of International Strategic Alliances

Type of Alliance	Purpose
Production alliance	Partners' motivation may include the desire to acquire complex manufacturing expertise and know-how from each other as well as reducing the costs of production.
Research and development alliance	The partners conduct joint research to develop new products, services, or technologies (i.e., pooled resources are more likely to lead to breakthroughs).
Financial alliance	The partners reduce their financial exposure with particularly expensive and risky projects by sharing the costs involved (e.g., jointly building a $1 billion chip manufacturing facility).
Marketing alliance	Partners share services or expertise in marketing related areas in ways that generate additional profits for both.

Chapter Summary

We began this chapter by considering the *six stages* that companies may go through in their international development. In *stage 1*, a domestic company begins internationalizing by exporting its products or services to foreign customers. Once it has opened overseas offices or sales subsidiaries in a foreign country, a company has moved to *stage 2*. As you might expect, *stage 3* involves the actual production of a significant amount of product overseas. In *stage 4*, a company recognizes the need for headquarters to make strategic decisions, even if local operations are largely staffed by local employees. A more global or transnational orientation occurs in *stage 5*. Finally, *stage 6* highlights the fact that firms are increasingly linking up to leverage their combined resources.

We then considered various options for entering foreign markets, starting with entry modes that don't require ownership of foreign facilities. This includes *exporting*, sending goods or services to foreign countries where they can be sold. Several types of exporting exist, including: (1) *direct exporting*; (2) *indirect exporting*; and (3) *intracorporate transfers*.

Licensing involves selling the right to use a firm's intellectual property (e.g., brands, technology) to a foreign company (the *licensee*). In many cases, the license granted comes with specific restrictions regarding where products can be sold and for how long. The firm providing the license (the *licensor*) obtains quick access to foreign markets and an immediate benefit in the form of royalties or other fees are paid by the foreign licensee. Licensing can be a very risky proposition, especially when proprietary technology is involved. *Franchising* involves the contractual right to operate a business using the methods, procedures, products, trademarks, and marketing strategies created by another company. The company offering the methods, trademarks, products, and so on is the *franchisor*, while the firm that agrees to run the business using those methods and products is the *franchisee*. Service firms, partic-ularly in the food and lodging industries, are most likely to enter foreign markets as franchisors. *Management contracts* and *turnkey projects* are also examples of entry modes not requiring any ownership responsibilities. Turnkey projects typically involve a contract to design and build a facility in a foreign country. When the project is complete, the facility may be run for a short time by the contractor, often under a management contract, to ensure smooth operations.

We then considered modes of entry involving ownership, like *wholly owned foreign subsidiaries*. This includes subsidiaries whose facilities are built from scratch (the *greenfield approach*) as well as subsidiaries that are purchased from foreign companies (the *acquisition approach*). A greenfield approach offers companies maximum control but is often time consuming and very expensive to execute. Acquisitions typically allow for speedier entry into foreign markets. That said, the acquiring firm is also buying all the problems that the acquired company had, such as poor labor-management relations, debt, and inferior product quality. On top of that, differences in cultural values and management styles can complicate prospects for an acquisition.

A form of entry that only requires partial ownership is the *joint venture*. A joint venture is a specific type of strategic alliance between two companies that is set up as a separate legal entity. Ownership of this entity can be split 50/50 between the parent companies, or one firm can have a more dominant stake. A common goal for many international joint ventures is to market, produce, and distribute a product in a particular foreign country or region. Often the partners are a large multinational and a smaller local company. In these circumstances, the multinational might provide the basic product design and technological expertise, while the local partner might provide knowledge of local culture, laws, and business practices. Of course, a variety of challenges, conflicts, and management hassles often come with joint ventures as well as other types of strategic alliances. Other types of alliances include *production alliances*, *research and development alliances*, *financial alliances*, and *marketing alliances*.

Discussion Questions

1. What are the different stages that companies may pass through as they develop internationally? Can you think of examples of firms that have progressed through all the stages? What about examples of firms that have remained very successful in a particular stage?

2. Compare and contrast the various foreign market entry options that do not involve ownership. Under what circumstances would each option be ideal?

3. Likewise, compare and contrast the various foreign market entry options that involve ownership. Under what circumstances would each option be ideal?

4. Describe the different types of international alliances that may exist between firms. What are some of the major management headaches associated with such alliances?

Up to the Challenge?

*Ford Buys Brands while GM and
Toyota Build Alliances*

BACK AT THE beginning of the chapter we described GM's alliance-based strategy for becoming the world's leading automobile company. We also intimated that Ford and Toyota are taking somewhat different routes to the same goal. So what are Ford and Toyota doing?

In a nutshell, Toyota is also constructing a global network of allied companies. But Toyota is organizing its alliance network differently. Toyota believes that its prowess in high-quality, flexible manufacturing is a core competence and wants to leverage it. The firm aims to have only one or two suppliers for every manufactured part. Wherever Toyota assembles cars, it wants to have locally owned suppliers nearby. Those local suppliers will only enjoy Toyota's continued business if they submit to rigorous ongoing inspections and take advice from Toyota about how to improve their manufacturing operations. So in a sense Toyota manages these independently owned suppliers. And to that extent, Toyota is like GM in taking a controlling approach based on management rather than ownership.

In contrast, Ford has used an acquisition strategy to keep up with, if not best, its competitors in the international car race. Over the past several years, several premium nameplates have been added to the Ford stable. Ford now owns upscale nameplates Volvo, Jaguar, and Land Rover outright. Indeed, at one point Ford was rumored to be interested in buying BMW. Ford also owns a significant piece of Mazda and has moved aggressively in recent years to shake up and essentially take over what was originally an "alliance partner." And in 2002, Ford said it would close several plants and spend $2 billion to make the rest more flexible and efficient. Some experts noted that Ford seemed to be embracing Honda's and Toyota's more flexible manufacturing approach. Others believe that Ford, and perhaps some of the other big auto players, will eventually focus on brand management and little else (ie., they will design and market vehicles, but outsource all other key tasks).

In any case, Ford's recent moves have doubtlessly made GM focus on what it will take to make its alliance-based strategy work. GM needs to effectively manage a broad confederation of companies, a tough challenge without majority ownership control. Another challenge for GM will be to somehow spread the product development benefits and technology advances it gleans from its various alliances across its product lines while still capitalizing on partners' expertise in specific markets.

One way GM is trying to do that is by allowing alliance partners to access its computerized design

system. For instance, that's how employees at partner Suzuki and GM were able to simultaneously draft and develop a new design for a small car, despite the 6,000-mile distance between them. GM has also designated specific units to take on primary liaison roles with particular partners. For example, GM's European subsidiary Opel is charged with taking the lead on relations with alliance partners Isuzu and Suzuki, among others.

What GM ultimately wants is for the companies in its alliance network to jointly develop whole families of vehicles that have common platforms, components, and general designs, all of which would be manufactured using similar processes. This advance would provide un-precedented flexibility (e.g., by allowing a dozen different cars to roll off the same assembly line) and economies of scale for GM while still allowing sufficient tailoring for local customers. And that would allow GM to respond quickly when market demands change. For example, Volkswagen's profit picture perked up when it was able to produce over fifty models from just four basic platforms.

That said, turning GM's dream into reality is a daunting endeavor. Alliances are notoriously tough to manage and partnering means giving up some control in any case. Disagreements and cross-cultural spats can flare into counterproductive grudge matches that ultimately doom the alliance. What's more, common platforms and shared components aren't a cure-all, particularly if customers feel that they're being offered similar, cookie-cutter products. And in recent years, automotive demand has been relatively weak worldwide, falling well short of the industry's capacity to churn out 80 million cars, trucks, and vans annually. On top of that, for years both Ford and GM have been offering costly incentives (e.g., rebates and cheap financing) to move cars, with profits coming from a narrow range of vehicles (e.g., SUVs, minivans, and crossovers) that are now under assault from foreign competitors, including Toyota and Honda.

And that's not all. Some smaller foreign firms dream of breaking into the ranks of the "biggest and best" global car companies. Consider Hyundai. Over the past several years, Hyundai's quality has risen twice as fast as the industry average. Its reputation and sales have been rising too, especially in the United States. The Korean automaker wants to be one of the top five auto companies in the world by 2010. The company has been designing vehicles in the United States for years and in 2001 began scouting locations for its first American assembly plant.

In this competitive environment, which approach—Ford's, Toyota's, or GM's—has the best chance of succeeding long term in your opinion? What are the pros and cons of each? Can you think of any alternatives that might drive each company to where it wants to go? And what about the competitive threats posed by upstarts like Hyundai? How should the global car giants respond?[77]

International Development
Using the Global Practices Instrument

Purpose

To help you reflect on your company's international operations and hone your ability to assess the internal corporate environment from a strategic perspective. This instrument measures the extent to which corporate practices embrace an international perspective and reflect a clear international strategy. We think it may be particularly useful now that you've read Chapters 8 and 9, which both deal with international strategy issues.

Instructions

Answer the following questions for *your* firm by circling the appropriate number. If you're not employed or the company you work for doesn't do business internationally, then pick a company on the Fortune Global 500 list and do library research to answer the questions (alternatively, your instructor may assign a company to you).

Of course, whether a particular international strategy orientation is appropriate for a specific company is another matter entirely. Likewise, a company may have a reasonable international strategy but may not execute it very well. These are issues that you should consider once all the answers are in.

In other words, how well do you think the company's existing strategy matches what it should be doing? If the match is poor, what recommendations would you have? If the match is good, what suggestions, if any, do you have for improving the firm's execution (e.g., in terms of market entry options or other management-related issues)?

A. *Management Team*

1. The firm's vision and culture is:

Domestic   1   2   3   4   5   Global

2. The senior management team . . .

| Doesn't include foreigners | 1 | 2 | 3 | 4 | 5 | Includes many foreigners |

3. Key jobs in all countries are held by . . .

| Home country employees | 1 | 2 | 3 | 4 | 5 | Local employees |

4. Top managers travel the world . . .

Rarely   1   2   3   4   5   Often

5. Top management familiarity with culture in key markets:

Unfamiliar   1   2   3   4   5   Familiar

6. Number of foreign nationals on company's board of directors:

None   1   2   3   4   5   Three or more

B. *Strategy*

1. Firm strategy for each country, region, or profit center:

| Separate, independent | 1 | 2 | 3 | 4 | 5 | Governed by one global plan |

2. Firm philosophy about alliances or coalitions abroad:

| "Go it alone;" relies on controlling subsidiaries or acquisitions in new markets | 1 | 2 | 3 | 4 | 5 | "Share to gain;" relies on foreign alliances to meet threats |

3. Units in specific foreign locations . . .

| Operate as separate companies | 1 | 2 | 3 | 4 | 5 | Operate as one global company |

4. In the company, environmental scanning of foreign markets is . . .

| Somewhat important | 1 | 2 | 3 | 4 | 5 | Extremely important |

5. The decisions made in the company reflect . . .

| Home country concerns and control | 1 | 2 | 3 | 4 | 5 | No preferential treatment to any country |

C. *Operations and Products*

1. The primary focus of the company is . . .

| Exporting | 1 | 2 | 3 | 4 | 5 | Full global operations |

2. The company's major operating facilities are located:

| In the home country | 1 | 2 | 3 | 4 | 5 | In North America, Japan, Europe, and elsewhere |

3. Production processes and product design decisions are . . .

Decentralized; each major country makes its own decisions

Centralized, though minor local changes are okay

1 2 3 4 5

D. *Scoring*
   Add up the points for each area:

   A. Management team (score range is 6–30):
      _____, divide by 6 = _____ average
   B. Strategy (score range is 5–25): _____, divide by 5 = _____ average
   C. Operations/Products (score range is 3–15): _____, divide by 3 = _____ average

To see where the firm is on the continuum between purely domestic and fully global, compare averages with the following scores.

Domestic	Moving toward Global		Approaching Global	Global

1.0   1.5   2.0   2.5   3.0   3.5   4.0   4.5   5.0

Source: Adapted from Lussier, R. N., Baeder, R. W., & Corman, J. (1994). Measuring global practices: Global strategic planning through company situational analysis. *Business Horizons*, September-October, 58–60.

From Theory to Practice
Critical Incidents in International Strategy

Purpose
To come up with strategies and implementation solutions to deal with problems facing various international corporations.

Instructions
Please read all four of the critical incidents that follow and develop a strategy for solving the problems presented (done *before* class). Your instructor will divide the class into groups. Each group should identify the strategic issues in all four incidents and try to achieve some kind of consensus on which strategy to implement (20 minutes).

Your instructor will lead a discussion on strategic issues. Are there some common issues which need to be addressed in international dealings? How can managers be more sensitive to these issues? (20 minutes) As an option, your instructor may ask each group to make a brief presentation on their respective findings (another 20 minutes).

Critical Incidents
Although strategic decision making is often quite complex and filled with many issues, the situations here are simplified examples of composite companies, based on true business cases. The idea is to discuss the few issues in these critical incidents without all the complexity that occurs in longer cases.

1. A clothing manufacturer has been losing business because of a competitor's lower prices and must take some action soon before the balance sheet looks worse. One idea would be to locate a new plant in Mexico, where wages are cheaper. It has been estimated that this could save the company enough to reduce the price of clothing by 15 percent, which would once again make it competitive. However, one of the top managers has mentioned that a shoe factory was just recently relocated to the area in question, and it has been hit with higher turnover and lower productivity than expected. He read that the shoes are expected to cost 12 percent more than former estimates had predicted. Should the company relocate this factory to Mexico? If not, what other strategies could be employed?

2. Equip, Inc. is interested in buying 70 percent of a large heavy machinery company in one of the former Soviet bloc countries. With a purchase price of $40 million and updating costs of $10 million, Equip figures it can realize a profit within three years, with a decent return for investors. However, the government has balked at Equip owning 70 percent, and instead wants to sell 35 percent at $20 million and expects the company to put in $8 million for renovations. Although it has not been explicitly stated (and no direct answer to questions has been given), the international department expects the company to resist laying off part of the inflated workforce. This would greatly change the profit picture. Still, if the market proceeds as expected, the company could be earning a respectable profit within five years. Inside information suggests that the government will not sell more than 49 percent, no matter what. Yet this is the type of machinery you want to get into, and you know you can develop this market further than almost any other company.

3. Your development and construction company put in a $60 million bid to build the new airport in one of the South American capital cities. The government has decided to privatize the airport. You know the other companies who bid and know that you are the most competent. Your idea is to reduce the number of employees at the airport from 2,000 to 85, with most work being contracted out to small businesses. Calculations show this to be the most efficient way to run the airport. Figures show that this project will mean a net profit of $2 million for the company, assuming no major unforeseen problems. However, a Canadian firm is given the job, a company you know is on the brink of bankruptcy. You also know that the government minister in charge of awarding the contract had spent six months in Canada a couple of years ago. Two years later you are not awarded the contract, and after the Canadian firm goes under, the government comes back to you and offers you the contract. However, because the Canadian firm made promises to keep the 2,000 employees and to hire several less than efficient subcontractors, you are not certain you can make a profit on this venture (for it looks quite difficult to get out of those promises). It even looks as if you will lose about $1 million. However, you know that several other major governments considering new airports around the world are looking at this project to see who does it and with what quality, and they are also looking at a few other similar projects now under construction by other companies.

4. You run a large mail order and television ordering business that has enjoyed enormous success in recent years. However, several of your key managers feel it is time to branch out into lesser developed countries, for there is virtually no competition in these places. They argue that even though profits would be low for several years, your company would have itself firmly established when the market surges (assuming it in fact would). Other managers do not disagree with that. On the contrary, they feel these are strong reasons to enter such markets. What they argue against are basically the problems of low income and uncertain economic futures in these countries, particularly in four of the countries. Two of the eight countries proposed even have some political instability (though admittedly not much). They also argue that these countries have poor phone systems, making it difficult for phone calls to get through and most of them do not have any capability of an 800-type system, though a few governments are said to be "thinking it over." Two of the countries are in the Pacific Rim region and are projecting tremendous rates of economic growth in the next five years. However, they are not yet consumer societies, and there is some disagreement when and if they will become so. What will you do?

Chapter

10

Making It Work: Effective International Operations

International Challenge

Exide Corporation Needed a Jump Start

LEARNING OBJECTIVES

After reading this chapter, you should be able to

- Appreciate the general challenges involved in managing strategic alliances.

- Identify the major types of organizational structures used by international firms and their respective strengths and weaknesses.

- Understand the various formal and informal approaches to coordination.

- Realize the importance of getting a technological edge and keeping it once you have obtained it.

EXIDE CORPORATION desperately needed a jump start. The Bloomfield Hills, Michigan, company was one of the world's largest makers of batteries, but this hardly made them immune to problems. In early 1999, for example, the company confronted any number of challenges. First, they were facing mounting losses after a relatively long history of success. This situation was compounded by a depressed share price ($5 versus $15 a year earlier) and a heavy debt burden. Worse yet, they faced a growing set of allegations about their business practices. Among other things, they were accused via shareholder lawsuits, and by the Florida State Attorney General's office, of selling used batteries as new and of some significant accounting irregularities. The AG's office also accused Exide's chief executive of perjury in his affidavits submitted in the state's case. The company was close to reaching a settlement with Florida, one that was made possible by the resignation of the management team that Florida accused of wrongdoing. In fact, Exide's chairman and chief executive, Arthur Hawkins, quit along with a key lieutenant in charge of North American operations. These abrupt departures followed earlier resignations by the chief financial officer and treasurer. In fact, two Exide board members had assumed day-to-day operations for the several months prior to the arrival of a new CEO, Robert Lutz.

In addition to turning his attention to these salient issues, Lutz also began to bore deeper into some more fundamental concerns about the business. He noted that the company had a booming European business, yet it missed profit targets for the previous fiscal year. And losses in U.S. operations had also mounted. Mr. Lutz began to look at the organizational structure of the firm as a possible cause and eventual remedy. Exide's structure was basically multidomestic, with about ten separately organized country operations. Shortly after his arrival, Lutz became convinced that this arrangement simply did not make sense. In fact, he felt that it actually encouraged the various European managers to compete with one another—in effect, to undercut each other's prices. Indeed, prices were falling. Lutz himself said, "Our country managers were exporting into each other's territories. . . the prices we had to meet were our own."

As it turned out, several of those country managers were responsible for businesses that Exide had acquired over time. Managers could earn a sizeable bonus if they met their country-specific target goals. As a result, in looking to expand their businesses, they went poaching into other Exide territories. As Lutz said, "They were driven to maximize their own results"—even if it was at the price of undercutting their Exide "cousins." These country managers were like "warlords" or barons, said one of those managers responsible for Britain, Mark Stevenson. Mr. Stevenson himself once battled with a German colleague over the same issue. He was selling batteries in Austria at 15 percent less than what the German unit charged in that country. While he felt that his prices fairly reflected the market there, he also recognized the problem.[1]

We think you, too, recognize the problem. We would like you to think about the organizational structure issues presented in this situation as you read through this chapter on making strategy work through effective operations. Think about the options available to Exide and then read about what Exide did to address the problems they faced in the Up to the Challenge box at the end of this chapter.

Making It Work: Effective International Operations

The last two chapters examined international strategy—the first assessing international strategy itself and the second examining various approaches to implementing the strategy. Assuming a firm has both assessed and implemented a strategy, its next goal is to stay afloat internationally. Accordingly, we now extend our discussion to the steps firms take to ensure that their international strategies work. First, we'll talk about general challenges in managing strategic alliances. We then turn our attention to a key mechanism through which firms implement their strategy—organizational structure, or the basic pattern of the firm's components, including various forms of organizational design and related coordinating tools. Today, any good strategy and structure must incorporate the impact of technology. Clearly, it's important to get a technological edge and to keep it once you have obtained it. Getting and keeping the edge is the subject of the last section of this chapter.

Challenges in Managing Strategic Alliances

Chapters 8 and 9 reviewed the strategic options available to firms and what a firm might do to bring those various strategic alliances into play. Deciding among options is one thing, but executing and managing them is quite another. In particular, there are any number of challenges to be faced and considered before venturing into an alliance with a foreign partner. These issues are summarized in Exhibit 10.1. First, it must be determined if an alliance is really the best strategic option for a given multinational. This usually involves making judgments about some of the control-benefit tradeoffs we have been talking about. Drawing on partners' capabilities and competencies has strategic advantages, but it often comes at the price of dependency, management headaches, and higher costs.

Next comes the thorny issue of selecting a partner. Ideally, partners should have similar operating philosophies and management styles. Common ground is often quite

EXHIBIT 10.1

Key Issues in Managing Strategic Alliances

Issue	Description
The logic of collaboration	Identifying when, where, and why to form an alliance; are the costs (less control) worth it (acquired learning)?
Selecting partners	Picking partners that maximize benefits and minimize risks (compatible management, trust, and complementary needs and assets)
Structuring alliances	Providing a structure that gives incentives for success (contract or equity based)
Managing alliance dynamics	Being aware of the management adjustments needed as alliances evolve
Managing alliance networks	Creating a system of reinforcing alliances that avoids anarchy
Recognizing alliance limits	Alliances can create organizational constraints, strategic gridlock, and dependence
The role of governments	Understanding the impact of government policies and pressures

Source: Adapted from Gomes-Casseres, B. (1993). *Managing international alliances.* Publication No. 793–133. Boston, MA: Harvard Business School Publishing.

difficult to find in an international context. Instead of similarity, however, partners should have **complementary** needs, goals, and capabilities. For this part of the equation, the KLM-Northwest alliance made considerable sense. KLM has a strong route structure in Europe and Africa, while Northwest offers extensive service within the United States. Joining these complementary strengths creates a formidable service network that both sides can benefit from.

Failure to monitor the partners' relationship is one reason why alliances have a low survival rate. Such ongoing fine tuning can be especially challenging when the multinational has formed several alliances. In fact, some multinationals, such as Corning Glass, have deliberately formed **alliance networks** to build a portfolio of partners who can help provide competitive advantages at a relatively low cost. Managing these networks is very time consuming and creates a potentially dangerous level of dependency. At the same time, the increasing popularity of alliances is also making it harder for multinationals to find new partners. Indeed, in the airline industry it is hard to find a firm that is not already in an international partnership. Even Midwest Express—a small Milwaukee-based airline that offers luxury travel at coach fares—has a marketing alliance with London-based Virgin Atlantic Airways.

Another management challenge that multinationals need to be aware of is the extent to which governments can affect alliances.[2] For instance, McDonnell-Douglas's production agreement with its Chinese partner faltered when the Civil Aviation Administration of China (CAAC) decided to oppose the alliance. The CAAC used its regulatory power to cancel sales of jets assembled in China by the alliance. As a result, McDonnell-Douglas lost ground in a booming market. Despite having a ten-year

REALITY CHECK

Putting Strategy in Place for Various Product Lines and Countries

A chat with John Haley, Director of Materials Management worldwide, Day International Inc. (www.dayintl.com)

Tell us a little about your company.

I work for a company headquartered in the U.S. Midwest. Basically, we make products that are used in the printing and textile industries. The business can be broken down into three individual components. One we call Image Transfer, which is a consumable rubber product that goes on a printing press. The textile components business is also primarily a rubber-type product that goes on a spinning frame that makes thread and other products. The third area is chemicals that are specially formulated for use on printing presses. My job is tying together the three divisions at the corporate level so that we can get the best deal on buying raw materials. Most of our materials are technical and so we don't usually have a lot of available suppliers; in fact, in most cases we're single sourced or have only two or three suppliers. We also purchase the freight of raw materials moving to us as well as the freight moving our products to customers. We not only want to keep prices low, but also we cannot afford to have materials damaged during shipment. We'll have scheduling problems in manufacturing or customer service problems if we do.

Other than your three division structure, how are you set up?

Basically, our international operations are wholly our own businesses. And we have facilities in the United States, Europe, the Pacific, and one small operation in South Africa. So I would

say that we have at our core a geographic structure or strategy. And, we ship a fair amount of product among our facilities. Some operations ship half products to others. For example, a large portion of the products used or sold through our South Carolina plant start in Germany. The products are finished for the U.S. market, Latin America, and the Pacific. We have warehousing operations in France, Germany, and Hong Kong for our Image Transfer business. In chemicals, we create formulations in the United States and England and then send them to satellite mixing facilities in South Africa, Malaysia, and Hong Kong. We located these facilities there because (a) they are close to market, and (b) the costs of our chemical products are sensitive to freight. In our chemicals business, we have also chosen to locate our factories close to our customers. In other businesses, we are able to use a globalization approach by manufacturing in the United States and Europe and competing on a worldwide basis. We've got to be close to customers.

So you're saying that the type of business you're in has dictated your multidomestic strategy and structure? Are there other ways you've explored to structure your operations?

Yes, and your students probably know these. But we've been at this international business for a long time now. We started shipping overseas in the early 1950s and bought a facility in Scotland in the late 1950s. We've continued our international acquisitions ever since, with the most recent example being the chemical company we bought three years ago with facilities on four continents.

---

assembly history in China, McDonnell-Douglas sold only eighty-seven jets to Chinese airlines. In contrast, Boeing, which made a point of cultivating a close relationship with the CAAC, had sold 250. Ironically, Boeing's purchase of McDonnell-Douglas meant that they were no longer competitors in the Chinese market.[3]

Finally, experts suggest that one of the things multinationals have to consider before getting into a strategic alliance is how to get out of one. Alliances terminate for a variety of reasons. Partners' goals, opportunities, or financial situations may all change. The point is that the divorce can be a messy, costly, and unfriendly affair. Multinationals can protect themselves against such circumstances by including exit clauses in alliance agreements that clearly spell out (1) the conditions that permit each partner to dissolve the alliance, (2) how alliance assets will be liquidated and divided up, (3) how partners will handle alliance liabilities that might remain after termination, and (4) how disputes threatening the alliance will be resolved.[4]

Joint ownerships create interesting structural advantages. Why haven't you pursued these?

It's true that we by and large have not. Several exceptions come to mind, however, such as in Moscow, where we own a majority interest in a joint venture that is a selling arm in Russia for products we make in the West. Most of what they sell is our products, but they also sell products of other firms so they can offer a full line of items. Additionally, we have a joint venture in Beijing with one of the biggest printing press manufacturers around. This is a 50-50 venture.

What's the advantage of working with a Chinese company?

They are actually a U.S.-European company. Our partner has some of the highest-speed commercial printing press equipment that requires a specialized product that we make. They are consumable—they wear out. We love it. We have a dominant share of the worldwide market, partly because it is technically difficult to make and our competition can't do it well or consistently. We also have a lot of other ties with this company, including a project to develop digital printing that will replace some of the current presses. The technology is different, but the business model is the same. The biggest printers in the world will buy their presses, and they consume a lot of our product.

What are some of the challenging things (other than those you've already noted) you are confronted with on a day-to-day basis?

I'd probably have to say that strategy and structure are one thing, but running the business involves a lot of communication. We try to work as best we can to keep the lines of communication open and free flowing because of the critical nature of our suppliers. We also recognize that we deal with humans, not some abstract structure. Misunderstandings are going to happen. Most of our suppliers are ISO 9002 (a quality certification program), so the technical specs answer some of the communication problems. But there are no specs for some products and services, and there we have a lot of touch and feel, knowledge, and prayer! We are more libertarian in our structure. Either way, we work hard at communicating. We are also on a first-name basis with almost everyone we deal with, up to the president. It is a cultural thing in our business. The president goes by his first name.

Do you run into other cultures that have more formal structures?

Absolutely. In fact, one of the things I have the most experience at is trying to get English, French, and German people to work together and see something in common. You have to understand, these folks have been literally battling and warring with each other for a long time. Trying to get those three factions together is a challenge because they see things very differently. There are cultural differences about how people think about work. But, I enjoy this a lot. It's a joy to deal with people even if it involves complicated problems. The cross-fertilization of ideas is fantastic. It's what made our company successful. Of course, sometimes you have to say, "Do it a specific way" as a last resort. It may happen once out of a hundred times. But most of the time, it's diplomacy, BS, friendship, schmoozing, and calling in chips. We are an international business. And, when people are exposed to the international arena, they find domestic U.S. jobs are boring because all these complicating factors aren't there. I love it.

Factors Affecting International Market Entry Choice

We have reviewed a variety of foreign entry options and their pluses and minuses. In many cases, entry decisions come down to judgments about (1) **degree of control** (how much "say" an entry mode offers over strategic and operational decisions), (2) **resource commitment** (the resources required to pursue a particular entry mode), (3) **dissemination risk** (the risks of having proprietary technology or expertise fall into the hands of a foreign partner), and (4) **systemic risk** (economic and political risks present in foreign markets). These judgments are affected by a wide variety of factors. In fact, over twenty different factors have been linked to entry choice, sometimes in an inconsistent fashion.[5] Exhibit 10.2 summarizes what we believe are some key factors influencing entry choice.

For instance, the nature of a firm's core competencies often drives entry choices. Multinationals whose main competitive advantage is proprietary technology may avoid

EXHIBIT 10.2

Factors Affecting Choice of International Entry Mode

Type of Factor	Examples
Firm factors	International experience Core competencies National culture of home country Corporate culture Firm strategy, goals, and motivation
Industry factors	Industry globalization Industry growth rate Technical intensity of industry
Location factors	Extent of scale/location economies Country risk Cultural distance Knowledge of local market Potential of local market Competition in local market
Venture-specific factors	Value of firm assets risked in foreign location Extent to which know-how involved in venture is informal (tacit) Costs of making/enforcing contracts with local partners Size of planned foreign venture Intent to conduct research and development with local partners

Source: Adapted from Phatak, A. V. (1997). *International management: Concepts and cases.* Cincinnati, OH: South-Western.

licensing and other entry modes that make controlling technology difficult. If that technology is evolving or in flux, however, then a strategic alliance with another firm may aid in the development of new or improved technologies. In contrast, if competitive advantage is based on management expertise (as in the case of many service firms), then licensing, franchising, or management contracts may represent little risk. In such cases, a brand name often goes with that expertise, something that is reasonably well protected internationally and difficult to duplicate.[6]

International experience also can drive a firm's entry choices. Firms with limited experience often use entry strategies that allow for complete control. As firms gain experience, they tend to enter more culturally and geographically distant markets where full control is difficult, leading to a heavier reliance on alliances, licensing, and so on. However, very experienced multinationals may go back to high-control entry modes (such as acquisitions), perhaps in order to coordinate their vast global operations more tightly.[7] The nature of the industry that a firm is in may also affect entry decisions. For firms in global industries, worldwide coordination and control of foreign units is essential. This need may dictate a preference for high control, something that wholly owned subsidiaries provide.[8]

Things get pretty complicated, however, once combinations of entry factors are considered. For instance, research suggests that firm nationality and level of internationalization (the percentage of sales earned abroad) do not affect the entry choices of firms competing in global industries. One explanation is that global industries by definition go beyond national borders and that national culture therefore offers little of value as competition flows across countries.[9]

Other studies suggest that culture and national origin do affect firm entry decisions. For instance, Japanese multinationals are less likely to react to shifting assessments of risk in China by raising or lowering their equity stake in joint ventures than are their American or European counterparts. Likewise, relative to Japanese and European multinationals, U.S. multinationals are less likely to insist on a majority stake in Chinese joint ventures despite the fact that they tend to put more capital into such ventures than what their agreed-on equity share calls for. More research is needed to explain exactly why these patterns occur.[10]

Research also suggests that perceptions of cultural distance can affect choice of entry mode.[11] However, the direction of this effect varies across studies. For instance, one study found that U.S. manufacturing multinationals tend to rely more on entry options that involve ownership (such as acquisitions) when the cultural distance with the target country is high. The idea is that ownership allows for more control over key technologies and management practices when they will be used in a distinctly different cultural context. Conversely, lower levels of perceived cultural distance are more likely to result in a preference for licensing and other indirect forms of foreign investment.[12] Research on service firms has reached the opposite conclusion. One study found that in a service environment, increased cultural distance was associated with entry modes that do not require ownership (such as relying on a management contract to run a hotel in culturally distant location).

Another interesting study found that when the cultural distance between the parent and host country was high, barriers to success were most severe when the foreign venture required **double-layered acculturation**. In other words, success was less likely when a multinational had to confront both a strange national culture and a strange corporate culture. This situation would occur when the multinational entered the market by setting up a joint venture, as opposed to building a wholly owned greenfield facility where only national culture is relevant. Ironically, the results also suggested that joint ventures and foreign acquisitions were the entry modes most likely to improve multinationals' ability to learn about cultural differences. This learning could increase the likelihood of success in subsequent ventures.[13] Overall, these are complex results and it is by no means clear why some of these cultural or national differences exist. This underscores two basic points: (1) that the issue of how nationality and culture impact international strategy implementation needs additional research, and (2) that several variables may interact to affect entry choice.[14]

Structuring International Business Operations

Once an entry choice is analyzed and taken, a key decision then becomes how to structure international operations. **Structure** refers to the way an organization is set up. It is what the firm uses to allocate resources, coordinate employees, distribute tasks, implement procedures, and gather and transfer information used in decision making. There is no shortage of different methods of organizational structure, although some are tied to a specific entry choice. Nevertheless, as you might suspect, there are benefits and tradeoffs between various structures. To perform well, however, a firm's organizational structure should match the sophistication of its competitive environment.[15] This implies an evolutionary process. Organizational structure typically changes as firms expand their international operations or modify their strategic approach. As a result, we'll begin by examining simple organization structures and work our way up to structures used by firms pursuing global strategies.

Basic structures for international business   In most cases, firms new to the international arena start by exporting to foreign markets. Early on, exports will be processed and handled by existing staff in existing departments, such as marketing. As exports grow, however, this arrangement can prove burdensome or even overwhelming. As a consequence, firms may look to modify their organizational structures to better coordinate and manage export operations. A common first step is to hire an export manager. This individual may also have a small staff. Together, this group is often organized into an export department. If the company has only a few products, the export manager often reports to the top marketing executive. This is the approach used by Allen-Edmonds Corporation, a U.S.-based manufacturer of high-quality dress shoes. Export staff involved in the sales and marketing of the company's shoes in Europe and Asia report to the vice president of marketing. Alternatively, if a firm exports a broad range of products, the export manager and his or her staff may report directly to the CEO.[16] These two possibilities are presented in Exhibit 10.3. Either way, we don't mean

EXHIBIT 10.3

Typical Structures for Firms with a Primary Focus on International Exports

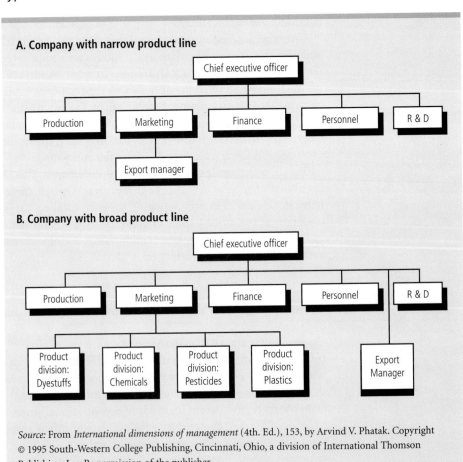

Source: From *International dimensions of management* (4th. Ed.), 153, by Arvind V. Phatak. Copyright © 1995 South-Western College Publishing, Cincinnati, Ohio, a division of International Thomson Publishing, Inc. By permission of the publisher.

to imply that these export processes are simple. Indeed, as we illustrate in the From Theory to Practice box at the end of the chapter, this structure and attending processes can be very complex.

As firms further expand internationally, so do pressures to become more knowledgeable about specific overseas markets. This is an issue that firms must confront once they start sending people abroad or begin operating foreign facilities. Generally speaking, a small export department is unlikely to be up to these challenges. In response to these strategic pressures, many firms at this stage turn to an international division structure. Basically, this involves splitting the company into domestic and international operations. The international division itself usually reports to a senior "international" executive at company headquarters (such as the vice president of

EXHIBIT 10.4

Examples of an International Division Structure

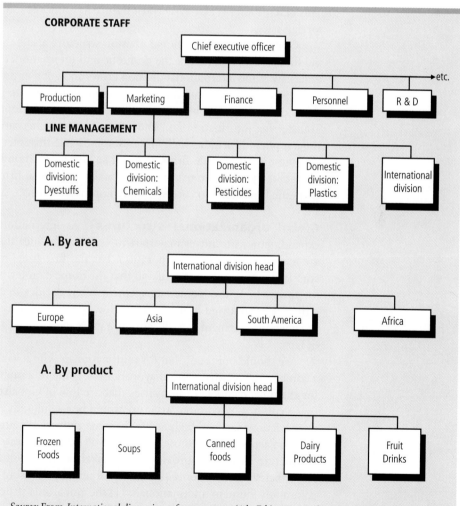

Source: From *International dimensions of management* (4th. Ed.), 155, 158, by Arvind V. Phatak. Copyright © 1995 South-Western College Publishing, Cincinnati, Ohio, a division of International Thomson Publishing, Inc. By permission of the publisher.

international operations) and provides the umbrella under which all international activities are conducted.17 For many companies, the resulting structure looks something like what you see in the top part of Exhibit 10.4. In this arrangement, a variety of domestic divisions are used to coordinate different product lines, with anything sold overseas lumped into the international division. The international division, however, may be further subdivided as overseas business expands. As you can see in the lower half of Exhibit 10.4, these subdivisions can be made either by geographic area or by product line. For instance, motorcycle maker Harley-Davidson essentially views international operations in geographic terms, with Europe and Asia treated as separate markets. As a result, different subunits within the international side of Harley-Davidson's business handle European and Asian operations.

One of the advantages of the international division structure is that it tends to concentrate managerial expertise and know-how. It also helps coordinate functions in overseas locations (such as purchasing, marketing, and sales) and serves as a reminder to top management that the firm has an international dimension. Companies that have a limited range of products, few senior managers with foreign experience, and a relatively small percentage of foreign sales are good candidates for this type of approach. This description fits Harley-Davidson since its domestic U.S. sales are twice that of total foreign sales.

Of course, the international division structure also has disadvantages. The potential for turf battles between the domestic and international sides of the business exist, especially as the international division grows and gobbles up more resources. The coordination of domestic and international operations can also prove troublesome. In fact, this can be a major problem as the firm moves toward adopting more global strategies. Transferring information and know-how between international and domestic operations is often difficult as well.[18] Interestingly, while this international division structure is common among U.S. firms, it is not so common among European multinationals. Undoubtedly, the main reason for this is that American firms rely more heavily on the domestic front than do corresponding European firms.[19]

Global organizational structures   As international operations continue to expand, senior executives may start to embrace the idea that international operations are a critical part of the corporation. For the first time, managers may feel that the company is truly international and that the home country is just one of many markets for the firm. At this point management often decides that an international division structure has outlived its usefulness.[20] However, as we discussed in Chapter 9, the extent to which management actually adopts a more global strategy depends on a wide range of factors.

We should point out that for multinationals with a variety of different businesses, a combination of structures may work best. Some of a multinational's businesses may, for example, compete in industries that are low in globalization potential, suggesting that a country-by-country structure would be useful. Other businesses may be subject to restrictions (such as high tariffs) in some countries, a situation that argues for coordination across units in those countries. Still other businesses and countries might need a structure that could provide both global coordination and local responsiveness.[21] Nevertheless, we are going to simplify things by focusing on three global structures commonly found in multinationals: (1) the global area structure, (2) the global product structure; and (3) the global matrix structure.

The **global area structure** is often a good choice for multinationals that have relatively few products and that compete in industries where a high degree of local responsiveness is required. This structure divides up the entire world into countries or regions, with each area having a fairly high degree of functional autonomy (they may have their own human resource, marketing, and production functions). Operational and strategic decision making is typically delegated to different regions or countries. The role of headquarters is to maintain overall strategic direction and control the multinational's finances. Of course, the main advantage of this structure is outstanding local responsiveness. Therefore, it is a good option for multinationals that view their businesses as essentially multidomestic. However, if local responsiveness becomes less critical or if location economies are more important (such as being able to chop production costs by moving manufacturing to a specific location), this structure can prove ineffective. The global area structure may also make it difficult to transfer learning, know-how, and competencies across borders.[22] Exhibit 10.5 illustrates the global area structure.

The **global product structure** organizes the multinational around what is usually a fairly diversified set of products or businesses. By *diversified* we mean that the products are made with different types of technology and have distinct sets of customers. Diversification often puts pressure on the multinational to coordinate and integrate key functions—such as marketing and production—that are specific to these products or businesses. In short, the global product structure uses separate divisions for each product line or business. These divisions have worldwide responsibilities for all functions associated with the product or business. Sometimes product divisions are further subdivided into areas or regions. Exhibit 10.6 illustrates the global product structure.

This structure works especially well for diversified multinationals when the pressures for local responsiveness are minimal. In other words, if the multinational

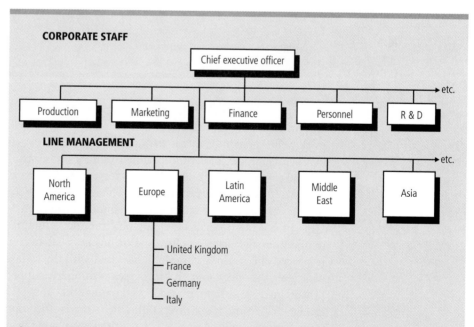

EXHIBIT 10.5

The Global Area Structure

Source: From *International dimensions of management*, (4th Ed.), 164, by Arvind V. Phatak. Copyright © 1995 South-Western College Publishing. Cincinnati, Ohio, a division of International Thomson Publishing Inc. By permission of the publisher.

EXHIBIT 10.6

The Global Product Structure

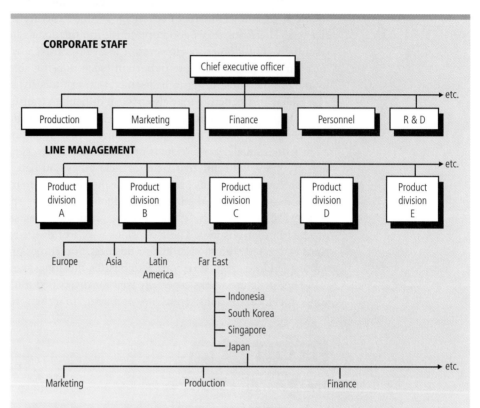

Source: From *International dimensions of management* (4th Ed.), 161, by Arvind V. Phatak. Copyright © 1995 South-Western College Publishing. Cincinnati, Ohio, a division of International Thomson Publishing Inc. By permission of the publisher.

competes in industries with truly global products (those that can be pretty much sold everywhere in the same form and in the same way), the global product structure can work well. Apparently, this is the case for the recently merged ExxonMobil company. Instead of adopting either the existing Exxon or Mobil structures, a new product-based structure was devised.[23] Likewise, Procter & Gamble's new "Organization 2005" plan acts to replace their area structures with global product structures that are tied to specific categories (e.g., paper goods, feminine protection, beauty care).[24]

At the same time, however, a global product structure does create a high level of duplication since each product line or business has to have its own facilities, human resources, and so on. ExxonMobil has dealt with this issue directly with their creation of a global services unit that provides centralized support in information systems, procurement, and human resources, among other things. Nevertheless, if local needs change or become more diverse, this structure is ill equipped to deal with it. In fact, local managers will often have a hard time even being heard since divisional product managers have more power and tend to focus on markets (often domestic ones) that account for the bulk of sales. Clearly, local responsiveness is not a strong point.[25] Indeed, this was the experience of P&G to their new structural plans. Thousands of managers were transferred or reassigned (over 1,000 European staffers to Geneva alone), creating considerable griping among middle and other management levels. These effects, in combination with weak earnings, were partly responsible for the CEO's departure after only a year and a half on the job. P&G has since reverted back to some of its original geographic structure in an effort to remain responsive to customers.[26]

Finally, the **global matrix structure** is an option that many multinationals are trying to pursue, especially those that compete in industries where both global integration and local responsiveness are required. Multinationals are also looking for a structure that will make it easier to take advantage of location economies and transfer learning and know-how throughout the entire organization. The global matrix tries to reconcile these often conflicting goals by having overlapping geographic and product division structures. In effect, decision making, control, and strategizing are shared between the product managers and geographic managers. In theory, both substructures (product based and geographic based) would have equal say; individual managers report to both a product executive and a geographic executive. The global matrix structure is illustrated in Exhibit 10.7.

While this structure has great potential, it is very difficult to implement in practice.[27] By definition, the global matrix blurs lines of authority and can create tremendous confusion and ambiguity if management does not have other mechanisms in place to help clarify things.[28] In fact, decision making can be much slower in a global matrix because managers from both the geographic and product substructures often need to spend time consulting and negotiating with each other to find common ground. Furthermore, holding managers accountable and staying free of destructive levels of conflict are often very tough to accomplish. With dual reporting arrangements,

EXHIBIT 10.7

The Global Matrix Structure

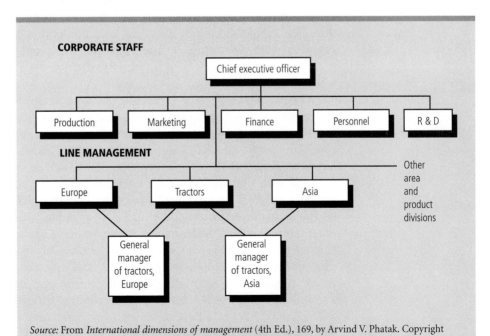

Source: From *International dimensions of management* (4th Ed.), 169, by Arvind V. Phatak. Copyright © 1995 South-Western College Publishing. Cincinnati, Ohio, a division of International Thomson Publishing Inc. By permission of the publisher.

managers under fire from a geographic executive can always blame the product side—and vice versa. Making the global matrix work requires a delicate balancing act by management. Ericsson's efforts to develop its matrix structure—a combination of customer units and geographic entities—was designed to bring the company close to customers. The financial markets, however, were relatively unimpressed and instead had additional suggestions for the troubled firm.[29] Nevertheless, if either the geographic or product side of the structure becomes too powerful, the matrix can collapse. This problem is a special challenge for Ciba-Geigy, a Swiss-based pharmaceutical firm, since along with its matrix structure based on product and geography, it has also added a third dimension of customer. One firm that has had considerable success with this structure is Asea Brown Boveri, featured in the following International Insights.

Other Relationships between Structure and Strategy

The functional or geographic setup is only one of many structural elements of a multinational. Another key element is *centralization,* or the locus of decision making in an organization. Centralization means that decision making is concentrated at the top of an organization or at its headquarters/home country. To some extent, the specific way an organization is differentiated (e.g., via products, geography, etc.) determines the degree of centralization, but there is more to decision making than this. The key question remains the extent to which a foreign operation or subsidiary is free to make decisions or whether that capability is centralized above the foreign operation.

In an earlier chapter, we referred to various strategies a firm could employ when it goes global. For example, a firm could adopt a globalization strategy that emphasizes similarity of products and services in various markets, or it could adopt a multidomestic strategy that focuses on tailoring. Typically, the choice is closely aligned with the amount of control over decisions. In Exhibit 10.9 we show the typical relationship between various strategies and aspects of structure, including this topic of centralization. That exhibit shows that the degree of centralization of decision making is often associated with the strategy a firm employs. For example, firms that use a multidomestic approach are likely to decentralize decision making to the national units in which they do business.

These conclusions about decision-making control are general, and many exceptions could be noted. For example, Deutsche Bank did not necessarily use a structure based on its strategy. Instead, it used a centralized approach common to German companies in its ill-fated acquisition of Bankers Trust, a U.S. company. Indeed, Deutsche Bank's chairman pointed out, "We don't believe in autonomy. We will continue with our centralized management."[33] Certain businesses may also have a tendency to exercise more control than others, even though their strategy might suggest otherwise. In the pharmaceutical business, for example, where control is critical, and in other technologically complex areas, where quality is of the highest importance (e.g., GE's aircraft engine business), a similar centralization effect is apparent.[34] There are also occasional efforts to adopt a less control-oriented structure than is probably necessary. A case in point is the BMW purchase of the British company, Rover. At first, to avoid attributions of a heavy-handed German approach to control and to keep its brand as a selling point, BMW gave Rover a relatively free hand. After four straight years of losses and lagging productivity, BMW exercised more centralized control and sold the operation about a year later.

As the BMW example suggests, the location of decision making within a company can change, sometimes dramatically, over time. This point is made further in the Up to

INTERNATIONAL INSIGHTS

Culture, People, and Structure Support Global Strategy at ABB

SUCCESSFULLY COMPETING against the likes of Siemens and General Electric is no small feat. Nevertheless, Zurich-based ABB Asea Brown Boveri AG has done well. The electrical equipment giant maintains 5,000 operations in 140 countries and is looking for more success. So how does ABB do it? In a nutshell, ABB's success is the result of a global matrix structure supported by a strong corporate culture and management team.

ABB's values come from the top. Executive Chairman Percy Barnevik led the merger joining Asea AB of Sweden and BBC Brown Boveri LTD of Switzerland in 1988. To guide the new firm, ABB, Mr. Barnevik wrote a 55-page document spelling out its values and policies. Today, ABB employees refer to this manifesto as the "bible." One of Mr. Barnevik's core ideas was that ABB should view itself as having no home base; rather, home was wherever ABB markets were. ABB's Zurich "headquarters" is staffed by 171 employees from nineteen different nations. This is also where ABB's executive committee, a collegial and international group that oversees global operations, is based. The idea is that ABB must prepare itself to tap good ideas and leverage expertise wherever it can be found. Indeed, even the new Internet-based strategy of CEO Jorgen Centerman is an example of such an approach.[30] But there is more to it than that.

To achieve a balance between global industry goals and local needs, ABB relies on a global matrix structure that combines business and geographic perspectives. ABB has four sets of businesses (Power Generation, Power Transmission/Distribution, Industrial and Building Systems, and Financial Services), each with several product or service lines. Geographically, the company is divided up into three major areas (Europe, the Americas, and Asia Pacific), each with a variety of country managers. This structure is illustrated in Exhibit 10.8.

As a result, local business managers have two bosses. For example, the plant manager of ABB's motor factory in Mexico (motors are part of the Industrial and Building Systems business segment) has two bosses: (1) the country manager for Mexico (part of the Americas geographic group); and (2) an Industrial and Building Systems manager responsible for global motor strategy. When local business managers have needs that conflict with ABB's global strategy for a particular product line, it's up to the country manager to sort things out. Usually, this involves negotiations with local management. Sometimes, however, things get rancorous. At one point, an ABB country manager had to threaten to move all work abroad before German unions would endorse a compromise plan that saved 1,500 jobs.

This incident underscores the critical nature of the country manager's job in ABB's matrix structure. Not surprisingly, ABB tries hardest to ingrain its values in these managers. The result is a 500-strong class of multilingual managers whose careers are spent moving from one foreign outpost to another. Their basic mission is to improve performance, cut costs, and get local managers to accept ABB's worldwide strategies while listening to local concerns at the same time. Being successful at this job requires strong identification with the corporation's worldview but also an extraordinary ability to understand local cultures. Benny Olsson, an ABB country manager for Mexico reflects this combination. Charged with pushing ABB's Mexican plants up to worldwide quality standards, Mr. Olsson—a blond, blue-eyed Swede—has an interesting answer when asked where he's from: "I'm Mexican".[31]

It remains to be seen what will happen to CEO Centerman's reorganization. He replaced the four industrial divisions with four new customer segments, two product-based divisions, and a new group to manage "corporate transformation"—a general shift to the Internet to respond more quickly to customers' needs.[32]

the Challenge box at the end of the chapter that features the structural changes the Exide Corporation has made in relatively short order over the last few years. Likewise, the formal decision chain may differ from the actual decision mode; moreover, actual decision making is less one-sided that we have implied. Both these points are also made by the Exide example. In general, all this suggests that a multinational possesses considerable informal structural control, a point we now turn to in greater depth.

EXHIBIT 10.8

ABB's Global Matrix Structure

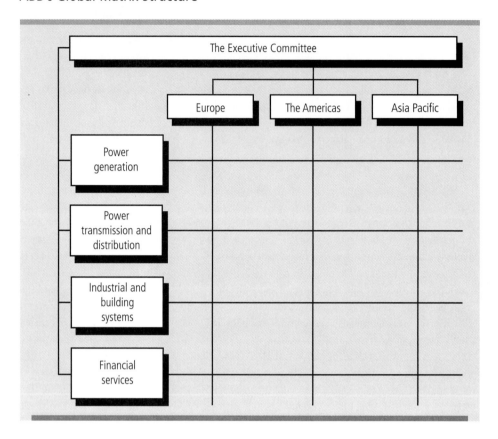

Formal and Informal Approaches to Coordination

There is more to strategy implementation than just pure organizational structure. Mechanisms have to exist that help coordinate the various pieces of the firm in ways that support its international goals. For instance, corporate culture, management processes, and human resources have to be appropriately aligned with firm strategy for it to be implemented successfully, especially in the case of global strategies (see also Exhibit 10.9 for other such differences across strategies). ABB's strong corporate culture and well-trained managers are examples of informal coordination mechanisms. These mechanisms support the firm's organizational structure as it pursues its international strategy. More formal coordination mechanisms also exist. For example, some multinationals use teams of managers from different units (either on a permanent or temporary basis) to improve coordination and increase information exchange across the organization. Other multinationals assign individual managers to act as a liaison between, say, a business area and a geographic area. Still other multinationals may have a policy whereby managers who have concerns or need information from another unit are told to contact their counterparts directly.[35]

Today, however, many experts are endorsing an interesting type of informal coordination mechanism known as the **lateral communication network**. This network can be defined as the informal set of interpersonal relationships that exists between

EXHIBIT 10.9

The Relationship between Structural Components and Strategy

	Type of Strategy			
Aspect of Structure	**Multidomestic**	**International**	**Globalization**	**Transnational**
Centralization	National/local Control	Core functions centralized; others under national control	Centralized at best global point	Combination of centralized/ decentralized
Division of labor	Global area	International division	Global product	Global matrix
Need for integrating mechanisms	Low	Medium	High	Very high
Organizational culture	Not important	Important	Important	Very important

Source: Adapted from Hill, C.W., & Jones, E. R. (1995). *Strategic management.* Boston: Houghton Mifflin; Deresky, J. *International management.* Upper Saddle River, NJ.: Prentice-Hall.

managers in different units of a multinational. When problems exist in one unit, managers can tap their informal networks for help. The attractiveness of such networks is that they can be a quick, flexible, and effective way to exchange information within multinationals. These attributes are especially valuable for two reasons: (1) information flow is needed to spread expertise and knowledge throughout the global organization, and (2) the global structures of large multinationals often impede this information flow. In fact, some experts argue that such interunit networking is even more important than formal structures. This implies that multinationals should see themselves more as a set of relational networks than as a rigid structure that distributes functions and responsibilities. Research tends to support this idea. One study found that foreign subsidiaries' decision-making autonomy (a structural variable) had little impact on the level of communications (1) between subsidiaries, or (2) between headquarters and subsidiaries. In both cases, however, the level of communications was positively affected by the extent to which managers engaged in informal networking with their peers.[36]

Unfortunately, their informality makes building lateral communications networks difficult by definition. Some multinationals, however, are trying to encourage managers to develop such networks. The idea is to create a patchwork quilt of relationships that will effectively cover and interconnect the entire organization. One way to support the development of informal networks is to encourage managers to use the sophisticated communications technology available to nurture their global contacts (such as electronic mail systems and telephone and video conferencing). Management development strategies that bring people together from around the world for face-to-face interactions and relationship building are another way that multinationals can encourage the formation of informal networks. Examples of multinationals that use this method to encourage the development of informal networks include Nokia, S. C. Johnson, and Unilever.

Informal networks among peers can be a powerful coordinating mechanism for multinationals. © Yang Liu/CORBIS

The Management of Technology by Multinationals

One advantage of such informal networks is the ability to make better decisions about entering or avoiding a particular country or about scaling back existing operations in risky locations. The issue of risk probably plays a larger role in the area of technology than any other. That is, today risk can increasingly be tied to threats to a firm's technological advantage—or its lack of advantage. Many of the better firms recognize that to survive and succeed, they must continually change and update their technological applications. There have been a number of dramatic technological changes and advances in the twentieth century, particularly in the areas of communications and transportation. And, of course, the rapid development of information technology has made many of these changes possible. On the other hand, some experts have also argued that instead of making strategy obsolete, the Internet actually has the opposite effect. Since it does not provide a proprietary operational advantage, this could make strategy all the more important.[37] Even wildly successful ventures are not necessarily seen as transforming their business, but instead reinforcing their core business. Nonetheless, it is probably fair to say that the competitive advantage offered by factoring technology, such as the Internet, into strategic initiatives can contribute to business success.

Getting a Technological Advantage

If the preceding statement is true, then how do firms develop a technological edge? There are several ways to gain a leg up on competition. One of the main ways is to develop a technological advantage entirely on your own. For example, a firm could assemble an in-house group of scientists and engineers to work on developing or altering a technology of importance to the firm. In many global industries, such as computers, communications, and oil/gas development, this is exactly what many do; in fact, it is common for such firms to have a stand-alone research and development arm. These companies are responsible for many of the important technological innovations of this century. Lucent Technologies, for example, maintained a large network of R&D units to provide solutions to problems and new product development (purchased from AT&T). In general, its investments in the former Bell Laboratories paid off. The complex in Homdel, New Jersey, is served by a large, unique-looking water tower built in the shape of a transistor, and it reminds one that this very important innovation was developed at the Labs (as were ten other Nobel Prize–winning innovations). As of the time of this writing, however, Lucent has more than its share of problems, and some predict that it may sell off some of its R&D units.

Although AT&T still retains an R&D unit, its budgets are much smaller now than a few years ago. Of course, not all R&D spending results in new, innovative, and marketable products. Nevertheless, the amount of R&D expenses and/or the percentage of scientists relative to the total number of employees is the main way that the technology intensity of firms is indexed. Since World War II, the United States on average has devoted a larger percentage of its gross domestic product to R&D than any other country. U.S. firms are still among the forefront in such investments. In 1992, for example, R&D expenditures as a percent of GDP were 3 percent in Japan, 2.7 percent in Germany, and 1.8 percent in the United States.[38] Exhibit 10.10 presents more recent data in regard to this point for a wide variety of countries.[39] As you can see, the Triad is responsible for most of this investment, with the United States, Japan, and European countries leading the way by a large margin. At the same time, if these expenditures come to fruition, then we can anticipate that countries such as Sweden, Korea, and Switzerland, among others, will be producing viable products or ventures based on advanced technology in the near future.

As these numbers suggest, acquiring a technological edge via in-house research facilities can be very expensive. And, as shown by the AT&T example, even some big firms have decided to cut back on their R&D. This "Lone Ranger" strategy, however, is not the only option. Firms from industries like semiconductors and telecommunications often decide to cost-share their R&D. Take, for example, the regional U.S. phone operating companies ("Baby Bells") that were created via a federal judicial decision that required AT&T to divest itself of its local phone service monopoly. At that time, seven new companies were created to deliver phone service to various regions of the United States. The ruling that created the firms stipulated that they could not compete with AT&T in certain business areas. However, many of those new companies felt that this stipulation would eventually be removed and that the Baby Bells (e.g., Ameritech, PacTel) would be able to develop all kinds of new products. Development costs in this area were seen as enormous; as a result the Baby Bells joined together to create one large R&D unit which would serve all seven companies. That company, Bell Communications Research, was very successful. Although there were some problems in information sharing, the cost savings to the consortium was great.

There is at least one other option, beyond developing it all yourself or in conjunction with others, for acquiring a technological edge. In some cases, a firm might simply purchase the technology that it needs. Ford, for example, recently bought a smaller company called Excell Industries that provided them a better way to make windows via a technology that would have been far more expensive for Ford to develop on its own.[40] This is a common strategy in the high technology and communications industry as well. For example, several years ago Acer Computers, Inc., the Taiwanese company that was among the first to make unique-looking PCs (e.g., different colors, rounded shapes, etc.), bought several U.S. firms. Acer's goal was to use the technology

EXHIBIT 10.10

Rankings of Various Countries on Total R&D Spending

Rank	Country	Expenditure (US$ millions)	Rank	Country	Expenditure (US$ millions)
1	United States	243,548	25	Russia	1,956
2	Japan	141,694	26	Singapore	1,567
3	Germany	50,262	27	Argentina	1,466
4	France	31,684	28	Poland	1,157
5	United Kingdom	25,750	29	Ireland	1,109
6	Italy	12,219	30	Turkey	935
7	Canada	10,034	31	South Africa	779
8	Korea	10,028	32	New Zealand	734
9	Sweden	8,776	33	Czech Republic	683
10	China	8,201	34	Portugal	660
11	Switzerland	8,083	35	Greece	614
12	The Netherlands	7,630	36	Chile	425
13	Taiwan	5,903	37	Colombia	374
14	Brazil	5,876	38	Hong Kong	354
15	Australia	5,570	39	Venezuela	341
16	Spain	5,383	40	Hungary	329
17	Belgium	4,490	41	Slovenia	300
18	Finland	4,003	42	Malaysia	287
19	Austria	3,786	43	Indonesia	187
20	Denmark	3,461	44	Iceland	162
21	Israel	2,841	45	Thailand	147
22	Norway	2,590	46	Slovak Republic	134
23	India	2,303	47	Philippines	51
24	Mexico	1,997	48	Estonia	30

Source: (2001). Total expenditure on R&D, 1999, ranking as of April 24, 2001. Http://www.imd.ch/wcy/criteria/4301.cfm

developed by these Silicon Valley companies to rapidly accelerate their North American business. This approach turned out to be less effective than they hoped, and in mid-2001, Acer turned from a manufacturer to a marketing and services provider, "making e-business the company's new core focus."[41]

As you have probably already gathered, even though acquiring existing technology may be cheaper (in the long run) than developing it on your own, acquisitions are still expensive. In fact, Acer paid over $100 million for those two American companies. In general, technology is just plain expensive, and this makes it extremely difficult for newly developing economies to catch up. New developments, such as powerful but inexpensive networked PCs, may offer opportunities for these countries (as the following International Insights illustrates).

Using Your Technological Edge

Once a company develops or acquires the technology it needs, it must then decide how to best use it. One way to do this is to try to keep the technology within the firm for its exclusive use. Usually those firms with large R&D arms try to keep their critical technology in house as they apply it to new products and services. Some firms seem to be especially good at new product development. The 3M Company of St. Paul, Minnesota, is particularly well known for its application of technology to new product development.[45] One of the main reasons seems to be that the marketing function of the firm has a close tie to the R&D group. This was certainly the case for the development of the Post-It product for which 3M is famous. Nevertheless, even among the best companies, most new products fail to become successful. In fact, economists estimate that about 80 percent of all new products fail in the marketplace.[46]

Once a new product is developed via R&D or other means, firms can choose to sell or transfer the technology to others. This can be a good source of revenue for the firm, but also a source of worry, as we will show. Probably the most common transfer of critical technology is from the multinational to one or more of its foreign subsidiaries (usually wholly owned). Obviously, one of the key advantages of this approach is that the multinational retains control over the important and proprietary technology. However, there are numerous other ways to transfer technology across borders. Since many of these were discussed in Chapter 9, we will only briefly mention them here.

One additional way that technology can be transferred is through franchising. Here a company sells another firm the right to use its products or services and the easily recognized company name. In return for all these benefits, the franchisee usually pays the company a fee based on the volume of business. There are many famous examples of U.S. businesses that transfer their technology in this way, including McDonald's, Holiday Inn, and Avis. Franchising offers less control over critical company technologies (in products or services) than if the multinational operated the business itself. But if the processes can be relatively easily copied anyway (e.g, the Burger King approach), then franchising may be the way to go. As we also know from Chapter 9, licensing and joint ventures are other ways that technological know-how can be shifted across borders. Each of these methods offers even less control by the multinational over important technology. Nevertheless, as we noted earlier, joint ventures are very common. One reason to risk proprietary technology by entering into an agreement with a foreign government is to get access to a market that is otherwise impenetrable. Joint ventures, for example, are a very common way to gain a foothold in China. Companies are stumbling over one another to enter China because of the size of this market, despite the fact that their technology is put at great risk.

INTERNATIONAL INSIGHTS

Downloading the Digital Bandwagon: Small Firms Bank on Technology to Create a Cultural Window of Opportunity

BILL GATES OF MICROSOFT is regularly seen on Brazilian television making a pitch for a home-banking program that is not one of his products. Looking straight at viewers, Mr. Gates gave the system developed by Uniao de Bancos Brasileiros SA a techie's highest praise: "It's really cool." Then, in Portuguese subtitles, Mr. Gates added, "Why didn't my bank think of that?"

One of the reasons this is noteworthy is that only seven years ago it was rare to see a PC in Brazil. Now, however, hundreds of thousands of Brazilians are banking at home—a rare event for most Americans still—and everybody recognizes Bill Gates. Brazil is apparently just one example of a global trend. Countries such as Hungary, Bangladesh, Poland, and Indonesia had historically been left out or have lagged far behind the technology revolution that has occurred over the last quarter century. The startup costs were enormous and these great sums of money were needed for other things. Now, however, these same countries are able to join the fray via the powerful—yet relatively affordable—PCs and networks.

And countries are jumping on this technology wagon. Many areas of the world are seeing growth in sales of PCs that is greater than the United States. Latin America, for example, saw a 24 percent growth spurt last year, up to 2 million machines. Some experts even feel that being a newcomer to the technology game pays a dividend. In the Czech Republic, for example, banks have purchased networks of PCs in droves. Unlike their Western counterparts, they do not worry about being tied to investments in older and more cumbersome mainframe systems. The Komercni Banka in Prague, for example, recently purchased a Dell Computer Corp. client-server network. This network allowed the bank to access a worldwide currency valuation system for the first time. It quickly brought them up to speed with foreign competition and did so in a relatively inexpensive way. "Some technology is now affordable by most people except the very, very poor nations," says Eduardo Talero, a technology specialist at the World Bank.

The spread of lower-cost but powerful computers has been a boon for small business. PC sales in Chile, for example, have increased over 350 percent in the last several years. The majority of this increase comes from small businesses. "There are a lot of people in Chile who started a company in their house and now are doing $1 million in sales every year," says Andres Rudolphy, president of Computek, Chile's largest PC company. Nevertheless, governmental policy also reflects an understanding of the importance of this trend. Santiago recently invested $3 million for school computers. And to help promote business, they have computerized trade and tariff data, company catalogs, and e-mailed sales brochures to potential customers around the world. This work may be responsible for Chilean success on the world market in products from kiwi fruit to tinned fish.

Although these are all positive trends, Chile and other developing countries have a good deal of ground to make up. For example, whereas the United States had sixty PCs for every 100 people in 2000, Chile had only about five.[42] Worse yet, Colombia had fewer than four per 100 and Venezuela and Brazil average about two PCs per 100 people. Data on the percent of people with Internet access at home show a similar disparity (e.g., 46% of U.S. households vs. 3% in Brazil).[43] However, if all these signs are any indication, less developed countries are catching up quickly. It may be one of the few times in history when this could happen, and many countries appear to be entering through this window of opportunity.[44]

Maintaining Your Edge

As we have said, the competitive advantage offered by technology is often a critical factor in the success of a multinational's products and services. Nevertheless, the process of transferring technology can put one's advantage at risk. As a result, many countries have developed laws that help their multinationals protect their technological edge. Although we have generally dealt with these issues in Chapter 2, here we can say that there are two main methods by which a multinational can protect its technology from abuse.

Maintaining a technological edge is a challenge for many multinationals.
© HMS Group/CORBIS

One mechanism that multinationals can use to protect their technology is a **patent**. A patent offers the developer monopoly rights for a certain period of time (e.g, seventeen years in the U.S.) for a new or substantially enhanced product or process. The justification for such a monopoly is that the originating firm spent a great deal of its time and money on the advancement and, as a result, they should be rewarded for their work. Proponents also argue that new product development would all but dry up if there were no such protection or incentive in the form of patents. Another type of protection is the **trademark**. Trademarks are the distinctive product designs, features, or logos that distinguish the product or service from others. Since people often buy a product because the trademark symbolizes an attractive, high-quality product (e.g., Hilfiger jeans, Reebok shoes, etc.), these designs also often receive protection from competition.

Although patents, trademarks, and other mechanisms do provide protection for the multinational, there are several issues here that make protection much less than complete. For one thing, there are some great differences among countries in how strictly they control the patent and trademark process. Exhibit 10.11, for example, compares these protections across a number of selected countries. As you will note, there is wide variance in the duration of a patent or trademark across countries as well as the amount of money a multinational can charge another company to use its technology (see "limits on royalties"). Perhaps the most important variable here, however, is whether the country is highly industrialized or in the process of developing. The latter type of country (e.g., Brazil, Egypt) is less likely to provide strong protection for technology than are industrialized countries (see left half of Exhibit 10.11).

Beyond cross-national differences in protection, another issue for multinationals is the ability to prevent misuse of legal mechanisms or the bypassing of them altogether

EXHIBIT 10.11

The Protection of Technology Across Borders

Country	Limit on Royalties	Highest Tax on Royalty (%)	Unpatentable Items	Patent Duration	Trademark Duration
Industrialized					
Canada	None	25	Chemicals for food and medicine; theories	17 yrs.	15 yrs. renewable
France	6% of sales, unless approved tech.	33.3	Nonindustrial items; animals, software, medical treatments	20	10 yrs. renewable
Germany	10% of sales	25	Medical treatments, software	20	10 yrs. renewable
Italy	None	21	Theories	20	20 yrs. renewable
Japan	None, but often 8% of sales	20	Nuclear transformations	20	10 yrs. renewable
United Kingdom	None, but often 7% of sales	25	Science discoveries; artistic	20	7 yrs. renewable
United States	None	46	Noncommercial items	17	20 yrs. renewable
Newly Industrialized/Developing					
Argentina	None	45	Drugs, nonindustrial items	5, 10, 15	10 yrs. renewable
Brazil	1–5% of sales to unrelated firms only	25	Drugs, foods; chemicals	15	10 yrs. renewable
Egypt	None	40	Any substance, only production processes are patentable	15 yrs., renewable	10 yrs. renewable
Mexico	None, but often	40	Food, drugs, agricultural items	14	5 yrs. renewable
Nigeria	1% of sales	15	Plants, animals, biological	20	7 yrs. renewable
Singapore	None	32	None	Only U.K. patents are valid	U.K. or Singapore registered. 7 yrs.

Source: Business International Corporation. (1990). Copyright © Investing, Licensing, and Trading Conditions. Reproduced by permission of the Economist Intelligence Unit.

(e.g, illegal pirating of products). Pirating was discussed in an earlier chapter. For now, however, we should point out that misuse of patent and trademark applications is also an issue. By this, we are referring to the legal but improper use of mechanisms like patents. For example, large firms sometimes engage in patent "flooding." This involves

INTERNATIONAL INSIGHTS

U.S. Firm Battled a Japanese Giant to Protect Its Technology

STEVEN CASE, founder and chair of a firm called Cyberoptics, has made a lot of good moves in his business career. But his invitation to Yamaha Motor Co. to visit Cyberoptics was not his best! Although the meeting initially was seen as very positive, their five-year alliance together ended up in U.S. District Court. Cyberoptics was suing Yamaha for contract and patent violations, charging that Yamaha, the maker of motorcycles and other vehicles, used a flood of patent filings to poach the technology Cyberoptics had developed.

A few years ago, it was common for many U.S. companies to worry that Japan would dominate lots of critical technology. Cases like that of Cyperoptics, however, show how worries about large foreign firms may still be warranted. In fact, the sheer number of similar cases a few years ago led the U.S. Trade Representative to raise the practice of "patent-flooding" by Japanese firms as an issue between countries, and the Cyberoptics case in particular. This practice caused much conflict in the late 1980s between Tokyo and Washington, and the issue has persisted despite a 1995 treaty designed to stop the practice.

Apparently, patent flooding is common in Japan; in the United States, however, it is often viewed as a questionable and potentially illegal business practice. Flooding occurs when a firm files for many separate but isolated patents that closely resemble a rival's patent that is larger in scope. As a result, the original innovating firm finds it difficult or impossible to bring the patented item to market. If it does, it finds itself slapped with lawsuits by the "flooder" claiming a patent infringement. To avoid all the problems and the costs, many firms (particularly smaller ones) are cornered into exchanging mutual patent rights.

The Cyberoptics case is much like this typical situation. And because of its relatively small size, there was a lot on the line. Mr. Case set up the company after leaving his teaching position at the University of Minnesota. His company makes products such as optical laser sensors and three-dimensional image analysis software that, among other things, help robots operate better. The firm started with

three employees but now has over 200 as well as revenues of over $64 million. Prior to this, however, Cyberoptics' problems began when Mr. Case met with Yamaha engineers at an Anaheim, California hotel. During the meeting, Cyberoptics demonstrated its new product. And Yamaha was impressed; they bought 500 of the systems over the next five years. What followed, however, did not impress an overly trusting and perhaps naive Cyberoptics.

Mr. Case said in his court affidavit that during a visit to Yamaha after his demonstration he came up with a way to improve the effectiveness of Yamaha's robots. In fact, he jotted down an outline of his invention right there on a napkin. Yahama engineers were impressed and told him so. In fact, the napkin is one of the many documents entered into evidence for this case. Mr. Case claims he signed and dated it for patent purposes. Other documents allegedly also support Cyberoptics' claim that Yahama made only slight changes to its inventions when they filed patents. Mr. Case says that without informing him, Yamaha filed twenty-six such patents in a number of countries that represent only slight variants of the Cyberoptics product. He claimed this was in violation of an agreement that neither company would file patents on their collaboration without mutual consent. Mr. Case says that he was not even aware of the Yamaha patents until another company pointed them out. The patents included were very similar to those he had sketched out on the napkin and in other places. For Yamaha's part, they denied the allegations. They claimed they informed Cyberoptics of the applications and that the napkin was nothing more than a duplication of existing Yamaha diagrams that their engineers showed Mr. Case. They did not remember seeing the napkin. Yahama countersued Cyberoptics for defamation, saying that the charges were false and slanderous. The record does show, however, that Yahama did apply for many related patents, and as early as 1996 Japan was added to the U.S. watchlist of countries with weak patent protection. While the facts were being sorted out in U.S. federal court, Cyberoptics continued to spend a lot of time and money to protect its technology.[47]

applying for many different patents dealing with small variations on technology origi-nally developed by one's competition. This practice handcuffs the innovating firm and ties them to the firm that "flooded" the patents. The following International Insights provides a specific example of how patent flooding affected a small U.S. firm.

Chapter Summary

In this chapter we extended our discussion of interna-tional strategy to a consideration of key ways that firms ensure that their international strategies work. First, we discussed the general challenges involved in managing *strategic alliances*. For example, we reviewed firm, industry, location, and venture-specific factors that can affect the choice of international entry modes. This led to a discussion of a key mechanism through which firms implement their strategy—*organizational structure*—the basic pattern or design of the firm's components.

We also considered the strengths and weaknesses of different types of structures. First, we discussed the *simple structures* that companies often use when they are first gaining experience in the international arena. These included hiring an export manager or setting up an export department. As international business grows, firms may split into domestic and international operations; the essence of the *international division structure*.

Organizations that see themselves as international companies and that have a substantial portion of their business overseas often turn to *global organizational structures*. We considered three examples: The *global area structure* divides up worldwide operations by geography. It is often a good choice when products need to be highly responsive to specific local needs. The *global product structure*, in contrast, divides up operations around product or business lines. This is a structure that works well for firms that have highly diversified products that can be sold anywhere in the world with little or no modi-fication. Finally, the *global matrix structure* relies on over-lapping product and geographic divisions. This structure tries to balance the needs of global integration with local

responsiveness. Although difficult to implement, it may be useful for multinationals that compete in global industries but still need to react effectively to local concerns. In addition, we included a discussion of the formal and informal coordination mechanisms—such as *lateral communication networks*—that support a multinational's structure and its international strategy.

Any time you add more complexity to a design or strategy, you open yourself up to potentially more prob-lems, and this is true in international operations as well. In particular, a firm that takes the international plunge subjects itself to more risk than others and probably more than many imagine. One of the biggest potential risk factors, and an issue any manager would need to monitor, has to do with technology. Clearly, it is important to get a technological edge and to keep it once you have obtained it. We completed the chapter with a discussion of this important issue.

Discussion Questions

1. What factors shape firms' foreign entry decisions?
2. What are the pros and cons associated with the various organizational structures used by interna-tional firms? How does structure relate to strategy?
3. What are some factors that could help a firm coordi-nate among the various strategies and structures used to conduct international business?
4. What are some of the management challenges in protecting and defending one's technological innova-tions? How might one or another organizational structure help a firm maintain its proprietary technology?

Up to the Challenge?

Robert Lutz and a New Structure May Recharge Exide's Batteries

You'll recall from the chapter opening box that Exide, one of the world's largest battery makers, faced some serious financial problems that seemed to be emanating in part from its organiza-tional structure. In short, its multidomestic structure encouraged intense competition within various country units of Exide, particularly in Europe, where they were

faced with meeting the prices of other Exide country units—an intolerable situation. What did Robert Lutz, chair, president, and CEO of the company, do?

The first thing Lutz did was to conduct a series of upper management retreats in order to build con-sensus for overhauling the company structure. In June 1999, barely six months on the job, Lutz convened a meeting of thirty senior executives in a hotel in Madrid, where he posed the question: "Does our future lie in country management or in global business units?" Some area managers were wary of change. This was true of German managers, whose region was in pretty good shape and who feared that a new structure might damage the German business. After the first meeting, a series of teams dealt with specific issues and then reported their findings at the next retreat, held in a converted castle in Florence. The team reports were hotly debated for two hours until Lutz stood up and announced, "We don't have 100% consensus, but I'm going to make a decision, and we're going to a global business structure." So global product lines were set to replace geographical fiefdoms.

Not all were happy, to say the least. Mr. Santigo Ramirez, European operations director in charge of some 10,000 executives, production workers, and salespeople, was disappointed. Lutz asked one of his executives, Eduardo Garnica, managing director of Spain, "Why don't you give it a try?" "No, I'm out of here," said Garnica, according to Lutz. Both Spanish managers left the company shortly after the reorganization. Another retreat three months later, this one at Amelia Island in Florida, revealed why there was resistance. "Being a country manager is my life," said Mr. Giovani Mele, managing director of Italy. "It's something I've worked for my whole life. I don't see how I'll have a role going forward" he said with a choked voice.

But, go forward is what Exide did. They initially formed six global business units organized around product lines. Many remaining country managers were demoted to a "local coordinator" role. A few, like Dr. Albrecht Leuschner, moved from German country manager to director of the global network power unit (this unit makes batteries for computers, phone systems, and the like). But, that did not last long.

"I was emperor of the world for six weeks," said Leuschner. In that interim period, Exide bought another battery maker, GNB Technologies, for $370 million in an effort to regain a preeminent position in North America. CEO Lutz feared that the president of GNB, the well-regarded Mitchell Bregman, would flee once that operation was fit into the global structure. So he made some moves back to the older geographic structure by allowing Bregman to retain control over the North American unit.

While this repositioning created some turmoil and turf battles, the newer, blended structure has worked well. In fact, although there are still separate North American and European battery groups, each has gotten together to make joint sales pitches to giant customers such as Ford. The company also inked a deal with Emerson to supply batteries, a deal Lutz believed would not have been made within the old organizational structure. And the results started to come in. Exide's operating results reversed themselves in the second half of the fiscal year 2001. Positive results were attributed to the GNB acquisition and the new structural approach. In fact, Lutz said the restructuring worked "far better" than they expected. But it wasn't seen as a permanent solution. Lutz vowed to change again if conditions warrant: "Come back a year from now and we will look different." But Exide will have to make future charges without Lutz, since he recently joined GM. Earlier in his career, as president of Chrysler, he made an impressive mark on that firm and probably will at GM as well.

International Development
A Detailed Look at Managing International Operations

Purpose

To work on skills in the area of recognizing and identifying operational plans based on particular strategic alliances for an international firm.

Instructions

Your instructor may place you in groups of four to six for this exercise. First, select a company that you are interested in, hopefully a firm that does business internationally. Research the firm on the Internet and through your online library resources, such as ABI Inform or LEXIS/NEXIS. Then identify the firm's main competitors or the two or three biggest players in that industry. Visit those websites and gather information about those firms as well.

Describe the international strategy used by your target firm and the main competitors in that industry. Do the following for each firm:

- Describe the international strategy taken by each firm. From your research, discuss the probable reasons for a firm's choice.
- Describe the form of organizational structure taken by each firm to run its international businesses. Evaluate some potential options for structuring international operations in their order of value.
- Evaluate the effectiveness of each firm's strategic approach compared to their competition.
- Provide a brief analysis of the risks faced by these firms using existing rating schemes available on the Internet (e.g., http://www.polrisk.com/)
- Are there any special technological issues or risks that may have determined (a) the particular strategy employed, and (b) the organizational structure used?

If the class is small enough, your instructor may have your group make a brief presentation (10 strategic minutes) about your findings to the class. This could be followed by a discussion about managing international operations. Alternatively, your instructor may make this an individual assignment and have students be prepared to take part in a general class discussion on the issues raised.

From Theory to Practice
Exporting Your Technology Products

For this exercise, we want you to assume that you work for a firm that makes equipment, and software to drive it, that is useful in the chemical and biological industries. Most of your sales are to various drug firms, academic institutions, and other research and development labs. And you wish to expand your business overseas. That means you will need to research issues related to the export of your products to other countries. Choose three countries from each continent that might be in a position to purchase your products/services. Your instructor may wish to put the class in groups to complete the project, in which case each person can be responsible for a continent. Once you target your countries, you should prepare a report that addresses the following items:

1. Do you need an export license for any of your products from the U.S. Bureau of Export Administration (BXA)? (Check with www.bxa.doc.gov)

2. To answer question 1, you may have to determine a commodity classification for your product. As it turns out, all commodities, technology, or software subject to the licensing authority of the BXA are included in the Commerce Control List (CCL). So please go to http://www.bxa.doc.gov/factsheets/facts2.htm and begin the classification process for at least two of your products.

3. According to U.S. law, the burden is on all exporters either to classify their products and services and then request a BXA review or to have the BXA do this for you prior to receiving their classification review. Look closely at the guidelines for preparing an export license after you classify your products (http://www.bxa.doc.gov/factsheets/pdf/cbwmtcr2.pdf) Then complete the application form (example forms are available as models at http://www.bxa.doc.gov/factsheets/pdf/cbwmtcr3.pdf). So this part of the assignment asks you to simulate the required application process but, of course, not to submit it to the BXA. Nevertheless, you can give an oral report of your findings to the class. The other groups will be familiar with these forms because they will have also completed them.

4. What are some examples of countries that are barred from possible exports from the United States? If none of the countries you have chosen is barred, be sure to note at least two countries that are. Conversely, if each of the countries you chose cannot receive your exported product, choose at least two countries that can. (One source for this is: http://www.bxa.doc.gov/Entities/Default.htm, although it is not a complete source.)

5. Finally, show that you have performed due diligence in familiarizing yourself with warning signs and possible red flags of possible problems with your export transaction partner (http://www.bxa.doc.gov/Enforcement/report.htm).

6. Another resource you might find useful in completing this project is the home page of the Trade Information Center of the U.S. Department of Commerce (http://www.unzco.com/basicguide/index.html) as well as the Export-Import Bank of the United States (http://www.exim.gov/).

Part

IV

Managing People in the International Arena

Chapter 11

Motivating and Leading across Cultures

International Challenge

Winning over the Bear: Can Western Firms Learn How to Motivate Russian Employees?

LEARNING OBJECTIVES

After reading this chapter, you should be able to

- Assess the cross-cultural applicability of various motivation theories.

- Describe how cross-cultural motivation strategies can be developed.

- Describe how a leader's behavior, power sources, and influence tactics can be modified to be effective across international environments.

- Describe the challenges facing international managers in multinationals and how more effective international leaders can be developed.

RUSSIA IS IN THE PROCESS of transforming itself into a market-based economy. Of course, there have been some hiccups along the way, including the challenges of using Western management and motivation practices with Russian employees. Those challenges have increased in recent years since most companies operating in Russia, including American firms with household names such as Coca-Cola and Pizza Hut, prefer local employees to expensive expatriates.

So which Western motivation tactics serve foreign companies best in Russia? This question was put to the test by researchers who pitted three popular motivation programs against each other in a Russian cotton mill. All three programs have been widely used in the United States.

- **Program 1 relied on the reinforcement theory concept of providing contingent rewards.** It involved giving Russian employees extrinsic rewards (e.g., valued American consumer goods, bonuses) in exchange for improvements in performance.
- **Program 2 also relied on reinforcement theory ideas but focused instead on behavior management tactics.** These tactics were used to shape employee behavior using verbal feedback. For instance, Russian supervisors were trained to praise workers when they improved their performance and to offer corrective suggestions when negative behaviors were displayed.
- **Program 3 was a job enrichment approach that relied on employee participation.** Here the researchers asked employees for suggestions about how their jobs and work might be changed and improved, without Russian supervisors being present. For instance, employees were solicited for suggestions

about how to improve procedures, increase their autonomy, and develop more skills. Employees were empowered to implement their suggestions, with the idea that doing so would improve their motivation and subsequent performance.

So here's your challenge. Which of these programs would most improve the motivation and performance of Russian employees? Why? If you can, do some research on how Russian history and culture might affect employee motivation. For answers about the research team's findings, take a look at the Up to the Challenge box at the end of the chapter.[1]

Motivating and Leading Abroad: Are All Bets Off?

Most American businesspeople think that effective motivation of employees is critical to management success. But adding cross-cultural issues to the mix makes understanding how to effectively motivate employees all the more complex. For example, what motivates employees and how they respond to feedback may vary dramatically depending on cultural factors, all the talk about "globalization" and "value convergence" notwithstanding.[2] In fact, cultural values (such as the value placed on hard work and thrift) may affect employee motivation in ways that can even help explain different economic growth rates across nations.[3]

Consequently, the first part of this chapter addresses the role of culture as a limiting factor in terms of the applicability of American approaches to motivation. Managers need to know which motivation strategies are applicable across cultures and which require culture-specific approaches.[4] Motivation appears to have only a few cross-cultural "universals." For instance, managers in most cultures would prefer to rely less on formal authority to motivate their employees.[5] But cultural values often have a large impact on leadership styles, a motivation-related topic we'll tackle later in this chapter. Overall, universal principles of motivation are few because there are few shared values across all cultures.[6] International managers must therefore work to understand how cultures and values can shape employee motivation in particular countries. On top of that, international managers also face the possibility that important regional differences in values exist *within* a country which impact both motivation and business performance. For instance, research shows that regional subcultures in Brazil have some distinct motivational tendencies which, in turn, may have implications for company sales.[7]

Motivation Theories and Their Applicability to Other Cultures

In this section we'll examine the cross-cultural applicability of several motivation theories. Many experts doubt that existing motivation theories have universal applicability.[8] In any case, two basic types of motivation theories exist. **Content theories** focus on what needs energize employee behavior. We'll look at two content theories: **Maslow's hierarchy of needs** and **Herzberg's two-factor theory**. **Process theories** of motivation, on the other hand, focus on how behavior becomes directed toward a particular need. We'll examine four process theories: **equity theory**, **reinforcement theory**, **goal theory** and **expectancy theory**.

Maslow's Hierarchy of Needs

Maslow said that people have five basic needs that are triggered in a hierarchical fashion.[9] At the most basic level are **physiological needs** (e.g., food and shelter). If these needs are met (e.g., through adequate wages) then employees should be motivated to satisfy **safety needs**. Benefits such as life insurance help provide safety. The next level up are **social needs**. These are satisfied when employees feel they "belong." **Esteem needs** are met when employees have self-respect and confidence. **Self-actualization** needs can be reached only after all other needs have been met and reflect employees' desire to reach their maximum potential. Some elements of this hierarchy lack consistent research support. For example, needs aren't always triggered in the order specified by the theory.[10]

Cross-cultural applicability   We would expect higher-order needs (e.g., esteem and self-actualization) to dominate in highly industrialized countries, with lower-order survival needs more prominent in less developed countries. Actually, this prediction is still consistent with the theory since lower-order needs should dominate behavior until they're satisfied. In other words, workers in poor countries don't have the luxury of pursuing self-actualization if their survival or safety is in question.[11]

Nevertheless, the needs hierarchy doesn't fit every culture. For instance, cooperative coworkers and other social needs may rank above self-actualization for some Chinese employees.[12] Other studies suggest that employees in individualistic societies (e.g., the U.S.) are likely to be more interested in pursuing personal accomplishment than employees in more collective societies (e.g., Japan).[13] Likewise, Germans raised in the formerly communist eastern part of the country may be more focused on existence needs and less concerned about personal achievement than Germans raised in the western half of the country. Although this difference is shrinking, it underscores the power of larger social institutions to affect individual motivation. In East Germany, subservience to the state was taught in schools and organizations. The effects of those teachings, while clearly fading, linger to some extent.[14]

In any event, this variability across countries is inconsistent with the idea that needs operate in a fixed hierarchy.[15] And some experts take the position that Maslow's needs hierarchy is nothing more than a philosophy reflecting American values. Its emphasis on higher-order growth needs is especially popular in the United States because American culture strongly values individualism and risk taking. Underscoring this is the fact that "achievement" is extremely difficult to translate into other languages.[16]

Herzberg's Two-Factor Theory

Herzberg claimed that without adequate **hygiene factors** such as good working conditions and pay, employees will be unhappy and unmotivated. If, on the other hand, hygiene factors are taken care of, this doesn't mean that employees will be highly motivated. To produce highly satisfied employees, **motivators** such as challenge and accomplishment are necessary. Providing motivators is referred to as **job enrichment**.[17]

Cross-cultural applicability   One study found that workers in Zambia generally matched Herzberg's two-factor model, with growth needs and other intrinsic factors associated with high motivation and poor relationships, company practices, and/or working conditions associated with dissatisfaction.[18] These results are summarized in Exhibit 11.1.

EXHIBIT 11.1

Sources of Work Motivation in Zambia

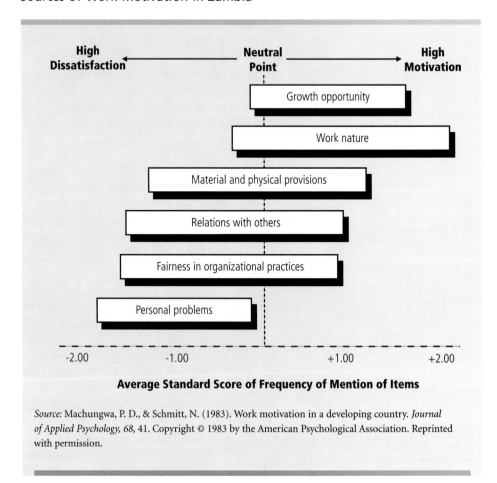

Average Standard Score of Frequency of Mention of Items

Source: Machungwa, P. D., & Schmitt, N. (1983). Work motivation in a developing country. *Journal of Applied Psychology, 68,* 41. Copyright © 1983 by the American Psychological Association. Reprinted with permission.

But other researchers have found differences across cultures. In one study, British managers were more interested in responsibility and autonomy than their French counterparts. The French, on the other hand, were more interested in security, fringe benefits, and good working conditions than their British colleagues. These results imply that generally speaking, job enrichment efforts are more likely to succeed in Britain than in France.[19] In fact, when cultural values include individualism, risk-taking (low uncertainty avoidance), and performance (masculinity), motivators may be viewed as a way to enhance individual achievement. Countries such as the United States and Britain fit this description. When the culture is individualistic and accepts risk but is relationship oriented (feminine), motivators may be seen as helping improve interpersonal harmony.[20] For instance, years ago Sweden's Volvo put workers into small, semi-autonomous teams to build cars. This job enrichment tactic was designed to increase cooperation among employees.[21]

Finally, job enrichment may be a tougher sell in developing countries such as Indonesia, India, and Pakistan. These countries tend to be collectivist, high in uncertainty avoidance and power distance, and low in masculinity. In high uncertainty avoidance cultures, some workers may be reluctant to make decisions because of the ambiguity inherent in doing so. Employees in collectivist cultures may also react negatively to efforts aimed at enriching jobs on an individual basis. High power distance discourages autonomous decision making. In feminine cultures, job enrichment efforts that focus on the job itself, without concern for personal relationships, may fail since employees' obligations to family or community are often paramount.[22] Nevertheless, there is clearly a worldwide trend toward increasingly complex or "enriched" jobs and the responsibility and control that go with them. But the ability of people to cope with such jobs may depend, at least in part, on the culture context in which they work.[23]

These cross-cultural differences also underscore one of the main criticisms of the two-factor approach—that hygiene factors do sometimes act as motivators. For instance, job security and pay (hygiene factors) often behave as motivators in developing countries, although the theory predicts they would not.[24] But the same may be true in many developed nations. For example, Jorma Ollila, CEO of Finnish telecommunications giant Nokia lobbied Finland's leaders to reduce income taxes in 2001. Apparently, Mr. Ollila was concerned that high taxes were cutting too deeply into paychecks, making it harder for Nokia to recruit key professionals. Exhibit 11.2 also

EXHIBIT 11.2

Where Are the (Un)happiest Employees?

Country	Employees Claiming They Are Very Satisfied with Their Current Job (%)
The Top Five	
Denmark	61
India (middle and upper classes only)	55
Norway	54
United States	50
Ireland	49
The Bottom Five	
Estonia	11
China	11
Czech Republic	10
Ukraine	10
Hungary	9

Source: Boyle, M. (2001). Nothing is rotten in Denmark. *Fortune,* February 19, 242. Reprinted with permission.

reports some results from a survey of employees in thirty-nine countries. It lists the countries with the highest and lowest percentage of employees who say that they're very satisfied with their jobs. Some experts claim Denmark snared the top spot in large measure because of outstanding relations between labor and management (including good pay, another hygiene factor). Ironically, this theme of getting along is reflected in one of Denmark's best known companies, toymaker Lego. The firm's name is derived from two Danish words that mean "play well." On the other hand, Hungary is at the bottom of the list in Exhibit 11.2, with less than 10 percent of its employees claiming to be very satisfied with their jobs. And experts point to two hygiene factors, lousy wages (the monthly wage averages about $300) and poor labor relations, as key reasons why Hungarian employees are a lot less happy than their Danish counterparts.[25] For another look at how a hygiene factor, money, is a big motivator for some Russian women, read the following International Insights.

Equity Theory

Equity theory focuses on how employees become motivated. It contends that when employees perceive that they've been treated unfairly, they are motivated to restore a sense of fairness.[27] This happens when employees compare themselves against other people in terms of **job outcomes** (e.g., pay, benefits) and **job inputs** (e.g., effort, skills). Specifically, employees compare their own **outcome/input ratio** against the outcome/input ratio of others. When the ratios are in balance, employees should feel satisfied. If they aren't, employees often try to restore the balance somehow. Studies done in the United States generally support equity theory.[28]

INTERNATIONAL INSIGHTS

Money Drives Russian Women Working for Mary Kay

DALLAS-BASED Mary Kay Cosmetics has been successful in Russia for years. Thanks to burgeoning demand for cosmetics, Russia ranks near the top of Mary Kay's more than two dozen foreign operations. But a big key to Mary Kay's success is its sales force of Russian women, some of whom routinely work 12 hours a day selling the company's products.

Most of these women are clearly motivated by money. Mary Kay provides sales training and sells its products to its Russian sales representatives at a 60 percent discount to retail prices. Typically, the Russian sales representatives then sell their Mary Kay products at full price, preferably to small groups of customers. On average, the women in Mary Kay's sales force make several hundred dollars a month. But Mary Kay's best Russian performers rake in thousands monthly. And some even have their own offices and secretaries.

Compare this to the low average monthly wage in Russia and you can see why turnover among Mary Kay's Russian sales force is so small.

Mary Kay is attractive to Russian women because it offers a shot at financial independence, something that is still relatively rare in Russia. Women sometimes feel that Russia's emerging market economy has left them behind. Two-thirds of Russia's unemployed are women, and some Russian organizations still reserve certain jobs for men. When they are employed, women in Russia are often stuck in low-paying positions and are the first to be laid off. Ironically, these same attitudes toward gender in Russia help make being a Mary Kay sales representative a socially acceptable job for Russian women as well as one that can pay well.[26]

Applying equity concepts in other cultures Experts contend that cultures that value individualism should embrace equity concepts. In such cultures, individual performance is important (inputs) and should be rewarded accordingly based on deservingness (outcomes). On the other hand, in collectivist cultures rewards are more likely to be distributed equally, regardless of performance, to preserve group harmony and cohesiveness.[29] In fact, as the following International Insights suggests, rewarding superior performance may sometimes create problems in China.

However, the link between culture and equity-based rewards is more complex than it appears. In one study, for example, Americans and Chinese were asked to evaluate hypothetical members of a work group. Although both Americans and Chinese tended to distribute rewards based on equity, the Chinese used a weaker equity standard to avoid creating conflict in the group. These results seem to confirm that collectivist cultures are less likely to apply equity concepts when distributing rewards than individualistic cultures.[31] Other experts, however, suggest that employees in collectivist cultures may use equity norms most when rewarding efforts to promote group cohesiveness.[32]

Another study illustrates how social changes may affect reward distribution preferences. In recent years, many Americans have become more concerned with cooperation and less concerned with wealth. The opposite trend is happening in China as it moves away from the egalitarian practices of the past. Both trends put pressure on traditional values in each country. In the study, Chinese and American managers read a scenario in which they had to distribute rewards among employees. Two types of rewards were examined—material rewards (e.g., pay raises) and socioemotional rewards (e.g., more supportive managers). Overall, Chinese managers preferred to use equity-based rules (e.g., performance) to distribute both types of rewards. Americans, however, based material rewards on performance but distributed socioemotional rewards equally. This pattern supports the idea that America is becoming less individualistic while China is moving in the opposite direction.

INTERNATIONAL INSIGHTS

Jacket Gesture Backfires in Shanghai

AMERICANS SOMETIMES forget that their approaches to motivation reflect American values. In one joint-venture plant in Shanghai, American managers gave leather jackets to a small group of Chinese employees. The idea was to recognize and encourage employee initiative. And this group had come up with the most suggestions for improving operations after being encouraged to do so.

But instead of serving as an example to the rest of the plant, one designed to promote employee initiative, the leather jackets created a backlash. Once they found out about the jackets, many Chinese employees in the rest of the plant wanted to know why they didn't get one. Management's explanation, that the jackets were a reward, went nowhere. Chinese employees continued their complaints, demanding equal treatment. At one point, the firm started getting calls

from local officials about the issue. After deciding things could spiral out of control, the Americans caved in and gave every Chinese employee a jacket (over 700 employees!).

Historically, Chinese employees expect to be taken care of by their bosses and offer loyalty and obedience in return. Tying rewards to performance was rarely part of that equation. Chinese companies also typically give workers benefits such as housing and food in addition to job security. Until recently, foreign companies that fired employees for lousy performance would be grilled by local officials concerned about the "social problems" caused by displaced workers. While China is changing and the use of performance-based rewards is rising, vestiges of the old "iron rice bowl" approach remain. And that's something to consider when it comes to motivating Chinese workers.[30]

So what do these complex findings on equity theory mean for international managers? Our advice is that managers should pay attention to (1) how their own cultural values might affect their willingness to use equity rules in reward allocations, and (2) how their subordinates' cultural values might affect their reaction to the use of equity rules. What's more, the world isn't a static place. As countries evolve, traditional values and practices may change in ways that affect how rewards should be allocated. Again, China may be a case in point. In recent years coastal firms in China could keep workers from the interior reasonably satisfied with little or no pay raises. Why? Because outside coastal cities, job prospects were often dim. As one production worker who had earned the same pay (about $60 per month) for three years put it, "What would I do back home?" But growing labor unrest in China is causing some to predict that this kind of reaction may soon be a thing of the past. Indeed, many low-paid employees in China already feel pangs of inequity, particularly if they compare themselves to others who seem better off.[33]

Reinforcement Theory

Reinforcement theory views motivation in terms of the consequences associated with behavior.[34] For example, managers can improve employee performance by applying **positive reinforcers** (e.g., bonuses) and eliminate poor performance by applying **punishment** (e.g., a pay cut). When used carefully, punishment can be effective.[35]

Cultural factors and reinforcement approaches   But managers need to know what employees value to use positive reinforcement effectively. However, this isn't as simple as it seems. For example, although apartheid has disappeared in South Africa, it still has motivational repercussions in the workplace. Many black employees are more motivated when their firm makes a real effort to help remove the social inequalities left over from apartheid (e.g., the inferior housing still plaguing much of the black majority). This connection between work and life outside of work also reflects African cultural values that emphasize the importance of community and family. Such values are seldom seen in Western management approaches.[36]

Culture may also affect how workers interpret the meaning of rewards and performance-related feedback. For instance, American employees tend to prefer positive feedback, while Japanese employees tend to embrace more critical feedback. The reasons may have to do with culture. Americans often like to revel in their triumphs, especially individual ones. Failure tends to be threatening and a challenge to individual self-worth. In Japan, however, critical evaluations may help people maintain a humble posture toward the wider group as well as offer suggestions for improving overall group performance.[37]

Along the same lines, American and Mexican workers may react differently when a supervisor gives positive performance feedback.[38] In one study, positive feedback after good performance seemed to stimulate the Americans' performance. For Mexican workers, however, there was no relationship between performance feedback and performance ratings. Americans may see praise as suggesting that even better performance is possible, while Mexicans may see it as an acknowledgment that their current performance is good. Mexican workers are also less likely to exceed the informal performance norms of their work groups no matter what feedback they receive from a supervisor. Compared to Americans, Mexicans tend to be more collectivist and, as such, are likely to pay close attention to group norms.[39]

The Mexican employees assembling these Chevy SUVs may react differently to performance feedback than their American counterparts.
© Danny Lehman/CORBIS

Cultural values can also present more fundamental hurdles for reinforcement strategies. For instance, performance-based pay may not motivate workers in high uncertainty avoidance cultures since a portion of pay is put at risk. Similarly, in highly collective cultures, individual merit pay may be less effective than pay based on group performance. Using large bonuses or hefty pay increases alone may also prove difficult in feminine cultures since loyalty to the boss, company, or coworkers is prized above performance. India is an example of a country where cultural values may limit reinforcement strategies. In fact, pay systems in some Indian companies violate principles of reinforcement theory. For example, compensation may reflect employee seniority as opposed to being contingent on behavior. Performance appraisal can be rudimentary and not timed to coincide with key tasks. So employees may see "merit pay" as something arbitrary. And this perception may reinforce many Indians' socialization experiences with family, religion, and other institutions. These experiences may lead some Indians to embrace a resigned fatalism and indifference to good performance (a state referred to *chalega*). Instead, effort may be directed to activities aimed at strengthening relationships with supervisors who offer valued rewards.[40]

Overall, research on reinforcement theory suggests that managers need to consider how culture affects what employees find motivating as well as how employees react to specific motivators. These factors will help determine what motivators will work best in a culture and what strategies will be most effective for using them.

Goal Theory

Establishing performance targets is the essence of goal setting. Many American studies show that specific and challenging goals improve motivation and performance, especially when employees have input into the targets that are set.[41]

Cultural barriers to using goal setting   Employee involvement in goal setting is popular in the United States. But goal setting assumes low power distance since employees must feel confident enough to negotiate goals with superiors. It also assumes low uncertainty avoidance. Reaching goals is rarely automatic, so employees must accept some level of risk. Finally, goal setting assumes a work environment that values high performance most.[42] The result is familiar. Goal setting has run into problems or taken different forms when used in different cultures. For instance, German goal setting usually involves more elaborate procedures and a stronger focus on team performance than American versions. This may reflect the German tendency to be higher in uncertainty avoidance. The more elaborate procedures and team focus in German goal-setting systems help reduce uncertainty.

Similarly, a "democratic" approach to goal setting may create problems in France. The strong chain of command orientation there reduces ambiguity and provides stability, arguably important values in a country with high power distance and high uncertainty avoidance. The employee involvement often required in American-style goal-setting threatens both the French desire for predictability and French managers' authority.[43] Similar hurdles may come up in developing countries (e.g., China, India) because of cultural values that are inconsistent with American assumptions about goal setting. Many developing countries score high on uncertainty avoidance, power distance, and collectivism and are low in masculinity. As a result, employees may be risk averse, dependent on supervisors, and fatalistic about their lives—a combination that makes for difficulties in goal setting.[44]

Expectancy Theory

Expectancy theory assumes that three factors determine employee effort in a given situation.[45] First, workers must believe that working hard will result in good performance. If, for example, workers feel it's impossible to hit production targets, they won't put out much effort. Second, workers must believe that rewards are associated with good performance. If this isn't the case, motivation will suffer. Finally, motivation and effort will also suffer if the rewards available to employees are unimportant to them.

The cultural assumptions of expectancy theory   As you've probably guessed, expectancy theory makes some now-familiar cultural assumptions. The theory emphasizes individualism and has a masculine orientation since it is focused on tasks rather than relationships. It also assumes that individual workers can control their lives to a great extent by manipulating effort. These assumptions fit American culture quite well. But many Chinese believe that fate helps determine events. Similarly, many Mexicans feel that being from the appropriate family is a real key to success. Likewise, many Saudi Arabians believe that what happens at work is a reflection of God's will. In each case, external forces are important.[46]

By saying that rewards have to be valued to produce motivation, expectancy theory implicitly suggests that reward systems need to be designed with cultural values in mind. One study of American, French, and Dutch managers helps make this point. The Americans felt that bonuses should be tightly connected to performance. This fits the expectancy theory assumption that people are achievement oriented and can tolerate the ambiguity that comes with fluctuating bonuses. In contrast, French and Dutch managers were less interested in money and were skeptical about linking pay and performance. The bonuses earned by French and Dutch managers were smaller and varied less than did the Americans'. These differences are predictable. Compared with their American counterparts, the Dutch tend to have a more feminine orientation and are less individualistic. As a consequence, Dutch managers are less likely to use pay as a way to "keep score" of individual achievement. Similarly, managers in high uncertainty avoidance cultures, such as France, may shy away from highly variable performance bonuses for executives.[47]

That said, values and sensibilities often change and evolve. For instance, rank and seniority once were all that mattered in German banks. Bonuses were unknown. But when German banks started losing talent to American and British rivals in recent years, they began fighting back. How? By using the common American tactic of offering bonuses in exchange for performance. Now banks such as Deutsche Bank and Bayerische Vereinsbank have bonus plans in place that can increase total compensation by 50 percent or more. But German banks aren't just copying American-style bonus plans. Many German banking executives remain uneasy about using big bonuses to publicize their individual achievements.

As a consequence, German banks tend to offer smaller bonuses than American banks for comparable positions. In a good year, for instance, currency traders in a U.S. bank might earn bonuses equal to 700 percent of their salaries. But Germans may feel that such huge bonuses prompt unnecessary risks and foster destructive competition among employees. As a consequence, some German banks try to encourage cooperation and teamwork by making part of the bonus contingent on an employee's ability to work well with colleagues. Nevertheless, Deutsche Bank and other German financial services firms seem to be slowly moving toward the more aggressive pay-for-performance management approaches found in U.S. banks.[48] For a closer look at how performance-reward linkages may be evolving in Japan, read the International Insights.

As interesting as this Japanese restaurant example is, major shifts in work attitudes about motivation will not happen overnight. Research, for instance, suggests that the perceived link between effort and performance is generally stronger for Americans than for Japanese. The longer history of performance-contingent reward systems in the United States may help explain this finding. Finally, Americans tend to see pay increases, promotions, and personal recognition as more desirable than do their Japanese counterparts. Cultural values that emphasize individual performance and achievement in the United States and group cohesion in Japan may account for this difference in perception. In any case, how fast and to what extent Japanese society will become more individualistic remains to be seen. But the government apparently wants to move in that direction. In 2002, Japan launched a new education policy designed to encourage children to adopt a more independent and individually-oriented mindset. Only time will tell whether this controversial policy has any significant impact in Japan.[50]

Some Conclusions about Motivation across Cultures

Overall, we suggest that international managers explicitly take cultural variables into account when designing reward systems and motivational strategies.[51] Granted, this is a tall order, one that is complicated by the fact that cultural values are a moving target. Plus, international managers may not recognize how their own values affect the motivation strategies they use. So it may be best to start with the idea that whatever motivational strategy is adopted, it should be **culturally synergistic**. In other words, it should complement rather than conflict with the various cultures involved. Developing such a motivation strategy involves four basic steps:

INTERNATIONAL INSIGHTS

Japanese Restaurant Chain to Employees: Perform or You're Chopped Liver

AMERICA'S "CUTTHROAT CAPITALISM" has been a tough sell in Japan. Contentious disputes about pay and performance have been virtually unknown, at least in traditional companies. But Japanese firms like Global Dining may provide a peek into the future. This restaurant chain has embraced three innovations that are shocking for many Japanese—plenty of conflict, do-or-die competition between employees, and brutally honest individual performance feedback.

How brutal? One cook sat in front of a group of bosses and peers to demand a sizeable pay increase. They immediately shouted out criticisms, including that his cooking was uneven and sales on his shift weak. A quick vote was taken and the answer to the humiliated cook was no, his pay would stand. In fact, all employees, from senior leaders to dishwashers, are evaluated against performance criteria in such face-to-face meetings. Employees who miss their performance targets get no bonuses. Managers who foul up are quickly demoted or fired. The flip side is that excellent performers are rewarded incredibly well. One young restaurant manager made over $150,000, considerably more than the average mid-career executive in large Japanese firms. Global Dining's CEO summed up the system's philosophy this way: "Just as sharks need to keep swimming to stay alive, we only want people who are constantly craving challenges."

The willingness to embrace such a demanding approach is part of a broader debate in Japan about traditionally cushy relationships between employees and big firms that often had little to do with performance (e.g., lifetime employment, seniority-based raises, etc.). Of course, Japan's prolonged economic difficulties and sagging international fortunes have been driving that debate. And Global Dining isn't alone. Firms such as Sony, clothing chain Fast Retailing, and machine parts firm Misumi Corporation are among the big Japanese companies that have brought in younger managers willing to live with the ups and downs of tough pay-for-performance schemes. Thanks to bonuses, one young Misumi manager pulled in almost $530,000, outearning the firm's president in the process.

But some workers at Global Dining worry about the stresses and pressures of life under such a ruthless performance management system. Even waiters watch each other closely since everyone votes on pay raises and bonuses for everyone else (one performance marker—how long it takes waiters to notice that a customer needs another drink). That said, Global Dining employees may have the last word since the system actually encourages criticism of superiors, right up to the CEO. In fact, at one point, employees complained to the CEO that the bonus formula made it too easy to get nothing at all. Eventually, employees demanded a vote on the issue; the CEO lost, and the formula was modified. One manager who left Global Dining to start his own restaurant said that while performance management was a good thing, his system would be less ruthless. As he put it, "There's a saying, 'too much is as bad as too little.'"[49]

1. **Describe the motivation situation.** How does the manager view the motivation issues? What perspectives do subordinates have? The purpose of this first step is to discover whether different motivational perspectives exist and whether they create conflict.

2. **Identify cultural assumptions about motivation.** The next step is to uncover the cultural values that help explain why different perspectives on motivation exist. The goal is to be able to reverse perspectives and see things from another culture's point of view.

3. **Generate culturally synergistic alternatives.** Once cultural assumptions have been identified, the next challenge is to develop motivation strategies that blend elements of the cultures involved or even go beyond them.

4. **Select and implement a synergistic strategy.** The final step involves picking what appears to be the best motivation strategy and implementing it. A key here is to

have all parties observe the strategy from their own cultural perspective. The chosen strategy may need to be fine-tuned based on any feedback received.

What Constitutes Effective Leadership in an International Context?

We've said that cultural values may affect employee behavior in ways that have implications for how companies should design work, manage performance, and provide rewards. We'll tackle these issues from management's perspective in this section on leadership.

Effective leadership in international companies requires incredible openness and an ability to appreciate cultural differences. But just defining "leadership" becomes more complex when cross-cultural issues are mixed in. The vast majority of research on leadership in the past fifty years originated in the United States, with all its accompanying cultural baggage. Only in the last ten to twenty years has interest in cross-cultural leadership issues risen significantly. Nevertheless, the knowledge base is expanding rapidly and offers some useful advice for international managers. In fact, the need for good advice is becoming more acute as companies increasingly pursue foreign markets.[52] Back in Chapter 4, we discussed how different cultures define leadership and the characteristics that effective leaders possess. But important questions remain. For instance, do managers behave differently across cultures in leadership roles? Do certain situations require similar leadership behaviors, regardless of culture? Can corporate culture override or weaken other cross-cultural effects with respect to leadership? This section will offer some answers to these questions.

When in Rome: Leader Behavior across Cultures

Our position is that leader behavior can vary dramatically across cultures and that effective international managers are aware of this. But like so many things in international management, leadership is something of a moving target. Leadership concepts, values, and styles continue to evolve around the world. This evolutionary process is probably most noticeable in nations that have undergone social and economic upheaval, such as Poland, the eastern half of Germany, and other parts of the old Soviet bloc.[53] However, the pace and extent of any change will vary across countries. For a closer look at how social changes have affected leadership in Russia, read the following International Insights.

In any case, research done in the United States reveals two basic types of leader behavior. **Task-oriented behavior** includes providing clear expectations for performance and outlining specific procedures to be followed. Other examples include planning, scheduling, providing technical help, and goal-setting. **Relationship-oriented behavior** includes showing personal concern for subordinates' feelings, needs, and well-being. Other examples include expressing empathy, warmth, encouragement, consideration, and trust to subordinates. But which type of leader behavior produces the best performance? In which countries? There's no simple answer. Depending on the circumstances, leaders may need to use different combinations of task-oriented and relationship-oriented behaviors to be effective.[55]

In India, for example, a **nurturant style**, which mixes empathy and concern for subordinates with an emphasis on getting the job done, often works best.[56] And in Japan, the **PM leader** is often most effective, especially when subordinate achievement

INTERNATIONAL INSIGHTS

The Evolving Russian Leadership Style

AMERICANS OFTEN feel that managers need motivation, drive, and self-confidence to be effective. So how do Russian business leaders compare? Exhibit 11.3 provides some answers for Russian managers across three time periods.

Leadership Motivation

For hundreds of years, village elders were the absolute authority in rural Russia. This autocratic leadership carried over into the Soviet system, with managers avoiding blame and refusing to take action without approval. But in a more open economy, Russian managers must shift from being authoritarian to being authoritative, providing vision and encouraging initiative. Although autocratic attitudes persist, many Russian managers now take responsibility and make strategic decisions on their own.

Leadership Drive

Russian villages focused on the community and treated individual achievement with contempt. They valued tenacity, hard work, and caution. These values helped Russians survive in a climate with short growing seasons and brutally cold winters. Under communism, Soviet managers focused on following rules, making connections, and demonstrating loyalty instead of developing new products or services. Today, most formal restrictions on individual ambition are gone and many Russians have started their own businesses. However, some Russians still see entrepreneurs and managers as immoral people who exploit others for personal gain.

The Honesty and Integrity of the Leader

A dichotomy exists in the area of corruption and integrity. Russians may feel it is acceptable to deceive strangers in business deals. But deceiving trusted friends is unethical. Russians may also use personal connections to obtain favors. For centuries, Russian villagers offered food to landowners in exchange for protection. These traditional values were reflected in the way Soviet managers operated. Stealing state property and deceiving superiors was acceptable because it helped Soviet managers protect their resources. Using personal connections to cut red tape was common under communism and persists to this day. Indeed, corruption increased with the collapse of the Soviet system. Today, some Russian entrepreneurs pay protection money to criminals just to stay in business.

The Leader's Self-Confidence

Russians have been described as both self-confident and fatalistic. Soviet leaders were sensitive to criticism about their product quality yet took great pride in running huge manufacturing plants. Today, Russian leaders often vacillate between feeling that they can't accomplish anything without foreign help to making grandiose promises to foreign partners.

Guidelines for Leading in Russia

Based on this evolutionary snapshot, here are some leadership guidelines for firms that want to do business in Russia:

● **Don't assume that Russian leadership is the same as it is in the West.** Encourage blended leadership approaches that take into account Russian history, character, and the changes that are taking place.

● **Avoid hubris and present a nonexploitative image.** Avoid actions that appear to exploit Russians to make money or that make managers appear too powerful. Instead, attempt to cultivate a caring and attentive leadership style.

● **Work to build trust.** To overcome Russians' traditional ambivalence to authority, strive to share information (including bad news) and encourage dissent. But recognize that building trust is a slow process.

● **Work to form strong personal relationships with Russian business partners.** Making an effort to develop personal relationships will improve the odds of being treated with trust and respect.

● **Instill respect for ethical practices in business.** Russians should be shown that Western business practices can protect against the excesses of Russia's emerging market economy.

● **Involve Russians in joint problem solving and action planning.** To overcome low self-confidence, involve Russian managers in problem solving. Likewise, Russian managers' expertise can be developed by involving them in the creation of action plans for achieving business goals.[54]

EXHIBIT 11.3

Russian Leadership across Eras

Leadership Trait	Village Elder (1400–1917)	Soviet Manager (1917–1991)	Market-Oriented Manager (1991–present)
Motivation			
Power	Autocrat	Centralized leadership	Moving to power sharing
Responsibility	Centralized	No action without permission	Learning to take responsibility
Drive			
Achievement	Don't make waves	Pawns of system	Unlimited potential
Ambition	Equal poverty for all	Serve party, collective good	Overcoming the sin of success
Initiative	Caution stressed	Follow rules, show loyalty	Fighting old values
Tenacity	Struggle to live	Struggle to accomplish anything	Struggle to accomplish something new
Honesty/Integrity			
Dual ethics	Deception in business, honesty with friends	Deceive bosses, personal integrity	Lawless capitalism, personal trust
Connections	Making deals with landowners	Cutting red tape of the state	Greasing palms, learning business practices
Self-confidence	Helplessness vs. bravado	Inferior quality vs. "big is best"	Need foreign help vs. overpromising

Source: Adapted from Puffer, S. M. (1994). Understanding the bear: A portrait of business leaders. *Academy of Management Executive, 8,* 41–54.

motivation is high. This leader combines concern about problem solving and motivation of group performance (**P**erformance leadership) with behavior designed to promote interdependence, avoid conflict, and maintain harmony within the work group (**M**aintenance leadership). These behaviors resemble the distinction between task- and relationship-oriented behaviors drawn by U.S. researchers.[57]

But lumping everything into two behavioral dimensions can mask important cross-cultural differences. For instance, the relationship-oriented behavior described by Western scholars is colder and more egalitarian than the more paternalistic Indian version.[58] In fact, international managers may get themselves into trouble by thinking about leadership in terms of "task-oriented" and "relationship-oriented" behaviors. This dichotomy may simply be inappropriate in many cultures.[59]

A study of Iranian employees illustrates this point nicely. The Iranians filled out a questionnaire that measured whether their immediate supervisor showed task-oriented and relationship-oriented behaviors. The results revealed that Iranian supervisors who acted in a benevolent and paternalistic way had the best performance ratings from subordinates. But forcing the Iranian data into task- and relationship-oriented factors produced no significant relationships with leader performance or subordinate satisfaction. This suggests that American definitions of leader behavior may make little sense in Middle Eastern cultures. In Iran, the boundary between work and family relationships is often ambiguous. The warm but firm father figure that plays such a prominent role in Iranian society translates into the supervisor who is directive but still shows respect for subordinates.[60]

Clearly, culture can impact how employees perceive leader style and behavior. Leaders also must express their behavior in culturally specific ways to be effective. So leadership style must be understood in terms of both its general underlying structure as well as its particular expression in certain cultures. For example, American and Japanese leaders might agree that relationship-oriented behavior is important for success. In the individualistic United States, however, a manager might express such behavior by showing respect for subordinates' ideas. In collectivistic Japan, in contrast, a manager might express support by spending more time with subordinates as a group.[61]

In fact, one study comparing managers from America, Britain, Japan, and Hong Kong found that while there was agreement on basic aspects of leadership style among managers, the specific expression of these behaviors varied across the four countries.[62] And these differences can explain the problems that managers run into when placed into foreign contexts. For instance, American and Japanese managers often encounter enormous difficulties leading in each other's "home" environment, often because of different conceptions of how leaders should actually behave. Overcoming this perception barrier may require a blending of leadership strategies that's akin to our synergistic recommendations on motivation.[63] For a look at how one manager views leadership, take a look at the following Reality Check on Heinrich von Pierer, the CEO of German engineering and electronics giant Siemens AG. One of Siemens' major competitors is U.S.-based General Electric.

Culture and the impact of leader behavior   Culture also affects the impact of leader behavior on the commitment and performance of subordinates. In collectivist, high power distance cultures such as Taiwan, task-oriented behavior may have a stronger positive impact on subordinates than in individualistic, low power distance cultures such as the United States.[65] For instance, research suggests that the criticism that Japanese managers often aim at subordinates would be viewed as punitive by most Americans, even though it works well in Japan. In their high power distance, collective context, Japanese managers usually balance their criticism with plenty of supportive behaviors and go to great lengths to minimize status symbols. On the other hand, Americans are more likely to use status symbols (e.g., a fancy office) to project authority.[66]

What happens, however, when American subordinates are exposed to Japanese leadership in a facility located in the United States? As we suggested earlier, this type of situation can prove challenging. In one study, Japanese managers had less impact on American than Japanese subordinates and had less influence overall than American supervisors. However, American subordinates performed better when a Japanese supervisor was friendly and supportive but worse when an American supervisor did basically the same thing. So supervisors' nationalities may affect how their behavior is interpreted by subordinates. Friendliness by an American supervisor may imply weakness, while the same behavior from a Japanese supervisor may imply a desire to get things done.

But can different leader behaviors have the same positive effects across cultural contexts? Yes, at least according to experts applying **Likert's System 4 theory**.[67] The theory says that four basic systems of leadership exist. In a **exploitative authoritative** (System 1) organization, decision making is confined to upper management, communication is top-down, and punishments are used to motivate. A **benevolent authoritative** (System 2) organization is also autocratic. However, managers are more

REALITY CHECK

Siemens CEO Heinrich von Pierer: A Leader on Leading

If there's a benchmark manager in your industry, then it's Jack Welch (former CEO of General Electric). How do you feel about that?

No one should be the benchmark 100 percent. But I have to say that we have taken a lot from GE, from Jack Welch. And it wasn't so easy in a company like Siemens to tell people to look around and see what we can learn from others. One example is benchmarking. Today it's part of our corporate culture. Jack Welch [used to] visit every division twice a year and speak to them for a whole day about management development. I do that, too.

But you also say that you can't become a "Neutron Heinrich"?

No, we have to do everything in the context of our European culture. If I had the nickname "Neutron Heinrich" . . . . You know how the name evolved? Go through the factory like a neutron bomb, the walls remain standing and the people are gone. Well, with that nickname I wouldn't get very far here.

What aspects of the American business model would you say aren't worth adopting?

The way one deals with people. One example is the German codetermination. Today I met with thirty representatives of works councils from all the operations in Berlin. In the Anglo-Saxon world, that always sounds so nice. But today the discussion focused on large drives, which we are

restructuring. That has massive consequences. The works council representative came and said, "We've taken a look at the master plan and we have suggestions from our plant, which is where our know-how lies, about where we could develop new business." That's great. That's also part of code-termination, that the people come with their own suggestions. Whether it's feasible, I can't say now. You have to understand, you come in to a German board meeting and there you have ten capitalists and ten labor representatives. That demands different behavior.

What kind of behavior? What's different?

That you talk to the people; that you include them; that we make decisions dependent on a broader consensus.

Is it a problem to manage a global company like Siemens when the management board is primarily made up of Germans?

First of all, you have to see the top Siemens 100. That consists of the management of the business divisions and the regional companies. And today, at this level, we have hardly any Germans. In the United States you'll find few Germans, nor in Spain, France, or Latin America. There are locals everywhere. And these people play a significant role in our top leadership. We have sufficient global input in the company to assure that the German influence isn't over-bearing.[64]

paternalistic, are interested in employees' needs, and may give employees limited decision-making freedom. In a **consultative** (System 3) organization, employees are even more involved in communicating, decision making, and working with managers. Still, management usually reserves the right to make the final decision. Finally, the **democrative** (System 4) organization involves employees heavily in decision-making in every-thing from problem solving to setting performance goals. Supervisors are supportive, the use of teams is widespread, and employees communicate laterally as well as vertically.

The theory argues that all companies should move toward System 3 and 4 leader-ship because a participative style results in the highest performance and morale. Studies of U.S. firms show that as companies move closer to System 4, various indicators of performance also increase.[68] These results aren't surprising since a participative approach like System 4 is a good match for a low power distance culture like the United States. By the same token, in a high power distance culture shouldn't a more autocratic leadership approach fit better and yield workers that are equally productive?

A comparison of managers in two manufacturing plants (one in Mexico, one in the U.S.) owned by an American firm suggests the answer is yes. Both plants produced the same product and were virtually identical. Interestingly, Mexican managers were more autocratic as leaders than their American counterparts. Overall, the Mexicans used System 2 (benevolent authoritative), whereas the Americans used System 3 (consultative). Nevertheless, both plants were equally productive and efficient, probably because the more autocratic Mexican style was a good match for the high power distance culture in Mexico. Likewise, the more participative System 3 approach was a good fit for the U.S. plant and its American values.[69]

The broader implication here is that foreign plants can match the level of performance attained in U.S. plants without using an "American" approach to leadership. Let's consider the U.S.-Mexico comparison in more detail. Many of the initial production problems facing American-owned plants in Mexico are traceable to American management techniques that are inconsistent with Mexican cultural values. These differences surface when U.S. multinationals send Americans to manage Mexican workers. Exhibit 11.4 describes the different management expectations that may separate Americans and Mexicans. Not surprisingly, Mexican workers sometimes appear passive to U.S. managers. In part, this may reflect a tradition that emphasizes jobs over profits. Moreover, compared to the United States, Mexico is less individualistic but higher in power distance and uncertainty avoidance. Many Mexicans embrace the view that conformity, respect, and personal loyalty to supervisors are important and should be rewarded. Indeed, the family may be the best analogy for the Mexican view of organizations. Just like in a family, people should work cooperatively but within a

EXHIBIT 11.4

Great Expectations:
The Gap between American and Mexican Managers

Leadership Issue	Management Expectations and Attitudes	
	American Managers	**Mexican Managers**
Valued employee behaviors	Initiative, achievement	Obedience, harmony
Key evaluation	Performance	Personal loyalty
Leadership style	Loose/informal, communicative power sharing possible	Close/formal, empathetic, use of directives, no power sharing
Basis of discipline/justice	Uniform application of rules and procedures	Personal relations
Work environment model	Competitive team	Cooperative family

Source: Adapted from de Forest, M. E. (1994). Thinking of a plant in Mexico? *Academy of Management Executive, 8,* 33–40.

prescribed role. The values Americans place on individual achievement and power sharing are often at odds with the Mexican emphasis on interdependence.

American managers also need to be sensitive about how they communicate with Mexican employees. For instance, honoring status is part of Mexican business rituals. At one U.S.-owned plant in Mexico, the ranking union leader was insulted when the American plant manager did not introduce him to visiting executives. The American saw the union leader as just another employee. The union leader, however, had a status that, under Mexican law, is equal to that of management. Formality is another way that Mexicans recognize status differences. Americans tend to be informal managers. One American manager in Mexico tried to break down status differences by wearing blue jeans and dispensing with titles. Mexicans thought he was unsophisticated. Distance between management and labor is expected.

Overall, Mexican workers often respond best to formal but empathetic supervisors. Traditionally, responsibility and autonomy aren't that important. Close supervision is expected, but leaders should also be personal and sensitive. Not surprisingly, American managers' efforts to share power and encourage problem solving are often confusing to Mexican workers, although this can be overcome with training and patience. Mexican supervisors are used to being obeyed without question. In fact, having to explain why an order is necessary can be seen as a weakness.

At the same time, American managers may feel that Mexican workers are undisciplined. Policies are sometimes loosely followed in Mexico. The problem is that Americans and Mexicans often view discipline differently. To the American manager, discipline results when policies are applied equally to all workers. To Mexicans, however, discipline is embodied in the form of loyalty to an authority figure, not a policy manual. One American plant manager learned this lesson the hard way. To prevent labor unrest, the American manager put together a sophisticated grievance system. Later, the manager was shocked when the entire workforce walked off the job without using the new system to air their complaints. But resolving worker grievances in Mexico may require a relationship-oriented approach, one where managers empathize with workers' needs in exchange for personal loyalty.[70]

Adapting leader behavior to the cultural context   Another implication of this discussion is that to be effective in other countries, managers may need to adapt their leadership style to match cultural expectations. For instance, consider a cultural mistake that American managers sometimes make in Japan. American managers may give pieces of a project to different individuals, feeling that clear assignments are the best way to organize work. In Japan, however, a better strategy would be to give the entire project to subordinates as a group and allow them to tackle it as they see fit. This would be more consistent with the Japanese view that interaction among employees provides the structure for organizing work.[71]

Nevertheless, many Americans continue to believe that if they are good managers in Los Angeles they can act the same way anywhere and succeed. One clever study debunked this idea by comparing Americans managing in Hong Kong and the United States on twelve different leader behaviors. As expected, the American managers behaved similarly in both places. But the relationship between behavior and performance was quite different. While eight of the leader behaviors were correlated with overall performance for Americans managing in the United States, only one behavior was correlated with performance for the Americans in Hong Kong. So the same behaviors that "worked" in the United States had no impact on performance in Hong Kong.[72]

The Impact of Culture on Leader Power and Influence

In addition to behaving in ways that show concern with performance or for people, leaders use their power to get subordinates to comply with various requests.[73] But do leaders in other countries rely on the same types of power, with the same results, as their American counterparts? Our discussion of power distance in Chapter 4 suggests that the answer in many cases is "no." For instance, as power distance increases, so might employees' tendency to attribute legitimate authority to those holding leadership positions. As a result, subordinates in high power distance societies (e.g., China) are likely to be more compliant than subordinates in low power distance societies (e.g., Sweden).

Even cultures with similar perspectives on power distance can differ in how legitimate power is viewed. For example, one American sent to manage an office in England observed that no one would come to see him directly. Instead, people went through the receptionist, secretary, and office manager before getting in to see him. Despite his protests that this was unnecessary and time consuming, his English employees continued to push visitors through the office's "chain of command." Although American and English employees are similar on power distance, there is greater formality and respect for managers' titles in England than in the United States.[74]

Another study comparing American and South Korean employees found that both groups defined their supervisor's power similarly. But American employees saw their supervisors as having more position power than personal power, while the opposite was true for Korean employees. In a collective culture like South Korea's, managers may have less position power than managers in individualistic cultures. As a result, managers in collective cultures may rely more on developing personal sources of power, such as expertise.[75]

Leaders also use various **social influence tactics** in actually attempting to affect subordinate behavior. These may include:

- **Assertiveness:** Forcefully presenting your position.
- **Friendliness:** Creating good feelings toward you.
- **Reasoning:** Using facts and logical arguments to support your position.
- **Bargaining:** Offering an exchange of benefits.
- **Sanctions:** Using threats and potential punishments.
- **Higher Authority:** Relying on leverage from managers farther up the hierarchy.
- **Coalition:** Using allies to apply unified pressure.[76]

Studies done in the United States suggest that leaders who rely on reasoning have more committed subordinates and are seen as more effective than leaders who use other tactics.[77] However, culture can affect the particular tactics leaders use and how effective they are in influencing others.[78]

For example, one study found that managers from America, Australia, England, Japan, and Taiwan all used the same basic influence tactics. However, in each country these tactics were defined differently and their relative importance varied (see Exhibit 11.5). Unlike managers from the three English-speaking countries, Taiwanese and Japanese managers both emphasized "assertive reasoning." This tactic essentially combines a "soft sell" (reasoning) with a harder edge (assertiveness). It is important in many Asian cultures for the leader to show concern for subordinates while at the same time underscoring his or her authority. However, the Taiwanese managers stood out by ranking sanctions first. This may reflect the greater focus in Chinese culture on the leader as a wise but autocratic father figure. In any case, more research is needed to document how leader influence tactics work across cultures.[79]

EXHIBIT 11.5

Ranking the Importance of Leader Influence Tactics across Countries

Tactic Rank	Manager's Nationality				
	American	**British**	**Australian**	**Taiwanese**	**Japanese**
1	Bargaining	Bargaining	Friendly reason	Sanctions	Assertive reason
2	Reason	Higher authority	Bargaining	Assertive reason	Higher authority
3	Higher authority	Coalition	Sanctions	Bargaining	Bargaining
4	Sanctions	Assertiveness	Higher authority	Higher authority	Assertive logic
5	Assertiveness	Sanctions	Coalition	Friendliness	Friendliness
6	Friendliness	Reason	Assertiveness	Coalition	Sanctions
7	Coalition	Friendliness		Assertiveness	Coalition

Source: Schmidt, S. M. & Yeh, R. (1992). The structure of leader influence: A cross-national comparison. *Journal of Cross-Cultural Psychology, 23,* 259. © 1992 by Sage Publications. Reprinted by permission of Sage Publications, Inc.

The Cross-Cultural Applicability of Transformational Leadership

In this section we consider **transformational leadership,** an increasingly popular perspective that espouses managers possess and use, to the extent that they can, a unique set of power and influence tactics. In general, the transformational leader is able to galvanize employees and help turn poorly performing companies into winners. In essence, this happens when the transformational leader creates an emotional bond with followers that inspires intense loyalty and outstanding performance. This bond is the result of the leader's:

- **Charisma:** The leader arouses intense emotions among followers based on absolute faith in and identification with the leader.
- **Use of inspirational appeals:** The leader communicates a clear and compelling vision for the future, one that entails extremely high performance expectations.
- **Intellectual stimulation:** The leader challenges subordinates to think about new ways to run the business, overcome problems, design products, and so on as they pursue the leader's vision.
- **Individualized consideration:** The leader gives subordinates personal attention, empathizes with their concerns, and communicates with them as individuals.[80]

Studies done on Americans show that transformational leaders can have positive effects on subordinate effort, performance, and satisfaction. That said, employees must want to follow a charismatic leader. Usually this requires a willingness to cede control to the leader, something that's more likely when subordinates feel vulnerable (e.g., during a business downturn). Small wonder that transformational leaders have the

Seen by many as a charismatic leader, Carlos Ghosn brought a transformational style to his management of Nissan (and its partnership with Renault, a point we noted back in Chapter 9).
© Reuters NewMedia Inc./CORBIS

greatest impact when a firm faces a crisis.[81] So is the world of international business, with its rapid changes and competitive threats, tailor-made for transformational leadership? Some experts say yes, arguing that the most successful international managers are transformational leaders.[82] They point to studies showing the positive impact of transformational leadership in places as diverse as Israel, New Zealand, and Singapore.[83]

But broad statements about the "global" value of transformational leadership should be treated cautiously.[84] For instance, transformational leadership may have more limited appeal in collective cultures where group harmony is highly prized. In countries like Japan, for instance, a charismatic leader who tries to galvanize individual performance may be seen as destructive to group cohesiveness. Nevertheless, Carlos Ghosn arguably is a charismatic leader who has largely succeeded in Japan. A foreigner who came from Renault to oversee the turnaround of a struggling Nissan, Ghosn has managed to do well with vision, tough performance expectations, and empathy. Whether Ghosn reflects shifting Japanese views about leadership or is merely the exception that proves the rule is unclear at this point. Nevertheless, what we can say is that everything else being equal, implementing a transformational approach to leadership is still more difficult in Japan than in the United States.

Toward Cross-Cultural Leadership: Adapting Path-Goal Theory

It's probably clear by now that there's no shortage of theories about how best to lead under different conditions. Unfortunately, when it comes to a comprehensive theory that can account for a variety of situational factors, including culture, we still have a long way to go. That said, one leadership model that might be adapted to include cultural variables is **path-goal theory**.[85] The theory says that there are four basic leadership styles:

- **Directive:** The leader provides clear procedures, guidelines, and rules for subordinates to follow when doing their jobs.
- **Supportive:** The leader focuses on subordinates' needs and overall well-being to maintain positive relationships.
- **Participative:** The leader consults with subordinates, solicits their opinions, and otherwise involves them in decision making.
- **Achievement-oriented:** The leader focuses on maximizing subordinate performance by setting lofty goals, providing challenges, and emphasizing excellence.

To be most effective, leaders should use the style that best fits the demands of a particular situation. In fact, several **contingency factors** may shape which style produces high motivation and performance among subordinates. For example, unstructured tasks (tasks that are poorly defined or unpredictable) may require more directive leadership, everything else being equal. On the other hand, highly structured tasks (tasks that are well defined, with clear guidelines for performance) may be a better fit for participative leadership. Similarly, immature subordinates (i.e., few skills, little experience) may benefit from directive leadership, while mature subordinates (i.e., plenty of experience, well-developed skills) may benefit from achievement-oriented leadership.

As it stands, path-goal theory is "culture free." But introducing Hofstede's cultural dimensions as a set of possible contingencies suggests some basic predictions. In general, participative leadership should work best in low power distance cultures, while directive leadership should work best in high power distance societies. Countries with moderate levels of power distance may find leadership that combines participation with some supportive behavior most attractive. A paternalistic style combining both supportive and directive behaviors should work best in collective societies (remember that collectivism is often associated with high power distance). Individualistic societies, which also tend to be low on power distance, should embrace participative leadership.

EXHIBIT 11.6

Introducing Cultural Contingencies into Path-Goal Theory:
Identifying Compatible Leadership Styles

Culture	Country Example	Most Compatible Leadership Style			
		Directive	**Supportive**	**Participative**	**Achievement**
Small PD*	Sweden			X	
Large PD	France	X			
Moderate PD	United States		X	X	
Collectivist	Taiwan	X	X		
Individualist	Denmark			X	
Moderate individualist	Argentina			X	
Strong UA	Greece	X			
Weak UA	England			X	X
Moderate UA	Germany			X	X

*PD = Power Distance, UA = Uncertainty Avoidance.

Source: Adapted from Rodrigues, C. (1990). The situation and national culture as contingencies for leadership behavior: Two conceptual models. *Advances in international comparative management, vol. 5,* ed. B. Prasad (Greenwich, CT: JAI Press), 51–68.

Finally, strong uncertainty avoidance cultures may prefer directive leadership, while in cultures more tolerant of ambiguity, participative and achievement-oriented styles might be better received. We've summarized these predictions in Exhibit 11.6.

Obviously, these are generalizations. A major goal for future research is to discover how important cultural values are relative to other contingency factors (e.g., task structure) in determining what type of leadership will be most effective in specific cultural contexts.[86]

Leadership Issues in Multinationals

In this last section, we'll consider international leadership from a corporate perspective. Doing so will underscore the difficulties that multinationals face with cross-cultural leadership issues. Just consider all the possible cross-cultural combinations. Leaders and subordinates who are from the country where the multinational is headquartered, a host country where the multinational does business, or a third country may all have to interact. Likewise, these interactions may happen in the headquarters country, a host country, or in a third country.

Some multinationals clearly hope that the increasing similarity of companies around the world in terms of structure, technology, and strategy will weaken or overcome cross-cultural differences. However, while companies around the world may look increasingly alike with respect to these macro-level factors, micro-level factors (such as leader behavior) may continue to be influenced by cultural values. As we've said, this implies that leaders must take cultural values into account to be effective.[87] In fact, some American, European, and Japanese multinationals have created comprehensive programs to develop more effective international managers. General Electric, Unilever, and Sony Corporation are three such examples.[88]

Other multinationals want to substitute their corporate values for the national values that they encounter in various countries. These multinationals believe that by emphasizing corporate values, a more homogeneous international workforce can be created. This would allow managers to use similar leadership strategies in all environments, even if the multinationals operate in dozens of countries and have thousands of foreign employees. The key, of course, is socializing employees to accept corporate values and to put their own cultural values aside if necessary.

The attraction of this strategy is obvious. It would make life a lot simpler. But building a global workforce with a common set of values is very difficult. Just working for a multinational may accentuate cultural values. In one study, cultural differences were more pronounced among employees working for a multinational than for employees working in their own countries for a local firm. So Italians acted more "Italian" when they worked for a foreign firm than when they worked for an Italian company. The same was true for the other nationalities in the study.[89]

Resistance can also occur when multinationals pressure foreign employees to accept corporate values that conflict with their national culture. For example, an American multinational's attempts to encourage participative decision-making among its European managers backfired. In fact, the multinational's training and indoctrination efforts only served to highlight the differences between corporate and local values. Opposition from European managers was the result.[90]

The skills needed for international leadership   As we've suggested, the best option for multinationals may be training and career development programs designed to build international leadership skills throughout the corporation.[91] But that's just part of the story. Companies need to identify their aspiring international managers early, using valid and reliable methods.[92] And once that happens, managers will need time to acquire the skills they need to be effective international leaders. For example, international managers should have a perspective on cultural issues that is not limited to a particular country or region. The continuing internationalization of business is increasing the frequency and variety of cross-cultural relationships that managers have to contend with. As a result, a country-based or regional set of experiences and skills is insufficient over the long haul. Ultimately, managers need transnational skills to be effective (these are listed in Exhibit 11.7).

At this point, however, few multinationals have made a sustained effort to develop transnational leadership skills in their managers. Fortunately, leadership development efforts are being implemented that can overcome the limitations inherent in the modest training programs now offered by most firms.[93] Chapter 12 will consider international employees in more detail and illustrate how firms can link leadership development to the business objectives they pursue abroad. For now, we'll leave you with some basic suggestions for implementing a transnational leadership development strategy. These are summarized in Exhibit 11.8. Companies that are serious about preparing their managers for international leadership challenges will take these ideas to heart.[94]

EXHIBIT 11.7

Comparing Transnational and Traditional Skills for International Managers

Transnational Skills	Transnationally Competent Managers	Traditional International Managers
Global perspective	Understand worldwide business environment from a global perspective.	Focus on a single foreign country and on managing relationships between headquarters and that country.
Local responsiveness	Learn about many cultures.	Become an expert on one culture.
Synergistic learning	Work with and learn from people from many cultures simultaneously. Create a culturally synergistic organizational environment.	Work with and coach people in each foreign culture separately or sequentially. Integrate foreigners into the headquarters' national organizational culture.
Transition and adaptation	Adapt to living in many foreign cultures.	Adapt to living in a foreign culture.
Cross-cultural interaction	Use cross-cultural interaction skills in a daily basis throughout one's career.	Use cross-cultural interaction skills primarily on foreign assignments.
Collaboration	Interact with foreign colleagues as equals.	Interact within clearly defined hierarchies of structural and cultural dominance.
Foreign experience	Transpatriation for career and organization development.	Expatriation or inpatriation primarily to get the job done.

Source: Adler, N. J., & Bartholomew, S. (1992). Managing globally competent people. *Academy of Management Executive, 6,* 54. © 1992 by the Academy of Management. Reprinted by permission.

Chapter Summary

In this chapter, we combined a discussion of motivation and leadership across cultures and countries. A key point that we made early on is that most research on these topics was done by Americans with all their accompanying cultural baggage. If managers need to know which motivational approaches and techniques work well overseas, then what they may take as common wisdom in the United States may be inappropriate in other countries. In fact, we reviewed some of the most common motivational theories and described research on their possible cross-cultural applicability. Overall, research shows that there are few motivational universals and that many approaches, including the tried and true reinforcement theory, can have very different effects when applied elsewhere. For example, employees in South Africa, Mexico, or Japan can react differently when a supervisor gives positive performance feedback. Whereas Americans gener-

ally are positively energized, the reactions of employees in these other cultures are far from simple nor consistent with those of American workers. Overall, we strongly suggest that managers explicitly take cultural variables into account in designing their reward systems and motivational strategies.

The same conclusions were reached about what makes for effective leadership in an international context. Similar to the work on motivation, research on leadership has also taken a decidedly Western or American bias. In the process of reviewing many different theories of leadership, we conclude that leader behavior can vary dramatically across cultures and that a manager's international effectiveness can be increased by awareness of this fact. We find that what constitutes effective leadership behavior and style can differ across countries and culture. A take-charge, aggressive style may work well in many situations in the United States, whereas in the Netherlands it is unlikely to be as successful. We completed the chapter by

EXHIBIT 11.8

Suggestions for Developing Leaders with Transnational Skills

Suggestion	Description/Explanation
Place a premium on experience	Research suggests that work experience is often the best way to develop international managers.
Make sure leadership development and other human resource practices are aligned	Building international skills into performance appraisal and establishing target assignments helps reinforce the importance of international executive development.
Create support mechanisms to help the development process	Develop methods for tracking career moves and the outcome of various developmental activities.
Ensure that senior executives take responsibility for international leadership development	Easier said than done, top management should work to monitor careers and plan assignments as a way of building visible and influential support for development efforts.
Educate top management about developmental information	If top management understands how development activities and evaluations work, they'll be more likely to support them.
Managers need to know how they are viewed and what their next career moves will be	Letting leaders with potential know that top executives are paying attention helps retain them and underscores their value to the firm.

Source: Adapted from Conner, J. (2000). Developing the global leaders of tomorrow. *Human Resource Management, 39,* 147–157.

advocating as close to a cross-cultural leadership approach as we can muster. Basically, this *path-goal model* suggests that to be most effective, leaders should use the style that best fits the demands of a particular situation and culture. The four basic leader styles suggested by the model are mapped onto common cultural dimensions that seem to suggest a better fit of one style over another in a particular culture.

Discussion Questions

1. How might Mexican, American, and Japanese managers try to tackle a motivation problem in, for example, the customer service area?
2. Think also how each of the managers in question 1 might approach the same problem if they were managing workers from and in those other two countries. What difficulties do you think they might have because of their cultural viewpoints?
3. Compare what might make for a good leadership style in China, Germany, and the United States. What sort of problems do you predict that a German leader might experience in a U.S. company? How would a typical German leader be perceived by his or her new U.S. employees?

Up to the Challenge?

Motivating Russian Employees

At the beginning of the chapter we described a study that put three American motivational approaches to the test with Russian mill workers. To refresh your memory, the first program involved giving workers valued extrinsic rewards (e.g., consumer goods, bonuses) in exchange for improvements in performance. The second program involved behavioral management, with Russian supervisors trying to shape employee behavior with praise for good performance and corrective suggestions when performance was below par. The third program borrowed a page from job enrichment ideas and relied on participative management tactics to improve motivation and performance. In a nutshell, employees were asked for suggestions about how to change their jobs and allowed to implement them.

Your challenge was to predict which of these three motivational approaches would work best with Russian employees. The research team felt that both the extrinsic reward and behavioral management programs would work well. Extrinsic rewards linked to performance complement the emphasis Russians place on hard work that is connected to material gains. And behavioral management lines up pretty well with Russian human resource management traditions that encourage feelings of accomplishment and taking responsibility for the common good.

But participative management was expected to encounter tough sledding, mainly because of Russian tradition and values. Although these values are changing, many Russians have worked for years in a traditional, "keep your mouth shut" environment. Asking questions and challenging authority was, and to some extent still is, a recipe for trouble in Russia. Instead, the Russian tradition of hard work was implemented in a communal context where strong, autocratic leadership was expected. In this tradition, employees are often very loyal to their work groups and colleagues while looking to management for approval and guidance on even trivial issues. Moreover, many Russian employees distrust outsiders and are hesitant to share information. So the research team believed that participative management, which requires employees who are willing to take the initiative, challenge the status quo, and communicate openly, would be hard for many Russians to swallow in the short term. Participative management tactics would undercut employees' traditional relationships with their bosses rather than motivate them.

To test these predictions, the researchers designed a clever real-life experiment. They randomly assigned Russian production employees to one of the three motivation programs. Before the programs started baseline performance data per worker (i.e., amount of cotton fabric produced) was collected for two weeks. Then the motivation programs ran in each group for the next two weeks, after which performance was measured again. Once the programs were stopped, performance was measured a final time after another two weeks. The idea was to see if performance improved after a program started but then slid back to baseline levels after it stopped. If that happened, the obvious conclusion would be that the program had caused the spike in performance.

The research team's predictions turned out to be on target. Production improved after extrinsic rewards were introduced but slid back after they were removed. The same basic pattern was seen for the behavioral management program. But the participative management program actually caused performance to drop. These results highlight both the benefits and risks associated with using Western motivation tactics in Russia, especially without extensive preparation and training. The extrinsic reward and behavioral management interventions appeared to work because they were consistent with Russian traditions and values, unlike participative management.

Consistent with these findings, reports from the field suggest that money and other extrinsic rewards are often powerful motivators for many Russian employees. And Russian employees tend to discuss pay and perks among themselves to a greater extent than their Western counterparts, perhaps because of communal traditions. Consequently, Western managers should expect to hear an earful if they pay and reward their Russian employees differently without clearly explaining the reasons for doing so. Today, many Western companies operating in Russia offer employees merit-based raises and bonuses as well as a full slate of perks and benefits, such as health care and pension plans, and, in a nod to the Soviet-practice of providing cheap meals for employees, free lunches.

But as the Russian economy evolves and begins to offer wider opportunities for employees, are there any risks and dangers for Western companies from a motivation standpoint? For one, there appear to be significant generational differences across the Russian employee population. For example, there are (1) older workers with excellent technical skills but no real understanding of Western business models; (2) Russians who have traveled abroad for business training if not business degrees in a variety of areas and who may have extensive experience working for international firms; and (3) younger employees who are inexperienced but open minded and willing to learn. Which type of employee would you want to hire if you were an international company setting up shop in Russia? And if you had all three types of employees on the payroll, how would you motivate them? Would your tactics vary across the three groups? If so, how?[95]

International Development

Testing Your Cross-Cultural Motivation Skills

Purpose

The goal of this exercise is to consider the challenge of motivating people from different cultures. Six short situations are presented about Egyptian, Chinese, Japanese, and American subordinates, along with alternative possibilities for motivating them.

Instructions

You can think about and select an answer for each situation either ahead of time or in class. Your instructor may ask you to break into small groups of four to eight and come up with a consensus answer for each example in class. Your group can then make a brief presentation (5 minutes) about your answers and rationales. In either case, your instructor can then lead a discussion about the most appropriate answers for each situation.

Motivation Situations

1. You would like to have a Saudi Arabian colleague's help so that you can finish a major assignment. You are most likely to get that help if you say:
   a. "In the name of God, please help me."
   b. "If you help me, I'll buy you dinner."
   c. "My friend, I need your help."
   d. "Let's be the first to finish this assignment."

2. You are a department manager in China. Which of the following would probably work best to motivate your production supervisor to improve performance?
   a. "If our department increases output by 20 percent, you'll get a 5 percent bonus."
   b. "I'm planning to reorganize the department and I'm thinking of promoting you if production increases."
   c. "If your team doesn't meet the quotas, you're fired."
   d. "Why don't you put in some overtime to help make the production quotas?"

3. You are a manager about to conduct a series of performance appraisals on your American subordinates. To motivate them, you will probably want to focus on recognizing the Americans'
   a. promptness.
   b. creativity.
   c. directness and openness.
   d. accomplishments.

4. Last month your Japanese team hit all production targets. Which of the following would be the best way to acknowledge their achievement?
   a. Treat them to a dinner where you give special recognition to the team leader.
   b. Don't mention it, because meeting targets is their job.
   c. Call the oldest team member aside and thank him or her.
   d. Thank the group at your next meeting and ask them to increase production even more.

5. You are managing a factory in Egypt. One supervisor's group is not meeting your production expectations. Which of the following might be the best way for you to draw the supervisor's attention to this problem?
   a. "Increase your group's productivity or you're fired."
   b. "Do you need any help with your group?"
   c. "You'd better take care of your group, or I may have to move you to another job."
   d. "Why don't you hold a meeting with your group to find out what's wrong?"

6. You are a manager in a large international company and are about to begin an important project. Mr. Hiro has been assigned to work for you on this project. Because Mr. Hiro is from Japan, which of the following is likely to motivate him?
   a. Being part of a strong, leading international firm.
   b. A good raise in his annual salary.
   c. A promotion to group leader and a better title.
   d. A trip to Hawaii for him and his wife after the project is completed.

Source: Based on materials from Elashmawi, F., and Harris, P. R. (1993). *Multicultural management: New skills for global business*, 148–151. © 1993 by Gulf Publishing Company. Used with permission. All rights reserved.

From Theory to Practice
Leadership Transitions in Emerging Market Economies

Purpose

To do a more detailed analysis of the type of leadership certain countries relied on when they were state dominated and the type of leadership they are now trying to embrace in a more market-oriented environment. Your instructor will assign specific countries to research.

This chapter discussed some of the leadership challenges facing Russian managers in their transition process. Other countries are going through similar transformations. These include the countries of eastern Europe (including what was once the Soviet Union), China, and Vietnam.

Instructions

Your instructor will place you into small groups (ideally 3–5) to do research on the basic approach to leadership used in a specific country that is trying to make the transition to a market economy. This research effort should be done outside of class and focus on: (a) the approaches to leadership used when the state controlled the economy; (b) the new approach to leadership that experts believe the country will need to be a competitive market economy; and (c) an assessment of progress and barriers to change that remain.

Your instructor may have each group make a presentation (15 minutes) about your findings to the class. This could be followed by a discussion about common and unique leadership themes in these transitioning economies as well as the role of cultural values. If your instructor decides to make this an individual assignment, be prepared to take part in a general class discussion on the issues raised.

Building an International Workforce: Strategy and Selection

Using Human Resources Strategically: Making the China Gambit Pay

LEARNING OBJECTIVES

After reading this chapter, you should be able to

● Explain why an international human resource management strategy is important for achieving a firm's international business goals.

● Identify the options for staffing international operations as well as their pros and cons.

● Discuss how culture impacts the selection and development of international employees.

● Understand how firms can manage equal opportunity and diversity issues in their international operations.

● Identify the major factors associated with the successful selection, preparation, adaptation, and repatriation of expatriates.

CHINA PRESENTS CHALLENGES for foreign companies. Among other things, corruption is fairly widespread and the long-term viability of China's political system is unclear. Nevertheless, many high-tech firms believe that China is a huge growth market for electronics. For instance, demand for mobile communications equipment and services is expected to increase 20 percent annually through 2005. On top of that, China is also a cheap export platform, thanks in part to its enormous supply of inexpensive labor (unskilled factory workers earn around 60 cents an hour). The combination of lost-cost production and high growth prospects is what prompts companies to take the risks that come with investing in China. And arguably the biggest risk taker among U.S. firms is Motorola. By the end of 2001, Motorola had invested over $3.4 billion in China, and announced that the firm, along with some partners and suppliers, planned to spend another $6.6 billion in the country through 2007. One of its biggest investments, the Motorola Tianjin Integrated Semiconductor Manufacturing Complex, began churning out product in the summer of 2001.

Already the biggest foreign investor in China when it comes to electronics, Motorola's $560 million Tianjin plant illustrates the firm's strategic desire to manufacture near the growing Asian markets it wants to serve. China alone already accounts for over 12 percent of Motorola's total sales, a figure that's expected to rise and that currently trails only the United States and Europe. Overall, Motorola has dozens of factories and sales offices in China that collectively employ over 6,000 people.

Nevertheless, Motorola has found that operating in China means responding to some unique (and changing) human resource management issues. Here's a partial list:

- China's workforce lags behind other industrialized countries in terms of education and skills. The government sees better training as a way to help transform China into a world-class competitor. And while efforts have been made to ramp up China's vocational education system, Chinese officials also believe that co-ownership speeds up the transfer of training, technology, and management know-how. That explains why China prefers that foreign firms establish joint ventures with local companies.

- While fading, vestiges of China's tradition of lifetime employment and extensive benefits for workers remain. Although wages are quite low by Western standards, employers typically provide benefits including child care, housing subsidies, and medical coverage. This traditional "iron rice bowl" system is less flexible than many foreign companies, especially those from the United States, are used to.

- Wage increases in state-owned companies are often small, infrequent, and not directly connected to individual or company performance. Likewise, promotions are often based on seniority or special connections (*guanxi*) rather than performance. The Chinese government frets about the stifling effect such approaches have on initiative and creativity. On the other hand, Chinese officials also are unlikely to do anything that might boost wages in a significant way, fearing that it could slow the foreign investment spigot. In any case, the upshot for foreign companies is that they must modify the incentive-laden human resource management practices that they often use in other countries (e.g., the U.S.).

- Although regulations have been loosened considerably in recent years, a complicated and centralized labor structure exists where the government has leverage over wages, labor movement, training regulations, and firing of workers. The Chinese government, however, continues to take steps to streamline the system.

For the most part, Motorola has met the human resource challenges it faced in China (sales have exceeded expectations in many cases). But what human resource strategies did Motorola use with its Chinese employees? If you had been advising Motorola, what recommendations would you have for hiring, developing, and retaining Chinese employees? Keep in mind that as far back as 1989, Motorola's plan was to manufacture its high-technology products inside China to world-class standards. Read through the rest of this chapter, do some research about Chinese human resource practices, and think about some options. Then read the Up to the Challenge box at the end of the chapter to learn about some of the key elements of Motorola's actual human resource management strategy in China.[1]

A Strategic Look at International Human Resource Management

In Chapter 11 we considered the motivation and leadership challenges facing managers in an international business environment. This chapter takes things to the next level by considering the broader role that human resource management plays in an international context. That strategy should shape the employee selection and development practices pursued by international firms. Traditionally, human resource management involves planning and executing activities that help select, train, develop, appraise, and reward employees. However, international human resource managers must also be able to contribute to the overall international strategic planning process for the business and think strategically within their own functional area in ways that help the firm achieve its international goals.[2] Ideally, human resource executives should be involved in all phases of the development and implementation of a company's international goals.[3]

Staffing and running foreign facilities, such as this factory in Mexico, present a variety of human resource management challenges to multinationals. © Danny Lehman/CORBIS

But why is a strategic perspective on international human resource management so critical? In a nutshell, companies with a highly trained, flexible, and motivated international workforce may have an advantage over competitors, especially if that workforce directly supports corporate goals.[4] What's more, developing such a workforce is much more difficult for a competitor to emulate than buying technology or securing capital.[5] Indeed, how well companies manage their human resources around the world can mean the difference between success and failure in international business. If you're still not convinced, consider the fact that compared to their competitors, firms that effectively manage their international human resources typically:

- do a better job of identifying new business opportunities around the world.
- have a satisfied and committed overseas staff with low turnover.
- are less likely to violate local cultural norms and values (and are less likely to lose business as a result).
- are better equipped to adapt to rapidly changing business conditions worldwide.[6]

And as we've seen, companies are more likely than ever to find themselves doing business in locations with diverse cultural, legal, economic, and political perspectives. The challenge for many firms is how to balance the need to coordinate units scattered around the world against the need for individual units to have the control necessary to deal effectively with local issues.[7]

By definition, this balancing act becomes more difficult to pull off as the level of diversity firms are exposed to increases. For example, when the parent firm's national culture differs dramatically from the cultures that prevail where its foreign subsidiaries are located, it may be harder for the parent firm to:

- share information and technology between the home office and foreign outposts.
- spread innovations and knowledge throughout the firm.
- promote needed organizational changes.
- minimize conflicts between employees in different countries.

Fortunately, human resource management strategies can be put in place to overcome such problems.[8] For instance, international human resource managers can take steps to ensure that senior executives understand the different cultures within the company workforce and around the world. They can also give advice about how the firm can coordinate functions across boundaries and create ways to develop outstanding cross-cultural skills in employees (e.g., through various training programs and career paths that involve significant overseas exposure).[9]

Of course, these are very general suggestions and a wide range of human resource practices might be used to implement them. As a starting point, some experts suggest companies should develop an international human resource philosophy that describes corporate values and attitudes about human resources. This philosophy will drive the development of core international human resource policies that define how employees all over the world should be treated. In other words, these policies will provide a broad outline of what constitutes acceptable international human resource practices. Under this broad umbrella, individual units will be able to fine-tune and select specific practices that best fit their local conditions.

However, executing this won't be easy, especially for firms operating in dozens of countries. Companies with heavy international exposure might find it extremely difficult, for example, to design a compensation system that is sensitive to cultural differences yet still meets general guidelines of being seen as fair and equally motivating by employees in a variety of countries. On top of that, how benefit packages are constructed, as well as the hiring, firing, and promotion practices used, can all be impacted by culture. Overall, developing a human resource management system that has universal elements, yet still allows for local flexibility, is a tall order.[10]

In any case, the suggestion to establish a basic set of corporate-wide policies first implies that corporate headquarters makes basic policy and philosophy decisions but gives individual units around the world at least some say over what human resource practices are actually implemented. In reality, however, firms organize their international human resource management activities in a variety of complex ways.[11] For example, some firms run virtually all international human resource functions out of corporate headquarters. Others centralize only general policy making and ask foreign units for advice about how to actually implement policies locally. Some firms are "integrative" in that they use what they feel are the most effective human resource practices on a worldwide basis, regardless of where they originally came from. These policies could be developed in the home country and then used in foreign subsidiaries or vice versa. In other cases, international human resource activities are divided up among corporate headquarters, regional areas, and individual subsidiaries, with each having specific responsibilities.

Finally, some firms organize international human resource functions around the type of employee. For instance, some large multinationals centralize human resource functions for parent-country nationals (PCNs) and third-country nationals (TCNs) but delegate decisions about host-country nationals (HCNs) to local units.[12] We'll have more to say about these different types of employees in the next section. But before we do, take a look at the following International Insights box. As you'll see, even a "simple" human resource task like screening job candidates is anything but when foreign prospects are involved.

INTERNATIONAL INSIGHTS

Hiring the Best and Brightest from Abroad Means Going the Extra Mile

IN MANY FIELDS such as computers, pharmaceuticals, and aerospace, finding the best employees with critical skills means scouring the world for talent. Consequently, American household names like Hewlett-Packard, Microsoft, Texas Instruments, and Pfizer have hired foreigners to fill key positions in the United States in recent years. And that's happened even in the face of substantial visa hurdles that must be cleared to legally bring foreigners into the United States to work.

But just screening potential foreign hires presents special issues and difficult challenges. Consider educational credentials. Verifying educational credentials is important regardless of where the job candidate is from. Things are more complicated, however, when the job candidate is a foreigner whose educational credentials were obtained outside the United States. Clearly, many overseas universities provide a superior education. The problem is that figuring out what's "superior" is rarely easy for American human resource professionals. Foreign universities usually have different standards, courses, and grading systems than their American counterparts. This can make it tough to interpret a foreign candidate's education against what American schools offer. Some U.S. firms use their own in-house tests to evaluate foreign applicants' education, skills, and abilities. A more common approach is to rely on consulting firms, such as New York–based World Education Services Inc., to assess the educational credentials of foreign job candidates.

But the challenges don't stop there. Assessing the work experience of foreign job applicants can also prove difficult, as does conducting background checks for criminal behavior. Once again, many U.S. firms turn to consultants who have the expertise and overseas contacts necessary to determine whether foreign candidates' experiences are accurately stated and how they compare against American candidates with similar backgrounds. Part of the challenge is language barriers. It's illegal for American firms to ask foreign job candidates about their language skills unless fluency in particular languages is necessary for performing the job. In most cases, however, language barriers come in to play when contacting references or foreign "gatekeepers" (e.g., administrative assistants, secretaries) who don't speak English. This means that whoever is conducting background checks needs to be fluent in the relevant foreign language.

When it comes to screening for past criminal behavior, the problem is that laws and legal systems vary. Consequently, what might be considered crimes in the United States aren't necessarily viewed as such in other countries. For instance, foreigners hired to work in the United States often seek permanent resident status. Doing so means that foreigners must present documents from their home countries that describe whether or not they have a criminal history. This procedure could cause an American firm to lose a foreign hire. Foreigners with clean records from their home countries may be barred from working in the United States because they've admitted behavior that is considered criminal under American law. A related problem is that criminal records may be inadequate in certain countries, making background checks more difficult.

Cultural differences can also make screening foreign candidates a challenge. Communication styles, expectations about performance feedback, and work values may all vary across countries. American human resource professionals should explain the company's work culture to foreign job candidates and do their homework about the candidate's culture before the interview takes place. The idea is to approach the job interview without preconceptions or inaccurate views of potential cultural differences. This preparation will make it easier to assess whether the foreign job candidate can successfully adapt to the American work environment. For instance, you might be surprised to learn that British employees in the United States appear to have higher rates of failure than foreign employees from any other country. This fact runs counter to most Americans' perceptions about the similarity of British and American work cultures.[13]

Basic Options for Staffing Foreign Operations

In this section, we'll begin our exploration of international human resource management approaches by examining the options for selecting and staffing international operations. Next, we'll investigate how firms can develop employees with global management skills. We'll wrap up the chapter by considering issues surrounding the selection, training, and repatriation of expatriates.

As we've suggested, firms should align their human resource management practices with their international business strategies. In other words, the strategic choices firms make to compete in the global economy should be supported by their international human resource practices.[14] For instance, a company that has significant interests and deep roots abroad will be well served by a top management team that has substantial international experience, one with a firsthand understanding of foreign markets, cultures, and business practices. In fact, since substantial international experience is still relatively difficult to obtain, executive teams that have it may offer their companies an important competitive advantage. That possibility has prompted many large U.S. firms in recent years to focus more on hiring and promoting top managers with international experience as well as offering international development opportunities to managers lower in the ranks. A good example is Richard Waggoner, who was instrumental in putting GM's South American operations back on track. That foreign experience was a key reason why GM named Waggoner CEO in 1998.[15]

But staffing international operations can be a complex proposition, with human resource managers facing a potentially confusing array of choices. For example, a traditional option is to recruit **parent-country nationals** (PCNs), especially for top management and important technical positions in foreign subsidiaries. PCNs have citizenship in the country where the hiring company is headquartered.

Once abroad, PCNs are usually referred to as **expatriates**. The reasons for using expatriates or PCNs could include one or more of the possible benefits summarized in Exhibit 12.1. As you can see, the expatriate function offers some pluses for the company as well as for individuals.[16] But the most common reasons for sending a PCN on an expatriate assignment may have to do with the lack of appropriate expertise (e.g., technical, managerial) where the foreign subsidiary is located or the belief that the PCN is the best option for effectively monitoring and controlling foreign operations.

On the other hand, sending a PCN abroad is typically an expensive proposition, at least compared with other staffing options. Adding to the expense is the fact that failure rates for expatriate assignments (i.e., the expatriate returns prematurely or otherwise fails to achieve desired objectives) are often quite high. Although estimates for failure rates vary considerably (from 15% up to 70%), a rough rule of thumb is that around 25 percent of expatriate postings end in some kind of failure.[17] We'll have more to say about the expenses associated with expatriates later. In many cases, however, the biggest drawback with PCNs is their limited understanding of a local culture and its business practices, especially early on in a foreign assignment.[18] To offset this, some firms recruit immigrants, or their adult children, for positions in foreign subsidiaries back in their ancestral homes. But as the following International Insights suggests, this option isn't as simple as it seems.

Consequently, many companies turn to **host-country nationals** (HCNs), especially to fill lower- and middle-level management jobs. HCNs are individuals from the foreign country where a multinational has decided to set up shop (e.g., a plant, a sales office, etc.). Some firms are reluctant to put HCNs in top management positions overseas because they feel it would dilute their ability to control foreign operations or to

EXHIBIT 12.1

Why Use Expatriates?
Possible Benefits for Companies and Employees

Possible Benefits for Companies	Possible Benefits for Employees
Key skills and expertise transferred to the foreign operation to address important issues	Skill development (e.g., culture, language, flexibility, adaptability)
Employee retention and commitment	Recognition, rewards, advancement
Know-how about local markets and practices transferred back to the parent company	Greater commitment to firm
Development of senior management team (building a broader international experience base)	Travel opportunities
Better overall performance of the foreign operation	Greater job and work life satisfaction

Source: Adapted from Downes, M., & Thomas, A. S. (2000). Managing overseas assignments to build organizational knowledge. *Human Resource Planning,* 20, 33–48.

maintain a unified corporate culture. Nevertheless, HCNs offer some potential advantages over PCNs. Not surprisingly, HCNs typically have a better grasp of the local culture, business practices, and language than anyone else. This knowledge has obvious implications for the success of a multinational's foreign operations. HCNs also tend to be cheaper for the company since expatriates usually entail expensive relocation costs and often higher salaries. Finally, hiring locals to staff foreign operations can bring public relations benefits and relieve the pressure that foreign governments often place on international firms to go local in staffing subsidiary operations.[20]

Another increasingly popular option is to use **third-country nationals** (TCNs) in foreign subsidiaries. As the name implies, TCNs enjoy citizenship in a country other than the foreign subsidiary where they work or the country where the parent company is based. Many firms are simply looking for a particular set of skills and find it in a TCN. For example, say a company wants someone with expertise in local culture and business practices to fill a specific management position in a foreign subsidiary. PCNs may have plenty of management experience but may lack local knowledge. Likewise, while HCNs may understand local conditions, they may lack the right combination of technical skills. A TCN may be the best option, especially if the goal is to groom someone for top management positions in foreign subsidiaries or to set up operations in developing countries that lack home-grown management talent. For instance, an American firm setting up manufacturing operations in Guatemala may find appropriate candidates in Mexico, a country with a large pool of Spanish-speaking management talent.

However, this example also underscores the fact that conflicts or rivalries between countries can jeopardize TCNs' chances for success. Mexico and Guatemala have been at odds because of Mexico's alleged mistreatment of Guatemalans caught illegally entering Mexico to find work. So when tensions run high, it could make life more difficult for a Mexican manager charged with supervising Guatemalan employees.

INTERNATIONAL INSIGHTS

Ethnic Expatriates: Straddling Cultural Boundaries

IT SEEMS LIKE a good idea. Recruit ethnic expatriates, people who immigrated to the United States or who lived there for years, and send them home to run your foreign operations there or to provide professional expertise in critical areas. What better way to fill important openings in markets that require both technical skills and a keen understanding of the local context? And many companies have found it to be an effective international human resource strategy. For instance, service firms like Hertz, McDonald's, and hotelier Cendant hire highly trained and well-educated immigrants who are comfortable straddling cultural boundaries and then export them to provide service support when foreign franchisees need help.

However, the outcomes aren't always so rosy. Ethnic expatriates may overestimate their ability to understand the culture in their ancestral homes, especially after spending years in the United States. Even if they do embrace the local culture, they may be seen as having betrayed corporate headquarters by going native. Furthermore, local employees may find ethnic expatriates' attempts to act like locals as flimsy impersonations that betray foreign influences and highlight their status as overpaid interlopers.

Consider some examples. After living in the United States for twenty-two years, Seiji returned to Japan to lead Apple Computer's Japanese subsidiary. He left after a year. Part of the reason was that his American colleagues saw him as too

Japanese, while his Japanese coworkers saw him as too American. Tanya immigrated to the United States at the age of 9. When she returned to her native Russia as a management consultant, she had an American MBA to go with her fluency in Russian. But in less than two years, she was back in the United States, weary of Russian women who were shocked by her ambition. More important, her local employees simply ignored the work deadlines she set. Danny spent twenty-eight years in the United States before returning to his birthplace, Taiwan, to lead Taiwan Aerospace. The move was a nightmare. Danny's Taiwanese colleagues resented him and saw him as an intruder. At one point, some of them even gave company secrets to competitors. Like the others, Danny soon gave up and returned to the United States.

So what can American firms do to improve ethnic expatriates' chances of success? One option is to hire locals as cultural translators to assist the ethnic expatriate. Another is to provide catch-up cross-cultural training for ethnic expatriates. For instance, after working in Mexico as a manager for Levi Strauss, Grace Canepa, a Peruvian educated in the United States, learned that Mexicans thought she was rude when she failed to use professional titles to address them. Unfortunately, less than 20 percent of ethnic expatriates receive any cross-cultural training.[19]

Although PCNs, HCNs, and TCNs represent three staffing categories, they don't describe all the possibilities. For instance, large multinationals increasingly want to maintain a talented **international cadre** of managers who can be plugged into any country and successfully represent the company's values. Doing this means selecting managers based on their potential and ability, regardless of their nationality, and exposing them to a variety of international experiences. Managers in the international cadre spend their careers jumping from one foreign assignment to the next. This group does not fit neatly into any of the three basic staffing categories we've described. Nevertheless, building such an international cadre seems to pay dividends. According to one study, multinationals that use regional transfers and TCNs extensively to build their international cadres tend to perform better than multinationals that rely more on traditional expatriates. And having an international cadre in place can help companies avoid expensive missteps, especially during a major push into new markets.[21]

By the same token, "PCN" doesn't really describe the **permanent expatriate**, an employee who stays on at a particular foreign subsidiary for an extended period of years. And how about an American who is hired directly by the French subsidiary of a U.S. multinational? Is the American a PCN or HCN? Neither, really. Finally, consider a Chinese

EXHIBIT 12.2

Types of International Staff and Their Potential Movement across Locations

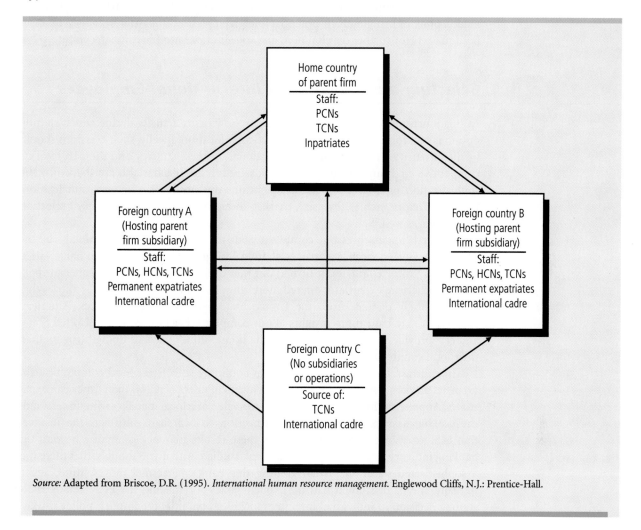

Source: Adapted from Briscoe, D.R. (1995). *International human resource management.* Englewood Cliffs, N.J.: Prentice-Hall.

employee working in the Beijing office of an American firm. The Chinese employee shows promise and a decision is made to send the employee to the United States to fill a temporary position at corporate headquarters. Such employees are sometimes referred to as inpatriates. Sending foreign employees to the home country is often done to develop specific skills, strengthen commitment to the parent firm, and to communicate corporate values more directly. Companies would also be wise to take advantage of what inpatriates can teach them about doing business in particular countries.[22]

Exhibit 12.2 illustrates some of this staffing complexity. It outlines the potential movement of employees between a firm's home country, countries hosting its foreign subsidiaries, and a country where no operations exist. In fact, we've seen all the staffing options described used simultaneously within a single company. For example, some years ago we visited foreign subsidiaries of S.C. Johnson, the U.S.-based firm that makes everything from shaving cream (Edge) to insecticide (Raid) all over the world. The Dutch managing director of S.C. Johnson's British subsidiary was essentially a permanent expatriate who had been running things in London for several years. In Spain, the company's top manager was an Australian who had been in several prior foreign postings. He was part of S. C. Johnson's international cadre. In China, we met an American executive in the company's Shanghai plant who had been continuously working in various overseas subsidiaries of S. C. Johnson for over twenty years! Finally, S. C. Johnson made a point of bringing high-potential foreign employees (inpatriates) to its Wisconsin headquarters for further development and socialization into the company culture.

Selecting and Developing International Employees

At this juncture, you're probably wondering how firms actually decide which staffing option is best for a particular job in a particular location. Ideally, such decisions should be directly tied to the company's international business strategy and the nature of its competitive environment. In many cases, selection approaches also are shaped by the sophistication of a firm's overseas operations and its level of internationalization. Likewise, factors such as firm size, market, industry, and culture can impact selection approaches as well.[23]

Research underscores this complexity. For instance, one study examined why the proportion of American expatriates staffing foreign positions for a U.S. bank varied across forty-three countries. It turned out that overseas branches with higher proportions of American expatriates offered more complex services and were in countries that were culturally distinct from the United States. In these circumstances, American expatriates may have more insights about complex services used in the United States and can provide more continuity with the home office's ways of doing business than their local counterparts.

In contrast, bank branches in foreign countries with fierce local competition for financial services relied more on local management talent (HCNs) than American expatriates. Apparently, in such circumstances the value of a local manager who understands the local business scene and has good connections to local firms outweighs the positives that U.S. expatriates possess. Of course, these results may not generalize beyond the banking industry or even the particular bank studied. And if you thought that there was a sophisticated selection system guiding this bank's personnel moves, think again. Actually, the bank studied had no explicit policy for making the PCN versus HCN staffing decision in individual foreign branches. Apparently the implicit policy worked well enough.[24]

Formal or not, companies often embrace a particular philosophy in making international staffing decisions. For instance, a **geocentric philosophy** means that the firm stresses ability and performance when selecting international staff, without regard to nationality. The goal is to develop and socialize managers who can be good corporate citizens anywhere in the world. Standards for performance are determined collaboratively between headquarters and operations around the world. At the other extreme is an **ethnocentric philosophy**. In this case, headquarters makes all key decisions and foreign subsidiaries have little autonomy or input. All important jobs at headquarters and in all foreign operations are held by PCNs (home country expatriates).

In between these two extremes are two other philosophies. A **polycentric philosophy** places human resource management control in the hands of the foreign subsidiary, although headquarters still makes broad strategic decisions. In other words, each subsidiary is set up as a semi-independent entity that controls its own staffing needs. As a result, HCNs usually hold top jobs in foreign subsidiaries. However, these same HCNs rarely move beyond the boundaries of the foreign subsidiaries to headquarters or other foreign locations. Similarly, with a **regiocentric philosophy**, most foreign employees will not move into headquarters positions. Nevertheless, employees can move from country to country in a particular region. And there may be quite a bit of collaboration among subsidiaries in a particular region (e.g., Europe or South America) to determine a common set of hiring and evaluation standards. Overall, the goal is to develop outstanding people to serve anywhere within a particular region.[25]

Developing Managers with International Skills

Many firms move toward a geocentric philosophy as they become more sophisticated in their international operations. And it can take years to build an internationally competent workforce, one where key employees know the business and are flexible, open minded, and experts in several different cultures and languages. Since big multinationals operate in dozens of countries, virtually all aspects of the business involve international contact. Such firms can no longer rely on just a few managers with international experience or a few experts on a particular country to succeed. In short, all employees must be able to recognize cultural differences that may affect business communications and working relationships.[26] Take a look at Exhibit 12.3 for a summary of the skills that international managers need to be successful. If you're not quite sure why some of these skills are necessary, read the following International Insights on the challenges facing today's international managers.

The big question, however, is how firms should go about developing employees with an appropriate set of international skills. While there's no precise recipe for success, many companies rotate promising managers through different types of foreign assignments over several years. This strategy produces managers with experience across a variety of countries and organizational circumstances, such as managing a start-up operation, an ongoing joint venture, a restructuring, and so on. Another strategy is to recruit foreign students who have come to the United States for an education and want to work in their home country after graduation. That gives firms well-educated employees who also have the language and cultural skills to succeed in their home countries. Likewise, some firms will recruit Americans in a similar fashion, hiring only those who are fluent in another language, open to other cultures, and are willing to embrace overseas assignments.

Finally, some U.S. companies have had success with training programs that bring high-potential managers from all over the world to work together on a variety of projects in a simulated environment. Such programs help build a network of relationships across nationalities and improves cross-cultural problem-solving skills. For example, Motorola annually puts hundreds of up-and-coming international managers through a business simulation that can last anywhere from days to a few weeks. As one Motorola manager who went through the simulation said, "It's surprising how realistic and demanding it is." And using such assessment tools can save companies money. French food giant Danone SA cut its failure rate among expatriate managers from 35 percent to 3 percent in three years by using simulations to evaluate international talent.[28]

In fact, some firms with extensive overseas operations have gone so far as to develop global training programs for employees. Sometimes, this includes training aimed at expatriates going to specific countries (which we'll discuss later). However, global training programs are mainly aimed at broader goals, such as developing overall cultural awareness, working effectively in cross-cultural teams, and building cross-cultural communication skills. Procter & Gamble, Intel Corporation, and Eastman Kodak are examples of U.S. firms that have successfully implemented global training programs.[29]

EXHIBIT 12.3

Do You Measure Up?
The Skill Profile for International Managers

Skill	Managerial Implication
Multidimensional perspective	Extensive multifunctional, multicountry, and multienvironment experience
Line management proficiency	Successful track record in overseas projects/assignments
Good decision making	Successful in making strategic decisions
Resourcefulness	Skilled in getting known and accepted by host country's government/business elite
Culturally adaptive	Quick and easy to adapt to foreign culture, with plenty of diverse cross-cultural experiences
Culturally sensitive	Can effectively deal with people from a variety of cultures, races, nationalities, and religions
Team-building skills	Able to create culturally diverse working groups that achieve organizational goals
Mental maturity	Endurance for the rigors of foreign posts
Negotiating skills	Track record of conducting successful business negotiations in multicultural environments
Change agent skills	Track record of successfully initiating and implementing organizational changes
Visionary ability	Quick to spot and respond to political or economic threats and opportunities in the host country

Source: Adapted from Howard, C.G. (1992). Profile of the 21st-century expatriate manager. *HR Magazine,* June, 93–100.

Cultural Differences in Selection and Development Procedures

Earlier we suggested that cultural values can shape how firms approach the selection and development of their international staff. That seems to be the case, for instance, among large multinationals, with American and British firms using somewhat different procedures to select and manage expatriates than their German and Japanese counterparts.[30] But perhaps the best illustration of this effect occurs when cultures collide. Consider what American Thomas Dimmick experienced when he was hired by Samsung, the South Korean electronics company, to help set up a plant in New Jersey:

> The hiring process was unique. Many people attended the interviews. Side conversations in Korean were the norm. Decision making inched forward as consensus was painstakingly achieved. The senior people did not commit themselves to a position until their respective

INTERNATIONAL INSIGHTS

Globetrotting Lessons in International Management

INTERNATIONAL MANAGERS are adaptable people who can cope with frequent overseas travel. Sound glamorous? Maybe. But the pace can be frenetic and exhausting. In fact, the tendency to send managers on short-term trips (i.e., less than a year) instead of traditional expatriate assignments (which typically last several years) has been accelerating recently. According to one survey of 500 global companies, nearly 80 percent expect to increase their use of shorter overseas assignments in the future. Another survey found that short-term assignments were the fastest-growing type of overseas experience. As one expert put it, "The growth in short-term assignments is really quite astounding." The reasons for this trend include lower costs and the success that companies feel they've had in developing "global managers" with broad international skills. In other words, companies often feel that their best managers can work effectively anywhere in the world. So why park them in one place for three years?

Short-term assignments mean that international managers often end up flitting around the world on short, grueling trips. Even jaunts that used to last weeks or months are now crammed into a few days. Also common are compressed overseas trips that include several stops. One manager's four-day itinerary out of New York included visits to Helsinki, London, and San Paulo. Total frequent flyer miles earned: 17,000.

And don't assume that the allure of flashy cities like Paris or Hong Kong will help you overcome jet lag. As international markets expand, managers are increasingly finding themselves in underdeveloped and sometimes risky locations where they face dirt roads, lousy hotels, and the occasional hair-raising event. One manager ended up using buckets of sea water for washing (and flushing) in Papua New Guinea after the hotel's water main was blown up by local guerrillas.

Speaking of risk, in the wake of the terrorist attacks of September 11, 2001, many companies were rethinking the need for international face time, particularly the long-term variety. Consequently, some firms began turning more to technological substitutes (e.g., video conferencing) and reserving travel for only the most important tasks or relationship-building efforts. Clearly, travel will remain an important part of international business. That said, companies these days may pay more attention to the reasons for international travel as well as employee safety and security.

In any case, on top of safety-related concerns are the personal and family hardships associated with frequent international travel. Consider Peter McAteer, an executive at Boston-based Giga Information. Three out of four weeks, Mr. McAteer is away from home, mostly out of the country. When asked what he wanted for Christmas, Mr. McAteer's son replied that he wanted his father to be home. Likewise, John Aliberti's wife says that "China has taken over our lives." His two children miss their father and endure the taunts of schoolmates about the dad who is never around. Why? Because Mr. Aliberti makes up to ten trips to China every year to drum up business for his firm, Pittsburgh-based Union Switch & Signal.

Of course, there are positives associated with all this short-term globetrotting. Mr. Aliberti thrives on the feeling he gets of being "on the frontier" in China. Another big plus for Aliberti is that he can act like a CEO in China, signing contracts and making decisions on the spot. The Chinese also fuss over Aliberti, providing limousines, luxury hotels, and respect.

Nevertheless, balancing the positives and negatives of frequent international travel requires enormous flexibility and adaptability. Consider Joaquin Carbanel. He had to adapt early when, at the tender age of nine, his Cuban parents sent him to live in the United States. After earning a law degree, Mr. Carbanel joined BellSouth Corporation and subsequently spent much of his time in airplanes. When BellSouth was pushing hard in Latin America, Mr. Carbanel shuttled between Atlanta and various South American countries. Mr. Carbanel says that being able to adapt your style to whatever culture you're in today is essential for survival as an international manager. Over time, Mr. Carbanel learned to handle big differences in business styles across three continents. Also important: foreign language skills, having a mentor to keep you "tuned in" at company headquarters, and resistance to jet lag. After all of his experiences, Mr. Carbanel says that "you feel at home wherever you are."[27]

staffs had fully and freely expressed their support or concerns for my candidacy. Personal issues were critical. Those items went beyond my wife and me. They penetrated into realms of what my father had done for a living, whether or not my mother worked outside of the home, and what my brothers and sister were doing. They all seemed to have a significance I could not fathom."[31]

Mr. Dimmick was dumbfounded because this hiring process was so different from what usually happens in American firms. Plus, as Mr. Dimmick admitted, his own ignorance of Korean culture and hiring practices prevented him from understanding what was happening. And we can say the same thing about Samsung's Korean managers since they weren't aware that Americans would be shocked by the personal questions they asked. In the United States, such questions are off limits and are perceived as irrelevant, discriminatory against certain groups, or both. In fact, simply asking some of these questions is illegal in the United States. Nonetheless, foreign managers may be unaware of these restrictions, be they legal or cultural, or may simply find them hard to grasp. Korean managers may feel that a good hire can't be made without some understanding of candidates' home life, religious orientation, and family members.[32]

Fortunately, selection procedures can be modified to better fit a cross-cultural environment. For example, traditional American selection and job analysis procedures can be adapted to Japanese cultural values, arguably a necessity in the many U.S. plants that Japanese firms have built in the past decade. How? It isn't easy. In one such auto parts plant, the plant's Japanese management wanted to stress team skills, consensus building, harmonious relationships, and other "Japanese values" when hiring American workers. But these same values make the U.S. practice of openly testing and comparing individual applicants an uncomfortable event for some Japanese. Since Japanese schools often provide companies with job candidates for specific openings, managers can avoid the bad feelings that might be created when comparing individuals. In contrast, American companies generally feel that it's their responsibility to pick the best candidate for a particular job, making comparisons between individuals difficult to avoid. Overall, the American and Japanese approaches to selection are clearly different. However, the eventual selection system developed at the American plant cleverly blended Japanese and American approaches.

Under that blended system, groups of job applicants are asked to assemble windshield wiper motors. Individuals' performance within groups is then graded by a group of trained assessors who reach a final score for each person using a consensus decision process. Applicants who reach a predetermined cutoff score are all considered qualified and are hired as needed to staff the plant. This system combines individual assessment (American) with consensus decision making for overall evaluation (Japanese). It also allows Japanese management to assess what they believe are important issues, such as the ability of a person to work in a team.[33]

Finally, the success of any selection or training program depends on whether it matches the culture of the employees being trained. For American managers, research found that self-focused training did more to improve performance than group-focused training. The opposite was true for Chinese managers. That's because information about their own capability to succeed at a task (self-focused training) may seem more "useful" to Americans than information about the capability of a group that they belong to (group-focused training). Self-focused information is valued in individualistic cultures since performance is often defined in terms of a single person's actions. In contrast, a Chinese manager may pay more attention to information that describes how a group that they belong to should approach a task. In collectivistic cultures, people view themselves as members of a group first and as individuals second. As a result, "performance" is defined in terms of shared responsibilities, making information about group performance more valuable. The upshot is that firms need to take the cultural values of the audience into account when designing training programs.[34]

For a deeper look at one American multinational's international human resource philosophies and practices, see the accompanying Reality Check box on NCR. This box underscores many of the points we've made so far in this chapter and foreshadows issues yet to come. As you read through the box, ask yourself how well NCR is doing to become more global and less American when it comes to human resource management.

Managing Equal Opportunity and Organizational Diversity

In this section, we'll consider the challenges companies face in managing diversity in their international human resources. Cultural norms, for example, can make it difficult for American firms to provide equal opportunities for potential expatriates, despite the legal requirement to do so. Consider the 1991 Civil Rights Act, which made it illegal for American firms to discriminate against U.S. citizens working abroad on the basis of color, sex, race, religion, or national origin. U.S. firms can sidestep this requirement only if complying with American law means a local law will be violated. For instance, if a foreign country's laws prohibit women from being managers, then U.S. civil rights legislation doesn't apply to American firms doing business there.[35]

Usually, however, American companies face cultural rather legislative hurdles. The American view that everyone deserves equal opportunity in the job market may be a cultural value not shared everywhere. U.S.-based Colgate-Palmolive found this out when Brazilian employees who were asked to fill out a survey about "equal opportunity" in the firm had no idea what it meant. The wording of the survey was changed as a result.[36]

Actually, some argue that sending women or minorities into certain cultural environments precludes their ability to be effective and sends a message that U.S. firms want to export their human resource management philosophies. Granted, some Saudi Arabian men would not seriously consider doing business with Saudi women. And an aspiring businesswoman in Saudi Arabia faces the fact that it's illegal for women to drive cars.[37] Likewise, women have traditionally been viewed as subordinate to men in many African countries.[38] In Russia, about 75 percent of the unemployed are female and few women have made it into senior management.[39]

Japan is also a country where women often are expected to be subordinate to men, although this situation is changing.[40] Women occupy about 43 percent of managerial positions in the United States, compared to only about 9 percent in Japan.[41] According to one survey, nearly 60 percent of Japanese women feel that men should provide income while women should take care of the house and children. The percentage of women agreeing with these ideas is much lower in North America and western Europe. For instance, only 24 percent of American women feel that men should be the breadwinner.[42]

In any case, American firms operating in places like Japan and Saudi Arabia sometimes refrain from sending female expatriates so as not to provoke a backlash, given local sensibilities. But legal challenges filed in U.S. courts have made it clear that American firms may lose lawsuits if they exclude women or minorities from overseas posts to avoid clashing with local cultural norms.[43] Of course, sexism may explain the reluctance of some U.S. companies to send women on overseas assignments. And this is hardly a phenomenon unique to American firms. European women also experience gender-related discrimination that makes it harder to land expatriate assignments compared with male counterparts of similar background and skills.[44]

REALITY CHECK

NCR and the Chinese Challenge

A chat with Jorg Kasparek, vice-president of compensation and benefits, NCR Corporation

Tell us a little about your role at NCR and the international strategy you use in pursuing it.

I'm responsible for NCR's worldwide benefit and compensation programs. My team consists of about thirty-five people who manage these policies worldwide. We also have managers in the field that support these functions locally. Our goal is to maintain a worldwide philosophy and level of consistency in the way we reward people, particularly in the benefits and compensation side. Although we set local rates for pay structures and align them to local conditions, everything else that we run, like our sales compensation programs, are structured on a worldwide basis. Having those programs aligned with our business strategies is critical. One of the challenges is that local laws and practices make it difficult to align pension and benefit plans with our business goals. But we still have a consistent philosophy underneath it all.

How would you describe NCR's international staffing strategy?

We operate in over one hundred countries and have been in the international market for a long time. So we rely heavily on local nationals. Having said that, our business model has shifted away from a country focus to one where business units operate using a regional approach. Particularly in markets like the European Union, North America, and parts of the Asia-Pacific region, we want to support customers on more of a regional basis. Of course, there are still the cultural or language issues to consider when servicing customers. We are not going to put a German, for instance, in a salesperson position if it's based in France. We'd want a French national for that. However, at the management level, the emphasis shifts away from local nationals to diverse teams of people from multiple countries working together in business units.

With management positions, we focus more on skill sets, knowledge of markets, and specific behavioral attributes. For example, a leader of a regional business unit might be located in Frankfurt, London, or Paris; her location is almost irrelevant. But she must understand the EU extremely well.

Adopting this regional approach has been a big shift for NCR over the last five years. We worry less about performance on a per-country basis than before and we've eliminated country managers. We're setting up regional centers for functions such as order processing, customer service, finance, and human resource support. And since we want employees with diverse language and cultural skills, we try to put those service centers in places where we can recruit different kinds of nationalities. So places like London, Amsterdam, and Sydney are great choices because they're teeming with people from a variety of cultural and linguistic backgrounds.

Can you share any challenging international staffing situations that you've dealt with?

Well, Japan represents an exception to our regional approach. It's more difficult for foreigners to succeed in Japan than in some other places. It's also difficult to find Japanese who have extensive regional experience. So with Japan, we're still country focused. Mainland China also presents challenges. Since they are just opening up, it's hard to find the right people. In addition, our business there is growing and we need to rapidly build an effective workforce. At times, we fill key positions in China with expatriates. Even then, we often bring people in from the region, like Taiwan or Hong Kong, who can adapt and assimilate more quickly and effectively.

What do you look for in international talent? How do you go about the selection process?

I deal with a lot of executive staffing issues. Invariably, what it comes down to is the right person for the job. That isn't necessarily a function of language or technical skills; rather,

Estimates of the percentage of North American expatriates who are women range from 10 percent to 13 percent, underscoring the possible role of gender discrimination in expatriate selection. Some experts, however, predict that the percentage will surpass 20 percent by 2005, as women continue to move slowly but surely into management ranks. Nevertheless, these numbers raise questions about what's going on. Some women undoubtedly lose out on overseas opportunities simply because their superiors assume

it's the ability to lead a diverse organization. I've seen people from all kinds of countries and cultures both excel and fail in these situations. Unfortunately, our ability to predict success could be better, despite our extensive interviewing and use of multiple selection tools. We're more comfortable working with an internal candidate because we know his or her strengths, weaknesses, and track record. The person also knows the organization. So it's usually less risky to put internal candidates into international leadership roles. On the other hand, staffing from within can perpetuate old cultural biases and may not inject new energy into the firm. The bottom line is that you have to strike a balance between those two approaches.

How do you develop international skills in your employees since you tend to hire locally?

The cost of expatriates is horrendous, particularly in cities like Tokyo, London, and Paris. What we are doing increasingly is moving people around and localizing them. This means that we drop them into a country on a local package so that they are paid like a local, have local health care coverage, arrange for their own housing, and so on. But we keep them tied to their original retirement plans so they have home country connections. We preach that to excel, employees must acquire more than one language, have diverse cultural experience, and be able to function in different business units. That's critical to our staff development.

Do you use short-term assignments to develop international employees?

This is a growing area. A lot of work today is done on a project basis. Short-term assignments also eliminate many of the issues associated with shutting down life in one location so you can move to another. With short-term assignments, a person can negate many of the personal issues with family that come up with longer postings. We see this as a positive from both a company and employee perspective. Here's one example. We've had a young African-American woman working with us for about five years now. Over that period she's spent a few months in the U.K. and in Sydney. Now she's

getting ready to go back to Europe for a couple of months. She's benefited tremendously from these experiences in other cultural environments and has developed relationships with colleagues in those countries that can be nurtured. So when business issues come up, she's able to go straight to the source for a first-hand perspective.

But we still use some long-term assignments. We recently brought a manager to Dayton from Argentina for two years. He provides HR support to the Latin American region. His predecessor was an American who didn't do that well. The new manager has made real progress because he understands the region and conducts all business in Spanish. Imagine how refreshing it must be for people across Latin America to call NCR headquarters and interact with someone who understands how they operate and communicates in their own language. And our manager gains insights into how the corporate level functions, which will ultimately benefit his career.

What big trends do you see in international human resources over the next five years?

It's difficult to talk about five-year horizons anymore. Certain technologies, particularly the Internet, have accelerated the way business operates. A long-range plan in our area is really eighteen months out. One of the biggest issues for the future is leadership development. How do we ensure that the next generation of business leaders is ready and prepared to take on the role? Another big question is: Where will they come from? I recently talked to a high-level headhunter based in London. He told me that for senior searches they won't even consider someone unless they speak more that one language, regardless of their experience. I asked him what he thought the profile of a senior human resource executive in a large multinational would look like in a few years. His response was that the prototype individual probably wouldn't be an American. Unfortunately, while the United States has an ethnically diverse population, it tends to be culturally and geographically isolated. This provides a very different experience from, say, a European who can jump on a train and arrive in another country and culture in an hour.

they're less interested in international careers than men, despite evidence to the contrary. Companies also may overstate the risks of sending women or minorities into supposedly hostile cultural environments overseas. The reality is that women posted abroad are usually seen as foreigners first and women second. Consequently, they're less likely to encounter the problems experienced by local women. Actually, gender may be an advantage to women in a foreign environment because it makes them so visible.

Many women in overseas postings say that their foreign counterparts were curious about them. The fact that they were women made them more memorable and gave them greater access to important people.[45]

So how can firms help women expatriates succeed overseas? Consider these suggestions:

- **Hiring:** Give women serious consideration for overseas assignments. It may help to root out inaccurate perceptions about the "handicaps" women face and stress that women may be more likely to succeed than men in certain situations.
- **Predeparture training:** Firms can train women to take advantage of cultural attitudes about gender and to use their unique position in certain countries to increase their effectiveness. Training can also educate women about sexist remarks and forms of harassment that they may encounter in certain countries and how best to respond.
- **On-site support:** Training on cultural and gender issues should continue for the first several months overseas. That way, training can be tried out in the foreign context, providing a forum for discussing any unexpected difficulties. Firms can also help female expatriates by providing clear job titles and duties. Ambiguity in these areas can undercut a woman's credibility, especially in countries like Japan.
- **Role modeling after repatriation:** After they return, female expatriates should be encouraged to serve as visible role models for other women considering international careers. The idea is to show other women that it's possible to succeed in an international assignment, even in a "hostile" environment.[46]

But how do multinationals juggle all the diversity issues they face when operating in dozens of countries? The possible combinations of interacting races, religions, and nationalities is virtually infinite. In essence, however, companies face two basic types of diversity issues. First, they have to effectively manage cross-national diversity (i.e., interactions between PCNs, HCNs, and TCNs). Then there's the interactions between employees from a specific country who represent different races, ethnic groups, and so on. This **intranational diversity** also has important implications for the organization. In fact, the continuing flow of immigrants into the U.S. job market has increased the intranational diversity challenges American firms face.

There are four strategies for dealing with both cross-national and intranational diversity issues in companies. The most functional strategy, **multiculturalism**, requires being open to the positive aspects of all cultures. These cultural elements can then be used to create new ways of interacting and doing business. The least functional approach, **separation**, involves the rejection of all cultural values except your own. As you might expect, this strategy makes it virtually impossible for people from different cultural backgrounds to work together without conflict. The other two strategies fall between these extremes. **Assimilation** requires that subordinate groups (e.g., foreign-born employees working for a U.S. firm) conform to the values of the dominant group (e.g., the firm's American managers) to get along. This strategy can produce distrust in the long run if no effort is made by the dominant group to understand the values of the subordinate group. The last strategy, **deculturation**, is really a benign form of separation. It occurs when each group maintains its own values without trying to influence anyone else (e.g., the expatriate who doesn't understand the host country's culture and has no desire to change that situation).[47]

But if multiculturalism is the best approach, how is it actually implemented? Some experts argue that firms should start by embracing a broader view of cultural diversity. Consider Colgate-Palmolive (yes, the firm with the Brazilian survey problem). Clearly the stakes are high for Colgate-Palmolive. With operations in over 170 countries,

Some multinationals overstate the risks of sending women into "hostile" cultures; these Westen women are merely asking for directions from police in Kuala Lumpur, Malaysia. © AFP/CORBIS

roughly 75 percent of the company's revenues come from foreign sources. Colgate-Palmolive's approach centers on respect. All managers experience a program, *Valuing Colgate People*, that shows how valuing differences can help organizational goals. The first part of the program focuses on the company's global values (e.g., caring for employees, building teamwork). Later, issues in specific countries are examined. For managers in the United States, this means looking at things like racial, gender, and age discrimination. In other countries, the issue might be religious or class discrimination. The idea is to focus on the problems in each corporate location that make it difficult for employees there to respect each other. The final goal of this training is to examine whether company policies, procedures, and systems support respect. For example, performance evaluations for Colgate-Palmolive's managers includes their efforts to model respect to their subordinates. Eventually, Colgate-Palmolive wants to extend this training to all employees everywhere.[48]

The Special Case of Expatriates

In this last section, we consider selection and development issues for expatriates. Despite the trend toward shorter overseas assignments, there's no doubt that expatriates are still important. In fact, expatriates often play a critical part in turning mere opportunities into viable overseas businesses. Specifically, expatriates may fulfill a variety of strategic roles for multinationals ranging from technical expert to subsidiary manager to relationship builder (perhaps as part of an informal coordination effort), either alone or in combination. Overall, there's simply no substitute for a long-term international assignment in many cases.

And the numbers are staggering. U.S. multinationals alone are estimated to employ 1.3 million expatriates of one kind or another. Also consider that roughly 80 percent of expatriates have a spouse or partner. Then throw children into the mix. For instance, of the 70 percent of expatriate managers who are dual career couples, some 60 percent have children under age 18. Taken together, a reasonable estimate might be that upwards of 3 million people are directly impacted by expatriate assignments in American multinationals. And for a snapshot of how pervasive expatriates can be in a large multinational, consider Royal Dutch/Shell. Although the firm uses local management talent extensively, it also has nearly 5,600 expatriates in some 120 countries.[49]

Of course, you may not find a three-year foreign assignment that appealing. Perhaps you'd worry about terrorism or your personal safety in general (those worries increased for many after the events of September 11, 2001). But maybe you just aren't the sort of person who would thrive in a challenging foreign environment in any case. Nevertheless, you may want to reconsider if your career goals include the executive suite. For instance, U.S. multinationals increasingly want their senior managers to have extensive foreign experience.[50] But expatriates can be risky for both companies and employees. The fact of the matter is that when companies make mistakes in selecting and managing their expatriates, the consequences can be disastrous. Exhibit 12.4 summarizes these consequences. As you can see, firms have a lot to worry about with expatriate assignments.

Simply put, expatriates are expensive even when things go well. Add up all the extras (e.g., higher pay, airfare for family members, moving expenses, housing allowances, education benefits for the kids, company car, taxes, home leave, etc.) and the first year abroad can end up costing 300 percent of the expatriate's base salary. The bill for an average overseas stay of three years can easily top $1 million per expatriate (Chapter 13 discusses expatriate costs in more detail).[51]

In any case, this underscores how important it is to do a good job when selecting and preparing expatriates. There are also problems associated with repatriation once the foreign assignment is complete. Next, we'll examine the factors that affect expatriate success and how companies can use this information to better manage expatriate assignments.

Selecting Expatriates

Companies often overemphasize technical skills, managerial qualifications, and the need to deal quickly with short-term problems overseas when selecting expatriates. While these problems occur in firms all over the world, European and Scandinavian companies tend to stress cross-cultural skills more and use a larger number of evaluation tools than their American counterparts. This suggests a more strategic selection process for European and Scandinavian firms, one in which viable candidates are matched with the goals and requirements of a specific foreign assignment. Indeed, relatively few American firms have a systematic way of linking their strategic international goals to the selection of expatriates. Moreover, psychological factors (e.g., open-mindedness, curiosity, sociability) and family dynamics (e.g., the spouse or partner's willingness or ability to adapt to a foreign environment) are often the most important predictors of expatriate success, particularly in certain locations.[52]

In any event, how do multinationals evaluate candidates for foreign assignments? As you might expect, practices vary. However, interviews (including spouses and partners in many cases), standardized tests (measuring personality characteristics such as adaptability and emotional maturity), performance in training exercises, and an

EXHIBIT 12.4

Expatriates: The Consequences of Failure

Consequence	Description/Implication
Premature return	Estimates of the percentages of expatriates who fail and are asked to come home (or request it), vary considerably (from 15–70%, depending on the type of assignment or the expatriate's situation). Regardless, a premature return potentially jeopardizes the firm's ability to compete effectively.
Wasted relocation costs	Sending an expatriate abroad (plus a partner, spouse, or children in most cases), not to mention belongings, is very expensive. Round-trip costs for a premature return can easily top $100,000.
Wasted preparation and support costs	A failed assignment means that the firm loses both the direct (e.g., training expenses, overseas pay premiums, housing allowances) and indirect costs (e.g., not getting the job done) spent on preparing and supporting expatriates.
Other indirect costs	Failure hurts the career and confidence of the expatriate and damages relations with local employees, officials, customers, and suppliers (all of which will take time to repair).
Ineffective performance	Even if expatriates stick out their assignments, up to 50 percent may not be performing well (e.g., making poor decisions, hurting local relations).
Turnover after repatriation	Some 25% of expatriates quit within one year of returning from a foreign assignment, which leaves the firm with no return on its $1 million investment for a typical three-year posting. Such turnover may reflect the fact that 75% of expatriates fail to receive a higher level position upon return.
Negative momentum	As word spreads of the problems that expatriates have (e.g., failure rates, "out-of-sight, out-of-mind" issues, lousy prospects after repatriation, etc.), recruiting new expatriates will become harder, making it more difficult to coordinate foreign operations and capitalize on overseas opportunities.

Sources: Adapted from Birdseye, M. G., & Hill, J.S. (1995). Individual, organizational/work and environmental influences on expatriate turnover tendencies: An empirical study. *Journal of International Business Studies, 41,* 787–806; Black, J. S., Gregersen, H. B., & Mendenhall, M. E. (1992). *Global assignments: Successfully expatriating and repatriating international managers.* San Francisco, CA: Jossey-Bass; Carpenter, S. (2001). Battling the overseas blues. *Monitor on Psychology,* July/August, 48–49; Hauser, J. (1999). Managing expatriates' careers. *HR Focus,* February, 11–12; Poe, A. C. (2000). Destination everywhere. *HR Magazine,* October, 67–75.

assessment of past accomplishments are often part of the screening mechanisms used to select expatriates. Interviews are almost always used by American firms in the selection process. Beyond job-specific qualifications, the purpose of these interviews should be to look for factors that predict expatriate success. These can include factors linked to the expatriate, the foreign location, and the firm itself. As you can see in Exhibit 12.5, the list of potentially important factors is formidable. What's more, these factors may interact in complex ways that aren't fully understood.[53]

Indeed, the factors that predict a successful expatriate assignment are not identical for everyone. For instance, American, Japanese, and European expatriates may adjust and adapt to foreign assignments in different ways. These differences reflect variations in expatriates' home cultures and the human resource management practices used by the companies they work for.[54]

EXHIBIT 12.5

Expatriate Assignments:
Factors That May Contribute to Success . . . or Failure

Firm Factors	Assignment Location Factors	Individual Factors
Nature of cross-cultural training	Cultural differences	Tolerance, flexibility
Communication/coordination mechanisms available to assist expatriates	Level of development (e.g., poverty, infrastructure, markets)	Coping skills, social orientation
Nature of the assignment (e.g., how clear, how difficult)	Climate and stability (e.g., level of political/business risk)	Language knowledge, prior international experience
Career development plan (e.g., for repatriation)	Government regulation (e.g., over product content, labor use)	Education, functional expertise
Incentives offered	Proximity to home country	Family dynamics
Mentor availability	Attitudes toward foreigners	Management skills

Source: Adapted from Downes, M., & Thomas, A. S. (2000). Managing overseas assignments to build organizational knowledge. *Human Resource Planning, 20,* 33–48.

But even if these complexities are somehow taken into account in the selection process, the person chosen may not accept. The financial package will need to be attractive. In addition, family issues will usually be a concern. For instance, spouses and partners may have to quit their own jobs to follow the expatriate. Some spouses may veto the foreign assignment if they're unable to pursue work or educational opportunities in the host country. Most candidates, once a position is offered, also want information about how the foreign posting will impact their careers.

And there's good reason to worry, since more expatriates are actually demoted than are given a higher-level job once they return. Many firms simply place returning expatriates in the positions that happen to be open at the time. Ideally, companies should be explicit about how the foreign assignment will help develop the expatriate's career. According to one survey, however, 75 percent of firms make no written promises up front regarding the job expatriates will have when they return. Clearly, these statistics are important warning flags for potential expatriates. But the news isn't all bad. Companies are slowly adapting to the evolving concerns of potential expatriates (although bigger firms are more likely to offer help than smaller ones). For instance, on the family assistance front, surveys report that between 1988 and 1998 the percentage of firms

- taking the loss of spouse or partner income into account when putting together an expatriate package jumped from 15 percent to nearly 26 percent.
- offering job search, résumé preparation, or career counseling to spouses and partners of expatriates rose from 7 percent to about 25 percent.
- allowing location visits before accepting an assignment increased from 65 percent to 91 percent.
- offering language training to family members accompanying expatriates rose from 18 percent to over 50 percent.[55]

EXHIBIT 12.6

A Recommended Process for Selecting Expatriates

Step	Description
1.	Create selection team.
2.	Define purpose of foreign assignment.
3.	Assess the foreign assignment context.
4.	Establish appropriate selection criteria.
5.	Define the candidate pool.
6.	Use multiple selection methods.
7.	Interview expatriate and spouse/partner.
8.	Make foreign assignment offer.
9.	Transition expatriate into training program.

Source: Black, J.S. Gregersen, H.B. & Mendenhall, M.E. (1992). *Global assignments: Successfully expatriating and repatriating international managers* (San Francisco, CA: Jossy-Bass), 83. Copyright © Jossey-Bass Inc. By permission of the publisher.

Finally, many experts recommend that firms develop a clear and coherent process for selecting expatriates along the lines presented in Exhibit 12.6. First, companies should create a selection team consisting of a home-country manager, a host-country manager, and a human resources professional. The role of the human resources professional is to identify potential candidates and make sure that valid selection tools are used. Likewise, the home- and host-country managers should ensure that the needs of both the parent company and foreign subsidiary are met. The next steps involve clarifying the purpose of the overseas assignment and assessing just how important cross-cultural skills will be in the foreign location. Once the first three steps are complete, then the selection team can develop criteria for success in the position. This will allow the team to identify potential candidates (through referrals, job postings, and other mechanisms). Next, candidates should be screened using a portfolio of tools (e.g., interviews, exercises, tests). Some experts suggest that companies encourage expatriate candidates and their families to think about whether the assignment is really a good fit for them throughout the process. The idea is to put the decision squarely where it belongs—with the expatriate.

Once the candidate pool has been narrowed down, more in-depth interviews can take place that lay out the assignment in detail. These interviews would include what expatriates can expect to find in the host country and the ramifications of the assignment for their careers. Especially important at this stage is to conduct interviews with spouses, partners, and other family members. Preassignment visits may also help family members develop a better feel for what life overseas will be like. Any concerns the candidate or family members have about the foreign assignment should be discussed in depth. Finally, the selection team can offer the position to the candidate with the best chances of success and, once accepted, start actual preparations for the foreign assignment.[56]

Training, Preparation, and Adjustment of Expatriates

That said, what constitutes effective preparation for an overseas assignment is a complex issue. Generally speaking, experts recommend that training and preparation be part of an ongoing process, with rigorous efforts made before, during, and after repatriation (expatriates often experience a kind of culture shock both when they begin an overseas assignment and after they return home). All training programs should have two basic goals: (1) to help employees be effective in their overseas jobs as quickly as possible; and (2) to minimize any adjustment problems expatriates and their families have in their new environment and after they return.[57]

But the unfortunate reality, at least according to some estimates, is that almost 40 percent of companies give expatriates no cross-cultural training prior to departure. Some experts suggest that when it comes to small- to mid-sized companies, the figure is closer to 90 percent. This flies in the face of evidence suggesting that cross-cultural training can improve the ability to adjust to new cultural environments as well as boost job performance.[58]

So how does training work and what should it include? Many experts believe a three-step process occurs during which expatriates actually learn from training. The first step involves **paying attention to cultural differences** that explain why foreigners think and behave the way they do. Next, expatriates must **retain knowledge about behavior that is culturally appropriate**. In other words, expatriates must think about the knowledge they have been exposed to and then use it to develop a mental framework for their own behavior. Such a framework helps expatriates remember how to behave in foreign settings and the consequences of making mistakes. The last step involves **practicing culturally appropriate behavior** that is consistent with the guidelines in expatriates' mental frameworks. This trying-it-out process helps expatriates fine-tune culturally appropriate behaviors and increases their confidence when interacting with foreign colleagues, clients, and suppliers.[59]

The training itself can range from superficial activities that can be covered in a few days to very rigorous efforts requiring substantial amounts of time and effort. In fact, some intensive training efforts may take months to complete. Exhibit 12.7 displays the range of training rigor possible and some associated activities. To determine the level of training rigor required, companies should take into account how important the assignment is, how long the assignment will last, and the extent to which expatriates must interact with the local population. Also important for determining training rigor is an assessment of cultural toughness (i.e., how different is the assignment location's culture from the home culture of the expatriates?). In general, the greater the difference from the home culture, the more difficult the expatriate's adjustment process in a foreign country will be. For instance, Americans will generally have more trouble adjusting in African, Middle Eastern, and Far Eastern countries than they would in western European countries. The cultural values Americans encounter in Kenya will probably seem more "foreign" than those encountered in Germany. In fact, cultural toughness shows up repeatedly as a factor that negatively affects expatriates' adjustment and even their willingness to accept a foreign assignment in the first place.[60]

EXHIBIT 12.7

Levels of Cross-Cultural Training Rigor

Level of Rigor	Time Duration	Activities Included
Low	4–20 hours	Lectures, films, books, area briefings
Moderate	20–60 hours	Everything above, plus role plays, cases, survival-level language training
High	60–180 hours	Everything above, plus assessment centers, simulations, field trips, in-depth language training

Source: Black, J.S. Gregersen, H.B. & Mendenhall, M.E. (1992). *Global assignments: Successfully expatriating and repatriating international managers* (San Francisco, CA: Jossey-Bass), 97. Copyright © Jossey-Bass Inc. By permission of the publisher.

But cultural toughness isn't just an issue for Americans and Europeans. Consider the Japanese executives in the following International Insights box as they prepare for assignments in the U.S. Overall, rigorous cross-cultural training is needed for employees headed to countries that, to them, are high in cultural toughness. Moreover, as we've said, the roles expatriates have should impact their training. For instance, communication styles vary across countries. So if an expatriate is in a job where extensive interactions with local people are required and communication norms in the foreign country are different, then more rigorous training in communication is advisable. Finally, take a look at Exhibit 12.8 for an overview of the various elements in the training process.

INTERNATIONAL INSIGHTS

Training Japanese Executives to Survive America

ACCORDING TO LEO LAWLESS, an American consultant, "About 98 percent don't have the foggiest idea what we're talking about." And just who is Mr. Lawless talking about? Try the Japanese executives in his sexual harassment training sessions who are headed to U.S. assignments. Many Japanese executives are baffled by U.S. laws and values about sexual harassment and other discrimination issues. Few Japanese executives have had extensive experience interacting with female managers. As a result, Japanese firms have been doing more to prepare their expatriates for postings in the United States, especially after losing sexual harassment lawsuits in American courts.

For instance, in one high-profile case, Mitsubishi Motors' American subsidiary was accused of widespread sexual harassment of female employees (mainly by American men, as it turns out). The allegations included sexually explicit jokes and the posting of nude pictures of women. Such behavior is relatively common in Japan. It's not unusual to see Japanese executives paging through lewd magazines in the office. Recruitment ads in Japan sometimes specify gender, age, and desired physical attributes. But today it's unlikely that a Japanese firm operating in the United States would repeat the mistake made by one Japanese expatriate some years ago in listing these requirements in a help-wanted ad for a receptionist: "taller than 5'8", 25–35 years old, breath-taking beauty."[61]

EXHIBIT 12.8

How It Works: The Cross-Cultural Training Process

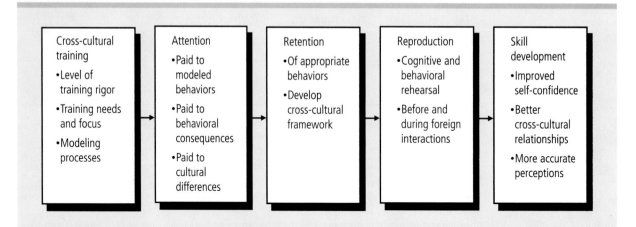

Source: Adapted from Black, J. S. & Mendenhall, M. R. (1990) Cross-cultural training effectiveness: A review and theoretical framework for future reasearch. *Academy of Management Review, 15,* 115–136.

Trends in expatriate preparation   To address the difficulties inherent in many foreign assignments, some multinationals are going to great lengths to create sophisticated training programs for expatriates. Royal Dutch/Shell, for instance, sent surveys to 17,000 former, current, and potential expatriates, as well as family members, to systematically assess the issues confronting employees in foreign assignments. The company used the results to create better training and career-management programs.[62]

Many training programs try to create open-mindedness by challenging expatriates' prejudices, assumptions, and attitudes about different cultures. This training goes beyond the short, superficial courses on business etiquette overseas that have often been used in the past. Today, firms are more likely to use training that emphasizes understanding and respecting all cultures. That's what Motorola had in mind when it built a cultural training center in Illinois. The center's courses are aimed at making Motorola's managers "transculturally competent."[63] But how well such extensive efforts actually work is open to debate. One expert put it this way: "We have a pretty good handle on what the skills and traits are that are necessary to do well in a cross-cultural environment, but we still don't really know whether we can effectively train people in those skills."[64]

Earlier we noted that firms also are doing more to address family and dual-career couple issues. In fact, 88 percent of Fortune 500 firms in one survey said that dual-career problems will create more expatriate selection and performance headaches in the years ahead. And some studies suggest that the expatriate's family situation is often the single most important predictor of success or failure—even more important than cultural skills, adaptability, or job knowledge.[65] The good news is that involving spouses, partners, and children in predeparture cultural training can have a positive effect on the adjustment of expatriates and their families, especially when combined with other forms of family assistance (e.g., help with spouse/partner job or education needs, lost income replacement).[66]

Nevertheless, when it comes to training and preparation, some experts urge expatriates to be cautious. As one expert put it, "It would still be rare to find a company that is utilizing everything that research has shown us about selecting, training, developing, and supporting expatriates."[67] Consequently, expatriates should consider taking steps on their own to prepare for overseas assignments. That may include signing up for local college courses to help build skills and abilities not included in company training. Along the same lines, expatriates may find it worthwhile to seek advice or suggestions about where to find resources from firms that specialize in cross-cultural training (e.g., Chicago-based Cendant Intercultural: www.cendantintercultural.com). Another option is to solicit insights from people who have been posted to the country where the expatriate will be sent. Finally, if not already provided by the employer, a predeparture visit to the host country (taking the family along) might prove very useful and help ease the settling-in process.[68]

Returning Home: Repatriation Issues

Unfortunately, the need for preparation, planning, and training doesn't end when the expatriate's plane takes off for some exotic foreign locale. A host of potential problems also await the expatriate when he or she returns. These repatriation problems help explain the high turnover rate among expatriates after they return home. Consider these common repatriation challenges:

● Changes in the home country and in the expatriate's values after several years abroad make returning home seem like a foreign assignment in itself.
● Changes in the home company (e.g., structure, people) require major adjustments and new learning upon return.
● Experiencing a new job after return is often difficult. (e.g., is it a demotion, unclear to begin with, disconnected from the overseas assignment, or not on a particular career track?)
● Having to reorient to living conditions in the home country can be tricky.
● Feeling unappreciated by the firm after performing well overseas is not uncommon.
● Adjusting to a lower standard of living after returning home (no more foreign premiums or fancy benefits) can be a letdown.[69]

Companies are beginning to realize how expensive it is to neglect repatriation issues. In fact, some firms address repatriation issues before the expatriate leaves. For instance, Monsanto, the pharmaceutical, chemical, and agricultural giant, started a repatriation program to combat high turnover among its expatriates. In large part, this problem was driven by expatriates' dashed expectations for promotions and advancement on return. Monsanto now does predeparture planning for the job expatriates will have when they return. The firm also gives returning expatriates opportunities to showcase their overseas accomplishments in public forums and provides counselors to help them overcome any readjustment problems. Such programs can improve the performance and adjustment of employees after an overseas assignment.[70]

Attacking the "out of sight, out of mind" problem is also a key issue. Some companies deliberately bring back expatriates several times a year to give them visibility and thank them for their work. Expatriates can meet with important managers and, ideally, a designated expatriate mentor. Return trips home serve to jump-start the adjustment process. And the longer expatriates are away, the more difficult they will find it to return. To combat this effect, firms can increase the frequency of home visits as the final return date approaches, especially for employees gone for more than two years.

For example, Coherent, Inc., a U.S.-based manufacturer with several overseas offices, has a formal program that brings employees home for short stints before their final return. Employees are brought back to the United States to complete small projects that last a few months. They then return overseas to conclude their affairs before coming home for good. This months-long period in the United States helps reacquaint expatriates with the office, their colleagues, and ongoing projects. It also gives expatriates an extended sample of life back in the United States. Overall, the program has helped cut down the repatriation adjustment period. Exhibit 12.9 lists some additional steps that firms can take to ease the repatriation process.

Finally, we want to point out that repatriation issues aren't the same everywhere. For example, Japanese expatriates tend to feel that international assignments are more valued by their companies than do their American colleagues. Cultural differences may have something to do with this effect. Research suggests that Americans tend to separate their commitment to the parent firm from their feelings about the job they have when they return home. This kind of compartmentalization can create turnover if Americans are unhappy with their new assignments. These problems seem less severe in Japanese expatriates, perhaps because of collectivistic values that encourage a more global view of commitment. In other words, Japanese expatriates may define commitment more in terms of the larger parent firm rather than the specific job they return to.[71]

Chapter Summary

We began this chapter by discussing the strategic value of international human resource management. However, developing specific human resource practices that support firm goals may require that companies develop an *international human resource philosophy* that will help shape *core international human resource policies*. We pointed out that the selection and development of international staff is a complex issue. In doing so, we examined the skills that international managers need to be successful.

Next, we considered the basic options for staffing foreign operations. These include *PCNs, HCNs,* and *TCNs*. Some firms are trying to develop an *international cadre* of managers who can be sent anywhere in the world. Companies are increasingly using *inpatriates,* foreign employees brought to the home country for various developmental assignments, to increase commitment. Sometimes firms embrace a particular selection philosophy in making staffing decisions. At one extreme is a *geocentric* approach—where ability is all that matters. An *ethnocentric* approach, in contrast, means that only PCNs will be posted in key overseas positions. *Polycentric* and *regiocentric* approaches fall between these two extremes. In a polycentric approach, human resource management control is in the hands of the foreign subsidiary, although headquarters still makes key decisions. Likewise, under a regiocentric approach, most foreign employees will not move into headquarters positions. However, employees can move from country to country in a particular region.

This chapter also examined the broader issue of managing both *cross-national* and *intranational diversity* in organizations. For instance, firm are sometimes reluctant to send women to certain countries because of local biases. But such concerns are overstated. Indeed, in certain foreign locations, women may actually be more likely to succeed than men because of local attitudes.

Finally, we considered several issues associated with *expatriates.* Clearly, the consequences of failed expatriate assignments are often severe. Therefore, companies need to use selection criteria that accurately predict expatriate success. Of course, expatriates also need to be prepared to deal with all the cultural and lifestyle changes that will be encountered abroad. The exact nature and level of training needed should be driven, in part, by the *cultural toughness* of the foreign location. Preparation is also needed if employees are to be successfully *repatriated* back to their home countries. Fortunately, companies are moving toward more sophisticated repatriation programs that kick in before the expatriate has even begun the foreign assignment. Such programs can have a positive impact on employees' adjustment and performance after returning home.

EXHIBIT 12.9

Steps for Improving the Repatriation Process

Time Frame	Steps/Description
Before departure	• Clearly communicate reentry job options. • Establish career development plan. • Appoint home and host country mentors to support expatriate. • Arrange home visits for visibility.
Six to nine months before return	• Narrow list of reentry job options. • Send expatriate job openings/listings • Ask expatriate to polish résumé. • Conduct home office visits to facilitate adjustment and schedule job interviews.
Three to six months before return	• Conduct briefings with employee and family about what they've learned. • Brief employee and family on changes in the U.S. that may impact their return. • Ask employee to list personal/professional expectations about the return to minimize misunderstandings and correct assumptions. • Explain firm's moving policies and repatriation programs—especially those dealing with financial issues.
Immediately upon return home	• Assign employee and family to a welcome home group consisting of former expatriates. • Match employee with a home sponsor who will cover changes in company structure, policy, technology, or products/services. • Provide returning spouse with career-related assistance (e.g., job-hunting help). • Offer counseling for more serious problems. • Show that the firm cares about overseas experiences.
Three to six months after returning home	• Provide training that discusses reentry shock, pace of adjustment, feelings. • Assess how employee's new skills and experience can be better used by the firm (ask employees for suggestions). • Reassess adjustment process to identify outstanding problems and offer assistance.

Sources: Adapted from Shilling, M. (1993). How to win at repatriation, *Personnel Journal* (September); Solomon, C. M. (1995). Repatriation: Up, down, or out? *Personnel Journal,* January, 28–37.

Discussion Questions

1. Why is having an international human resource management strategy important for companies?
2. What are some of the pros and cons associated with using PCNs, TCNs, and HCNs?
3. How does culture impact the selection and development of international employees?

4. What are some of the major approaches that companies can take to managing diversity? Which approach has the best chance of success in your view?
5. What should the basic elements of a successful program to select, prepare, and repatriate employees destined for foreign assignments look like? How can cultural toughness, family issues, and concerns about gender be dealt with?

Up to the Challenge?

Motorola's Human Resource Management Moves in China

A T THE BEGINNING of this chapter, we asked how Motorola might have responded to the human resource management challenges of doing business in China, especially given its large investment there. Clearly, Motorola has done many things right to adapt to the Chinese human resource management environment, one where practices continue to evolve as China becomes more dominant in the global economic mainstream.

Initially, Motorola had two major human resource problems in China. First, Motorola needed a local workforce that could meet the firm's world class quality standards. The company felt that the local labor pool lacked the requisite skills and the obsessive approach to quality that is a key element of Motorola's corporate culture. Motorola realized that it could intensively train workers in all aspects of its operations, something it has perfected in the United States and other countries, if it had 100 percent ownership of its Chinese plants. Fortunately, when former Motorola CEO Bob Galvin began negotiating with China in 1989, 100 percent ownership was something he bargained for and eventually won. In addition, Motorola realized that building training programs around its existing corporate slogans, like "Six Sigma" (meaning factories should have no more than four defects per million products shipped), would appeal to Chinese employees. After all, sloganeering is something that generally works well in China. And sure enough, it only took new Chinese employees at one Motorola plant six months to hit the Six Sigma quality target. Indeed, once properly trained, Chinese employees can produce high-tech products at world-class levels. One expatriate managing a plant churning out Motorola cell phones had this to say about China and its workers: "We can do anything here that we do anywhere else. The learning curve is a fast ramp."

The second major challenge for Motorola was to hold on to its highly trained Chinese workforce, an expensive investment that could be lost to competing companies' hiring forays. As a result, Motorola pays its entry-level production workers extremely well by Chinese standards. Plus, in a nod to China's "iron rice bowl" tradition of housing subsidies, Motorola built several hundred condos for Chinese employees. In fact, the company offers a cut-rate ownership deal to interested employees who can come up with the necessary down payment.

Although Motorola's investment gamble and Chinese human resources practices have generally worked well so far, whether the firm can stay the course remains to be seen. Competitors are taking aim at Motorola's Chinese operations and China's long-term political stability is somewhat murky in any case. On top of that, the Chinese human resource environment is in flux, with millions of employees and government bureaucrats laid off in recent years as authorities try to make the Chinese economy more competitive. Hopefully, proposals to make it easier for Chinese to buy homes will reduce the pressure on companies to provide employees with expensive housing benefits. Likewise, the government's interest in starting a national pension system suggests that companies can look forward to lower employee welfare costs in the future.

That said, the vast interior provinces of China remain overregulated and hamstrung by state-instituted controls and inefficiencies. While still a source of cheap labor for coastal cities, these regions also represent the next frontier. Eventually, foreign companies that have tended to hug the comparatively wealthy eastern coast of China will move inland. As one international agency put it, "a large reform agenda remains" for China. And that means that Motorola and other foreign companies still face plenty of challenges as they cope with the evolving human resource management scene in China.[72]

International Development
What Is Your International Orientation?

Purpose

To develop self-insight regarding your level of experience with and interest in other countries and cultures.

Instructions

The following sample items are taken from the International Orientation Scale. Answer each question and give yourself a score for each dimension. The highest possible score for any dimension is 20 points.

Dimension 1: International Attitudes

Use the following scale to answer questions Q1 through Q4:

> 1 *Strongly agree*
> 2 *Agree somewhat*
> 3 *Maybe or unsure*
> 4 *Disagree somewhat*
> 5 *Strongly disagree*

Q1. _____ Foreign language skills should be taught (as early as) elementary school.

Q2. _____ Traveling the world is a priority in my life.

Q3. _____ A year-long overseas assignment (from my company) would be a fantastic opportunity for my family and me.

Q4. ___ Other countries fascinate me.

Total Score for Dimension 1: _____

Dimension 2: Foreign Experiences

Q1. _____ I have studied a foreign language.

> 1 Never
> 2 For less than a year
> 3 For a year
> 4 For a few years
> 5 For several years

Q2. _____ I am fluent in another language.

> 1 I don't know another language.
> 2 I am limited to very short and simple phrases.
> 3 I know basic grammatical structure and speak with a limited vocabulary.
> 4 I understand conversation on most topics.
> 5 I am very fluent in another language.

Q3. _____ I have spent time overseas (traveling, studying abroad, etc.).

> 1 Never
> 2 About a week
> 3 A few weeks
> 4 A few months
> 5 Several months or years

Q4. _____ I was overseas before the age of 18.

> 1 Never
> 2 About a week
> 3 A few weeks
> 4 A few months
> 5 Several months or years

Total Score for Dimension 2: _____

Dimension 3: Comfort with Differences

Use the following scale for questions Q1 through Q4:

> 1 *Quite similar*
> 2 *Mostly similar*
> 3 *Somewhat different*
> 4 *Quite different*
> 5 *Extremely different*

Q1. _____ My friends' career goals, interests, and educations are . . .

Q2. _____ My friends' ethnic backgrounds are . . .

Q3. _____ My friends' religious affiliations are . . .

Q4. _____ My friends' first languages are . . .

Total Score for Dimension 3: _____

Dimension 4: Participation in Cultural Events

Use the following scale to answer questions Q1 through Q4:

> 1 *Never*
> 2 *Rarely*
> 3 *Sometimes*
> 4 *Often*
> 5 *Always*

Q1. _____ I eat at a variety of ethnic restaurants (e.g. Greek, Polynesian, Thai, German).

Q2. _____ I watch the major networks' world news programs.

Q3. _____ I attend ethnic festivals.

Q4. _____ I visit art galleries and museums.

Total Score for Dimension 4: _____

Self-Assessment Discussion Questions

Would you like to improve your international orientation? If so, what could you do to change various aspects of your life?

Source: This exercise was prepared by Paula Caligiuri, School of Management and Labor Relations. Rutgers University. Used with permission. As appeared in *Management international: Cases, exercises, and readings* by Dorothy Marcic and Sheila Puffer. Copyright © 1994 by West Publishing Company, Minneapolis/ St. Paul, Minn., a division of International Thomson Publishing Inc. Reprinted by permission.

From Theory to Practice
Learning More about International Human Resource Management

Purpose

To find out more about the human resource management issues facing companies in overseas subsidiaries and other international cooperative relationships, and to compare how different companies try to deal with the international human resource management challenges they face.

Instructions

Your instructor will divide the class into groups of three to six people. Each group should interview at least two managers (preferably ones with some human resource management responsibility) at a local company that has some international business activity, such as:

- having offices abroad to help market and sell products or services.
- running foreign subsidiaries or acting as a subsidiary for a foreign company that assembles or manufactures products.
- having joint ventures abroad or being part of a local joint venture.
- being part of an international alliance to develop technology, build a product, share information, or make international deals.

The purpose of the interviews should be to assess basic international human resource challenges facing the company and to determine what strategies the company is using to resolve them. Interviews should include these questions (as well as others that your group may wish to develop on its own):

- What is the nature of your involvement in international business/operations?
- What are the key human resources challenges facing your company in its international operations (e.g., staffing foreign operations, not having enough control to deal with local issues)? Why do these challenges exist? To what extent do they reflect cultural, legal, or political differences across countries?
- What human resource strategies, policies, and practices have been developed to overcome these challenges? By whom? Have they been successful? Why or why not?

Your group should make a 15-minute class presentation about their findings. If using small groups is impractical, your instructor may set up this activity as an individual assignment. Likewise, if interviewing managers is impractical, your instructor may treat this activity as a library research assignment designed to answer the questions raised. In any case, class discussion (another 15–20 minutes) will focus on three issues:

- To what extent do the human resource challenges reported reflect the type of international operations companies are engaged in?
- To what extent do the human resource challenges reported reflect country-specific factors (e.g., cultural differences)?
- Assess the quality and appropriateness of the human resource strategies being pursued by various companies. Are there any suggestions for improvement?

13 Evaluating and Rewarding International Employees

International Challenge

Receiving a Performance Evaluation Overseas

LEARNING OBJECTIVES

After reading this chapter, you should be able to

- Identify the purpose of performance appraisal across cultures.

- Understand the problems in evaluating performance and providing feedback to people of different cultures.

- Understand that compensation is one of the main reasons to evaluate performance and that this means more than just level of pay.

- Appreciate the fact that compensation has different inherent meaning across cultures.

- Understand the different models that are available for compensating expatriates and apply the best method.

You have been assigned by your firm to the People's Republic of China for an extended work assignment. You have never been to China before, but you feel your company did a very good job preparing you to live and be a manager in this new culture. You have learned a few words of Chinese and you think you will even get the tones correctly so that you will be understood. And despite getting sick the first two weeks of the assignment, you have bounced back quickly, working hard and avoiding the usual homesickness. After your first six months on assignment, you are evaluated. The evaluation, however, is very puzzling. You have done a good deal of reading and you are aware that China is a group-oriented (collective) culture. So during your first few months as manager, you tried some group involvement techniques. In particular, you tried to get your employees to participate in decision making about the production line setup and supply ordering system. In cases where this did not work out too well, you gave the team and its leaders quick and direct feedback in an effort to be useful. Apparently, these techniques and more backfired miserably, and you received a neutral or ambiguous evaluation by your host-country boss. Although you didn't realize it until months later, this evaluation turned out to be a very bad thing, likely to be a setback for potential promotions when you return to the United States. On top of this, you didn't realize how expensive good housing is in Shanghai. Your salary, while adjusted upward for this overseas assignment, does not make up for the high cost of living in the PRC. All this makes you wonder if you should have done what your peer group of managers did—turn down an assignment in China! What went wrong here? Think about possible explanations as you read this chapter and we will discuss our interpretations at the end.

Performance Appraisal

The performance evaluation is one of the most controversial (and probably hated) thing for most employees. Likewise, if you ask a group of practicing managers what they dislike most about their jobs, the task of evaluating employees is often at the top of their list. That annual (or more frequent) ritual of appraising performance is usually despised by both parties. Partly this distaste results from a general reluctance to directly provide employees with feedback about their performance. Few managers enjoy this process, especially when the performance feedback is negative. Furthermore, the process itself is inherently difficult.

Giving an Evaluation

Put yourself into a typical evaluation situation. As a manager, you may have six people who report directly to you. Your job is to determine how well these six people performed their job. Unless you took extensive notes on each employee as the year proceeded, this task (at a minimum) requires a pretty good memory. You have to recall the accomplishments and the limitations of each person. Then you might need to sum these pluses and minuses across the year-long evaluation period accurately, trying not to be overly influenced by recently occurring events or overly salient events. For some jobs (like sales), this summarizing may be easier than it is for others (research and development personnel). Nonetheless, you must then compare these summed and appropriately weighted evaluations across your six people. If you don't distinguish the six people from one another, your boss may wonder why you don't have the fortitude to give someone a negative evaluation. Further, your pool of rewards is very limited, so you have to rank your people from first to sixth. As if all of this isn't tough enough, now comes the hard part. You may have to meet with each person to give them the feedback and tell them what level of rewards you think they deserve. No wonder people dislike this whole process!

Now, however, imagine that your job is to evaluate one of your people who is on foreign assignment. You may have visited the foreign location during the year, but you did not have a chance to see and evaluate the manager's performance in the usual hands-on way that you are used to. Further, you have limited understanding of the environment they work in and the larger cultural and country impediments to their performance. In other words, we could take the usual level of dislike for performance evaluations and multiply it by two or three to approximate the difficulty in evaluating expatriate performance. The first half of this chapter details the problems and pitfalls that can occur when conducting performance evaluations of expatriates and foreign nationals that you may be working with. The second half of the chapter reviews the intricacies of compensation for this group of people.

Performance Evaluation for Expatriates

As we said, many companies are recognizing the value of a global perspective. In particular, they understand the value of learning and using new and customized training, motivation methods, negotiation techniques, and more. In order to do this, however, they must often send managers abroad to gain this type of knowledge. Research has shown that this technique is often successful.[1] In one study, 150 expatriate managers were surveyed about the skills they learned overseas. These managers reported that an overseas experience resulted in the following changes in their skills:

● An increased ability to manage cultural differences
● A better ability to understand the multinational firm and relations between domestic and international operations
● A more open mind about different problem-solving methods
● A more flexible approach to dealing with human resources

These are all valuable skills for the employee and positive outcomes for the company, but for a number of reasons they may not be realized in an international context. One reason is that few of these skills are usually assessed in a normal (domestic) performance appraisal. Second, even if the dimensions are considered, they are very difficult to evaluate. For example, how would you decide whether your employee has an "open mind" or can "better manage for cultural differences"? Third, the open-mindedness itself (and the other skills) almost has to be seen to be evaluated—often through repeated interactions with others (see Chapter 12). Fourth, people from different cultures give and take appraisal feedback in very different ways. One culture, for example, may value loyalty and commitment to the firm very highly, whereas others may not. Likewise, some cultures do not give feedback publicly, even if that feedback is positive. So in addition to the fact that performance evaluation is an unwanted but necessary part of the job for a manager to start with, more problems emerge when they are conducted from a distance—either a geographic distance or a cultural one.

Despite all these problems, most multinationals evaluate the performance of their expatriates, regardless of their country of origin or their assignment. The remainder of this section will deal with several important questions about performance appraisal: (1) Who should evaluate the performance of the expatriate? (2) When or how often should they be evaluated? and (3) What in the performance of an expatriate manager should be evaluated?

Who Should Evaluate Performance?

A company has a large number of options for evaluating domestic or expatriate employees. In addition to a traditional supervisor evaluation, performance could also be judged by one's peers, subordinates, and/or customers. In a global setting, however, there are often two different sources for each of these evaluators. For example, while an American manager assigned to the Netherlands may have a Dutch boss, he or she may still have a boss in the United States. There is much controversy about which evaluation source is better—the evaluation by the host manager or the evaluation by the home office manager. We will discuss the pros and cons of each of these sources in turn.

Evaluations by host/local managers   An expatriate will often have to be evaluated by local management. That manager or group may be familiar with the culture the expatriate comes from; indeed, that person may be a national of that country as well. Alternatively, the manager could be from virtually anywhere, including but certainly not limited to, the country in which he or she is now working. Nonetheless, that manager will probably appraise the expatriate's performance from his or her own cultural perspective. In a very large sense, this is a good thing. The expatriate was sent overseas to do a good job in that foreign country. As we have already stated, the quality of the expatriate's job in large part may revolve around how culturally aware and savvy he or she is. So a manager who is from the host country and thus is familiar with local cultural values and behaviors may be in a very good position to judge whether or not the expatriate is aware of those cultural norms and is using them to advantage. Likewise, having a host manager conduct evaluations takes advantage of that person's knowledge of the expatriate's performance that is based on daily interactions. The manager has seen more of the expatriate's performance than nearly anybody, and almost certainly more than the home office manager, who may be back in the United States.

The use of a host-country manager to conduct the appraisal, however, is not without problems. One source of the problems is the very thing we mentioned above as a possible advantage—the host managers' use of their own cultural frame of reference. An anecdote about an American working in India illustrates this point.[2] Following the current rage in the United States, this American manager tried to use some participative management by asking his Indian subordinates to provide input and new ideas about a project. While this technique may have worked well in the United States, it did not in India. As we noted in Chapters 4 and 11, Indian culture is high in power distance and more autocratic leadership is expected. Accordingly, the Indians felt that the U.S. manager did not know what he was doing. A good manager should not have to ask his employees for ideas. One result of this situation was that the expatriate received very negative performance evaluations from his host manager. And later, upon his return to the United States, this incident had a lingering effect on his career—it was one of the reasons he was denied a promotion.

Now you could argue that the manager's problem we just relayed is deserving of a negative evaluation. After all, if you are going to be an expatriate manager, then you should be aware of one of the primary cultural values that embodies the country to which you've been assigned. Perhaps the blame could also be placed on the home office having failed to provide cultural training for this manager. Regardless of where the blame lies, however, this can be an issue with the use of host country nationals as the source of a performance appraisal. If the home office manager had conducted the evaluation, the performance rating might not have been nearly so negative.

Of course, there are other potential problems associated with a host manager's performance evaluation. There is always the language problem; the manager may not be able to clearly communicate feedback to the expatriate. Also, as implied earlier, the dimensions of performance that are evaluated may be different for the host national and the expatriate/home office. Some things may just be more salient or important to the host manager and therefore those things may carry unusually heavy weight in the evaluation. An expatriate in China, for example, may learn over time to show considerable restraint in sharing her feelings, even if she is upset at one of her subordinates. This trait may count positively in an evaluation by a host Chinese manager. For a U.S. evaluator, however, not being frank may count negatively. Finally, an appraisal by a host-country manager may not be tied closely to the company's overall global strategy. So if the expatriate acts in a way that may not directly benefit the foreign subsidiary but does benefit the corporation as a whole, she or he may still receive a negative performance evaluation. In a case like this, we hope that the home office would recognize the overall benefit of the expatriate's performance, but they may not. Instead, they may simply focus on the easier piece of information to gather and digest—the appraisal by the host manager. Overall, then, the use of host-country managers to conduct appraisals has both pluses and minuses. A multinational may, therefore, want to consider using home office personnel for these reasons.

Evaluations by home office management   Clearly, there are advantages to using a home office manager to conduct a performance evaluation. For one, this person may be familiar with your work or pattern of work. The new information provided by your expatriate experience could be integrated and evaluated in this context. Second, this person presumably speaks the same language as you and thus could have a leg up on a host-country manager in communicating feedback. Third, this person probably shares many of the same cultural values and beliefs that you have. This **cultural identity** provides the capability for much to be shared and learned from a performance appraisal. Collectively, these characteristics appear to provide distinct advantages to the home office manager as the provider of performance evaluations.

On the other hand, however, there are also some disadvantages associated with using the home country manager as the source of the performance appraisal. Most of these problems result from the very thing that offers advantages to the home country manager—the fact that the manager is geographically and psychologically distant from the employee who works at a foreign location. Specifically, the home manager receives a dearth of feedback or information about the employee to be evaluated. And considering that the home office manager has little if any opportunity to observe the employee, there can be problems with the quality of the evaluation. In fact, in the study of overseas employees described earlier, expatriates reported that they did not have much contact at all with the home office during their overseas assignment. And what little contact that did exist was often not with their direct supervisor. It was the rare expatriate who had home office contact of even more than several times a year. Even worse yet, this sporadic contact was usually initiated by the expatriate. One can only presume that this contact resulted from encountering a big problem that required intervention by the home office. In other words, the nature of the little contact that did exist was probably not all that positive.

Another potential problem with the use of home office appraisals is these managers' relative lack of familiarity with the intricacies of the expatriates foreign posting. In fact, evaluators may not have any experience working in the country where the employee is assigned. As a result, they may not understand the pressures the expatriate experiences and the standard to use when evaluating their performance. Again, what is worse is the fact that about 67 percent of upper managers in U.S. corporations have no international experience whatsoever, let alone experience in the country in question.[3]

What's the solution? Some firms have tried to capitalize on the strengths offered by both host- and home-country evaluations by getting both types of managerial evaluations on the same employee. For example, firms such as AT&T and 3M Corporation have developed a "career sponsor" program to link the expatriate to the corporate office. The sponsor's job is to keep the expatriate in touch with what is going on at home and to act as a mentor. Many times, these sponsors will conduct performance evaluations using the cultural perspective of the home office, and assessments of such programs shows them to be successful.[4]

When Should Performance Be Evaluated?

As for a domestic performance evaluation, the question of *when* to do performance evaluations is not easily answered. In the United States, the most common interval used between evaluations is six months, while a nearly similar percentage conduct appraisals on an annual basis. As usual, however, when it comes to the international stage, things get considerably more complex. On one hand, it seems premature to conduct an appraisal after six months on a foreign assignment—even if the complete overseas assignment is only designed to last one year. After all, as we discussed in the previous chapter, expatriates need time to adjust to their very new and different surroundings. Likewise, considerable time is necessary for family adjustment. Thus, six months would appear to be too soon to conduct the first appraisal. On the other hand, if it is obvious that things are not going well, it would behoove management—in either the host or home country—to let the expatriate know as soon as possible. It seems inappropriate to let the problems fester for yet another six months before giving any feedback.

So what is the answer here? At first blush the answer would seem obvious: use a compromise strategy where expatriates get some informal feedback early on in their assignment period and wait until the end of the first year for the formal appraisal. The problems with this compromise have been detailed earlier. For one, the home office rarely contacts the expatriate as it is; accordingly, even the compromise strategy may actually be difficult to execute. Additionally, for the host-country manager, such informal feedback may be culturally difficult or inappropriate to deliver. Accordingly, that manager may be constrained to wait until the formal evaluation is scheduled. Finally, a six-month period that covers the necessary adjustment time may just not be enough time to see any effects of the expatriate's performance. So, as with domestic appraisals, the question of timing is not easily answered. As unsatisfying as it may be, the answer is probably a fuzzy one—that is, evaluate at the "right" time for the particular assignment.

What Should Be Evaluated?

In some ways the questions of "who" and "when" are much easier to answer than the issue of *what* should be evaluated.

Variables that affect the "what" question   Regardless of whether you choose a host or home country evaluator and regardless of when and how often the appraisal is conducted, exactly what should be evaluated? This is an extremely complicated question, and one for which there is also no single answer. Clearly, a sales job may involve different skills than may be involved in financial management or production management. Beyond this general blanket statement, however, there are some very important considerations to keep in mind when you are evaluating performance. There seems to be at least three important variables that can affect an expatriate's performance and that should be taken into account when constructing and delivering a performance appraisal: (1) the environment in which the job is done, (2) the task or tasks themselves, and (3) the personality of the expatriate.[5]

Environmental variables   Of course, the circumstances under which any job is performed can be more or less demanding. Working in a mine is more difficult than working in an office. This notion of **environmental variables**, however, expands greatly when we consider a cross-cultural performance appraisal. That is, working for a mine company in Zimbabwe is probably more difficult than working for one in Montana. In general, some environments are easier to work in than others, and this fact in turn may determine the performance level of an expatriate manager. Given the little time that is spent communicating with the expatriate, however, we assume that the full impact of these environmental variables will not be appreciated. For example, experts point out that you should probably not give an expatriate manager in Mexico a negative evaluation if the productivity of his employees is only half the average productivity of Americans.[6] Although this result seems indicative of poor managerial performance, it must be tempered in light of the Mexican work environment. In particular, if that performance level was observed, it would show that the expatriate manager actually has employees working at a level that is about four times higher than the usual Mexican plant! In short, we must appreciate that the expatriate manager is dealing with the constraints of working in Mexico, not the relative advantages of managing in the United States, Germany, or Japan.

Task variables   A second set of variables deals with the actual tasks themselves that are being undertaken. Close attention should be paid to the duties or types of job assignments that may importantly affect performance levels.[7] For example, certain tasks require a greater amount of interaction with others. Being adept in the area of cultural "awareness" or acumen is much more important in these tasks than it would be for other assignments. A software engineer, for example, is less likely to need these cultural skills to be successful than would a production manager. The latter must interact with a large number of foreign nationals in order to be successful. Likewise, during foreign assignments, middle-level managers might be responsible for interacting with local and regional government officials. In the United States, this function is usually reserved for the highest officers in the organization.[8] Thus, there are differences in the types of tasks expatriates and nationals perform in general, let alone the task variations across different foreign assignments. The manager who performs the appraisal might also not fully appreciate these task differences.

Personality variables   Finally, there are simply inherent differences among individuals in their abilities to handle a foreign assignment. Chapter 12 described in detail the research that looks at who may do better in a foreign assignment than others. In fact, otherwise good performers may be poor ones if their personality leads them to be closed to change or not sensitive to others. Clearly, traits like these could negatively impact their performance and perhaps derail a career that would have been otherwise successful without the foreign assignment. Since the choice of the person for the overseas assignment is one of the few variables that firms have a great deal of control over, personality predictors of adjustment should be considered important. Otherwise, the home office may in effect be dooming a particular type of manager to a poor performance evaluation.

Problems in Cross-Cultural Evaluations

Even if your firm has considered these three important constraints on performance overseas, they still may run into some problems with an appraisal system. Perhaps the biggest obstacle may be exactly what to measure about an employees' performance, constrained as it is by the variables just mentioned. You may say, "No problem. If the expatriate is a reasonably high-level manager, we could use a variety of financial measures to index the performance of the manager. After all, the reason we set up a foreign operation was to make money, not to break some culture barrier." Well, even with this straightforward logic in mind, things are not as easy as they seem. For one, most financial performance data are subject to a conversion problem, including amount of sales and some other important measures. Worse yet, some currencies are not convertible to other (foreign) currencies. As several authors pointed out, the fact that you made nearly 300 million yuan on your operations in China may be not that meaningful if it's not possible to bring that money out.[9]

A second reason to look closely at financial performance measures is that many multinationals use a variety of techniques to minimize their taxes and to avoid possible losses from fluctuations in the value of the foreign currency. Accordingly, the true contribution of the foreign subsidiary to the overall financial performance of a firm is often masked via these techniques. Experts recommend, therefore, that many traditional financial measures of performance not be used as the primary determinant of an expatriate's performance evaluation because they are certainly cruder than similar values measured domestically. If you still wish to use financial yardsticks to evaluate an expatriate's performance, some experts recommend that a second set of measures be calculated that purifies the influence of the financial differences across borders. Given that we already know that the home office maintains little contact with the expatriate, it seems unlikely that most companies would find the time and money to do this. Instead, a variety of other general guidelines should probably be considered in evaluating an expatriate's performance.

Guidelines for Expatriate Evaluation

We have said a lot about the problems and pitfalls involved in a performance appraisal for an expatriate. What are some of the practical implications of all this? What in the way of guidelines can we suggest for better appraisals of performance?

Rating an assignment   One suggestion is to do a thorough assessment of the general difficulty of the foreign assignment faced by the expatriate.[10] Then, a difficulty score could be used to weight the normal performance appraisal process. For example, if the expatriate has received a very difficult assignment, her usual evaluation could be multiplied by 2.0. If the foreign posting is only moderately difficult, then the process could be weighted by 1.5, and so on. Of course, the challenge for human resource personnel is to figure out which assignment is more difficult than others.

Factors that determine assignment difficulty   Experts point to at least three things that probably play a crucial role here. First, the extent of language adjustment—if any—would certainly add to assignment difficulty. An expatriate with Holiday Inn could have some assignments where the language of use is English (e.g., India), whereas for other assignments (e.g., Tibet) they may need several languages from the Sino-Tibetan family. Since Chinese and Tibetan are extremely difficult languages to speak, let alone write, this would certainly add to the difficulty of an assignment in Lhasa, Tibet. Although strongly related to language usage, the degree of **cultural toughness** can also affect difficulty of assignment. Clearly, an assignment in London or even Amsterdam would be easier for most American expatriates than would one in Quito, Ecuador, or Jakarta, Indonesia.

Finally, *economic and political stability* are factors that would determine difficulty. We discussed these issues in detail in Chapter 2. For now, however, we simply note that the political and economic problems in any one country can be very difficult for an expatriate manager to overcome. Those who do well in such environments are probably performing at very high levels. For example, one set of authors relate a story of a relatively high-ranking American expatriate who was instrumental in stopping a strike in the firm's Chilean plant. This strike would have shut down the plant and soured relations with the home office. They point out that stopping the strike was a very large accomplishment for an American, especially in a country that is used to such strikes. Clearly, the expatriate manager must have demonstrated a good deal of cultural acumen and insight. Because of the volatility in exchange rates in Chile, however, demand for the plant's product temporarily decreased by 30 percent. Rather than recognizing the excellent performance of the expatriate in averting the strike, the home office focused on the negative sales figures. As a result, the expatriate received an undesirable, lackluster performance evaluation.[11]

General guidelines   Beyond just rating the general difficulty of the assignment, an evaluator can also do the following:

- In general, place somewhat more weight on evaluations performed by home country managers; all in all, they are more familiar with actual performance.
- If the home office has responsibility for the evaluation, they should try to involve another person with expatriate experience in the same country in the appraisal process.
- If the host country has responsibility for the evaluation, those managers might be well-advised to seek input from the home office manager before conveying it to the expatriate employee.

Issues Involved in Evaluating Foreign-Born Employees

Until now, we have focused on the important task of doing a performance appraisal on an employee assigned overseas. Certainly you may run into a situation in which you are asked to evaluate the performance of a foreign expatriate, perhaps based in the United States. For example, a Chinese national may be assigned to work in one of your company's U.S. plants. Likewise, even if you are assigned overseas, it may be your job to conduct an evaluation of the performance of the foreign nationals working with you.

Under these circumstances, things get even more complex. Beyond all the other issues just discussed, you'll have to grapple with exactly how you should deliver feedback—regardless of whether it is good or bad news. There are very wide differences in the practice of giving people (employees in particular) feedback. For example, one study looked at the form of appraisal systems in five Arab countries.[12] It was found that the appraisal system itself was basically informal, with little evidence of forms, files, and documents that we are used to in the United States. As a result, feedback is largely subjective and informal, with an emphasis on the interpersonal aspects of performance on the job. One is unlikely, therefore, to see papers change hands during a performance appraisal and even less likely to see written documents enter a file for future reference. This presents an interesting situation because many multinational firms simply export their formal and explicit performance appraisal forms to their foreign subsidiary.[13] Clearly, there is great potential for a culture clash when an implicit and informal culture meets an explicit and formal evaluation system.

Even the feedback itself is likely to be moderated by culture. For example, given that we know Japan to be a collectivist culture, we should not be surprised to find that performance appraisal is likely to be done in a group setting. Of course, such a venue for delivering feedback is rare in the individualistic United States. Although some argue that the popularity of team approaches in the U.S. has many firms thinking about group evaluations,[14] they certainly are not the major way evaluations are conducted. Further, the effects of various types of praise or criticism—whether delivered in a group or alone—vary considerably among cultures.

Perhaps the best way to illustrate these differences is to consider England—a country that has all the appearances of being culturally similar to the United States. One study did just that by looking at how performance feedback would affect the behavior of Americans and the English.[15] It was found that Americans became more productive after receiving either praise or criticism. In general, the more feedback they received, the higher their subsequent performance. This finding was observed for the English only after they received praise for their behavior; they did not respond well to criticism.[16] In fact, criticism is a type of feedback that is not often delivered effectively in England. Apparently, German workers are similar on this count—in general, they are often resentful of feedback because they believe it makes them admit failures and shortcomings.[17] Likewise, other research showed there can be wide differences in reactions to performance appraisals among Southeast Asian countries (e.g., Indonesia, Malaysia, the Philippines, and Thailand), even though we may be tempted to group these cultures together.[18]

So feedback is not equally effective in different cultures. Exhibit 13.1 presents an analysis of these and other differences one is likely to see in performance appraisal systems and feedback across three different cultures. This figure shows that there is wide variance in how an appraisal is conducted and what is (and is not!) said during the appraisal. In the United States, for example, the emphasis in the appraisal is on evaluation, not on development or improvement per se. Accordingly, if necessary, criticism is direct with little eye toward saving the face of the person receiving the evaluation. In other cultures, however, the process of providing the feedback is monitored much more carefully for its effect on the recipient. In Korea, for example, feedback is very indirect, with great concern for saving face. Despite this admonition to pay close attention to cultural differences, even among apparently similar countries there are some general things to keep in mind when delivering performance feedback. The following International Insights provides some very general guidelines that are probably instructive for all of us to be aware of, even if there are specific and important differences among cultures.

EXHIBIT 13.1

Differences in Performance Evaluation Systems across Three Countries

Appraisal Characteristic	Country		
	United States	Saudi Arabia	Korea
General emphasis	Evaluation	Evaluation/coaching	Coaching
Amount of feedback	High	High	Low
Delivery method	Individual	Individual	Individual
Emphasis on face saving	Low degree	High degree	High
Level of employee involvement	Medium to high	High	Low
Type of feedback	Criticism is direct	Criticism less direct	Criticism very indirect
Level of formality	Formal; probably written	Informal; not written	Informal; not written
Determinant of positive appraisal	Visible performance criteria	Seniority/connections	Seniority

Source: Harris, P. R., & Moran, R. T. (1991). *Managing cultural differences* (3rd Ed.). Houston, TX: Gulf. Reprinted by permission.

INTERNATIONAL INSIGHTS

Giving Performance Feedback to Foreign-Born Employees

IN THE UNITED STATES, managers are often told to reward in public and criticize in private. This advice, however, may not always be the best for your foreign-born employees. One expert provides the following specific recommendations for crafting feedback that you might deliver through a performance evaluation.[19] Although this advice does not always hold true for every foreign national, the following suggestions are very good starting points for the American manager:

- **Give feedback through a third party:** In many cultures, direct feedback—even if it is positive in form—can be very uncomfortable. If you belong to a collectivistic culture, being singled out for feedback can be very disconcerting. Accordingly, feedback may often be best delivered (even in individualistic cultures) through a trusted third party.
- **Communicate to the whole group:** In addition to this suggestion, another way to blunt the effect of direct feedback is to gather the work group together. One can then provide the gathering as a whole the set of feedback you wish to communicate. Since some work today is team

based, this method is probably a good technique for individualistic cultures as well.

- **Change the form of the feedback:** Almost always there are several ways of saying the same thing. Try several different approaches, even if the employee gives the appearance of understanding what you are saying.
- **Simplify the feedback:** This recommendation applies to feedback for any employee, but especially a foreign-born one. And it refers to the fact that we can almost always simplify and clarify what we mean. For example, you can eliminate or replace needless words. For example, the phrase "in spite of the fact that ..." could be simplified to *though* or simply *although*. (Other examples: "the reason why is that" to *because*; "This is a subject that" to *this subject*.)
- **Avoid slang:** Phrases like "the bottom line," "they'll eat this one up," "the home stretch," "I'm all ears," and "let's get rolling" are difficult to interpret. Although these phrases are so common to us that they are obvious, consider the perspective of someone from another culture.

Compensation of International Employees

One of the main reasons that companies spend time conducting appraisals and developing their unique cultural approaches is the effect the appraisal has on compensation. And often one's compensation is inextricably tied to one's future with the company. Thus, we will discuss a number of important issues about compensation across borders and cultures. As you will note, there is a wide disparity across countries in pay levels—for workers and executives alike. This alone is an important area to study, but it is further complicated by a cross-national assignment. Wage and benefit differences across countries present a set of practical and important problems for international human resource personnel. We will discuss both these issues in the last half of this chapter.

Compensation Systems

Probably the first (and only) thing most people think of when they hear the word *compensation* is their level of pay. However, companies compensate us in many ways for our work beyond actual pay. For one, health insurance coverage is one of the relatively hidden parts of our paycheck. As you probably know, health care costs represent a large and increasing cost to firms, especially those with an international presence. Additionally, pension plans, vacation and personal time off, and recreation/health facilities are all other sources of substantial cost to firms. Certainly, there are other sources of compensation as well. Nevertheless, there are points raised here about compensation that you perhaps hadn't thought about. For one, compensation must be thought of as more, in some cases much more, than just level of pay. Second, this perspective indirectly shows that there is considerable variation in compensation methods across jobs within our culture alone. All this must be layered on top of the differences that exist across cultures as well. How do companies in other countries and cultures compensate their employees, including the leaders of their companies?

The Meaning of Compensation

One important thing to consider before discussing specific differences in various types of compensation is the meaning of compensation across culture. That is, compensation in the United States is thought of as the exchange of our effort and output for wages and benefits. Clearly, the exchange model of compensation is common among many Western individualistic cultures. But even among these cultures, compensation may mean more than just exchange. In Germany, for example, the word for compensation implies achievement. Apparently, the word originated among shoemakers who custom-fit shoes to the buyer's feet. Shoes that "measured up" were ones that deserved compensation.[20] The Japanese word for compensation suggests a protection or safety net. The notion of trust inherent in this perspective makes the paternalistic Japanese employment system easier to understand. These examples suggest that compensation as a simple exchange may be specific to the United States and similar cultures. Accordingly, issues such as entitlement and obligation may play a more important role when compensation is delivered across cultures. Surely, you are bound to encounter some of these various expectations about the employment relationship when doing business across borders.

Pay Levels across Countries

Wage levels vary across country and culture. In fact, it is common to read about companies that have or are considering moving their facilities offshore because of wage differentials. Beyond any social issues raised by such practices, we presume that these plant closures are intended to save (or make) money. We used to live in Milwaukee, Wisconsin, and while there saw our share of companies who folded up their operations and moved elsewhere. For instance, Briggs & Stratton, the company that makes small engines for lawnmowers, moved some of their operations in Wisconsin to Mexico, where labor costs—pay levels in particular—are lower.

Data show that there are many countries with labor costs that are similar to the United States (e.g., Canada, France, the U.K.) or even higher than the United States (e.g., Belgium, Germany, the Netherlands, and Sweden). Germany, for example, has costs that are approximately 152 percent of the costs for U.S. production workers. Certainly, these data do not paint the complete cost picture for a firm that is considering a relocation, but they are instructive. These cost differences partly explain why some foreign firms have built factories in the United States (e.g. BMW, Honda, Nissan, Toyota) and why some firms, such as Briggs & Stratton, are leaving the United States. The Bureau of Labor Statistics (BLS) reported that Mexican labor costs in the late 1990s were only 25 percent of those in the United States. Certainly, this figure in large part can explain why thousands of U.S. firms have established *maquiladoras*—plants set up just across the U.S. border within Mexico.[21]

It should be noted that these data are rough estimates; there are large differences within countries in compensation rates (witness some companies moving from Michigan and Wisconsin to Kentucky). Likewise, the in-country data are also subject to some further interpretation. For example, while the BLS estimates that Mexican wages are only 25 percent of U.S. costs, other estimates put this ratio at closer to 40 percent. Nevertheless, even the higher estimate produces an effective labor cost of $6/hour in Mexico relative to $16.70 in the United States.[22] Apparently, the difference in these figures results from extra-production costs that are not reflected in the BLS estimates. For example, it is customary in Mexico to pay a Christmas bonus of one month's pay. Likewise, it is common and expected that Mexican workers receive 80 percent of their base pay for vacation bonuses in addition to bonuses paid for being punctual. Also, the Mexican government requires that firms distribute 10 percent of pretax profits to employees. Although this can be unequally distributed among workers, an estimate of the average cost per employee can be built in to these estimates. Finally, Mexican law mandates that workers be paid 365 days a year.[23]

CEO Compensation across Countries

Cross-national differences also emerge when we consider the compensation of managers and CEOs of U.S. firms versus the leaders of foreign companies.[24]

Relative compensation   Exhibit 13.2 presents data regarding the average compensation of CEOs from various countries for firms with annual revenue of 500 million dollars or more.[25] This figure is important since it shows a more complete compensation picture than we have focused on thus far. That is, the figure shows not only the base salaries of the CEOs, but it also provides estimates of incentive packages that include shares and share options. Some that claim the high base salaries paid to U.S. executives is misleading. Indeed, U.S. CEOs do have very high base salaries—they are the highest in the world. But the total compensation package also far and away favors U.S. executives. The CEO of Computer Associates, Charles Wang, took home a base salary of (only) $4.6 million in 2000, but he pocketed over $650 million in long-term compensation. It may be that the marginal tax rates in the United States lead Americans to be cash crazy, but they don't explain the massive CEO–average worker pay discrepancy. Nevertheless, we can see why one observer noted, "In America, cash is king and everybody wants it up front."[26]

Perks and other compensation   Indeed, the compensation policies of many countries recognize the bite taken by taxes and as a result try to reimburse their CEOs in nontaxable ways. For example, consider the package received by a Portuguese executive who may be earning a mere $35,000 a year. This person may have a maid, a gardener, and a washerwoman. In addition, he or she will probably be given a company car (with gas), housing, a monthly expense allowance (about $500), and his/her utilities will be paid. Likewise, a Mexican executive with a base pay of $30,000 will receive a company-supplied car and chauffeur along with a certain amount of groceries and liquor delivered to his or her home twice a month.[27] Because of tax rates, the Japanese executive may receive among the best set of perquisites. In fact, a Japanese firm often pays up to 50 percent of mortgage interest for all employees, and as they move up, they

EXHIBIT 13.2

Oceans Apart:
CEO Compensation in Several Countries*

Country	CEO Pay	Country	CEO Pay
United States	475	Italy	20
Venezuela	50	Canada	20
Brazil	49	Belgium	18
Mexico	47	Spain	16
Singapore	44	Netherlands	16
Argentina	44	France	14
Malaysia	42	New Zealand	13
Hong Kong	41	Sweden	12
United Kingdom	24	Germany	12
Thailand	24	Switzerland	11
Australia	23	Japan	11
South Africa	22	South Korea	8

*Average CEO pay is reported as a multiple of average manufacturing employees' pay.
Source: Adapted from————. (2000). Chief executives' pay. *The Economist*, September 30, 110.

get much more. Managers may also get a car/chauffeur, a bigger expense account, and paid memberships in exclusive golf and social clubs (known in Japan as "castles"). In fact, an American working in Japan said this about one of his Japanese colleagues: "Each time he got promoted, he moved to a better house. And as his expense account grew, the bars he'd visit would get better."

Total compensation   In spite of the higher level of perks paid to executives in most other countries, the overall package clearly favors Americans. In fact, in terms of total compensation, American CEOs far outpace the other countries listed in Exhibit 13.2. A comparable Italian executive receives only 20 percent of the compensation that an American CEO receives on average. And while it is not shown in this exhibit, there is much greater emphasis in the United States on variable forms of compensation. In other words, bonuses and incentives based on performance account for about 50 percent or more of the total compensation of U.S. executives, whereas for the other countries this percentage reached a high of only about 23 percent. All in all, we see a dramatic difference that favors U.S. chief executives.[28]

Vacation Time

Exhibit 13.2 also does not include one other very important thing—vacation time. Perhaps you've heard about the vaunted vacation time received by many European workers and executives alike. Exhibit 13.3 shows that there are indeed large differences in the number of paid vacation days per year across countries. As with our discussion of how CEO compensation is driven by tax codes, vacation time is also affected by legal regulations. For example, whereas Sweden mandates a minimum of thirty paid vacation days per year, Hong Kong only requires seven paid days and there is no minimum at all in the United States or the United Kingdom. Likewise, there is some variation in the number of holidays observed in various countries. Collectively, this shows that the typical number of paid vacation days ranges from a low of about thirty in the United States to a high of forty-six or forty-seven in France, Germany, and Hong Kong. This is quite a range.

All these figures suggest that one needs a complete understanding of a country's laws and customs to fully understand the compensation costs associated with doing business there. We do not, however, wish to overstate the impact of the laws and customs of each individual country. Indeed, some evidence suggests that there is increasing similarity in compensation practices (e.g., in wages, benefits, and other legally required compensation) among countries with similar cultures. In fact, one study analyzed the effect of both country and cultural categorization on compensation

EXHIBIT 13.3

Paid Vacation Days in Various Countries

Country	Lawfully Required Number of Days	No. of Days Usually Given	Legal Holidays	Total Paid Vacation Days
Canada	10	20	11	33
France	25	25–30	16	46
Germany	15	30	16	46
Hong Kong	7	20–30	17	47
Japan	19	20	16	36
Mexico	14	15–20	19	39
Sweden	30	30	14	44
United Kingdom	0	25–30	9	39
United States	0	20	10	30

Source: Milkovich, G. T., & Newman, J. M. (1999). *Compensation.* Chicago: Irwin. Reprinted by permission.

practices.[29] These researchers found that cultural grouping (e.g., Asian, Latin, European, etc.) explained compensation patterns much better than country-level customs and laws.

The Basis for Compensation across Countries

We know from the foregoing that there are differences in compensation across both country and culture. On what basis do various countries and cultures provide compensation? The study just discussed suggests that cultural practices are important to consider. To answer this question fully, however, we refer back to our earlier discussion of the meaning of compensation across culture. Some countries, such as the United States, refer to compensation as an exchange. This label suggests that the notion of **equity** is a major basis for determining level of compensation. Equity prescribes that those who contribute more are deserving of greater compensation. As we discussed in Chapter 11 on motivation, U.S. firms are more likely to operate on this equity principle than perhaps any other country.

This equity standard, however, is not the only one used to determine compensation levels. Consider the French as an example. Like most European countries, their traditional bonus system is not tied closely to performance. In fact, in France it is common for many employees to receive an extra month's salary before their traditional vacation time in July or August and once again before Christmas. This pattern leads many French to think in terms of net pay. In fact, when they are offered a monthly salary, the French quite automatically ask, "Is it net or gross?" and "How many times a year do I get this salary?"[30] As a result, the French have gotten very used to these bonuses, so much so that they really consider them as part of their base pay. In fact, there have been cases of companies that introduced additional equity-based pay opportunities but then who quickly regretted it. In one French company, for example, a performance-based bonus was paid for two straight years because the company did well. The third year, however, saw a drop in performance and no such bonus was paid. The work's council (a union-like organization in France), however, did not accept this and threatened to close down the plant. Apparently, the "bonus" had become viewed as an entitlement and strong feelings were expressed. As a result, the company paid the bonus. Mexico carries this practice a step further by systematizing worker acquisition of compensation extras. In particular, Mexico has an "acquired rights" law that mandates that if a bonus or benefit is given out at least two years in a row, it becomes the employee's right to receive it in the future.[31]

The Japanese view of compensation is paternalistic—one that implies rewards for loyalty and commitment. So one would predict that performance is determined by these more long-term concerns and is indexed by things like ability to get along with others, longevity, and seniority. As a result, Japanese firms are more likely to compensate their employees for seniority than are U.S. firms. One study, for example, examined the pay raise decisions of a group of Japanese and American managers.[32] These managers were asked to allot pay raises to a group of employees, including people described as low and high performers. The results were consistent with what we might expect. The U.S. managers gave much higher raises to the high performers and much lower raises to the poor performers than did the Japanese managers. For example, the Japanese gave about twice as much of a raise to low performers than did the Americans. Likewise, they gave about 80 percent less to high performers than did the U.S. managers. Thus, there appears to be a much higher link between performance and pay decisions for U.S. than Japanese managers.

Although these findings are probably true of many Asian firms that share the Confucian tradition, that tradition may be in the process of changing. Exhibit 13.4, for example, shows the results of a survey of 1,900 Japanese human resource officers. These people judged the relative impact of seniority to merit in determining pay raises, and they were surveyed across a number of years. As the exhibit shows, Japanese firms do indeed use seniority as a major mechanism by which to determine a pay raise. Nevertheless, the weight that seniority has received has dropped over the nine year period covered by the survey. One can only guess that the current rate is significantly less than the 46 percent reported over a decade ago in this study.[33] The following International Insights suggests that if Toyota is any indicator, then the change is even more dramatic. It also shows, however, that Japanese who openly advocate equity as the basis of compensation can still attract considerable notice and resistance.

INTERNATIONAL INSIGHTS

Hiroshi Okuda—
A Nail That Stuck Out At Toyota

THE PRESIDENT OF TOYOTA until recently (now chairman) was Hiroshi Okuda, and apparently he stood out in a crowd. For one thing, his appearance was different from that of most Japanese executives—he is over 6 feet tall and stood out in a crowd whether he is in Detroit or Tokyo. More importantly, he was very outspoken and frank. An example was a dinner he held with American journalists recently, where he more than held his own in English. One question about his competition prompted Mr. Okuda to say, "I don't understand why Ford chose that kind of styling for the Taurus; it is too round. In Japan that styling was popular four or five years ago." Similarly frank comments about the superiority of Toyota's Lexus operation in Japan over that in Kentucky also drew attention. Toyota's own PR department muttered off record that if you stick out all over the place, you are going to get banged. Even a friend said of Okuda, "He sticks out all over the place."

There is no doubt that he stuck out at Toyota. For one thing, Okuda was the first person outside the Toyoda family to run the company. Technically he was not the CEO—that position during his tenure was still held by 71-year-old Shoichiro Toyoda. Everyone, knew who was in charge, however—Mr. Okuda. He changed many things about the company, much of which appeared to be for the better. Toyota was due for a shakeup, given their erratic performance the last few years. Beyond the many problems with the Japanese economy, Toyota was also dealing with a common problem for family-run companies. Sometimes a family member whose time has come to lead just isn't up to the task. Apparently, this was the case when Tatsuro Toyoda ascended to Toyota CEO in 1992. A close company observer said, "Tatsuro was very civilized but a lousy businessman." Toyota by then had become big and lethargic. Mr. Okuda was brought in to change entrenched management attitudes. He believed that only younger executives had the vigor and imagination to run a big company like Toyota. Accordingly, he announced a new policy that took titles away from general managers at age 55 and managers at age 50. They were allowed to stay on with the firm, but with seriously reduced responsibilities.

With these and other actions, Mr. Okuda completely overhauled Toyota's traditional seniority-based promotion system and remodeled it with a new emphasis on merit. "I had no choice," he said. "Employing young people is vital to any company." Mr. Okuda also cleared away the dead wood from the board of directors and retired about a third of Toyota's top executives. Although the normal retirement age is 60 in Japan and most of these people were over that age, it is still unusual to force such guidelines on top management because of the reverence for seniority. Nevertheless, younger men were put in their place, some jumping several grades with one promotion—again, a highly unusual move in Japanese corporations. In a *Fortune* interview a few years ago, Mr. Okuda said, "So far we have not been able to rejuvenate the workforce as I had hoped. The general impression is that Toyota is old and conservative." Apparently, this means that more than the traditional seniority system is going to change at Toyota in the near future.[34]

EXHIBIT 13.4

The Relative Impact of Seniority versus Merit on Pay Raises
in Japanese Firms

Year	Seniority (%)	Ability/Merit (%)
1978	57.9	42.1
1983	54.4	45.6
1984	49.0	51.0
1987	46.0	54.0

Source: Adapted from Mroczkowski, T., & Hanaoka, M. (1989). Continuity and change in Japanese management. *California Management Review,* Winter, 39–52.

Other research also reports that the number of British firms that have implemented similar equity compensation systems had increased by a factor of about 5 from 1978 to 1990.[35] Additionally, they also showed that international compensation systems are becoming more and more similar.[36] Nevertheless, as implied by other research just discussed, we still see differences. In fact, in Exhibit 13.5, expected differences in compensation methods across three of Hofstede's most important cultural dimensions are presented.[37]

Expatriate Compensation

Thus far we have reviewed differences among countries and cultures in various types of compensation. It is also important, however, to consider the compensation packages and necessities of an expatriate employee and executive.

Expatriate costs   As we discussed in Chapter 10, when U.S. multinationals establish a presence overseas, they often send over their own teams of managers to run that unit. And as discussed, there are a variety of reasons for using expatriates, including familiarity with company methods, greater technical skill, and a generally higher trust level for the expatriate. Although we don't know a good deal about when one or more of these reasons predominates, we do certainly know one thing—the use of expatriates is expensive! The average annual cost to send an employee overseas is about $300,000.[38] In fact, this figure is about five times as high as a domestic relocation. What accounts for all these costs? Well, there are the usual things involved in a move, including interviewing and hiring and actual moving costs themselves. Each of these factors, however, is certainly more expensive than it would be for a domestic relocation. A majority of companies, however, go well beyond this by providing a large number of costly benefits. These can include financial allowances and assistance with acclimating to the foreign culture. Exhibit 13.6 presents some examples of additional costs that could be incurred with an expatriate.

EXHIBIT 13.5

Predicted Compensation Practices across Culture

Cultural Dimensions	Sample Countries	Characteristics of Compensation System
Individualism–Collectivism		
Individualist	United States Canada New Zealand United Kingdom	Performance-based compensation schemes; equity for distribution; rewards given for individual efforts
Collectivist	Indonesia Japan Korea Singapore	Extra performance variables; group compensation scheme likely to be successful; equality/need rule important
Power Distance		
Low	United States United Kingdom Denmark Australia	Wage gap between lowest & highest job not often great; profit sharing/gain sharing likely to be successful
High	Malaysia Mexico Philippines Spain	Hierarchical compensation; compensation tied to one's place in the social structure; large salary gap between workers and management
Uncertainty Avoidance		
Low	Singapore Sweden Canada United States	Lots of variable/contingent compensation; bonuses/pay at risk, dependent on performance
High	Greece Japan Korea Portugal	Highly structured, lock-step compensation plans; centralized decision making and evaluation; discretionary pay minimized

Sources: Adapted from Gomez-Mejia, L. R., & Welbourne, T. (1991). Compensation strategies in a global context. *Human Resource Planning*, 14, 29–41; Hodgetts, R. M., & Luthans, F. (1993). U.S. multinationals' compensation strategies for local management: Cross-cultural interpretations. *Compensation and Benefits Review*, 42–48.

Despite the fact that some companies are aware of the many additional costs faced by expatriates, a surprisingly high percentage (77%) of those who return from an assignment are dissatisfied with the compensation they received.[39] This unhappiness can make the expatriate less willing to adjust to a new culture, less productive, and more willing to leave the firm after they return from a foreign assignment. Accordingly, it is worth looking at the main goals and components of the expatriate compensation package in order to improve on expatriate satisfaction.

EXHIBIT 13.6

Potential Sources of Costs Associated with Expatriation

Direct Payments/Reimbursements	Support for Adjustment to Global Assignment
Tax reduction/equalization	Home leave (4–6 weeks)
Housing allowance	Emergency leave
Furnishing allowance	Personal security
Education allowance	Car/driver
Hardship/Foreign service premium	Domestic help
Currency protection	Spouse employment
Goods and services differential	Child care provider
Temporary living allowance	Language/translation services
Car/Transportation allowance	Cultural training
Assignment completion bonus	Repatriation assistance
Extension bonus	Social club fees
Help renting U.S. home	Imported food and other goods

Source: Adapted from Milkovich, G. T., & Newman, J. M. (1999). *Compensation.* Chicago: Irwin.

Models for compensating expatriates   As detailed in Chapter 12, an expatriate assignment can, and more likely than not will, be a difficult one. There are cultural, language, and environmental adjustments, among others, to be made. These difficulties are no secret to the potential expatriate. Accordingly, a firm must design a compensation plan that will be enough of an incentive to attract good people. There are a variety of ways to classify the methods that multinationals use to devise such plans. One main method is the ***ad hoc* approach**, in which individual employees negotiate with their firm for covering the costs inherent in a foreign assignment.[40] While this approach has some merit, the drawbacks include potential unequal treatment of expatriates and a lack of country-specific knowledge (e.g., taxes, cost of living, etc) on the part of both the firm and the employee. Although a firm may be able to successfully negotiate down their costs with an expatriate, several experts have pointed out that this strategy may be shortsighted. An employee who takes the foreign assignment, may quickly find out that the compensation (in total or parts) is inadequate or is different from that of others. This discovery can lead to an early termination of an expatriate assignment, which in turn is expensive for a firm (see Chapter 12).

Another more systematic approach is called **localization**. Basically, this approach involves paying the expatriate essentially the same as the local nationals in similar positions. This approach may be especially useful when an employee is going to be a career internationalist, because the permanent expatriate probably does not keep the home country standard in evaluating their compensation. The model is also used for the more typical expatriate as well. Localization, however, is much easier to apply when an expatriate moves to a country with a higher standard of living. It is difficult to accept a lower level of compensation because the standard of living is less expensive in Mexico than in the United States. The localization approach is rarely used without adjustments being made (base pay, allowances, etc.), but it still has serious limits.[41]

The balance sheet method By far the most popular approach is called the **balance sheet** (or build-up) model. The philosophy of this approach is that the expatriate should not suffer a loss as a result of transfer. This general goal of trying to "keep the expatriate whole" is the stated objective of many multinational companies, as found in a recent survey.[42] Accordingly, it is a system that is designed to keep expatriates' standard of living on a par with that of their contemporaries at home. Although Exhibit 13.6 shows that there are potentially many costs associated with expatriation, the balance sheet approach commonly divides expenses into four categories. Beyond the base salary, major expenses are usually considered in the categories of housing, income taxes, good/services, and a reserve or discretionary component. First, however, let's consider the issue of base salary. Using this balance sheet approach, salary would be determined in the same way as for domestic employees. That is, if domestic employees receive average raises of about 5 percent, then so do the expatriates. The particular economic conditions in the foreign posting are not germane to the expatriate's base salary.

Likewise, it is common for a multinational to pay a premium or incentive to the expatriate for taking the foreign assignment. As we mentioned here and earlier in Chapter 12, there are some distinct disadvantages of expatriation—not the least of which are a "career interrupt" and the hardship of living in a foreign country. And firms often make compensation adjustments to account for this hardship. These adjustments can represent a sizeable cost to a firm. In fact, most companies pay a foreign service premium, and these often range from 10 to 30 percent of base pay.[43] Some companies go beyond this amount to pay a hardship allowance as well for locations that are undesirable because of extreme weather, safety concerns, or limited access to goods or medical services. An American expatriate assigned to Amsterdam, for example, would receive a lower allowance than for an assignment in Tehran, Iran, where some still celebrate Death to Americans as a national holiday.[44] So whereas the monthly allowance for an assignment in Seoul might be $300, the same allotment for Chengdu could be as much as $1,000. It is difficult to make such hardship judgments, even for firms that have considerable experience with the international domain. Accordingly, many look to easily available rating schemes, such as the U.S. Department of State's *Hardship Post Differentials Guidelines*.[45] This is a guide that is updated periodically to reflect the degree of hardship experienced by foreign service personnel and is used by many multinationals for the same purpose.

Purchase power and the balance sheet Beyond these base payments, however, the balance sheet approach is mainly concerned with a set of expenses that are common in any family budget. The main purpose of the balance sheet approach is to protect or equalize expenses in the foreign country to the home country for each category, and Exhibit 13.7 depicts this approach.[46] The first column of this figure presents the base costs in the home country—say, the United States. Of course, the home country purchasing power changes depending on one's income, size of family, and other variables. But for purposes of discussion, let us consider how purchasing power at home

EXHIBIT 13.7

The Balance Sheet Approach to Expatriate Compensation

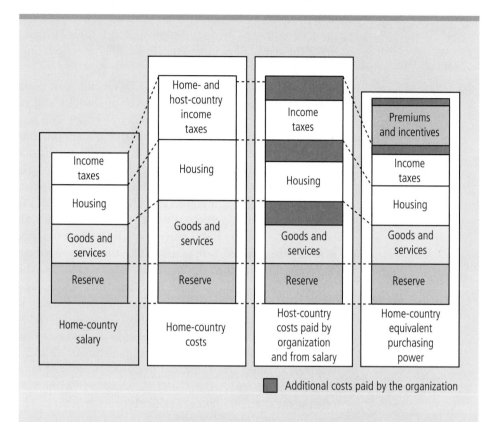

Source: Reynolds, C. (1994). Compensation basics for North American expatriates: Developing an effective program for employees working abroad. *American Compensation Association.* Reprinted from ACA Building Block #15. 1994 with permission from the American Compensation Association (ACA). 14040 N. Northsight Blvd., Scottsdale, Ariz. U.S.A. 85260; © ACA.

might be translated to purchasing power abroad. As shown in column 2 of this figure, most categories of costs tend to be higher overseas than at home.

Housing costs   Housing, for example, usually involves considerably higher expenses than you might think, even in what might be considered a generally low-cost country. There are several reasons for this. For one, housing is typically rented and this is often covered by a shorter-term lease, which drives up costs. Second, if we consider U.S. expatriates, it is important to recognize that what they are used to in terms of housing is very different than most of the rest of the world. Americans expect larger and more luxurious digs than their counterparts in a foreign country (unless those Americans are from Manhattan or San Francisco!). In fact, some human resource personnel have noted that it is sometimes impossible to even find comparable housing for a U.S. expatriate in a city like Tokyo or Beijing, let alone pay for it!

The costs for housing expatriates around the world can vary dramatically. Exhibit 13.8 presents some estimates of housing costs in various cities in the world. As you can see in the figure, housing in many cities is outrageously expensive. Even Chicago or

EXHIBIT 13.8

Expatriate Housing Costs in Ten Foreign Cities*

Location	Estimated Yearly Housing Costs
Beijing	$158,400
Hong Kong	$156,000
Tokyo	$153,600
Shanghai[2]	$120,000
Moscow	$108,000
Seoul	$102,000
London	$93,600
Ho Chi Minh City	$86,400
Singapore	$85,200
New York	$72,000

*This figure presents an estimate of the average yearly housing costs for a typical expatriate family of four. Estimates are taken from a sample of comparable homes or apartments that would be available to rent. These costs are based on rents for a home/apartment with 3–4 bedrooms, in safe and accessible neighborhoods, and they include costs for utilities, insurance, maintenance, and taxes.
[2] Estimate for three-bedroom apartment, since that is the only reasonably available housing source.
Source: Adapted from————. (1997). Housing costs in foreign cities. *Wall Street Journal*, January 24, B8.

New York, which some Americans might consider expensive, looks like a real bargain relative to some foreign cities. Column 2 of Exhibit 13.7 reflects the fact that host-country housing costs are often more expensive than at home for U.S. expatriates. With the balance sheet approach, if we assume your housing costs are about $2,500 per month in Chicago ($28,894/12 months) and about $4,300 in London, the company would make up the $1,800 per month.[47]

Taxes   A second major category of expatriate expenses is taxes, which is also reflected in the balance sheet approach in Exhibit 13.7. This area of compensation is among the most technical and difficult for a multinational to deal with. In part, this is a consequence of the large number of tax, securities, and currency control rules both in the United States and in foreign countries.[48] Exhibit 13.9 presents only one such complication—the different corporate and marginal income tax rates in several countries where U.S. expatriates are commonly sent. As you can see, the marginal tax rates of these countries varies markedly: Britain and Ireland are quite low, whereas France and the Netherlands are relatively high. Of course, the United States has agreements with some countries about social security surcharges. France and Belgium, for example, are leaders in making "totalization" agreements in their laws. France has included the following items in their laws regarding expatriates:[49]

EXHIBIT 13.9

Tax Rates around the World

Country	Corporate Tax Rate*	Top Marginal Income Tax Rate
United Kingdom	30	40
France	40	57
Germany	50	52
Ireland	29	44
Italy	41	46
Japan	42	49
Netherlands	38	60
Spain	37	48
Sweden	28	58
Switzerland	30	57
United States	40	40

*includes local and state taxes.
Source: Adapted from————. (2000). Whose burden is heaviest? *The Economist*, September 9, 53–54.

- An agreement that companies with an office in France can avoid French taxation of an expatriate's housing, schooling, and other allowances.
- Provisions to eliminate taxes (in France) of expatriate income from sources such as dividends, interest, and capital gains
- A totalization agreement to eliminate social security taxes in France
- A system to greatly reduce French taxes on income from stock options

However, even when foreign tax rates are lower (e.g., in Canada), the total tax burden for an expatriate may be higher. This is the case for several reasons. For one, many countries tax not only income but also all allowances, adjustments, and incentives. Worse yet, the United States is among the very few countries in the world (the only industrialized one!) to tax expatriate income.[50] So even if a company executive is paying relatively low taxes while on an Irish assignment, he or she will probably also have a tax due in the United States (income below a certain amount is excluded). If you are an Irish expatriate working in the United States, however, you may not be taxed by your government. Therefore, with the balance sheet approach, the firm will either pay a differential to the expatriate to account for the increased tax burden (protection), or it will pay directly to the other country an amount that ensures equivalent purchasing power for the expatriate (equalization). Regardless of how these additional costs are paid out, the goal is to make up the difference in costs incurred by the expatriate.

These Munich window-shoppers might be concerned about their goods and service adjustment if they were expatriates. © Adam Woolfitt/CORBIS

Living expenses   A final but important category of expenses typically included in the balance sheet approach are those caused by living expenses—the goods and services that you will buy when living in a foreign country. Some of these expenses include food, transportation, clothing, and entertainment items, among many others. This category of expenses may be the most difficult to estimate since this category shows more fluctuation in price than any of the others. Additionally, the currency exchange rate is more likely to be felt here than in other expatriate expense categories. In housing, for example, one often signs a year-long lease with the annual price predetermined.

Despite these difficulties, we can still get estimates of the difference in prices of a collection of goods and services. Various companies publish a survey of costs of goods and services in many world cities, data that are regularly collected all around the world (as we show in the Reality Check interview later in the chapter). Exhibit 13.10 shows what an expatriate might face while spending a year or two in Tokyo or Hong Kong. Clearly, the cost of goods and services in Japan and many other Asian cities is high. On the other hand, some other cities on this list are surprisingly inexpensive (e.g., Frankfurt, Prague, Manila). Johannesburg, for example, is a relatively cheap place to live; an expatriate's living expenses here are about 60 percent below those of the Big Apple.[51]

If this list is hard to swallow for an expatriate, consider the Big Mac economic index that is reported annually by *The Economist* magazine.[52] Their rationale—partly tongue in cheek—is to provide a quick and easily digestible (even if you think the product is not) method that can be used to compare costs across countries. For your interest, we present these data in Exhibit 13.11. China appears to be a relative bargain (Big Mac only $1.20), whereas your wallet will be lighter in Zurich ($3.65). While this is hardly a perfect index of purchasing power parity, it certainly is food for thought.[53] Regardless of what index you use, it appears that a basket of goods and services in some countries is expensive, whereas in others it may be relatively cheap.[54] What is especially interesting

EXHIBIT 13.10

Cost Estimates for Goods and Services in Various World Cities*

City	Cost of Living	City	Cost of Living
Tokyo	162	Caracas	76
Belgrade	124	Frankfurt	75
Hong Kong	120	Sao Paulo	69
Seoul	105	Santiago	67
Taipei	105	Lima	67
New York	100	Istanbul	63
London	100	Jakarta	62
Tel Aviv	98	Kuala Lumpur	61
Singapore	97	Warsaw	61
Beijing	93	Bangkok	56
Buenos Aires	92	Prague	52
Paris	88	Johannesburg	50
Mexico City	87	Budapest	47
Moscow	84	Manila	47
Lagos	81	Karachi	47
Cairo	79	Mumbai	40

*The ratings, using New York City as the base rating of 100, were estimated using the average price of over 100 goods and services that you would commonly buy (these include food, clothing, entertainment, and transportation costs).

Source: Adapted from————. (2002). Cost of living index. *The Economist*, January 6, 196.

is that even in those countries that have inexpensive goods and services, purchases by expatriates end up being higher anyway. One expert points out that most expatriates keep their relatively high-living home-country consumption tastes even in a foreign country. They are willing and anxious to buy expensive imports from their home country, a habit that in turn drives up the expense index much higher than the estimates.[55]

Presumably, expatriates would receive an adjustment to their average domestic living expenses while on foreign assignment. If the readily available adjustment indexes are not appropriate (perhaps because expatriates want to import goods they are used to at home), then a firm may wish to conduct its own cost survey. Nonetheless, the survey results could rapidly become useless because of inflation or changes in exchange rates.

EXHIBIT 13.11

Do You Want Fries with That Foreign Assignment?
The Big Mac in Various Countries

	Big Mac Prices				
Country	**Local Currency**	**US$**	**PPP of $***	**Exchange Rate**	**Over/under Valuation against Dollar (%)**
United States	$2.54	—	—	—	—
Australia	A$3.00	1.52	1.18	1.98	−40
Brazil	R3.60	1.64	1.42	2.19	−35
United Kingdom	£1.99	2.85	1.28	1.43	12
China	Y9.90	1.20	3.90	8.28	−53
Czech Republic	K56.00	1.43	22.0	39.0	−44
Denmark	DKr24.75	2.93	9.74	8.46	15
Germany	DM5.10	2.30	2.01	2.22	−9
Hong Kong	HK$10.70	1.37	4.21	7.80	−46
Japan	Y294	2.38	116	124	−6
Mexico	Peso21.9	2.36	8.62	9.29	−7
Russia	R35.00	1.21	13.8	28.9	−52
South Korea	Won3,000	2.27	1,181	1,325	−11
Sweden	Skr24.0	2.33	9.45	10.28	−8
Switzerland	SFr6.30	3.65	2.48	1.73	44
Taiwan	NT$70.0	2.13	27.6	32.9	−16
Thailand	Baht55.0	1.21	21.7	45.5	−52

*Purchasing power parity, or ppp = local price divided by U.S. price.
Source: ———. (2001). *The Economist,* April 21. Reprinted by permission.

This is a case where a firm would probably wish to pay the employee allowance in local currency and at monthly intervals. [56]

The balance sheet on balance   All in all, you can see that the major goal of the balance sheet approach is to treat the expatriate fairly. Certainly, the effect of many of the adjustments made is to make a foreign posting less of a hardship for an employee;

REALITY CHECK

What Do Zippers, Tabasco, Prozac, and Golf Balls Have in Common? They're All in a Day's Survey [57]

A Wall Street Journal interview with Megan Lipman, research analyst with Associates for International Research (Air-Inc.) of Cambridge, Massachusetts.

Background Information

Megan Lipman works for Air-Inc., one of the largest international survey research companies. The firm collects data on the prices of goods and services in many countries all around the world. (Readers may be aware that the U.S. Consumer Price Index is also based on surveys done in supermarkets, malls, and the like in order to monitor prices.) They sell this information to their clients, the largest of whom is the European Union. But Air-Inc also has lots of other companies and government agencies as clients as well—all of whom use this information to compute expatriates' cost of living adjustments. Demand for their services is on the rise as employers try to keep close accounting of expatriate expenses.

What does Ms. Lipman do for Air-Inc?

Like most of Air-Inc's surveyors who are in the 22 to 33 age range, Ms. Lipman (age 25) flies around the world from city to city for about six weeks at a time. Once there, she spends about three days pegging costs by visiting supermarkets, gas stations, theaters, and beauty salons—among other places. During this interview, for example, Megan Lipman had flown to Malta, where she was tracking down prices for a 20-centimeter zipper, 20 mgs of Prozac, a sleeve of golf balls, a 14-carat gold wedding ring, Tabasco sauce, a dozen red roses, and the cost of repairing a washing machine. She has a regular schedule of items to price, and this list was not that unusual.

How does she get her data?

When she gets to a location, such as a supermarket, she presents her business card to the manager and asks if she can carry out a pricing survey. She then heads up and down the aisles recording price after price. Most managers are very friendly and helpful. But in some shops, managers resent young foreigners nosing around the store, partly because they think the survey is being done by their competition. In those cases, Air-Inc's surveyors often covertly wander the store with smaller notebooks and surreptitiously make their

notes. While she was in a Malta pharmacy, one manager sternly pulled her aside and asked "Can I have a word with you?" Concerned that she'd be kicked out of the store and lose her hard-earned data, she was relieved when he asked instead if his son could get an internship with Air-Inc.

She also spends a good deal of time in the many (luxury) hotel rooms in which she stays, collecting even more data. There she or a translator she hires uses the phone directory to make calls to physicians, insurance and real estate agents, and repair shops for more prices. And even when she returns home to Cambridge, she analyzes the reams of data she collected, determines an average price for various items, and tracks these prices to those of the last several surveys. Air-Inc. then makes recommendations to raise or lower cost of living allowances for its clients.

How did she get the job? What's her training? And does she like it?

First, she loves it. "I never in my life could have dreamed that such a job existed," she said. After graduating from the College of the Holy Cross in Worcester, Massachusetts, with dual majors in art history and Spanish, she worked two years as a translator. Then she responded to a newspaper ad even though it seemed dull: "Responsibilities include data collection, analysis, and preparation of various statistical data for cost of living analysis." But it was the last sentence that made her send in the résumé: "Will spend at least one-third of time in international travel." The interviewers fired questions at her such as, "What would you do if you were stranded in a central African nation with three days until the next flight?" Her answer: "If there were no other safe ways to get out, I'd get as much work done on the phone as possible." (How's that for a new twist on the "I work too hard" response to the usual "Tell us about your weak points" interview question?). Now she spends about half the year traveling to Qatar, the United Arab Emirates, Bangladesh, New Zealand, Cyprus, Venezuela, and dozens of other places. She makes about $40,000/year, has a very generous expense account, and enjoys her traveling. The drawbacks? The many travel hassles (delays, missed connections, etc.) and a lot of time spent alone. It's also tough to maintain a relationship, although she has dated her Boston boyfriend for over a year now, sees him during her six-week stays at home, and meets him in romantic places, as in London recently.

sometimes they may even help to make expatriation a pleasure. This is not to say, however, that the balance sheet approach is without its problems. For one, the approach is difficult for a firm to administer and is complex to explain. As suggested, the balance sheet approach often requires either collecting or buying sets of data on cost of living and housing. Likewise, the transfer of payments for the various adjustments is also difficult both to explain to the expatriate and to monitor fiscally.

Some very practical problems could also emerge. Earlier, we implied that expenses in the three major categories will be greater for the overseas employee. What if costs are less for an expatriate who transfers, say, to Mexico? Should the payments to the employee be reduced to reflect a lower cost of living in Mexico? While the balance sheet system would function to eliminate such "windfalls" to the employee, many firms do not do so.[58] Indeed, most balance sheet users are now using some modified version that makes these adjustments.[59] But in principle, the balance sheet would allow for the reduced compensation to the expatriate in a low-cost country. Along the same lines, others have noted a significant change in the number of companies that even consider a foreign assignment as something deserving of a special premium.[60] In fact, the number of firms that do not pay any incentive premium at all to work overseas has nearly doubled in recent years.[61] So although firms may adjust compensation for the increased cost of overseas living, increasingly they feel that some of the best jobs are there. With increasing globalization, their rationale is that employees should relish an opportunity to work overseas. If a firm makes the foreign assignment a real part of the career track of its management, this is probably a reasonable position to take. Time will tell on this point. For now, however, we encourage you to complete the hands-on exercise at the end of this chapter. There we ask you to put together a fair compensation package for expatriate employees in several different foreign assignments; we think you will find that this is no easy task.

Compensating Foreign Country Nationals

Of course, one of the very many things multinational management has to think about is the specific mix of U.S., local-country, and third-country nationals in the staffing of a foreign office or plant. The strategic issues involved in these and other decisions have been discussed earlier (Chapters 8, 9, and 12), but for now we can certainly remind you that there are many good reasons for hiring local-country nationals. Obviously, there would be minimal relocation costs for such personnel. And many of the adjustment problems resulting from cultural differences that we have outlined would presumably be averted. Likewise, if the operation is a joint venture—as, say, many enterprises are in the People's Republic of China—you may earn the approval of that government by hiring their citizens.[62]

Compensation methods   Regardless of the reason they are hired, it is clear that many local and third-country nationals are employed by U.S. multinationals. And there are a variety of different models for compensating those foreign nationals. For one, a company could peg salaries at the level of the U.S. expatriate with whom they may work side by side. As it turns out, few U.S. firms use this approach.[63] More often than not, salaries of local nationals are set to their prevailing country standards. In general, local nationals receive the fewest elements of compensation of the three groups.[64] This does not necessarily mean that it will always be cheaper for the U.S. firm to hire local nationals. For example, the firm may save money using an expatriate in Belgium and France because of savings earned by avoiding the social security premiums that are necessary for their citizens. Conversely, the high tax equalization and other costs for expatriates in Britain and Germany may make a local national a relative bargain.[65] In some countries, however, this situation is changing dramatically and it is therefore necessary for the human resources professional to stay abreast of the current employment situation. Surprisingly, China appears to be one of these countries where compensation may be more complex (and changing) than you think, as shown in the following International Insights.

INTERNATIONAL INSIGHTS

Chinese Managers Know Their Way around the Labor Market[66]

COMPANY-PAID APARTMENTS and houses, 20 percent or more salary increases, food and clothing allowances, fully paid maternity leave, paid day care, retirement, saving, and medical benefits . . . even a laundry allotment. We know what you're thinking—who can I call, and where can I send my résumé? As it turns out, you would not be calling a Silicon Valley company. Unfortunately, you'd have to make a very long distance call, and even then they don't want your résumé! What we've described is actually a typical compensation package provided to Chinese citizens who work for joint ventures of foreign-owned businesses in the People's Republic of China.

These data are based on a survey of human resource personnel from fifty-eight offices throughout the PRC. The main reason for these very attractive compensation packages is the immense amount of competition for well-educated and savvy Chinese nationals, many of whom speak very good English. These types of people make excellent managers in joint venture operations. For one, their dual language skills represent an excellent asset—one that few American businesspersons have. While some firms provide Chinese language training, the demands of the job and the relatively short time frame for the assignment make mastery of the difficult Chinese language nearly impossible. Additionally, they are obviously privy to the home culture and often have more than a passing familiarity with U.S. culture—many having been educated here. Third, the Chinese government mandates the hiring of a percentage of their nationals in these joint ventures. Finally, these people are just plain smart. This combination of skills makes them a hot commodity among the many U.S. and other foreign companies that have established joint ventures in China. We recently visited the Shanghai plant of a major U.S. personal product manufacturer, S. C. Johnson & Son ("Johnson Wax"). Many of their Chinese managers fit this profile. We spent some time with one manager and got a chance to

speak with him (in English). As it turns out, he had been employed with several similar firms in the last several years, including some of S. C. Johnson's competitors in China, such as Procter & Gamble, Kimberly Clark, and others. He said it was not uncommon to receive multiple offers at any one time.

Now, despite what seems like generous pay raises and perquisites, pay in China is definitely low by U.S. standards. The typical manager working for a joint venture office gets about $7,000 a year (including allowances). Perhaps more surprising is that the typical joint venture manager earns only $2,500 per year. The average industrial worker for a state factory earns only $500 per year (not including state subsidies). "Pay and benefits packages reflect a mixture of old ways and emerging capitalism," says Paula DeLisle, a consultant in Hong Kong for the Wyatt Co. International, based in Washington, D.C. Indeed, this appears to be the case, because in the shadow of this services-to-the-highest-bidder phenomenon, there are some legal guidelines on wage payments. Although the Provisions for Labor Management stipulate that compensation is at the discretion of the board of directors, there are also more direct regulations on wages. Article 8 of the Sino-Foreign Joint Ventures Provisions sets wage levels at 120 to 150 percent of the real wages of local staff and workers in similar state enterprises. Later, however, article 39 of this document states that the salary and bonus system should adhere to principles of "each according to his work" and "more pay for more work."[67] It remains to be seen what happens in the interplay between these two objectives—market and bureaucratic regulations. They may continue to function side by side. As Ms. DeLisle says, "On one hand, the paternalistic employer will earmark specific allowances, and on the other the free market enterprise uses discretionary bonuses to motivate performance."

How to pay local and foreign employees is a challenge, particularly when they are doing similar work. © Adam Woolfitt/CORBIS

Despite these examples, there will certainly be many times when the multinational will employ an expatriate and a local national in the same position and where they will work closely with each other. Of course, it is probably inevitable that these groups of personnel will compare their compensation packages, and sometimes the difference will be all too apparent (chauffeured car, etc.). Since locals average lower compensation, this situation appears destined to have problems. A survey of 225 human resource managers and directors of U.S. multinationals looked at the problems they have experienced in compensating their international managers.[68] A variety of different problems were mentioned, but the single most important one was the discrepancies among compensation programs for expatriates, local, and third-country nationals. These were identified as the source of significant or very significant problems for 80 percent of the sample! The *Wall Street Journal* recently reported that 100 percent of a sample of forty-five large U.S. multinationals reported that different compensation levels were their biggest international problem. Incidentally, third-country nationals (e.g, a Dutch manager working in Britain for a U.S. firm) typically fare better in terms of total compensation than local nationals. These people may need a salary and living adjustment to attract them to a different location, whereas the local national is already there. Once there, all have to work together because it is common to mix these three groups of employees in any one location. The issues of how this cultural diversity of groups and teams mix together and the problems they might present, however, is the topic of our next and last chapter.

Chapter Summary

Few people enjoy conducting performance evaluations on their employees, and adding foreign employees in the mix only makes the task more distasteful. There are many problems associated with the appraisal of the expatriate's performance, and they are not easily overcome. These basic questions loom large: *who* will evaluate the expatriate, *how often* will the evaluation be done, and most importantly, *what* will be evaluated and how. The "who" question involves tradeoffs between whether the evaluation is conducted by a local manager or the home office. We detailed some of the problems faced by both parties and present general guidelines for delivering feedback in an international context (the what/how question).

One main reason to evaluate is eventually to compensate. We also dealt with this topic in detail, pointing out along the way that compensation means more than just pay level. Nevertheless, there are differences in pay levels across countries. American CEOs seem to have the best deal, with their pay far outstripping that of typical workers, and compared with CEOs in all other countries.

We also discussed the complex issues involved in compensating expatriate employees. The *balance sheet* approach to compensation is among the most popular. Its goal is to maintain the same lifestyle for the foreign employee as she or he would enjoy at home. This is difficult to do because adjustments due to housing, taxes, and goods and services, among other things, need to be considered. Firms will often pay a consulting firm for data on housing costs, living and other expenses that vary over time. Expatriation is a large expense for an employer, but the benefits of having a cadre of managers and executives with international experience may prove to be worth the cost.

Discussion Questions

1. What are some of the problems in evaluating employee performance, and how are these problems complicated by an international setting?
2. How might cultural beliefs about the basis for compensation affect your approach to rewarding expatriates and host-country/third-country nationals in the same firm?
3. What are some of the ways that employees and executives alike can be compensated for their international service?
4. How should expatriates be compensated? What is the best approach, and why?

Up to the Challenge?

Performance Evaluation Overseas

At the start of this chapter, we asked you to put yourself in place of an expatriate assigned to the People's Republic of China. You tried to use your management knowledge about employee participation techniques in an effort to improve performance on one of the production lines for which you are responsible. Unfortunately, this and several related techniques, such as providing rewards for good performance, did not work well. Because of the language barrier, you have not made much headway in terms of diagnosing what went wrong. At your six-month review, you received a decent evaluation, although it was somewhat neutral and open to interpretation.

What you should know now is that language is probably not the only problem. Even if you spoke Chinese well, the Chinese would probably not give you direct feedback about the cause of the problems with your implementations. As we know from Chapter 5, such feedback to a superior may cause that person to lose face. In fact, this effect is probably the source of the problem with the participation and feedback techniques that were tried. The Chinese employees are unlikely to provide suggestions for improving the production process because it could have the related effect of showing you (the manager) up. In cultures like these, the manager is presumed to have the necessary expertise, and attempts to show otherwise often result in loss of face. Incidentally, this may also be the reason you received an ambiguous evaluation rather than a more direct and somewhat negative appraisal. If a local or third-country national delivered the feedback, that person would also be reluctant to provide the direct feedback that you as an American might be used to. As we saw in this chapter, preferences for feedback and ways that it is provided differ a good deal among cultures. This is why a further evaluation provided by one's home-country manager might yield valuable information for the expatriate. Finally, as we found out in the second half of this chapter, the PRC can be a surprisingly expensive place for an expatriate to live. If your firm did not use the balance sheet model of compensation, then you may suffer financial as well as performance problems.

International Development
Giving Negative Feedback across Cultures

Purpose

To explore the managerial task of giving performance feedback to employees; to consider how to make feedback useful, especially across cultures; and to practice the skills of giving helpful feedback.

Instructions

This year your company, after careful consideration, has instituted a 360-degree feedback performance evaluation system. It was agreed that one of your jobs as a manager would be to meet with each employee individually to go over his or her results.

You are about to meet with Chris Damone, a line supervisor who has been with the company for seven years. A review of Chris's past performance evaluations indicates an employee who has been reliable and has had above-average productivity. Results from Chris's 360, however, have a definitely negative consistency, i.e., avoids trying new ideas, uses coercion with peers and subordinates, doesn't listen well, ignores feedback, often fails to return phone calls or other inquiries, blames mistakes on others or tries to cover them up, and is often unavailable when questions arise. In addition to this feedback, you are aware that Chris has been an outspoken opponent of the company's affirmative action policy and was particularly angry to have been passed over for a recent promotion in favor of a minority employee.

Part A: Evaluations of Americans

Prepare an action plan regarding this situation (15 minutes). Working in groups of three to five, prepare a plan that will help Chris improve. It might be useful to assign someone in your group to be the spokesperson who will eventually summarize your plan to the class.

Consider some of all of these questions as you work on the plan:

1. What could the manager have done differently, if anything, to clearly present the problems with Chris's behavior? Did the manager check frequently with Chris to be sure that the message being sent was the one being received?
2. Were Chris and the manager able to listen to one another without becoming confrontational or defensive?
3. Are the goals of the action plan clear and helpful?
4. How should the manager proceed as the goals set with Chris are met or fail to be met?

Part B: Cross-Cultural Evaluation

Now prepare your plan to help present feedback to an employee in the Middle East. Consider the situation regarding Chris to apply here. As you prepare your action plan and recommendations, consider some or all of these questions:

1. What could/should the manager have done differently with this employee from the Middle East?
2. What are the key differences between this plan and the one you devised for the U.S. employee?
3. What were the cultural differences that led you to make changes in the plan here?

Source: French, W. (1998). *Human resources management* (4th Ed.), 362–363. Boston: Houghton Mifflin. This exercise was originally prepared by Janet W. Wohlberg, The Rappay Group, 1075 Main Street, Williamstown, MA 01267. Used with permission.

From Theory to Practice
Assembling an Expatriate Compensation Package

Purpose

To improve your understanding of how salary, tax, and living cost differentials across countries make it very difficult to put together an expatriate compensation package.

Instructions

This exercise involves completing a report that summa-rizes your research on the compensation of expatriates assigned to different countries. Depending upon your instructor's directions, this exercise can be completed in small groups or as an individual exercise/case. Regardless, imagine that an American firm has plans to send a manager on an expatriate assignment to one of two foreign countries and would like your advice about how to structure a compensation package. Your instructor will indicate which pairs of cities and countries are being considered for the expatriate's posting. Unless your instructor specifies otherwise, you can assume that the potential expatriate is based in Chicago, is married with two school-age children, and has a base salary of $150,000. Of this amount, approximately 60% is spent on living expenses, about 30% goes to cover various taxes, and the remaining 10% is allotted to savings.

As noted in the chapter, living expenses are complex and vary dramatically from country to country. Your report will certainly have to account for transportation, clothing, housing, food, and the many other elements that could play a role in this category. Remember that the tax situation for many foreign assignments is complex, and this will have to be factored into your report. All in all, how should the compensation packages differ across the two countries (if at all)? Along the way, be sure to describe why there are differences across countries (or why not) in the specific aspects of the package. In addition to the text and other reference sources, you may find many of the web sites below useful for completing your report:

1. **The U.S. Department of State Foreign Per Diem Page**

   http://www.state.gov/m/a/als/prdm/

   This site provides cost estimates for living in almost every country in the world. A related site presents more detail on indexes of living costs, cost differentials, housing, and more (see http://www.state.gov/www/perdiems/quarterly_reports).

2. **STAT-USA/Internet (a service of the U.S. Department of Commerce)**

   http://www.stat-usa.gov/tradtest.nsf

   Here you'll find country and market research information as well as detailed summaries of

general background information on most countries in the world.

3. **International Tax and Accounting Site Directory**

   http://www.taxsites.com/international.html#countries

   This is an international tax site directory, with country-specific information.

4. **OECD Data Site, Purchase Power Parity**

   http://www.oecd.org/pdf/M00009000/M00009294.pdf

   This site presents data that allows one to compare the cost of a basket of consumer goods and services across a number of countries.

5. **Global Relocation Survey (sponsored by GMAC and SHRM)**

   http://www.windhamint.com/Surveys.asp

   A nearly 80-page report on trends and costs in relocating personnel all over the globe.

6. **W. M. Mercer Companies, Worldwide Quality of Living Survey**

   http://www.wmmercer.com/global/english/resource/index4.html

7. **The Expat Forum**

   www.expatforum.com

Managing Work Groups across Cultures: From Small Teams to Large Labor Forces

International Challenge

Teams at BP

LEARNING OBJECTIVES

After reading this chapter, you should be able to

- Recognize the impact of groups in a multicultural environment.

- Identify the various meanings that cultures place on groups.

- Be aware of the promise and pitfalls presented by diversity in and among groups.

- Appreciate the importance of relations between groups of employees and management across cultures/countries.

- Understand the various forms and effects of unions across a large number of countries.

- Identify several forms of employee input, beyond unions, that can lead to agreements.

LIKE MANY FIRMS headquartered in the European Union, British Petroleum (BP) has to be concerned with how teams of workers from different countries and cultures get along with each other. In their relatively new finance center in Brussels, they asked about forty professionals from thirteen different countries to work closely together. Prior to this effort, they had been fairly autonomous, working within their own countries and providing their own finance and accounting services internally. BP had successfully experimented with a multicultural group in its London operations and wished to extend this effort to serve its European operations. Rob Ruijter, a Dutchman, was appointed team leader. Mr. Ruijter, himself an experienced expatriate, knew that the going would not be easy. He recognized that there were opportunities offered by diversity, and he wished to capitalize on these. He also knew that these cultural differences had great potential for creating problems that can reduce group productivity. He wanted to avoid this potential disaster by making sure the team became closeknit as soon as possible. As you read this chapter, think about some of the practical things that Mr. Ruijter and BP could do to avoid problems and to capitalize on the possibilities offered by group diversity.[1]

Groups are the basic building blocks of organizations. A group is defined as two or more people who interact together in order to pursue common goals. This is a very broad definition that could apply to everything from a small group of friends who gets together socially all the way to a world wide labor union comprising thousands of people. And this is in fact the scope of Chapter 14, which we will approach in two main parts. First, we will focus on smaller work groups and the impact that culture may have on the way that they function. For example, we will look at how work teams might operate differently in various cultures. The question of how to manage a culturally diverse group or workforce is very important. We will review a variety of different team-building methods that can be used to make these diverse groups function better.

The second half of this chapter, while still concerned with how groups operate across culture, will shift gears. In particular, we will focus on the larger issue of relations between groups of workers and management, within and across countries and cultures. First, we will look at the myriad different approaches that are taken to labor relations across borders. One of the most important group issues in labor relations is the connection between management and unions. In some countries, maintaining this link has been a smoother and more successful process than in others. We will also look at the general issue of employee participation—or, as it is often called around the world, industrial democracy. We will look at different forms of industrial democracy, their effectiveness, and the cultural setting in which they take place. Finally, we'll examine how frequently conflict, such as strikes and lockouts, can occur in different countries. In doing so, we will look at the export and import of industrial relations policies by both the United States and foreign countries.

Managing Groups across Cultures

Groups are important to the life of most organizations—whether those groups and firms are multinational or not. There are task forces, cross-functional teams, self-directed work teams, special committees, boards, production crews, and many more kinds of groups that people get together in to accomplish goals. Why do we have so many different organizational forms for interacting with other people? One major reason is probably that groups offer extraordinary opportunity to get something done; they may offer more than the sum of their parts. Groups offer the potential for pooling knowledge, better decision making, and more; the result can be a harder-working, smarter, and more productive set of people. This is the promise that a group holds. Many of us, of course, have had group experiences that have been singularly unproductive. The real challenge for the manager is to avoid the latter and instead set the stage so that the promise of groups can be realized. As we have pointed out in earlier chapters on communication, training, and performance appraisal, the challenge that a manager ordinarily faces in these areas is magnified several fold in multicultural groups. We will review cultural differences in the ways groups typically operate and then outline a set of variables and techniques that allow managers to build more effective cross-cultural work groups.

Differences in Group Behavior across Cultures

There are differences among cultures in how important groups are to the lives of people. Let's explore the relative strength of the group in various cultures.

Individuals and collectivists   As you may remember from Chapters 4 and 11, one of the most important cultural distinctions is the difference between individualism and collectivism. To refresh your memory, examples of individualistic countries include the United States, Britain, Netherlands, and Belgium, whereas collectivist countries include Taiwan, Mexico, the Philippines, Japan, and many South American countries. You will also recall that in the collectivist countries people see group goals as more important than individual goals. Of course, the definition of a group can range from a

These Chinese business people may draw sharper distinctions between in-groups and out-groups than their American counterparts.
© Yang Liu/CORBIS

family, a clan or tribe, to an organization, and different effects may be found for each type of group. In individualistic countries, people are expected to take care of themselves and much emphasis is placed on autonomy, individual achievement, and privacy. People in individualistic cultures tend to apply the same value standards to everyone, whereas collectivists apply different standards to their in-groups and out-groups.

In-groups and out-groups   Some see this last point as the key element that distinguishes individualistic from collectivist cultures.[2] Collectivists put great emphasis on the needs of the in-group over those of the individual person, and they value cooperation with in-group members over their own self-interest. Of course, all groups are not the same for collectivists. Some, for example, place their family first (e.g., the Chinese), whereas others place their organization first (perhaps the Japanese). Regardless of how the in-group is defined, collectivists draw much sharper boundaries between their own in-group and out-groups than do individualists. The distinction between family and neighbors in collectivistic cultures is large, whereas in individualistic cultures it is relatively small. In fact, we have already reviewed some research that speaks to these points. Recall, for example, that the self-attitudes of collectivists seem to be more influenced by their standing in groups than is true for individualists. When they are asked to describe themselves, collectivists are much more likely to use group-based descriptions (e.g., "I am happy when I work with friends") than are individualists ("I am a happy person"). Likewise, we also discussed perceptual and motivational differences between cultures that differ in level of individualism.

One thing we did not discuss in detail was the pervasive effect of this cultural norm regarding groups on the lives of people in collectivist cultures. We do not mean to imply that individualists do not group together to accomplish tasks. Clearly they do. What we do mean is that when people get together, the process of group interaction differs substantially between these two types of cultures. And, apparently, one learns early on in life how this group process is supposed to proceed. One study, for example, looked at group interaction patterns of 10–12-year-old Chinese and American children.[3] Even though both groups worked on the same type of task, the Chinese children approached the task in a cooperative, group-enhancing way, whereas the American kids chose strategies that reflected self-enhancing, competitive motives. This is consistent both with our American upbringing and with the traditional Chinese saying, "Friendship first and competition second."[4]

Group Productivity across Cultures

How might groups affect the process, quality, and quantity of work done in various cultures? The findings in this area are complex, but there are some general results that can be summarized.

Social loafing   In research done in the United States, people are more productive when working alone than when they work together with others in groups. This phenomena is known as **social loafing**. Apparently people loaf or freeload because they assume the group will get the job done and because they can then redirect their effort toward their own goals—even if that just involves relaxing. Similar results have been found in over fifty different studies, encompassing many different types of jobs and organizations but comprising mostly American workers.

INTERNATIONAL INSIGHTS

Just in Case You Were Napping the Day They Talked about Collectivism: Hell Camp for Japanese Managers

AS WE HAVE SAID, Japan is a culture that emphasizes collectivism—smooth and harmonious interpersonal relations. In spite of this emphasis, most of which starts early in life, some Japanese managers are sent "back to school" to get more group/collectivism training. This training is often known as Hell Camp, and it involves some very rough treatment that Japanese managers often submit to in order to move ahead in their organizations.

Hell Camp is a mix of boot camp and Outward Bound. It is designed to toughen up employees and to tighten the bonds between employee and company. The camps are run by private companies and involve a two-week long series of often humiliating exercises. For example, a group of employees might be sent down to a very busy train station and told to sing out their company song (yes, some companies have their own songs). Additionally, if they do not sing loud enough, they are berated by their trainer, often to the point of tears. The sight of some of these relatively high-ranking employees crying publicly because their trainer is not pleased is something to be seen!

If their trainer is pleased, however, they might be permitted to remove one of the many badges of shame they must put on at the beginning of the training. They must successfully remove all the badges in order to graduate from the program. Graduation means a successful reentry into the company with new and better heights to be reached. Failure to graduate often means returning to camp sometime later and starting the training again from scratch. After several failures, an employee will not be permitted to retry. This is a very sad occasion for those people because it also signals an end to their rise in the company.[5]

But is this social loafing phenomenon a uniquely American effect? There is good reason to believe it is, because Americans have had their trouble with teams and teamwork, and because of the great emphasis U. S. culture places on individuality. Other cultures (e.g., Japan) are apparently much more team oriented and their work is organized in this manner. Research supports this idea. A group of Japanese researchers, for instance, found the opposite of what was typically found with American groups: Japanese perform better in groups than when working alone.[6] Other studies show that social loafing occurs among Americans (individualists) but not among Chinese (collectivists).[7]

In-groups and social loafing   One researcher took these findings one step further.[8] The social loafing research that we have discussed thus far only compared people who were working alone or in groups. And at least one of these studies reported social loafing effects for collectivists (Taiwanese) in addition to their other findings.[9] Moreover, "group" effects do not always favor collectivists. For example, research shows that there is surprisingly poor communication among employees of the same company who are members of different in-groups.[10] Likewise, another study found that collectivists were actually more competitive than individualists when facing members of out-groups.[11] All this led one researcher to wonder about how the type of group would affect social loafing. He observed that in some of the existing studies, groups were assembled from a set of people with no real connection (out-group), whereas other research studied intact groups that existed prior to their participation in the study (in-groups such as intact work groups or an existing class of students). He predicted that collectivists would be more likely to loaf when they participate in a group that is of no special significance to them (out-group).

To examine this question, the performance of over 160 managers from China, Israel, and the United States was studied.[12] Some of these managers were asked to work alone, whereas others were placed in two different group situations. An **in-group** situation was created by leading those groups to believe that they shared a number of similar characteristics that usually lead to close friendships. An **out-group** condition was also created by telling managers that other group members had very different traits and characteristics and that they came from very different backgrounds. In all cases, the managers worked on simulated management tasks such as rating job applications. When they did work with a group, the managers always worked with their fellow nationals because the researcher wanted to study the effect of country or culture on performance in groups. Chinese and Israelis were chosen to participate because they come from collectivist cultures and Americans were chosen because they are the prototypic individualistic culture.

The findings were interesting. First, the results of earlier studies were replicated by showing that there was a reduction in group performance (loafing) for Americans but not for the Israeli or Chinese managers. What's more, the collectivists also showed social loafing when they performed with an out-group. The collectivists (from China and Israel) were likely to reduce their input into a work team when that group held few ties of any importance to them. When the collectivists worked with an in-group, however, their performance was not reduced.

Implications of social loafing research   What does this all mean for the practicing manager? This line of research has a number of interesting practical implications. First, work strategies that are based on individual performance may not be effective in collectivist cultures. For example, the belief that individually based incentives would be maximally effective in China or Israel fails to recognize the impact and importance of groups to these cultures. Importing an American pay-for-performance approach to individuals in China, for example, may be counterproductive. The research also shows that adopting any old group incentive plan could also be shortsighted. The study clearly found that the type of group in which collectivists worked, not just being in a group per se, affected performance. A natural collection of individuals, an in-group, is where you're likely to see the performance jumps in a collectivist culture.[13]

On the surface, you probably would expect many work groups in collectivist cultures such as China would be composed of in-group members. This would be expected because in-groups hire people who are similar to them; once hired, they tend to be committed and stay with this group much longer than with an out-group. Based on this reasoning, an American expatriate manager might be wise, for example, to employ group-based incentive schemes (see Chapter 11, where we discussed motivation). In many rapidly developing economies like India, in contrast, work and travel patterns are changing in response to job opportunities. In China, for example, although one needs a work permit to move from a rural location to a city like Shanghai or Guangzhou, there is still remarkable (albeit, illegal) movement of the labor force. Therefore, one would likely expect an increasing diversity of work groups, even in a country such as China. This means that American expatriate managers will have to be especially clever and insightful when they seek to introduce new group techniques in such settings.[14]

Finally, it is interesting to reflect on the use of group-based management schemes in the highly individualistic United States. Various team approaches to work in the United States appear to be increasing; current estimates are that about 10 percent of employees in U.S. firms are organized into units or self-directed work teams.[15] One implication of the group research we discussed is that these team-based schemes are less likely to be successful than the old-fashioned person-based approaches common in the United States. On the other hand, the United States has a great deal of cultural heterogeneity and there will be even more through the next decade. So a great challenge for U.S. managers (and foreign expatriate managers) is to understand and match methods and tasks together. One area where this cultural mix has already taken place is among flight crews of commercial airlines. The following International Insights illustrates some of the challenges presented to such groups.

Diversity: When Different Cultural Groups Come into Contact

Until now, we have talked about differences in group behavior across cultures. There are many times, of course, when different cultural groups come into contact with one another, such as during negotiations or when they're members of the same flight crew. There are and will continue to be times when you will have to form and lead an intercultural group as a manager.

Diversity in work groups   As implied by the material in the last two chapters, as an expatriate you will most certainly be asked to manage a diverse group of workers, including local nationals, third country nationals, and perhaps other U.S. expatriates. Likewise, you don't have to be an expatriate to deal with these intercultural problems; issues of diversity are important for a manager dealing with foreign nationals, immigrants at home, and members of minority groups.

Assumptions about diversity   This does not mean, however, that U.S. companies and managers are the best at dealing with diversity issues. One main reason that the

INTERNATIONAL INSIGHTS

The Best Care in the Air Might Be Cross-Cultural

ONE ACTIVITY THAT is naturally group oriented is the operation of large commercial jet aircraft. The flight crew of some modern aircraft can reach and exceed twenty people, not counting the ground crew that is necessary to operate smoothly. Interestingly, an analysis of commercial aviation accidents from 1959 through 1990 showed that flight crew behavior, rather than technical failures, have been the cause of about 70 percent of all accidents! Increasingly, interpersonal topics such as communication, leadership, and decision making have been studied in an attempt to reduce problems that lead to accidents. And as we have documented, many of these interpersonal topics are affected by culture.

Following this reasoning, one study looked at the attitudes of flight crews from eight different countries (the U.S. and seven Asian/collectivist countries).[16] Commercial aviation is a highly regulated industry, and as a result, flight crews perform very similar tasks in very similar environments. So, because their job differences are minimized across culture, any differences in attitudes noted among these workers are probably culturally based. The researchers asked all crew members, including pilots and flight attendants, to complete a standardized questionnaire about what is optimal behavior on the flight deck. The results were very interesting. For one, Asian pilots and flight attendants were more similar in their attitudes than were these same American groups. This finding might reflect the now familiar need for social harmony among collectivist cultures—in this case manifested in similar attitudes. As a result, there was more consistency in attitudes among Asian flight crews.

Additionally, the results showed that U.S. flight attendants preferred a captain who encouraged their questions but who also took charge in any emergency. U.S. pilots actually stood out from all the other groups, including the U.S. flight attendants. They generally showed highly individualistic attitudes, reflective of the solo flyer of the old days of aviation. In the Asian cultures, however, both the attendants and pilots preferred to see an autocratic but communicative captain in almost all circumstances.

These differences present problems for the most common training method for today's flight crews. This approach, called *crew resource management* (CRM), emphasizes recognition and acceptance of crew/team interconnection and the free flow of information among the crew. Accordingly, CRM appears to reflect collectivism and low power distance. As such, the technique may create problems or be an advantage, depending upon the culture of the crew being trained. Highly individualist U.S. pilots are asked to forego their "flyboy" images and work more in teams. Although this may be tough for them, CRM training can capitalize at the same time on the American orientation toward low power distance via their natural tendency to share flight information. And although Asian crews appear to be more team oriented and thus compatible with CRM training, their high-power-distance orientation may discourage the open sharing of information. As the authors of the study point out, CRM training in forceful action by junior officers may be too foreign for a Chinese flight crew to adopt. At the same time, the CRM concept of group input may be too difficult for American pilots to accept. So in an emergency both groups have both assets and liabilities to fall back on. The challenge for crew resource management is to make sure all aspects of the training sink in to crews from all cultures.

United States may be behind other countries in dealing with diversity issues is the philosophy or assumptions we hold about the topic. Exhibit 14.1 presents a set of assumptions about diversity that an expert contends are common but misguided in considering the issue of diversity.[17] The exhibit also presents more appropriate assumptions that better characterize the impact of diversity. It is common in the United States (and other countries as well) to assume similarity in behavior and attitudes (see the first column of Exhibit 14.1). For instance, in response to a story about how we were befriended on a recent trip to China by a local resident, one person responded, "It just goes to show you that people are the same everywhere."

EXHIBIT 14.1

Philosophies about Diversity

Common and Misleading Assumptions	Uncommon but More Applicable Assumptions
Homogeneity: The melting pot. We are all the same.	**Heterogeneity:** Cultural complexity. There are many different cultural groups; people have similarities to and differences from me.
Parochialism: There is only one way. We neither recognize nor entertain other ways of working or doing things.	**Compound:** Our way is not the only way. There are many culturally different ways of reaching the same goal and living life.
Ethnocentrism: There is one best way. Our way is the best way and all other ways are inferior to ours in reaching a goal.	**Contingency:** Our way is one possible way. There are many other different but equally good ways (culturally contingent) to reach the goal.

Source: Adler, N. J. (1991). *International dimensions of organizational behavior.* Boston: PWS-Kent. Reprinted by permission.

Now, while he may be partially correct, and while he was certainly trying to be complimentary, this statement represents the **homogeneity** perspective. Applied to multicultural groups, it would suggest that with enough interaction, the group itself would blend many different perspectives into one. (The *E pluribus unum* motto that appears on U.S. coins illustrates this philosophy since it means "out of many, one."). This could be a very misleading assumption if widely and uniformly applied.[18] A less commonly held assumption, but probably more appropriate, is that of **heterogeneity**. This refers to a situation of cultural pluralism or multiplexity. Even if homogeneity eventually does come about in your particular multicultural group, it is probably best to assume heterogeneity to start with. Likewise, issues of **parochialism** and **ethnocentrism** can also be problematic and are best approached by more open and different paths to a goal (see Exhibit 14.1).

Minuses and pluses of diversity   As Exhibit 14.1 suggests, managers who are responsible for building work groups that are composed of people from different cultures have their hands full. In fact, beyond one's philosophical perspective, a large number of practical problems need to be overcome in order for groups to run smoothly and effectively. Exhibit 14.2 lists some of these road blocks. Some could be predicted simply from a consideration of the word *diversity* itself. Our dictionary defines the word as "varied, dissimilar, and divergent." In general, these three adjectives conjure up images of heavy sledding for a manager. In fact, one expert reports that while all sixty of the international executives in her study could list a disadvantage associated with cultural diversity in groups (many offered multiple negatives), less than one-third could think of even one advantage. One French executive said, "I have been involved in many situations over the years, but I can't think of one made easier because it involved more than one culture." Likewise, a Danish executive stated "I can think of no situation . . . where managing became easier or more effective because it involved people from more than one culture."

Perhaps one reason that disadvantages are easy to recall is that they are so salient. Exhibit 14.2, for example, points out that communication itself is more problematic in such groups. Likewise, the potential confusion and possible, even outright, conflict that

EXHIBIT 14.2

Cultural Diversity in Groups: Advantages and Disadvantages

Advantages	Disadvantages
Better understanding of foreign employees	Increased ambiguity/confusion re: norms and leadership
More effective work relations with foreign clients	Greater potential for miscommunication
Better marketing ability to foreign customers	More time needed to manage cultural differences
More creative ideas produced over time	Potential for lower group cohesion
Decisions stand the test of time and and location	Harder to agree on specific decision

Source: Adler, N. J. (1991). *International dimensions of organizational behavior.* Boston: PWS-Kent. Reprinted by permission.

can emerge with cross-cultural groups stands out and is easy to remember. In contrast, the benefits associated with group diversity (see Exhibit 14.1 also) take longer to manifest and are more difficult to observe.

Since the advantages are more difficult to think of even for professionals, let us spend a minute discussing Exhibit 14.2. Imagine two different types of groups, each working on developing a new type of computer chip. One group consists of about twenty-five American scientists who are working on the project in upstate New York. While there are some women on the project, most of the team members are men and all are Americans. Will there be problems among these relatively homogenous project team members? Yes, undoubtedly. There are the usual problems we are all familiar with when we work closely with other people. Now, however, consider the same problem, but with a change of players. Let's say that this project is being tackled as a cooperative alliance among three multinationals—German, Japanese, and American. As shown in column 2 of Exhibit 14.2, now we can expect many more problems. For one, we know from our discussion of communication in Chapter 6 that there will be difficulties in this area. Likewise, each culture has different ways of working and of leading the work that is done. Finally, sorting out all these things will take more time than if most people already abide by the same norms and speak the same language. On the other hand, the diversity brought to the computer chip project offers the potential for many creative and inventive design solutions. The many different perspectives brought to the problem offer a kind of built-in brainstorming—the very kind of activity that can lead to creative ideas.[19] Likewise, if the product is marketed, it will likely have wide appeal. The following International Insights, in fact, presents more detail about this very real situation faced by Siemens, Toshiba, and IBM in their recent joint project.

Using diversity to your advantage   There are now a very large number of research studies on the effects of group diversity on productivity. What we know is that

INTERNATIONAL INSIGHTS

Cross-Cultural Teams Open in the Catskills

A FEW YEARS AGO, three companies who ordinarily competed with one another entered into a strategic alliance to develop a revolutionary computer memory chip. The Triad (as they call themselves) is composed of employees from Siemens AG of Germany, Toshiba of Japan, and IBM of the United States and they work in upstate New York at an IBM facility. The Triad has undertaken a joint project that is relatively unprecedented in its scope. Nearly 100 scientists were formed into teams to represent the three companies (and three continents) in this project. Initially, some of the originators of the project were worried that the teams' diverse cultural backgrounds might create problems. It turns out that they had reason to worry.

Take, for example, the Toshiba scientists. The Germans were shocked to find them closing their eyes and apparently sleeping during important meetings. This, however, is a common practice for overburdened Japanese workers when the discussion doesn't center on them. The Japanese themselves, who ordinarily work in large teams, found it very difficult to sit in small, individual offices and speak English. As a result, they often withdrew when they could to the more comfortable confines of all-Japanese groups. Further undercutting any team synergy were the feelings of the American scientists. They felt that the Germans planned way too much and that the Japanese—who typically like to review proposals constantly—wouldn't make a specific or clear decision. The Germans and the Japanese complained that their American counterparts didn't spend enough time getting to know them, either at work or in socializing after work.[20] Unfortunately, all this led to a climate of misunderstanding and mistrust. There were even some suspicions that information and progress were being held back from the group by various company cliques.

In theory, the pooling of a diverse and intelligent group of people together to design new advanced technology is supposed to work. These are exactly the circumstances that are likely to produce major creative insights. The reason it hasn't worked, says management, is that people have wanted and been able to stay in and around their separate groups. The project is not doomed, however, nor is it considered a failure. Work is on schedule and in some smaller areas is a little bit ahead of schedule. But management is disappointed that they haven't seen the kind of major creative leaps that they were hoping for. In fact, a senior manager said that if it weren't for the financial savings inherent in joint projects like this, he thinks that IBM might be able to do as well or better on their own.

In analyzing the situation, the lack of attention to group interaction and team building variables is seen as the culprit. Apparently, although there was great effort on the technical and logistical side of things, there was little if any attention paid to team building and understanding different approaches to work. Instead, the three companies gave their employees the normal courses on working and living abroad. Mr. Takaaki Tanaka, a human resources executive for Toshiba, said, "We should have done more cooperative efforts with HR people from Siemens and IBM to develop joint training programs." Siemens also briefed their employees on living abroad and a bit on what they call the American "hamburger style of management." Americans, they said, start their criticism gently. They start with a "how's the family" smalltalk; that's the "top of the hamburger bun." Then they go right to the meat, namely, the criticism; it's then topped with more bun (words of encouragement). With Germans, they go on, it's all meat, and with Japanese you have to learn to smell the meat. Despite all the obstacles, work is underway to try to overcome their differences. And team members say that they have learned a lot—both about technology and about cooperating with different groups of people.[21]

---

the particular composition of a group does impact performance. Across a number of ways of defining diversity (gender, age, culture), the more varied a group is, the more difficult time they have (at least initially).[22] More diverse groups have trouble communicating with one another, they have more difficulty working as a unit (becoming cohesive), and they take longer to set up a useful structure or way of doing things than do more homogenous groups.[23] Nevertheless, once an understanding and structure gets in place, the diverse group becomes as effective as the homogenous group. Because of their ability to bring more to the group table, however, diverse groups sometimes perform even better than other groups. This is particularly the case when the group is working on projects requiring creativity and problem solving rather than simple routine tasks.[24] This is exactly what one study of the functioning of top management teams found— that cultural diversity was responsible for higher team performance and that when conflict did occur, it was also more functional.[25]

Finally, another set of studies suggests that the extent of differences in the group should be studied over time.[26] These researchers found that while homogeneous teams (similar on demographic characteristics and nationality) outperformed diverse groups at first, over time the performance of highly heterogeneous teams improved and equaled that of the less diverse teams. Interestingly, teams defined as "moderately" heterogeneous did not perform nearly as well as the other two types of teams. Apparently, teams consisting of two main subgroups don't appear to be particularly motivated to integrate with one another, but instead rely on the presence of others in their subgroup for information, company, and the like. In contrast, multiple subgroups (very heterogeneous teams) don't allow people to fall back so easily on the comfort of their familiar in-group. Gradually, people move their focus from their individual group to that of a larger whole. Apparently, even the addition of a third subgroup can offset any negative effects that might occur with just two main subgroups.[27] What all this means is that the clever manager can possibly offset some of the short-term problems associated with group diversity and reap the more long-term benefits.

How can you cleverly manage diversity to your advantage? It is no easy task, to be sure. Many of us might naturally use demographic and other obvious differences as "psychological fault lines," akin to the same concept in geology. If these differences become too salient or important, they may act as dividing lines that split a team into a bunch of subgroups.[28] But many people agree that to be effective, multicultural teams must be able to capitalize on their chief advantage—the ability to produce creative solutions to problems. One expert suggests several guidelines that should be considered to get the most out of multicultural teams:[29]

- **Choose appropriate tasks:** It would be a mistake to choose members of a multicultural team based solely on their ethnicity. Instead, members who have similarly high ability levels but diverse attitudes and behaviors, should be chosen.
- **Explicit recognition of differences:** Instead of minimizing or overlooking cultural differences, members should be encouraged to recognize and describe those differences. This will get team members on the road to understanding those differences. Hopefully, the group can then start to be open to what team members of different cultures can contribute. A corresponding disadvantage of this technique is that it may accentuate the fault lines we just discussed. So this must be done carefully.
- **Adoption of a Vision/Mission:** Because multicultural teams come from diverse backgrounds, they often have difficulty agreeing on how to focus their efforts. There may be as many targets are there are group members; this is in fact the creative possibility of the multicultural team. A side effect of this advantage is that such teams may flounder aimlessly. Accordingly, specific meetings and time spent on hashing out a broad goal that goes beyond individual differences will go a long way toward making the multicultural team effective.
- **Equal Status among Team Members:** Unequal status or power among team members can be a problem. Under these circumstances, we know that the very

creativity that is sought from a multicultural team could be stifled because of pressures (implicit or otherwise) from more powerful members. It is common among international teams to make someone from the parent company the leader of the team. Although there may be good reason to make a manager from headquarters the leader, doing this can make the parent culture dominate the proceedings. This kind of domination is even more likely to happen if the team is composed of people from high-power-distance cultures. Although the team may have a lot to contribute, the strong norm of deferring to the leader in most matters will suppress their potential contribution.[30]

● **Feedback:** Culturally diverse teams have difficulty agreeing on the benefit of various ideas—perhaps because the methods they use to gauge the benefits are so different. Accordingly, to develop similar judgment criteria, it helps to give frequent feedback on their ideas and progress to produce greater cohesion and speed along this process.

Managing the diversity that comes with using multicultural teams is difficult. Nevertheless, there is the promise that, managed correctly, these teams could have much to contribute. It is important to recognize that these teams are only a small part of the much larger organizational and labor "team." We will now turn our attention to these related but larger issues.

Labor Relations in and across Cultures

Working with smaller multicultural teams is difficult enough. But often there are even larger group issues to deal with. These may involve groups within whole companies, industries, or even countries. The relations between and among these groups are much more complex for several reasons. For one, these groups are often much larger than the multicultural teams we have been discussing thus far. Also, the relationships among these larger groups are often very highly regulated. There are constraints over what groups of workers are legally allowed to do, and there are similar rules governing what companies—multinational or otherwise—can do. Finally, even beyond the legal constraints on these groups, there may also be alliances or connections that have to be kept in mind. For example, if your employee union is international, the specific negotiating tactics with your company might be directed or obliged to follow the overall guiding principles of the union. Or, from a multinational's perspective, they might be able to secure concessions from employees and their unions if they have a credible threat of moving their operations elsewhere.

These topics are of central concern to the field of labor or industrial relations. In the most general sense, this topic deals with employee-employer relationships, which can vary dramatically across countries. For example, the regulations and practices of labor relations are very different in France than they are in Spain, even though these countries share a border. To address these topics, we will first outline the perspectives of management and workers. We will then discuss agreements or structures that have been devised for soliciting employee input or control. These methods include not only labor unions, but also many other agreements and mechanisms that companies have devised or been forced to adopt. Despite the sometimes best intentions of firms, unions, and governments, there are times when conflicts arise. Sometimes agreement just can't be reached and the conflict reaches the point where action is taken, either by workers (strikes) or by management (lockouts). We will discuss each of these topics in turn.

Management and Worker Perspectives on Labor Relations

Workers in many different countries and cultures are concerned with issues such as pay level, job security, benefits, and working conditions. They often form unions with other employees in order to have power over these important work outcomes. And they often wish to extend this power in order to have a say in important decisions facing the firm, such as whether a particular unit should be cut back. In other cases, complex laws control firms in ways that effectively serve the function of a union—even when no organized labor groups exist.

Either way, groups of workers have basically one main method of getting their way on key issues—by threatening to reduce work output or stop it all together. This threat may be less credible, however, when the employer is a multinational. A large multinational has many resources at its disposal and thus may be able to outlast a union strike by simply absorbing losses at a particular location. Or, if they are flexible enough, they may be able to increase production temporarily at another facility so that little if any loss needs to be absorbed. Worst yet, from the employees' perspective, the firm may threaten to move its operations to another country in response to the strike, or it may proactively do so in order to reduce wages or benefits. The multinational, therefore, has considerable power—more than a solely domestic firm—in controlling employees.

Hyster Corporation of Portland, Oregon is a case in point. This firm had a forklift-truck plant in Irvine, Scotland. They had some good news for their 500 employees—with a grant from the British government they were ready to invest $60 million in the Irvine plant, creating another 100 jobs for Scottish workers. There was a big catch, however, and this is the problem that unions face when dealing with a large multinational. The catch was that the increase in production would create an overcapacity in its European operations. To reduce the overcapacity, Hyster would have to cut back production at its factory in the Netherlands and move that to Irvine. However, workers at Hyster-Scotland would have to take a 14 percent pay cut. They had 48 hours to decide.

As if this weren't enough, the next day each employee got a letter from the company. The letter said, "Hyster is not convinced at this time that Irvine is the best of the many alternatives open to it. It has not made up its mind. The location of the plant to lead Europe is still open." At the bottom of the page was a spot asking them to vote yes or no for the proposition. Only eleven people voted no. Workers complained that they had had no warning and no input. Although Hyster's employees were not unionized, many felt it would not have made a difference: "It was an industrial rape," "It was do-or-else," said some employees.[31]

To combat this considerable power of the multinational, unions and other employee groups have tried to get control via legal means. Many countries, for example, have enacted permanent employment laws. After a probationary period, it becomes extremely difficult to discharge an employee. And even if those difficult circumstances are realized, the employee is often due large amounts of severance pay. The following International Insights illustrates this situation for German workers. In Belgium, for example, an employee making $50,000 a year would be entitled to termination benefits of nearly $100,000 (see Exhibit 14.3).[32] Likewise, companies must often obey other nationally mandated rules regarding treatment of employees. Even beyond these, however, unions may have some power to wield. For example, if the parts produced in an English factory are necessary for production to continue in the firm's Belgian plant, then the union has a source of power. This is exactly what happened to Ford. A strike in Britain forced an almost immediate shutdown of its plant in Belgium. Some feel that this interconnection among plants forced Ford to a rapid settlement.[33]

EXHIBIT 14.3

Severance Payments Required for European Employees

Country	Payments (US$) by Seniority of Employee	
	Younger Employee*	**Middle-Aged Employee***
Italy	45,000	130,000
Spain	56,000	125,000
Belgium	40,000	95,000
Portugal	38,000	83,000
Greece	28,000	67,000
Germany	15,000	25,000
United Kingdom	12,000	19,000
Ireland	8,000	13,000

*Younger employee assumes age 35, fifteen years' service, earning $30,000; Middle-aged employee assumes age 45, twenty years' service, earning $50,000. Each country may require additional benefits that are not specified here.

Source: ———. (1992). Employee dismissals can prove costly for companies in Europe. *HR Focus*, August, 18. Reprinted by permission © IOMA.

Labor Unions across Countries

We have shown that both groups—employees and firms—have some ways to exert influence over the other. Despite this give and take, most experts feel that the MNC has significantly greater overall influence than any employee group or union.[35] Like many other things we have studied, however, this influence varies among countries. Accordingly, in this next section we want to review some of the differences among countries in the structure of employee input and control.

As suggested, there are many mechanisms by which employees try to wrest control of the workplace away from management. Of course, the first method we all probably think of is a union. Unions in the United States were originally established to bring about reform in the workplace before laws existed to protect worker interests and rights. Now, U.S. unions have a relatively high profile, and that profile is not altogether positive. In fact, national surveys indicate a relatively negative view of unions by Americans. Perhaps this attitude can partly explain why union membership in the United States has been steadily declining in recent years. In fact, today only about 14 percent of the total United States workforce are union members.

While other industrialized countries have also seen a general decline in union membership, the overall percentage in still high. Among the U.S.'s seventeen largest industrialized competitors, union participation rates average over 50 percent.[36] Exhibit 14.4 presents data on union "density" rates in a large number of countries. As you can see, the percentage of workers who are unionized varies greatly across countries.

INTERNATIONAL INSIGHTS

Mandatory Payments for Dismissed German Workers

MULTINATIONALS OPERATING AROUND the world can be forced to pay large severance or termination benefits to their employees. In Europe, for example, there are extensive laws and requirements regarding termination. The average laid-off worker in the United States gets one week's severance pay for every year of service. German workers, however, get more than four times as much on average—ranging from one month of pay for every year of employment on up. Also, Germans often get as many as seven months to find a new job, again compared to less than one month in the United States. When you add in other mandated benefits like relocation and retraining that are available in Germany, termination costs in the United States have to be considered modest. Of course, this even assumes that you are permitted to let a worker go in Germany. Bernard Mahlow, an executive recruiter in Germany, says, "U.S. firms that establish themselves here are shocked by the termination rules. The possibility of firing someone quickly without cause is impossible."

Colgate-Palmolive ran into some of these rules in the late 1990's after it announced plans to close its factory in Hamburg and the 500 jobs it represented. Colgate initially offered German employees a severance plan that cost the company 30 million marks ($20.5 million); this was an average of $40,000 per employee. Colgate strongly argued that the plan was similar or better than what other firms in the area had recently provided. However, to workers this was nothing more than a starting offer. German law gives the union an opportunity to approve such decisions, and they felt the offer was far too low. Tom Kovacs, the union officer, pointed out that this operation was profitable for Colgate (the company had to release this information to the union). The union attracted a good deal of public attention to their plight, including stories in local papers about how employees and their families had worked for Colgate for three generations. Eventually, the mayor of Hamburg publicly condemned the company for its move and the union threatened to drag out the negotiation process. Additional German law stipulated that if the issue could not be settled before the end of the year, Colgate must keep workers for three more months, a move that would cost Colgate another $6 million. Eventually, Colgate raised its offer and agreed to a settlement just before Christmas. The agreement provided that neither side would disclose the terms.[34]

The oldest and most well developed union systems occur in the EU countries. Even among these countries, however, there are differences in the percentage of workers covered by unions. France, for example, has only about 11 percent of its workforce covered by unions, whereas Britain has a relatively large percentage of workers who are union members (nearly 40%). These national differences have been tied to a number of factors, including the political leanings of the government, how wages are determined, and the size of the public employment sector.[37]

It is important to note that these union density rates should not be taken completely at face value. For one thing, the raw percentage of union members is not all important. Often, the bargaining agreements reached by the union and management end up covering many more employees than just union members.[38] More importantly a high union density does not necessarily mean that unions are more effective or influential. In fact, in some cases, a relatively low density rate (e.g., France at 11%) may belie the true degree of union influence. Also, in some countries, labor may be represented by a whole political party, thereby also increasing union influence. Clearly, however, not all unions across borders are structured the same nor are they equally influential. We will discuss the nature and impact of unions in a number of important countries around the globe. This discussion is more detailed about Western countries, reflecting the fact that they were industrialized before other areas and thus have had greater opportunity for employee groups to form unions.

EXHIBIT 14.4

Union Density Rates around the World*

Country	Density (%)	Change Last Decade (%)	Country	Density (%)	Change Last Decade (%)
Australia	35.2	−35.2	South Korea	18.0	—
Belgium	51.9	−0.2	Mexico	26.0	—
Canada	37.4	1.8	Netherlands	25.6	−11.0
Denmark	80.1	2.3	Poland	33.8	−42.5
France	9.1	−37.2	Singapore	17.0	—
Germany	28.9	−17.6	Spain	18.6	62.1
Greece	24.3	−33.8	Sweden	91.1	8.7
Iceland	83.3	6.3	Switzerland	22.5	−21.7
Ireland	48.9	−12.6	United Kingdom	32.9	27.7
Italy	44.1	−7.4	United States	14.2	−22.1
Japan	24.0	−16.7	Venezuela	25	—

*Rates are estimates of the percentage of wage and salary workers who are union members.
Source: Adapted from———. (1999). Human Development Report, 1999: United Nations Development Program, Profile of People in Work (www.undp.org).

Unions among EU Countries

Because the notion of union influence is mostly indexed by perceptions, there is some debate about who is influential and why. Nevertheless, it appears, at least among EU countries, that union power has not withered away over the last five years.[39]

Unions in Germany Unions in Germany have been strong over the years. There is only one union for workers in most major industries, and membership in that organization is entirely voluntary. Unions will typically bargain with a group or federation of employers in an industry. As in the United States, the contract will include most major work issues, including pay, benefits, and conditions of employment. As such, the main goals of the union are economic in form, as opposed to some of the more politically motivated union activity found in countries such as France or Italy.

The nature of the relation between unions and management has been fairly cooperative over the last twenty years or so. One reason is that workers have a number of avenues of input into how the business is run, including representation on the board of directors! This latter situation, unique to Germany, is called **codetermination**. This policy, set up by the Allies after World War II, was designed to prevent industrial might from lining up completely with a potentially threatening government, as had happened before the war. The system is most predominant in the steel and coal industries, sectors that were critical pre- and postwar enterprises.[40] Here, unions select five board members, shareholders select another five members, and this body then selects an eleventh member. Outside of steel and coal, union membership on boards varies by industry size. They receive one-third of the board seats in firms of 500–2000 employees, and equal representation if the firm has over 2,000 employees.

In the last decade or so, unions have been willing to trade concessions in working conditions and pay for job security and reduced working hours. The desire to keep working hours short is very important for Germans. In fact, in 1989, when Germany introduced Thursday night shopping as the first excursion into after-hours work schedules, the retail workers went out on strike. The International Insights box elaborates on this obsession with free time for Germans compared to Americans. More recently, German unions are becoming increasingly hostile as firms act to remove restrictions on employment, ones that produce among the most restricted labor markets in Europe.[41] This resistance has not, however, produced stronger unions; instead, both membership and influence have weakened as many see the downside of the lack of flexibility that German union activity has in part produced.[42] Indeed, while German unions are still strong relative to other countries in the world, participation has dropped from about 33 percent in 1990 to about 25 percent in 2000 (compared to 14% in the U.S.).

Unions in the United Kingdom   The union movement in the United Kingdom has a very long history—among the longest of any country. British unions are also relatively powerful, although their influence has waned a bit the last decade or so. The union movement can also be seen as political in Britain, although not as political as some other countries (see the discussion of France later). In fact, the desire for unions to push their political agenda led to the formation of the Labour Party in Britain in 1883. Since then, the trade unions have played a significant role in this political party and to this day provide the vast majority of financial support for the party.

Union density in the U.K. is about 2.5 times that of the United States. Union participation, however, has seen a big dip recently. At the height of its influence in 1979, membership was around 57 percent, whereas the density rate now is just about 40 percent. There are a number of reasons for the drop in participation in unions, but perhaps the biggest reason has to do with the political environment. The conservative governments that have dominated Britain during the last fifteen years passed legislation that reduced the power of the unions. Additionally, the economy fared quite well during this period, thereby reducing the appeal of union membership.[47] Nevertheless, unions still wield considerable power and influence. A large firm usually negotiates with anywhere from five to seven unions; thus there is great complexity in these dealings. Cross-union dealings can be fractionated. This situation has played into the hands of companies, who have successfully pushed collective bargaining down from a national to a business level. Likewise, many new businesses have tried to maintain a nonunion status consistent with the "enterprise culture" of the conservative Tory governments of Margaret Thatcher and John Major. In short, British unions have taken it on the chin lately and are still searching for a new strategy.[48]

Unions in France   French unions have been dominated by five main national unions. As in Japan, most large employers also have a company union. These unions are among the most political in the world. In fact, the chief distinction among these unions is not the industry or occupations they cover, but instead their political/social leanings.[49] The development of these five confederations can be clearly traced to ideological issues

INTERNATIONAL INSIGHTS

Germans Think Americans Work Too Hard

ANGIE CLARK AND Andreas Drauschke have similar managerial jobs for similar pay (about $33,000 a year) in department stores in Washington and Berlin. Apparently, however, the comparison ends there. Mr. Drauschke's job is contractually set at a 37-hour work week with six weeks annual paid leave. His store closes at 2 P.M. on Saturday, is never open on Sunday, and stays open one night (Thursday) each week. "I can't understand that people go shopping at night in America . . . logically speaking, why should someone need to buy a bicycle at 8:30P.M.?" (he manages the auto and bicycle division of the store).

Ms. Clark, on the other hand, works at least 44 hours a week, including evening shifts and weekend stints. She often brings work home with her and has never taken off more than one week at a time. While most Americans admire the stereotypic German industriousness, Ms. Clark—born in and a frequent visitor to Germany—has a different view. U.S. workers average about 20 percent more working hours per week than Germans. And the disparity is increasing, growing in the year 2000 to a difference of about 1,970 hours per year for Americans compared to about 1,525 for Germans.[43] "Germans put leisure first and work second," said Ms. Clark. Many of her employees and fellow managers at the store work second jobs and rack up 60 hours or more per week of work. Mr. Drauschke, however, has a different perspective; he has no interest in working beyond the mandated 37 hours per week, even for more money. "Free time can't be paid for," said the German. Mr. Drauschke finds the American penchant for a second job simply unthinkable. In fact, it is **illegal** for Germans to work at other jobs during their six-week (and sometimes longer) vacation; it is seen as a time for recovering.

Apparently, the long and irregular work hours come at a price for Americans. Turnover at the German store is nearly zero, whereas it is nearly 40 percent a year in the U.S. store. Likewise, because of the several-year apprenticeships they serve, German workers know their products in and out. Training for Ms. Clark's U.S. workers is about two days.

Despite these advantages, many—including former German Chancellor Kohl and current Chancellor Schroeder—are worried that the short weeks, many holidays, and other perks are crimping German competitiveness. Schroeder went as far as to say, "A successful industrial nation doesn't allow itself to be organized as a collective amusement park." Industry leaders have started taking Schroeder's advice to heart and have begun to pull out of the employer federations that they feel are responsible for giving in to workers, and they have begun to cut side deals by themselves.[44] The future of German unions is in great flux now, and the German worker's penchant for leisure time could be at risk.[45] This could be a special problem given some of the issues faced by the German economy these days (e.g., continued integration of the east) and the market initiatives undertaken by the government in response.[46] And it may be an especially important issue in light of a recent study that concluded that it is not cultural differences so much as pay policies that may be behind these work hour differences. One study found that workers in both countries work more hours when pay scales are unequal—thereby galvanizing effort. But in Germany, where pay scales are tighter and other benefits are guaranteed, the motivating potential is lower! Whatever the reason, Germans still think Americans work too hard.

and conflicts, and they reflect the pattern of social division in France.[50] These five major confederations have competed with one another for membership, and it is common for all five to be present in any one work setting. Employees may choose to join one or the other depending on their political viewpoint.

Membership in any of these unions is not large by the standards of other countries. The largest union—the CGT, a largely industry/public service union with a communist leaning—has only about 675,000 members.[51] In general, France, at about 11 percent, has among the lowest levels of union density of all industrialized countries (see Exhibit 14.5). Partly, this low density reflects the fact that they really didn't have to push for new members. For much of the time since the mid-1970s, the French government has been socialist in form. And the socialists often protected or enhanced the rights of employees. Likewise, there has been a long government tradition of extending collective

Although France has a low union density rate, French unions tend to be influential and unafraid to take action. © Peter Turnley/CORBIS

agreements to companies and industries who were not party to the accord. Thus, a worker could benefit from the union's influence without having to be a union member. Accordingly, union influence is much greater than the 11 percent density figure would suggest.

Other European Unions   As mentioned earlier, the extent of union structures and activities in Europe runs the gamut of options. Because Europe was the first continent to industrialize, there is great complexity and variety of union representation. If you're not yet convinced of this from the foregoing discussion, just a brief review of some other countries may do the job. In the Netherlands, for example, the trade unions were initially formed and developed by religious and political groups. And, this is still true today. A good case in point is the largest union in Holland, the FNV; it is a merger between a socialist union and a Catholic union. These unions, however, are not as ideological as French unions and have participated with the government in many initiatives—including the formation of the Dutch welfare state. Unions are important in the Netherlands, and several experts have claimed that their influence is much greater than their 25 percent density rate suggests.[52] Likewise, Dutch employees can exert control over the workplace via other unique outlets (see later).

Unions in Sweden, as in most other European countries, began as a socialist movement among manual workers. And because of a largely friendly government, they flourished in a mutually cooperative environment. This can perhaps account for why Sweden has such a high density rate (83%). Although there has been some hostility between government and the unions lately, membership rates have not dropped off.[53] In fact, unions have been in the forefront of recognizing global competitive pressures. As a result, they have embraced many management initiatives to improve productivity, such as technological advances.[54] Belgium also has a relatively high union density rate (about 55%). It might be even higher, however, if there were fewer laws governing labor relations. In fact, the workplace in Belgium is one of the most highly controlled in the world. We have already pointed out that there are a large number of laws governing compensation, severance pay, and other human resource issues in Belgium. Despite the fact that the most important unions are organized around religious/political bases, there is a "culture of compromise" in their interactions.[55] Spain is perhaps on the other end of the regulated spectrum. Recently, there has been more unified union activity, especially in response to the great financial gains made by corporations. There is a great deal of flux in unions relations and attempts are made to develop new union policy and strategy in the face of the economic gains.

In general, the long history of union organizing has left many European workers covered by an extensive set of regulations and protections, especially by U.S. standards. Many multinationals have complained about this state of affairs, but their options are limited, as illustrated in the following International Insights.

Unions in Asia

There is also union influence in Asia, although this varies from country to country.

Japanese unions   There are over 60,000 unions in Japan, the vast majority of which are called *enterprise unions*.[59] That is, while there are some large national unions in the public and private sectors (e.g., Municipal Workers; Teachers' Union; Iron & Steel Workers' Union; Railway Workers' Union), nearly 95 percent of all unions are enterprise, or in-house, unions. The tradition has been to follow the principle of "one company, one union." In other words, these in-house unions represent only the employees of their respective companies. Membership in these unions is limited to regular and permanent employees. A large number of workers in any given company are part time or temporary and are covered neither by unions nor by the human resource practices that are closely associated with Japanese firms (e.g., lifetime employment, value of seniority, etc.).

As might be expected from our many discussions of Japanese culture, the relationship between union and management is harmonious. This wasn't always the case. In fact, after World War II, many Japanese unions were both militant and violent. The labor movement was often led by radical and militant union organizers whose agendas often included socialist revolution. One of the worst strikes—called the 100-day strike—came in 1953 at Nissan, when management locked employees out of plants for over three months. After many long and back-breaking strikes like this one, major Japanese employers basically struck a deal: We'll give you lifetime employment and good benefits for a promise of no labor strife.

Apparently, both groups have kept the bargain to an extent, because there is little if any labor strife in Japan. This is partially the case because junior management often provides the enterprise union leadership. In fact, the training received in these union positions is seen very favorably by management and is taken into account for future promotions.[60] Observers often criticize this relationship as being too cozy; they maintain that the union is a management control mechanism rather than a way to represent workers. For example, it has been pointed out that even when Japanese unions go out on strike, they do so for very short periods of time—often a half day or less. What's more, a striker may often work his full shift after he walks a picket line. Further, productivity often shows no change during a strike. There is some cross-union cooperation, but not much. For example, several enterprise unions coordinate their bargaining activities during a traditional Spring Wage Offensive (*shunto*) to establish a national pattern

INTERNATIONAL INSIGHTS

Europe's Response to Restrictive Labors Laws? One Word . . . Temps![56]

HOW WOULD YOU LIKE nearly six weeks of paid vacation and several other national holidays sprinkled in right after you start your first job? Not enough to sell you? How about only 37 hours per week of work—and none on weekends or at night? Still not good enough? Let's also say that you'll be informed of and involved in major financial and other decisions made by the company. And how about great job security, because the company has to be in extreme financial straits before it can let you go? And, even then they must give you seven months to look for a new job and $120,000 to ease your pain (though your salary is only $50,000). Does this sound like every worker's pipe dream?

Well, it's no dream. This situation is characteristic of the labor situation in many Western European countries. A long history of union organizing and socialist-leaning governments have resulted in labor laws that make it very expensive to hire European workers. These laws, however, mostly affect permanent workers. If you are willing to take temporary or part-time work, firms are still hiring! In France, for example, temporary employment has risen by 50 percent since the late 1980's—one in five workers are now part-timers.

Of course, most workers would much prefer permanent employment, but in hard times temporary work is certainly better than nothing. Many firms point out that such work keeps many off the public dole—especially young workers, among whom unemployment is a big problem. Governments are going along with this trend, if only begrudgingly. In Germany, for instance, a legal ban on temporary agencies was lifted only in 1994. In two years, the American temporary firm, Manpower International, has seen revenues grow by 35 percent there. Spain is another example of this trend—seven out of every ten jobs created in the mid-1990s were for temporary workers. This is easily understood when you consider that employers can be required to pay those thrown out of work for up to three and a half years afterward. In Britain there is more of the same: 30 percent of the workforce is temporary.

Many predict that this trend will only increase unless there is a major shift in workplace legal regulation. And, a good deal of this is being enacted. In Spain, for example, the center-right government of José Anzar cut this severance pay nearly in half, and he is going after more. Unemployment has decreased from 22 percent in 1996 to 13 percent in 2001, accounting partially for Mr. Anzar's reelection.[57] And Sweden, of all countries, is starting to cut the dole as well. While workers have traditionally been guaranteed 80 percent of their last net pay—indefinitely—a new law there permits the ability to reduce benefits after a worker refuses a job referral and to remove them altogether after three refusals. The law also specifies that after 300 days of jobless benefits, the person must enter a skills-training course full time—and they can't leave until they get a job! France recently enacted a similar law, and Dutch law cuts all benefits if one job referral is refused. Finally, Denmark also cut its benefit time to three months down from eighteen months.[58] Maybe one word ("temps") won't work too much longer—maybe you'll need three in Europe soon – ("back to work!")

or rate of wage increases. The individual enterprise unions then use this rate as a standard for their own bargaining.

Unions in China   Like most other aspects of business—and culture, for that matter—China is unlike any other country. Their imperial history as well as their revolutionary one has put a special flavor on labor relations in general and worker representation in particular. Even though we're skipping about 3,000 years or so of Chinese history, labor relations in China since the liberation in 1949 have been complex in and of themselves.

One of the hallmarks of the communist approach has been the full employment policy. This employment relationship has been referred to as the *iron rice bowl.* Employee's needs and jobs were taken care of; they were secure and permanent. An employee could not be fired for any reason and pay and housing were guaranteed. As you might imagine, such a situation is not conducive to what an American might consider good service. Many foreigners have complained about the poor level of service they receive. This is not because of a lack of staffing. A visit to any department store in Hangzhou or Changsha would certainly convince you of this. Full employment means that even in small departments, like the baby section of a store, one person will be responsible for diapers, another person two feet away will be responsible for formula, and yet another not three feet away will get you baby food. Recently, with the adoption of several new laws, workers can now be laid off (made "redundant"). The law provides for treatment of laid-off workers and also provides a system for arbitrating any disputes that occur in this process. Little is known, however, about how such processes are actually handled.[61] Nevertheless, although the full employment policy is beginning to change, especially among joint venture businesses, it is still very prevalent.

Partly as a result of this situation, union activity is certainly not of the variety we see elsewhere in the world, especially in western Europe and the United States. Nevertheless, there are unions in the PRC. As might be expected, however, they play a supporting role when they play any role at all. Communist ideology is consistent with the notion of union activity in that it dictates that "workers are masters of the house."[62] And although unions are ostensibly the link between the party and the masses, they are often ridiculed as unnecessary (*pao loong tau,*—"a body to fill a temporary vacancy"). Although PRC leader Deng Xiaoping once said that economic changes have resulted in unions "no longer being the unnecessary organizations that some believe," they are unlikely to replace the influence exerted by the party.[63] After all, the union movement is officially obligated to work with management and the party to resolve problems. Further, it is barred entirely from dealing with worker grievances against management; this is a party responsibility.

One area where this situation may be different is in joint ventures. Joint ventures are owned by the central government and a foreign enterprise, and their management is governed by a very complex set of laws and regulations. Generally, though, management is directed to "positively support" the work of trade unions in joint ventures. In fact, they are required by law to set aside 2 percent of all wages paid in order to fund programs to educate and train union members. Further, unions have the right to sit on the board of directors to air opinions and complaints. They do not, however, have the right to vote. Thus, via this mechanism and others, unions deal directly with the foreign partners of the joint venture to solve their mutual problems. Unfortunately, perhaps because of their inexperience and lack of negotiating skills, unions often don't do very well in this direct relationship. The International Insights that follows highlights some of the resulting problems faced by Chinese workers involved in joint ventures.

Unions in other Asian countries   There are widely varying practices in other Asian countries. Countries such as India, Indonesia, the Philippines, Thailand, and Vietnam are examples of economies—and labor relations—in a state of transition. Hong Kong, which returned to the PRC in 1997, is yet another. Hong Kong is a part of the PRC with virtually no unemployment, and very low levels of union activity. Despite their Confucian tradition, many have characterized the attitude of Hong Kong workers as an "everyone for himself" approach.[65] This attitude obviously hinders any substantial union participation. And Hong Kong managers capitalize on it in their dealings with labor, as evidenced by their resolution of the Cathay Pacific Airline crew strike. Of course, the long-term effect of returning to China on its highly skilled and comparatively well-off workforce will be interesting to follow.

INTERNATIONAL INSIGHTS

Unions in the Middle Kingdom— Not Forbidden, But Not That Useful, Either[64]

NOT LONG AGO, China ordered all foreign-funded companies to enroll their workers in official trade unions—and to do it within six months time. And many workers think that such an order is way overdue. The number of fatal accidents, layoffs, and labor conflicts in China is at an all-time high. As a result, the central government is faced with a major labor backlash resulting from its growth and foreign venture policies.

According to workers and many others, the need for action is clear. In the foreign-funded factories—estimated to employ about 10 million Chinese—accidents abound and treatment is poor. In some factories, workers are strip-searched, beaten, and even forbidden to use the bathroom during work hours. At a foreign-owned factory in the Fujian province city of Xiamen, forty workers (one-tenth of the workforce) have had fingers crushed by obsolete machines. According to official reports, there were over 45,000 industrial accidents in the booming Guangdong province alone last year—claiming more than 8,700 lives!

Zhang Dinghua, vice chair of the national union and representing the National Council, said that 88 percent of foreign companies operating in China have no unions. This is in spite of the fact that joint venture contracts require union representation. Mr. Zhang, however, says that the government intends to follow through on its union requirement this time. In particular, they are singling out Hong Kong, Taiwanese, and other Asian investors as the main culprits. The government came under particularly close scrutiny last year when a fire at a Hong Kong–owned toy factory in Shenzhen destroyed the plant and eighty-four people lost their lives. Mr. Zhang said that the owner was at least partially responsible because he ordered the exits locked for fear that workers would steal his toys.

Even the normally passive (by Western standards) unions are upset. Since the central government has given greater control of commerce to provincial and regional authorities, workers say that safety and job assurance have dipped markedly. The government got a taste of worker anger recently in Heilongjiang (a northeastern province), where some 2 million workers lost their jobs in the mid-1990s. Western sources say that over 100,000 workers took to the streets in the province's major cities to protest pay cuts and job losses. Although the provincial governor was sacked as a result, workers continued their protests with work slowdowns and unpublicized strikes (which are illegal in China).

The central government is in a difficult position as its growth policies have deliberately fostered entrepreneurial activity but have also raised accident rates and labor strife. The government is also worried about the reactions of foreign investors to their moves to quell the labor strife. For example, an unnamed executive with an American company in Shanghai said, "I don't consider it an appetizing prospect. We've been here for years without any union demands, and now they're telling us we have to start negotiating pay with the Communist party." In response, the Chinese government has moved to try to assure foreign business that unions won't be detrimental to their interests. At the same time they have made a more traditional move, trying to prevent the spontaneous rise of solidarity-type labor movements by suppressing activists. For example, 120 labor leaders who signed a worker protection charter were recently arrested. How this will all play out remains to be seen—as is always the case in China. One thing is certain, however—the challenges of dealing with the world's largest workforce will only increase.

The other so-called "Asian Tigers," the countries of Singapore, South Korea, and Taiwan, have become major influences in the world economy. Although a good deal of government and multinational control and influence is exerted on labor relations in these countries,[66] there are big differences in the state of their labor relations. Whereas labor issues in Singapore and to an extent Taiwan have been relatively calm, relations in Korea have been more confrontational. A particularly well-publicized strike against Hyundai in 1993 illustrates this high level of union activity.[67] The length of the strike and the poor manner in which it was handled by the company was reminiscent of the infamous Homestead strike in Pittsburgh around the turn of the century. Many predict that relations between firms and workers will get worse before it gets better.[68] And if events at Daewoo are any sign of this, then the predictions have already come true.[69] Korean workers violently resisted GM's initial efforts to make a bid for the troubled Korean car firm. Some have echoed arguments that were similar to those raised about Japanese bids on United States firms a decade earlier: "Selling the company to GM would mean handing over a piece of Korea to the United States," said one Daewoo worker.

Central/South American Unions

With the passage of the North American Free Trade Agreement, much attention has been focused on Mexico. A good deal of federal law governs labor relations in Mexico, and many of those regulations favor labor. As we have already noted, there are a large number of guarantees in terms of wages and benefits provided by law. As a result, Mexico is a country with a relatively high degree of union participation. In fact, only twenty employees are necessary in order to form a union in Mexico. As a result, Mexican firms are used to negotiating with many different unions within one unit or factory. If the official union declares a strike, all personnel—including management—must vacate the premises. Flags are stationed at each locked entrance signifying that the plant is under strike. Union members receive pay during the time at which they are out on a (legal) strike.[70] Unions have won a large number of worker rights, mostly through federal legislation rather than direct union activity. On the other hand, the Labor Secretariat has considerable discretionary power to allow strikes at all. Additionally, in the *maquiladoras*, which employ over 1.3 million Mexicans, companies are often free to choose submissive, government-affiliated unions for their factories.[71] It remains to be seen now what will happen with President Fox's initiatives along these lines. Other major South American economies (Brazil, Argentina) have varying levels of government control and input into labor relations activity.

African Unionism

Generally, union activity in Africa is somewhat like the continent itself—underdeveloped. In general, labor relations in developing countries are very different from those of industrialized ones. The major reason seems to be that most Third World countries have targeted industrial development as their major national priority. Thus, unlike the laissez-faire approach of many Western countries, Third World states have great involvement in labor relations.[72] Nevertheless, there is some range in styles across countries, from the relatively compliant approach in Kenya[73] to a more active approach in South Africa.[74]

South African labor relations are especially interesting given the apartheid policy that was followed. In the 1970s, when apartheid was at its height, there was relative peace among groups. Whites, Asians, and black groups were permitted to form unions and allowed to engage in collective bargaining agreements. Blacks, the vast majority of citizens, however, were denied similar rights. In 1980, African groups gained limited union rights, and the number of union members nearly tripled in five years. Despite the fact that apartheid still existed, the power of the black unions grew quickly. Strike activity increased greatly in the 1980s, some of it very violent. The effect of this organizing was dramatic. In fact, one study showed that the increased wage effects for black workers due to union membership approached the percentage gains realized by American workers, and these gains (again, in terms of percentage) were greater than for European workers.[75] The main thrust of these gains was for poorer, low-skill workers, whose minimum wages increased much more than any other category of workers. This study was especially interesting because it showed that even five years before negotiation became commonplace for the white majority government (1985) and with Nelson Mandella still in jail, black union workers won concessions of dramatic size.

As president of South Africa, Mr. Mandela's challenge became the need to balance the increasingly strident demands made by both unions and businesses—especially foreign ones. Several years ago, the country's big national union federation (COSATU) staged a one-day nationwide strike against a provision in the new constitution that allowed companies to lock out striking workers. President Mandela appeared with workers wearing COSATU colors and the provision was deleted. Big businesses in South Africa are pursuing the matter in the courts. More important, businesses and foreign investors say that the incident underscores their concern that South African unions have too much influence over government policies. To be more competitive globally, companies want the government to adopt more flexible labor rules and dump state-run enterprises. The unions counter that in the short term this policy will create even more unemployment aand that many of apartheid's inequities (such as low pay and poor living conditions for black citizens) remain and must be addressed.[76] These are some big hurdles for President Mbeki to jump.

International Employee Unions

As noted, unions have had varying degrees of membership and success in recent years. Perhaps the largest challenge to domestic unions, however, is the multinational itself. As detailed in a earlier International Insights box, multinationals have great power that they can wield against any one union or even sets of unions within a country. One of the main cards companies can play is the threat to move some or all of their operations to another, more friendly country. Since unions almost always represent workers in one country, they are relatively powerless in the face of this threat.[77]

There have been a variety of responses by unions to this perceived threat, but perhaps the most noteworthy has been the development of international organizations of workers and their interests. In fact, as far back as 1919, the League of Nations, as part of the peace agreement ending World War I, created the International Labor Organization (ILO).

The ILO is composed of representatives from employees, employers, and governments, and each group has a say in policies that are developed.[78] There are now over 170 member countries in this organization. The ILO has mainly been responsible for developing guidelines and standards for labor conditions and treatment. These guidelines, however, have the same legal status as an international treaty. Accordingly, they must be ratified and agreed to on a nation-by-nation basis. Given the controversial issues that the ILO deals with (equal pay, child labor, discrimination of various groups, etc.) and this ratification scheme, it should not be surprising to hear that many countries don't become party to all guidelines. Even if a country ratifies a guideline, making sure they comply with its stipulations is even tougher.[79] In many ways, the ILO operates like its larger parent organization, the United Nations. Other important international organizations also have similar goals, including arms of the European Union and the Organization for Economic Cooperation and Development (OECD).

REALITY CHECK

Running Global Teams at Citigroup

A chat with Jonathan J. Bhushan, Vice President, Global Corporate and Investment Banking, Citigroup, U. K.

Can you tell us what you do?

At Citigroup (www.citigroup.com) I am a regional account manager, and I focus on the foreign subsidiary business for the automotive and retail industries. I cover Europe, including central and eastern parts of the continent. Our job is to match banking products with customer requirements. This could occur in a number of areas, including structured/corporate finance, risk management, fixed income, e-business, and more. We also cooperate with our consumer bank and other product sectors (e.g., card and leasing programs). So we handle a number of diverse companies who have subsidiaries here in Europe. They may not be United States based; they could be from Canada, Japan, or Korea, among others; our customer base is very diverse culturally.

How do you deal with diversity?

Here at Citi, we try to reflect the diversity by assigning various members of our team to work with those diverse clients. For example, my colleague from Japan handles most of the Japanese clients, my associate from Korea works with those companies, and I focus mainly on U.S. customers. And we have a number of Europeans here, not only from the United Kingdom but also from Italy, central, and eastern Europe. So our internal and external constituents are very diverse. We try to mirror the customer in our approach.

What in your background prepared you for such a job?

This is a good question because I think background/experience is invaluable. Actually, I went to the Czech Republic for the first time in 1991 with a backpack to teach English. Then, I went back to intern there at a joint venture. After that, I spent a year in Gambia with the Free Market Development Advisor's program. In the interim I came back to the U.S. to finish my MBA at Columbia but headed right back to the Czech Republic when I finished. In 1997, I moved to the U. K., where I am now. This experience gives me a better idea of where my colleagues are coming from and allows me to serve as kind of a "border crosser." In fact, I remember learning Czech from friends and being immersed in that environment—I never had any formal training. Like all languages there is a formal and informal usage; I learned the informal. And when I entered the business world there, I would use informal Czech in situations when it should have been formal. But the Czechs really appreciated my attempts and sensed that I knew and understood a little about their perspective.

There is also a group of unions with international membership. One of the most important of these is the International Confederation of Free Trade Unions (ICFTU), and its goal is to help national unions in their dealings with multinationals. The membership of the ICFTU is concentrated in North America and Europe and thus is a force to be reckoned with by firms. Closely associated with these groups are International Trade Secretariats (ITSs), which often cover each major industry type (e.g., the International Metal Workers Federation). There are also some ITSs at the company level such as the General Motors Council, which includes union members from many GM plants around the globe. Regardless of the form these many organizations take, their general goals are the same. They are trying to emulate the organization of a multinational itself and to develop a transnational bargaining system.

Despite all this activity, most observers of the international scene suggest that international unions have been largely ineffective.[80] There are a number of complex reasons for this fact, including the unique laws of any one country and multinational

What are some pluses of working within such a diverse team?

I think that this is one of the defining factors of our bank. To appreciate my perspective, it's important to understand that I came to Citigroup in an unusual way. I joined the bank in the Czech Republic, so I never worked for them in the U.S. At the time, I was working on a report on the Czech banking system for the U.S. Department of State. I noticed that when I went to German or French banks there, all the top management were expatriates from those countries and middle management was mainly Czech. But at Citigroup, the CEO was German, the head of Cash Management was from South Africa, the Operations head was from Egypt, the Treasury head was from India, and so on. I looked around and said, "Where's the American?" They offered me a job after I finished the report and I decided to join because I like the cultural diversity and the enormous pluses it can offer in terms of creativity and productivity.

What about this? How do you get the creativity and productivity from such a diverse group?

On the creativity side, we've organized along industry lines, but as I mentioned, my colleagues from Japan and Korea handle customers in their respective countries. All three of us, however, explicitly share ideas and develop a lot of creative views of the industry (worldwide) and generally learn from each other. An example of the creative/productive balance might be that my Japanese colleague might take an idea that we use with an American client, tailor and develop it into a parallel idea from the Japanese client, and see it through in that country.

Within my own group, which itself is diverse, you just have to do a lot of work as a manager. I think most of your students don't appreciate that all this stuff is really what managing is all about. You have to build individual relationships in order to really get to know your people, and this is hard and takes a lot of time. Fortunately, Citigroup gives us the leeway and flexibility to do this.

What are the key issues in creating an effective global team?

First, understand local markets and customs and make sure you have people with the skills to deal with that. Of course, having the right technical skills is critical. The other big thing is communication skills. I'm not necessarily saying someone needs to speak English, Czech, or French, but I'm talking about having team players who work well with others and appreciate what they bring to the team.

What advice would you give to students who want to work on an international team?

Well, now that I'm getting older, I think the best advice is to think long term about where you want to be. Students sometime go for the best offer after graduation. It wasn't that long ago, so I do remember these pressures and attractions, but I had faith in my international objectives. I ended up taking a rather low-paying job to study the Czech banking system because I knew that long term I wanted to be in the global environment. Too many students don't consider where they want to be in five to ten years. Preparation always meets opportunity. I find myself in a great work environment and my work has purpose. It can't get much better than that.

opposition. One of the most insidious reasons, however, has been the ability of such firms to play one country and its unions or set of unions against another. There are some examples of cross-border coordination among unions, such as the financial and other support provided by IG Metall (the largest German union) to striking workers at British Aerospace during their four-month strike.[81] Also, the United Electrical Workers union in the United States recently supported a Mexican union's efforts to organize a General Electric plant in Mexico.

These events, however, are unusual. Many powerful unions within countries are in effect political groups and thus more concerned with national issues, not international labor organizations. In fact, the most common occurrence is for one country's union to gain jobs by dealing with a multinational that is having labor trouble in another country. This competitive attitude is summed up by a Canadian union member: "An American union is not going to fight to protect Canadian jobs at the expense of American jobs."[82] British and French unions are also battling about the transfer of jobs across the channel. Several large American and other multinationals are laying off high-cost French workers and taking their operations to Britain. For example, Hoover Appliances (owned by Maytag Corporation) had announced plans to close a 600-employee factory in Dijon, France, and move its operations to Glasgow, Scotland. Interestingly, Hoover's Scottish workers accepted changes in work conditions for job security and the 400 new jobs that would result. The French were outraged and took to the streets to protest. They also crossed the channel to take part in a TV debate, during which they accused their Scottish colleagues of taking their jobs. British government officials were rather pleased about their success, with then Prime Minister John Major saying "Others recognize the virtues of Britain." British union leaders were quieter about the incident, except to say that "we have nothing to be ashamed of."[83]

It is clear that most workers probably see their foreign counterparts as competitors, not as allies in the same struggle. Thus, international unions have at least one large obstacle to overcome in order to be successful. A recent trend might help their cause.[84] Several American unions have begun to join forces with their European and international counterparts. The AFL-CIO, for example, has made connections with European unions, something it rarely has done, and has also taken nontraditional positions (e.g., supporting President Bush's call for an immigration amnesty).[85]

Other Forms of Employee Control/Input

Our discussion up until this point may have led you to believe that unions are the primary and perhaps only method by which employees can obtain desired outcomes. Unions are not the complete story by any means. There are a large number of mechanisms by which employees can glean benefits, both within and beyond union structures. These methods are known by a variety of different terms, including *industrial democracy, self-management,* and *worker participation.* The last term is probably most appropriate here since we are referring to methods by which workers participate in the management of the firm. This participation can include many different forms of input, ranging from no input at all to sharing of business information to consultation committees, all the way to worker's veto rights over a decision. Although there are many forms of worker participation in management (including unions themselves), we will discuss three different varieties: (1) joint consultation committees (JCCs), (2) works councils, and (3) board membership.[86]

Joint consultation committees   First, *joint consultation committees* are common in many countries, especially Western ones. As the name implies, these are groups of workers who sit on a committee that deals with topics of mutual interest to workers and management. Their charge can range all over the board, from a concern with improving quality (such as quality circles) to a concern with working hours, safety issues and the general quality of work life (as in Sweden). Typically, committee members make suggestions that may or may not be taken up by management. In turn, management is often expected to keep workers informed about developments via the committee. Obviously, the effectiveness of such committees depends on the goodwill and intentions of a firm and is most likely to be successful in paternalistic companies with relatively good employee relations.[87]

Works councils   are another form of worker participation and are common in many European countries (e.g., Belgium, France, Germany, the Netherlands). These groups are similar to JCCs in many ways but the essential difference is that works councils often have significant power to combat management decisions and actions. Often, these councils exist as a result of national laws that mandate the creation of these groups. Equally often, their creation is deemed necessary because of what is seen as a social obligation to seek employee input rather than as a means to improve competitiveness or the bottom line.[88]

In the Netherlands, for example, Dutch law requires that any firm with thirty-five or more employees must create a works council. The council is a body of members, elected by employees, that must be consulted in decisions of importance to the organization. These issues are often related to personnel policy (e.g., safety and training programs, pay and benefits issues, relocation of work, plant closures, etc.). If a firm has 100 or more employees, this consultation could include major financial decisions (new capital investments, business acquisitions, etc.). Theoretically, the works council should represent the interest of employees. Members of the council, however, may be managers or production employees. In reality, councils can be coopted by management via this and other means.[89]

In powerful works councils, as in Germany, an employee may effectively hold two jobs—their regular job and their job as council representative. Thus, it's not uncommon to have a second office and perhaps even two staffs, right on company grounds. The council representative may be similar to a shop steward in the U.S. union environment. The difference is that the former has more real input into company decisions.

Board membership   is a third, less common mechanism by which workers have input into the business. In this case, input is often extensive. In seven European countries (Austria, Denmark, France, Germany, Luxembourg, Norway, and Sweden) law dictates that workers must have some kind of representation on the board of directors of firms. In most cases, these boards are supervisory boards—the group that selects the management board who is responsible for running day-to-day operations. For example, we have already talked about the notion of codetermination in German industry, and this is an example of a board membership method. Typically, workers have only a minority membership on the board (the exception being large German firms). And despite what appears to be such a radical idea, research shows that board memberships for workers generally have little negative or positive effect on the business. Typically, they meet very infrequently (often just a few hours a year), and equally often, when talk does turn to substantive issues, worker representatives feel at a disadvantage. Many feel they lack the background to fully evaluate the complex financial and other information discussed in these meetings. Nevertheless, in other groups they are believed to be responsible for providing valuable input that changed health, safety, and investment decisions by the firm. At the minimum, they appear to provide a symbolic function for workers, and some unions (such as the British and Swedish) view them as a valuable information source rather than a power-wielding group.

Putting Agreements into Practice

As we have discussed here, there are many ways that agreements between management and workers can evolve, including via unions, national legislation, and the many participation systems that are available. Unfortunately, there are even a larger number of ways that disagreement can come about. As a result, there can be and is conflict and strife between management and labor.

EXHIBIT 14.5

Rankings of the General Climate of Industrial Relations in Thirty-Seven Countries

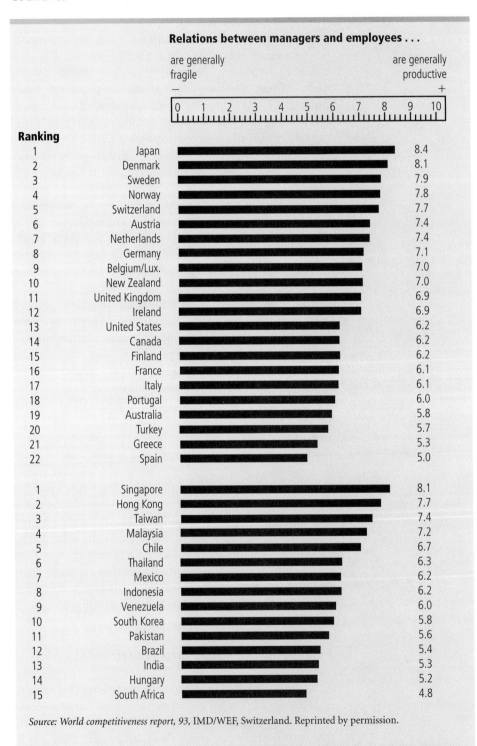

Relations between managers and employees . . .

are generally fragile — / are generally productive +

Ranking		
1	Japan	8.4
2	Denmark	8.1
3	Sweden	7.9
4	Norway	7.8
5	Switzerland	7.7
6	Austria	7.4
7	Netherlands	7.4
8	Germany	7.1
9	Belgium/Lux.	7.0
10	New Zealand	7.0
11	United Kingdom	6.9
12	Ireland	6.9
13	United States	6.2
14	Canada	6.2
15	Finland	6.2
16	France	6.1
17	Italy	6.1
18	Portugal	6.0
19	Australia	5.8
20	Turkey	5.7
21	Greece	5.3
22	Spain	5.0
1	Singapore	8.1
2	Hong Kong	7.7
3	Taiwan	7.4
4	Malaysia	7.2
5	Chile	6.7
6	Thailand	6.3
7	Mexico	6.2
8	Indonesia	6.2
9	Venezuela	6.0
10	South Korea	5.8
11	Pakistan	5.6
12	Brazil	5.4
13	India	5.3
14	Hungary	5.2
15	South Africa	4.8

Source: World competitiveness report, 93, IMD/WEF, Switzerland. Reprinted by permission.

Relations between management and labor   Multinationals consider the general relations between management and employees when they choose to invest in a foreign subsidiary. And although this topic was covered in detail in earlier chapters, here we can say that those relations show great variability. Exhibit 14.5, for example, shows data collected by the World Economic Forum that ranks 37 different countries on the degree of productive relations between management and employees. On a 1 to 10 scale, there are only three countries in this survey with ratings over an "8"—Japan, Denmark and Singapore. While there may certainly be other reasons not to locate a plant in these and other countries (such as Sweden, Norway, and Switzerland, all with high ratings but also high labor costs), poor employee relations is not one of those! The United States ends up being tied for twenty-second place among these thirty-seven countries, a relatively low showing, but perhaps not that surprising.

Deterioration of relations   Sometimes these poor relations can deteriorate even further, resulting in work slowdowns, sabotage, and even violence. These events, however, are either difficult to track or are not that common. More common and easier to observe is the strike. Here we can look at easily documented features of strikes, such as their frequency, size, and length. Just because these variables seem relatively objective, however, does not mean that there are no problems with making direct comparisons of strikes across countries.[90] For one thing, there are many nation-specific definitions of what constitutes a strike or other type of work stoppage. Danish statistics, for example, exclude any disputes during which fewer than 100 days are lost from their reports.[91] Despite this, Denmark ranks high on work days lost because of strikes. Nevertheless, some groups, including the ILO and the OECD, have worked to clear up this issue. Strike data are usually based on the number of strikes and the number of work days lost because of the strike. Based on these data, researchers have reached three main conclusions about the nature of strike action:[92]

● There has been a general decline in strikes since the 1970s.
● The number of days lost because of strikes has declined sharply; in the EU, strike activity fell by nearly a half in the 1990's.[93]
● There has been a shift in the nature of strikes toward political objectives, the public/service sector, and work process issues (security, participation) rather than outcomes per se (e.g., pay level).

Exhibit 14.6 presents a ranking of a large number of countries on the volume of strike activity—the number of working days that are lost by strike. There are a number of interesting things about this list. For one, there appears to be a very general relationship between country wealth and strike activity. It is generally observed that strikes decline during economic downturns and increase in times of prosperity.[94] The figure shows that countries that are doing well generally have a relatively high level of strike activity—Italy, Spain, and Korea are a few countries that fit this pattern. Clearly, however, other countries do not fit this pattern—including Hong Kong, Japan, Malaysia, and France. These countries are well off, yet strike activity is low. There are other cultural and legal structures in place that can further help explain this variance in strikes across countries. We next provide a more detailed discussion of the nature of strikes in several key countries.

Japan   As we have already mentioned, union-management relations in Japan are quite good (also see Exhibit 14.5). Accordingly, most disagreements are settled amicably. It is quite rare for relations to get caustic enough to result in a strike. And even when they do, the strike is brief and not bitter—often it is undertaken to either embarrass

INTERNATIONAL INSIGHTS

Japanese Firms Have a Friend in the Unions[96]

JAPAN'S NORMALLY vigorous economy has taken its lumps in recent years. In 1986, for example, it faced its worst slowdown in nearly two decades, and in the early to mid-1990s the value of the dollar impacted Japan very negatively. In most countries, firms would face these troubled waters alone. In Japan, however, management knows that they have a friend they can turn to—the unions!

In the late 1980s, for example, the government pushed corporations to raise wages in order to spur the economy. Corporations worried about their profit levels, however, refused to do so, and labor unions supported management. In their annual negotiations that year, steelworkers accepted their smallest raises in their history without a fight, and the largest two shipbuilding unions didn't even ask for a raise. It is this kind of cooperation that Japanese management counts on and that eases their worries during down times.

Consider the perspective of Shinichi Tsuji, a leader of one of the most radical of the three unions at a Japanese subsidiary of Royal Dutch/Shell. When interviewed, Mr. Tsuji was demonstrating in a Tokyo street with a sign fastened to his body that claimed the company was trying to bust his union. However, he claimed the union was also getting tough. "We went on strike the day before yesterday. We stayed out for 45 minutes. Yesterday we struck again for 15 minutes." The following day they struck briefly again (for higher wages), but the strike was held at lunchtime so that the demonstrators would not have to miss any work.

This attitude characterizes most Japanese unions. The average Japanese employee strikes about 5 minutes a year, a rate far below that for the United States. As Karuki Shimizu—the head of the Nissan Motor Co's union—says "union members want to protect their jobs and preserve their livelihood. The best way to do that is to cooperate with the company." Mr. Shimizu boasts that his union has not struck since 1953. Likewise, the Kawasaki Steel Corporation is getting help from its union to restructure in the face of declining demand. They are closing an old production line in central Japan's rust belt and opening a new automated line in the less-developed east coast area. Nine hundred employees will be losing their jobs, and the union did not raise an eyebrow. The company is not firing anyone; the slack will be taken up by retirements and reassignments. Such action in western Europe or the United States might result in a pitched battle in the streets. Not in Japan, however, where labor conflict of any significance is largely a thing of the 1940s and 1950s.

management or to bring to their attention a matter of importance. Lockouts by management are extremely rare. In fact, even though the sometimes emotional and expressive behavior of union members is tolerated, management is expected to always be courteous and civil in their language and behavior.[95] The accompanying International Insights provides further detail about the meaning and enactment of strikes in Japan.

Germany   As mentioned earlier, unions have a tradition of strength in Germany. However, strike activity is not at all frequent (see Exhibit 14.6). Partly this is due to the many input and control mechanisms that workers have in German enterprises. As we discussed earlier, Germans have input in the form of work's councils and the codetermination process, among others. In addition, however, German labor relations are also covered by many legal regulations, making more extreme steps like strikes and lockouts less necessary. For example, laws prohibit either strikes or lockouts when a contract is in effect. Thus, if there is a strike, it typically happens when contracts with workers have expired and negotiations are still continuing over a new contract. There have been times when Germans have struck with an existing contract in place, as in the early 1980s. This was a period of high inflation and workers wanted to raise wages to keep up with this inflation—even though that strike activity was illegal. These situations, however, are rare in Germany.

EXHIBIT 14.6

Strike Activity in a Variety of Countries*

Country	Days Lost to Strike	Country	Days Lost to Strike
Iceland	375	New Zealand	65
Spain	320	Sweden	50
Canada	220	United States	40
Turkey	185	Portugal	36
Denmark	179	United Kingdom	25
Finland	178	Belgium	25
Italy	175	Netherlands	20
Australia	120	Germany	14
Ireland	115	Austria	6
Norway	83	Switzerland	3
France	75	Japan	1

*Entries reflect the number of working days lost per 1,000 employees, annual average from 1989–1998. *Source:* Adapted from———. (2001). *The Economist,* May 12, 108, based on data from the British Office for National Statistics.

The United Kingdom   As we've said, unions are fairly common in Britain, and they are relatively powerful. As Exhibit 14.6 also shows, strike activity is also quite high. The reason for this high frequency might be exactly opposite to the explanation of low German activity—the government has taken a "hands-off" approach to labor relations. Their laissez-faire approach has resulted in fewer legal constraints on labor relations than many other EU countries. For example, labor contracts do not prohibit strikes. As a result, they happen more often, and so frequently that the public gets used to them. Strikes usually occur during a deadlock in negotiations, although no one type of strike (in terms of frequency or style) seems to predominate in Britain—there are just a lot of them.[97]

The United States   Exhibit 14.6 shows that the United States has a relatively high amount of strike activity. U.S. labor contracts typically prohibit strikes during the period of the agreement. Thus, once a contract is in place, a strike (called a "wildcat" strike) is rare and usually not authorized by the union. As in Germany, once a contract expires and a new one is not yet approved, a strike becomes a viable option—an option that is exercised frequently. Employees may sometimes choose to continue to work during the negotiation period, while threatening a strike. Lockouts by management are not unheard of, but they are also relatively rare.

Effect of Unions on Strikes

An important question from management's perspective is the overall effect or return from a unionized workforce. As we have mentioned throughout this chapter, with some exceptions most managers find dealings with unions, whether they be in China or the United States, to be difficult. Nevertheless, there are some benefits from a unionized workforce, including a structured bargaining system and some contractual obligations that must be fulfilled.

Perhaps a more subtle benefit of union membership, however, is that it may quell more extreme and militant worker action. For instance, the data presented in Exhibit 14.7 show the relation between overall level of worker militancy and union density in twelve EU countries. Militancy is defined as a combination of variables that are indicative of labor strife and unrest. In general, the exhibit shows a negative relation between militancy and union density. In other words, the greater the tendency toward unionization, the lower the incidence of violence. For example, the five countries on the right portion of Exhibit 14.7 (the United Kingdom, France, Greece, Italy, and Spain) all have high levels of militancy and a low percentage of workers who are unionized. The left side of this graph shows the opposite relationship for several countries (e.g., the Netherlands). So despite all the management resistance to unions and some levels of conflict that result, there may be a silver lining. Organized employee input—perhaps in many forms—may actually act to make management-worker relations smoother than would otherwise be the case.

Chapter Summary

In this chapter we looked at the value and influence of *groups*—both small and large—across cultures. First, we examined smaller work teams and considered the impact of culture on how these function. We reviewed research that shows that national and cultural differences have the potential to be both problematic and promising. For example, groups are more important in collectivist countries than they are in individualistic ones. But even in a collectivist culture in-groups and out-groups vary dramatically in their value. Social loafing, a common effect in individualistic countries, also tends to occur among collectivists but only in groups that are unimportant to them (out-groups). They pitch in whole-heartedly when working in groups that are important (in-groups).

We also raised the general issue of diversity in cross-cultural groups. Diversity means that there are sometimes widely differing ways of doing things. These differing styles can be a hindrance to group effectiveness if not recognized and managed correctly. We discussed specific cases of diverse cross-cultural teams and offered suggestions for benefitting from the promise of diversity.

In the second half of the chapter, we shifted our discussion to larger groups and broadened the discussion. There we focused on the relations between two important groups—management and employees. There are many differences across countries in the presence and influence of unions. Nevertheless, employee interests are often represented to management by unions, although we showed that the percentage of workers who are union members varies across countries. One reason for the variance is that worker interests in some of those countries is ensured by other mechanisms, such as laws or political forms of worker input. Worker input can range from mild forms of control—such as having some say or input into work procedures—all the way to having voting rights over important firm decisions. Despite these available communication and input methods, sometimes management and employees just cannot agree. Labor strikes are one response to a lack of agreement although we have discussed many ways throughout the book by which understanding and accord can be reached.

Discussion Questions

1. What are the effects of groups on productivity for various cultures. What would increase productivity for American, Chinese, or German groups?
2. What factors could explain why a multicultural group might experience tough going?
3. Why might multinationals have the upper hand in dealing with workers, even if those workers are unionized?
4. How do U.S. unions differ from those in Western Europe, Asia, or Latin America?
5. What is the relationship between the presence of unions and the level of hostility among workers? Why is this the case?

EXHIBIT 14.7

The Relationship Between Worker Militancy and Union Representation*

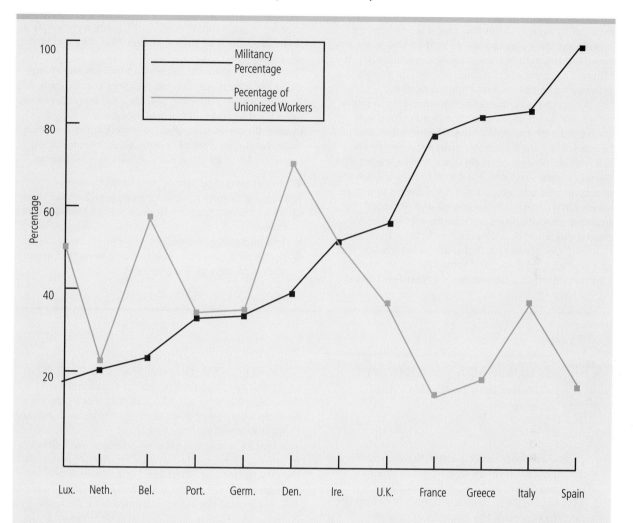

* Spanish labor relations were considered the most militant and thus assigned 100%; other countries' rankings are reported relative to this figure.

Source: Sparrow, P., and Hiltrop, J.M., (1994). *European human resource management in transition.* New York: Prentice-Hall. Reprinted by permission.

Up to the Challenge?

Cultural Diversity among Work Teams at BP [98]

WHEN PEOPLE FROM different cultural traditions come into contact—as with the work teams created by BP—many of the issues we have discussed thus far in this book come into play. Communication becomes critical, perception plays a role, decision-making styles can produce conflict, and more. Mr. Ruijter's challenge was to gain the trust and commitment of the team members so that he could capitalize on their strengths. One of the first things he did was to organize a two-day seminar on team building. All team members attended and were encouraged to participate via techniques that would uncover their approach to groups. As you might have predicted from your reading, the training led off with an exercise designed to uncover beliefs and philosophies that each member may have had about cultural differences. As discussed in this chapter, this technique is highly recommended by experts. After this one, a series of more specific exercises was completed that helped team members understand their preferences and those of others. Communication techniques were practiced in order to make this understanding concrete.

Along the way, the various groups learned many things. For example, early on the Dutch group was concerned with the style of management that would be used. They were used to an open style in which lthey would be able to freely share their opinions. The Germans were very concerned that proper operations procedures be put into place quickly. Even some more minor differences were discovered and discussed. For example, the Americans were surprised that the French shook hands with everyone in their team every morning. Discussion revealed that the French saw this as a sign of friendliness and informality. The Americans said they felt that a handshake is a relatively formal

sign of politeness. Likewise, the Germans did not wish to be addressed by their first names (even if you knew them well), whereas the Scandinavians wanted to be addressed by last name only. Many of these cultural differences were brought out in the open during the seminar. It appeared that all participants were eager to share the aspects of their culture which they thought were valuable.

As this experience suggests, if there is one thing that goes a long way toward building a team spirit, it is simply discussing differences—bringing them out in the open for discussion. This is not, however, as easy as it sounds. BP seems to have done it well, for their Brussels team developed a set of ground rules for interacting together. Some of these rules include the following:

- Do not prejudge people, functions, cultures.
- Create a climate in which people aren't afraid to ask.
- Try not to make assumptions; if you do, though, check them!
- Talk and discuss issues.
- Agree on a common objective and keep that in mind during periods of disagreement.

International Development

Japanese Decision-Making Exercise

Purpose

1. To give students the opportunity to work through a meaningful task in the manner of Japanese consensual decision making
2. To compare their own experiences of group decision making with the Japanese approach

Instructions

Your instructor will explain the processes of Ringi and Nemawashi and will set up the structure of the exercise. Group composition includes leaders (Kacho) and student manager (Bucho). Then your instructor will divide the class into groups of four to six members. Your group will design a final exam format that is likely to be a valuable learning tool and basis of evaluation. (20 minutes).

Now your instructor will divide the class into new groups of four to six members (the Kacho groups). In your new group you will continue with the task, using the results of the primary group as a starting point. After this meeting, groups can choose their own venue for future meetings. Your instructor will give advice during one or two open-ended class sessions. Outside class meetings occur at the instiga-

tion of the group and student leaders (20 minutes).

Now the whole class will generate a Ringi document that specifies the content of the exam. This document must be signed by all students in the class. Your instructor will discuss what problems, if any, the Ringi document might cause.

Finally, the whole class will discuss the following questions: How much did your experience resemble the descriptions of Ringi and Nemawashi found in the literature? (Background reading: Chapter 3 of *The false promise of the Japanese miracle* by P. Sethi, N. Namiki, and C. Swanson.) What difficulties did you encounter? Were those difficulties likely to be present in the Japanese context? If so, how would they probably be managed?

Source: Van Buskirk, B. (1994). Japanese decision making. In D. Marcic and S. Puffer (eds.), *Management International: Cases, Exercises, and Readings.* Minneapolis, MN.: West Publishing Company. Reprinted by permission.

From Theory To Practice
The Blanchworth China Company

Purpose
To illustrate the complexities involved in dealing with labor and unions across borders.

Background
The Blanchworth China company was founded in the British Isles in the eighteenth century and has established a world wide reputation for premium quality china designed and handcrafted in the United Kingdom. The china always has sold well in the United States and in the early 1980s, fueled by a strong dollar, it experienced an explosive growth in sales. However, as the dollar went into a long decline through the mid- and late 1980s, sales of Blanchworth china dropped by 25 percent in the United States. This decline is particularly important to Blanchworth because the U.S. market accounts for approximately 90 percent of the company's output.

The premium quality china market is roughly divided into two segments based on price: the high segment is priced from US$75 to US$300 per plate, while the lower segment ranges from US$25 to US$75 per plate. Blanchworth has always dominated the high segment with approximately 85 percent market share, but the company had no presence in the lower segment. Unfortunately, it was the high segment of the market that decreased 25 percent in sales dollars in the late 1980s, while the lower segment had grown by 50 percent during the same period. It was clearly a worldwide trend, not only in Blanchworth's market, but also for most other discretionary income items.

In addition to the falling value of the U.S. dollar and the shrinking market for higher-priced china, several other factors helped to create a severe financial crisis for Blanchworth by the end of the 1980s. During the "good times" of the 1980s, when demand and profits were high, Blanchworth's skilled worker's union made heavy wage and work-rule demands. The company's managers acceded to these demands in order to avoid any work stoppages. As a result, Blanchworth's crafters became some of the highest paid skilled workers in the British Isles. Workers' salaries increased from 60 percent of the cost of product to nearly 80 percent by the late 1980s. These high labor costs, coupled with company debt incurred by the acquisition of a premium crystal manufacturer, prevented Blanchworth from lowering its prices when U.S. demand decreased.

In 1988, management was forced to propose immediate cost-reducing measures in order to save the company. Among other things, they determined to reduce their labor force by 25 percent and to purchase new equipment that would make the remaining workers more productive. After heated encounters between management and union leaders, the union finally became convinced that the labor force cuts were necessary in order to save the company. The union also agreed to rescind work rules that had worked to preclude higher worker productivity. The union made these concessions in order to prevent the company from declaring bankruptcy and to save the most union jobs.

After a year of operation with the new equipment, Blanchworth management found that increases in productivity were offset by the larger than expected number of senior crafters taking advantage of the early retirement package. This package was offered as one means of reducing the labor force by the targeted 25 percent. Profits continued to slide after the work force reduction, and Blanchworth management finally decided the company would have to enter the lower segment of the premium quality china market. While Blanchworth managers realized it would face many more competitors in this lower segment of the market than in the high-price segment, they believed the company's well-respected name and other marketing strengths would allow it to make a quick entry into this segment.

In late 1990, Blanchworth introduced a new line of products lighter in weight and less ornate than its original china place settings. This entire product line is produced in Eastern Europe at a fraction of the labor cost associated with the Blanchworth U.K. plant. Preliminary market research show that this line has stronger appeal for the younger, first-time china buyers who see themselves as more contemporary and value conscious than traditional Blanchworth customers; moreover, these younger buyers are generally less brand loyal. Blanchworth called it new line *Krohn China*.

Krohn is carried by the same distribution channel as Blanchworth, but it has its own logo, package design, advertising agency, and display case. Management felt that the name Blanchworth associated with the name Krohn would help to establish an image of high quality, but, at the same time, the name Krohn would differentiate the new line from traditional Blanchworth china. This name association has helped to gain the reseller support necessary in making the new line readily accessible to a large market.

As a result of Blanchworth management's decision to locate its new operations in Eastern Europe, members of the union and residents of the community in which the Blanchworth factory is located felt betrayed. Union leaders were never informed about the new product line that could have meant rehiring many Blanchworth skilled workers. In addition, the move to Eastern Europe has caused ill-will among many consumers throughout the United Kingdom and has resulted in some critical editorial articles in the local and national press.

The union contends that most U.S. customers are brand loyal to Blanchworth because it is made by skilled workers in the United Kingdom. They argue that this loyalty stems from the fact that many Americans trace their ancestry to one or more countries in the United Kingdom. Management counters that Blanchworth has never been sold specifically as a U.K. product and that most U.S. buyers neither know nor care where their china products are made. Although many bitter feelings arose between management and the union, no work stoppages occurred during 1991.

In early 1992, management announced that after the first year of sales, Krohn generated twice as much profit per plate as Blanchworth. Also, they asserted that Blanchworth employees in the United Kingdom were still not productive enough to offset the high wages these workers earned. As a result, management representatives opened discussions with union leaders about how to solve the continuing low-profit problem. Management suggested that the only solution was a further reduction in wages and benefits, as well as another major change in work rules. The union disagreed with this perspective and countered that the low level of profitability actually resulted from poor management, rather than "overpaid, unproductive workers" as suggested by management.

Although never openly stated, union leaders suspect that management may be considering moving all Blanchworth operations to Eastern Europe. The union continues to argue that U.S. customers will not accept Blanchworth china that is not made by U.K. crafters. They cite the fact that 100,000 tourists tour the U.K. plant each year and that at least half of these tourists are Americans. Many of these American tourists purchase over US$1,000 in china products during their visit to the plant. The union contends that the tourists who come to the plant feel a strong affinity for Blanchworth china because it is a product of the United Kingdom, and most of these on-site sales would be lost if the plant were moved to Eastern Europe. To further strengthen this argument, the union cites the U.S. Census Bureau 1990 statistics giving the following breakdown of U.S. citizens by U.K. ancestry: England 32.6 million, Scotland 5.4 million, Ireland 38.7 million, and Wales 2.0 million.

Instructions

You are a business consultant who has been brought in to assist Blanchworth's top management with strategic decision making in several areas. During the briefing you are given additional information:

- Management is serious considering moving all Blanchworth factory operations to Eastern Europe while keeping its other functions in the United Kingdom. They make it clear that the design and quality assurance operations would remain in the United Kingdom. The concern is about how quickly the new Eastern European plant and workers could achieve full quality production, especially if the U.K. workers shut down the British plant before the new plant is on line.
- Management is concerned about political instability in Eastern Europe. If they move both Krohn and Blanchworth, their entire production could be compromised, with little chance of reopening a plant in the United Kingdom.
- Sales of Krohn in the United Kingdom are extremely sluggish, but are doing well on the continent. Krohn does seem to be gaining acceptance slowly in the United States, mostly among young couples buying it for themselves rather than receiving it as gifts from parents or friends and relatives.
- The union and the community have threatened to discredit the firm if it moves to Eastern Europe by taking their case directly to the U.K and U.S. customers.

Answer the following questions about this case:

1. The management believes its foreign sales will be unaffected by moving all operations to Eastern Europe. What research should be done before making this decision? Which research methodology do you recommend?
2. Try to anticipate the ways in which the union and the community could discredit the company name if it leaves the United Kingdom. Will Americans boycott the company after the move? Will Americans voice their disapproval in large numbers before the move? How will you get these answers?
3. What specific measures can management take to "inoculate" the firm against the union actions that you anticipated in question 2? Should it take these steps rather than dealing with the problem after it is a reality?
4. Should management ask for concessions in order to keep the firm in the United Kingdom? Make a list of possible concessions and tell who should provide them, for example, the union, community, national government, and so on. Concentrate on the long-term solutions when sketching out a plan for how a win-win situation can be reached in this case.

Source: Catlin, L. B., & White, T. F. (2001). *International business: Cultural sourcebook and cases studies,* 47–50. Cincinnati, OH: South-Western. Reprinted by permission.

1

On a Global Stage: The Context of International Management
Fighting Twenty-first Century Pirates: The Business Software Alliance in Hong Kong

Fighting software piracy is a goal of every software developer I have ever met in my life. No matter what country they are from. So I think the aims and the mission statement and the goals of the BSA are identical to non-members', software firms.

– KEVIN HENSHAW, DIRECTOR BSA (ASIA)

For computer software firms, software piracy represented a large loss of potential revenues. In response to the trade in pirated software, computer software companies banded together in 1988 into an international political lobby organization, the Business Software Alliance (BSA). Individual charter versions of the BSA were established in countries around the world to press governments to tighten intellectual property legislation and pursue anti-piracy measures. By the mid-1990s, Asia had become one of the largest regions for pirated computer software, and Hong Kong was the epicentre of the regional trade in piracy. However, Hong Kong was also the commercial and financial hub for Asia and the major computer hardware distribution center for both China and the region. This made Hong Kong an important market for the BSA's member companies. For the BSA in Hong Kong, then, the task they were presented with was to clamp down on software piracy and illegal software distribution while simultaneously increasing the size of the local software market. How could they encourage notoriously protectionist Asian governments to open their computer sectors to free and transparent trade while simultaneously getting them to strike hard at the illicit trade that threatened mostly large U.S. firms?

Hong Kong's Computer Software Industry

In spite of economic difficulties in Asia overall, few sectors of the economy can expect to exceed the performance of the software industry. The software industry is the heart of the "Information Society"—that culmination of information technology and communications developments now heralding a new industrial revolution.

—PRICEWATERHOUSECOOPERS [1]

The computer software industry was widely recognised as an engine of economic development and growth in a modern economy. In Hong Kong, the computer software industry stimulated growth through the creation of highly skilled and highly paid jobs, substantial tax revenues, and the development of tools needed to enable local industries to compete effectively in the global market.

In a report commissioned by the Business Software Alliance (BSA) in 1997 (and released in 1998), international consulting firm PricewaterhouseCoopers (PwC) found that the 1996 computer software market in Hong Kong had a retail value of more than US$279 million, and generated some

Peter Lovelock and Katherine Lo prepared this case under the supervision of Dr. Ali F. Farhoomand for class discussion. This case is not intended to show effective or ineffective handling of decision or business processes. This case is part of a project funded by a teaching development grant from the University Grants Committee (UGC) of Hong Kong. "Fighting 21st Century Pirates: The Business Software Alliance in Hong Kong" by Peter Lovelock and Katherine Lo. Copyright © 1999 The University of Hong Kong. No part of this publication may be reproduced or transmitted in any form or by any means—electronic, mechanical, photocopying, recording, or otherwise (including the Internet)—without the permission of The University of Hong Kong. Used by permission.

US$570 million in total economic activity.² At a time of significant economic uncertainty, this sector of the market was expected to grow at an annual average rate of 21.2 per cent between 1996 and 2001, resulting in a market generating purchases worth US$729.7 million, and US$1.4 billion in total economic activity by 2001 (see Exhibit 1).³

To arrive at these numbers, the PwC survey focused on "packaged software." The packaged software market covers a diverse range of products, including personal computer business software—such as operating systems, word processors, spreadsheets, graphics, database management, computer-aided design (CAD) and computer-aided engineering (CAE) products, and networking software. Packaged software also covers entertainment, educational and other leisure programs (see Exhibit 2).

EXHIBIT 1

Growth of Hong Kong's Computer Software Market

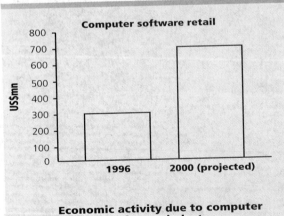

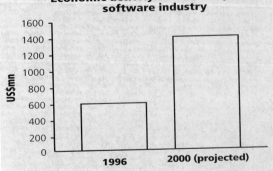

Source: BSA, *Contribution of the Packaged Software Industry to the Hong Kong Economy*, May 1998.

EXHIBIT 2

Software Product-Market Segments

Software Application	PC Business Software	Packaged Software
Operating Systems	PC only	Inet, Servers, Mainframes
Word Processing	✓	✓
Spreadsheets/Statistics	✓	✓
Graphics	✓	✓
Accounting	✓	✓
Communications	✓	✓
Databases	PC only	✓
CAD—Computer Aided Design	✓	✓
CAE—Computer Aided Engineering	✓	✓
Utilities	✓	✓
Decision Making Software	✓	✓
Networking Software	—	✓
Entertainment	—	✓
Educational Programmes	—	✓
Enterprise-wide Systems (SAP, Baan, etc.)	—	✓

Source: BSA, *Contribution of the Packaged Software Industry to the Hong Kong Economy*, May 1998.

In 1996, the packaged software industry was estimated to have directly generated well over 4,000 jobs in Hong Kong.⁴ However, direct employment by software publishers was only one component of job creation stimulated by the computer industry in Hong Kong. For example:

- "Downstream" distribution and retailing of computer software resulted in the employment of a wide variety of sales, marketing and systems integration personnel.

● Downstream consulting services also generated employment and economic activity through: software installation and integration; software customization; systems maintenance and translation services.

● "Upstream" job creation boosted the local economy through employment related to market research, technical research, translation and localisation services, the supply of raw materials (such as diskettes, CDs, printed matter, packaging) and a host of advertising, marketing and other functions.

● Further economic activity was generated by software publishers, original equipment manufacturers (OEMs), distributors, resellers and service providers purchasing business services, which ranged from additional information technology (IT) purchases to professional services such as accounting and legal advice, financial services and buildings and infrastructure services (see Exhibit 3).

In terms of the direct fiscal benefits to the Hong Kong economy, the packaged software industry generated some US$37 million in tax contributions in 1996.[5] The benefits provided to the Hong Kong economy by the computer software industry were not, however, limited to the number of jobs created, or the tax revenues generated. The infrastructure and accompanying skills added value to the development process, providing a broader economic stimulus. The use and dissemination of computer technologies (and hence computer software) provided the underlying "intellectual infrastructure" to Hong Kong's development as a services center. The deployment of computers increased the automation of repetitive, labour-intensive tasks. As a result, organizations were able to employ increasingly skilled staff to build on substantive, rather than administrative, work. Of even greater importance for Hong Kong as a regional financial hub was its ability to provide the latest financial services rapidly and efficiently, or risk losing ground to neighboring "world" cities such as Singapore, Tokyo or Shanghai.

Packaged and Customised Software

Two types of computer software could be found in use in Hong Kong. The first was that upon which the PwC survey (cited above) was based: packaged software. In Hong Kong, the packaged software available

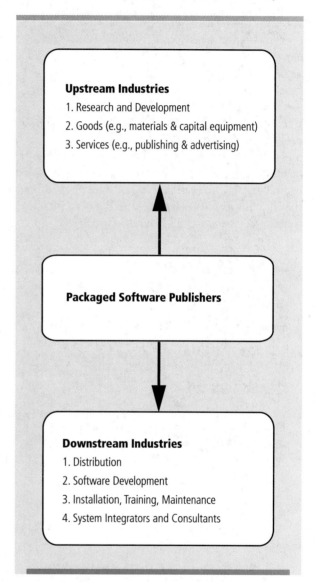

EXHIBIT 3

Stucture of the Packaged Software Industry

Upstream Industries
1. Research and Development
2. Goods (e.g., materials & capital equipment)
3. Services (e.g., publishing & advertising)

Packaged Software Publishers

Downstream Industries
1. Distribution
2. Software Development
3. Installation, Training, Maintenance
4. System Integrators and Consultants

originated mostly from America or Taiwan. The second type of software in Hong Kong was proprietary software with commercial applications. This was software written by software houses or consultancies, tailored to the specific needs of individual companies or discrete industries. While this latter work occurred in Hong Kong, it was largely based on adaptation and customization of foreign-derived software. In other words, Hong Kong did not possess a software development industry to speak of.

For those involved in the anti-piracy lobby movement, this presented several problems. Where the message elsewhere focused upon the damage that piracy inflicted upon the development of the local industry, there was very little software development taking place in Hong Kong. Furthermore, there was very little momentum for software research and development (R&D) to take place. With the Hong Kong Government's long-established policy of non-intervention, original R&D was left to the private sector. For many years, the Government had been loathe to involve itself in developmental projects such as technology parks or software development programs—meaning that the usual anti-piracy message fell upon deaf ears. Finally, there appeared to be little incentive for Hong Kong people to take notice of, and react to, an issue such as software piracy when they did not see themselves as suffering from piracy. Indeed, they would suffer from the curtailment of piracy, with prices for legitimate software often 100 times or more than those of the counterfeit copies.

Software Piracy in Hong Kong

The rate of software piracy in Hong Kong was estimated to have been 64 per cent in 1996, meaning that 64 per cent—or more than six out of every 10—programs sold in Hong Kong were illegitimate or counterfeit copies.[6] This was estimated to have cost the local industry some US$129 million in direct revenue losses. Software piracy further cost Hong Kong in excess of 5,700 jobs and US$51 million in tax revenues in 1996, according to the same estimates (see Exhibit 4). Reducing the illegal copying of software would have obviously increased the fiscal

EXHIBIT 4

Outputs Projected to 2001

	Economic Contribution: Existing Piracy Rate			Projected Economic Contribution: Estimated Reduction in Piracy Rate			Comparisons	
	A	**B**	**(B-A)**	**C**	**D**	**(D-C)**	**(C-A)**	**(D-B)**
	1996	**2001**	difference	**1996**	**2001**	difference	**1996**	**2001**
Direct Sales and Output								
Final Packaged Software Sales (US$000s)	279,000	729,665	450,655	662,904	1,733,659	1,070,755	383,904	1,004,004
Software Publishing & Value-Added Downstream Activity (US$000s)	330,534	864,429	533,895	785,349	2,053,884	1,268,535	454,815	1,189,455
Supporting Business Activity: Indirect + Induced (US$000s)	199,583	521,960	322,377	474,210	1,240,176	765,966	274,627	718,216
Total Economic Activity (US$000s)	530,117	1,368,389	856,272	1,259,559	3,294,060	2,034,501	729,442	1,907,671
Direct Employment								
Software Publishing Activity	1,118	1,850	732	2,656	4,396	1,740	1,538	2,546
Downstream Activity	1,481	2,451	970	3,519	5,824	2,305	2,038	3,373
Supporting Employment: Indirect + Induced	1,600	2,648	1,048	3,802	6,292	2,490	2,202	3,644
Total Employment by Software Industries	4,199	6,949	2,750	9,977	16,512	6,535	5,778	9,563

continued...

EXHIBIT 4

Outputs Projected to 2001 (Continued)

	Economic Contribution: Existing Piracy Rate			Projected Economic Contribution: Estimated Reduction in Piracy Rate			Comparisons	
	A	**B**	**(B-A)**	**C**	**D**	**(D-C)**	**(C-A)**	**(D-B)**
	1996	**2001**	**difference**	**1996**	**2001**	**difference**	**1996**	**2001**
Government Revenues								
Software Publishing (US$000s)	11,160	29,168	18,026	26,516	69,346	42,830	15,356	40,160
Downstream Activity (US$000s)	16,176	42,303	26,127	38,433	100,513	62,080	22,257	58,210
Indirect + Induced Effects (US$000s)	9,597	25,098	15,501	22,802	59,633	36,831	13,205	34,535
Total Fiscal Contributions (US$000s)	36,933	96,587	59,654	87,751	229,492	141,741	50,818	132,905
Assumptions								

Growth rate: sales and taxes	21.2%
Growth rate: employment	10.6%
Estimated piracy rate, PC business software, 1996	64.0%
Reduced piracy scenario, PC business software	27.0%

Source: BSA, Contribution of the Packaged Software Industry to the Hong Kong Economy, May 1998.

contributions produced by the software industry. The Government would have benefited from the higher direct and indirect taxation resulting from higher sales and profits. Personal taxation and social contribution receipts from the enlarged workforce would also have risen. It would therefore appear to have been strongly in the Government's interest to limit software piracy, and yet for many years they had refused to respond to the complaints from the anti-piracy lobby.

Admittedly, the rate of software piracy in Hong Kong (67 percent in 1997) looked *comparatively* low, given the situation in China (96 percent), Vietnam (98 percent), Indonesia (93 percent), and elsewhere (see Exhibit 5). The dollar losses attributable to software piracy were also small when compared to the top-ranked offending countries (see Exhibit 6). But Hong Kong's software piracy rate was significantly higher than the estimated rates in other developed countries such as Japan, Australia and even Singapore. Furthermore, while the rate of software piracy in a market such as Japan had fallen from 41 percent in 1996 to 32 percent in 1997, Hong Kong's rate of software piracy, by contrast, had continued increasing, from 62 percent in 1995 to 67 percent in 1997. Why was this the case?

Hong Kong was the leading transhipment point for pirated goods travelling from the PRC and other parts of Asia across the region and elsewhere across the world. One report, for example, noted that the "BSA continues to find counterfeit CD-ROMs throughout much of Asia, Eastern Europe, Latin America, and even in the United States. BSA investigations have revealed that Hong Kong is being used as the transhipment point through which pirates export their illegal goods to major world markets."[7] In another, from Bangkok, the following extract was recorded:

EXHIBIT 5

1997 BSA/SPA Piracy Study Results

	Piracy Rates (%)				Retail Revenue (Pirated) US$1000			
	1994	1995	1996	1997	1994	1995	1996	1997
Western Europe								
Austria	47	47	43	40	41,223	66,994	50,267	41,620
Belgium/Luxembourg	53	48	38	36	75,973	78,210	49,197	51,485
Denmark	48	47	35	32	67,300	82,670	37,531	45,787
Finland	53	50	41	38	56,081	80,603	36,335	37,754
France	53	51	45	44	421,145	537,567	411,966	407,900
Germany	48	42	36	33	671,069	775,898	497,950	508,884
Greece	87	86	78	73	28,845	40,573	45,802	44,546
Ireland	74	71	70	65	30,590	40,640	45,650	46,847
Italy	69	61	55	43	288,490	503,648	340,784	271,714
Netherlands	64	63	53	48	206,706	275,320	221,144	195,098
Norway	53	54	54	46	80,092	96,981	103,852	104,337
Portugal	65	61	53	51	36,091	50,230	36,183	40,991
Spain	77	74	65	59	190,746	229,933	148,823	167,288
Sweden	54	54	47	43	151,993	206,332	112,498	127,051
Switzerland	38	47	43	39	65,842	132,779	99,545	92,898
United Kingdom	42	38	34	31	370,793	444,561	337,344	334,527
Total Western Europe	52	49	43	39	2,782,978	3,642,938	2,574,871	2,518,726
Eastern Europe								
Bulgaria	94	94	98	93	19,269	20,394	9,594	13,171
CIS-less Russia	95	94	95	92	311,471	37,033	49,469	44,276
Czech Republic	66	62	53	52	97,150	56,108	69,212	51,972
Hungary	76	73	69	58	101,902	55,086	42,987	25,488
Poland	77	75	71	61	208,176	150,287	169,202	107,625
Romania	93	93	86	84	19,025	20,163	8,380	15,297
Russia	95	94	91	89	516,254	301,076	383,304	251,837
Slovakia	66	62	56	58	23,683	13,678	14,055	17,018
Slovenia	96	96	91	76	19,082	20,174	8,666	9,198
Other Eastern Europe	82	84	73	62	64,779	74,078	27,639	25,474
Total Eastern Europe	85	83	80	77	1,100,792	748,077	782,509	561,355
North America								
U.S.	31	26	27	27	3,589,512	2,940,294	2,360,934	2,779,673
Canada	46	44	42	39	341,637	347,085	357,316	294,593
Total North America	32	27	28	28	3,931,150	3,287,379	2,718,251	3,074,266
Latin America								
Argentina	80	80	71	65	160,769	151,814	122,389	105,194

continued...

EXHIBIT 5

1997 BSA/SPA Piracy Study Results (Continued)

	Piracy Rates (%)				Retail Revenue (Pirated) US$1000			
	1994	**1995**	**1996**	**1997**	**1994**	**1995**	**1996**	**1997**
Bolivia	93	92	89	88	3,314	4,017	3,527	3,853
Brazil	77	74	68	62	293,757	441,592	356,370	394,994
Chile	74	68	62	56	39,717	47,920	39,960	33,147
Columbia	80	72	66	62	84,861	103,288	85,920	65,085
Ecuador	90	88	80	75	13,715	15,460	12,852	13,236
El Salvador	97	97	92	89	11,439	13,207	11,489	10,419
Guatemala	94	94	89	86	8,745	10,095	8,675	7,867
Honduras	89	88	83	78	4,221	4,592	3,918	3,468
Mexico	78	74	67	62	192,361	135,905	105,909	133,102
Nicaragua	94	92	89	83	5,791	6,529	5,763	5,010
Panama	78	77	64	60	6,457	7,330	5,528	4,867
Paraguay	95	95	89	87	5,144	6,327	5,408	5,029
Peru	89	84	74	66	33,436	40,522	32,437	31,017
Uruguay	87	84	79	74	16,879	18,876	16,116	13,613
Venezuela	72	72	70	64	46,211	57,968	51,272	54,905
Other Latin America	69	77	54	47	54,407	76,074	43,230	34,848
Total Latin America	78	76	68	62	981,223	1,141,516	910,763	919,653
Asia/Pacific								
Australia	37	35	32	32	158,678	198,146	128,267	129,414
China	97	96	96	96	364,021	443,933	703,839	1,449,454
Hong Kong	62	62	64	67	64,495	122,938	129,109	122,169
India	79	78	79	69	103,054	155,645	255,344	184,664
Indonesia	97	98	97	93	104,452	150,921	197,313	193,275
Japan	66	55	41	32	1,399,813	1,648,493	1,190,323	752,598
Korea	75	76	70	67	510,605	675,281	515,547	582,320
Malaysia	82	77	80	70	66,704	80,596	121,488	82,552
New Zealand	43	40	35	34	25,970	26,083	29,271	20,284
Pakistan	95	92	92	88	10,881	14,233	23,144	20,395
Philippines	94	91	92	83	40,647	45,022	70,735	49,151
Singapore	61	53	59	56	37,252	40,374	56,553	56,599
Taiwan	72	70	66	63	112,005	165,462	116,980	136,850
Thailand	87	82	80	84	67,834	99,146	137,063	94,404
Vietnam	100	99	99	98	3,910	35,076	15,216	10,132
Other Asia/Pacific	96	95	86	83	74,157	90,053	49,113	31,974
Total Asia/Pacific	68	64	55	52	3,144,478	3,991,399	3,739,304	3,916,236
Middle East/Africa								
Bahrain	92	92	90	89	3,614	4,243	4,495	3,576
Cyprus	77	77	70	68	2,169	2,566	2,540	1,809
Israel	78	75	69	54	41,380	55,639	77,261	57,060
Jordan	87	87	83	80	2,194	2,567	2,659	1,883

continued...

EXHIBIT 5

1997 BSA/SPA Piracy Study Results (Continued)

	Piracy Rates (%)				Retail Revenue (Pirated) US$1000			
	1994	1995	1996	1997	1994	1995	1996	1997
Kuwait	91	91	89	88	8,697	10,300	10,817	7,889
Lebanon	80	79	73	79	1,221	1,419	1,422	1,796
Malta	77	77	70	64	1,678	1,975	1,956	1,299
Mauritius	90	90	88	77	1,375	1,562	1,646	1,070
Oman	96	96	95	93	6,304	7,397	7,905	5,682
Qatar	91	91	89	87	2,569	3,033	3,206	2,760
Reunion	70	72	66	59	1,612	1,894	1,860	1,232
Saudi Arabia	78	77	79	74	22,251	29,619	32,562	22,541
Turkey	90	90	85	84	69,298	95,249	90,717	64,306
UAE	89	89	72	60	7,792	9,866	8,653	5,325
Other Middle East	79	78	73	73	34,246	37,491	37,822	27,774
Total Middle East	84	83	79	72	206,400	264,820	285,522	206,003
Egypt	84	84	88	85	8,244	10,674	18,128	12,890
Kenya	82	82	77	72	338	437	443	302
Morocco	82	82	77	72	5,069	6,579	6,675	4,559
Nigeria	82	82	77	72	2,787	3,620	3,673	2,509
South Africa	64	58	49	48	68,528	88,323	43,783	69,833
Other Africa	87	87	83	71	114,500	146,878	152,531	95,414
Total Africa	77	74	70	60	199,466	256,512	225,234	185,507
Total MidEast/Africa	80	78	74	65	405,866	521,332	510,756	391,510
Total World	49	46	43	40	$12,346,487	$13,332,640	$11,236,454	$11,381,746

Source: BSA/SPA, 10 December, 1998, *1997 Global Software Piracy Report*, http://www.bsa.org/statistics/97ipr.pdf

"What is it you desire?" asks the Indian gentleman, "Business software," I reply. "Of course," he says, "I have the latest from Hong Kong, all on one disc. It is called an installer. This is version 10." It was a little pricey, about US$60, but I bought it anyway, since he had gone to the trouble of reaching under the counter for the disc. On it I found Lotus SmartSuite, Adobe Illustrator, PC File, a soft-porn screen saver from Germany, the Physicians Desk Reference, and Norton PC Anywhere—64 programs in all.[8]

With software "theft" in Asia responsible for almost US$4 billion of the estimated US$11 billion lost to the software industry worldwide in 1997, Hong Kong was not only helping to stimulate this demand, it was playing a major role in facilitating such trade.

The Role of Hong Kong in Software Piracy

Vendors of pirated copies of computer software in Hong Kong made no secret of their locations, and areas where counterfeit software could be purchased were common knowledge to the computer-literate population. Pirated software could, for example, be bought in various well-known shopping arcades throughout Hong Kong, with Sham Shui Po's "Golden Arcade" being the most infamous.

> I prowl the aisles of the software piracy mother lode, the Golden Shopping Arcade in Hong Kong's Sham Shui Po district. All around me in the basement of this dingy, block-long urban warehouse, eager shoppers paw through the bins and tables of the densely packed stalls. Inside a stall called the Everything CD Shop . . . I buy the first of my installer discs, Volume 2. This tribute to pirate technology costs the same as all the other CD-ROMs at Golden Arcade, about 9 bucks or three for US$25. Incredibly, this disc has 86 programs on it, each compressed with a self-extracting installation utility. Volume 2 has a beta copy of Windows 95 as well as OS/2 Warp, CorelDraw! 5, Quicken 4.0, Atari Action Pack for Windows, Norton Commander, KeyCad, Adobe Premier, Microsoft Office, and dozens of other applications, including a handful written in Chinese. Connoisseurs of the genre compare the different versions of the installer discs like fine wines. Someone from Microsoft later tells me that the retail value of the disc is between (US)$20,000 and (US)$35,000.[9]

The low prices at which the software was sold fuelled demand, with branded software, such as that developed by Microsoft or Lotus, sold at a fraction of the legitimate price–often as much as 100 times cheaper. Pirated CD-ROM versions of well-known software, whether business applications or leisure software, could regularly be bought for HK$50, or HK$100 for three.

As was noted in a 1995 article in the *New York Times,* "what sets Hong Kong apart . . . is the pervasiveness of pirated material throughout all segments of society here, from the back alleys of Kowloon to the executive suites of major companies."[10] In other words, the problem of piracy in Hong Kong could not be solely attributed to those responsible for selling and counterfeiting, but was a far more pervasive aspect of the society and the commercial culture. Moreover, there was wide recognition that much of what was on sale was generated by large foreign demand, as well as by local needs. It was not uncommon for Westerners from places such as America, Canada and Australia to travel to Hong Kong specifically for the purchase of cheap counterfeit computer software, which were pirated copies of mostly American products. In a trip to any one of the more prominent shopping arcades where pirated software was on sale it would not be unusual to see

---

EXHIBIT 6

BSA Estimates of Revenues Lost to Piracy and Illegal Software's Market Share

	Total loss, US$ bn	Piracy rate, %
United States	2.8	27
China	1.4	96
Japan	0.8	32
Korea	0.6	67
Germany	0.5	33
France	0.4	44
Brazil	0.4	62
Italy	0.3	43
Canada	0.3	39
Britain	0.3	31

Source: BSA, March 1999.

Americans purchasing a huge catalogue of software. The difference between the total price of the counterfeit software and the price of the legitimate software was considered sufficient to cover the cost of the trip.[11]

The Business Software Alliance

Alarmed by the rise of computer software piracy globally, a group of large U.S. software publishers joined forces in 1988 to combat the growth of the illegal software market. The result, the BSA, was a consortium of like-minded computer software and hardware companies. It represented software publishers for personal computers and the Internet, including Microsoft, Adobe, Novell, Lotus and Symantec. Members of its Policy Council included Apple Computers, Compaq Computers and Intel (see Exhibit 7). In 1992, the Hong Kong office of the BSA

EXHIBIT 7

BSA Members

BSA Worldwide Members

Adobe Systems	http://www.adobe.com
Autodesk	http://www.autodesk.com
Bentley Systems	http://www.bentley.com
Filemaker (Europe)	http://www.filemaker.com
Inprise (Asia)	http://www.inprise.com
Lotus Development	http://www.lotus.com
Macromedia (Asia)	http://www.macromedia.com
Microsoft	http://www.microsoft.com
Novell	http://www.novell.com
Symantec	http://www.symantec.com
Visio	http://www.visio.com

BSA Policy Members

Apple	http://www.apple.com
Compaq	http://www.compaq.com
IBM	http://www.ibm.com
Intel	http://www.intel.com
Intuit	http://www.intuit.com
Sybase	http://www.sybase.com

Source: BSA, *About BSA,* http://www.bsa.org/about/
index.html, March 1999.

was established. By 1997 there were four BSA offices
in Asia: Hong Kong, Beijing, Singapore and Kuala
Lumpur. Regional members included Inprise (Asia),
Macromedia (Asia) and Filemaker (Europe).

Since its establishment, the BSA had been aggressive in promoting software copyright protection
through education and enforcement programs worldwide. The organization had conducted frequent advertising, direct mail, media relations and school-level
education programs to raise awareness about copyright
laws. Businesses and organizations were able to obtain
free advice on effective software management from
the BSA. To ensure that software copyrights were
adequately protected, the BSA conducted enforcement
programs in over 65 countries, with actions instigated
against organizations that had violated software copyright laws. These included actions against software
resellers and dealers, counterfeit producers and end-
user organizations that made unauthorized copies of
software. Companies found infringing software copyrights were required to compensate the software
industry for losses and all legal fees, besides making
a commitment to comply with copyright laws.

However, while the BSA was a non-profit
industry association, its members were almost exclusively publicly traded software firms. Thus, while the
BSA had a commitment to increasing the size of the
software market, its membership was driven by a
"clear profit motivation".[12] Obviously, these two
agendas—while complementary for the membership—did not always go hand-in-hand.

In the first instance of combating software piracy
in developing economies, the overall market size
would quite obviously *decrease*—perhaps dramatically—as individuals and companies (particularly
small- and medium-sized companies) would be
unable to afford to purchase legitimate copies,
lowering demand. Also excluded from the market
would be those consumers who would later have
upgraded to a legitimate version of the software.
(Once, for example, they had satisfied themselves that
the utility of the software justified the price.)

Thus, while the argument often put forward was
that piracy eroded the profits of software companies,
discouraging them from entering certain markets, the
first issue for all of these companies was to create a
market. It was for this reason that many software
companies turned a blind eye to piracy in small and
developing economies so that the demand for their
product could be generated. Once the demand had
been created, the software vendors were much more
intent on protecting their property rights and
pursuing profit maximization.

Fighting Software Piracy

It's just a matter of necessity. We want the software and we want it now. We need it. But we can't get it any other way: the real stuff is overpriced, and there's zero support.[13]

—AMERICAN COMPUTER ENTREPRENEUR IN ASIA

The software industry covered a wide variety of categories, including output from the music industry (audio cassettes, records and CDs), the film industry (video cassettes, VCDs and laser discs) and the computer industry (computer software on "floppy" diskettes, CD-ROMs and, more recently, via the Internet). Software piracy is defined as the unauthorized copying and distribution of copyrighted software products. Software anti-piracy guidelines were originally based upon copyright laws that were designed to protect the intellectual rights inherent in scientific and manufacturing patents. For the purposes of worldwide trade, these were enshrined in the Berne Convention. Significantly, the U.S., now the world's policeman and enforcement champion in intellectual property rights, did not join the Berne Convention as a signatory until 1989—one year after the formation of the BSA!

The Berne Convention

The Berne Convention—the oldest and most widely approved international copyright treaty[14]—was first adopted on September 9, 1886, in Berne, Switzerland.[15] The agreement grew out of a perceived need in the late nineteenth Century to protect authored works from international pirating, or unauthorized copying.[16] A growing demand for new printed materials during the late nineteenth Century motivated many publishers to reprint unauthorized versions of foreign works. Authors whose works were pirated had little recourse against the publisher because copyright laws were typically enacted on a national basis. Such laws gave copyright protection only to authors who were nationals of the country in which the laws were enacted.

The Berne Convention established several principles of international copyright that have remained through each version of the treaty: the principle of national treatment (under which a country extends the same protection to foreigners that it accords to its own authors); minimum standards of protection that all signatories must meet; automatic protection of copyrighted works as soon as they are created,

without any formalities required such as notice or registration.

However, because it was a net importer of copyrighted materials, the U.S. resisted joining the Berne Convention for over a century. Adherence to the treaty's conventions would have required U.S. publishers of foreign works—many of whom produced pirated copies—to pay royalties and fees to foreign copyright holders. Prior to World War II, U.S. trade representatives argued that ideas were free and should not be regulated by such restrictive practices. However, by the end of World War II, the U.S. had become a major exporter of copyrighted materials, and by the late-1970s the U.S. had acquired substantial trade dominance in what are known as "cultural" industries—film and music software and publishing, to the extent that by the late-1980s approximately 70 percent of the U.S. software industry's revenues were generated from foreign markets. It had long become clear that it would be to the country's economic advantage if its own authors and copyright holders could be assured of receiving royalties from overseas publishing.[17]

By the 1980s, the U.S. was still one of the few major developed countries not abiding by the Berne Convention. When it became clear that the U.S.'s role as a pariah in international copyright had begun to erode its position in reaching other trade agreements concerning intellectual property, Congress finally passed the Berne Convention Implementation Act of 1988. This act made the U.S. a party to the Berne Convention beginning in 1989, officially ending U.S. copyright isolation.

To attack the growth of computer software piracy, the BSA, upon establishment, worked in conjunction with the U.S. Government through the U.S. Trade Representative (USTR). The BSA provided a list of countries requiring U.S. attention under the Special 301 provisions of the U.S. Trade Act of 1974, based on inadequate levels of copyright protection within those nations.[18] "Special 301" authorized the U.S. Government to impose unilateral trade sanctions against countries that had failed to provide adequate and effective protection for intellectual property owners.

Special 301

The "Special 301" provisions of the Trade Act of 1974 (as amended) allowed the USTR to "determine whether the acts, policies and practices of foreign countries deny adequate and effective protection of intellectual property rights or fair and equitable market access for U.S. persons that rely on intellectual property protection."[19] Special 301 was further amended in the Uruguay Round Agreements Act (of the General Agreement on Tariffs and Trade (GATT)) to clarify that a country can be found to deny adequate and effective intellectual property protection even if it is in compliance with its obligations under the TRIPS (Trade Related Intellectual Property in Services) Agreement. It was also amended to direct the USTR to take into account a country's prior status and behaviour under "Special 301." Once a pool of countries has been determined,[20] the USTR was required to decide which if any of these countries should be designated as "Priority Foreign Countries."

Priority Foreign Countries were those countries that: (i) had the most onerous and egregious acts, policies and practices, with the greatest adverse impact (actual or potential) on relevant U.S. products; and, (ii) were not engaged in good-faith negotiations or making significant progress in negotiations to address such problems. If a country was identified as a Priority Foreign Country, the USTR would then decide within 30 days whether to initiate an investigation of the acts, policies and practices that were the basis for identifying the country as a Priority Foreign Country.[21] Once listed as a Priority Foreign Country, the country in question received "priority attention," which could include trade sanctions, market restrictions or other such like-minded unilateral trade responses.

In 1995, under recommendation from the BSA, the U.S. placed Hong Kong on its trade provisions watchlist, threatening the territory with sanctions under "Special 301" if the situation in software piracy did not improve in the territory. Raids were conducted by the Hong Kong Customs and Excise Department (CED), and CD reproduction plants were shut down. The BSA suggested that the response by Hong Kong authorities was good—but not good enough. Subsequently, Hong Kong remained on the U.S. trade watchlist.

From the BSA's perspective, the focus upon Hong Kong was warranted for several reasons. In comparison to developed markets within the Asia-Pacific region, such as Japan or Singapore, the level of software piracy remained high. Second, in contrast to most other localities in the region, the relative level of piracy was increasing. Third, the role of the Hong Kong market was not simply as a separate individual market, but as a point of trans-shipment, particularly to and from mainland China.

By 1995, 26 factories had been identified in southern China as being responsible for the production of some 75 million compact discs each year (even though the local market could only absorb approximately five million).[22] Copies produced in China had been identified as passing through Hong Kong to places as far away as Latin America and Europe. Many of these plants were known to be state-owned.[23] Thus the production of pirated computer software could be—at least in part—attributed to the "support" of the Chinese Government. Moreover, the counterfeit factories were inevitably owned or run by Chinese businessmen who were well connected to the regional or city governments. The situation was further complicated by the fact that most plants operated as legitimate businesses, producing compact discs and computer software for foreign buyers. They simply did not ask many questions on the legitimacy of the production or on the possible violation of copyright.[24]

Though the Hong Kong Government was able to make some progress in fighting against software piracy, the software piracy rate kept increasing. In May 1997, the BSA recommended that Hong Kong be put on a watch list with a scheduled out-of-cycle review.[25] Hong Kong would be removed from the list only if it had achieved distinct improvements in the anti-piracy situation. For many in Hong Kong, the question by this time was: Which market was being targeted?

By 1997, Hong Kong policy-makers were trying to boost the territory's "high-tech" capabilities. High software prices threatened to drive down computer sales, as most new PCs already came with thousands of dollars worth of software pre-installed, reducing exposure to cutting-edge software for young programmers. It also threatened to reduce the amount of computer trade in and through the territory. The factories that produced illegitimate CD-ROMs in China were almost all located in the province of Guangdong. Costing several million dollars and, in many cases, using sophisticated Philips replicating equipment, the enterprises were usually joint ventures with Hong Kong businessmen.

The BSA, therefore, had been forced to move away from its traditional emphasis upon local market potential and the damage that piracy was doing to local development, as there simply was very little software development taking place in Hong Kong.

Indeed, they had shifted focus to Hong Kong's traditional role as a trade entrepot, and as a "gateway" into China. With Hong Kong having built much of its contemporary success by being able to exploit "gray" market areas between Western and Chinese legal and commercial interpretations, software piracy was itself stimulating significant economic activity: from production and transportation, to sales and even "protection." It was upon this economic chain and Hong Kong's role as China's "window on the world" that the BSA in conjunction with the U.S. Commercial Service sought to attack the flow of software piracy. Unless Hong Kong was able to use its position and influence to curb the flow of pirated goods, the U.S. would attack Hong Kong's position as a regional trade center.

BP Amoco: Financing Development of the Caspian Oil Fields

One of the many challenges facing the Finance Group after the BP/Amoco merger in 1998 was to evaluate and, if necessary, restructure the company's global investment portfolio, including its 34 percent share of the Azerbaijani International Oil Consortium (AIOC). The 11-firm consortium was in the process of developing oil fields in the Azerbaijani sector of the Caspian Sea (Exhibit 1 identifies the AIOC members). As of March 1999, AIOC had completed the $1.9 billion Early Oil Project, which was producing 100,000 barrels of crude oil per day (bpd). The next three stages, known as the Full Field Development Project, were expected to cost an additional $8 to $10 billion and would bring total production to 800,000 bpd by 2005. [1]

Before the merger, BP and Amoco held the two largest interests in AIOC (17 percent each), yet they had chosen different strategies for funding their shares of the Early Oil Project. Whereas BP had used general corporate funds, Amoco was one of five AIOC partners that had raised $400 million of project finance with assistance from two multilateral agencies. Now, as a merged entity, the Finance Group had to reassess the firm's financial strategy for the Early Oil Project and determine the best way to finance the Full Field Development Project. While it was possible to continue with a dual financing strategy, such an approach could complicate BP Amoco's management of the asset as well as impair its effectiveness as the *de facto* leader of the joint venture.

Caspian Oil and the AIOC

The Caspian Basin (see the map in Exhibit 2) had been the site of significant oil production since the middle of the nineteenth century. Although the fields had, at one time, provided as much as 70 percent of the former Soviet Union's output, production had fallen to only 8 percent by the late 1980s. [2] Despite the decline, many industry experts believed the region held from 50 to 200 billion barrels of undeveloped oil and gas reserves, an amount equal to the reserves in the North Sea. [3]

With the transformation of the Soviet Union into the Commonwealth of Independent States in 1991, Azerbaijan and the other Soviet republics became independent countries. Azerbaijan, on the western shore of the Caspian Sea, had a population of 8 million and a land area slightly smaller than the state of Maine. About 90 percent of the population were Azeri, an ethnic and linguistic group with mixed Turkish and Iranian heritage. In common with the other Caspian Sea littoral states, it had a majority Muslim population, a high unemployment rate, a low standard of living, and an economy that was dependent on oil (Exhibit 3 provides data on

Dean's Research Fellow Michael Kane and Professor Benjamin Esty prepared this case. HBS cases are developed solely as the basis for class discussion. Cases are not intended to serve as endorsements, sources of primary data, or illustrations of effective or ineffective management. "BP Amoco (B): Financing Development of the Caspian Oil Fields." Copyright © 2002 by the President and Fellows of Harvard College. Harvard Business School Case 9-201-067. This case was prepared by Professor Benjamin Esty and Dean Michael Kane as the basis for class discussion rather than to illustrate either effective or ineffective handling of an administrative situation. Reprinted by permission of Harvard Business School.

EXHIBIT 1

Azerbaijan International Operating Committee (AIOC) Members as of 12/31/98 (except Itochu Corp—FYE 3/31/99)

Company	Country	AIOC Share	Assets (billions)	Net Worth (billions)	Debt to Total Capital	S&P Debt Rating[a]	Revenues (billions)	Net Income (billions)	Capital Expend. (billions)	Owner-ship	Reserves (barrels in billions)[b]
BP Amoco p.l.c[c]	U.K.	34.1%	$84.5	$41.8	24.0%		$68.0	$3.3	$10.4	public	15.2
Amoco Corp.	U.S.	17.0				AAA					
British Petrol.	U.K.	17.1				AA					
Statoil	Norway	8.6	18.6	5.3	47.0	AA	14.1	0.0	2.8	government	4.6
Turkish Petroleum	Turkey	6.8	0.3	0.2	34.0	unrated	0.3	0.0	0.1	government	n/a
Amerada Hess	U.S.	1.7	7.9	2.6	44.2	BB–	6.6	(0.5)	1.4	public	1.0
Unocal	U.S.	10.0	7.6	2.2	54.3	A	5.0	0.1	1.7	public	1.6
Exxon	U.S.	8.0	92.6	43.8	16.2	AAA	118.0	6.4	8.8	public	14.1
Pennzoil	U.S.	4.8	n/a	n/a	44.9	n/a	1.8	0.0	n/a	public	n/a
Ramco PLC	U.K.	2.1	0.1	0.1	0.0	unrated	0.0	0.0	0.0	public	10.9
LUKoil	Russia	10.0	3.9	2.1	33.0	unrated	1.9	(0.1)	0.8	government	10.7
Itochu Corp.	Japan	3.9	56.9	2.6	85.0	unrated	108.7	(0.3)	0.7	public	n/a
Socar	Azerbaijan	10.0	n/a	n/a	n/a	unrated	n/a	n/a	n/a	government	n/a

Source: Company Annual Reports.

a. Senior unsecured debt rating, except in the case of Amerada Hess which is an issuer rating.

b. Reserves of crude oil and natural gas in billions of barrels or oil equivalent.

c. British Petroleum plc and Amoco Corporation became subsidiaries of BP Amoco on 12/31/98.

Azerbaijan and other AIOC member countries).

The years following independence were marked by coup attempts, terrorist activities, declining GDP—GDP fell by more than 60 percent between 1988 and 1994, and external conflicts with neighboring countries. In fact, Azerbaijan and Armenia had been fighting over disputed border provinces since the early 1990s. A 1994 cease-fire had ended the war, but other border conflicts with Russia to the north and Iran to the south remained a threat. As one author noted, the region "almost seems to have been made for war" with more than 50 ethnic groups living along the 900-mile Caucasus mountain range.[4]

Heydar Aliyev, a former head of the KGB in the Brezhnev administration, was elected President in 1993. In 1994, he signed a Production Sharing Agreement (PSA) for Caspian oil as a first step towards developing Azerbaijan's natural resources. This "Deal of the Century," as it was called in the popular press, created a 30-year agreement between the Azerbaijani government and AIOC, a joint venture including SOCAR (the State Oil Company of Azerbaijan), BP, Amoco, Russia's and Turkey's national oil companies, and several other foreign oil companies. The PSA gave AIOC exclusive rights to develop three geologically connected oil fields—

EXHIBIT 2

Map of the Caspian Region

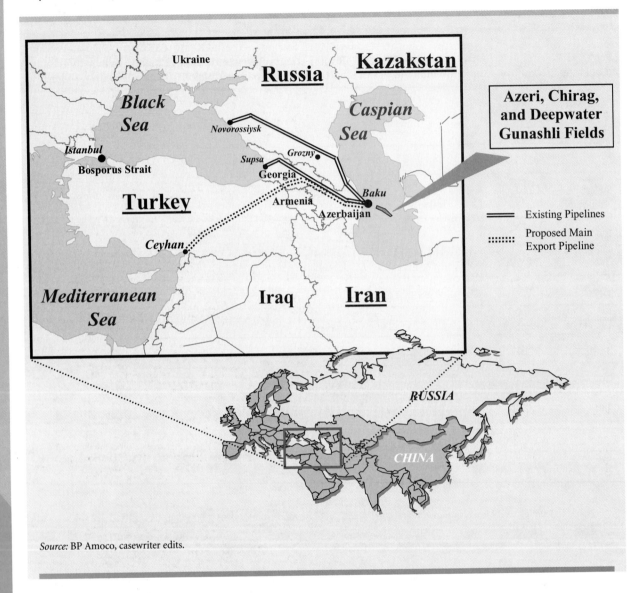

Source: BP Amoco, casewriter edits.

Azeri, Chirag, and deepwater Gunashli—in the western part of the Caspian Sea. SOCAR had discovered, but only partially developed, the fields between 1979 and 1987. According to AIOC, the fields contained between 4.5 and 5.0 billion barrels of oil.[5]

The diversity of AIOC's membership reflected Aliyev's development strategy. One industry analyst wrote, "President Heydar Aliyev's goal has been to attract as wide as possible a variety of oil companies to the tiny Caspian state, so as to anchor Azerbaijan firmly within the Western powers' interest and assure

its political future."[6] By early 1999, Azerbaijan had signed 17 similar agreements with potential capital spending of $40 billion.[7] During this period, BP, Amoco, and other foreign oil companies were negotiating similar concessions with other Caspian states.

The Caspian Oil Fields

AIOC had the exclusive right to develop the Azeri, Chirag, and deepwater Gunashli fields subject to

EXHIBIT 3

Statistics on Caspian Countries and AIOC Member Countries (1998)

Country	Population (millions)	GNP (billions)	GNP per Capita Rank	Euromoney Country Investment Risk[a]	S&P Sovereign Debt Rating[b]	Institutional Investor Risk Rating[c]
Armenia	3.8	$1.7	162	29.6	unrated	unrated
Azerbaijan	7.9	3.8	161	33.4	unrated	unrated
Georgia	5.4	5.3	139	25.7	unrated	10.8
Japan	126.4	4,089.1	7	90.9	AAA	86.5
Kazakstan	15.6	20.9	126	40.3	B+	29.7
Norway	4.4	152.0	4	94.0	AAA	87.7
Russia	146.9	331.8	101	23.0	CCC	19.3
Turkey	63.5	200.5	89	48.5	B	38.9
Turkmenistan	4.7	n/a	n/a	31.8	unrated	unrated
United States	270.3	7,903.0	10	94.5	AAA	90.9
United Kingdom	59.1	1,264.3	22	91.2	AAA	90.2
Uzbekistan	24.1	22.9	141	28.8	unrated	18.9

Sources: WorldBank, *World Development Indicators*, 2000 ; Euromoney, Institutional Investor.

a. 27th Annual Rating, March 1999. The Euromoney risk rating measures the relative risk of investing in 180 countries, based on surveys of economists and analysts, and runs on a scale from 0 (high risk) to 100 (low risk).

b. The S&P sovereign debt rating measures the capacity and willingness of host governments to repay their foreign currency debt when due.

c. The *Institutional Investor* risk rating measures the risk of government default on debt, and runs on a scale from 0 (high risk) to 100 (low risk).

certain conditions. It had to complete a seismic survey, an environmental impact study, and a series of test wells. Based on the findings, AIOC then had to submit a detailed plan of development to SOCAR. The actual development plan consisted of four parts, the Early Oil Project followed by the three-stage Full Field Development Project. Both AIOC and SOCAR had the right to approve each stage, based on the results of the previous stage. In addition to laying out these rights and obligations, the PSA created a revenue sharing agreement for the output and established a special tax regime for AIOC in lieu of other local taxes.[8]

The Early Oil Project involved developing the Chirag Field by refurbishing an offshore production platform, drilling new wells, and constructing a 105-mile sub-sea pipeline to an onshore terminal. It also involved rebuilding two export pipelines to the Black Sea—a 750-mile northern route to the Russian port of Novorossiysk and a 550-mile western route to the Georgian port of Supsa—and constructing an export terminal at Supsa. As of March 1999, Early Oil was complete except for the pipeline through Georgia. It was producing 100,000 bpd as planned and shipping the oil via the northern pipeline to Novorossisyk (see

Exhibit 2). Originally estimated to cost $1 billion, the final cost came in at $1.9 billion primarily due to greater than expected expenditures on the western pipeline.[9]

Having essentially finished the Early Oil Project, AIOC began to concentrate on developing the full field. The first stage, development of the Azeri field, would begin in early 2000, cost $2.6 to $3.1 billion, and bring total production to 300,000 bpd by 2003.[10] The second stage, planned for 2002, would develop the deepwater Gunashli field at an estimated cost of $3 billion. The third and final stage, planned for 2003 and 2004, targeted further development of the Azeri field at an estimated cost of $2 billion.[11] The final stages would increase production by 300,000 bpd and 200,000 bpd, respectively, for a total production rate of 800,000 bpd by 2005. The fields would produce at this rate until 2011, at which time output would gradually decline as the reserves were depleted.[12] According to the plan, the refurbished pipelines from the Early Oil Project could transport the production through Stage 1, but additional production would require a new pipeline that was not currently part of the AIOC investment budget.[13]

AIOC had recognized the need for a new pipeline since the very first PSA negotiations in the early 1990's because the Caspian Sea and the former Soviet republics of Azerbaijan, Kazakstan, Turkmenistan and Uzbekistan were landlocked. A banker from Citibank summed up the political and transportation issues this way:

> It is hard to find a more geo-politically challenging territory than the homes of Caspian Basin oil, and not surprisingly, investors have been reluctant to take the risky bet that the oil can be developed, produced and, crucially, transported to safer shores without wars or government action getting in the way.[14]

Driven by these concerns, oil companies and governments engaged in an active debate over the route, timing, cost, and financial responsibility for a Main Export Pipeline (MEP). The U.S., Turkish, Georgian, and Azerbaijani governments became advocates for a 1,080-mile pipeline from Baku through Georgia and Turkey to the Mediterranean port of Ceyhan, thereby avoiding both Russia and Iran (see Exhibit 2). With cost estimates ranging from $2.6 to $4 billion, additional reserves from other Caspian producers would be needed to justify the investment.[15] By one estimate, the MEP would be economical only if there were at least 6 billion barrels of proven reserves to transport.[16] At the time, however, it was not clear who was going to build the MEP, where it would go, or when it would be completed.

Financing Early Oil

AIOC was organized as an unincorporated joint venture between subsidiaries from each member company.[17] Each subsidiary was responsible for funding a certain percentage of the capital expenditures and was entitled to receive an equivalent percentage of the output. The obligations to provide funds were several, meaning that members were responsible for only their shares of the total. Members achieved limited liability by incorporating special purpose subsidiaries as their investment vehicles and created centralized project management by forming a joint operating company with staff and funds contributed by the members.

Under this structure, each partner had a choice in how to finance its share of the $1.9 billion Early Oil Project. Six members with combined interests of 48.2 percent chose to use internal funds. For example, BP contributed approximately $325 million to cover its share (17.1% × $1.9 billion). In contrast, five members of AIOC (Amoco, Exxon, Unocal, LUKoil, and Turkish Petroleum) formed a Mutual Interest Group (MIG) for the purpose of obtaining a project loan with assistance from two multilateral agencies, the International Finance Corporation (IFC) and the European Bank for Reconstruction and Development (EBRD).[18] The multilaterals not only provided access to long-term funds that banks were often unwilling to provide, but also helped mitigate political risks because of their roles as development banks and lenders of last resort. The MIG's creation surprised many analysts because "Exxon could clearly fund its 8 percent share comfortably on balance sheet, and Unocal could do the same with its 10 percent holding. (And the) appetite among banks for a non-recourse debt package for Russia's LUKoil and Turkish Petroleum . . . (was) likely to be limited.[19] According to a senior project finance banker:

> These are tougher countries from a political risk point of view than such countries as Chile and the Philippines. Some are quite new as autonomous countries, some harbor long standing border tensions, others have less than stable governments or

economic policies. So it will not be an easy process for lenders to get comfortable.[20]

In February 1999, the IFC, EBRD, and MIG members closed a $400 million, limited recourse project financing with an effective interest rate of less than 10 percent, representing a spread of 350–400 basis points over the current 6-month LIBOR rate.[21] Traditionally, the multilateral agencies funded projects in one of three ways: direct lending ("A loans"), indirect lending as agent for a syndicated bank loan ("B loans"), or equity contributions. In this case, the financing was structured as ten A loans and ten B loans—each agency (IFC and EBRD) made an A and a B loan to special purpose subsidiaries at each of the five MIG partners.[22]

Syndication of the $200 million in B loans proved difficult, yielding commitments totaling $75 million from three commercial banks. Concurrently, the IFC and EBRD funded $150 million out of the $200 million in A loans, yet hoped to raise the rest of the money once the "appetite" for emerging market debt improved.[23] Even though the financing was not complete, it was seen as an important milestone for the region in general and for AIOC in particular. The deputy director of the EBRD's natural resources group said:

> The kind of long-term financing that the EBRD and the International Finance Corporation (IFC) has provided . . . has not been previously made available to the region. The commitment of the EBRD and IFC will send a positive signal about financing projects in the region.[24]

The Finance Group's Decisions

In March 1999, BP Amoco's Finance Group needed to resolve two issues: first, whether to refinance Amoco's project loan from the Early Oil Project; and second, how to finance BP Amoco's share of the Full Field Development Project, currently estimated at approximately $2.8 billion ($8.1 billion of expenditures × 34.1 percent share). In deciding whether to prepay the IFC/EBRD loans, the Group had to consider the costs and benefits of prepayment. While BP Amoco could lower its funding cost by prepaying the loan, the total amount outstanding was only $73.8 million ($225 million of loans × 32.8%, representing BP Amoco's proportionate share of the MIG loans). Historically, BP had been able to issue medium-term bonds at

40–80 basis points over equivalent government bonds, issue long-term bonds at 80–120 basis points over government bonds, and obtain bank loans at LIBOR. (In March 1999, the 10-year U.S. Treasury yield was 5.20 percent and the current 6-month LIBOR rate was 5.30 percent.) Because of the cost advantage it had in raising corporate debt, BP preferred to use internal funds rather than project loans to finance its oil and gas investments. Prepayment, however, would not relieve BP of its administrative and reporting duties as the project operator. More importantly, it might send a negative signal to the other MIG members and could jeopardize AIOC's relationship with the IFC and EBRD.

The second decision, how to finance the Full Field Development Project, was more critical because capital expenditures for Stage 1 were projected to start in less than a year. BP Amoco could finance its $1.0 billion obligation (34.1% × $3.0 billion) for Stage 1 in several ways. Like the Early Oil Project, it could use a dual financing strategy, whereby half its commitment would come from internal funds and half from a project loan. The advantage of this approach was that it gave them the best of both worlds; the disadvantage was that it also gave them the worst of both worlds.

Alternatively, BP Amoco could join some or all of the AIOC members and try to arrange a project loan following the IFC/EBRD model used for Early Oil. This strategy allowed BP Amoco to leverage its investment with outside funds and extended the multilaterals' commitment to the project. The real question was how much protection was needed? Did the existing commitment provide sufficient protection against political risks, or did they need more? The main concerns with this option, particularly given the incomplete syndication, were the time needed to close a deal and the cost associated with project debt.

The third option for Stage 1 was to fund it entirely using internal funds. Like each of the options, this one had drawbacks. For example, by stepping away from the IFC/EBRD process, BP Amoco could be perceived as making it harder for the remaining members to negotiate a good deal—BP Amoco was, after all, the consortium's largest investor and project operator. Having weaker consortium members negotiate with lenders might result in a deal that unduly hindered BP Amoco's operational and managerial flexibility. More importantly, it could establish disadvantageous precedents for future financings. A related problem involved decision making at the consortium level. If, as expected, at least some partners partici-pated in another project loan, would the dual financing strategy create an environment prone to disagreement? A final concern was that other AIOC partners might accuse BP Amoco of free riding on their efforts to set up and carry the more expensive financing, while sharing in the political risk protec-tion it provided. Whether these arguments against the use of internal funds outweighed the advantages from BP Amoco's perspective was not clear.

A final, though not immediate, concern was how BP was going to finance later stages of Full Field Development. Its ability to participate in project financings for later stages might be affected by how it decided to finance the earlier stages. Specifically, if by abstaining from an IFC financing for Stage 1, BP Amoco was perceived to make the financing more difficult, or if the financing actually failed, then the IFC might be unreceptive to later requests for financing. For the Finance Group, the question boiled down to one of perspective. Should they view the Full Field Development as a single project or a series of projects?

Project Risks

The oil industry was notorious for reserve, price, and, in certain cases like Azerbaijan, transportation risks. Compounding these risks was the fact that it was an especially volatile period for emerging market invest-ments. As the Finance Group contemplated their options, they had to consider how these risks affected their current and future AIOC commitments, and the probability they would earn an acceptable rate of return. But they could not restrict their attention to AIOC assets alone because BP Amoco was, concur-rently, the largest foreign investor in four unrelated exploration concessions in Azerbaijan alone.[25] As exploration projects, these investments were much smaller (e.g. $100 million) than the investment in a typical development project such as the Full Field Development Project (e.g. several billion).

1. Political Risks

Political instability in Azerbaijan was an immediate concern because success hinged upon local support for the project. Although the 76-year old Aliyev was in control in early 1999, the Economist Intelligence Unit noted the precarious situation that existed at the time:

> The sudden departure of the president, Heydar Aliyev, for medical treatment in Turkey on January 17th (1999) reopens the issue of the succession in Azerbaijan . . . . There are real questions about whether a transition, especially one prompted by the sudden incapacitation of Mr. Aliyev, could be effected peacefully.[26]

A change in leadership could easily exacerbate exist-ing disputes. For example, the ownership of oil and gas in the Caspian Sea was hotly contested between all of the countries bordering the Sea. Russia and Iran both rejected Azerbaijan's claims to reserves, contending that the Caspian was a lake and, therefore, its oil should be under international law. Without the Azeri government to enforce its claims, AIOC could lose its exclusive right to develop the fields. In addi-tion, there was the smoldering dispute with Armenia, which could re-ignite at any moment.

Another dimension of political risk was the region's new and essentially untested legal infrastruc-ture. Russia and the former Soviet republics had, to varying degrees, recently adopted new corporate, securities, and bankruptcy laws. Yet as one AIOC partner cautioned:

> Azerbaijan lacks a fully developed legal system, which could result in legal uncertainties and, ulti-mately, investment risks . . . Effective redress in Azeri courts for a breach of law or regulation may be diffi-cult or impossible to obtain, particularly against state agencies.[27]

BP Amoco had good reason to be concerned about these risks because of its $571 million invest-ment OAO Sidanko, Russia's fifth largest oil and gas company. Sidanko had declared bankruptcy in January 1999, and was presenting a high-profile test case of Russia's new bankruptcy law. While some argued the Russian legal system was plagued with asset stripping, tainted court rulings, and corruption, others argued the new system might actually work in a fair and efficient manner, albeit with some growing pains.[28]

2. Financial Risks

The financial crisis that began in Thailand in 1997, and spread to Russia in the fall of 1998, was now affecting emerging markets around the world. A project finance banker said: "Everything has stopped in Russia. It is becoming increasingly difficult to open credit lines for Russian projects, even with the support of the multilaterals."[29] The crises would surely affect both the availability and cost of funds. As evidence, the MIG financing was the first significant syndication of long-term debt to the oil and gas sector in the former Soviet Union, and even this financing was incomplete.[30] Previous loans were small, short-term, and expensive with rates up to 450 basis points over LIBOR.[31]

The Russian crisis also increased the likelihood that government–owned AIOC member LUKoil might have trouble raising the funds required for its 10 percent participation. If such an event occurred, it would create a difficult situation for the other partners in deciding how to proceed.

3. Transportation Risks

The northern and western pipelines to the Black Sea could handle the production levels projected through Stage 1, but presented operational and economic risks that made them an unsatisfactory long-term solution. The northern route was owned and operated by SOCAR on the Azerbaijan side and by Transneft, the Russian state-owned pipeline system, on the Russian side. Thus, Transneft controlled pricing and service decisions for a pipeline that was already more expensive to use than the western pipeline.[32] Perhaps even more troubling was the fact that the pipeline crossed through Chechnya where a civil war had been raging for years. Commenting on these risks, *The Economist* wrote: "Azerbaijan is worried that the Russians will have a stranglehold, and the oil companies fret about security: even with a bypass (around Chechnya), the pipeline will still be within shooting distance of the unpredictable Chechens."[33]

Even if the oil did reach the Black Sea, it still had to get through the Bosporus Straits before it reached western markets. As part of its on-going campaign to bring the Main Export Pipeline through Turkey to Ceyhan, the Turkish Government had taken an increasingly restrictive stance against tanker traffic through the Straits. The Turkish Minister for Maritime Affairs had recently warned the Caspian oil producers that Turkey was ready to raise transit fees fivefold, and reportedly said, "Then they will see what happens to their dreams of cheap oil."[34]

4. Industry Risks

Like all upstream investment projects, the Caspian development projects were subject to reserve and commodity price risk. Both the level of actual reserves in the three fields and the ability to get them out of the ground were still largely unknowns. In fact, other exploration ventures in the Azeri sector of the Caspian had come up short:

> CIPCO, a consortium led by the U.S. company Pennzenergy, has decided to wind up operations next month after discovering an offshore field that was uneconomic. The North Absheron Operating Company led by Unocal and BP Amoco, which is drilling on the same structure, may not have found enough oil to justify exploiting the field.[35]

Besides reserve risks, AIOC also had to contend with volatility in crude oil prices. In early 1999, the price of oil had collapsed to $10.00 per barrel, a 25-year low (Exhibit 4a shows historical prices for Brent Crude, a roughly comparable grade of oil.) Low oil prices in 1998 had dramatically affected the reported earnings, market values, and capital spending programs of oil companies around the world. For example, BP Amoco's net income was down by almost 50 percent (from $6.0 to 3.3 billion) and its capital expenditures were down by almost 10 percent (from $11.4 to 10.4 billion) in 1998. In response to falling oil prices, David Woodward, AIOC president, announced a 20 percent cut in the consortium's budget for the coming year and warned: "With oil prices hovering around the US$10 a barrel mark, the high cost of [getting and] shipping oil from the Caspian region—on average US$7 a barrel—is threatening the viability of much existing production, never mind new investment."[36] In its analysis of the Caspian oil projects, BP Amoco had used $14.00 per barrel as its benchmark price, well above the current price.[37]

According to traded futures contracts, however, market participants were expecting prices to rise in the coming years (see Exhibit 4b). Given the project's cost structure and expected production levels, AIOC's financial returns would clearly be a function of the existence of reserves and the price at which they could be sold (Exhibits 5a and 5b present estimates of project economics and production levels, respectively.)

Historical Price Per Barrel of Brent Crude (January 1982 to March 1999)

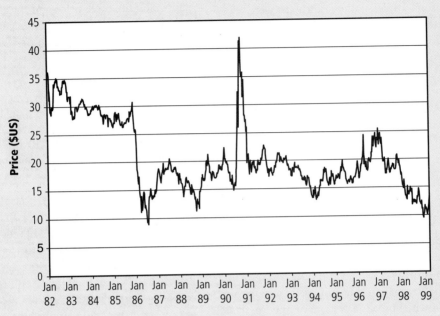

Source: Datastream.

Capital Markets Data as of March 15,1999

Maturity	U.S. Treasury Yields	Brent Crude Future Prices ($ per bbl)	Light Sweet Crude Oil Futures Prices ($ per bbl)	Projected Prices for World Oil ($ per bbl)[a]
1 month		$12.56	$14.49	
3 months	4.60%	12.61	14.40	
6 months	4.69	12.65	14.28	
1 year	4.75	12.83	14.31	$16.55
2 years	4.95	13.45	14.60	16.85
3 years	5.10	13.65	14.95	17.24
4 years			15.35	17.48
5 years	5.06		15.90	17.80
7 years	5.29			18.15
10 years	5.14			18.64
20 years				20.46
30 years	5.51			

Sources: Datastream, *The Wall Street Journal,* and case writer analysis.

a. Based on projections from the Energy Information Administration's *Annual Energy Outlook,* 2000 (in constant 1998 $US). The World oil price is an annual average acquisition cost of imported crude oils to U.S. refiners.

EXHIBIT 5a

Estimated Project Economics for the Azeri, Chirag, and Deepwater Gunashli Fields

	Project Economics (per barrel)			
Oil prices (assumed)	**$10.00**	**$15.00**	**$20.00**	**$25.00**
Production costs[a]	4.00	4.00	4.00	4.00
Transportation costs[b]	3.00	3.00	3.00	3.00
Gross profit	3.00	8.00	13.00	18.00
AIOC cost recovery[c]	1.50	4.00	6.50	9.00
Pre-tax profit	1.50	4.00	6.50	9.00
AIOC share[d]	1.05	2.80	4.55	6.30
Azerbaijani taxes[e]	0.26	0.70	1.14	1.58
After tax profit to AIOC	0.79	2.10	3.41	4.72
Total available to AIOC for cost recovery and profit[f]	**$2.29**	**$6.10**	**$9.91**	**$13.72**

Source: Casewriter estimates based on public information.
a. Production costs are assumed higher than BP Amoco's world average of $3.05/bbl (Amoco Corp., Form 8K, 8/12/98).
b. The PSA contemplates transportation costs to the Mediterranean of $3.00/bbl (Ramco Energy Prospectus, 3/10/97, p. 40).
c. The PSA allocates 50% of gross profit for cost recovery (Ramco Energy Prospectus, 3/10/97, p. 40).
d. Initially, there is a 70/30 split between AIOC and SOCAR (Ramco Energy Prospectus, 3/10/97, p. 40).
e. The Azeri tax rate for the AIOC is 25% (Ramco Energy Prospectus, 3/10/97, p. 47).
f. Includes the AIOC cost recovery plus the after-tax profit to AIOC, but excludes certain bonus payments due to SOCAR. This number is approximately equal to the free cash flow AIOC could expect to receive per barrel.

EXHIBIT 5b

Estimated Production Volumes for Azeri, Chirag, and Deepwater Gunashli Project

Year		Average Daily Production (barrels of oil)	Production (millions of barrels per year)	Capital Expenditures ($ millions)
1998				$1,900
1999	Early Oil Complete	100,000	36.5	$1,000
2000		100,000	36.5	$1,000
2001		100,000	36.5	$1,100

continued...

EXHIBIT 5b

Estimated Production Volumes for Azeri, Chirag, and Deepwater Gunashli Project (Continued)

Year		Average Daily Production (barrels of oil)	Production (millions of barrels per year)	Capital Expenditures ($ millions)
2002		200,000	73.0	$1,000
2003	Stage 1 Complete	200,000	73.0	$1,500
2004	Stage 2 Complete	400,000	146.0	$1,500
2005	Stage 3 Complete	600,000	219.0	$1,000
2006		800,000	292.0	
2007		800,000	292.0	
2008		800,000	292.0	
2009		800,000	292.0	
2010		800,000	292.0	
2011		800,000	292.0	
2012		700,000	255.5	
2013		700,000	255.5	
2014		700,000	255.5	
2015		600,000	219.0	
2016		600,000	219.0	
2017		600,000	219.0	
2018		500,000	182.5	
2019		500,000	182.5	
2020		500,000	182.5	
2021		300,000	109.5	
2022		200,000	73.0	
2023		0	0.0	0.0
Total			**4,526.0**	**$10,000**

Source: Casewriter estimates assuming reserves of 4.5 billion barrels of oil and $10 billion total development cost.

3

Interacting Effectively in an International Environment
Grupo Financiero Inverlat

By October 1996, it had been four months since management at the Bank of Nova Scotia (BNS) increased its stake in the Mexican bank, Grupo Financiero Inverlat (Inverlat), from 8.1 percent, to an equity and convertible debt package that represented 54 percent ownership of the bank. A team of Canadian managers had been sent to Mexico to assume management of the ailing financial institution immediately after the deal was struck. Jim O'Donnell, now Director General Adjunto (DGA)[1] of the retail bank at Inverlat, had been there from the beginning.

Jim was a member of the original group that performed the due diligence to analyze Inverlat's finances before negotiations could begin. Later, he and his wife Anne-Marie (also an executive with the bank) were the first Canadians to arrive in Mexico in May 1996. Since then, 14 additional Canadian managers had arrived, and restructured the four most senior levels within Inverlat. The pace of change had been overwhelming. Jim now wondered how successful his early efforts had been and what could be done to facilitate the remaining restructuring.

A Brief Inverlat History

In 1982, in his last days as leader of the Mexican Republic, President Lopez Portillo announced the nationalization of Mexico's banks. They would remain government institutions for the next 8 to 10 years. Managers characterized the years under government control as a period of stagnation in which the structure of the Mexican financial institutions remained constant despite substantial innovations in technology and practice in the banking industry internationally.

Many Inverlat managers claimed that their bank had generally deteriorated more than the rest of the banking sector in Mexico. Managers believed that there was no overall strategy or leadership. Lacking a strong central management structure, each of the bank's geographic regions began to function independently, resulting in a system of control one manager described as "feudal". The eight regions developed such a level of autonomy that managers commonly referred to Inverlat not as a bank, but as eight small banks. The fragmented structure made new product development almost impossible. When the central corporate offices developed a new product, they had no guarantee that it would be implemented in the regions and ultimately, the branches. The power struggle within the regions

Richard Ivey School of Business
The University of Western Ontario

Daniel D. Campbell prepared this case under the direction of Professors Kathleen Slaughter and Henry W. Lane solely to provide material for class discussion. The authors do not intend to illustrate either effective or ineffective handling of a managerial situation. The authors may have disguised certain names and other identifying information to protect confidentiality. Ivey Management Services prohibits any form of reproduction, storage or transmittal without its written permission. This material is not covered under authorization from CanCopy or any reproduction rights organization. To order copies or request permission to reproduce materials, contact Ivey Publishing, Ivey Management Services, c/o Richard Ivey School of Business, The University of Western Ontario, London, Ontario, Canada, N6A 3K7; phone (519) 661-3208, fax (519) 661-3882, e-mail cases@ivey.uwo.ca. Copyright © 1997 Ivey Management Services. One-time permission to reproduce granted by Ivey Management Services on April 15, 2002.

demanded such loyalty that employees often had to say: "I cannot support you (in some initiative) because my boss told me not to."

In 1990, an amendment to the Mexican constitution allowed majority private sector ownership of Mexican commercial banks. Between 1990 and 1992, eighteen banks were privatized by the Mexican government including Inverlat. BNS, looking to expand its interests in Latin America, purchased 8 percent of the company in 1992 for C$154 million.

Under the structure of the newly privatized bank, there were three corporate cultures: that of the original bank; that of the Casa de Bolsa, the bank's brokerage house; and that of the new chair of the bank, an executive from Banamex, Mexico's largest financial institution. Many senior Banamex executives were invited to join Inverlat, some even came out of retirement to do so. The Banamex culture soon dominated the organization, as senior management tried to create a "Little Banamex." Inverlat managers without a history in Banamex said that the strategy could never function because Inverlat did not have the clients, technology, or financial resources of Banamex.

Inverlat's leaders did recognize, however, that the years of stagnation under nationalization had created a bank that had failed to create a new generation of bankers to reflect the changing times. They realized that the bank required a rejuvenation, but the managers did not have the knowledge or the capacity to effect the change.

Nowhere was the lack of development more prominent, and ultimately more devastating, than in the credit assessment function. The banks pursued a growth strategy dependent on increased lending but, unfamiliar with the challenges of lending to the private sector, failed to collateralize their loans properly or to ensure that covenants were being maintained. In early 1995, following a severe devaluation of the Mexican peso, Mexico's credit environment collapsed; so did the bank. The Mexican government assumed responsibility for the bank, and BNS was forced to write down its original investment by almost 95 percent to C$10 million.

Negotiations with BNS

Management at BNS chose to view the loss in value of their investment as a further buying opportunity and, in early 1996, they began negotiations with the Mexican government. BNS contributed C$50 million for 16 per cent of new stock in the bank and C$125 million in bonds convertible on March 31, in the year 2000 for an additional 39 percent of equity. If, in the year 2000, BNS decided not to assume ownership of the bank, they could walk away without converting the debt and retain a much smaller portion of ownership.

As the majority shareholder until the year 2000, the Mexican government contracted BNS to manage the bank. A maximum of 20 BNS managers would be paid by the Mexican government to manage Inverlat on the government's behalf. If BNS wanted more Canadian managers to work in the bank, BNS would have to pay for them. It was intended that the Canadian managers would remain at Inverlat only until the Mexican managers developed the skills to manage the bank effectively on their own.

With the exception of a handful of the most senior officers in the bank, employees at Inverlat had no direct means of receiving information about the progression of the negotiations with BNS. Instead, they were forced to rely on often inaccurate reports from the Mexican media. As the negotiation progressed, support among Inverlat employees for a deal with BNS was very strong. Inverlat employees did not want to become government bureaucrats and viewed BNS as a savior that would bring money, technology and expertise.

Employee Expectations

Soon after the deal was completed with BNS, however, the general euphoria was gradually replaced by the fear of actions the Canadians were likely to take as they assumed their management role. Senior managers were worried that they would be replaced by someone younger, who spoke English and had an MBA. Rumors, supported by inaccurate reports in local newspapers, ran rampant. One newspaper reported that as many as 180 senior level managers would be imported to Inverlat from BNS in Canada.

Anxiety mounted as speculation increased about the magnitude of downsizing that BNS would implement as it restructured the bank in its turnaround. Although BNS had purchased banks in other Latin American countries, few Inverlat employees, including the most senior management, had any knowledge about the strategies that BNS management had used. Inverlat managers felt that their employees viewed BNS as a "gringo" corporation, and expected them to take the same actions other U.S.

companies had taken as they restructured companies they had purchased in Mexico. Most believed that if any foreign bank purchased Inverlat, most of the senior management team would be displaced and up to half of the bank staff would be let go. Similarly, very few managers knew the details of the contract that limited the number of managers that could come to the bank from Canada.

Very few of the Mexican employees had had any significant contact with Canadian managers, but the majority expected behavior similar to that of U.S. managers. Only a handful of senior level managers had been in contact during the due diligence and the Canadians realized that they required greater insight into the Mexican culture if they were to manage effectively. As a result, the members of the senior team that were going to manage the Mexican bank arrived in Mexico one month in advance to study Spanish. The Canadian managers studied in an intensive program in Cuernavaca, a small city 80 km southwest of Mexico City. During the three-week course, lectures were available on the Mexican culture. Mexican managers were extremely impressed by this attempt by the Canadians to gain a better understanding of the situation they were entering and thought the consideration was very respectful. One manager commented that:

> At the first meeting, the Canadians apologized because it would be in English, but promised that the next would be in Spanish. The fact is, some are still in English, but the approach and the attempt were very important.

Four months later, the Canadian team was still undergoing intense tutorial sessions in Spanish on a daily basis with varying levels of success.

Canadian managers said they were trying to guard against putting people into positions simply because they were bilingual. A Canadian manager, expressing his commitment to function in Spanish, commented that:

> There are 16 Canadians down here and 10,000 Mexicans. Surely to God, the 16 Canadians can learn Spanish rather than trying to teach the 10,000 Mexicans English or having people feel that they are being left out of promotions or opportunities just because they don't speak English. This is a Spanish-speaking country and the customers speak Spanish.

Inverlat and BNS Cultures

In Canada, BNS was considered the bank with the most stringent financial control systems of the country's largest banks. Stringent, not only in deciding not to spend money in non-essential areas, but also in maintaining a tough system of policies and controls that ensured that managers held to their budgets.

Inverlat executives, on the other hand, were accustomed to almost complete autonomy with little or no control imposed on their spending. Very little analysis was done to allocate resources to a project, and adherence to budget was not monitored. Mexican managers believed that greater controls such as the ones used by BNS should be implemented in Inverlat, but they also felt that conflicts would arise.

An early example experienced in the bank was a new policy implemented by BNS management to control gifts received by managers from clients. BNS managers imposed a limit of 500 pesos[2] for the maximum value of a gift that could be received by an executive. Gifts of larger value could be accepted, but were then raffled off to all employees of the bank at Christmas. Some Mexican managers took offense at the imposition of an arbitrary limit. They felt that it was an indication that BNS did not trust their judgment. Managers thought that it would be better if the bank communicated the need for the use of good judgment when accepting gifts and then trusted their managers to act appropriately.

Mandates of BNS

Two months after the arrival of the Canadian executive team, the new bank chairman, Bill Sutton gave an address to 175 senior executives within Inverlat. The purpose of the address was threefold: to outline management's main objectives in the short term; to unveil the new organizational structure of senior level managers; and to reassure employees that no staff reductions would be undertaken for the first year.

The primary objectives, later printed in a special company wide bulletin were the following:

1. Identify all non-performing loans of the bank.
2. Develop an organization focused on the client.
3. Improve the productivity and efficiency of all operations and activities.

4. Improve the profitability of the 315 branches.
5. Develop a liability strategy.
6. Improve the integrity of the financial information.

These objectives were generally well received by the Mexican managers. Some criticized them as being too intangible and difficult to measure. Most, however, believed that the general nature of the objectives was more practical, given the type of changes that were being made in the first year. They did agree that the goals would need to be adjusted as planning became more focussed during the 1997 budget planning process.

The new management structure differed sharply from the existing structure of the bank. The original eight geographic regions were reduced to four. Managers were pleased to see that the head of each of these divisions was Mexican and it was generally viewed as a promotion for the managers.

The second change was the nature in which the Canadians were added to the management structure. The senior Canadian managers became "Directores Generales Adjuntos (DGAs)" or senior vice presidents of several key areas, displacing Mexican managers. The Mexican DGAs not directly replaced by Canadians would now report to one or more of the Canadian DGAs, but this was not reflected in the organization chart (see Exhibit 1). Mexican DGAs retained their titles and formally remained at the same level as their Canadian counterparts.

EXHIBIT 1

Grupo Financiero Inverlat Organization Chart (Post-reorganization)

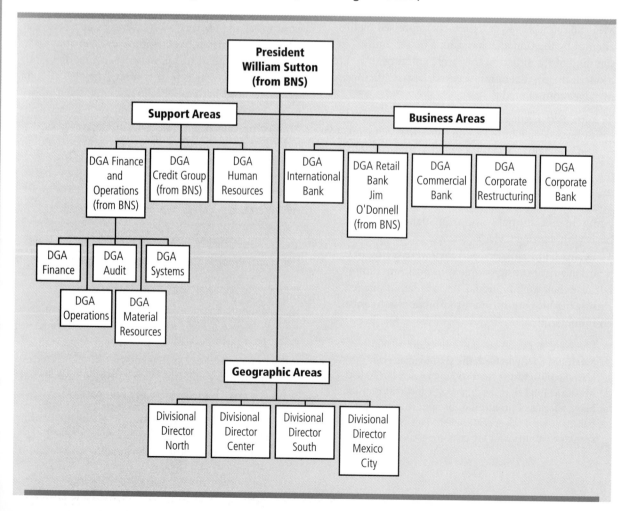

Mexican managers later reported mixed feelings by employees about whether or not they worked under a Canadian or Mexican DGA. Many felt that a Mexican DGA and his (there were no female DGAs working within the bank) employees were more "vulnerable" than a Canadian; however, senior managers also felt that they had an opportunity to ascend to the DGA position when it was being held by a Mexican. Many felt that Canadian managers would always hold the key positions in the bank and that certain authority would never be relinquished to a Mexican. This was not the message that BNS manage-ment wanted to convey. One of Jim O'Donnell's first comments to his employees was that he would only be in Mexico until one of them felt confident that they could fill his shoes.

The last message was the new management's commitment not to reduce staff levels. A policy of "no hires, no fires" was put in place. Employees were able to breathe a sigh of relief. Many had expected the Canadian management team to reduce staff by 3000 to 5000 employees during the first several months after their arrival.

The Communication Challenge

Canadian and Mexican managers already experienced many of the difficulties that the two different languages could present. Many of the most senior Mexican managers spoke English, but the remaining managers required translators when speaking with the Canadians. Even when managers reporting directly to them spoke English, Canadians felt frustra-tion at not being able to speak directly to the next level below. One manager commented that "some-times, I feel like a bloody dictator" referring to the need to communicate decisions to his department via his most senior officers.

Meetings

Even when all managers at a meeting spoke English, the risk of mis-communication was high. A Mexican manager recalled one of the early meetings in English attended by several Mexicans. Each of the Mexican managers left the meeting with little doubt about what had been decided during the meeting. It was only later, when the Mexicans spoke of the proceed-ings in Spanish, that they realized they each had a different interpretation about what had transpired. What they found even more alarming was that each manager had heard what he had wanted to hear, clearly demonstrating to themselves the effect of their biases on their perception of events.

This problem might have been exacerbated by the way some of the Canadians chose to conduct meetings. Mexican managers were accustomed to a flexible atmosphere in which they were free to leave the room or carry on side-conversations as they saw fit. Canadian managers became frustrated and changed the meeting style to a more structured, controlled atmosphere similar to what they used in Canada. The Mexican managers were told that breaks would be scheduled every two hours and that only then should they get up from the table or leave the room.

Canadian managers believed that the original conduct of the Mexican managers during meetings was due to a lack of discipline and that the new conduct would lead to higher productivity. The Canadians did not recognize the negative impact that could result from the elimination of the informal interactions that had occurred in the original style.

Beyond Language

Despite the cross-cultural training received in Cuernavaca, some Canadians still felt they had a lot to learn about the cultural nuances that could create major pitfalls. Jim O'Donnell recalled a meeting at which he and several Mexican managers were having difficulty with some material developed by another Mexican not present at the meeting. Jim requested that this manager join them to provide further expla-nation. Several minutes later, as this person entered the room, Jim said jokingly, "OK, *here's* the guy that screwed it all up." The manager was noticeably upset. It was not until later, after some explaining, that Jim's comment was understood to be a joke. Jim said it brought home the fact that, in the Mexican culture, it was unacceptable, even in jest, to be critical of someone in front of other people.

This was easier said than done. Often, what the Canadians considered a minor difference of opinion could appear as criticism that Mexican managers would prefer be made behind closed doors when coming from a more senior manager. One Mexican manager commented on the risks of disagreeing with an employee when others were present:

When someone's boss is not in agreement, or critical of actions taken by an employee and says something during a meeting with other employees present, other managers will use it as an opportunity to also say bad things about the manager. Instead, when a disagreement arises in an open meeting, the senior manager should say, "see me later, and we will discuss it."

To the contrary, the Canadian managers were trying to encourage an environment in which all managers participated in meetings and positive criticism was offered and accepted.

Mexican Communication Style

On verbal communication, one of the original Inverlat managers commented:

In Mexico, interactions between individuals are extremely polite. Because Mexicans will make every effort not to offend the person they are dealing with, they are careful to "sugar-coat" almost everything they say. Requests are always accompanied by "por favor," no matter how insignificant the request.

Mexicans often speak the diminutive form. For example: *Esperame* means *Wait for me. Esperame un rato* means *Wait for me a moment.* A Mexican would more often say *Esperame un ratito.* "Ratito" is the diminutive form meaning "a very short moment". It is not as direct.

This politeness is extended into other interactions. Every time a Mexican meets a coworker or subordinate, a greeting such as "Hello, how are you?" is appropriate, even if it is the fourth or fifth time that day that they have met. If you don't do this, the other person will think you are angry with him or her or that you are poorly educated.

One Canadian manager explained that some of the Mexican managers he dealt with went to great lengths to avoid confrontation. He was frustrated when the Mexicans would "tell him what he wanted to hear." Often these managers would consent to something that they could or would not do, simply to avoid a confrontation at the time.

Other Messages: Intended or Otherwise

Due to the high level of anxiety, Mexican managers were very sensitive to messages they read into the actions taken by the Canadians. This process began before the Canadians made any significant changes.

As the Canadians began to plan the new organizational structure, they conducted a series of interviews with the senior Mexican managers. The Canadians decided who they would talk to based on areas where they believed they required more information. Unfortunately, many managers believed that if they were not spoken to, then they were not considered of importance to the Canadians and should fear for their positions. Even after the organizational structure was revealed and many Mexican managers found themselves in good positions, they still retained hard feelings, believing that they had not been considered important enough to provide input into the new structure.

Similarly, at lower levels in the bank, because of the lack of activity in the economy as a whole, many employees were left with time on their hands. Because many employees feared staff reductions at some point, they believed that those with the most work or those being offered new work were the ones that would retain their jobs.

Communications as an On-going Process

When Jim held his first meeting with the nine senior managers reporting to him, he began by saying that none of them would have their jobs in two months. Realizing the level of anxiety at that point, he quickly added that he meant they would all be shuffled around to other areas of the retail bank. Jim explained that this would give them an opportunity to learn about other areas of the bank and the interdependencies that needed to be considered when making decisions.

Jim stuck to his word, and within two months, all but one of the managers had been moved. Some, however, had experienced anxiety about the method by which they were moved. Typically, Jim would meet with an employee and tell him that in two or three days he would report to a new area (generally, Mexican managers gave at least a month's notice). When that day arrived, Jim would talk to them for 30 to 45 minutes about their new responsibilities and goals, and then he would send them on their way.

For many of the Mexicans, this means of communication was too abrupt. Many wondered if they had been moved from their past jobs because of poor performance. More senior Mexican managers explained that often these managers would come to them and ask why Jim had decided to move them. Most of the Mexicans felt that more communication was required about why things were happening the way they were.

Accountability

Early on, the Canadian managers identified an almost complete lack of accountability within the bank. Senior managers had rarely made decisions outside the anonymity of a committee and when resources were committed to a project, it was equally rare for someone to check back to see what results were attained. As a result, very little analysis was done before a new project was approved and undertaken.

The first initiative taken by the Canadians to improve the level of analysis, and later implementation, was the use of what they called the "business case." The case represented a cost benefit analysis that would be approved and reviewed by senior managers. Initially, it was difficult to explain to the Mexican managers how to provide the elements of analysis that the Canadians required. The Mexicans were given a framework, but they initially returned cases that adhered too rigidly to the outline. Similarly, managers would submit business cases of 140 pages for a $35,000 project.

Cases required multiple revisions to a point of frustration on both sides, but it was only when an analysis could be prepared that satisfied the Canadians and was understood by both parties, that it could be certain that they all had the same perception of what they were talking about.

Some of the Mexican managers found the business case method overly cumbersome and felt that many good ideas would be missed because of the disincentive created by the business case. One manager commented that "It is a bit discouraging. Some people around here feel like you need to do a business case to go to the bathroom."

Most agreed that a positive element of the business case was the need it created to talk with other areas of the bank. To do a complete analysis, it was often necessary to contact other branches of the bank for information because their business would be affected. This was the first time that efforts across functional areas of the bank would be coordinated. To reinforce this notion, often Canadian managers required that senior managers from several areas of the bank grant their approval before a project in a business case could move forward.

Matrix Responsibility

Changes in the organizational structure further complicated the implementation of a system of accountability. Senior management had recognized a duplication of services across the different functional areas of the bank. For example, each product group had its own marketing and systems departments. These functions were stripped away and consolidated into central groups that would service all areas of the organization.

Similarly, product groups had been responsible for the development and delivery of their products. Performance was evaluated based on the sales levels each product group could attain. Under the initial restructuring, the product groups would no longer be responsible for the sale of their products, only for their design. Instead, the branches would become a delivery network that would be responsible for almost all contact with the client. As a result, managers in product groups, who were still responsible for ensuring the sales levels, felt that they were now being measured against criteria over which they had no direct control. The Canadian management team was finding it very difficult to explain to the Mexicans that they now had to "influence" instead of "control." Product managers were being given the role of "coaches" who would help the branch delivery network to offer their product most effectively.

As adjustments were made to the structure, the Mexican manager's perception of his status also had to be considered. In the management hierarchy, the Mexican manager's relationships were with the people in the various positions that they dealt with, not with the positions themselves. When a person was moved, subordinates felt loyalty to that individual. As a result, Mexican managers moving within an organization (or even to another organization) often did so with a small entourage of employees who accompanied them.

Staff Reductions

As services within the bank were consolidated, it was obvious that staff reductions would be required. Inverlat staff were comforted by the bank's commitment to retain all staff for the first year, particularly when considering the poor state of the economy and the banking sector; but, even at lower levels of the organization, the need for reductions was apparent. Some managers complained that the restructuring process was being slowed considerably by the need to find places for personnel who were clearly no longer required.

Motivations for retaining staffing levels were twofold. First, BNS did not want to tarnish the image of its foreign investment in Mexico with massive reductions at the outset. When the Spanish bank, Banco Bilbao Viscaya (BBV), purchased Banca Cremi the previous year, they began the restructuring process with a staff reduction of over 2000 employees. BNS executives thought that this action had not been well received by the Mexican government or marketplace.

The second reason BNS management felt compelled to wait for staff reductions was that they wanted adequate time to identify which employees were productive and fit into the new organizational culture, and which employees would not add significant value. The problem was, quality employees were not sure if they would have a job in a year, and many managers thought that employees would begin to look for secure positions in other organizations. One Canadian manager commented that even some employees who were performing well in their current postions would ultimately lose their jobs. Many thought action needed to be taken sooner than later. A senior Mexican manager explained the situation:

Take the worst case scenario, blind guessing. At least then, you will be correct 50 percent of the time and retain some good people. If you wait, people within the organization will begin to look for other jobs and the market will choose who it wants. But as the market hires away your people, it will be correct at 90 percent of the time and you will be left with the rest.

Until that point, not many managers had been hired away from the bank. Many felt that this was due to the poor condition of the banking sector. As the economy improved, however, many believed that the talented managers would begin to leave the bank if job security could not be improved.

Jim felt that something was needed to communicate a sense of security to the talented managers they could already identify, but he was not certain how to proceed.

Conclusion

Jim felt that the Canadian team had been relatively successful in the early months. Many managers referred to the period as the "Honeymoon Stage." It was generally felt that the situation would intensify as managers looked for results from the restructured organization and as staff reductions became a reality. Jim then wondered how he could best prepare for the months ahead. Much of the communication with employees to date had been on an ad hoc basis. Jim did not feel they could take the risk of starting reductions without laying out a plan. The negative rumors would cause the bank to lose many of its most valued Mexican managers.

4

Luna Pen

A Puzzling Request

Erika Graeper absently twirled the Luna in her fingers. It was not as massive as the Mont Blanc's Meisterstück or the most expensive Pelikans, but the Luna had a comfortable heft and balance. It was handsome, as well. The pen's midnight blue barrel was accented by a gold clip, and an elegant crescent moon was inlaid at the top of the cap.

Erika smiled to herself, as the Luna tripped memories of both pleasure and small embarrassment. It had been given to her by her grandmother a dozen years ago when she had been about to start university. Erika had promptly used the pen to write a thank you note on crisp white stationery and had solemnly said that it would be a great help in her studies. Once at school, however, she had reverted to ball point pens and mechanical pencils. Since then, the Luna had been tucked, unused, in the back of a desk drawer.

The gift certainly would still have been forgotten had not an odd letter happened to come to her desk at DGG the first month she started to work for that company. Judging by the notes that had been scribbled on it, the letter had gone past three other people before being forwarded to her. Her immediate boss, Wilhelm Mann, had scribbled a cryptic instruction that said in its entirety: "Please Respond—Luna out of production for years."

Mann was out of the office and was unavailable to provide more information, so Erika had turned to the letter itself. It was from Cecil Armstrong, president of Queensland Office Supply, Ltd., in Brisbane, Australia, and was addressed to Herr Heinrich Dumart, president of Luna, in Frankfurt, Germany. Armstrong's letter complained of difficulties in obtaining Luna pens for the retailers with whom he dealt. "Small wonder," Erika thought to herself, "since Lunas aren't made any more." But as she read further, she became perplexed. Armstrong had written: "Your representative, Mr. Alven Feng, assures me that manufacturing is being stepped up to meet increased demand, but his deliveries often are late and are insufficient to satisfy my customers' needs."

Erika checked back to see the date of the letter— January 12, 2000. It had probably taken less than a week to arrive from Australia, but another three months had passed as the letter had bounced from one office at DGG to another until it found its way to Erika. Nevertheless, Armstrong was writing as if the Luna were still being made. It seemed unlikely, but perhaps her boss had been wrong about the pen being out of production.

Armstrong's letter went on to praise the pen and to encourage the Luna company to take full advantage of its growing market. "I do not know the nature of your relationship with Mr. Feng, but if he does not have exclusive rights to represent you in this part of the world, I would very much like to pursue that possibility for Australia."

Armstrong had attached a copy of a letter he had written a year earlier, likewise asking about distribution rights. Attached, as well, was a letter dated November 5, 1999, from Alven Feng to Cecil Armstrong. He promised new pens would be delivered shortly, but stated that while Luna was striving to meet increased demand, it did not want to compromise quality to do so. Feng's letterhead identified him as "Managing Director" of Global Service Company, Taipei, Republic of China. Erika recalled that meant Taiwan, not mainland China, but never had heard of Feng's company.

"Please respond," Erika's boss had directed her. But how was she to reply to a request from someone halfway around the world regarding a product that was no longer made?

Erika Graeper

Erika's only knowledge of the Luna pen came from the fact that her grandmother happened to have given her one long ago. Erika had been trained in electrical engineering, had worked for a German audio speaker manufacturer for three years, then earned her MBA from the University of Texas, Austin, in 1997. Her decision to attend professional school in the United States surprised her friends and family, but Erika had wanted to see more of the world. She chose Texas specifically because of the university's ambitious partnership with private corporations to spawn new computer technology.

As she had hoped, business school expanded her interests beyond engineering; somewhat to her surprise, she became particularly fascinated with marketing. Upon graduation, Erika went to work for Dell Computer right in Austin, Texas. Dell had grown enormously in just a few years, by assembling quality products and selling many of them through technical product centers on university campuses throughout the United States. Erika's timing in joining the company had not been good, however. Technical problems with some of its notebooks and aggressive competition from Compaq and IBM had blocked Dell's growth. Repositioning itself, Dell followed the lead of Gateway by adopting a direct telephone sales strategy.

Erika enjoyed her two years at Dell, but with the changes at the company she felt the job was not giving her the kind of experience she had hoped for. While on a brief vacation to her family's home outside of Frankfurt, she happened to hear of an interesting position that had opened up at DGG, a fast-growing distributor of computer peripherals and related supplies. DGG had started as a small greeting card company, the Deutsche Grusskarte Gesellschaft, but through a series of acquisitions and mergers, it moved into stationery and, then, office products. When it expanded beyond Germany, the name was formally trimmed to its bare initials. Admirers of its fat earnings statements (net earnings averaged 15 percent of revenue over the past five years) sometimes still refer to DGG as "Die Goldene Gans"—the golden goose. DGG's annual revenues in the previous year, over DM1.27 billion (US$580 million), resulted in net earnings of DM194 million (US$88 million).

Erika interviewed with many people at DGG, and was specifically hired by Wilhelm Mann, who had been impressed with the depth of her technical and business experience. In her new position, Erika was to work with several of the company's Asian suppliers who produced printer cartridges, diskettes, and other products on to which DGG put its label.

While not really a marketing position, the assignment would certainly broaden her perspective. Mann had said, apparently seriously, "One reason we are hiring you is your experience with dealing with non-European cultures." Erika was not about to contradict him, but she doubted that her experience in Austin, Texas, with country music, barbecue, and Lone Star beer would have much relevance to doing business in Singapore or Hong Kong. Still, she had confidence in her personal ability to adapt to different customs and be alert to possible misunderstandings. Nothing in all of her background, however, had given her even an inkling about the business of fountain pens.

Luna Eclipse?

Erika discussed the Luna Pen puzzle with three of her new colleagues before finding someone who could explain why a letter to Heinrich Dumart should be forwarded to her at DGG. Her company had been growing quickly and many of its employees had come on board just recently. Few knew more than she did about DGG's past, but Dieter Bauer had been there for many years and was able to provide some history.

Luna was a small company that had been owned and operated by the Dumart family for almost 60 years, Bauer had explained. Annual revenues in the 10 years between 1978 and 1988 were approximately DM21.8 million (US$10 million). In the 1980s, when the then-senior Dumart was approaching retirement age, he sold the firm's stock to a larger stationery company, though he stayed on to manage the pen business. Three years later, in turn, DGG acquired that stationery company as a vehicle for manufacturing and marketing copy and printer paper. Luna was not central to the deal, and DGG had made some efforts to spin it off. With the death of Herr Dumart several months earlier, and Luna showing annual losses, there was little interest.

"Luna is in corporate Valhalla now," Bauer said. When Erika did not seem to understand his reference, he explained that Luna was now in whatever afterlife companies experience when they die. "We tore down the little factory where the pens were made on the other side of the city maybe five or six years ago. There's a warehouse there now. If Luna Pen exists today, it's just on paper."

Erika nodded with a slight smile. Bauer was from Bonn and seemed very formal, but perhaps his word play was intentional. "But why did this matter end up on my desk?" she asked.

"Oh, that's easy," he replied, "You're our new expert on the mysterious Orient." Now Erika felt comfortable enough to respond, "Maybe no one else new wanted to be bothered with the problem."

"That may be true," Bauer agreed, "and as the newest person here, you can't bump it to someone else." That reality gave Erika little comfort.

Erika was tempted at first to write Cecil Armstrong and simply tell him that Luna had gone out of business years ago, but she remained puzzled by the fact that he was somehow still getting supplies from Alven Feng of Global Service. Erika did not want to get deeply distracted by this small transaction, as she was about to leave for her first trip to Asia. Out of courtesy she wrote Armstrong, acknowledging his letter and apologized for the delayed response. She explained that Luna had been acquired by DGG and that she had "only recently assumed some responsibilities" in its regard. She thanked him for his kind words about the product and promised to contact him again after she had a chance to look into things.

Luna Rising?

One week later Erika was in Malaysia, having just finished an exhausting round of meetings with several of DGG's suppliers there. With other meetings to prepare for in Hong Kong and Seoul, and flight delays out of the Kuala Lumpur airport, the Luna puzzle was the furthest thing from Erika's mind when she happened to spot a handsome indigo pen in the display at the duty-free shop.

"Please show it to me," she asked the clerk. The dark blue box had LUNA written on it in discreet gold letters. Inside, there was a set of directions for filling the pen and a warranty which identified Global Service of Taipei as the repair facility. Erika carefully looked at the pen itself. To her eye, it seemed identical to the one her grandmother had given her. There on the golden nib was the familiar word, Luna.

The clerk mistook Erika's scrutiny for dissatisfaction and perhaps inferring too much from the fine quality of her suit, said, "I think you would like better this special edition Hemingway by Mont Blanc." The clerk offered the impressive red pen almost as if it were a religious artifact, but Erika barely gave it a glance.

"No, no. I'm sorry. I want the Luna," she said.

The look of disappointment on the clerk's face was obvious. The Luna was priced at DM92 (US$40), while the Hemingway was ten times as much, but it was clear that Erika knew what she wanted.

It was clear to Erika, as well, that she had just solved the mystery of the fountain pens: she was buying a counterfeit. Mr. Feng—or somebody behind him—had neatly stepped into the vacuum that had been left when DGG tore down the Luna factory.

Erika felt a flash of exhilaration and indignation. How dare someone appropriate her company's good name and property! Then she laughed at herself. "I've barely worked for DGG a month," she thought. "How quickly one develops loyalties. Perhaps instead I should ask how we overlooked the potential value of the Luna brand name." According to Armstrong's letter, the pen enjoyed some popularity in Australia, and here it was in faraway Malaysia, too.

Erika's flight was called and she was on the plane to Hong Kong before she realized that she should have asked the clerk where the shop got the pens, though the warranty slip suggested that Global Service was a likely answer. When she finished her appointments in the city, she went on an exploration of local stationery stores. The first two had heard of Luna, but did not stock them, but a third shop had a good supply. Here the price was equivalent to DM115 (US$50), but after only a moment's hesitation, Erika bought an identical twin of the fountain pen she had purchased in Kuala Lumpur two days earlier. It, too, carried a warranty from Global Service. Erika took care to obtain a detailed receipt. For good measure, she also bought a bottle of Luna brand ink.

In Seoul, the last stop of her trip, she set out on a similar expedition, though this time without success. One older shopkeeper remembered the Luna quite well. "Oh, yes. Made in Germany. Not so expensive. But you can't get them any more." Apparently Feng had yet to tap the Korean market.

DGG's Options

On her return to Frankfurt, Erika wrote a detailed memo to Wilhelm Mann summarizing the results of her scheduled meetings. She added a short postscript stating, "I've come across some interesting information on the Luna matter you referred to me."

Two days later she met with Mann who was quite impressed with her general report. After the scheduled topics had been covered, Erika reached into her handbag. "I picked up a couple of souvenirs that you might like to see. This one is from Malaysia," she noted as she slid a small blue box across his desk, "and here is its twin from Hong Kong."

Mann opened the first one in puzzlement, then the second. When he spotted the Luna name, a smile of recognition broke over his face. "So it's a fine little company we have, Luna. No factory, no workers, no inventory, but somehow we still produce fountain pens. And, look, now we are making ink, too!"

Erika showed Mann the correspondence with Cecil Armstrong in Brisbane. Her letter in response had only been intended to buy a little time. Some mysteries had been resolved, but a lot of questions remained unanswered, not the least of which was the identity of Alven Feng and Global Service. Before investing any serious effort, Mann suggested that they review DGG's options. "Let's just say we confirm that Global Service has made a tidy little business selling counterfeit Lunas. What should we do about it—if anything?"

Erika had anticipated the question and imagined several alternatives. "My first reaction," she admitted, "was to bring a lawsuit for violating our trademark, though I expect that might be expensive and time-consuming. Of course, we always could use the threat of a suit as bargaining leverage."

"Check with Gunther Schmidt in our legal department," Mann interrupted. "We need to know where we stand in that regard."

"Also, we'd need to think about what such a suit would get us," Erika continued. "I suppose we might collect royalty damages, but putting Global out of business doesn't really help us in any way—unless we want to get back into fountain pens."

"I can't see doing that," Mann mused. "It's just too far removed from our core business. We didn't make anything of Luna when we had it and the big accounts we serve today buy printer ribbons by the truck load. They're not asking for fountain pens. Am I wrong?"

Erika did not feel she knew Mann well enough to challenge such a statement directly. Moreover, she suspected that he was probably right on this issue. Still she told him about some quick research she had done on the fountain pen market. Most of the sources she was able to find through LEXIS/NEXIS described the burgeoning market in the United States, though clearly fountain pens were reappearing everywhere. Annual sales in America had bottomed out at 6.4 million units in 1978 after the onslaught, first, of ball point pens, then felt tips. But the trend reversed itself in the 1980s, notably with the sales of luxury writing instruments. In 1990, 25.5 million fountain pens were sold in the United States. Germany's own Mont Blanc apparently had half of the American high-end market, Erika added. Overall sales continued to grow, more than doubling since 1990.

"So Luna got out—not in—on the ground floor?" Mann asked.

"It would seem so, yes," Erika said. "Luna would probably be in a niche with Osmiroid, Platignum, and some of the lower-priced Parkers. I don't have any sense of production costs, but it certainly looks as if these companies are doing very well. Even if it's not the right business for us, Luna may well be valuable to someone else."

Mann thought for a moment, then neatly arranged the Luna boxes side by side on his desk. Even if DGG could find someone else to manufacture the pens, he speculated, he still worried that his company was poorly positioned to promote and distribute them. "Let me check that option with some other people here, but I don't think we want to be in the fountain pen business."

With the hour growing late, the two of them quickly sketched some options. First, DGG could bring suit against Feng and Global to recover damages for past trademark violations. Second, it could negotiate some sort of settlement with Feng in respect to prior royalties and the right to future use of the Luna name, either through some sort of on-going licensing arrangement or an outright sale. Third, of course, DGG might find some other enterprise that would be interested in buying Luna's goodwill.

"Would you be willing to handle this?" Mann asked.

Erika was delighted at the prospect of having a project that was entirely her own, though Mann cautioned her not to get too deeply entangled. "We have much bigger things on our agenda. Anything you can get out of this will be a windfall."

DGG's Legal Position

Within the week, Mann confirmed that his superiors did not want to resurrect its fountain pen activities, though DGG would be glad to get whatever value was represented by the Luna name. In the meantime, Erika had also received a written legal opinion from Gunther Schmidt. He had found the old Luna files and confirmed that the Luna name had been duly registered internationally, though he cautioned that this might have more significance in Europe and North America than in certain Asian countries. Countries that once were notorious for counterfeiting, he noted however, were now starting to crack down—in order to become better trading partners—but there still were some differences from place to place. In particular, he added, there might be a question of whether the Luna name had been "abandoned," and thus could be appropriated by another company. Although DGG had never formally dissolved the Luna firm, the reality was that it had been out of business for several years.

There were practical problems of greater concern, he added. First, in a typical trademark violation case, the complaining party measures its damages in terms of lost market share and tarnished reputation. As DGG had voluntarily left the market, could it really be said to have lost anything? There was still the possibility that some sort of punitive damages might be won. Second, prosecuting such a suit would be expensive, Schmidt warned. It would be necessary to hire local counsel, perhaps in each of the countries in which the Lunas were being illegally sold. The advocates would want to be paid up front, while any award—and subsequent collection—of damages

could take years. And should DGG not prevail in court, it might be liable to pay the legal costs of the winning parties. On the other hand, Schmidt acknowledged that the threat of litigation might be the only way of bringing Feng to the bargaining table.

Erika was not surprised by the tone of Schmidt's memo, though it deepened her realization that she was not in the strongest bargaining position, either with Global or with other potential buyers who might be worried about the legitimacy of the Luna name. Schmidt had offered no support for an aggressive legal campaign to vindicate DGG's rights, nor could Erika herself recommend such action, at least not at the outset.

The situation seemed to call for some negotiated solution. To that end, Erika got authorization from Mann to hire an investigator in Taipei to learn more about Global Service and Alven Feng.

It took several weeks to find someone in Taipei to prepare a report, and then another two before the information was on Erika's desk. She learned that Global Service was a legitimate company founded in the late 1950s in Taipei by the Feng family. It was still privately held, so financial information was not available, but knowledgeable observers estimated that its trade activities were in excess of DM45.4 million (US$21 million) annually. Profit figures were even harder to obtain, but the investigator suggested that the usual return for this type of firm was between 8 percent and 13 percent of revenues. Global had done some limited manufacturing over the years, but typically acted as the middleman, distributing other companies' products. At the outset, Global had opportunistically traded in small goods to America; in the 1970s, for example, it was very active in the export of toys made in Taiwan and elsewhere. It was now out of that business entirely; with growing prosperity in the Pacific Rim, it had turned east to do its business. One of its more lucrative activities was said to be the Asian distributorship of Luna pens, which it both manufactured and distributed. Without providing an exact figure, the investigator estimated that Luna pens and other Luna brand products accounted for approximately one-quarter of Global's sales.

Alven Feng, the report concluded, was the 58-year-old managing director of Global and eldest son of its founder. Other family members were involved in the business, including a brother based in Malaysia, but Alven Feng was said to rule the enterprise with an iron hand. A recent newspaper article on the company, which included a photograph of Feng receiving a community service award, was attached. The copy was not good and Erika could only make out the image of a serious looking man, a bit stout, wearing glasses. The translation of the article itself provided a laudatory account of Feng's public service and speculated that Global, with large cash reserves, was poised for a major expansion.

Preparing to Negotiate

Erika needed to make another trip to Southeast Asia on other important business. At some point, it would be necessary to deal with Mr. Feng and Global Service and now seemed to be as good a time as any. "But how should I start the discussions?" she thought to herself.

From her days in Texas, she remembered the American saying, "shoot first, ask questions later." Maybe she should have Schmidt retain a Taiwanese lawyer to file a trademark suit, even if she didn't plan to prosecute it fully. She was confident that she could win Schmidt's and Mann's support for this strategy, particularly if it seemed like the only realistic way of getting Feng's attention.

Or perhaps she should not start so aggressively. She drafted several different letters for comparison. One summarized the Luna situation as she understood it and threatened legal action if Global did not pay damages for past infractions. Another version was more conciliatory in tone and hinted at a possible joint venture. Still another said nothing about Luna pen, but suggested that in light of DGG's growing Asian presence, she wished to discuss a possible relationship with Global to handle computer products.

Erika thought fleetingly about whether there was any way or advantage in having Alven Feng come to her, so she would be operating on familiar territory. Perhaps that might happen at some stage, but she decided that there was more to be learned about Global from being on site.

Back when she had been interviewed for her new position at DGG, Wilhelm Mann had flattered her ability to deal with people from other cultures and she had not demurred. Her recent trip to Asia on other business had been merely introductory; ideas were explored, but no firm agreements were negotiated. This time Erika would likely have to make a deal with Feng and any others who might be involved. She

was not comfortable with the fact that she knew little about him, and even less about how he bargained.

In her apartment, Erika had cartons of books that she still hadn't unpacked from her time in the United States. Among them were some negotiation texts and books on working in unfamiliar cultures. She had greatly enjoyed browsing in the bookstores of Austin. With the best of intentions Erika had picked up things that she meant to read but too rarely had the chance to open. Now it was time to do some research.

One book[1] included a collection of short "dialogues," many of which demonstrated how easily people from different countries could talk past one another and not even know it. Erika scanned the pages quickly for conversations with the Chinese. One particularly telling example had a westerner insistent on getting down to the "basics" of the detail at hand while her Chinese counterpart wanted to talk at length about the history of both companies.

Another book on differences in body language warned that when the Chinese "suck air in quickly and audibly around the teeth," it is a sign that you should modify your request "rather than risk having your Chinese counterpart face the highly embarrassing (for them) situation of having to say 'no.'"[2] Silence, she read, could be a sign of polite contemplation, but direct eye contact was uncommon.

Were such rules of behavior and communication always accurate, Erika wondered? She recalled that when she was in Austin, various well-meaning classmates had remarked on how much more friendly and outgoing she seemed than most Germans. "Well, the people from the north are more formal," she had usually explained, "but I'm from Munich and we're much more outgoing." Reflecting on her own experience, she wondered if people were wrong when they stereotyped all Germans, what could she confidently expect to know about anyone else just from their nationality?

Erika read further and found a few useful observations. Nevertheless, her research left her less confident than when she began. How should she initiate a meeting with Alven Feng? Should she be aggressive or conciliatory? Would her being female have any bearing on the negotiation?

Erika's schedule called for her to be in Taipei in exactly one week. For a brief moment, she regretted ever having opened up the Luna question. A simple bureaucratic reply to Mr. Armstrong would have ended the matter and spared her all this uncertainty. She quickly regained her resolve, however, remembering Mann's comment that anything she won from Alven Feng and his Global Service would be a pure windfall. Still, this would be the first deal she had made for DGG and she wanted to make a good impression.

Erika centered several sheets of unlined paper on her desk, removed the cap from the pen her grandmother had given her, and began to sketch her negotiation strategy.

Assignment

This background material brings Erika Graeper to the point where she had to make some key decisions. Going forward, this case asks you to step into her shoes and deal with the issues as they develop.

Before reading the rest of this page, please take several minutes to outline a negotiation strategy. If you were in Erika's position, for example, what steps might give you the best chance of achieving your goals? What further information might you need before contacting Feng; and how might you realistically obtain it?

After outlining your strategy, please read the following scenario and tentatively choose one of the options which is offered. In your next class session, discuss the possible advantages and drawbacks of various options. You will then learn what Erika herself did in this situation and what transpired next.

Luna Situation 1 Imagine you are Erika Graeper. What would be your initial approach to the negotiation with Alven Feng?

Please read the alternative approaches listed below. Although none of the alternatives may be exactly what you would do, circle the letter (A, B, etc.) of the approach that you would be most likely to take if these were your only options. Next, select the one you would be least likely to take, and put an X over the corresponding letter.

A. Fax Feng requesting a meeting with him in Taipei next week. Outline your understanding that Global Service Company has built a considerable business using the Luna name without DGG's permission. Raise the issue of back payments for past misuse of the name, and a possible license or sale for future use.

B. Write Feng that DGG is prepared to file lawsuits in the Republic of China and elsewhere to protect its rights in the Luna trademark. Unless your company assert its rights, Feng has no reason to negotiate.

C. Contact other companies in Southeast Asia that might be potential buyers of the Luna name, in order to determine their possible interest. Also, write Feng and tell him DGG is planning on selling the rights to the Luna name. Request that he come to Frankfurt in the near future to discuss the settlement of this matter.

D. Fax Feng, introduce yourself, and tell him that you will be in Taipei next week. Ask if there is any convenient time to discuss your recent discovery that the Luna pen is selling well in the Far East, under his company's marketing strategy. Let him know that DGG is interested in some form of partnership with Global Service.

5

Capitalizing on International Opportunities
Go Global—or No?

For two years, DataClear has had the data analysis market to itself. But now a British upstart is nipping at its heels. Should DataClear continue to focus on its strong domestic prospects or expand overseas to head off the nascent international threat?

"Why aren't they biting?" wondered Greg McNally as he laid down another perfectly executed cast. He was fly-fishing in the most beautiful spot he had ever seen, on the Alta in Norway—reputedly the home of Scandinavia's worthiest salmon. And he had plenty of opportunity to admire the view. No fish were getting in the way.

What a difference from the luck he'd had a couple of weeks earlier trout fishing at Nelson's Spring Creek in Montana. It seemed like so much more time had passed since the two-day off-site he had called there, designed to be part celebration of the past, part planning for the future.

Some celebration had definitely been in order. The company, DataClear, was really taking off, fueled by the success if its first software product, ClearCloud. In 1999, its first full year of operation, DataClear's sales had reached $2.2 million. Now, the following September, it was looking like 2000 sales could easily reach $5.3 million. At the all-staff meeting on the Friday before the off-site, Greg had announced the company's success in recruiting two more great executives, bringing the staff to 38. "I'm more confident than ever that we'll hit our goals: $20 million in 2001 and then $60 million in 2002!"

Clouds on the Horizon

A New Jersey native, Greg held an MSc from Rutgers and then went West to get his PhD in computer science from UC Berkeley. He spent the next 15 years at Borland and Oracle, first as a software developer and then as a senior product manager. He started DataClear in Palo Alto, California, in the spring of 1998.

At that time, Greg realized that companies were collecting information faster than they could analyze it and that data analysis was an underexploited segment of the software business. It was at a seminar at Northwestern University that he saw his opportunity. Two researchers had developed a set of algorithms that enabled analysts to sift through large amounts of raw data in powerful ways without programmers' help. Greg cashed in his Oracle options and, in partnership with the two researchers, created DataClear to develop applications based on the algorithms.

His partners took responsibility for product development and an initial stake of 20 percent each; Greg provided $500,000 in financing in return for 60 percent of the shares and the job of CEO. A year later, Greg offered David Lester, founder of DL Ventures and a former Oracle executive, 30 percent of the company in return for $5 million in additional funding.

In his previous positions, Greg had shown a

knack for leading "fizzy" technical teams, and under his leadership, the two researchers came up with a state-of-the-art data analysis package they dubbed ClearCloud (from the clarity the software brought to large data clouds). Two versions, one for the telecommunications industry and the other for financial services providers, were officially launched in September 1998. ClearCloud had a number of immediate and profitable applications. For instance, it could be used to help credit card companies detect fraud patterns more quickly in the millions of transactions that occurred every day. Greg conservatively estimated the annual demand from the U.S. telecommunications and financial services sectors to be around $600 million. The challenge was to make potential users aware of the product.

ClearCloud was an instant hit, and within just a month of its launch, Greg had needed to recruit a dozen sales staffers. One of the first was Susan Moskowski, a former sales rep at Banking Data Systems, who had worked successfully with Greg on several major joint pitches to financial institutions. She had spent two years at BDS's Singapore subsidiary, where she had laid the groundwork for a number of important contracts. She had left BDS to do an MBA at Stanford and jointed DataClear immediately on graduating as the new company's head of sales. She was an immediate success, landing DataClear's first major contract, with a large West Coast banking group.

Greg realized that ClearCloud had huge potential outside the telecommunications and financial services industries. In fact, with relatively little product development, Greg and his partners believed, ClearCloud could be adapted for the chemical, petrochemical, and pharmaceutical industries. Annual demand from customers in those sectors could reach as high as $900 million.

But accessing and serving clients in those fields would involve building specialized sales and service infrastructures. Just two months ago, to spearhead that initiative, Greg recruited a new business-development manager who had 20 years' experience in the chemical industry. A former senior R&D manager at DuPont, Tom Birmingham was excited by ClearCloud's blockbuster potential in the U.S. market. "The databases can only get bigger," he told Greg and Susan. Greg had asked Tom to put together a presentation for the off-site in Montana on the prospects for expanding into these new sectors.

Just two weeks before the outing, however, Susan burst into Greg's office and handed him an article from one of the leading trade journals. It highlighted a British start-up, VisiDat, which was beta testing a data analysis package that was only weeks away from launch. "We're not going to have the market to ourselves much longer," she told Greg. "We need to agree on a strategy for dealing with this kind of competition. If they start out as a global player, and we stay hunkered down in the U.S., they'll kill us. I've seen this before."

The news did not take Greg altogether by surprise. "I agree we've got to put together a strategy," he said. "Why don't we table the domestic-expansion discussion and talk about this at our off-site meeting, where we can get everyone's ideas? Unlike the rest of us, you've had some experience overseas, so perhaps you should lead the discussion. I'll square things with Tom."

Go Fish

In Montana, Susan kicked off the first session with the story of GulfSoft, a thinly disguised case study of her former employer. The company had developed a software package for the oil and gas exploration business, which it had introduced only in the United States. But at almost the same time, a French company had launched a comparable product, which it marketed aggressively on a global basis. A year later, the competitor had a much larger installed base worldwide than GulfSoft and was making inroads into GulfSoft's U.S. sales. When she reached the end of the story, Susan paused, adding ominously, "Today, we have 20 installations of ClearCloud outside the U.S.—15 in the U.K. and five in Japan—and those are only U.S. customers purchasing for their overseas subsidiaries."

At Susan's signal, the room went dark. Much of what followed, in a blizzard of overhead projections, was market research showing a lot of latent demand for ClearCloud outside the United States. The foreign markets in telecommunications and financial services were shown to be about as large as those in the U.S.—that is, another $600 million. The potential in pharmaceuticals, petrochemicals, and chemicals looked to be about $660 million. Taken altogether that meant a potential market of $1.5 billion domestically and $1.26 billion abroad.

In ending, Susan drew the obvious moral. "It seems pretty clear to me that the only defense for this kind of threat is to attack. We don't have any international sales strategy. We're here because we need one—and fast."

She glanced at Greg for any hint of objection, didn't see it, and plunged ahead "We know we can sell a lot of software in the U.S., but if we want DataClear to succeed in the long run, we need to preempt the competition and go worldwide. We need a large installed base ASAP.

"I propose that for the afternoon we split into two groups and focus on our two options for going forward. Group A can consider building our own organization to serve Europe. Group B can think about forming alliances with players already established there. Based on what you can come back with tomorrow, we'll make the call."

As the lights came back on, Greg blinked. He was dazzled. But he sensed that he needed to do some thinking, and he did his best thinking knee-deep in the river. After lunch, as the two groups got to work, Greg waded into Nelson's Spring Creek. The fish seemed to leap to his hook, but his thoughts were more elusive and ambivalent.

Money, Money, Money

Greg decided he needed a reality check, and that night he called David Lester to review the day's discussion. Not too surprisingly, Lester didn't have a lot of advice to give on the spot. In fact he had questions of his own. "Instead of focusing on foreign markets in our core industries, what if we focus on developing ClearCloud for the domestic pharmaceutical, chemical and petrochemical industries and capitalize in the $900 million U.S. market?" he asked. "How much would that cost?" Greg offered a best guess of $2 million for the additional software-development costs but hadn't yet come up with a number for marketing and sales; the industries were so different from the ones DataClear currently focused on. "Whatever the cost turns out to be, we're going to need another round of financing," Greg allowed. "Right now we're on track to generate a positive cash flow without raising any additional capital, but it won't be enough to fund a move beyond our core industries."

"That's not where I was headed," Lester replied.

"What if we went out and raised *a lot* more money and expanded the product offering and our geographic reach at the same time?"

Greg swallowed hard; he was usually game for a challenge, but a double expansion was daunting. He couldn't help thinking of the sticky note he'd posted on the frame of his computer screen a few days after he started DataClear. It clung there still, and it had just one word on it: "Focus."

Lester sensed Greg's hesitation: "Look. We're not going to decide this tonight. And really, at the end of the day it's up to you, Greg. You've done the right things so far. Keep doing them." Hanging up, Greg was reminded how pleased he was with Lester's hands-off approach. For the first time, he wondered what things would be like if he had a more hands-on venture capitalist as an investor—maybe one with some experience in international expansion.

Greg was also reminded of his own lack of international management experience. Eight years earlier, he had politely turned down an opportunity to lead a team of 50 Oracle development engineers in Japan, primarily because he had been unwilling to relocate to Tokyo for two years. His boss at the time had told him: "Greg, software is a global business, and what you don't learn early about cross-border management will come back to haunt you later."

Options on the Table

At ten o'clock the next morning, Group A took the floor and made their recommendation right off the bat: DataClear should immediately establish an office in the U.K. and staff it with four to six salespeople. Britain would be a beachhead into all of Europe, but eventually there would also be a sales office somewhere on the Continent, maybe in Brussels. They had even drafted a job description for a head of European sales.

Greg was impressed, if a little overwhelmed. "Any idea how much this would cost us in terms of salaries and expenses over the first year?" he asked.

"Conservatively, about $500,000 a year, probably more," the group leader replied. "But cost is not so much the point here. If we don't make this move, we'll get killed by VisiDat—or some other competitor we don't even know about yet. Imagine if SAP introduced a similar product. With their marketing machine, they would just crush us."

Tom Birmingham started to object. "Where are we going to find local staff to install and support the product?" he wanted to know. "I mean, this is not just about setting up an office to sell: ClearCloud is a complex product, and it needs a service infrastructure. We'd have to translate the interface software, or at least the manuals, into local languages. We'd need additional resources in business development and product support to manage all this. Selling ClearCloud in Europe is going to cost a lot more than $500,000 a year—"

Susan was quick to jump in. "Good point, Tom, and that isn't all we'll need. We also have to have somebody in Asia. Either Singapore or Tokyo would be an ideal base. Probably Tokyo works better because more potential clients are headquartered there than in the rest of Asia. We need at least four people in Asia, for the time being." Tom frowned, but, feeling that Susan had the momentum, decided to hold his fire.

After lunch, it was Group B's turn. They suggested using autonomous software distributors in each country. That would help DataClear keep a tight grip on expenses. Greg spoke up then. "What about teaming up with some local firm in Europe that offers a complementary product? Couldn't we get what we need through a joint venture?"

"Funny you should mention that, Greg," said the presenter from Group B. "We came up with the idea of Benro but didn't have time to pursue it. They might be willing to talk about reciprocal distribution." Benro was a small software shop in Norway. Greg knew it had about $5 million in sales last year from its data-mining package for financial services companies. Benro was very familiar with European customers in the financial services sector but had no experience with other industries. "Working with Benro might be cheaper than doing this all on our own, at least for now," the presenter said.

Susan chose that moment to speak up again. "I have to admit I'm skeptical about joint ventures. I think it will probably take too long to negotiate and sign the contracts, which won't even cover all the eventualities. At some point we will have to learn how to succeed in each region on our own."

That's when Greg noticed Tom studying Susan, his eyes narrowing. So he wasn't surprised—in fact he was a little relived—when Tom put the brakes on: "I guess I don't see how we can make that decision until we gather a little more input, Susan," Tom said. "At the very least, we need to have a conversation with Benro and any other potential partners. And I know I'd want to meet some candidates to lead a foreign sales office before I'd be comfortable going that route. But my real concern is more fundamental. Are we up to doing all this at the same time we're building our market presence in the U.S.? Remember, we don't yet have the capability to serve the chemical and pharmaceutical industries here. There are still only 38 of us, and I estimate that building the support infrastructure we need just for domestic expansion could cost as much as $2 million—on top of product development."

Before Susan could object, Greg struck the compromise. "Tell you what. Let's commit to making this decision in more than three weeks. I'll clear my calendar and connect with Benro myself. At the same time, Susan, you can flush out some good candidates for a foreign sales office and schedule them to meet with Tom and me."

Casting About

And that's how Greg McNally found himself up a creek in Norway that Sunday morning. Benro's CEO had been interested; Greg was confident that the meeting with him on Monday would yield some attractive options. And once the trip was booked, it didn't take Greg long to realize that he'd be near some fabled fishing spots.

He also realized it would be a great chance to pick the brain of his old Berkeley classmate, Sarah Pappas. A hardware engineer, Sarah had started her own company, Desix, in Mountain View, California, in 1993. The company designed specialty chips for the mobile communications industry. Within seven years, Desix had grown into one of the most successful specialized design shops around the world, with about 400 employees. Like Greg, Sarah had received funding from a venture capitalist. Since a lot of demand for Desix's services was in Scandinavia and to a lesser degree in Japan as well, Sarah had opened subsidiaries in both places and even decided to split her time between Mountain View and Oslo.

Greg arrived in Oslo on Thursday morning and met Sarah that evening at a waterfront restaurant. They spent the first half-hour swapping news about mutual friends. Sarah hadn't changed much, thought Greg. But when the conversation turned to potential geographic expansion and he asked about her experience, Greg saw her smile grow a little tense. "Ah, well," she began. "How much time do you have?"

"That bad?"

"Actually, to be honest, some things were easier than we thought," she allowed. "Recruiting, for example. We never expected to get any great engineers to leave Nokia or Hitachi to join us, but we ended up hiring our Oslo and Tokyo core teams without much trouble. Still, some things turned out to be hard—like coordinating the three sites across the borders. There were so many misunderstandings between Oslo and Mountain View that at first our productivity went down by 40 percent."

The story got worse. Sarah explained how, in 1998, her venture capitalist sought to exit its investment. Since an IPO seemed inadvisable for various reasons, the parties agreed to sell the company to Pelmer, a large equipment manufacturer. Sarah agreed to stay on for three years but couldn't do much to keep the engineers in her Oslo and Tokyo subsidiaries from leaving. No one had fully anticipated the clash between Pelmer's strong U.S. culture and Desix's local cultures in Oslo and Tokyo. By this point, Sarah felt, the merger had destroyed much that had gone into making Desix a small multinational company.

"I can tell I've been a real buzz killer," she laughed apologetically, as Greg picked up the check. "But if I were you, given what I've been through, I'd stay focused on the U.S. for as long as possible. You might not build the next Oracle or Siebel that way, but you'll live a happier life."

"So you think you made the wrong choice in expanding internationally?"

"Well, no," said Sarah, "because I don't think we had a choice. You, on the other hand, can sell much more product in the U.S. than we could have."

Up to His Waist

The next day brought its own worries, as Greg met with Pierre Lambert, a candidate for head of European sales, whom Susan had identified through a headhunter. Lambert had graduated from the Ecole des Mines in Paris and then worked for four years at Alcatel and five years at Lucent. As they talked, it occurred to Greg that he had no experience in reading résumés from outside the States. Was Ecole des Mines a good school? He noted that Lambert had worked only in France and the U.S. How successful would he be in the U.K. or Germany? As he wrapped up the interview, Greg figured he would need to see at least five candidates to form an opinion about the European labor market. And Asia would be even harder.

That evening, he compared notes with Tom, who had interviewed Lambert by phone the previous day. Tom expressed some doubts: he suspected Lambert wasn't mature enough to deal with the level of executives—CIOs and chief scientists—that DataClear would be targeting. That call only just ended when the cell phone rang again with Susan on the line. "Greg—I thought you would want to know. VisiDat just made its first significant sale—to Shell. The deal is worth at least $500,000. This is huge for them."

And now, two days later, here he stood in the glorious, frustrating Alta. He could see the salmon hanging out under the surface. He cast his line again, an elegant, silvery arc across the river and maneuvered the fly deftly through the water. Nothing.

Greg slogged back to shore and peered into the box housing his extensive collection of hand-tied salmon flies. Was it just that he was so preoccupied? Or were the conditions really so different here that none of his flies would work? One thing was for sure: it was a lot chillier than he'd expected. Despite the liner socks, his feet were getting cold.

6

Philips versus Matsushita: A New Century, a New Round

Throughout their long histories, N. V. Philips (Netherlands) and Matsushita Electric (Japan) had followed very different strategies and emerged with very different organizational capabilities. Philips built its success on a worldwide portfolio of responsive national organizations while Matsushita based its global competitiveness on its centralized, highly efficient operations in Japan.

During the 1990s, both companies experienced major challenges to their historic competitive positions and organizational models, and at the end of the decade, both companies were struggling to reestablish their competitiveness. At the turn of the millennium, new CEOs at both companies were implementing yet another round of strategic initiatives and organizational restructurings. Observers wondered how the changes would affect their long-running competitive battle.

Philips: Background

In 1892, Gerard Philips and his father opened a small light-bulb factory in Eindhoven, Holland. When their venture almost failed, they recruited Gerard's brother, Anton, an excellent salesman and manager. By 1900, Philips was the third largest light-bulb producer in Europe.

From its founding, Philips developed a tradition of caring for workers. In Eindhoven it built company houses, bolstered education, and paid its employees so well that other local employers complained. When Philips incorporated in 1912, it set aside 10 percent of profits for employees.

Technological Competence and Geographic Expansion

While larger electrical products companies were racing to diversify, Philips made only light-bulbs. This one-product focus and Gerard's technological prowess enabled the company to create significant innovations. Company policy was to scrap old plants and use new machines or factories whenever advances were made in new production technology. Anton wrote down assets rapidly and set aside substantial reserves for replacing outdated equipment. Philips also became a leader in industrial research, creating physics and chemistry labs to address production problems as well as more abstract scientific ones. The labs developed a tungsten metal filament bulb that was a great commercial success and gave Philips the financial strength to compete against its giant rivals.

This case derives from an earlier case, "Philips versus Matsushita: Preparing for a New Round," HBS No. 399-102, prepared by Professor Christopher A. Bartlett, which was an updated version of an earlier case by Professor Bartlett and Research Associate Robert W. Lightfoot, "Philips and Matsushita: A Portrait of Two Evolving Companies," HBS Case No. 392-156. The section on Matsushita summarizes "Matsushita Electric Industrial (MEI) in 1987," HBS Case No. 388-144, by Sumantra Ghoshal (INSEAD) and Christopher A. Bartlett. Some early history on Philips draws from "Philips Group—1987," HBS Case No. 388-050, by Professors Frank Aguilar and Michael Y. Yoshino. This version was also prepared by Professor Bartlett. HBS cases are developed solely as the basis for class discussion. Cases are not intended to serve as endorsements, sources of primary data, or illustrations of effective or ineffective management. "Philips versus Matsushita: A New Century, a New Round." Copyright © 2001 by the President and Fellows of Harvard College. Harvard Business School Case 9-302-049. This case was prepared by Professor Christopher Bartlett as the basis for class discussion rather than to illustrate either effective or ineffective handling of an administrative situation. Reprinted by permission of Harvard Business School.

Holland's small size soon forced Philips to look beyond its Dutch borders for enough volume to mass produce. In 1899, Anton hired the company's first export manager, and soon the company was selling into such diverse markets as Japan, Australia, Canada, Brazil, and Russia. In 1912, as the electric lamp industry began to show signs of overcapacity, Philips started building sales organizations in the United States, Canada, and France. All other functions remained highly centralized in Eindhoven. In many foreign countries Philips created local joint ventures to gain market acceptance.

In 1919, Philips entered into the Principal Agreement with General Electric, giving each company the use of the other's patents. The agreement also divided the world into "three spheres of influence": General Electric would control North America; Philips would control Holland; but both companies agreed to compete freely in the rest of the world. (General Electric also took a 20 percent stake in Philips.) After this time, Philips began evolving from a highly centralized company, whose sales were conducted through third parties, to a decentralized sales organization with autonomous marketing companies in 14 European countries, China, Brazil, and Australia.

During this period, the company also broadened its product line significantly. In 1918, it began producing electronic vacuum tubes; eight years later its first radios appeared, capturing a 20 percent world market share within a decade; and during the 1930s, Philips began producing X-ray tubes. The Great Depression brought with it trade barriers and high tariffs, and Philips was forced to build local production facilities to protect its foreign sales of these products.

Philips: Organizational Development

One of the earliest traditions at Philips was a shared but competitive leadership by the commercial and technical functions. Gerard, an engineer, and Anton, a businessman, began a subtle competition where Gerard would try to produce more than Anton could sell and vice versa. Nevertheless, the two agreed that strong research was vital to Philips' survival.

During the late 1930s, in anticipation of the impending war, Philips transferred its overseas assets to two trusts, British Philips and the North American

Philips Corporation; it also moved most of its vital research laboratories to Redhill in Surrey, England, and its top management to the United States. Supported by the assets and resources transferred abroad, and isolated from their parent, the individual country organizations became more independent during the war.

Because waves of Allied and German bombing had pummeled most of Philips' industrial plant in the Netherlands, the management board decided to build the postwar organization on the strengths of the national organizations (NOs). Their greatly increased self-sufficiency during the war had allowed most to become adept at responding to country-specific market conditions—a capability that became a valuable asset in the postwar era. For example, when international wrangling precluded any agreement on three competing television transmission standards (PAL, SECAM, and NTSC), each nation decided which to adopt. Furthermore, consumer preferences and economic conditions varied: in some countries, rich, furniture-encased TV sets were the norm; in others, sleek, contemporary models dominated the market. In the United Kingdom, the only way to penetrate the market was to establish a rental business; in richer countries, a major marketing challenge was overcoming elitist prejudice against television. In this environment, the independent NOs had a great advantage in being able to sense and respond to the differences.

Eventually, responsiveness extended beyond adaptive marketing. As NOs built their own technical capabilities, product development often became a function of local market conditions. For example, Philips of Canada created the company's first color TV; Philips of Australia created the first stereo TV; and Philips of the United Kingdom created the first TVs with teletext.

While NOs took major responsibility for financial, legal, and administrative matters, fourteen product divisions (PDs), located in Eindhoven, were formally responsible for development, production, and global distribution. (In reality, the NOs' control of assets and the PDs' distance from the operations often undercut this formal role.) The research function remained independent and, with continued strong funding, set up eight separate laboratories in Europe and the United States.

While the formal corporate-level structure was represented as a type of geographic/product matrix, it was clear that NOs had the real power. NOs reported directly to the management board, which Philips enlarged from 4 members to 10 to ensure that top management remained in contact with and control of the highly autonomous NOs. Each NO also regularly sent envoys to Eindhoven to represent its interests. Top management, most of whom had careers that included multiple foreign tours of duty, made frequent overseas visits to the NOs. In 1954, the board established the International Concern Council to formalize regular meetings with the heads of all major NOs.

Within the NOs, the management structure mimicked the legendary joint technical and commercial leadership of the two Philips brothers. Most were led by a technical manager and a commercial manager. In some locations, a finance manager filled out the top management triad that typically reached key decisions collectively. This cross-functional coordination capability was reflected down through the NOs in front-line product teams, product-group-level management teams, and at the senior management committee of the NOs' top commercial, technical, and financial managers.

The overwhelming importance of foreign operations to Philips, the commensurate status of the NOs within the corporate hierarchy, and even the cosmopolitan appeal of many of the offshore subsidiaries' locations encouraged many Philips managers to take extended foreign tours of duty, working in a series of two- or three-year posts. This elite group of expatriate managers identified strongly with each other and with the NOs as a group and had no difficulty representing their strong, country-oriented views to corporate management.

Philips: Attempts at Reorganization

In the late 1960s, the creation of the Common Market eroded trade barriers within Europe and diluted the rationale for maintaining independent, country-level subsidiaries. New transistor- and printed circuit-based technologies demanded larger production runs than most national plants could justify, and many of Philips' competitors were moving production of electronics to new facilities in low-wage areas in East Asia and Central and South America. Despite its many technological innovations, Philips' ability to bring products to market began to falter. In the 1960s, the company invented the audiocassette but let its

Japanese competitors capture the mass market. A decade later, its R&D group developed the V2000 videocassette format—superior technically to Sony's Beta or Matsushita's VHS—but was forced to abandon it when North American Philips decided to outsource, brand, and sell a VHS product which it manufactured under license from Matsushita.

Over three decades, seven chairmen experimented with reorganizing the company to deal with its growing problems. Yet, entering the new millennium, Philips' financial performance remained poor and its global competitiveness was still in question. (See Exhibits 1 and 2.)

Van Reimsdijk and Rodenburg Reorganizations, 1970s

Concerned about what one magazine described as "continued profitless progress," newly appointed CEO Hendrick van Reimsdijk created an organization com-mittee to prepare a policy paper on the division of responsibilities between the PDs and the NOs. Their report, dubbed the "Yellow Booklet," outlined the disadvantages of Philips' matrix organization in 1971:

> Without an agreement [defining the relationship between national organizations and product divisions], it is impossible to determine in any given situation which of the two parties is responsible. . . . As operations become increasingly complex, an organizational form of this type will only lower the speed of reaction of an enterprise.

On the basis of this report, van Reimsdijk proposed rebalancing the managerial relationships between PDs and NOs—"tilting the matrix" in his words—to allow Philips to decrease the number of products marketed, build scale by concentrating production, and increase the flow of goods among national organizations. He proposed closing the least efficient local plants and converting the best into International Production Centers (IPCs), each supplying many NOs. In so doing, van Reimsdijk hoped that PD managers would gain control over manufacturing operations. Due to the political and organizational difficulty of closing local plants, however, implementation was slow.

In the late 1970s, his successor CEO, Dr. Rodenburg, continued this thrust. Several IPCs were established, but the NOs seemed as powerful and independent as ever. He furthered matrix

EXHIBIT 1

Philips Group Summary Financial Data, 1970–2000 (millions of guilders unless otherwise stated)

	2000	1995	1990	1985	1980	1975	1970
Net sales	F83,437	F64,462	F55,764	F60,045	F36,536	F27,115	F15,070
Income from operations (excluding restructuring	NA	4,090	2,260	3,075	1,577	1,201	1,280
Income from operations (including restructuring)	9,434	4,044	−2,389	N/A	N/A	N/A	N/A
As a percentage of net sales	11.3%	6.3%	−4.3%	5.1%	4.3%	4.5%	8.5%
Income after taxes	12,559	2,889	F−4,447	F1,025	F532	F341	F446
Net income from normal business operations	NA	2,684	−4,526	n/a	328	347	435
Stockholders' equity (common)	49,473	14,055	11,165	16,151	12,996	10,047	6,324
Return on stockholders' equity	42.8%	20.2%	−30.2%	5.6%	2.7%	3.6%	7.3%
Distribution per common share, par value F10 (in guilders)	F2.64	F1.60	F0.0	F2.00	F1.80	F1.40	F1.70
Total assets	86,114	54,683	51,595	52,883	39,647	30,040	19,088
Inventories as a percentage of net sales	13.9%	18.2%	20.7%	23.2%	32.8%	32.9%	35.2%
Outstanding trade receivables in month's sales	1.5	1.6	1.6	2.0	3.0	3.0	2.8
Current ratio	1.2		1.4	1.6	1.7	1.8	1.7
Employees at year-end (in thousands)	219	265	273	346	373	397	359
Wages, salaries and other related costs	NA	NA	F17,582	F21,491	F15,339	F11,212	F5,890
Exchange rate (period end; guilder/$)	2.34	1.60	1.69	2.75	2.15	2.69	3.62
Selected data in millions of dollars							
Sales	$35,253	$40,039	$33,018	$21,802	$16,993	$10,098	$4,163
Operating profit	3,986	2,512	1,247	988	734	464	NA
Pretax income	5,837	2,083	−2,380	658	364	256	NA
Net income	5,306	1,667	−2,510	334	153	95	120
Total assets	35,885	32,651	30,549	19,202	18,440	11,186	5,273
Shareholders' equity (common)	20,238	8,784	6,611	5,864	6,044	3,741	1,747

Sources: Annual reports; Standard & Poors' *Compustat*; Moody's Industrial and International Manuals.
Note: Exchange rate 12/31/00 was Euro/US$: 1.074.

simplification by replacing the dual commercial and technical leadership with single management at both the corporate and national organizational levels. Yet the power struggles continued.

Wisse Dekker Reorganization, 1982

Unsatisfied with the company's slow response and concerned by its slumping financial performance,

upon becoming CEO in 1982, Wisse Dekker outlined a new initiative. Aware of the cost advantage of Philips' Japanese counterparts, he closed inefficient operations—particularly in Europe where 40 of the company's more than 200 plants were shut. He focused on core operations by selling some businesses (for example, welding, energy cables, and furniture) while acquiring an interest in Grundig and Westinghouse's North American lamp activities.

EXHIBIT 2

Philips Group, Sales by Product and Geographic Segment, 1985–2000 (millions of guilders)

	2000		1995		1990		1985	
Net Sales by Product Segment:								
Lighting	F11,133	13%	F8,353	13%	F 7,026	13%	F 7,976	12%
Consumer electronics	32,357	39	22,027	34	25,400	46	16,906	26
Domestic appliances	4,643	6	—	—	—	—	6,644	10
Professional products/Systems	—	—	11,562	18	13,059	23	17,850	28
Components/Semiconductors	23,009	28	10,714	17	8,161	15	11,620	18
Software/Services	—	—	9,425	15	—	—	—	—
Medical systems	6,679	8	—	—	—	—	—	—
Origin	1,580	2	—	—	—	—	—	—
Miscellaneous	4,035	5	2,381	4	2,118	4	3,272	5
Total	83,437	100%	64,462	100%	F 55,764	100%	F 64,266	100%
Operating Income by Sector:								
Lighting	1,472	16%	983	24%	419	18%	F910	30%
Consumer electronics	824	9	167	4	1,499	66	34	1
Domestic appliances	632	7	—	—	—	—	397	13
Professional products/Systems	—	—	157	4	189	8	1,484	48
Components/Semiconductors	4,220	45	2,233	55	−43	−2	44	1
Software/Services	—	—	886	22	—	—	—	—
Medical systems	372	4	—	—	—	—	—	—
Origin	2,343	25	—	—	—	—	—	—
Miscellaneous	−249	−3	423	10	218	10	200	7
Increase not attributable to a sector	−181	−2	(805)	(20)	−22	−1	6	0
Total	9,434	100%	4,044	100%	2,260	100%	F3,075	100%

Source: Annual reports.

Conversion rate (12/31/00): 1 Euro: 2.20371 Dutch Guilders.

Totals may not add due to rounding.

Product sector sales after 1988 are external sales only; therefore, no eliminations are made; sector sales before 1988 include sales to other sectors; therefore, eliminations are made.

Data are not comparable to consolidated financial summary due to restating.

Dekker also supported technology-sharing agreements and entered alliances in offshore manufacturing.

To deal with the slow-moving bureaucracy, he continued his predecessor's initiative to replace dual leadership with single general managers. He also continued to "tilt the matrix" by giving PDs formal product management responsibility, but leaving NOs responsible for local profits. And, he energized the management board by reducing its size, bringing on directors with strong operating experience, and creating subcommittees to deal with difficult issues. Finally, Dekker redefined the product planning process, incorporating input from the NOs, but giving global PDs the final decision on long-range direction. Still sales declined and profits stagnated.

Van der Klugt Reorganization, 1987

When Cor van der Klugt succeeded Dekker as chairman in 1987, Philips had lost its long-held consumer electronics leadership position to Matsushita, and was one of only two non-Japanese companies in the world's top ten. Its net profit margins of 1 percent to 2 percent not only lagged behind General Electric's 9 percent, but even its highly aggressive Japanese competitors' slim 4 percent. Van der Klugt set a profit objective of 3 percent to 4 percent and made beating the Japanese companies a top priority.

As van der Klugt reviewed Philips' strategy, he designated various businesses as core (those that shared related technologies, had strategic importance, or were technical leaders) and non-core (stand-alone businesses that were not targets for world leadership and could eventually be sold if required). Of the four businesses defined as core, three were strategically linked: components, consumer electronics, and telecommunications and data systems. The fourth, lighting, was regarded as strategically vital because its cash flow funded development. The non-core businesses included domestic appliances and medical systems which van der Klugt spun off into joint ventures with Whirlpool and GE, respectively.

In continuing efforts to strengthen the PDs relative to the NOs, van der Klugt restructured Philips around the four core global divisions rather than the former 14 PDs. This allowed him to trim the management board, appointing the displaced board members to a new policy-making Group Management Committee. Consisting primarily of PD heads and funtional chiefs, this body replaced the old NO-dominated International Concern Council. Finally, he sharply reduced the 3,000-strong headquarters staff, reallocating many of them to the PDs.

To link PDs more directly to markets, van der Klugt dispatched many experienced product-line managers to Philips' most competitive markets. For example, management of the digital audio tape and electric-shaver product lines were relocated to Japan, while the medical technology and domestic appliances lines were moved to the United States.

Such moves, along with continued efforts at globalizing product development and production efforts, required that the parent company gain lfirmer control over NOs, especially the giant North American Philips Corp. (NAPC). Although Philips had obtained a majority equity interest after World War II, it was not always able to make the U.S. company respond to directives from the center, as the V2000 VCR incident showed. To prevent replays of such experiences, in 1987 van der Klugt repurchased publicly owned NAPC shares for $700 million.

Reflecting the growing sentiment among some managers that R&D was not market oriented enough, van der Klugt halved spending on basic research to about 10 percent of total R&D. To manage what he described as "R&D's tendency to ponder the fundamental laws of nature," he made R&D the direct responsibility of the businesses being supported by the research. This required that each research lab become focused on specific business areas (see Exhibit 3).

Finally, van der Klugt continued the effort to build efficient, specialized, multi-market production facilities by closing 75 of the company's 420 remaining plants worldwide. He also eliminated 38,000 of its 344,000 employees—21,000 through divesting businesses, shaking up the myth of lifetime employment at the company. He anticipated that all these restructurings would lead to a financial recovery by 1990. Unanticipated losses for that year, however—more than 4.5 billion Dutch guilders ($2.5 billion)—provoked a class-action law suit by angry American investors, who alleged that positive projections by the company had been misleading. In a surprise move, on May 14, 1990, van der Klugt and half of the management board were replaced.

Timmer Reorganization, 1990

The new president, Jan Timmer, had spent most of his 35-year Philips career turning around unprofitable businesses. With rumors of a takeover or a government bailout swirling, he met with his top 100 managers and distributed a hypothetical—but fact-based—press release announcing that Philips was bankrupt. "So what action can you take this weekend?" he challenged them.

Under "Operation Centurion," headcount was reduced by 68,000 or 22 percent over the next 18 months, earning Timmer the nickname "The Butcher of Eindhoven." Because European laws required substantial compensation for layoffs—Eindhoven workers received 15 months' pay, for example—the first round of 10,000 layoffs alone cost Philips $700 million. To spread the burden around the globe and

EXHIBIT 3

Philips Research Labs by Location and Specialty, 1987

Location	Size (staff)	Specialty
Eindhoven, The Netherlands	2,000	Basic research, electronics, manufacturing technology
Redhill, Surrey, England	450	Microelectronics, television, defense
Hamburg, Germany	350	Communications, office equipment, medical imaging
Aachen, W. Germany	250	Fiber optics, X-ray systems
Paris, France	350	Microprocessors, chip materials, design
Brussels	50	Artificial intelligence
Briarcliff Manor, New York	35	Optical systems, television, superconductivity, defense
Sunnyvale, California	150	Integrated circuits

Source: Philips, in *Business Week*, March 21, 1988, p. 156.

to speed the process, Timmer asked his PD managers to negotiate cuts with NO managers. According to one report, however, country managers were "digging in their heels to save local jobs." But the cuts came—many from overseas operations. In addition to the job cuts, Timmer vowed to "change the way we work." He established new performance rules and asked hundreds of top managers to sign contracts that committed them to specific financial goals. Those who broke those contracts were replaced—often with outsiders.

To focus resources further, Timmer sold off various businesses including integrated circuits to Matsushita, minicomputers to Digital, defense electronics to Thomson and the remaining 53 percent of appliances to Whirlpool. Yet profitability was still well below the modest 4 percent on sales he promised. In particular, consumer electronics lagged with slow growth in a price-competitive market. The core problem was identified by a 1994 McKinsey study that estimated that value added per hour in Japanese consumer electronic factories was still 68 percent above that of European plants. In this environment, most NO managers kept their heads down, using their distance from Eindhoven as their defense against the ongoing rationalization.

After three years of cost-cutting, in early 1994 Timmer finally presented a new growth strategy to the board. His plan was to expand software, services, and multimedia to become 40 percent of revenues by 2000. He was betting on Philips' legendary innovative capability to restart the growth engines. Earlier, he had recruited Frank Carrubba, Hewlett-Packard's director of research, and encouraged him to focus on developing 15 core technologies. The list, which included interactive compact disc (CD-i), digital compact cassettes (DCC), high definition television (HDTV), and multimedia software, was soon dubbed "the president's projects." But his earlier divestment of some of Philips' truly high-tech businesses and a 37 percent cut in R&D personnel left the company with few who understood the technology of the new priority businesses.

By 1996, it was clear that Philips' HDTV technology would not become industry standard, that its DCC gamble had lost out to Sony's Minidisc, and that CD-i was a marketing failure. While costs were lower, so too was morale, particularly among middle management. Critics claimed that the company's drive for cost-cutting and standardization had led it to ignore new worldwide market demands for more segmented products and higher consumer service.

Boonstra Reorganization, 1996

When Timmer stepped down in October 1996, the board replaced him with a radical choice for Philips—an outsider whose expertise was in marketing and Asia rather than technology and Europe. Cor Boonstra was a 58-year-old Dutchman whose years as CEO of Sara Lee, the U.S. consumer products firm, had earned him a reputation as a hard-driving marketing genius. Joining Philips in 1994, he headed the Asia Pacific region and the lighting division before being tapped as CEO.

Unencumbered by tradition, he immediately announced strategic sweeping changes designed to reach his target of increasing return on net assets from 17 percent to 24 percent by 1999. "There are no taboos, no sacred cows," he said. "The bleeders must be turned around, sold, or closed." Within three years, he had sold off 40 of Philips' 120 major businesses—including such well known units as Polygram and Grundig. He also initiated a major worldwide restructuring, promising to transform a structure he described as "a plate of spaghetti" into "a neat row of asparagus." He said:

> How can we compete with the Koreans? They don't have 350 companies all over the world. Their factory in Ireland covers Europe and their manufacturing facility in Mexico serves North America. We need a more structured and simpler manufacturing and marketing organization to achieve a cost pattern in line with those who do not have our heritage. This is still one of the biggest issues facing Philips.

Within a year, 3,100 jobs were eliminated in North America and 3,000 employees were added in Asia Pacific, emphasizing Boonstra's determination to shift production to low-wage countries and his broader commitment to Asia. And after three years, he had closed 100 of the company's 356 factories worldwide. At the same time, he replaced the company's 21 PDs with 7 divisions, but shifted day-to-day operating responsibility to 100 business units, each responsible for its profits worldwide. It was a move designed to finally eliminate the old PD/NO matrix. Finally, in a move that shocked most employees, he announced that the 100-year-old Eindhoven headquarters would be relocated to Amsterdam with only 400 of the 3000 corporate positions remaining.

By early 1998, he was ready to announce his new strategy. Despite early speculation that he might abandon consumer electronics, he proclaimed it as the center of Philips' future. Betting on the "digital revolution," he planned to focus on established technologies such as cellular phones (through a joint venture with Lucent), digital TV, digital videodisc, and web TV. Furthermore, he committed major resources to marketing, including a 40 percent increase in advertising to raise awareness and image of the Philips brand and de-emphasize most of the 150 other brands it supported worldwide—from Magnavox TVs to Norelco shavers to Marantz stereos.

While not everything succeeded (the Lucent cell phone JV collapsed after nine months, for example), overall performance improved significantly in the late 1990s. By 1999, Boonstra was able to announce that he had achieved his objective of a 24 percent return on net assets.

Kleisterlee Reorganization, 2001

In May 2001, Boonstra passed the CEO's mantle to Gerald Kleisterlee, a 54-year-old engineer (and career Philips man) whose turnaround of the components business had earned him a board seat only a year earlier. Believing that Philips had finally turned around, the board challenged Kleisterlee to grow sales by 10 percent annually and earnings 15 percent, while increasing return on assets to 30 percent.

Despite its stock trading at a steep discount to its breakup value, Philips governance structure and Dutch legislation made a hostile raid all but impossible. Nonetheless, Kleisterlee described the difference as "a management discount" and vowed to eliminate it. The first sign of restructuring came within weeks, when mobile phone production was outsourced to CEC of China. Then, in August, Kleisterlee announced an agreement with Japan's Funai Electric to take over production of its VCRs, resulting in the immediate closure of the European production center in Austria and the loss of 1,000 jobs. The CEO then acknowledged that he was seeking partners to take over the manufacturing of some of its other mass-produced items such as television sets.

In mid 2001, a slowing economy resulted in the company's first quarterly loss since 1996 and a reversal of the prior year's strong positive cash flow. Many felt that these growing financial pressures—and shareholders' growing impatience—were finally leading Philips to recognize that its best hope of survival was to outsource even more of its basic manufacturing and become a technology developer and global marketer. They believed it was time to recognize that its 30-year quest to build efficiency into its global operations had failed.

Matsushita: Background

In 1918, Konosuke Matsushita (or "KM" as he was affectionately known), a 23-year-old inspector with the Osaka Electric Light Company, invested ¥100 to start production of double-ended sockets in his modest home. The company grew rapidly, expanding into battery-powered lamps, electric irons, and radios. On May 5, 1932, Matsushita's 14th anniversary, KM announced to his 162 employees a 250-year corporate plan broken into 25-year sections, each to be carried out by successive generations. His plan was codified in a company creed and in the "Seven Spirits of Matsushita" (see Exhibit 4), which, along with the company song, continued to be woven into morning assemblies worldwide and provided the basis of the "cultural and spiritual training" all new employees received during their first seven months with the company.

In the post-war boom, Matsushita introduced a flood of new products: TV sets in 1952; transistor radios in 1958; color TVs, dishwashers, and electric ovens in 1960. Capitalizing on its broad line of 5,000 products (Sony produced 80), the company opened 25,000 domestic retail outlets. With more than six times the outlets of rival Sony, the ubiquitous "National Shops" represented 40 percent of appliance stores in Japan in the late 1960s. These not only provided assured sales volume, but also gave the company direct access to market trends and

---

EXHIBIT 4

Matsushita Creed and Philosophy (Excerpts)

Creed

Through our industrial activities, we strive to foster progress, to promote the general welfare of society, and to devote ourselves to furthering the development of world culture.

Seven Spirits of Matsushita

Service through Industry
Fairness
Harmony and Cooperation
Struggle for Progress
Courtesy and Humility
Adjustment and Assimilation
Gratitude

KM's Business Philosophy (Selected Quotations)

"The purpose of an enterprise is to contribute to society by supplying goods of high quality at low prices in ample quantity."

"Profit comes in compensation for contribution to society. . . .[It] is a result rather than a goal."

"The responsibility of the manufacturer cannot be relieved until its product is disposed of by the end user."

"Unsuccessful business employs a wrong management. You should not find its causes in bad fortune, unfavorable surroundings or wrong timing."

"Business appetite has no self-restraining mechanism. . . .When you notice you have gone too far, you must have the courage to come back."

Source: "Matsushita Electric Industrial (MEI) in 1987," Harvard Business School Case No. 388-144.

consumer reaction. When post-war growth slowed, however, Matsushita had to look beyond its expanding product line and excellent distribution system for growth. After trying many tactics to boost sales—even sending assembly line workers out as door-to-door salesmen—the company eventually focused on export markets.

The Organization's Foundation: Divisional Structure

Plagued by ill health, KM wished to delegate more authority than was typical in Japanese companies. In 1933, Matsushita became the first Japanese company to adopt the divisional structure, giving each division clearly defined profit responsibility for its product. In addition to creating a "small business" environment, the product division structure generated internal competition that spurred each business to drive growth by leveraging its technology to develop new products. After the innovating division had earned substantial profits on its new product, however, company policy was to spin it off as a new division to maintain the "hungry spirit."

Under the "one-product-one-division" system, corporate management provided each largely self-sufficient division with initial funds to establish its own development, production, and marketing capabilities. Corporate treasury operated like a commercial bank, reviewing divisions' loan requests for which it charged slightly higher-than-market interest, and accepting deposits on their excess funds. Divisional profitability was determined after deductions for central services such as corporate R&D and interest on internal borrowings. Each division paid 60 percent of earnings to headquarters and financed all additional working capital and fixed asset requirements from the retained 40 percent. Transfer prices were based on the market and settled through the treasury on normal commercial terms. KM expected uniform performance across the company's 36 divisions, and division managers whose operating profits fell below 4 percent of sales for two successive years were replaced.

While basic technology was developed in a central research laboratory (CRL), product development and engineering occurred in each of the product divisions. Matsushita intentionally under-funded the CRL, forcing it to compete for additional funding from the divisions. Annually, the CRL publicized its major research projects to the product divisions, which then

provided funding in exchange for technology for marketable applications. While it was rarely the innovator, Matsushita was usually very fast to market—earning it the nickname "Manishita," or copycat.

Matsushita: Internationalization

Although the establishment of overseas markets was a major thrust of the second 25 years in the 250-year plan, in an overseas trip in 1951 KM had been unable to find any American company willing to collaborate with Matsushita. The best he could do was a technology exchange and licensing agreement with Philips. Nonetheless, the push to internationalize continued.

Expanding Through Color TV

In the 1950s and 1960s, trade liberalization and lower shipping rates made possible a healthy export business built on black and white TV sets. In 1953, the company opened its first overseas branch office—the Matsushita Electric Corporation of America (MECA). With neither a distribution network nor a strong brand, the company could not access traditional retailers, and had to resort to selling its products under their private brands through mass merchandisers and discounters.

During the 1960s, pressure from national governments in developing countries led Matsushita to open plants in several countries in Southeast Asia and Central and South America. As manufacturing costs in Japan rose, Matsushita shifted more basic production to these low-wage countries, but almost all high-value components and subassemblies were still made in its scale-intensive Japanese plants. By the 1970s, protectionist sentiments in the West forced the company to establish assembly operations in the Americas and Europe. In 1972, it opened a plant in Canada; in 1974, it bought Motorola's TV business and started manufacturing its Quasar brand in the United States; and in 1976, it built a plant in Cardiff, Wales, to supply the Common Market.

Building Global Leadership Through VCRs

The birth of the videocassette recorder (VCR) propelled Matsushita into first place in the consumer electronics industry during the 1980s. Recognizing the potential mass-market appeal of the VCR—developed by Californian broadcasting company, Ampex, in 1956—engineers at Matsushita began developing VCR technology. After six years of development work, Matsushita launched its commercial broadcast video recorder in 1964, and introduced a consumer version two years later.

In 1975, Sony introduced the technically superior "Betamax" format, and the next year JVC launched a competing "VHS" format. Under pressure from MITI, the government's industrial planning ministry, Matsushita agreed to give up its own format and adopt the established VHS standard. During Matsushita's 20 years of VCR product development, various members of the VCR research team spent most of their careers working together, moving from central labs to the product divisions' development labs and eventually to the plant.

The company quickly built production to meet its own needs as well as those of OEM customers like GE, RCA, and Zenith, who decided to forego self-manufacture and outsource to the low-cost Japanese. Between 1977 and 1985, capacity increased 33-fold to 6.8 million units. (In parallel, the company aggressively licensed the VHS format to other manufacturers, including Hitachi, Sharp, Mitsubishi and, eventually, Philips.) Increased volume enabled Matsushita to slash prices 50 percent within five years of product launch, while simultaneously improving quality. By the mid-1980s, VCRs accounted for 30 percent of total sales—over 40 percent of overseas revenues—and provided 45 percent of profits.

Changing Systems and Controls

In the mid-1980s, Matsushita's growing number of overseas companies reported to the parent in one of two ways: wholly owned, single-product global plants reported directly to the appropriate product division, while overseas sales and marketing subsidiaries and overseas companies producing a broad product line for local markets reported to Matsushita Electric Trading Company (METC), a separate legal entity. (See Exhibit 5 for METC's organization.)

Throughout the 1970s, the central product divisions maintained strong operating control over their offshore production units. Overseas operations used plant and equipment designed by the parent company, followed manufacturing procedures dictated by the center, and used materials from Matsushita's domestic plants. Growing trends toward local sourcing, however, gradually weakened the divisions' direct control. By the 1980s, instead of controlling inputs, they began to monitor measures of output (for example, quality, productivity, inventory levels).

About the same time, product divisions began receiving the globally consolidated return on sales reports that had previously been consolidated in METC statements. By the mid-1980s, as worldwide planning was introduced for the first time, corporate management required all its product divisions to prepare global product strategies.

Headquarters-Subsidiary Relations

Although METC and the product divisions set detailed sales and profits targets for their overseas subsidiaries, local managers were told they had autonomy on how to achieve the targets. "Mike" Matsuoko, president of the company's largest European production subsidiary in Cardiff, Wales, however, emphasized that failure to meet targets forfeited freedom: "Losses show bad health and invite many doctors from Japan, who provide advice and support."

In the mid-1980s, Matsushita had over 700 expatriate Japanese managers and technicians on foreign assignment for four to eight years, but defended that high number by describing their pivotal role. "This vital communication role," said one manager, "almost always requires a manager from the parent company. Even if a local manager speaks Japanese, he would not have the long experience that is needed to build relationships and understand our management processes."

Expatriate managers were located throughout foreign subsidiaries, but there were a few positions that were almost always reserved for them. The most visible were subsidiary general managers whose main role was to translate Matsushita philosophy abroad. Expatriate accounting managers were expected to "mercilessly expose the truth" to corporate headquarters; and Japanese technical managers were sent to transfer product and process technologies and provide headquarters with local market information. These expatriates maintained relationships with senior colleagues at headquarters, who acted as career mentors, evaluated performance (with some input

EXHIBIT 5

Organization of METC, 1985

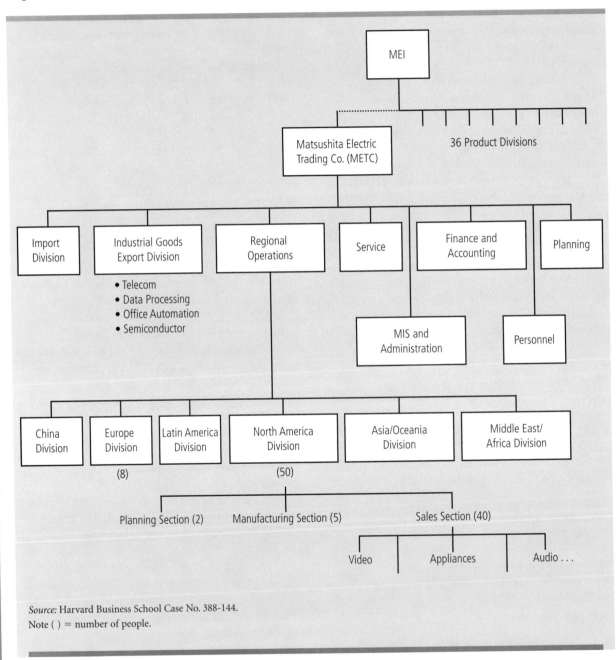

Source: Harvard Business School Case No. 388-144.
Note ( ) = number of people.

from local managers), and provided expatriates with information about parent company developments.

General managers of foreign subsidiaries visited Osaka headquarters at least two or three times each year—some as often as every month. Corporate managers reciprocated these visits, and on average, major operations hosted at least one headquarters

manager each day of the year. Face-to-face meetings were considered vital: "Figures are important," said one manager, "but the meetings are necessary to develop judgment." Daily faxes and nightly phone calls between headquarters and expatriate colleagues were a vital management link.

Yamashita's Operation Localization

Although international sales kept rising, as early as 1982 growing host country pressures caused concern about the company's highly centralized operations. In that year, newly appointed company President Toshihiko Yamashita launched "Operation Localization" to boost offshore production from less than 10 percent of value-added to 25 percent, or half of overseas sales, by 1990. To support the target, he set out a program of four localizations—personnel, technology, material, and capital.

Over the next few years, Matsushita increased the number of local nationals in key positions. In the United States, for example, U.S. nationals became the presidents of three of the six local companies, while in Taiwan the majority of production divisions were replaced by Chinese managers. In each case, however, local national managers were still supported by senior Japanese advisors, who maintained a direct link with the parent company. To localize technology and materials, the company developed its national subsidiaries' expertise to source equipment locally, modify designs to meet local requirements, incorporate local components, and adapt corporate processes and technologies to accommodate these changes. And by the mid-1980s, offshore production subsidiaries were free to buy minor parts from local vendors as long as quality could be assured, but still had to buy key components from internal sources.

One of the most successful innovations was to give overseas sales subsidiaries more choice over the products they sold. Each year the company held a two-week internal merchandising show and product planning meeting where product divisions exhibited the new lines. Here, overseas sales subsidiary managers described their local market needs and negotiated for change in features, quantities, and even prices of the products they wanted to buy. Product division managers, however, could overrule the sales subsidiary if they thought introduction of a particular product was of strategic importance.

President Yamashita's hope was that Operation Localization would help Matsushita's overseas companies develop the innovative capability and entrepreneurial initiatives that he had long admired in the national organizations of rival Philips. (Past efforts to develop such capabilities abroad had failed. For example, when Matsushita acquired Motorola's TV business in the United States, its highly innovative technology group atrophied as American engineers resigned in response to what they felt to be excessive control from Japan's highly centralized R&D operations.) Yet despite his four localizations, overseas companies continued to act primarily as the implementation arms of central product divisions. In an unusual act for a Japanese CEO, Yamashita publicly expressed his unhappiness with the lack of initiative at the TV plant in Cardiff. Despite the transfer of substantial resources and the delegation of many responsibilities, he felt that the plant remained too dependent on the center.

Tanii's Integration and Expansion

Yamashita's successor, Akio Tanii, expanded on his predecessor's initiatives. In 1986, feeling that Matsushita's product divisions were not giving sufficient attention to international development—in part because they received only 3 percent royalties for foreign production against at least 10 percent return on sales for exports from Japan—he brought all foreign subsidiaries under the control of METC. Tanii then merged METC into the parent company in an effort to fully integrate domestic and overseas operations. Then, to shift operational control nearer to local markets, he relocated major regional headquarters functions from Japan to North America, Europe, and Southeast Asia. Yet still he was frustrated that the overseas subsidiary companies acted as little more than the implementing agents of the Osaka-based product divisions.

Through all these changes, however, Matsushita's worldwide growth continued generating huge reserves. With $17.5 billion in liquid financial assets at the end of 1989, the company was referred to as the "Matsushita Bank," and several top executives began proposing that if they could not develop innovative overseas companies, they should buy them. Flush with cash and international success, in early 1991 the company acquired MCA, the U.S. entertainment giant, for $6.1 billion with the objective of obtaining a media software source for its hardware. Within a year, however, Japan's bubble economy had burst, plunging the economy into recession. Almost overnight, Tanii had to shift the company's focus from expansion to cost containment. Despite his best efforts to cut costs, the problems ran too deep. With 1992 profits less than half their 1991 level, the board took the unusual move of forcing Tanii to resign in February 1993.

Morishita's Challenge and Response

At 56, Yoichi Morishita was the most junior of the company's executive vice presidents when he was tapped as the new president. Under the slogan "simple, small, speedy and strategic," he committed to cutting headquarters staff and decentralizing responsibility. Over the next 18 months, he moved 6,000 staff to operating jobs. In a major strategic reversal, he also sold 80 percent of MCI to Seagram, booking a $1.2 billion loss on the transaction.

Yet the company continued to struggle. Japan's domestic market for consumer electronics collapsed—from $42 billion in 1989 to $21 billion in 1999. Excess capacity drove down prices and profits evaporated. And although offshore markets were growing, the rise of new competition—first from Korea, then China—created a global glut of consumer electronics, and prices collapsed.

With a strong yen making exports from Japan uncompetitive, Matsushita's product divisions rapidly shifted production offshore during the 1990s, mostly to low-cost Asian countries like China and Malaysia. By the end of the decade, its 160 factories outside Japan employed 140,000 people—about the same number of employees as in its 133 plants in Japan. Yet, despite the excess capacity and strong yen, management seemed unwilling to radically restructure its increasingly inefficient portfolio of production facilities.

In the closing years of the decade, Morishita began emphasizing the need to develop more of its technology and innovation offshore. Concerned that only 250 of the company's 3,000 R&D scientists and engineers were located outside Japan, he began investing in R&D partnerships and technical exchanges, particularly in fast emerging fields. For example, in 1998 he signed a joint R&D agreement with the Chinese Academy of Sciences, China's leading research organization. Later that year, he announced the establishment of the Panasonic Digital Concepts Center in California. Its mission was to act as a venture fund and an incubation center for the new ideas and technologies emerging in Silicon Valley. To some it was an indication that Matsushita had given up trying to generate new technology and business initiatives from its own overseas companies.

Nakamura's Initiatives

In April 2000, Morishita became chairman and Kunio Nakamura replaced him as president. Profitability was at 2.2 percent of sales, with consumer electronics at only 0.4 percent, including losses generated by one-time cash cows, the TV and VCR divisions. (Exhibits 6 and 7 provide the financial history for Matsushita and key product lines.) The new CEO vowed to raise this to 5 percent by 2004. Key to his plan was to move Matsushita beyond its roots as a "super manufacturer of products" and begin "to meet customer needs through systems and services." He planned to flatten the hierarchy and empower employees to respond to customer needs, and as part of the implementation, all key headquarters functions relating to international operations were transferred to overseas regional offices.

But the biggest shock came in November, when Nakamura announced a program of "destruction and creation," in which he disbanded the product division structure that KM had created as Matsushita's basic organizational building block 67 years earlier. Plants, previously controlled by individual product divisions, would now be integrated into multi-product production centers. In Japan alone 30 of the 133 factories were to be consolidated or closed. And marketing would shift to two corporate marketing entities, one for Panasonic brands (consumer electronics, information and communications products) and one for National branded products (mostly home appliances).

They were radical moves, but in a company that even in Japan was being talked about as a takeover target, observers wondered if they were sufficient to restore its global competitiveness.

EXHIBIT 6

Matsushita, Summary Financial Data, 1970–2000[a]

	2000	1995	1990	1985	1980	1975	1970
In billions of yen and percent:							
Sales	¥7,299	¥6,948	¥6,003	¥5,291	¥2,916	¥1,385	¥932
Income before tax	219	232	572	723	324	83	147
As % of sales	3.0%	3.3%	9.5%	13.7%	11.1%	6.0%	15.8%
Net income	¥100	¥90	¥236	¥216	¥125	¥32	¥70
As % of sales	1.4%	1.3%	3.9%	4.1%	4.3%	2.3%	7.6%
Cash dividends (per share)	¥14.00	¥13.50	¥10.00	¥9.52	¥7.51	¥6.82	¥6.21
Total assets	7,955	8,202	7,851	5,076	2,479	1,274	735
Stockholders' equity	3,684	3,255	3,201	2,084	1,092	573	324
Capital investment	355	316	355	288	NA	NA	NA
Depreciation	343	296	238	227	65	28	23
R&D	526	378	346	248	102	51	NA
Employees (units)	290,448	265,397	198,299	175,828	107,057	82,869	78,924
Overseas employees	143,773	112,314	59,216	38,380	NA	NA	NA
As % of total employees	50%	42%	30%	22%	NA	NA	NA
Exchange rate (fiscal period end; ¥/$)	103	89	159	213	213	303	360
In millions of dollars:							
Sales	$68,862	$78,069	$37,753	$24,890	$13,690	$4,572	$2,588
Operating income before depreciation	4,944	6,250	4,343	3,682	1,606	317	NA
Operating income after depreciation	1,501	2,609	2,847	2,764	1,301	224	NA
Pretax income	2,224	2,678	3,667	3,396	1,520	273	408
Net income	941	1,017	1,482	1,214	584	105	195
Total assets	77,233	92,159	49,379	21,499	11,636	4,206	2,042
Total equity	35,767	36,575	20,131	10,153	5,129	1,890	900

Sources: Annual reports; Standard & Poors' *Compustat*; Moody's Industrial and International Manuals.

[a]Data prior to 1987 are for the fiscal year ending November 20; data 1988 and after are for the fiscal year ending March 31.

EXHIBIT 7

Matsushita, Sales by Product and Geographic Segment, 1985–2000 (billion yen)

	2000		1995		FY1990		FY1985	
By Product Segment:								
Video and audio equipment	¥1,706	23%	¥1,827	26%	¥2,159	36%	¥2,517	48%
Home appliances and household equipment	1,306	18	—	—	—	—	—	—
Home appliances	—	—	916	13	802	13	763	14
Communication and industrial equipment	—	—	1,797	26	1,375	23	849	16
Electronic components	—	—	893	13	781	13	573	11
Batteries and kitchen-related equipment	—	—	374	4	312	5	217	4
Information and communications equipment	2,175	28	—	—	—	—	—	—
Industrial equipment	817	11	—	—	—	—	—	—
Components	1,618	21	—	—	—	—	—	—
Others	—	—	530	8	573	10	372	7
Total	¥7,682	100%	¥6,948	100%	¥6,003	100%	¥5,291	100%
By Geographic Segment:								
Domestic	¥3,698	51%	¥3,455	50%	¥3,382	56%	¥2,659	50%
Overseas	3,601	49	3,493	50	2,621	44	2,632	50

Source: Annual reports.
Note: Total may not add due to rounding.

Managing People in the International Arena
The Case of the Floundering Expatriate

At exactly 1:40 on a warm, sunny Friday afternoon in July 1995, Frank Waterhouse, CEO of Argos Diesel, Europe, leaves his office on the top floor of the Argos Tower, overlooking the Zürichsee. In the grip of a tension headache, he rides the glass elevator down the outside of the mirrored building.

To quiet his nerves, he studies his watch. In less than half an hour, Waterhouse must look on as Bert Donaldson faces the company's European managers—executives of the parts suppliers that Argos has acquired over the past two years. Donaldson is supposed to give the keynote address at this event, part of the second Argos Management Meeting organized by his training and education department. But late yesterday afternoon, he phoned Waterhouse to say he didn't think the address would be very good. Donaldson said he hadn't gotten enough feedback from the various division heads to put together the presentation he had planned. His summary of the company's progress wouldn't be what he had hoped.

It's his meeting! Waterhouse thinks, as the elevator moves silently down to the second floor. How could he not be prepared? Is this really the man who everyone at corporate headquarters in Detroit thinks is so fantastic?

Waterhouse remembers his introduction to Donaldson just over a year ago. Argos International's CEO and chairman, Bill Loun, had phoned Waterhouse himself to say he was sending the "pick of the litter." He said that Donaldson had a great international background—that he had been a professor of American studies in Cairo for five years. Then he had returned to the States and joined Argos. Donaldson had helped create the cross-divisional,

cross-functional teams that had achieved considerable cost reductions and quality improvements.

Loun had said that Donaldson was just what Argos Europe needed to create a seamless European team—to facilitate communication among the different European parts suppliers that Waterhouse had worked so hard to acquire. Waterhouse had proved his own strategic skills, his own ability to close deals, by successfully building a network of companies in Europe under the Argos umbrella. All the pieces were in place. But for the newly expanded company to meet its financial goals, the units had to work together. The managers had to become an integrated team. Donaldson could help them. Together they would keep the company's share of the diesel engine and turbine market on the rise.

Waterhouse deserved to get the best help, the CEO had said. Bert Donaldson was the best. And later, when the numbers proved the plan successful, Waterhouse could return to the States a hero. (Waterhouse heard Loun's voice clearly in his head: "I've got my eye on you, Frank. You know you're in line.")

Waterhouse had been enthusiastic. Donaldson could help him reach the top. He had met the man several times in Detroit. Donaldson seemed to have a quick mind, and he was very charismatic.

But that wasn't the Donaldson who had arrived in Zürich in August 1994 with his wife and two daughters. This man didn't seem to be a team builder —not in this venue. Here his charisma seemed abrasive.

The elevator comes to a stop. Waterhouse steps into the interior of the building and heads toward the seminar room at the end of the hall.

Waterhouse keeps thinking of his own career. He has spent most of his time since Donaldson's appointment securing three major government contracts in Moscow, Ankara, and Warsaw. He has kept the ball rolling, kept his career on track. It isn't his fault that Donaldson can't handle this assignment. It isn't his fault that the Germans and the French still can't agree on a unified sales plan.

His thoughts turn back to Donaldson. It can't be all Bert's fault, either. Donaldson is a smart man, a good man. His successes in the States were genuine. And Donaldson is worried about this assignment; it isn't as though he's just being stubborn. He sounded worried on the phone. He cares. He knows his job is falling apart and he doesn't know what to do. What can he return to at Argos in the States if he doesn't excel here in Europe?

Let Donaldson run with the ball—that's what they said in Detroit. It isn't working.

Waterhouse reaches the doorway of the seminar room. Ursula Lindt, his executive assistant, spots him from the other side. Lindt is from a wealthy local family. Most of the local hires go to her to discuss their problems. Waterhouse recalls a few of her comments about Donaldson: Staff morale on the fifth floor is lower than ever; there seems to be a general malaise. Herr Direktor Donaldson must be having problems at home. Why else would he work until midnight?

Waterhouse takes a seat in the front row and tries to distract himself by studying the meeting schedule. "Managing Change and Creating Vision: Improving Argos with Teamwork" is the title. Donaldson's "vision" for Argos Europe. Waterhouse sighs. Lindt nears him and, catching his eye, begins to complain.

"A few of the managers have been making noises about poor organization," she says. "And Sauras, the Spanish director, called to complain that the meeting schedule was too tight." Her litany of problems continues: "Maurizio, the director in Rome, came up to me this morning and began to lobby for Donaldson's replacement. He feels that we need someone with a better understanding of the European environment." Seeing Waterhouse frown,

Lindt backs off. "But he's always stirring up trouble," she says. "Otherwise, the conference appears to be a success." She sits down next to Waterhouse and studies her daily planner.

The room slowly fills with whispers and dark hand-tailored suits. Groups break up and reform. "Grüss Gott, Heinz, wie geht's?" "Jacques, ça va bien?" "Bill, good to see you...Great." Waterhouse makes a perfunctory inspection of the crowd. Why isn't Donaldson in here schmoozing? He hears a German accent: "Two-ten. Ja ja. Amerikanische Pünktlichkeit." Punctuality. Unlike Donaldson, he knows enough German to get by.

A signal is given. The chitchat fades with the lights. Waterhouse turns his gaze to the front as Donaldson strides up to the podium.

Donaldson speaks. "As President Eisenhower once said, 'I have two kinds of problems, the urgent and the important. The urgent are not important, and the important are never urgent.'" He laughs, but the rest of the room is silent save for the sound of paper shuffling.

Donaldson pauses to straighten his notes and then delivers a flat ten-minute summary of the European companies' organizational structure. He reviews the basics of the team-building plan he has developed—something with which all the listeners are already familiar. He thanks his secretary for her efforts.

Then he turns the meeting over to Waterhouse, who apologizes for not having been able to give the managers any notice that this session would be shorter than planned. He assures them that the rest of the schedule is intact and asks them to take this time as a break before their 4 p.m. logistics meeting, which will be run by the French division head.

The managers exchange glances, and Waterhouse detects one or two undisguised smiles. Walking out of the seminar room, he hears someone say, "At least the meeting didn't run overtime." Waterhouse fumes. He has put in four years of hard work here in Europe. This is the first year of his second three-year contract. He is being groomed for a top management position back in the States. The last thing he needs is a distraction like this.

He remembers how Detroit reacted when, a little over a month ago, he raised the issue of Donaldson's failure to adjust. He had written a careful letter to Bill Loun suggesting that Donaldson's assignment might be over his head, that the timing wasn't right. The

CEO had phoned him right away. "That's rubbish, Frank," his voice had boomed over the line. "You've been asking for someone to help make this plan work, and we've sent you the best we've got. You can't send him back. It's your call—you have the bottom-line responsibility. But I'm hoping he'll be part of your inner circle, Frank. I'd give him more time. Make it work. I'm counting on you."

More time is no longer an option, Waterhouse thinks. But if he fires Donaldson now or sends him back to Detroit, he loses whatever progress has been made toward a unified structure. Donaldson has begun to implement a team-building program; if he leaves, the effort will collapse. And how could he fire Donaldson, anyway? The guy isn't working out here, but firing him would destroy his career. Bert doesn't deserve that.

What's more, the European team program has been touted as a major initiative, and Waterhouse has allowed himself to be thought of as one of its drivers. Turning back would reflect badly on him as well.

On the other hand, the way things are going, if Donaldson stays, he may himself cause the plan to fail. One step forward, two steps back. "I don't have the time to walk Donaldson through remedial cultural adjustment," Waterhouse mumbles under his breath.

Donaldson approaches him in the hall. "I sent a multiple-choice survey to every manager. One of them sent back a rambling six-page essay," he says. "I sent them in April. I got back only 7 of 40 from the Germans. Every time I called, it was 'under review.' One of them told me his people wanted to discuss it—in German. The Portuguese would have responded if I'd brought it personally."

Waterhouse tells Donaldson he wants to meet with him later. "Five o'clock. In my office." He turns away abruptly.

Ursula Lindt follows him toward the elevator. "Herr Direktor, did you hear what Herr Donaldson called Frau Schweri?"

Bettina Schweri, who organizes Donaldson's programs, is essentially his manager. She speaks five languages fluently and writes three with style. Lindt and Schweri have known each other since childhood and eat lunch together every day.

"A secretary," Lindt says, exasperated. "Frau Schweri a secretary? Simply not to believe."

Back in his office, Waterhouse gets himself a glass of water and two aspirin. In his mind, he's sitting across from Donaldson ten months earlier.

"Once I reach a goal," Donaldson says, "I set another one and get to work. I like to have many things going at once—especially since I have only two years. I'm going for quick results, Frank. I've even got the first project lined up. We'll bring in a couple of trainers from the Consulting Consortium to run that team-skills workshop we talked about."

Waterhouse comes back to the present. That first workshop hadn't gone too badly—at least he hadn't heard of any problems. But he, Waterhouse, had not attended. He picks up the phone and places a call to Paul Janssen, vice president of human resources for Argos Europe. Paul is a good friend, a trusted colleague. The two men often cross paths at the health club.

A few seconds later, Janssen's voice booms over the line. "Frank? Why didn't you just walk down the hall to see me? I haven't seen you at the club in weeks."

Waterhouse doesn't want to chat. "Donaldson's first training weekend, in February," he says. "How'd it go? Really."

"Really. Well, overall, not too bad. A few glitches, but nothing too out of the ordinary for a first run. Bert had some problems with his assistant. Apparently, Frau Schweri had scheduled the two trainers to arrive in Zürich two days early to prepare everything, recover from jet lag, and have dinner at the Baur au Lac. They came the night before. You can imagine how that upset her. Bert knew about the change but didn't inform Frau Schweri."

Waterhouse has the distinct impression that Janssen has been waiting for a chance to talk about this. "Go on," Waterhouse says.

"Well, there were a few problems with the workshops."

"Problems?"

"Well, yes. One of the managers from Norway—Dr. Godal, I believe—asked many questions during Bert's presentation, and he became rather irascible."

"Bert?" Waterhouse asked.

"Yes. And one of the two trainers wore a Mickey Mouse sweater—"

"Mickey Mouse?" Waterhouse laughs without meaning to.

"A sweater with a depiction of Mickey Mouse on the front."

"What on earth does that have to do with Bert?"

"Well, Bert offered them a two-year contract after

Frau Schweri advised him not to. He apparently told her he was satisfied with the trainers and, so far as he was concerned, questions about their personal habits and clothing weren't worth his time."

"Yes, and—"

"Well, there were complaints—"

"They all went to Frau Schweri?" He is beginning to see.

"One of the managers said the trainers provided too much information; he felt as though they were condescending to him. A bombardment of information, he called it. Other managers complained that Bert didn't provide enough background information. The French managers seemed to think the meeting was worthwhile. But Bert must think that because his style works with one group, the others will fall into place automatically. And everyone was unhappy with the schedule. The trainers always ran overtime, so everybody was displeased because there weren't any coffee breaks for people from various offices to network. Oh, and the last thing? All the name cards had first names and last names—no titles."

"No titles," Waterhouse says, and lets out a sigh. "Paul, I wish you'd told me all this earlier."

"I didn't think you needed to hear it, Frank. You've been busy with the new contracts." They agree to meet at the club later in the week, and they hang up. Waterhouse stares down at Donaldson's file.

His résumé looks perfect. He has a glowing review from the American University in Cairo. There, Donaldson earned the highest ratings for his effectiveness, his ease among students from 40 countries, and his sense of humor. At Argos in the United States, he implemented the cross-divisional team approach in record time. Donaldson is nothing short of a miracle worker.

Waterhouse leans back in his swivel-tilter and lets the scuttlebutt on Donaldson run through his mind. Word is that he's an *Arbeitstier*. "Work animal" is the direct, unflattering translation. He never joins the staff for a leisurely lunch in the canteen, preferring a sandwich in his office. Word is he can speak some Arabic from his lecturing days in Cairo but still can't manage a decent "good morning" in Swiss German. Word is he walks around all day—he says it's management by walking around—asking for suggestions, ideas, plans, or solutions because he can't think of any himself.

Waterhouse remembers an early conversation with Donaldson in which he seemed frustrated. Should he have paid more attention?

"I met with Jakob Hassler, vice president of human resources at Schwyz Turbines," Donaldson had said, pacing the office. "I wanted some ideas for the training program. Schwyz is the first company we acquired here; I wanted to show Hassler that I don't bite. When I opened the door, he just stood there. I offered him a chair beside the coffee table, told him to call me Bert. He nodded, so I asked him about his family and the best place to buy ski boots, and he answered but he acted so aloof. I took a chair across from him, listened to ten minutes of one-word answers, and then I finally asked him how things were going in general, to which he said, 'Everything is normal.' Can you beat that, Frank? I told him I was interested in his ideas, so he pushed his chair back and said, 'Please let me know what you expect.' I reminded him that we're all on the same team, have only two years for major change, gave him a week to get back to me with a few ideas, and you know what he said? He said, 'Ja ja.'"

At the time, Donaldson's frustration seemed to stem from the normal adjustment problems that expatriates face. But he never did adjust. Why doesn't he just give Hassler what he needs to know and get out? Waterhouse knows this; why hasn't Donaldson figured it out?

His phone rings—the inside line. It's Ursula Lindt. "Frau Direktor Donaldson just called. She said Herr Direktor Donaldson was expected home at 4. I told her you had scheduled a meeting with him for 5." She waits. Waterhouse senses that there is more to her message. "What else did she say, Frau Lindt?"

"I inquired after her health, and she said she's near the end of her rope. Bored without her work. She said they thought Zürich would be a breeze after Cairo. Then she went into a tirade. She said that they're having serious problems with their eldest daughter. She'll be in grade 12 at the international school this fall. She's applying to college. Frau Donaldson said her daughter's recommendations from her British teachers are so understated that they'd keep her out of the top schools, and she keeps getting C's because they're using the British grading scale. She reminded me that this is a girl with a combined SAT score of over 1350."

Lindt is done. Waterhouse thanks her for the information, then hangs up. Julie Ann is usually calm, collected. She has made some friends here. Something must have pushed her over the edge. And their daughter is engaging, bright. Why is this all coming to a head now?

Waterhouse recalls his most recent meeting with Donaldson, a couple of days before Donaldson's vacation in May.

"I've tried everything, Frank. I've delegated, I've let them lead, I've given them pep talks." Waterhouse remembers Donaldson sinking deep into his chair, his voice flat. "No matter what I do—if I change an agenda, if I ask them to have a sandwich with me at my desk—someone's always pissed off. We're talking about streamlining an entire European company and they're constantly looking at their watches. We run ten minutes overtime in a meeting and they're shuffling papers. I tell you, Frank, they're just going to have to join the rest of us in the postindustrial age, learn to do things the Argos way. I worked wonders in Detroit . . ."

The clock in Waterhouse's office reads 4:45. What can he do about Donaldson? Let him blunder along for another year? And take another 12 months of . . . he closes the door on that thought. Send him back and forget? Morale on the fifth floor will improve, the Europeans will be appeased, but with Donaldson will go the training program, such as it is. Corporate will just think that Waterhouse has forgotten how to play the American way. They'll think that he mistreated their star. Can he teach Donaldson cultural awareness? With the Ankara, Moscow, and Warsaw projects chewing up all his time? You can't teach cultural savvy. No way.

He hears Donaldson enter the outer office. A hanger clinks on the coat tree. How can he work this out?

Hewlett-Packard Barcelona Division

In February 1995, the Barcelona Division of Hewlett-Packard (BCD) celebrated its 10th anniversary and the official opening of its expanded facilities. The fiscal year 1994 had closed with sales 87 per cent up on the previous year at 106,473 million pesetas, of which 58,958 million pesetas' worth of production was exported (see Exhibit 1—Sales and Exports 1991–1994).

> We often use the example of a growing child to describe BCD. If you ever play sports with your kids you know that as a child grows into adolescent, it master the skills, sometimes even outstripping the skills of the parents. But you can still dominate for some time because the adolescent lacks judgement. That's the stage we're at now; we do what we do very well, but decision-making must be tuned, and BCD staff need to learn when to be fast and when to be calm and slow, how and when to use their capabilities (A BCD Manager)

> We're going to have to learn big and fast. The rapid growth means our experienced people are spread throughout the organization to train the new staff. We're moving into new markets and we'll have to concentrate on developing our core capabilities. This means we must learn to manage external partnerships for sub-contracting other activities. (A BCD Manager)

> The transition has been even more successful than expected. We originally planned to keep a group in San Diego, but we've been able to transfer everything, just leaving the marketing centre. All the linkages are well established. (Rich Raimondi, General Manager, Hewlett-Packard, Barcelona Division)

> What takes up most of my time and thoughts now is working towards making the future of BCD both viable and exciting. (Rich Raimondi BCD GM)

History of Hewlett-Packard

Dave and Bill tossed a coin to decide the name of their new business partnership. It came up "Hewlett-Packard." The partnership became official on January 1, 1939 and began business with US$538 in working capital. From a rented garage . . . in Palo Alto, California, they offered one product. Known as the 200A audio oscillator . . . [1]

This is how HP describes the formal confirmation of what Dave Packard and Bill Hewlett had been planning for 5 years—to set up their own business. They had a good product that soon caught the attention of important customers such as Walt Disney, who used it to produce the stereophonic sound presentation of "Fantasia."

As sales passed the US$1 million mark in 1943, the company employed 100 people on two shifts a day. At that time the founders took key decisions to influence the relationships of the company and HP people. They avoid large contracts that could lead to a "hire-and-fire" operation and destroy employment stability. They chose to finance growth on a "pay-as-we-go" basis. The Christmas bonus of 1940 was the forerunner to subsequent production

---

Case of the Research Department at IESE. "Hewlett-Packard Barcelona Division" by Paddy Miller. Copyright © 1995 IESE. Used by permission.

bonuses, profit-sharing and employee stock-purchase plans. Health insurance was added and social events became traditional.

> Those decisions arose from a deliberate effort "to get out and learn as much as we could about management"—how to produce good results through teamwork. (Dave Packard)

In 1957, Dave Packard summarized HP's operating philosophy in a document called "Hewlett-Packard Corporate Objectives" (See Exhibit 2—HP Corporate Objectives).

> These [corporate objectives] represented the distilled wisdom of the first 18 years in business. Since then our key objectives have changed little. They have stood the test of time (John Young, former HP president)[2]

By 1994, Hewlett-Packard had reached net revenue for the year, from worldwide activities, of US$25,000 million, 23 percent up on the previous year, giving profits of US$1,600 million, 36 percent more than in 1993 (see Exhibit 3—Selected Financial Data 1990–1994). The company was operating in 110 countries and employed a total or 97,900 people worldwide.

From the 200A audio oscillator, Bill Hewlett and Dave Packard continued to develop high-quality, innovative electronic measuring instruments for broad application by engineers and scientists. By

EXHIBIT 1

**Hewlett-Packard Barcelona Division
(Hewlett-Packard Española, S.A.)
Sales and Exports 1991–1994 (millions of pesetas)**

1991	
Local sales	31,881
Exports	9,124
Total sales	41,005
1992	
Local sales	32,821
Exports	12,871
Total sales	45,692
1993	
Local sales	37,190
Exports	20,074
Total sales	57,264
1994	
Local sales	47,515
Exports	58,958
Total sales	106,473

EXHIBIT 2

Excerpts from HP's Statement of Corporate Objectives

The achievement of an organization are the result of the combined efforts of each individual in the organization working toward common objectives. These objectives should be clearly understood by everyone in the organization, and should reflect the organization's basic character and personality.

If the organization is to fulfill its objectives, it should strive to meet certain other fundamental requirements:

. . . highly capable, innovative people at all levels of the organization;
. . . objectives and leadership which generate enthusiasm at all levels; there can be no place, especially among . . . management, for halfhearted interest or halfhearted effort;
. . . uncompromising honesty and integrity;
. . . all levels work in unison . . . through effective, cooperative effort.

Objectives

1. *Profit:* To achieve sufficient profit to finance our company growth and to provide the resources we need to achieve our other corporate objectives.

. . . It is the one absolutely essential measure of our corporate performance over the long term . . .

continued...

EXHIBIT 2

Excerpts from HP's Statement of Corporate Objectives (Continued)

... Our long-standing policy has been to reinvest most of our profits and to depend on this ... to finance our growth. This can be achieved if our return on net worth is roughly equal to our sales growth rate.

... Profits vary from year to year ... our needs for capital also vary, and we depend on short-term bank loans to meet those needs ... However, loans are costly and must be repaid; thus, our objective is to rely on reinvested profits as our main source of capital.

Meeting our profit objective requires that ... every product ... is considered good value ... yet is priced to include an adequate profit.

2. *Customers:* To provide products and services of the greatest possible value to our customers, thereby gaining and holding their respect and loyalty.

... products that fill real needs and provide lasting value ...

3. *Fields of interest:* To enter new fields only when the ideas we have, together with our technical, manufacturing and marketing skills, assure that we can make a needed and profitable contribution to the field.

... The key to HP's prospective involvement in new fields is contribution. This means providing customers with something new and needed, not just another brand of something they can already buy ...

4. *Growth:* To let our growth be limited only by our profits and our ability to develop and produce technical products that satisfy real customer needs.

5. *Our people:* To help HP people share in the company's success, which they make possible; to provide job security based on their performance; to recognize their individual achievements; and to help them gain a sense of satisfaction and accomplishment from their work.

... Relationships within the company depend upon a spirit of cooperation among individuals and groups, and an attitude of trust and understanding on the part of managers toward their people. These relationships will be good only if employees have faith in the motives and integrity of their peers, supervisors and the company itself.

... Job security is an important HP objective ... the company has achieved a steady growth in employment by consistently developing good new products, and by avoiding the type of contract business that requires hiring many people, then terminating them when the contract expires ...

6. *Management:* To foster initiative and creativity by allowing the individual great freedom of action in attaining well-defined objectives.

... insofar as possible, each individual at each level in the organization should make his or her own plans to achieve company objectives and goals. After receiving supervisory approval, each individual should be given a wide degree of freedom to work within the limitations imposed by these plans, and by our general corporate policies ...

7. *Citizenship:* To honor our obligations to society by being an economic, intellectual and social asset to each nation and each community in which we operate.

... to make sure that each of these communities is better for our presence.

Source: Taken from case study 482-125, *Human Resources at Hewlett-Packard.*

1948, when the first of it's highly successful line of microwave measurement products was launched, the market had grown to include manufacturing and processing customers, in addition to electronics and science.

In the 1960s, with growing markets around the globe, HP set up its sales organization structured along regional and national lines. In time, over a hundred local sales teams were created, each one committed to local customers. It also diversified into new markets with products such as the first HP minicomputer and the first high-tech desktop calculator.

The U.S. government had been a major customer since World War II and this relationship continued, with HP diodes, switches and atomic clocks contributing to space travel.

As the range of products and market diversified, HP restructured into product divisions, so that efforts would be concentrated on maintaining leadership

EXHIBIT 3

Hewlett-Packard
Selected Financial Data, *Unaudited*

In millions except per share amounts and employees	For the years ended October 31				
	1994	**1993**	**1992**	**1991**	**1990**
U.S. orders	$ 11,692	$ 9,462	$ 7,569	$ 6,484	$ 6,143
International orders	13,658	11,310	9,192	8,192	7,342
Total orders	$ 25,350	$ 20,772	$ 16,761	$ 14,676	$ 13,485
Net revenue	$ 24,991	$ 20,317	$ 16,410	$ 14,494	$ 13,233
Earnings from Operations	$ 2,549	$ 1,879	$ 1,404	$ 1,210	$ 1,162
Earnings before effect of 1992 accounting change	$ 1,599	$ 1,177	$ 881	$ 755	$ 739
Net earnings	$ 1,599	$ 1,177	$ 549	$ 755	$ 739
Per share:					
Earnings before effect of 1992 accounting change	$ 6.14	$ 4.65	$ 3.49	$ 3.02	$ 3.06
Net earnings	$ 6.14	$ 4.65	$ 2.18	$ 3.02	$ 3.06
Cash dividends paid	$ 1.10	$ 0.90	$ 0.725	$ 0.48	$ 0.42
At year-end:					
Total assets	$ 19,567	$ 16,736	$ 13,700	$ 11,973	$ 11,395
Employees	98,400	96,200	92,600	89,000	92,200

Source: Extract from Hewlett-Packard 1994 Annual Report.

and competitive advantage in each of its markets (see Exhibit 4—HP Corporate Organization Chart).

History of BCD

Although HP's sales organization first set up in Spain in 1971, it was not until 1985 that manufacturing started in the pen plotter facility in Terrassa.

We had to find a suitable property to lease and equip, negotiate agreements with local suppliers and get production started so that the first shipments could be made within 6 months. (A BCD Manager involved in the start-up)

Our first GM was German, but not bureaucratic in the way we typically expect German managers to be. He was a "bulldozer," not afraid to break the rules,

EXHIBIT 4

Hewlett-Packard Corporate Organization, March 1995

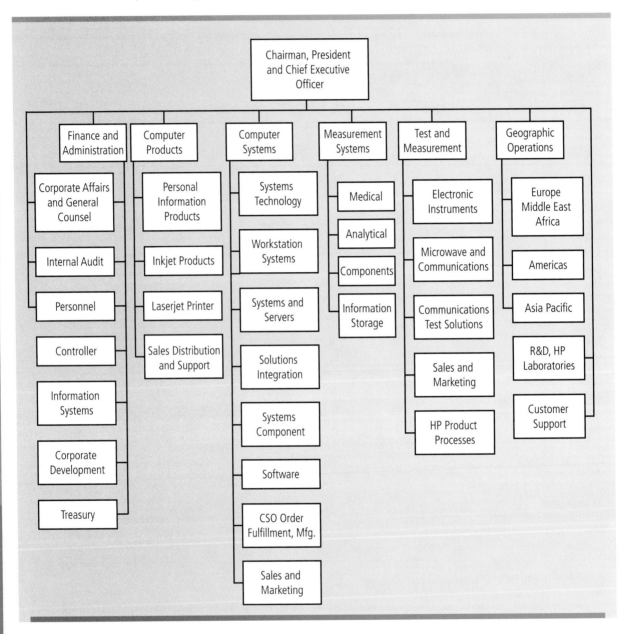

not scared of risk. He came with a manufacturing background and all the energy needed for the start-up phase. (A BCD Manager)

Each phase in a company's evolution needs a particular type of general manager. It's like road building—you need both bulldozer and graders, depending on the stage you're at. (A BCD Manager)

The Terrassa facility manufactured pen plotters under license from HP San Diego. The one objective of this first phase was to develop manufacturing competencies and processes.

By 1987, R&D and marketing skills were being added so that the Spanish operation could increase its involvement in product development and getting its products to market.

We needed a new General Manager with a different style to develop our design capabilities. The new GM came from an R&D background, was American, and process oriented. He taught us to define and analyze problems and laid the foundations of many of the processes we still use today. (A BCD Manager)

Our Marketing skills were still weak and our product (pen plotters) was quickly being made obsolete by the new inkjet technology being developed in San Diego. Our people were committed, but our business wasn't exciting enough to attract the best people available in HP and the company felt stifled. We were still only contributors to someone else's P&L and what we needed was full responsibility for a product line. (A BCD Manager)

We were in a rut, without a charter for the future. Our third General Manager had worked his way up through the sales organization in Germany. He's a person of great vision and business instincts. He was good at identifying problems or opportunities based on very little information. (A BCD Manager)

Because he was Spanish, he had an understanding of the local situation, but also the contracts about HP to be able to attract the foreigners needed for developing the business. He was able to convince the rest of HP that we could take on a product line. (A BCD Manager)

His style was informal and spontaneous, with less process, in line with his marketing perspective. He put great emphasis on accountability. (A BCD Manager)

By 1990, there were 182 employees producing 7 products. The first 3 products designed in BCD were launched and the company moved to its new purpose-built 2,643 million peseta facility in Sant Cugat.

The decision to grant the worldwide charter for plotters was made public in March 1993 (see Exhibit 5—Press release). Work on the transition had already started in San Diego two years earlier. Both the new General Manager and a new head of R&D were being prepared for the next stage of BCD's development.

I was approached about going to BCD with the business a year before the move. This gave me plenty of time to prepare. I didn't know Rich before his appointment, but we've since worked closely together on the transfer both in San Diego and then in BCD. (A BCD Manager)

The General Manager's Role

When I first came to BCD 3 years ago there was a strong manufacturing process that we had to change to a business process, incorporating information on customer needs and product development. My three main aims were to bring about successful transition of the large format plotter business from San Diego to BCD, to develop the business for its long-term survival and to develop the people and skills.

(RICH RAIMONDI, *BCD GENERAL MANAGER*)

Rich brought better business management knowledge and his personal leadership style. Rich's style is different from the previous GM's style. He is rigorous with the process. This is important for the division's maturity.

(A BCD MANAGER)

Transferring responsibility

Product Division status in HP is only granted when the company has fully developed Marketing, R&D, and Manufacturing capabilities. A Division has full worldwide responsibility for all activities relating to its product line, using the sales and marketing centers around the world as the main channel to the end customer.

Marketing, R&D, and Manufacturing are the drivers of the business, supported by the service functions of Quality, Personnel, and Control. However, they all have equal value in the staff team. (Rich Raimondi)

We have a number of Foreign Services Executives in the core functions because it takes much longer to prepare local staff to take over these responsibilities. It's very rare for HP to recruit at management level from outside. The level of interdependency between HP organizations makes it difficult for outsiders to adapt. (Rich Raimondi)

The transfer of responsibilities was a slow and gradual process. Each core function was introduced into the network in a progressive, overlapping process so that no risk was involved until the BCD staff were ready and experienced enough to take over. (A BCD Manager)

BCD has a framework to guide it through the steps of the product life cycle. The model describes each area's contribution to each of the stages of development from innovation to design, prototype,

EXHIBIT 5

Hewlett-Packard Barcelona Division Press Release

Hewlett-Packard's Barcelona site to expand operations with worldwide charter for plotters and production of inkjet printers

Company to expand manufacturing facilities and employment

BARCELONA, Spain, March 3, 1993—Hewlett-Packard has announced plans to expand its operations here by shifting worldwide responsibility for research and development, marketing and production of its entire range of large-format pen and inkjet plotters to Spain from its San Diego, California, site. Additionally, within two years, HP plans to manufacture all its DeskJet family of inkjet printers for the European market at the Barcelona site.

HP will invest more than 1,800 million pesetas ($15.3 million) over the next two years for an additional 8,000 square-meter (86,000 square-foot) plant and equipment at the present Sant Cugat, Barcelona, site. HP also foresees a doubling of its R&D expenditure over the next three years and a 50 percent increase of its present employment of about 300 by the end of 1994. The new building is slated to be completed in the spring of next year.

The move is also expected to increase local jobs substantially as local suppliers increase the number of parts for the planned printer production. At present, more than a third of the suppliers to the plant are based in Spain, providing plastic parts, metal components, cables and packaging. HP aims to increase collaboration with local companies, thus promoting technology transfer and the creation of additional employment.

"This year, the Sant Cugat site takes over worldwide responsibility for the large-format pen and inkjet plotters from San Diego operations," said Juan Soto, HP's general manager, Iberia. "And, with the transfer of HP DeskJet printer production, this facility is elevated to a strategic site within HP's InkJet Product Group." HP's Vancouver, Wash. (USA) and Singapore facilities will continue to build HP DeskJet printer products for the rest of the world.

At present, the HP site manufactures a range of large-format and desktop plotters, inkjet color printers as well as fiber-tip and roller-ball plotter pens. In fiscal year 1992, HP Spain, with shipments of 12,871 million pesetas ($109.5 million), ranked second among Spain's computer exporters. The shipments represent a 14 percent increase over the previous year.

Hewlett-Packard began to manufacture plotters in Barcelona in 1985. With the completion of the present expansion plan, the company will have invested a total of more than 4,500 million pesetas ($38.3 million) in the Sant Cugat facility.

HP's Inkjet Products Group (IPG), the world's leading supplier of inkjet printers, has sold more than 6.5 million printers since the first one was introduced in 1984. HP inkjet technology, which is used in a variety of products from facsimile machines to plotters, was developed at HP Laboratories and HP Inkjet Technology Centers. IPG's products are sold worldwide through computer dealers and value-added resellers. IPG has divisions in Barcelona, Spain; Singapore; and Corvallis, Ore., San Diego, Calif. and Vancouver, Wash. in the U.S.A.

Hewlett-Packard is an international manufacturer of measurement and computation products and systems recognized for excellence in quality and support. The company's products and services are used in industry, business, engineering, science, medicine and education in approximately 110 countries. HP has 93,100 employees and had revenue of $16.4 billion in its 1992 fiscal year.

testing, manufacture, maturity, and decline. This is one of the tools used throughout HP to coordinate projects.

> We first got involved in a product enhancement, working with San Diego, based on the product life cycle process. We've been through 3 trial runs of product enhancement, so that we're now practiced in the process and experienced enough to embark on our own product development. (A BCD Manager)

Networks

The development of innovative technology and products in BCD depends on complex networks and relationships between clients, suppliers, and HP personnel.

> Perhaps the biggest challenge in my work is communications. When you need a face-to-face meeting to understand feelings and personalities, it means international travel. Most of our development partners are in the U.S. (An FSE Manager)

> The FSEs act as linkages with other HP sites, but it's also their responsibility to transfer this role to local staff. Managers are assigned responsibilities to develop these linkages. In one R&D project a specific group has been formed whose sole purpose in life is to ensure that the linkage is successful. (An FSE Manager)

Working at a distance and in different time zones makes you prepare better for telephone and video-conferencing. But it's a considerable burden that we have to carry. I hadn't realized this before I came to BCD. (An FSE Manager)

Based on the inkjet technology developed in San Diego, BCD was replacing the obsolete pen plotter technology and researching new applications that would take it into new markets.

External networks have always been important because a plotter is only part of the client's needs. We have to work closely with hardware and software developers to make sure our product is compatible. Standardisation of operating systems, new markets and new customer requirements mean we'll have to develop new external partnerships for the future. (A BCD Manager)

Resources

BCD's workforce increased for 300 to 800 people in 1994. This was partly due to the growing transferred large format plotter business and to taking on the manufacturing, under license from Vancouver, of the DeskJet product line for the European market. The manufacturing area was increased to 10,000 sq. m. with 4,000 sq. m. of office space.

We chose Sant Cugat because of its location in relation to the rest of Europe. Also, the Generalitat (Regional government), unlike other areas of Spain, was willing to help smooth our path. We're an important employer in the area. (A BCD Manager)

The Barcelona area offered a range of advantages that were attracting foreign investment. HP hoped that the promised "Silicon Vallés" would materialise, with other information technology companies setting up in the area to provide a competitive and dynamic environment. Major investment was underway to update the area's communications systems. The reputation of the local universities and business schools indicated that they would be a good source of young professionals.

This is an attractive company, so it can attract people from the top 10 per cent, particularly English-speaking MBAs. (A BCD Manager)

HP is very selective in considering job candidates. There is great emphasis on adaptability and cultural fit. Psychometric testing is not used, although some specialised skills tests are used when necessary. Selection is based on behavioral interviewing.

We look for three main qualities. We look for innovation and creativity, we believe in learning from our mistakes—no risk means no fun. We look for indications that this person has made a specific contribution to improving something in a work situation or elsewhere.

We look for commitment. Every employee is the real driver and decision-maker to achieve his or her objectives—and even for his or her own development.

We look for people who can work in teams. Big contributions always come from team efforts and our evaluation procedures reflect this. (BCD Personnel Manager)

Process

The Corporate Objectives spelled out in 1957 have been reinforced with strategies and practices for achieving the objectives (see Exhibit 6—HP Way, Strategies and Practices). This process is based on communication, management by objectives, an open-door policy and total quality.

Rich brought me to BCD a year ago. His most important role for me has been as mentor. He's taken time to help me with my first steps. (A BCD Manager)

BCD has a formal meetings structure that can take up to 30–40 percent of each manager's time each week. The GM and his staff team meet every Monday for the full day. Strategic issues and new product development rather than operational issues occupy progressively more of their time. Each manager has a 1-on-1 meeting with the GM almost every week for 2 hours to discuss issues relating to their areas that they consider important. The GM meets with all managers and supervisors twice a year to keep them informed and to answer questions. Informal coffee talks with smaller groups take place about twice a month.

Process implies accessibility and permanent contact. Rich operates an excellent balance between business, people and cultures. He's constantly communicating to all levels; there's a permanent flow and sharing of information. (A BCD Manager)

EXHIBIT 6

Free Translation of "El Estilo HP—Estrategias y prácticas"

The HP Way—Strategies and Practices

HP's value and objectives guide us in the process of creating strategies and practices to manage a dynamic business such as ours in a constantly changing world.

Direct Management

This is an informal HP practice to keep up-to-date with individual work and with the company's activities through both informal and structured communication. Direct management implies trust and respect for the individual, such as recognizing each person's contribution and listening to their ideas and initiatives.

This management style is reflected in the following practices:

- Managers always have time to observe what's happening in their departments. They're always available to discuss any problems that arise.
- Individuals working in teams within the organization.
- Informal coffee sessions, inter-departmental lunches, informal conversations.

Management by Objectives

HP management is participative. Employees contribute to developing the objectives that then form part of the management processes and are an integral part of all HP departments. Flexibility and innovation in looking for alternative ways of meeting these objectives offer an effective way of satisfying customers' needs.

Management by objectives can be found in:

- Documentation relating to the organization's strategies.
- The extra effort put in by all departments.
- The shared plants and objectives.

Open Door Policy

This ensures that there will be no adverse consequences when problems are presented in a responsible manner. Trust and integrity are important aspects of the open door policy.

The open door policy can be particularly useful:

- To share feelings and frustrations constructively.
- To understand alternatives clearly.
- To discuss different professional options, business practices and communication deficiencies.

Total Quality Control

Total Quality Control is a management philosophy, together with the operating method, aimed at improving quality and satisfying customers' needs. Our successes reflect the way TQC has contributed to offering the best possible products and services to our customers.

Total Quality Control encourages:

- The continuous improvement of processes using scientific methods.
- Participation in quality and satisfying customers' needs.
- Satisfying both internal and external customers' needs.

The HP Way is based on respect for the integrity of the individual—Bill Hewlett, 1987.

Rich looks for consensus. If there are conflicts between departments, he expects you to solve the problem between you. He'll only intervene if you can't find a solution. (A BCD Manager)

Rich looks for consensus—his main function is as a facilitator. This is a multicultural organization that sometimes needs a "referee" to cope with the diversity and turn it into an enriching factor. (A BCD Manager)

Process is a way of getting people to cover systematically all the steps necessary to make a decision. Data is turned into information on which decisions are made and implemented. (A BCD Manager)

The process that BCD has experienced during this phase of its evolution can be summarized by the "Decision-Making Values" which Rich and his management team have devised to guide them.

The essence of these values is summarized as follows:

- Decisions should be made by the fewest people and at the lowest level.
- Always challenge and test who needs to be involved and at what level.
- Make the most important decision first.
- Look for issues. Don't hide them. Don't wait for them.
- Communicate clearly what the expectations, objectives and boundaries are when delegating/empowering.
- Get closure on other functions' concerns before key decisions.
- It is unacceptable not to support a decision once it is made.
- Consensus is good, but not mandatory.
- Feedback should be given courageously, freely, and constructively, and received openly, even after decisions, but best done directly to the manager.
- We will support fully our subordinates' decisions.
- Encourage and support risk-taking and learning.
- Trust first, seek to understand second, challenge third.

Other GMs have had a more driving style and have imposed their processes. Rich has involved us in designing the process. It's changed 3–4 times already to manage change. There's no right answer, so leaving the process open means it's easy to modify when necessary. It has been very much a team effort. (A BCD Manager)

HP believes that it is important to give every individual the tools with which to work. Total Quality Management is one of the ways the HP Way is reinforced by providing those tools. A deployment plan is part of every performance evaluation that gives access to courses on the specific techniques. The main focuses are on planning, process management, dealing

---

EXHIBIT 7

Quality Strategy: Characteristics of a TQM Organization

TQM Dimension	Applications
Strategic and Customer Focus	• Uses knowledge of customer and market needs to drive business strategies and their implementations. • Strategies address ways to optimize relationships with suppliers, partners, and customers. • Analyzes markets, channels, and competition to anticipate future needs. • Measures and manages customer satisfaction. • Instills passion for customer service in the organization. The organization focuses on understanding and satisfying the needs of both external and internal customers.
Planning	• Aligns plans at all levels of the organization; involves partner organizations, if appropriate. • Links day-to-day activities to plans. • Uses the business planning process to produce a road map for achieving business objectives. • Develops plans at the process level which yield output targets. • Produces a road map for improving the key processes.

continued...

EXHIBIT 7

Quality Strategy: Characteristics of a TQM Organization (Continued)

TQM Dimension	Applications
Process Management	● Aligns, manages, and improves processes within the framework of business objectives. ● Manages cross-organizational processes across functional and organizational boundaries. ● Leverages customer satisfaction results to improve key processes. ● Uses data and statistical techniques to manage processes and to drive corrective action.
Improvement	● Continuously improves processes. ● Employs improvement projects to systematically resolve critical business issues. ● Applies systematic process improvement techniques to improvement activities. ● Leverages lessons learned from improvement projects across the organization. ● Standardizes, manages, and improves the improvement process over time.
Leadership and Participation	● Focuses, motivates, and improves the organization's efforts to achieve business objectives. ● Models and promotes quality principles to improve the organization's effectiveness and efficiency. ● Models and promotes quality principles to improve the organization's effectiveness and efficiency. ● Empowers individuals with the opportunity and responsibility to maximize their contribution. ● Encourages open communications; shares ideas within and across organizational boundaries.

with customers, improvement, and team work (see Exhibit 7—Characteristics of a TQM Organization from "A Guide to Quality at Hewlett-Packard).

The Future

The new inkjet technology had opened up a wide range of applications for large format plotters. The ability to innovate with color made these products attractive to new markets. The emphasis in the past had been on meeting the needs of professionals such as architects and draughtsmen in reproducing plans and drawings to high standards of accuracy and reliability, with minimum color requirement.

The new technology offered cost-effective solutions to the print industry and alternatives to traditional methods such as offset lithography.

> We'll need new skills for the future. Our color imaging expert is already working with the UPC (Universidad Politecnica de Catalunya). We have a CAD room there and we sponsor a prize for student innovation projects. (A BCD Manager)

> It's proving difficult to get the staff to move out of the comfort zones they've become used to. Good solid processes have been developed, but some of

these now need to be broken and the processes changed if progress is to happen. (An FSE Manager)

> You have to give your teenagers roots, so that they know where they come from and wings so that they can learn independence. Working on delegation skills is currently one of my biggest issues. Management tends to be protective, but we have to move decision-making 2 or 3 levels down the organization. (An FSE Manager)

> Two years ago we were nobody in terms of value added to the community, now we're one of the most important companies in the area. It's something that comes with volume and we're not getting the right level of recognition. We'd like the government to listen to our concerns and take them into account for such issues as labor legislation and tax regulations. (A BCD Manger)

> New product and market development is our major objective for the year. We've moved it into first place on our weekly agenda. I read everything I can find related to our situation, but I expect the staff team to be better prepared than I am. (Rich Raimondi)

> We're at the stage where our parents have said, "Son, You're grown up now, it's time you got to work to fend for yourself." (A BCD Manager)

Chapter Endnotes

Chapter 1

1. Bernstein, A. (2001). Low-skilled jobs: Do they have to move? *Business Week,* February 26, 94–95.
2. Engardio, P. (2000). The barons of outsourcing. *Business Week,* August 28, 177–178.
3. ———. (2000). Globalization: Threat or opportunity? An IMF issues brief. (www.imf.org/external/np/exr/ib/2000/042100.htm).
4. Gleckman, H., & Carney, D. (2000). Watching over the world wide web. *Business Week,* August 28, 195–196.
5. ———. (2001). China and the WTO: Ready for the competition? *The Economist,* September 15, 35–36; ———. (2001). Playing by the rules. *The Economist,* July 28, 67; Cooper, H. (2001). U.S., E.U. end trans-Atlantic banana war. *The Wall Street Journal,* April 12, A2; Winestock, G., & Leggett, K. (2001). China to enter WTO; Dispute on insurance to be first test. *The Wall Street Journal,* September 17, A16, A17; Wonacott, P. (2001). China braces for changes ahead of WTO. *The Wall Street Journal,* July 23, A12.
6. ———. (2000). A different, new world order. *The Economist,* November 11, 83–85; Bernstein, A. (2000). Backlash: Behind the anxiety over globalization. *Business Week,* April 24, 38–44.
7. ———. (2001). When the economy held its breath. *The Economist,* September 15, 65–66.
8. Carpenter, M. A., & Fredrickson, J. W. (2001). Top management teams, global strategic posture, and the moderating role of uncertainty. *Academy of Management Journal, 44,* 533–545.
9. ———. (2001). Let the bad times roll. *The Economist,* April 7, 63; Oyama, D. (2001). Cisco aims to train 100,000 workers in India by 2006. *The Wall Street Journal,* January 16, A19.
10. Davis, B., & Harper, L. (1995). Middle class's fears about coming years may be misguided. *The Wall Street Journal,* March 29, pp. A1, A9.
11. Edmondson, G., Capell, K., Moore, P. L., & Burrows, P. (2000). See the world, erase its borders. *Business Week,* August 28, 113–114.
12. ———. (2001). The cutting edge. *The Economist,* February 24, 80.
13. Engardio, P. (2001). America's future: Smart globalization. *Business Week,* August 27, 132–137.
14. Deans, B. (2001). Popular resistance barrier to trade pact. *Dayton Daily News,* April 22, 16A.
15. ———. (2001). Trade in the Americas: All in the familia. *The Economist,* April 21, 19–22.
16. ———. (2000). Emerging market indicators: Trading partners. *The Economist,* December 2, 106; Wysocki, B. (1996). Imports are surging in developing nations. *The Wall Street Journal,* July 8, p. A1.
17. Farrell, C. (1994). The triple revolution. *Business Week,* November 18, pp. 16–25.
18. Engardio, P. (2001). America's future: Smart globalization. *Business Week,* August 27, 132–137.
19. Barrett, A. (1995). It's a small (business) world. *Business Week,* April 17, pp. 96–101.
20. Dempsey, D.(2001). YSI: Blending business, nature. *Dayton Daily News,* April 22, F1.
21. Smith, G., Malkin, E., Wheatley, J., Magnusson, P., & Arndt, M. (2001). Betting on free trade: will the Americas be one big market? *Business Week,* April 23, 60–62.
22. ———. (2001). Trade in the Americas: All in the familia. *The Economist,* April 21, 19–22; Whalen, C. J., Magnusson, P., & Smith, G. (2001). NAFTA's scorecard: So far, so good. *Business Week,* July 9, 54–56.
23. ———. (1999). A survey of Canada: Holding its own. *The Economist,* July 24, 1–18; Thomas, G. S. (2001). Asia, Canada comprise bulk of U.S. trade deficit. *Dayton Business Journal,* April 20, 16.
24. ———. (2000). A survey of Mexico: After the revolution. *The Economist,* October 28, 1–16; Whalen, C. J., Magnusson, P., & Smith, G. (2001). NAFTA's scorecard: So far, so good. *Business Week,* July 9, 54–56.
25. ———. (2000). A survey of Mexico: After the revolution. *The Economist,* October 28, 1–16; Millman, J. (2000). The world's new tiger on the export scene isn't Asian, it's Mexico. *The Wall Street Journal,* May 9, A1, A10.
26. ———. (2000). A survey of Mexico: After the revolution. *The Economist,* October 28, 1–16; Borrus, A., & Smith, G. (2001). Spotlight on the border. *Business Week,* September 10, 40–43; Millman, J. (2000). A new future for Mexico's workforce. *The Wall Street Journal,* April 14, A15, A16.
27. ———. (2001). Slowing economy, quickening politics. *The Economist,* May 19, 33–34; ———. (2001). Fox and Bush, for richer, for poorer. *The Economist,* February 3, 37–38; ———. (2000). A survey of Mexico: After the revolution. *The Economist,* October 28, 1–16; Millman, J. (2001). Mexico braces for drop-off in auto sector. *The Wall Street Journal,* January 23, A17, A18; Thomas, G. S. (2001). Asia, Canada comprise bulk of U.S. trade deficit. *Dayton Business Journal,* April 20, 16.
28. ———. (2002). The economy: ON steroids. *The Economist,* January 26, 51–52; ———. (2001). When the economy held its breath. *The Economist,* September 15, 65–66; ———. (2001). United States: The kiss of life? *The Economist,* April 21, 23; Sapsford, J., & Barta, P. (2002). Despite the recession, Americans continue to be avid borrowers. *The Wall Street Journal,* January 2, A1, A20.
29. Porter, M. E. (2001). Japan: What went wrong. *The Wall Street Journal,* March 21, A22.
30. ———. (2000). Creativity. *The Economist,* September 23, 128.
31. ———. (2001). The great merger wave breaks. *The Economist,* January 27, 59–60; ———. (2001). Survey of corporate finance: The party's over. *The Economist,* January 27, 1–20.
32. Thomas, G. S. (2001). Asia, Canada comprise bulk of U.S. trade deficit. *Dayton Business Journal,* April 20, 16.
33. ———. (2002). Is Latin America losing its way? *The Economist,* March 2, 11; Baker, S., Weiner, E., Smith, G., Charters, A., & Jacobson, K. (1992). Latin America: The big move to free markets. *Business Week,* June 15, 50–55; Johnson, M. (1996). Untapped Latin America. *Management Review, 85,* 31–34.
34. ———. (2000). Latin America: The slow road to reform. *The Economist,* December 2, 23–26.
35. ———. (2000). Latin America: The slow road to reform. *The Economist,* December , 23–26; Smith, G., Goodman, J., Lindblad, C., & Robinson, A. (2002). Argentina: A wrong turn? *Business Week,* January 21, 42–44; Druckerman, P. (2001). Argentina's new peso plan draws mixed response. *The Wall Street Journal,* April 17, A15; Goodman, J. (2001). Beyond the default drama. *Business Week,* September 3, 49; Hanke, S.H. (2001). Argentina is no Turkey. *The Wall Street Journal,* March 2, A11; Larroulet, C. (2001). Look to Chile for an answer to the Latin malaise. *The Wall Street Journal,* August 24, A9; Moffett, M. (2001). Argentina pins all its hopes on harsh plan. *The Wall Street Journal,* July 23, A10; Moffett, M., & Bussey, J. (2001). The Argentine economy: A tough nut for a tough man. *The Wall Street Journal,* April 4, A17.

36. Karp, J. (2002). Brazilian growth is below expectations. *The Wall Street Journal,* March 1, A11; Jordan, M. (2001). Auto makers slow production in Brazil. *The Wall Street Journal,* July 23, A10; Jordan, M. (2000). Multinationals bet on Brazil's recovery. *The Wall Street Journal,* September 5, A25, A30; Karp, J. (2001). Signs point to interest-rate rise in Brazil. *The Wall Street Journal,* April 17, A15.

37. ———. (2001). Another blow to Mercosur. *The Economist,* March 31, 33–34; Harbrecht, D., Smith, G., & DeGeorge, G. (1994). Ripping down the walls across the Americas. *Business Week,* December 26, 78–79.

38. Einhorn, B., & Borrus, A. (1996). Why the WTO is stuck in the mud. *Business Week,* December 16, 50.

39. ———. (2001). In praise of rules: A survey of Asian business. *The Economist,* April 7, 1–18; ———. (2000). Asian economies: Happy neighbors. *The Economist,* August 26, 63; Weidenbaum, M. (1996). The Chinese family business enterprise. *California Management Review, 38,* 141–156.

40. Bremner, B., Balfour, F., Shari, M., Ihlwan, M., & Engardio, P. (2001). Asia: The big chill. *Business Week,* April 2, 48–50.

41. Barnathan, J., & Roberts, D. (1996). A hard "soft" landing: China's state industries are sputtering. *Business Week,* October 21, 50–51; Biers, D. (1996). Weaker Asian exports are prompting lower forecasts for region's economy. *The Wall Street Journal,* August 7, A8; Biers, D. (1996). Asian exports show signs of reviving as global demand for electronics rises. *The Wall Street Journal,* December 26, 8; Engardio, P. (1996). Is the East Asian juggernaut sputtering? *Business Week,* August 26, 44; Engardio, P., Moore, J., & Hill, C. (1996). Time for a reality check in Asia. *Business Week,* December 2, 58–67; Kahn, J. (1996). China's markets: Big but often saturated. *The Wall Street Journal,* August 5, A1; Lehner, U. C. (1995). Is the vaunted "Asian miracle" really just an illusion? *The Wall Street Journal,* October 20, A10; McDermott, D. (1996). Singapore's economy loses some juice. *The Wall Street Journal,* August 21, A10.

42. ———. (2001). Now comes the hard part: A survey of China. *The Economist,* April 7, 1–15; ———. (2001). China's economic power: Enter the dragon. *The Economist,* March 10, 23–25; Schlevogt, K. A. (2000). The business environment in China: Getting to know the next century's superpower. *Thunderbird International Business Review, 42* (January–February), 85–111.

43. Schlevogt, K. A. (2000). The business environment in China: Getting to know the next century's superpower. *Thunderbird International Business Review, 42* (January–February), 85-111.

44. ———. (2001). In praise of rules: A survey of Asian business. *The Economist,* April 7, 1–18; ———. (2001). China's economic power: Enter the dragon. *The Economist,* March 10, 23–25; Brown, O., & Chang, L. (2002). China says growth slowed to 7.3% in 2001. *The Wall Street Journal,* March 1, A7; Clifford, M., Roberts, D., Engardio, P., & Webb, A. (2001). China: Coping with its new power. *Business Week,* April 16, 28–34; Schlevogt, K. A. (2000). The business environment in China: Getting to know the next century's superpower. *Thunderbird International Business Review, 42* (January–February), 85–111.

45. Clifford, M. L., & Roberts, D. (2001). Downturn? What downturn? *Business Week,* April 9, 44; Clifford, M., Roberts, D., Engardio, P., & Webb, A. (2001). China: Coping with its new power. *Business Week,* April 16, 28–34; Wonacott, P. (2001). China plans a more market-oriented economy. *The Wall Street Journal,* March 6, A10.

46. ———. (2001). India's sluggish privatization: Unproductive. *The Economist,* September 8, 65–66; ———. (2001). A billion Indians now. *The Economist,* March 31, 39; ———. (2001). India's breakthrough budget? *The Economist,* March 3, 37;

Pearl, D. (2000). The rigors of cracking India's markets. *The Wall Street Journal,* November 27, A25, A28.

47. Einhorn, B., Kripalani, M., & Engardio, P. (2001). India 3.0. *Business Week,* February 26, 44–46; Kripalani, M., & Clifford, M. L. (2000). India wired. *Business Week,* March 6, 82–91.

48. Clifford, M. L., & Kripalani, M. (1996). Modern India has been put on hold. *Business Week,* April 29, 54–55; Jordan, M. (1996). In India, repealing reform is a tough sell. *The Wall Street Journal,* May 22, A16; Khalilzadeh-Shirazi, J., & Zagha, R. (1994). Economic reforms in India. *Columbia Journal of World Business, 29,* 24–31; Kripalani, M. (1996a). Walking a fine line on reform. *Business Week,* June 17, 60; Kripalani, M. (1996b). A traffic jam of auto makers. *Business Week,* August 5, pp. 46–47; Martin, T. (1994). The world economy in charts. *Fortune,* July 25, 118–124; Thomas, T. (1994). Change in climate for foreign investment in India. *Columbia Journal of World Business, 29,* 32–41.

49. ———. (2001). Japan: The shadow of joblessness. *The Economist,* September 1, 11; ———. (2001). Japan's economy: Another false dawn? *The Economist,* March 24, 79–81; Belson, K. (2001). Japan: This time it could get nasty. *Business Week,* January 15, 52; Porter, M. E. (2001). Japan: What went wrong. *The Wall Street Journal,* March 21, A22.

50. ———. (2002). Economics focus: checking the slumpometer. *The Economist,* March 2, 72; Porter, M. E. (2001). Japan: What went wrong. *The Wall Street Journal,* March 21, A22.

51. Bremner, B., & Belson, K. (2001). Dark before dawn? *Business Week,* March 19, 54–55; Dvorak, P., Guth, R. A., Singer, J., and Zaun, T. (2001). Frayed by recession, Japan's corporate ties are becoming unraveled. *The Wall Street Journal,* March 2, A1, A6; Ono, Y., & Zaun, T. (2001). Wall street intensifies Japan's woes, but they all trace back home. *The Wall Street Journal,* March 16, A1, A6.

52. Porter, M. E. (2001). Japan: What went wrong. *The Wall Street Journal,* March 21, A22; Schoenberger, K. (1996). Has Japan changed? *Fortune,* August 19, 72–82.

53. ———. (2001). China's man pushes out Hong Kong's woman. *The Economist,* January 10, 35; ———. (2000). Meddling in Hong Kong. *The Economist,* September 30, 22; ———. (2000). Hong Kong: Atonement day. *The Economist,* February 26, 50; Balfour, F., & Clifford, M.L. (2001). Hong Kong: A city under siege. *Business Week,* July 23, 48–49; Clifford, M. (2001). Hong Kong: Another body blow to the rule of law? *Business Week,* January 29, 55.

54. Flannery, R. (2000). Taipei eases stance on China business. *The Wall Street Journal,* August 3, A9; Roberts, D., Webb, A., Clifford, M., & Hannon, B. (2000). Uneasy collaborators. *Business Week,* August 14, 52–55.

55. ———. (2001). Singapore: Death by a thousand cuts. *The Economist,* September 15, 38; ———. (2000). A survey of Southeast Asia: The tigers that changed their stripes. *The Economist,* February 12, 1–16.

56. ———. (2001). South Korea: Entrepreneurial fresh air. *The Economist,* January 13, 60; Ihlwan, M. (2001). So long, corporate reform. *Business Week,* January 22, 52–53; ———. (2000). South Korea dumps the past, at last. *The Economist,* November 11, 75–76; Booth, J. (2002). South Korean economy gets more diverse. *The Wall Street Journal,* February 7, A14; Bremner, B., & Ihlwan, M. (2000). Korea's digital quest. *Business Week,* September 25, 68–76.

57. ———. (2000). A survey of South-east Asia: The tigers that changed their stripes. *The Economist,* February 12, 1–16; ———. (2001). Indonesia: The odd couple. *The Economist,* February 17, 27–30; ———. (2001). After the B movie, a new main attraction

for Filipinos. *The Economist,* January 27, 37–38; Frank, R. (2000). In Subic Bay's decline, Filipinos see return of familiar problems. *The Wall Street Journal,* September 20, A1, A6; Schuman, M. (2001). Indonesia's economy is now sputtering. *The Wall Street Journal,* April 17, A17; Shari, M. (2001). Indonesia: Will rising chaos cripple the economy? *Business Week,* March 26, 66.

58. ———. (2001). Business pains in Vietnam. *The Economist,* March 24, 48; Cumming-Bruce, N. (2001). Vietnam party congress could produce new leadership. *The Wall Street Journal,* April 18, A19.

59. ———. (2001). Europe: The Balkan jigsaw. *The Economist,* April 28, 47–48; Chazan, G. (2001). A Ukraine in deepening turmoil stands at a crossroads—and takes a step to the east. *The Wall Street Journal,* March 6, A18; Child, J., & Czegledy, A. P. (1996). Managerial learning in the transformation of eastern Europe: Some key issues. *Organizational Studies, 17,* 167–179; Luthans, F., & Riolli, L. T. (1997). Albania and the Bora Company: Lessons learned before the recent chaos. *Academy of Management Executive, 11,* 61–72.

60. ———. (2001). The Swiss say no. *The Economist,* March 10, 22; Costin, H. (1996). *Managing in the global economy: The European Union.* Fort Worth, TX: Dryden Press.

61. ———. (2001). A survey of European enlargement: Europe's magnetic attraction. *The Economist,* May 19, 1-16; ———. (2001). Permanent revolution for Europe's union? *The Economist,* February 3, 49–50; ———. (2001). The European central bank: The terrible twos begin. *The Economist,* January 6, 63–66; ———. (2000). The Nice summit: So that's all agreed, then. *The Economist,* December 16, 25–28; Hofheinz, P. (2002). One currency, many voices: Issues that still divide Europe. *The Wall Street Journal,* January 2, A6.

62. ———. (2001). The world economy: Waiting for growth. *The Economist,* April 28, 76; ———. (2000). Europe's economies: Stumbling yet again? *The Economist,* September 16, 77–80; Rhoads, C., & Sims, T. (2001). Why Europe may resist the economic bug. *The Wall Street Journal,* March 29, A10, A11; Fairlamb, D. (2001). Back from the depths. *Business Week,* January 8, 52–53.

63. ———. (2001). Unwelcome to Iberia. *The Economist,* February 10, 51–52; Edmondson, G., & Malkin, E. (2000). Spain's surge. *Business Week,* May 22, 73–80.

64. ———. (2001). Will western Europe receive the great unwashed—one day? *The Economist,* April 21, 43–44; ———. (2000). Poverty in eastern Europe: The land that time forgot. *The Economist,* September 23, 27–30.

65. ———. (2001). More cash, please. *The Economist,* May 12, 55; ———. (2000). Togetherness: A balance sheet. *The Economist,* September 30, 25–28; ———. (2000). Eastern Germany's slow revival. *The Economist,* May 27, 51; Ewing, J. (2000). What Germany can teach the rest of Europe. *Business Week,* October 16, 72.

66. ———. (2001). Investment in Eastern Europe. *The Economist,* November 17, 102; Michaels, D. (1996). Booming economy in Poland brings jobs, wealth and apathy. *The Wall Street Journal,* November 25, A1, A10; Miller, K. L., Simpson, P., & Schiller, Z. (1996). Piling into central Europe. *Business Week,* July 1, 42–44.

67. ———. (2001). The changing Poles. *The Economist,* October 14, 59–60; Kaminski, M. (2000). Poland presses to meet EU requirements. *The Wall Street Journal,* September 7, A21.

68. ———. (2002). Emerging market indicators: Russia. *The Economist,* February 23, 110; ———. (2001). The smell test. *The Economist,* February 24, 71; ———. (2000). The Russian economy: Boom and gloom. *The Economist,* November 25, 97;

Banerjee, N. (1996). Russian economy showing signs of life as some major firms post hefty profits. *The Wall Street Journal,* June 5, A11; Starobin, P., & Tavernise, S. (2000). A new home for Russian capital—Russia. *Business Week,* March 6, 58.

69. Starobin, P., & Kravchenko, O. (2000). Russia's middle class. *Business Week,* October 16, 78–84; Starobin, P., & Kravchenko, O. (2000). So far, the mobility is all upward. *Business Week,* July 24, 85.

70. ———. (2001). Investment in Eastern Europe. *The Economist,* November 17, 102; ———. (2001). A survey of Russia: Putin's choice. *The Economist,* July 21, 1–16; ———.(2000). The Russian economy: Boom and gloom. *The Economist,* November 25, 97; Starobin, P., & Belton, C. (2002). Russia: Cleanup time. *Business Week,* January 14, 46–47; Starobin, P., & Belton, C. (2000). The crumbling of Russia. *Business Week,* September 11, 60.

71. ———. (1999). Crime without punishment. *The Economist,* August 28, 17–19; ———. (1999). A krisha over your head. *The Economist,* August 28, 17; Starobin, P., & Belton, C. (2002). Russia: Cleanup time. *Business Week,* January 14, 46–47; Belton, C. (2000). The friends of Vladimir. *Business Week,* December 4, 56–58; Starobin, P., & Belton, C. (2000). Tycoon under siege. *Business Week,* July 24, 48–50.

72. ———. (2001). Economic pain, unequally spread. *The Economist,* August 11, 35–36; ———. (2001). Appendix 1: Regional economic prospects (in World Bank's *Prospects for Development:* www.worldbank.org); ———. (2001). Pink hotels on Syria's hills. *The Economist,* March 24, 54; Reed, S. (2000). Saudi Arabia. *Business Week,* July 31, 70–74.

73. ———. (2001). Africa's elusive dawn. *The Economist,* February 24, 17; Holmes, K. R., & Kirkpatrick, M. (1996). Freedom and growth. *The Wall Street Journal,* December 16, p. A16.; Lansner, T. R. (1996). Out of Africa. *The Wall Street Journal,* December 10, p. A22; O'Reilly, B. (2000). Death of a continent. *Fortune,* November 13, 259–274.

74. ———. (2001). Afrabet soup. *The Economist,* February 10, 77; ———. (2001). Africa's elusive dawn. *The Economist,* February 24, 17.

75. ———. (2001). Africa's plan to save itself. *The Economist,* July 7, 44; ———. (2001). Africa's elusive dawn. *The Economist,* February 24, 17; Zachary, G. P. (2001). African leaders stress benefits of self-reliance, *The Wall Street Journal,* February 7, A22.

76. ———. (2001). Appendix 1: Regional economic prospects (in World Bank's *Prospects for Development:* www.worldbank.org); Cooper, H. (2002). Can African nations use duty-free deal to revamp economy? *The Wall Street Journal,* January 2, A1, A4. Drum, B. (1993). Privatization in Africa. *The Columbia Journal of World Business,* Spring, 145-149; Greenberger, R. S. (1996). New leaders replace yesteryear's "big men," and Tanzania bene-fits. *The Wall Street Journal,* December 10, A1, A15.

77. ———. (2000). From apartheid to welfare state. *The Economist.* April 1, 42–43; ———. (2000). South Africa: Pay packets. *The Economist,* July 29, 45–46; ———. (2000). South Africa: The left kicked into touch. *The Economist,* September 16, 56–57; ———. (2001). Africa's great black hope: A survey of South Africa. *The Economist,* February 24, 1–16; Fine, A. (1994). The color of money is starting to change. *Business Week,* March 14, 42; Thurow, R. (2000). South Africans who fought sanctions now scrap for investors. *The Wall Street Journal,* February 11, A1, A4.

78. ———. (2001). When the economy held its breath. *The Economist,* September 15, 65–66; Phillips, M. M. (2001). Global economy appears to be facing 'most challenging' environment in years. *The Wall Street Journal,* April 18, A4.

79. Edmondson, G. (2000). See the world, erase its borders. *Business*

Week, August 28, 113–114.

80. ———. (2001). Geography and the net: Putting it in its place. *The Economist,* August 11, 18–20; ———. (2000). The global battle: Technology and innovation. *The Wall Street Journal,* September 25, R6; Koretz, G.(2001). The net hauls in a big catch. *Business Week,* March 12, 32.

81. ———. (2000). A survey of e-management: Inside the machine. *The Economist,* November 11, 5–6; Vickery, L. (2001). "Cultural portal" could translate way to profit. *The Wall Street Journal,* February 12, B6.

82. Hitt, M. A., Keats, B. W., & DeMarie, S. M. (1998). Navigating in the new competitive landscape: Building strategic flexibility and competitive advantage in the 21st century. *Academy of Management Executive, 12,* 22–42.

83. Glasgall, W. (1995). Hot money. *Business Week,* March 20, 46–50; Luhnow, D. (2001). Mexican peso holds its own against U.S. dollar. *The Wall Street Journal,* April 12, A14; Schlesinger, J. M. (1996). IMF drafts plan to avert another Mexico. *The Wall Street Journal,* December 31, A4.

84. Phillips, M. M. (2001). Financial contagion knows no borders. *The Wall Street Journal,* July 13, A2; Glasgall, W. (1995). Hot money. *Business Week,* March 20, 46–50.

85. Cooper, H., & Blumenstein, R. (1996). As U.S. firms gain on rivals, the dollar raises pesky questions. *The Wall Street Journal,* August 16, A1, A4.

86. Bianco, A., & Moore, P. L. (2001). Downfall: The inside story of the management fiasco at Xerox. *Business Week,* March 5, 82–90.

87. Hilsenrath, J. E. (2001). Die-hard dollar damages U.S. exporters. *The Wall Street Journal,* March 20, A2; Miller, S., & Champion, M. (2000). Will Japan's car makers leave the U.K.? *The Wall Street Journal,* September 5, A28.

88. Zaun, T.(2001). As the yen weakens, Japan's car makers smile. *The Wall Street Journal,* April 10, A15, A19.

89. Sparks, D. (2000). Business won't hedge the euro away. *Business Week,* December 4, 157; Zaun, T.(2001). As the yen weakens, Japan's car makers smile. *The Wall Street Journal,* April 10, A15, A19.

90. Katz, I. (2000). Adios, Argentina—hello, Brazil. *Business Week,* January 17, 56.

91. Aeppel, T. (2002). The dollar's strength tests the ingenuity of U.S. manufacturers. *The Wall Street Journal,* January 22, A1, A10; Cooper, C.(2000). Euro's drop is hardest for the smallest. *The Wall Street Journal,* October, 2, A21, A24.

92. ———. (2000). A survey of the new economy: Knowledge is power. *The Economist,* September 23, 27; Siekman, P. (2000). The big myth about U.S. manufacturing. *Fortune,* October 2, 244C–244E.

93. ———. (2001). Outsourcing to India: Back office to the world. *The Economist,* May 5, 59–62; Lavin, D. (2002). Globalization goes upscale. *The Wall Street Journal.* February 1, A18; Clifford, M., & Kripalani, M. (2000). Different countries, adjoining cubicles. *Business Week,* August 28, 182-184; Koretz, G. (2000). Solving a global growth enigma. *Business Week,* November 20, 32.

94. Clifford, M., & Kripalani, M. (2000). Different countries, adjoining cubicles. *Business Week,* August 28, 182–184.

95. Borrus, A. (2000). Give me your tired, your poor—and all your techies. *Business Week,* November 13, 48; Koretz, G. (2000). The economy's Achilles' heel? *Business Week,* November 13, 42.

96. Baker, S., & Armstrong, L. (1996). The new factory worker. *Business Week,* September 30, 59–68.

97. Montgomery, C. (2002). Chief: No delivery from labor pains. *Dayton Daily News,* March 2, 1E, 8E; Sasseen, J. A. (1994). Which country has the most qualified workforce? *Business Week,*

October 17, 92–93.

98. Ewing, J., Carlisle, K., & Capell, K. (2001). Help wanted: Germany starts wooing skilled workers. *Business Week,* September 17, 52–53; Valbrun, M. (2000). Immigrants find economic boom brings more than higher pay. *The Wall Street Journal,* August 16, B1, B4.

99. Coy, P. (2000). The creative economy. *Business Week,* August 28, 76–82.

100. Malpass, A. (1998). Ready for that job on the street? *Business Week,* March 16, 118.

101. Gentile, M. C. (1996). *Managerial excellence through diversity.* Chicago, IL: Irwin; Joplin, J. R. W., & Daus, C. S. (1997). Challenges of leading a diverse workforce. *Academy of Management Executive, 11,* 32–47.

102. Robinson, G., & Dechant, K. (1997). Building a business case for diversity. *Academy of Management Executive, 11,* 21–31.

103. Phatak, A. V. (1997). *International Management: Concepts and Cases.* Cincinnati, OH: South-Western College Publishing.

104. Stanek, M. B. (2000). The need for global managers: A business necessity. *Management Decision, 38,* 232–242; Roberts, K., Kossek, E.E., & Ozeki, C. (1998). Managing the global workforce: Challenges and strategies. *Academy of Management Executive, 12,* 93–106.

105. Murray, M. (2001). As huge companies keep growing, CEOs struggle to keep pace. *The Wall Street Journal,* February 8, A1, A6.

106. Dwyer, P., Engardio, P., Schiller, Z., & Reed, S. (1994). Tearing up today's organization chart. *Business Week,* November 18, 80–90; Stanek, M. B. (2000). The need for global managers: A business necessity. *Management Decision, 38,* 232–242; Roberts, K., Kossek, E. E., & Ozeki, C. (1998). Managing the global workforce: Challenges and strategies. *Academy of Management Executive, 12,* 93–106.

107. Birkinshaw, J., & Hood, N. (2001). Unleash innovation in foreign subsidiaries. *Harvard Business Review* (March), 79, 131–138; Shrader, R. C. (2001). Collaboration and performance in foreign markets: The case of young high-technology manufacturing firms. *Academy of Management Journal, 44,* 45–60; Harris, T. G. (1993). The post-capitalist executive: An interview with Peter Drucker. *Harvard Business Review* (May–June), 71, 115–122; Hitt, M. A., Keats, B. W., & DeMarie, S. M. (1998). Navigating in the new competitive landscape: Building strategic flexibility and competitive advantage in the 21st century. *Academy of Management Executive, 12,* 22–42.

108. Hofstede, G. (1993). Cultural constraints in management theories. *Academy of Management Executive, 7,* 81–94; Triandis, H. C. (1996). The psychological measurement of cultural syndromes. *American Psychologist, 51,* 407–415.

109. Hordes, M. W., Clancy, J. A., & Baddaley, J. (1995). A primer for global start-ups. *Academy of Management Executive, 9,* 7–11.

110. Bernstein, A. (2001). Low-skilled jobs: Do they have to move? *Business Week,* February 26, 94–95.

Chapter 2

1. Yatsko, P. (2000). Knocking out the knockoffs. *Fortune,* October, 2, 216.

2. Yatsko, Knocking out the knockoffs, 213–218; Behar, R. (2000). Beijing's phony war on fakes. *Fortune,* October 30, 189–208; ———. (1996). Chinese piracy: A case for copying. *The Economist,* November 23, p. 73; Faison, S. (1996). Copyright pirates prosper in China despite promises. *The New York Times,*

February 20, 1996; Kraar, L. (1995). The risks are rising in China. *Fortune,* March 6, 179–180.

3. Richards, E. L. (1994). *Law for global business.* Boston, MA: Irwin.

4. Czinkota, M. R., Ronkainen, I. A., Moffett, M. H., & Moynihan, E. O. (1995). *Global business.* New York: Dryden Press.

5. Czinkota, Ronkainen, Moffett, & Moynihan, *Global business.*

6. Richards, *Law for global business.*

7. Tillinghast, E. (1992). A survey of the legal profession. *The Economist,* July 18, 1–18.

8. Cullison, A. E. (1991). Product-liability claims hard to win in Japan. *Journal of Commerce,* August 9, 2A.

9. Darlin, D. (1989). Foreign lawyers in Japan chafe under restrictions. *The Wall Street Journal,* February 7, B1; Flom, J. (1991). Home court is best advantage. *Financial Times,* June 27, 10; Work, C. P., Peterson, S., & Tanakadate, H. (1985). Two air disasters, two cultures, two remedies. *U.S. News and World Report,* August 26, 25–26.

10. Schaffer, R., Earle, B., & Agusti, F. (1993). *International business law and its environment.* Minneapolis, MN: West.

11. Rao, N. V. (1992). Islamic interest rule threatens Pakistan's bid for aid. *The Journal of Commerce,* January 29, p. 2A.

12. Brown, K. (1994). Banking on laws of Islam: Interest-free loans, investments grow. *Houston Chronicle,* April 10, B4; ———. (1996). Islamic finance: Turning the Prophet's profits. *The Economist,* August 24, 58–59.

13. Richards, *Law for global business.*

14. Zamet, J. M., & Bovarnick, M. E. (1986). Employee relations for multinational companies in China. *Columbia Journal of World Business, 21,* 13–19.

15. Pincus, L. B., & Belohlav, J. A. (1996). Legal issues in multinational business strategy: To play the game, you have to know the rules. *Academy of Management Executive, 10,* 52–61.

16. Pincus & Belohlav. Legal issues in multinational business strategy.

17. Richter, I. (2000). Legal colossus may be forged between U.K., German firms. *The Wall Street Journal,* April 10, A25; ———. (2000). Lawyers go global: The battle of the Atlantic. *The Economist,* February 26, 79–81.

18. Wessel, D. (2001). The legal DNA of good economies. *The Wall Street Journal,* Sept. 6, A1.

19. ———. (2001). Unprofitable policies: Insurance in Asia. *The Economist,* August 11, 57–58.

20. Zachary, G. P. (2000). Who's holding the strings? A reckoning for the WTO. *The Wall Street Journal,* October 5, A21.

21. Phillips, M. M. (2000). Can World Bank lend money to third world without hurting poor? *The Wall Street Journal,* August 14, A1, A8.

22. Schaffer, Earle, & Agusti. *International business law and its environment.*

23. Dichtl, E., & Koeglmayr, H. G. (1986). Country risk ratings. *Management International Review, 26,* 4–11.

24. Kobrin, S. J., & Punnett, B. J. (1984). The nationalization of oil production. In D. W. Pearce, J. Siebert, & I. Walter (Eds.), *Risk in the political economy of resource development.* London: McMillan.

25. Richards, *Law for global business.*

26. Richards, *Law for global business*

27. Harbrecht, D. (1996). Dodging danger while doing business abroad. *Business Week,* May 27, 151.

28. Griffin, R. W. & Pustay, M. W. (2000). *International Business: A Managerial Perspective.* Reading, Mass.: Addison Wesley.

29. Kahn, J. (1996). China's "greens" win rare battle on river: For now, many factories are closed on putrid Huai. *The Wall Street Journal,* August 2, A8.

30. Richards, *Law for global business.*

31. U.S. Department of State. (1995). U.S. Exports: Non-proliferation and foreign policy controls. *U.S. Department of State Fact Sheet,* December 6, 1995, 1–2.

32. Hufbauer, G. C., & Schott, J. J. (1984). Economic sanctions: An often used and occasionally effective tool of foreign policy. In M. R. Czinkota (Ed.), *Export Controls.* New York: Praeger.

33. Schaffer, Earle, & Agusti, *International business law and its environment.*

34. Richards, *Law for global business,* 325.

35. Burton, T. M. (1992). Baxter made cut-rate deal with Syria to escape blacklist, US probe finds. *The Wall Street Journal,* December 22, A3,A4; Burton, T. M. (1993). How Baxter got off the Arab blacklist and how it got nailed. *The Wall Street Journal,* March 23, A1; Shellenbarer, S. (1990). Did hospital supplier dump its Israel plant to win Arabs favor? *The Wall Street Journal,* May 1, A1, A10.

36. Pesta, J. (2001). India braces for brave new drug world. *The Wall Street Journal,* March 7, A17.

37. Kraar, The risks are rising in China.

38. Kraar, The risks are rising in China.

39. ———. (1996). Chinese piracy: A case for copying. *The Economist,* November 23, 73; Faison, S. (1996). Copyright pirates prosper in China despite promises. *The New York Times,* February 20, 1996; Kraar, The risks are rising in China.

40. Spaeth, A., & Naj, A. K. (1988). PepsiCo accepts tough conditions for the right to sell cola in India. *The Wall Street Journal,* September 20, 44.

41. Seyoum, B. (1996). The impact of intellectual property rights on foreign direct investment. *Columbia Journal of World Business, 31,* 51–59.

42. Greenberger, R. S. (1996). Software theft extends well beyond China. *The Wall Street Journal,* May 20, 1996, A1.

43. Lehman, B. A. (1996). Intellectual property: American's competitive advantage in the 21st century. *Columbia Journal of World Business, 31,* 7–16.

44. Gregory, A. (1989). Political risk management. In A. Rugman (Ed.), *International business in Canada.* Scarborough, ON: Prentice-Hall.

45. Bennett, J. (2001). Small businesses abroad get a big hand from OPIC. *The Wall Street Journal,* May 14, B10.

46. Rugman, A. M., & Verbeke, A. (1990). *Global corporate strategy and trade policy.* New York: Routledge; Yoffie, D. B. (1988). How an industry builds political advantage. *Harvard Business Review,* May–June, 82–89.

47. Frank, R. (2001). Thai food for the world: Government of Thailand plans to open 3,000 restaurants to promote nation abroad. *The Wall Street Journal,* Feb 6, B1, B4.

48. Marsh, D. (1992). The European market: Political worries fail to deter western investors. *Financial Times,* October 12, 3.

49. Yatsko, Knocking out the knockoffs, 213–218.

Chapter 3

1. King, N, & Bravin, J. (2000). Call it mission impossible Inc.— Corporate-spying firms thrive. *The Wall Street Journal,* July 3, B1, B4; Crock, S., Smith, G., Weber, J., Melcher, R. A., & Himelstein, L. (1996). They snoop to conquer. *Business Week,* October 28, 172–176.

2. Wood, D. J. (1991). Corporate social performance revisited.

Academy of Management Journal, 16, 691–718.

3. Gottlieb, J. Z., & Sanzgiri, J. (1996). Towards an ethical dimension of decision making in organizations. *Journal of Business Ethics, 15,* 1275–1285.

4. Amba-Rao, S. C. (1993). Multinational corporate social responsibility, ethics, interactions and third-world governments: An agenda for the 1990s. *Journal of Business Ethics, 12,* 553–572.

5. L'Etang, J. (1995). Ethical corporate social responsibility: A framework for managers. *Journal of Business Ethics, 14,* 125–132; Reidenbach, R. E., & Robin, D. P. (1990). Toward the development of a multidimensional scale for improving evaluations of business ethics. *Journal of Business Ethics, 9,* 639–653; Velasquez, M. (1995). International business ethics: The aluminum companies in Jamaica. *Business Ethics Quarterly, 5,* 865–881; Wood, Corporate social performance revisited.

6. Cohen, J. R., Pant, L. W., & Sharp, D. J. (1992). Cultural and socioeconomic constraints on international codes of ethics: Lessons from accounting. *Journal of Business Ethics, 11,* 687–700; Schlegelmilch, B. B., Robertson, D. C. (1995). The influence of country and industry on ethical perceptions of senior executives in the US and Europe. *Journal of International Business Studies, 26,* 859–879.

7. ———. Business Ethics: Doing well by doing good. (2000). *The Economist,* April 22, 65–67.

8. DeGeorge, R. T. (1993). *Competing with integrity in international business.* New York: Oxford University Press.

9. Buller, P. F., Kohls, J., J., & Anderson, K. S. (1991). The challenge of global ethics. *Journal of Business Ethics, 10,* 767–775; Frederick, W. C. (1991). The moral authority of transnational corporate codes. *Journal of Business Ethics, 10,* 165–177; Velasquez, M. (1995). International business ethics: The aluminum companies in Jamaica. *Business Ethics Quarterly, 5,* 865–881.

10. Donaldson, T. (1989). *The ethics of international business.* New York: Oxford University Press.

11. Jackson, Jurisprudence and the interpretation of precepts for international business. *Business Ethics Quarterly, 4,* 291–320.

12. Jackson, K. T. (1994). Jurisprudence and the interpretation of precepts for international business.

13. Borrus, A., Javetski, B., Parry, J., & Bremner, B. (1996). Change of heart. *Business Week,* May 20, 48–49; Cooper, H. and Bahree, B. (1996). World's best hope for global trade topples few barriers. *The Wall Street Journal,* December, 3, A1, A8.

14. Baron, D. P. (1996). *Business and its environment.* Upper Saddle River, NJ: Prentice-Hall.

15. Hinson, H. (1990). Movie stars. *Esquire,* December, 120–126.

16. Kaltenheuser, S. (1995). China: Doing business under an immoral government. *Business Ethics,* May/June, 20–23; Kelly, M. (1996). Is Pizza Hut Burma's keeper? *Business Ethics,* July/Aug, 73–75.

17. Sethi, S. P. (1993). Operational modes for multinational corporations in post-Apartheid South Africa: A proposal for a code of Affirmative Action in the marketplace. *Journal of Business Ethics, 12,* 1–12.

18. Kelly, Is Pizza Hut Burma's keeper?

19. Bardacke, T. (1997). PepsiCo joins list of groups quitting Burma. *Financial Times,* January 28, 1, 18.

20. Kaltenheuser, China: Doing business under an immoral government.

21. Shari, M. (2001). Staying the course. *Business Week,* September 24, 112.

22. Bernstein, A. (1999). Sweatshop reform: How to solve the standoff. *Business Week,* May 3, 186–190; Friedland, J., & Pura, R.

(1996). Troubled at home, Asian timber firms set sights on the Amazon. *The Wall Street Journal,* November 11, A1, A; ———. (1996). The fun of being a multinational. *The Economist,* July 20, 51–52; ———. (1996). Who's next? *The Economist,* July 13, 48–49; ———. (1999). Sweatshop wars. *The Economist,* Feb. 27, 62–63.

23. Schlegelmilch, B. B., Robertson, D. C. (1995). The influence of country and industry on ethical perceptions of senior executives in the US and Europe. *Journal of International Business Studies, 26,* 859–879.

24. Becker, H., & Fritzsche, D. J. (1987). A comparison of the ethical behavior of American, French, and German managers. *Columbia Journal of World Business, 22,* 87–95.

25. Borrus, A., Toy, S., & Salz-Trautman, P. (1995). A world of greased palms: Inside the dirty war for global business. *Business Week,* November 6, 36–38; ———. (1997). Enron and On and On. *The Economist,* June 14, 74; Jordan, M. (1996). Indian leader Rao quits post to face charges. *The Wall Street Journal,* September 23, A17; Steinmetz, G., & Greenberger, R. S. (1997). US embassies give American companies more help overseas. *The Wall Street Journal,* January 21, A1, A6.

26. Dolecheck, M. M. (1992). Cross-cultural analysis of business ethics: Hong Kong and American business personnel. *Journal of Managerial Issues, 4,* 288–303; Dubinsky, A. J., Jolson, M. A., Kotabe, M., & Lim, C. U. (1991). A cross-national investigation of industrial salespeople's ethical perceptions. *Journal of International Business Studies, 22,* 651–670; Kennedy, E. J., & Lawton, L. (1996). The effects of social and moral integration on ethical standards: A comparison of American and Ukrainian business students. *Journal of Business Ethics, 15,* 901–911; McCabe, D. L., Dukerich, J. M., & Dutton, J. (1993). Values and moral dilemmas: A cross-cultural comparison. *Business Ethics Quarterly, 3,* 117–130.

27. Husted, B. W., Dozier, J. B., McMahon, J. T., & Kattan, M. W. (1996). The impact of cross-national carriers of business ethics on attitudes about questionable practices and form of moral reasoning. *Journal of International Business Studies, 27,* 391–411.

28. Moore, R. S., & Radloff, S. E. (1996). Attitudes towards business ethics held by South African students. *Journal of Business Ethics, 15,* 863–869.

29. ———. (1990). Hey, America, lighten up a little. *The Economist,* July 28, A5.

30. Transparency International website (2000) www.transparency.de.

31. ———. (2000). Business ethics: doing well by doing good. *The Economist,* April 22, 65–67.

32. Langlois, C. C., & Schlegelmilch, B. B. (1990). Do corporate codes of ethics reflect national character? Evidence from Europe and the United States. *Journal of International Business Studies,* Fourth Quarter, 519–539.

33. Langlois & Schlegelmilch, Do corporate codes of ethics reflect national character?

34. Langlois, & Schlegelmilch, B. B. (1990). Do corporate codes of ethics reflect national character?; Schlegelmilch, B. (1989). The ethics gap between Britain and the United States: A comparison of the state of business ethics in both countries. *European Management Journal, 7,* 57–64.

35. DeGeorge, *Competing with integrity in international business.*

36. Feder, B. J. (1994). Honeywell's route back to South Africa market. *The New York Times,* January 31, C1, C4; Templin, N. (1988). They're getting out of South Africa. *USA Today,* June 14, 7B.

37. Feder, Honeywell's route back to South Africa market.

38. Sethi, S. P. (1993). Operational modes for multinational corporations in post-Apartheid South Africa: A proposal for a code of

Affirmative Action in the marketplace. *Journal of Business Ethics, 12,* 1–12.

39. McFarlin, D. B., Coster, E. A., & Mogale-Pretorius, C. (1999). Management development in South Africa: Moving toward an Africanized model. *Journal of Management Development,* July, 33–41.

40. Rossouw, G. J. (1998). Establishing moral business culture in newly formed democracies. *Journal of Business Ethics, 17,* 1563–1571.

41. Kaltenheuser, China: Doing business under an immoral government, 20–23.

42. Vance, C. M., & Paderon, E. S. (1993). An ethical argument for host country workforce training and development in the expatriate management assignment. *Journal of Business Ethics, 12,* 635–641.

43. Kaltenheuser, China: Doing business under an immoral government.

44. Beaver, W. (1995). Levi's is leaving China. *Business Horizons, 38,* 35–40.

45. Beaver, Levi's is leaving China.

46. Zachary, G. P. (1994). Levi's tries to make sure contract plants in Asia treat workers well. *The Wall Street Journal,* July 28, A1, A6.

47. Buller, P. F., Kohls, J. J., & Anderson, K. S. (2000). When ethics collide: Managing conflict across cultures. *Organizational Dynamics, 28,* 52–66.

48. Clifford, M. L. (1996). Keep the heat on sweatshops. *Business Week,* Dec. 3, 90.

49. Singer, A. W. (1996). Levi Strauss' global sourcing guidelines come of age. *Ethikos,* May/June, 4–12.

50. Ortega, B. (1995). Conduct codes garner goodwill for retailers, but violations go on. *The Wall Street Journal,* July 3, A1, A4.

51. Edmondson, G., Carlisle, K., Resch, I., Anhalt, K., & Dawley, H. (2000). Workers in bondage. *Business Week,* November 27, 146–162.

52. Donaldson, T. (1994). Global business must mind its morals. *The New York Times,* February 13, E11.

53. Noonan, J. (1984). *Bribes.* New York: Macmillan.

54. Jacoby, N. H., Nehemkis, P., & Eells, R. (1977). *Bribery and extortion in world business: A study of corporate political payments abroad.* New York: Macmillan.

55. Jacoby, Nehemkis, & Eells, *Bribery and extortion in world business.*

56. Jacoby, Nehemkis, & Eells, *Bribery and extortion in world business.*

57. Schaffer, Earle, & Agusti, *International business law and its environment.*

58. ———. (2000). Shenanigans in France. *The Economist,* November 4, 53; ———. (1996). Who's next? *The Economist,* July 13, 48–49; Toy, S. (1996). Under suspicion: Le tout business elite. *Business Week,* Jan. 22, 58; Toy, S., Edmondson, G., & Javetski, B. (1995). Will les affaires lead to reform in la France? *Business Week,* Feb. 27, 56–57.

59. Kamm, T, Rohwedder, C., & Trofimov, Y. (2000). Europe can't decide whether dirty money in politics is a problem. *The Wall Street Journal,* February 9, A1; ———. (2000). Stopping the rot in public life. *The Economist,* September 16, 41–43; ———. (2000). Bill, borrow and embezzle. *The Economist,* February 17, 48; Reed, J., & Portage, E. (1999). Bribery, corruption are rampant in Eastern Europe, survey finds. *The Wall Street Journal,* November 9, A21.

60. Bremner, B. (1996). How the mob burned the banks. *Business Week,* January 29, 42–47; ———. (2001). Another bad apple in Japan. *The Economist,* January 27, 39.

61. Lee, C. K. (1996). Unfinished business: Kim sends the chaebol a message. *Business Week,* September 9, 56–57; Nakarmi, L. (1995). The slush fund that's shaking up Seoul. *Business Week,* November 13, 60.

62. Wrong, M. (1996). Tanzania's egalitarian dream now nightmare of corruption. *Financial Times,* October 4, 6.

63. Berkowitz, B. D. (1996). The irony of the Huang affair. *The Wall Street Journal,* November 6, A20; Dwyer, P., Shari, M., & Moore, J. (1996). Did Clinton's Indonesian friends have a grip on policy? *Business Week,* November 4, 40–42.

64. Pope, H. (2000). Corruption stunts growth in ex-Soviet states. *The Wall Street Journal,* July 5, A17; Galuszka, P., & Brady, R. (1996). The battle for Russia's wealth. *Business Week,* April 1, 50–52.

65. Czinkota, M. R., Ronkainen, I. A., Moffett, M. H., & Moynihan, E. O. (1995). *Global Business.* New York: Dryden Press.

66. Singer, A. W. (1991). Ethics: Are standards lower overseas? *Across the Board, 28,* 31–34.

67. DeGeorge, *Competing with integrity in international business.*

68. Cohen, J. A. (1976). Japan's Watergate. *The New York Times Magazine,* November 21, 104–119.

69. Kotchian, C. A. (1977). The payoff: Lockheed's 70-day mission to Tokyo. *Saturday Review,* July 9, 7–16.

70. Boulton, D. (1978). *The grease machine.* New York: Harper & Row.

71. Kim, S. H., & Barone, S. (1981). Is the foreign corrupt practices act of 1977 a success or failure? A survey of members of the Academy of International Business. *Journal of International Business Studies, 12,* 123–126.

72. Fadiman, J. A. (1986). A traveler's guide to gifts and bribes. *Harvard Business Review,* July/Aug., 122–136; Singer, Ethics: Are standards lower overseas?

73. Graham, J. L. (1984). The foreign corrupt practices act: A new perspective. *Journal of International Business Studies, 15,* 107–121

74. Graham, The foreign corrupt practices act: A new perspective.

75. Vogel, T. T. (1997). Foreigners rang early alarm on Ecuador. *The Wall Street Journal,* February 10, A14.

76. Engardio, P., & Shari, M. (1996). The Suharto empire. *Business Week,* August 19, 46–50.

77. Singer, Ethics: Are standards lower overseas?

78. Donaldson, Global business must mind its morals.; Schlegelmilch, B. (1989). The ethics gap between Britain and the United States: A comparison of the state of business ethics in both countries. *European Management Journal, 7,* 57–64.

79. ———. (1996). Operating an ethics hotline: Some practical advice. *Ethikos,* Mar./Apr., 11–13.

80. Graham, G. (1993). US seeks OECD foreign bribes ban. *Financial Times,* December 6, 3; Keatley, R. (1994). U.S. campaign against bribery faces resistance from foreign governments. *The Wall Street Journal,* February 4, A6.

81. Dunne, N. (2000). Bribery helps win contracts in developing world. *Financial Times,* January 21, 6; Graham, U.S. seeks OECD foreign bribes ban; Keatley, U.S. campaign against bribery faces resistance from foreign governments; Milbank, D., & Brauchli, M. W. (1995). How U.S. concerns compete in countries where bribes flourish. *The Wall Street Journal,* September 29, A1, A14; Greenberger, R. S. (1995). Foreigners use bribes to beat U.S. rivals in many deals. *The Wall Street Journal,* October 12, 3.

82. Quench, J., & Austin, J. (1993). Should multinationals invest in Africa? *Sloan Management Review,* Spring, 107–118.

83. Miffed, S. (1996). Asia stinks. *Fortune,* December 9, 120–132; Devraj, R. (2000). Development India: Thousands of jobless question green concerns. *Interpress Service,* December 29, 7–8.

84. ———. (1996). The global poverty trap. *The Economist,* July 20, 34.

85. Fath, J. (1994). Industrial policies for countries in transition? *Russian and East European Finance and Trade, 30,* 38–77; Godfrey, M. (1995). The struggle against unemployment: Medium term policy options for transitional economies. *International Labour Review, 134,* 3–15; O'Leary, C. J. (1995). Performance indicators: A management tool for active labour programmes in Hungary and Poland. *International Labour Review, 134,* 729–753.

86. Woodruff, D. (1996). East Germany is still a mess—$580 billion later. *Business Week,* June 17, 58.

87. Friedland, J. (1996). Latin America resists reform backlash. *The Wall Street Journal,* August 5, A8.

88. Quench, & Austin, Should multinationals invest in Africa?

89. Smith, C. S., & Brauchli, M. W. (1995). Despite rapid growth of China's economy, many are suffering. *The Wall Street Journal,* October 18, A1, A16.

90. Chen, K. (1995). As millions of Chinese try to get rich quick, values get trampled. *The Wall Street Journal,* May 2, A1, A16.

91. Roberts, D. (2000). The great migration: Chinese peasants are fleeing their villages to chase big-city dreams. *Business Week,* December 18, 176–188; Chen, K. (1996). A teenager's journey mirrors inner migration that's changing China. *The Wall Street Journal,* October 29, A1, A4.

92. Singh, J. B., & Carasco, E. F. (1996). Business ethics, economic development and protection of the environment in the new world order. *Journal of Business Ethics,* 15, 297–307.

93. Kirkpatrick, D. (2001). Looking for profits in poverty. *Fortune,* February 5, 176–177.

94. Ball, D. A., & McCulloch, W. H. (1999). *International business: The challenge of global competition.* Burr Ridge, IL: Irwin McGraw-Hill; King & Bravin, Call it mission impossible Inc.

95. King, & Bravin, Call it mission impossible Inc.

Chapter 4

1. Filipczak, B. (1992). Working for the Japanese. *Training, 26,* 23–29; Linowes, R. G. (1993). The Japanese manager's traumatic entry into the United States: Understanding the American-Japanese cultural divide. *Academy of Management Executive, 7,* 21–40.

2. Hofstede, G. (1993). Cultural constraints in management theories. *Academy of Management Executive, 7,* 81–94; Triandis, H. C. (1996). The psychological measurement of cultural syndromes. *American Psychologist, 51,* 407–415.

3. Adler, N. J. (2002). *International dimensions of organizational behavior* (4th Ed.). Cincinnati, OH: South-Western; Shenkar, O. (2001). Cultural distance revisited: Towards a more rigorous conceptualization and measurement of cultural differences. *Journal of International Business Studies, 32,* 519–535.

4. Granato, J., Inglehart, R., & Leblang, D. (1996). The effect of cultural values on economic development: Theory, hypotheses, and some empirical tests. *American Journal of Political Science, 40,* 607–631.

5. Earley, P. C., & Singh, H. (2000). New approaches to international and cross-cultural management research. In P. C. Earley & H. Singh (Eds.), *Innovations in international and cross-cultural management,* 1–14. Thousand Oaks, CA: Sage.

6. Begley, T. M., & Tan, W. L. (2001). The socio-cultural environment for entrepreneurship: A comparison between East Asian and Anglo-Saxon countries. *Journal of International Business Studies, 32,* 537–553.

7. Newman, K. L., & Nollen, S. D. (1996). Culture and congruence: The fit between management practices and national culture. *Journal of International Business Studies,* Fourth Quarter, 753–779.

8. Morris, M. W., Podolny, J. M., & Ariel, S. (2000). Missing relations: Incorporating relational constructs into models of culture. In P. C. Earley & H. Singh (Eds.), *Innovations in international and cross-cultural management,* 52–90. Thousand Oaks, CA: Sage; Sampson, E. E. (2000). Reinterpreting individualism and collectivism. *American Psychologist,* 55, 1425–1432.

9. Shenkar, Cultural distance revisited: Towards a more rigorous conceptualization and measurement of cultural differences.

10. Osland, J. S., & Bird, A. (2000). Beyond sophisticated stereotyping. Cultural sensemaking in context. *Academy of Management Executive, 14,* 65–79.

11. Hall, E. T. (1976). *Beyond culture.* Garden City, NY: Anchor Press; Hall, E. T., & Hall, M. R. (1990). *Understanding cultural differences.* Yarmouth, ME: Intercultural Press.

12. Trompenaars, F. (1993). *Riding the waves of culture.* London: Brealey.

13. Ronen, S. & Shenkar, O. (1985). Clustering countries on attitudinal dimensions: A review and synthesis. *Academy of Management Review, 10,* 435–454.

14. Shenkar, Cultural distance revisited: Towards a more rigorous conceptualization and measurement of cultural differences.

15. Alston, J. P. (1989). Wa, Guanxi, and Inhwa: Managerial principles in Japan, China, and Korea. *Business Horizons,* March-April, 26–31.

16. ———. (2002). Japanese careers: Show me the money. *The Economist,* January 26, 56; ———. (2000). In search of the new Japanese dream. *The Economist,* February 19, 59–63; ———. (2000). Child's play. *The Economist,* February 19, 60; ———. (2000). Survey of the young: Tomorrow's child. *The Economist,* December 23, 11–14; Meek, C. B. (1999). Ganbatte: Understanding the Japanese employee. *Business Horizons,* January-February, 27–35; Ono, Y., & Spindle, B. (2000). Japan's long decline makes one thing rise: Individualism. *The Wall Street Journal,* December 29, A1, A4.

17. Alston, Wa, Guanxi, and Inhwa: Managerial principles in Japan, China, and Korea.; Bond, M. H. (1991). *Beyond the Chinese face.* Hong Kong: Oxford University Press; Chen, M. (1995). *Asian management systems: Chinese, Japanese and Korean styles of business.* London: Routledge.

18. Chen, *Asian management systems: Chinese, Japanese and Korean styles of business.*

19. Bass, B. M. (1990). *Stogdill's handbook of leadership: A survey of theory and research.* New York: Free Press; McFarlin, D. B., Sweeney, P. D., & Cotton, J. C. (1992). Attitudes toward employee participation in decision-making: A comparison of European and American managers in a U.S. multinational. *Human Resource Management, 31,* 363–383.

20. Adler, *International dimensions of organizational behavior;* Cox, T. & Blake, S. (1991). Managing cultural diversity: Implications for organizational competitiveness. *Academy of Management Executive,* 5, 45–56.

21. Kumbula, T. S. (1993). As apartheid falls, black education becomes (at last) a serious issue. *Black Issues in Higher Education, 10,* September 23, 15–18.

22. McFarlin, D. B., Coster, E. A., & Mogale-Pretorius, C. (1999). Management development in South Africa: Moving toward an Africanized framework. *Journal of Management Development, 18,* 63–78.

23. Sivakumar, K., & Nakata, C. (2001). The stampede toward Hofstede's framework: Avoiding the sample design pit in cross-cultural research. *Journal of International Business Studies, 32,* 555–574.

24. Hofstede, G. (1980). Motivation, leadership, and organization: Do American theories apply abroad? *Organizational Dynamics,* Summer, 42–63; Hofstede, G. (2001). *Culture's consequences* (2nd Ed.). Thousand Oaks, CA: Sage; Hofstede, G. (1984). *Culture's consequences.* Newbury Park, CA: Sage; Hofstede, Cultural constraints in management theories.; Hofstede, G. (1991). *Cultures and organizations: Software of the mind.* London: McGraw-Hill U.K.; Hofstede, G. (1996). An American in Paris: The influence of nationality on organization theories. *Organizational Studies, 17,* 525–537.

25. Morris, Podolny, & Ariel, Missing relations: Incorporating relational constructs into models of culture.

26. Bond, *Beyond the Chinese face.*; Hofstede, Cultural constraints in management theories.

27. Dowling, P. J., & Nagel, T.W. (1986). Nationality and work attitudes: A study of Australian and American business majors. *Journal of Management, 12,* 121–128.

28. Used by permission. (Company to remain anonymous.)

29. Trompenaars (1993). *Riding the waves of culture;* Trompenaars, F., & Hampden-Turner, C. (1998). *Riding the waves of culture: Understanding cultural diversity in global business* (2nd Ed.). New York: McGraw-Hill.

30. Ali, A. (1988). A cross-national perspective of managerial work value systems. In R. N. Farmer & E. G. McGoun (Eds.), *Advances in international comparative management,* vol. 3, 151–170. Greenwich, CT: JAI Press; Trompenaars, *Riding the waves of culture.*

31. MOW International Research Team (1987). *The meaning of working.* London: Academic Press.

32. Meek, Ganbatte: Understanding the Japanese employee.; Zimmerman, M. (1985). *How to do business with the Japanese.* New York: Random House.

33. Lincoln, J. R. (1989). Employee work attitudes and management practice in the U.S. and Japan: Evidence from a large comparative survey. *California Management Review, 32,* 89–106; Meek, Ganbatte: Understanding the Japanese employee.

34. Grant, L. (1997). Unhappy in Japan. *Fortune,* January 13, 142; Meek, Ganbatte: Understanding the Japanese employee.

35. MOW International Research Team, *The meaning of working.*

36. Sherer, P. M. (1996). North American and Asian executives have contrasting values, study finds. *The Wall Street Journal,* March 6, B11.

37. Hofstede, Cultural constraints in management theories.

38. See Greenberg, J., & Baron, R. A. (2000). *Behavior in organizations* (7th Ed.). Englewood Cliffs, NJ: Prentice-Hall.

39. Hofstede, G. (1993). Cultural constraints in management theories.

40. Laurent, A. (1983). The cultural diversity of western conceptions of management. *International Studies of Management and Organization, 13,* 75–96.

41. Ali, A. (1988). A cross-national perspective of managerial work value systems. In R. N. Farmer & E. G. McGoun (Eds.), *Advances in international comparative management,* vol. 3, 151–170. Greenwich, CT: JAI Press; Bass, B. M. (1990). *Stogdill's handbook of leadership: A survey of theory and research.* New York: Free Press.

42. Ayman, R., Kreicker, N. A., & Masztal, J. J. (1994). Defining global leadership in business environments. *Consulting Psychology Journal, 46,* 64–73; Dorfman, P. (1996). International and cross-cultural leadership. In B. J. Punnett & O. Shenkar (Eds.), *Handbook for international management research,* 267–350. Cambridge, MA: Blackwell.

43. Yeung, A. K., & Ready, D. A. (1995). Developing leadership capabilities of global corporations: A comparative study in eight nations. *Human Resource Management, 34,* 529–547.

44. Okechuku, C. (1994). The relationship of six managerial characteristics to the assessment of managerial effectiveness in Canada, Hong Kong, and People's Republic of China. *Journal of Occupational and Organizational Psychology, 67,* 79–86.

45. Geppert, M. (1996). Paths of managerial learning in the east German context. *Organization Studies, 17,* 249–268; Kostera, M., Proppe, M., & Szatkowski, M. (1995). Staging the new romantic hero in the old cynical theatre: On managers, roles and change in Poland. *Journal of Organizational Behavior, 16,* 631–646.

46. Osland & Bird, Beyond sophisticated stereotyping: Cultural sense-making in context.

47. Filipczak, B. (1992). Working for the Japanese. *Training, 26,* 23–29; Linowes, R. G. (1993). The Japanese manager's traumatic entry into the United States: Understanding the American-Japanese cultural divide. *Academy of Management Executive, 7,* 21–40.

48. Gutner, T. (1996). Never give a Mandarin a clock and other rules. *Business Week,* December 9, 192; Murphy, K. (1999). Gifts without gaffes for global clients. *Business Week,* December 6, 153.

Chapter 5

1. Webb, J. (2000). History proves Vietnam victors wrong. *The Wall Street Journal,* April 28, A19; ———. (2000). Vietnam then and now. *The Wall Street Journal,* April 8, A18.

2. Smith, E. D., & Pham, C. (1996). Doing business in Vietnam: A cultural guide. *Business Horizons, 39,* 47–51.

3. Smith & Pham, Doing business in Vietnam.

4. McArthur, L. Z., & Brown, R. M. (1983). Toward an ecological theory of social perception, *Psychological Review, 90,* 215–238.

5. Bond, M. H., & Forgas, J. (1984). Linking person perception to behavioral intention across cultures. The role of cultural collectivism. *Journal of Cross-Cultural Psychology, 15,* 337–353.

6. This comment applies equally to cultures that may share fundamental similarities, such as the United States and Australia. Simply sharing characteristics does not imply that one culture understands the other, as is apparently the case with the United States. Bryson, for example, shows that Australia has a very low profile among Americans and they generally know little of the country (Bryson, B. (2000). The land down where? *The Wall Street Journal,* September 15, A18.)

7. Bond, M. H., & Wan, K. C., Leung, K. & Giacalone, R. A. (1985). How are responses to verbal insult related to cultural collectivism and power distance? *Journal of Cross-Cultural Psychology, 16,* 111–127.

8. Forgas, J. P., & Bond, M. H. (1985). Cultural influences on the perceptions of interaction episodes. *Personality and Social Psychology Bulletin, 11,* 75–88.

9. Hall, E. T. (1983). *The dance of life.* Garden City, NY: Anchor Press; Hall, E. T., & Hall, M. R. (1990). *Understanding cultural differences.* Yarmouth, ME: Intercultural Press.

10. Gudykunst, W., B., & Ting-Toomey, S. (1988). Culture and affective communication. *American Behavioral Scientist, 31,* 384–400; Scherer, K. R., & Wallbott, H. G. (1994). Evidence for universality and cultural variation of differential emotion response patterning. *Journal of Personality and Social Psychology, 66,* 310–328.

11. LaFrance, M., & Mayo, C. (1978). Cultural aspects of nonverbal

communication: A review essay. *International Journal of Intercultural Relations, 2,* 71–89; Ramsey, S. J. (1979). Nonverbal behavior: An intercultural perspective. In M. Asante et al. (Eds.), *Handbook of Intercultural Communication.* Newbury Park, CA: Sage.

12. Archer, H. (2001). Doing business in Japan: The secrets of meishi. www.shinnova.com/part/99-japa.

13. Sweeney, P. D., & McFarlin, D. B. (2002). *Organizational behavior: Solutions for management.* McGraw-Hill Irwin: Burr Ridge, Il.

14. Hall, E. T. (1976). *Beyond culture.* Garden City, NY: Anchor Press.

15. Hall & Hall, *Understanding cultural differences.*

16. Levine, R. V., & Wolff, E. (l985). Social time: The heartbeat of culture. *Psychology Today,* March, 28–35.

17. Levine, R. V., & Bartlett, K. (l984). Pace of life, punctuality, and coronary heart disease in six countries. *Journal of Cross-Cultural Psychology, 15,* 233–255.

18. Hall, *The dance of life.*

19. Hall & Hall, *Understanding Cultural Differences.*

20. Usunier, J-C., G. (1991). Business time perceptions and national cultures: A comparative survey. *Management International Review, 31,* 197–217.

21. Hall, E. T. (l960). The silent language in overseas business. *Harvard Business Review,* May-June, 87–96.

22. Bluedorn, A. C., Kaufman, C. F., & Lane, P. M. (l992). How many things do you like to do at once? An introduction to mono-chronic and polychronic time. *Academy of Management Review, 6,* 17–26; Kaufman, C., Lane, P., & Lindquist, J. (1991). Exploring more than 24 hours a day: A preliminary investigation of poly-chronic time use. *Journal of Consumer Research, 18,* 392–401.

23. Chandler, T. A., Sharma, D. D., Wolf, F. M., & Planchard, S. K. (1981). Multi-attributional causality: A five cross-national samples study. *Journal of Cross-Cultural Psychology, 12,* 207–221; Choi, I., Nisbett, R. E., & Norenzayan, A. (1999). Causal attribu-tion across cultures: Variation and universality. *Psychological Bulletin, 125,* 47–63.

24. Kashima, Y., & Triandis, H. C. (l986). The self-serving bias in attributions as a coping strategy: A cross-cultural study. *Journal of Cross Cultural Psychology, 17,* 83–97.

25. Smith, S. H., Whitehead, G. I., & Sussman, N. M. (l990). The positivity bias in attributions: Two cross-cultural investigations. *Journal of Cross-Cultural Psychology, 21,* 283–301.

26. Smith, Whitehead, & Sussman, The positivity bias in attributions.

27. Bond, M. H., Leung, K., & Wan, K. (l982). The social impact of self-effacing attributions: The Chinese case. *Journal of Social Psychology, 118,* 157–166.

28. Morris, M. W., & Peng, K. (1994). Culture and cause: American and Chinese attributions for social and physical events. *Journal of Personality and Social Psychology, 67,* 949–971.

29. Barnum, C., & Wolniansky, N. (1989). Taking cues from body language. *Management Review,* June, 59–60.

30. Miller, J. G. (1988). Bridging the content-structure dichotomy: Culture and self. In M. H. Bond (Ed.), *The cross-cultural chal-lenge to social psychology,* vol. 11. Beverly Hills, CA: Sage.

31. Weisz, J. R., Rothbaum, F. M., & Blackburn, T. C. (l984). Standing out and standing in: The psychology of control in America and Japan. *American Psychologist, 39,* 955–969.

32. Markus, H. R., & Kitayama, S. (1998). The cultural psychology of personality. *Journal of Cross-Cultural Psychology, 29,* 63–87; Markus, H. R., & Kitayama, S. (1991). Culture and the self: Implications for cognition, emotion, and motivation. *Psychological Review, 98,* 224–253.

33. Bond, M. H., & Cheung, T. (1983). College students' sponta-

neous self-concept. *Journal of Cross-Cultural Psychology,* June, 153–171.

34. Triandis, H. C. (1989). The self and social behavior in differing cultural contexts. *Psychological Review, 96,* 506–520.

35. See also Cousins, S. D. (1989). Culture and self-perception in Japan and the United States. *Journal of Personality and Social Psychology, 56,* 124–131.

36. Schweder, R. A., & Bourne, E. J. (1982). Does the concept of the person vary cross-culturally: In R. A. Schweder & R. A. Levine (Eds.) *Culture Theory: Essays on Mind, Self, and Emotion.* New York Cambridge University Press (158–199).

37. Miller, J. G. (1984). Culture and the development of everyday social explanation. *Journal of Personality and Social Psychology, 46,* 961–978. See also a study by Stipek, D., Weiner, B., & Li, K. (1989). Testing some attribution-emotion relations in the People's Republic of China. *Journal of Personality and Social Psychology, 56,* 109–116. Based on a carefully done study, these researchers concluded that there is little support for characteri-zations of Chinese as being particularly other oriented and of Americans as being relatively more self-focused. The difference in results is difficult to explain. The only real difference of note is that this study is the newest of the lot and thus may reflect some of the recent changes occurring in China, particularly among the young and educated. Regardless, the general pattern of findings we present in this section appears to reflect some differing views of the self, perhaps reflective of a Western inde-pendent self and a non-Western interdependent self.

38. Sweeney & McFarlin, *Organizational behavior: Solutions for management.* Originally based on Reeder, J. A. (1987). When West meets East: Cultural aspects of doing business in Asia. *Business Horizons,* Jan.-Feb., 69–74.

39. Redding, S. G., & Ng, M. (1983). The role of "face" in the organi-zational perceptions of Chinese managers. *International Studies of Management & Organization, 13,* 92–123.

40. Reeder, When West meets East: Cultural aspects of doing busi-ness in Asia.

41. Reeder, When West meets East: Cultural aspects of doing busi-ness in Asia.

42. Mabe, P. A., III, & West, S. E. (1982). Validity and self-evaluation of ability: A Review and meta-analysis. *Journal of Applied Psychology, 42,* 280–297.

43. Farh, J-L., Dobbins, G. H., & Cheng, B-S. (1991). Cultural rela-tivity in action: A comparison of self-ratings made by Chinese and U.S. workers. *Personnel Psychology, 44,* 129–147.

44. Kelly, L., Whatley, A., & Worthley, R. (1993). Self-appraisal, life goals and national culture: An Asian-Western comparison. *Asia Pacific Journal of Management, 7,* 41–58.

45. Yu, J., & Murphy, K. R., (1993). Modesty bias in self-ratings of performance: A test of the cultural relativity hypothesis. *Personnel Psychology, 46,* 357–363.

46. Furnham, A., Bond, M., Heaven, P, Hilton, D., Lobel, T., Masters, J., Payne, M., Rajamanikam, R., Stacey, B., & Daalen, H. V. (1992). A comparison of Protestant work ethic beliefs in thirteen nations. *Journal of Social Psychology, 133,* 185–197.

47. Furnham et al., A comparison of Protestant work ethic beliefs in thirteen nations.

48. Lynn, R. (1991). *The secret of the miracle economy: Different national attitudes to competitiveness and money.* Exeter, UK: Social Affairs Unit.

49. Furnham, A. (1992). Just world beliefs in twelve societies. *Journal of Social Psychology, 133,* 317–329.

50. Hymowitz, C. (2000). U.S. executives reply to criticism leveled by foreign counterparts. *The Wall Street Journal,* Sept. 19, B1;

Hymowitz, C. (2000). Companies go global, but many managers just don't travel well. *The Wall Street Journal*, August 15, B1.

51. Neff, R. (1989). Japan's hardening view of America. *Business Week*, December 18, 62–64.

52. Stening, B. W., Everett, J. E., & Longton, P. A. (1981). Mutual perception of managerial performance and style in multinational subsidiaries. *Journal of Occupational Psychology, 54*, 255–263.

53. ———. (1986). *Time*, June 16, p. 52. Reprinted by permission.

54. Almaney, A. J. (1982). How Arabs see the West. *Business Horizons*, Sept.-Oct. 11–17.

55. Sheehan, J. G. (1978). The Arab: TV's most popular villain. *Christian Century*, December 3, 1214–1218.

56. ———. (1980). The other anti-semitism. *New Republic*. March 6, 22.

57. Almaney, How Arabs see the West.

58. Hastings, E. H., & Hastings, P. K. (1993). *Index to international public opinion 1992–1993*. Westport, CT: Greenwood Press.

59. Oreskes, M. (1990). Poll detects erosion of positive attitudes toward Japan among Americans. *The New York Times*, February 6, B7.

60. Bizman, A., & Amir, Y. (1982). Mutual perceptions of Arabs and Jews in Israel. *Journal of Cross-Cultural Psychology, 13*, 461–469; Brofenbrenner, U. (1961). The mirror image in Soviet-American relations: A social psychologist's report. *Journal of Social Issues, 17*, 45–56.

61. Berrien, F. K. (1969). Familiarity, mirror imaging and social desirability in stereotypes: Japanese vs. Americans. *International Journal of Psychology, 4*, 207–215; Haque, A., & Lawson, D. L. (1980). The mirror image phenomenon in the context of the Arab-Israeli conflict. *Journal of Intercultural Relations, 4*, 107–115; Shari, M. (2000). Wages of hatred: Indonesia's hostility of a minority costs the country dearly. *Business Week*, October 9, 71–74.

62. Lee, Y-T., & Ottati, V. (1993). Determinants of in-group and out-group perceptions of heterogeneity: An investigation of Sino-American stereotypes. *Journal of Cross-Cultural Psychology, 24*, 298–818.

63. Iwao, S. & Triandis, H. C. (1993). Validity of auto- and heterostereotypes among Japanese and American students. *Journal of Cross-Cultural Psychology, 24*, 428–444; Vassiliov, V., Triandis, H. C., Vassiliov, G., & McGuire, H., (1972). Interpersonal contact and stereotyping. In H. C. Triandis (Ed.), *The Analysis of Subjective Culture*. New York: Wilby (pp. 89–115).

64. Omens, A. E., Jenner, S. R., & Beatty, J. R. (1987). Intercultural perceptions in United States subsidiaries of Japanese companies. *International Journal of Intercultural Relations, 11*, 249–264.

65. Bond, M. H. (1986). Mutual stereotypes and the facilitation of interaction across cultural lines. *International Journal of Intercultural Relations, 10*, 259–276.

66. Lee & Ottati, Determinants of in-group and out-group perceptions of heterogeneity.

67. Bond, Mutual stereotypes and the facilitation of interaction across cultural lines.

68. Khanna, S. R. (1986). Asian companies and the country stereotype paradox: An empirical study. *Columbia Journal of World Business*, Summer, 29–38.

69. Shimp, T. A. & Sharma, S. (1987). Consumer ethnocentrism: Construction and validation of the CETSCALE. *Journal of Marketing Research, 24*, 280–289.

70. Archer, R. (1992). Want to "buy American"? It's a lot easier said than done. *The Arizona Republic*, March 2, 1992, A6.

71. Lincoln, J. R., (1989). Employee work attitudes and management practice in the U.S. and Japan: Evidence from a large compara-

tive survey. *California Management Review*, Fall, 89–106; Lincoln, J. R., & Kalleberg, A. L. (1990). *Culture, control, and commitment: A study of work organization and work attitudes in the U.S. and Japan*. Cambridge: Cambridge University Press; Near, J. P. (1986). Work and nonwork attitudes among Japanese and American workers. *Advances in International Comparative Management*, vol. 2, 57–67; Near, J. P. (1989). Organizational commitment among Japanese and U. S. workers. *Organization Studies*, 10, 281–300.

72. Azumi, K. & McMillan, C. J. (1976). Worker sentiment in the Japanese factory: Its organizational determinants. In L. Austin (Ed.), *Japan: The paradox of progress*, 215–229. New Haven, CT: Yale University Press; Cole, R. E. (1979). *Work, mobility and participation*. Berkeley: University of California Press; Lincoln, J. R., Hanada, M., & Olson, J. (1981). Cultural orientations and individual reactions to organizations: A study of employees of Japanese-owned firms. *Administrative Science Quarterly, 26*, 93–115; Lincoln, J. R., & McBride, J. (1987); Naoi, A. & Schooler, C. (1985). Occupational conditions and psychological functioning in Japan. *American Journal of Sociology, 90*, 729–752; Pascale, R. T., & Maguire, M. (1980). Comparison of selected work factors in Japan and the United States. *Human Relations, 33*, 433–455.

73. Kunungo, R., Wright, R. (1983). A cross-cultural comparative study of managerial job attitudes. *Journal of International Business Studies, 14*, 115–129.

74. Hui, C. H., Yee, C., & Eastman, K. L. (1995). The relationaship between individualism-collectivism and job satisfaction. *Applied Psychology: An International Review, 44*, 276–282.

75. Randall, D. M. (1993). Cross-cultural research on organizational commitment: A review and application of Hofstede's value-survey module. *Journal of Business Research, 26*, 91–110.

76. Luthans, F., McCaul, J. S., & Dodd, N. G. (1985). Organizational commitment: A comparison of American, Japanese, and Korean employees. *Academy of Management Journal, 28*, 213–219.

77. Lincoln & Kalleberg, *Culture, control, and commitment*.

78. England, G. W., & Misumi, J. (1986). Work centrality in Japan and the United States. *Journal of Cross-Cultural Psychology, 17*, 399–416.

79. Gomez-Mejia, L. R. (1984). Effect of occupation on task-related, contextual, and job involvement orientation: A cross-cultural perspective. *Academy of Management Journal, 27*, 706–720.

80. Gomez-Mejia, Effect of occupation on task-related, contextual, and job involvement orientation.

Chapter 6

1. Dawson, C. (2001). What Japan's CEOs can learn from Bridgestone. *Business Week*, January 29, 50; Kunii, I., & Foust, D. (2000). "They just don't have a clue how to handle this." *Business Week*, September 18, 43; Zaun, T., Dvorak, P., Shirouzu, N., & Landers, P. (2000). Bridgestone boss has toughness, but is that what crisis demands? *The Wall Street Journal*, September 12, A1, A18.

2. Adair, C. (2000). Don't get into cultural hot water. *The Toronto Star*, August 9, G6.

3. Jandt, F. E. (2001). *Intercultural communication: An introduction*. Thousand Oaks, CA: Sage.

4. Tung, R. L. (1984). How to negotiate with the Japanese. *California Management Review, 26*, 62–77.

5. Adair, Don't get into cultural hot water.

6. ———. (1999). Chinese whispers. *The Economist,* January 30, 77–79.

7. Dulek, R. E., Fielden, J. S., & Hill, J. S. (1991). International communication: An executive primer. *Business Horizons, 34,* 20–25.

8. Fox, J. (2000). The triumph of English. *Fortune,* September 18, 209–212.

9. ———. (2001). English is still on the march. *The Economist,* February 24, 50–51; ———. (2001). You have ways of making us talk. *The Economist,* February 24, 50; Fox, The triumph of English.

10. Halpern, J. W. (1983). Business communication in China: A second perspective. *Journal of Business Communication, 20,* 43–55; Ling, C. (2001). Learning a new language. *The Wall Street Journal,* March 12, R18; Zong, B., & Hildebrandt, H. W. (1983). Business communication in the People's Republic of China. *Journal of Business Communication, 20,* 25–32.

11. ———. (2001). Tongue-tied. *The Economist,* April 7, 83.

12. Glain, S. (1994). Language barrier proves dangerous in Korea's skies. *The Wall Street Journal,* October 4, B1.

13. Fixman, C. S. (1990). The foreign language needs of U.S.-based corporations. *The Annals of the American Political and Social Science Association, 511,* 25–46.

14. Dulek, Fielden, & Hill, International communication: An executive primer.

15. ———. (1987). Viewpoint: Letters. *Advertising Age,* June 29, 20; Ricks, D. A. (1983). *Big business blunders: Mistakes in multinational marketing.* Homewood, IL: Dow Jones Irwin.

16. Clark, D. (1996). "Hey, #!@*% amigo, can you translate the word 'gaffe'?" *The Wall Street Journal,* July 6, B6.

17. Victor, D. A. (1992). *International business communication.* New York: Harper Collins.

18. Koide, F. (1978). Some observations on the Japanese language. In J. C. Condon & M. Saito (Eds.), *Intercultural encounters with Japan. Communication—contact and conflict,* 173–179. Tokyo, Japan: Simul Press; Weitz, J. R., Rothbaum, F. M., & Blackburn, T. C. (1984). Standing out and standing in: The psychology of control in America and Japan. *American Psychologist, 39,* 955–969.

19. Barnlund, D. C. (1989). Public and private self in communicating with Japan. *Business Horizons, 32,* 32–40; Tung, R. L. (1984). How to negotiate with the Japanese. *California Management Review, 26,* 62–77.

20. Barnlund, D. C. (1989). Public and private self in communicating with Japan. *Business Horizons, 32,* 32–40; Haneda, S., & Shima, H. (1982). Japanese communication behavior as reflected in letter writing. *Journal of Business Communication, 19,* 19–32.

21. Imahori, T. T., & Cupach, W. R. (1994). A cross-cultural comparison of the interpretation and management of face: American and Japanese responses to embarrassing predicaments. *International Journal of Intercultural Relations, 18,* 193–219; Sueda, K. & Wiseman, R. L. (1992). Embarrassment remediation in Japan and the United States. *International Journal of Intercultural Relations, 16,* 159–173.

22. Barnlund, D. C., & Yoshioka, M. (1990). Apologies: Japanese and American styles. *International Journal of Intercultural Relations, 14,* 193–206.

23. Tata, J. (2000). Toward a theoretical framework of intercultural account-giving and account evaluation. *The International Journal of Organizational Analysis, 8,* 155–178.

24. Dvorak, P. (2000). Japanese dairy pours on the apologies: Snow Brand puts humility first after big recalls. *The Wall Street Journal,* July 12, A21.

25. Barnlund, D. C., & Araki, S. (1985). Intercultural encounters: The management of compliments by Japanese and Americans. *Journal of Cross-Cultural Psychology, 16,* 9–26.

26. Almaney, A., & Alwan, A. (1982). *Communicating with Arabs.* Prospect Heights, IL: Waveland Press, cited in Nelson, G. L., El Bakary, W., & Al Batal, M. (1993). Egyptian and American compliments: A cross-cultural study. *International Journal of Intercultural Relations, 17,* 293–313.

27. Copeland, L., & Griggs, L. (1985). *Going International.* New York: Random House.

28. Copeland & Griggs, *Going International;* Victor, *International business communication.*

29. Gudykunst, W. B., Gao, G. E., Nishida, T., Bond, M. H., Leung, K., Wang, G., & Berraclough, R. A. (1989). A cross-cultural comparison of self-monitoring. *Communications Research Reports,* 7–14.

30. Hymowitz, C. (2000). Flooded with e-mail? Try screening, sorting, or maybe just phoning. *The Wall Street Journal,* September 26, B1.

31. Kilpatrick, R. H. (1984). International business communication practices. *Journal of Business Communication, 21,* 33–44.

32. Varner, I. I. (1988). A comparison of American and French business correspondence. *Journal of Business Communication, 25,* 55–65.

33. Haneda, S., & Shima, H. (1982). Japanese communication behavior as reflected in letter writing. *Journal of Business Communication, 19,* 19–32; Johnson, J. (1980). Business communication in Japan. *Journal of Business Communication, 17,* 65–70.

34. Kilpatrick, R. H. (1984). International business communication practices. *Journal of Business Communication, 21,* 33–44.

35. Sullivan, J. J. & Kameda, N. (1983). The concept of profit and Japanese-American business communication problems. *Journal of Business Communication, 19,* 33–39.

36. Rajan, M., & Graham, J. L. (1991). Nobody's grandfather was a merchant: Understanding the Soviet commercial negotiation process and style. *California Management Review,* Spring, 223–239.

37. Stewart, T. A. (2000). Knowledge worth $1.25 billion. *Fortune,* November 27, 302–303.

38. Knapp, M. (1980). *Essentials of nonverbal communication.* New York: Holt, Rinehart and Winston.

39. Barnlund, D. C. (1975). *Public and private self in Japan and the United States: Communication styles of two cultures.* Tokyo: Simul Press; Barnlund, Public and private self in communicating with Japan.

40. Collett, P. (1971). Training Englishmen in the nonverbal behavior of Arabs: An experiment on intercultural communication. *International Journal of Psychology, 6,* 209–215.

41. Lee, H. O., & Boster, F. J. (1992). Collectivism-individualism in perceptions of speech rate: A cross-cultural comparison. *Journal of Cross-Cultural Psychology, 23,* 377–388.

42. Peng, Y., Zebrowitz, L. A., & Lee, H. K. (1993). The impact of cultural background and cross-cultural experience on impressions of American and Korean male speakers. *Journal of Cross-Cultural Psychology, 24,* 203–220.

43. We thank an anonymous reviewer for these comments and insights.

44. Limaye, M. R., & Victor, D. A. (1991). Cross-cultural business communication research: State of the art and hypotheses for the 1990s. *Journal of Business Communication, 28,* 277–299.

45. Haneda & Shima, H. Japanese communication behavior as reflected in letter writing.

46. Kume, T. (1985). Managerial attitudes toward decision-making: North America and Japan. In W. B. Gudykunst, L. P. Steward,

S. Ting-Toomey (Eds.), *Communication, culture, and organizational processes*, 231–251. Beverly Hills, CA: Sage.

47. Elliot, S., Scott, M. D., Jensen, A. D., & McDonough, M. (1982). Perceptions of reticence: A cross-cultural investigation. In M. Burgoon (Ed.), *Communication Yearbook 5*. New Brunswick, NJ: Transaction Books.

48. Triandis & Albert, Cross-cultural perspectives.

49. Victor, *International business communication*.

50. Zaun, T. (2001). Bridgestone lets Firestone be Firestone. *The Wall Street Journal*, May 24, A14.

Chapter 7

1. Heydenfeldt, J. A. G. (2000). The influence of individualism/collectivism on Mexican and U.S. business negotiation. *International Journal of Intercultural Relations, 24,* 383–407.

2. Saner, R., Yiu, L., & Sondergaard, M. (2000). Business diplomacy management: A core competency for global managers. *Academy of Management Executive, 14,* 80–92.

3. Thomas, K. W., & Schmidt, W. H. (1976). A survey of managerial interests with respect to conflict. *Academy of Management Journal, 10,* 315–318.

4. Ricks, D. A. (1983). *Big business blunders: Mistakes in multinational marketing.* Homewood, IL: Dow Jones Irwin.

5. Thomas, K. W. (1976). Conflict and conflict management. In M. D. Dunnette (Ed.), *Handbook of industrial and organizational behavior,* 889–935. Chicago: Rand McNally.

6. Prunty, A. M., Klopf, D. W., & Ishii, S. (1990). Argumentativeness: Japanese and American tendencies to approach and avoid conflict. *Communication Research Reports, 7,* 75–79.

7. Klopf, D. W. (1991). Japanese communication practices: Recent comparative research. *Communication Quarterly, 39,* 130–143.

8. Ting-Toomey, S., Gao, G., Trubinsky, P., Yang, Z., Kim, H. S., Lin, S. L., & Nishida, T. (1991). Culture, face maintenance, and styles of handling interpersonal conflict: A study in five cultures. *International Journal of Conflict Management, 2,* 275–296; Tse, D. K., Francis, J., & Walls, J. (1994). Cultural differences in conducting intra- and inter-cultural negotiations: A Sino-Canadian comparison. *Journal of International Business Studies, Autumn,* 537–555; Trubisky, P., Ting-Toomey, S., & Lin, S. L. (1991). The influence of individualism-collectivism and self-monitoring on conflict styles. *International Journal of Intercultural Relations, 15,* 65–84.

9. Kirkbride, P. S., Tang, S. F. Y., Westwood, R. I. (1991). Chinese conflict preferences and negotiating behavior: Cultural and psychological influences. *Organization Studies, 12,* 365–386; Tang, S. F. Y., & Kirkbride, P. S. (1986). Developing conflict management skills in Hong Kong: An analysis of some cross-cultural implications. *Management Education and Development, 17,* 287–301.

10. Kozan, M. K. (1989). Cultural influences on styles of handling interpersonal conflicts: Comparisons among Jordanian, Turkish, and U.S. managers. *Human Relations, 42,* 787–799.

11. Leung, K., & Iwawaki, S. (1988). Cultural collectivism and distributive behavior. *Journal of Cross-Cultural Psychology, 19,* 35–49.

12. Victor, D. A. (1992). *International Business Communication.* New York: HarperCollins.

13. Tata, J. (2000). Toward a theoretical framework of intercultural account-giving and account evaluation. *International Journal of Organizational Analysis, 8,* 155–178.

14. Yang, N., Chen, C. C., Choi, J., & Zou, Y. (2000). Sources of work-family conflict: A Sino-U.S. comparison of the effects of work and family demands. *Academy of Management Journal, 43,* 113–124.

15. Pornpitakpan, C., & Giba, S. (1999). The effects of cultural adaptation on business relationships: Americans selling to Japanese and Thais. *Journal of International Business Studies, 30,* 317–338; Tata, J. (2000). Toward a theoretical framework of intercultural account-giving and account evaluation. *International Journal of Organizational Analysis, 8,* 155–178.

16. Weiss, S. E. (1996). International negotiations: Bricks, mortar, and prospects. In B. J. Punnett & O. Shenkar (Eds.), *Handbook for international management research,* 209–265. Cambridge, MA: Blackwell.

17. Stoever, W. A. (1981). *Renegotiations in international business transactions.* Lexington, MA: Lexington Books; Weiss, S. E. (1996). International negotiations: Bricks, mortar, and prospects. In Punnett & Shenkar, *Handbook for international management research,* 209–265.

18. Graham, J. L. (1983). Brazilian, Japanese, and American business negotiations. *Journal of International Business Studies, 14,* 47–62; Weiss, S. E. (1996). International negotiations: Bricks, mortar, and prospects. In Punnett & Shenkar, *Handbook for international management research,* 209–265.

19. Thomas, G. S. (2001). Asia, Canada comprise bulk of U.S. trade deficit. *Dayton Business Journal,* April 20, 16; Van Zandt, H. F. (1970). How to negotiate in Japan. *Harvard Business Review,* (November-December), 45–56.

20. Gulbro, R., & Herbig, P. (1996). Negotiating successfully in cross-cultural situations. *Industrial Marketing Management, 25,* 235–241.

21. Graham, J. L., & Herberger, R. A. (1983). Negotiators abroad—Don't shoot from the hip. *Harvard Business Review,* (July-August, 160–168.

22. Gulbro, & Herbig, Negotiating successfully in cross-cultural situations; Tung, R. L. (1984). How to negotiate with the Japanese. *California Management Review, 26,* 62–77; Van Zandt, H. F. (1970). How to negotiate in Japan. *Harvard Business Review,* (November-December), 45–56; Volkema, R. J. (1999). Ethicality in negotiations: An analysis of perceptual similarities and differences between Brazil and the United States. *Journal of Business Research, 45,* 59–67.

23. Tung, R. L. (1984). How to negotiate with the Japanese. *California Management Review, 26,* 62-77; Van Zandt, H. F. (1970). How to negotiate in Japan. *Harvard Business Review,* (November-December), 45–56.

24. Grindsted, A. (1994). The impact of cultural styles on negotiation: A case study of Spaniards and Danes. *IEEE Transactions on Professional Communication, 37,* 34–38. Pornpitakpan, C., & Giba, S. (1999). The effects of cultural adaptation on business relationships: Americans selling to Japanese and Thais. *Journal of International Business Studies, 30,* 317–338.

25. Gulbro & Herbig, Negotiating successfully in cross-cultural situations.

26. Graham, J. L., & Sano, Y. (1986). Across the negotiation table from the Japanese. *International Marketing Review, 3,* 58–71.

27. Graham, J. L., & Mintu-Wimsat, A. (1997). Culture's influence on business negotiations in four countries. *Group Decision and Negotiation, 6,* 483–502.

28. Herbig, P. A., & Kramer, H. E. (1992). Do's and don't of cross-cultural negotiations. *Industrial Marketing Management, 21,* 287–298.

29. Banthin, J., & Steizer, L. (1988/89). "Opening" China:

Negotiation strategies when East meets West. *Mid-Atlantic Journal of Business, 25,* 1–14; Tung, R. L. (1982). U.S.-China trade negotiations: Practices, procedures, and outcomes. *Journal of International Business Studies,* Fall, 25–37.

30. Campbell, N. C. G., Graham, J. L., Jolibert, A., & Meissner, H. G. (1988). Marketing negotiations in France, Germany, the United Kingdom, and the United States. *Journal of Marketing, 52,* 49–62; Tung, How to negotiate with the Japanese.

31. Campbell, N. C. G., Graham, J. L., Jolibert, A., & Meissner, H. G. (1988). Marketing negotiations in France, Germany, the United Kingdom, and the United States. *Journal of Marketing, 52,* 49–62; Graham, J. L., Mintu, A. T., & Rodgers, W. (1994). Explorations of negotiation behaviors in ten foreign cultures using a model developed in the United States. *Management Science, 40,* 72–95.

32. Graham, J. L. (1983). Brazilian, Japanese, and American business negotiations. *Journal of International Business Studies, 14,* 47–62; Tung, How to negotiate with the Japanese.

33. Graham, J. L. (1988). Negotiating with the Japanese: A guide to persuasive tactics (Part I & II). *East Asian Executive Reports, 10,* Nov. v. 6, 19–21; Dec. v. 8, 16–17.

34. Barnum, C., & Wolniansky, N. (1989). Why Americans fail at overseas negotiations. *Management Review,* October, 56–57.

35. Herbig & Kramer, Do's and don't of cross-cultural negotiations.

36. Volkema, R. J. (1999). Ethicality in negotiations: An analysis of perceptual similarities and differences between Brazil and the United States. *Journal of Business Research, 45,* 59–67.

37. Stewart, S., & Keown, C. F. (1989). Talking with the dragon: Negotiating in the People's Republic of China. *Columbia Journal of World Business, 24,* 68–72.

38. Weiss, J. (1988). The negotiating style of the People's Republic of China: The future of Hong Kong and Macao. *Journal of Social, Political and Economic Studies, 13,* 175–194.

39. Graham & Herberger, Negotiators abroad—Don't shoot from the hip.

40. Graham, J. L. (1985). The influence of culture on the process of business negotiations: An exploratory study. *Journal of International Business Studies, 16,* 81–96; Graham & Herberger, Negotiators abroad—Don't shoot from the hip.

41. Graham, Negotiating with the Japanese: A guide to persuasive tactics (Part I & II); Graham & Herberger, Negotiators abroad—Don't shoot from the hip.

42. Graham, Negotiating with the Japanese: A guide to persuasive tactics (Part I & II).

43. Oh, T. K. (1984). Selling to the Japanese. *Nation's Business,* October, 37–38.

44. Banthin, J., & Steizer, L. (1988/89). "Opening" China: Negotiation strategies when East meets West. *Mid-Atlantic Journal of Business, 25,* 1–14.

45. Pettibone, P. J. (1990). Negotiating a joint venture in the Soviet Union: How to protect your interests. *Journal of European Business, 2,* 5–12.

46. Adler, N. J., Graham, J. L., & Gehrke, T. S. (1987). Business negotiations in Canada, Mexico, and the United States. *Journal of Business Research, 15,* 411–429.

47. Heydenfeldt, The influence of individualism/collectivism on Mexican and U.S. business negotiation.

Chapter 8

1. Bainbridge, A. (2001). Jollibee reports 3.3% income drop. *Philippine Daily Inquirer,* February 17; ———. (2002). A busy bee in the hamburger hive. *The Economist,* March 2, 62; Filman, H. (1996). Happy meals for a McDonald's rival. *Business Week,* July 29, 77; Marozzi, J. (1997). Jollibee disappoints despite 12% climb. *Financial Times,* January 31, 26; Prasso, S. (1999). "Hamburgers, they appeal to any culture." *Business Week Online International Edition,* June 14; Visaya, M. G. (2000). Jollibee opens 5th branch in California. *Asian Journal Online,* July 10–13; www.jollibee.com; www.mcdonalds.com.

2. Phatak, A. V. (1995). *International dimensions of management* (4th Ed.). Cincinnati, OH: South-Western.

3. Ghemawat, P. (2001). Distance still matters: The hard reality of global expansion. *Harvard Business Review,* September, 137–147.

4. Byrne, J. A. (1996). Strategic Planning. *Business Week,* August 26, 46–52; Porter, M.E. (1998). Clusters and the new economics of competition. *Harvard Business Review,* November-December, 77–90.

5. Phatak, *International dimensions of management.*

6. Gary, L. (2001). Strategy as process. *Harvard Management Update,* July, 8; Griffin, R. W., & Pustay, M. W. (1996). *International business: A managerial perspective.* Reading, MA: Addison-Wesley; Porter, M. E. (1990). The competitive advantage of nations. *Harvard Business Review, 90,* 73–93.

7. Hamel, G. (2001). Innovation's new math. *Fortune.* July 9, 130–131.

8. Byrne, J. A. (1996). Strategic Planning. *Business Week,* August 26, 46–52; Brews, P. J., & Hunt, M. R. (1999). Learning to plan and planning to learn: Resolving the planning school/learning school debate. *Strategic Management Journal, 20,* 889–913.

9. ———. (2001). Economic size. *The Economist,* May 12, 110.

10. Mehta, S. N. (1994). Small companies look to cultivate foreign business. *The Wall Street Journal,* July 7, B2; Rose, R. L., & Quintanilla, C. (1996). More small U.S. firms take up exporting, with much success. *The Wall Street Journal,* December 20, A1, A11.

11. Smith, L. (1995). Does the world's biggest company have a future? *Fortune,* August 7, 124–126.

12. Porter, M. E. (1990). The competitive advantage of nations. *Harvard Business Review, 90,* 73–93.

13. Hill, C. W. L. (1994). *International business: Competing in the global marketplace.* Burr Ridge, IL: Irwin.

14. Porter, M. E. (1998). Competing across locations: Enhancing competitive advantage through a global strategy. *Harvard Business School Press,* Product #2026.

15. Porter, Competing across locations.

16. Lodge, G. C., & Bell, M. (1995). Is the United States competitive in the world economy? *Harvard Business School* (Publication 9-795-129). Boston, MA: Harvard Business School.

17. Porter, The competitive advantage of nations, 73–93.

18. See Grant, R. M. (1991). Porter's "competitive advantage of nations": An assessment. *Strategic Management Journal, 12,* 535–548; Luo, Y., & Park, S. H. (2001). Strategic alignment and performance of market-seeking MNCs in China. *Strategic Management Journal, 22,* 1411–155; Mueller, F. (1994). Societal effect, organizational effect and globalization. *Organization Studies, 15,* 407–428; Murtha, T. P., & Lenway, S. A. (1994). Country capabilities and the strategic state: How national political institutions affect multinational corporations' strategies. *Strategic Management Journal, 15,* 113–129.

19. Daniels, J. D., & Radebaugh, L. H. (2001). International business: Environments and operations (9th Ed.). Upper Saddle River, NJ: Prentice-Hall.

20. Li, P. P. (1993). How national context influences corporate strategy: A comparison of South Korea and Taiwan. In

S. B. Prasad & R. B. Peterson (Eds.), *Advances in international comparative management* (Vol. 8, pp. 55–78). Greenwich, CT: JAI Press.

21. Craig, C. S., & Douglas, S. P. (1996). Developing strategies for global markets: An evolutionary perspective. *Columbia Journal of World Business*, Spring, 70–81.

22. Ghoshal, S., & Bartlett, C. A. (1990). The multinational organization as an interorganizational network. *Academy of Management Review, 15,* 603–625.

23. Malnight, T. W. (1996). The transition from decentralized to network-based MNC structures: A evolutionary perspective. *Journal of International Business Studies, 27,* 43–65.

24. See Bartlett, C. A., & Ghoshal, S. (1989). *Managing across borders: The transnational solution.* Boston, MA: Harvard Business School Press; Hout, T., Porter, M. E., & Rudden, E. (1982). How global companies win out. *Harvard Business Review,* September-October, 9–108; Lovelock, C. H., & Yip, G. S. (1996). Developing global strategies for service businesses. *California Management Review, 38,* 64–85; Prahalad, C. K., & Doz, Y. L. (1987). *The multinational mission: Balancing local demands and global vision.* New York: The Free Press; Tomlinson, R. (2000). Can Nestle be the very best? *Fortune,* November 13, 353–360.

25. Prahalad, C. K., & Doz, Y. L. (1987). *The multinational mission: Balancing local demands and global vision.* New York: The Free Press; Wheelen, T. L., & Hunger, J. D. (1995). *Strategic management and business policy* (5th Ed.). Reading, MA: Addison-Wesley.

26. Morrison, A. J., Ricks, D. A., & Roth, K. (1991). Globalization versus regionalization: Which way for the multinational? *Organizational Dynamics, 19,* 17–29.

27. Schiller, Z., Burns, G., & Miller, K. L. (1996). Make it simple: That's P&G's new marketing mantra—and it's spreading. *Business Week,* September 9, 96–104.

28. Wheelen, T. L., & Hunger, J. D. (1995). *Strategic management and business policy* (5th Ed.). Reading, MA: Addison-Wesley.

29. Bartlett, C. A., & Ghoshal, S. (1989). *Managing across borders: The transnational solution.* Boston, MA: Harvard Business School Press.

30. Birkinshaw, J., Morrison, A., & Hulland, J. (1995). Structural and competitive determinants of a global integration strategy. *Strategic Management Journal, 16,* 637–655.

31. Morrison, A. J., Ricks, D. A., & Roth, K. (1991). Globalization versus regionalization: Which way for the multinational? *Organizational Dynamics, 19,* 17–29.

32. Birkinshaw, J., Morrison, A., & Hulland, J. (1995). Structural and competitive determinants of a global integration strategy. *Strategic Management Journal, 16,* 637–655.

33. Johansson, J. K., & Yip, G. S. (1994). Exploiting globalization potential: U.S. and Japanese strategies. *Strategic Management Journal, 15,* 579–601; Yip, G. S. (1995). *Total Global Strategy.* Englewood Cliffs, NJ: Prentice-Hall.

34. Mosakowski, E. (2000). Strategic colonialism in unfamiliar cultures. In P. C. Earley & H. Singh (Eds.), *Innovations in international and cross-cultural management,* 311–337. Thousand Oaks, CA: Sage Publications; Rosenstein, J., & Rasheed, A. (1993). National comparisons in strategy: A framework and review. In S. B. Prasad & R. B. Peterson (Eds.), *Advances in international comparative management,* vol. 8, 79–99. Greenwich, CT: JAI Press.

35. Haley, G. T., & Tan, C. T. (1999). East vs. West: Strategic marketing management meets the Asian networks. *Journal of Business & Industrial Marketing,* 14, 91–101; Jain, S. C., &

Tucker, L. R. (1995). The influence of culture on strategic constructs in the process of globalization: An empirical study of North American and Japanese Multinationals. *International Business Review,* 2, 19–37; Wacker, J. G., & Sprague, L. G. (1998). Forecasting accuracy: Comparing the relative effectiveness of practices between seven developed countries. *Journal of Operations Management,* 16, 271–290.

36. Horning, C. (1993). Cultural differences, trust and their relationships to business strategy and control. In S. B. Prasad & R. B. Peterson (Eds.), *Advances in International Comparative Management,* Vol. 8, 175–197. Greenwich, CT: JAI Press.

37. O'Grady, S., & Lane, H. W. (1996). The psychic distance paradox. *Journal of International Business Studies, 27,* 309–333.

38. Erramilli, M. K. (1996). Nationality and subsidiary ownership patterns in multinational companies. *Journal of International Business Studies, 27,* 225–248; Tse, D. K., Pan, Y., & Au, K. Y. (1997). How multinationals choose entry modes and form alliances: The China experience. *Journal of International Business Studies, 28,* 779–803.

39. Mehta, S. N. (1994). Small companies look to cultivate foreign business. *The Wall Street Journal,* July 7, B2; Rose, R. L., Quintanilla, C. (1996). More small U.S. firms take up exporting, with much success. *The Wall Street Journal,* December 11, A1, A11.

40. Baird, I. S., Lyles, M. A., & Orris, J. B. (1994). The choice of international strategies by small businesses. *Journal of Small Business Management, 32,* 48–59.

41. Mascarenhas, B. (1996). The founding of specialist firms in a global fragmenting industry. *Journal of International Business Studies, 27,* 27–42.

42. Yukl, G. (2002). *Leadership in organizations* (5th edition). Englewood Cliffs, NJ: Prentice Hall.

43. Atwater, L.E., & Atwater, D.C. (1994). Strategies for change and improvement. In B. M. Bass & B. J. Avolio (Eds.), *Improving organizational effectiveness through transformational leadership,* 146–172. Newbury Park, CA: Sage Publications.

44. Griffin & Pustay, *International business: A managerial perspective;* Phatak, *International dimensions of management.*

45. Jacob, R. (1994). The big rise. *Fortune,* May 30, pp. 74–90; Phatak, *International dimensions of management.*

46. Forster, J., & Gaylord, B. (2001). Can Kraft be a big cheese abroad? *Business Week,* June 4, 63–64.

47. Friedland, J. (1996). In this "great game," no holds are barred: U.S. power companies seek to dominate Latin gas markets. *The Wall Street Journal,* August 14, A10; Vogel, T. T. (1996). Foreign funds buoy Colombian leader. *The Wall Street Journal,* August 20, A6.

48. Kahn, J. (1996). China finds a promising market in Africa. *The Wall Street Journal,* July 19, A9.

49. Pearl, D. (1996). Saudis, of all people, find industry hobbled by a lag in electricity. *The Wall Street Journal,* August 20, A1, A8.

50. Sawyer, O. O. (1993). Environmental uncertainty and environmental scanning activities of Nigerian manufacturing executives: A comparative analysis. *Strategic Management Journal, 14,* 287–299.

51. Garland, J., Farmer, R. N., & Taylor, M. (1990). *International dimensions of business policy and strategy* (2nd Ed.). Boston, MA: PWS-Kent.

52. Phatak, *International Dimensions of Management.*

53. Ortega, B. (1994). Wal-Mart is slowed by problems of price and culture in Mexico. *The Wall Street Journal,* July 29, A1, A5.

54. Griffin, & Pustay, *International business: A managerial perspective;* Phatak, *International dimensions of management.*

55. Barney, J. B. (1995). Looking inside for competitive advantage. *Academy of Management Executive, 9,* 49–61.

56. Schlender, B. R. (1994). Matsushita shows how to go global. *Fortune,* July 11, 159–166.

57. Phatak, *International dimensions of management.*

58. Griffin & Pustay, *International business: A managerial perspective.*

59. Choi, A. (1995). For Mercedes, going global means being less German. *The Wall Street Journal,* April 27, B4; Taylor, A. (2000). Bumpy roads for global automakers. *Fortune,* December 18, 278–292.

60. Griffin & Pustay, *International business: A managerial perspective.*

61. Gupta, A. K., & Govindarajan, V. (2001). Converting global presence into global competitive advantage. *Academy of Management Executive, 15,* 45–56.

62. Burrows, P., Bernier, L., & Engardio, P. (1995). Texas Instruments' global chip payoff. *Business Week,* August 7, 64–66.

63. Phatak, *International dimensions of management.*

64. Naughton, K., & Borrus, A. (1996). America's no. 1 car exporter is . . . Japan? *Business Week,* February 26, 113; Taylor, A. (2001). Imports to Detroit: Eat our dust. *Fortune,* June 11, 150–154.

65. ———. (2001). Nokia succumbs. *The Economist,* June 16, 65; ———. (2000). A Finnish fable. *The Economist,* October 14, 83–85; Baker, S. (2001). Outsourcing alone won't save Nokia's rivals. *Business Week,* February 12, 38; Baker, S., Shinal, J., & Kunii, I. M. (2001). Is Nokia's star dimming? *Business Week,* January 22, 66–72; Capell, K., Echikson, W., & Elstrom, P. (2001). Surprise! Nokia doesn't walk on water. *Business Week,* June 25, 49; Edmondson, G., Elstrom, P., & Burrows, P. (1996). At Nokia, a comeback—and then some. *Business Week,* December 2, 106; Jacob, R. (1996). Nokia fumbles, but don't count it out. *Fortune,* February 19, 85–88; Moore, S. D. (1996). Finland's Nokia, in turnaround, posts 14% rise in pretax quarterly profit. *The Wall Street Journal,* November 15, A7A.

66. Yip, G. S. (1995). *Total global strategy.* Englewood Cliffs, NJ: Prentice-Hall.

67. Johansson, J. K., & Yip, G. S. (1994). Exploiting globalization potential: U.S. and Japanese strategies. *Strategic Management Journal, 15,* 579–601.

68. Yip, *Total global strategy.*

69. Snow, C. C., Snell, S. A., Davison, S. C., & Hambrick, D. C. (1996). Use transnational teams to globalize your company. *Organizational Dynamics, 24,* 50–67.

70. Bartmess, A., & Cerny, K. (1993). Building competitive advantage through a global network of capabilities. *California Management Review, 35,* 2–27.

71. Kim, W. C., & Mauborgne, R. A. (1991). Implementing global strategies: The role of procedural justice. *Strategic Management Journal, 12,* 125–143; Kim, W. C., & Mauborgne, R. A. (1993). Making global strategies work. *Sloan Management Review,* Spring, 11–25.

72. ———. (2002). A busy bee in the hamburger hive. *The Economist,* March 2, 62; Bainbridge, A. (2001). Jollibee reports 3.3% income drop. *Philippine Daily Inquirer,* February 17; Filman, H. (1996). Happy meals for a McDonald's rival. *Business Week,* July 29, 77; Marozzi, J. (1997). Jollibee disappoints despite 12% climb. *Financial Times,* January 31, 26; Prasso, S. (1999). 'Hamburgers, they appeal to any culture.' *Business Week Online International Edition,* June 14; Visaya, M. G. (2000). Jollibee opens 5th branch in California. *Asian Journal Online,* July 10–13; www.jollibee.com.ph; www.mcdonalds.com.

Chapter 9

1. ———. (2002). General Motors and Fiat: A duo of dances, *The Economist,* March 9, 63–64; ———. (2002). Incredible shrinking plants. *The Economist,* February 23, 71–73; ———. (2001). A survey of the near future: Will the corporation survive? *The Economist,* November 3, 14–18; ———. (2000). The global gambles of General Motors. *The Economist,* June 24, 67–70; Roberts, D., & Webb, A. (2001). China's carmakers: flattened by falling tariffs. *Business Week,* December 3, 52; Taylor, A. (2000). Bumpy roads for global automakers. *Fortune,* December 18, 278–292; White, G. L. (2001). GM finally nails down deal with Daewoo. *The Wall Street Journal,* September 21, A21.

2. Negandhi, A. (1987). *International management.* Boston, MA: Allyn & Bacon; Welch, L.S., & Luostarinen, R. (1988). Internationalization: Evolution of a concept. *Journal of General Management, 14,* 55–71.

3. Rohwer, J. (2000). GE digs into Asia. *Fortune,* October 2, 165–178.

4. Milliman, J., Von Glinow, M.A., & Nathan, M. (1991). Organizational life cycles and strategic international human resource management in multinational companies: Implications for congruence theory. *Academy of Management Journal, 16,* 318–339.

5. Black, J. S., Gregersen, H. B., & Mendenhall, M. E. (1992). *Global assignments: Successfully expatriating and repatriating international managers.* San Francisco: Jossey-Bass.

6. Landers, P. (2001). Penney blends two business cultures. *The Wall Street Journal,* April 5, A15, A17.

7. ———. (2001). Wal around the world. *The Economist,* December 8, 55–57; Ellison, S. (2001). Carrefour and Ahold find shoppers like to think local. *The Wall Street Journal,* August 31, A5; Zellner, W., Schmidt, K. A., Ihlwan, M., & Dawley, H. (2001). How well does Wal-Mart travel? *Business Week,* September 3, 82–84.

8. Rohwer, J. (2000). GE digs into Asia. *Fortune,* October 2, 165–178.

9. Tse, D. K., Pan, Y., & Au, K. Y. (1997). How MNCs choose entry modes and form alliances: The China experience. *Journal of International Business Studies, 28,* 779–803.

10. Briscoe, D. R. (1995). *International human resource management.* Englewood Cliffs, NJ: Prentice-Hall; Ball, J., Zaun, T., & Shirouzu, N. (2002). Daimler explores idea of "world engine." *The Wall Street Journal,* January 8, A3.

11. Dyer, J. H. (2000). Examining interfirm trust and relationships in a cross-national setting. In P. C. Earley & H. Singh (Eds.), *Innovations in international and cross-cultural management,* 215–244. Thousand Oaks, CA: Sage.

12. Bogner, W. C., Thomas, H., & McGee, J. (1996). A longitudinal study of the competitive positions and entry paths of European firms in the U.S. pharmaceutical market. *Strategic Management Journal, 17,* 85–107.

13. Burpitt, W. J., & Rondinelli, D. A. (2000). Small firms' motivations for exporting: To earn and learn? *Journal of Small Business Management, 38,* 1–18.

14. Hill, C. W. L. (1994). *International business: Competing in the global marketplace.* Burr Ridge, IL: Irwin.

15. Updike, E. H., & Vlasic, B. (1996). Will Neon be the little car that could? *Business Week,* June 10, 56.

16. ———. (2002). Steel: Rust never sleeps. *The Economist,* March 9, 61–62; Holmes, S., & Belton, C. (2001). Boeing: In search of a big bear hug. *Business Week,* November 12, 71.

17. Griffin, R. W., & Pustay, M. W. (1996). *International business: A*

managerial perspective. Reading, MA: Addison-Wesley.

18. Wong, M. (2000). Law's land mines trip up exporters. *Dayton Daily News,* September 17, 1F, 4F.

19. Barringer, B. R., Macy, G., & Wortman, M. S. (1996). Export performance: The role of corporate entrepreneurship and export planning. *Journal of International Management, 2,* 177–199; Dosoglu-Guner, B. (2001). Can organizational behavior explain the export intention of firms? The effects of organizational culture and ownership type. *International Business Review, 10,* 71–89.

20. Griffin & Pustay, *International business: A managerial perspective.*

21. Montgomery, C. (2001). This car company knows (and grows) beans. *Dayton Daily News,* December 9, 1F, 8F.

22. Hill, *International business: Competing in the global marketplace.*

23. Griffin, & Pustay, *International business: A managerial perspective.*

24. Hill, *International business: Competing in the global marketplace.*

25. Price, R. M. (1996). Technology and strategic advantage. *California Management Review, 38,* 38–55.

26. Updike, E. H., & Nakarmi, L. (1995). A moveable feast for Mitsubishi. *Business Week,* August 28, 50–51.

27. Engardio, P., & Roberts, D. (1996). Microsoft's long march. *Business Week,* June 24, 52–54.

28. Clifford, M. L., Roberts, D., Trinephi, M., & Kerwin, K. (1996). Where's that pot of gold? *Business Week,* February 3, 54–58; Naughton, K., Engardio, P., Kerwin, K., & Roberts, D. (1995). How GM got the inside track in China. *Business Week,* November 6, 56–57; Templeman, J., Woodruff, D., Roberts, D., & Engardio, P. (1995). How Mercedes trumped Chrysler in China. *Business Week,* July 31, 50–51.

29. Hill, *International business: Competing in the global marketplace.*

30. Griffin & Pustay, *International business: A managerial perspective.*

31. Frank, R. (2000). Big Boy's adventures in Thailand. *The Wall Street Journal,* April 12, B1, B4.

32. Jordan, M. (2000). McDonald's strikes sparks with fast growth in Brazil. *The Wall Street Journal,* October 4, A23.

33. Hill, *International business: Competing in the global marketplace.*

34. Deogun, N. (1997). PepsiCo draws new battle plan to fight Coke. *The Wall Street Journal,* January 27, B1, B10; Frank, R. (1996). PepsiCo's critics worry the glass is still half empty. *The Wall Street Journal,* September 30, B10; Tannenbaum, J. A. (1996). Franchisees see opportunity in PepsiCo restructuring. *The Wall Street Journal,* October 15, B2.

35. Griffin & Pustay, *International business: A managerial perspective.*

36. Solis, D., & Friedland, J. (1995). A tale of two countries. *The Wall Street Journal,* October 2, R19, R23.

37. Matthews, R. G. (2000). U.S. Steel's plunge into Slovakia reflects urgent need to grow. *The Wall Street Journal,* October 12, A1, A10.

38. Hill, *International business: Competing in the global marketplace.*

39. ———. (2001). Red tape and blue sparks. *The Economist,* June 2, 9–10; ———. (2001). India's economy: Unlocking the potential. *The Economist,* June 2, 13; Kumar, S., & Thacker-Kumar, L. (1996). Investing in India: Strategies for tackling bureaucratic hurdles. *Business Horizons, 39,* 10–16.

40. ———. (2001). The amazing disintegrating firm. *The Economist,* December 8, 61–62; ———. (2001). Red tape and blue sparks. *The Economist,* June 2, 9–10; Ewing, T. (1996). Enron resumes building Dabhol plant in India, finishes a phase of financing. *The Wall Street Journal,* December 11, A4; Kripalani, M., & McWilliams, G. (1996). Enron's ordeal may not be over. *Business Week,* June 10, 59; Kripalani, M. (2001). Enron switches signals in India. *Business Week,* January 8, 58.

41. Yip, G. S. (1995). *Total global strategy.* Englewood Cliffs, NJ: Prentice-Hall.

42. Lublin, J. S. (1995). Too much, too fast. *The Wall Street Journal,* September 26, R8, R10.

43. Bannon, L., & Pereira, J. (1996). No. 1 toy maker Mattel agrees to buy no. 3 Tyco in $755 million stock deal. *The Wall Street Journal,* November 19, A3, A6.

44. ———. (2001). Red tape and blue sparks. *The Economist,* June 2, 9–10; Wonacott, P. (2001). China's privatization efforts breed new set of problems. *The Wall Street Journal,* November 1, A15.

45. Hill, *International business: Competing in the global marketplace.*

46. Schweiger, D. M., Csiszar, E. N., & Napier, N. K. (1993). Implementing international mergers and acquisitions. *Human Resource Planning, 16,* 53–70.

47. Calori, R., Lubatkin, M., & Very, P. (1994). Control mechanisms in cross-border acquisitions: An international comparison. *Organizational Studies, 15,* 361–379; Olie, R. (1994). Shades of culture and institutions in international mergers. *Organizational Studies, 15,* 381–405.

48. Matthews, R. G. (2000). U.S. Steel's plunge into Slovakia reflects urgent need to grow. *The Wall Street Journal,* October 12, A1, A10.

49. Allen, M. (1995). What is privatization anyway? *The Wall Street Journal,* October 2, R4; Barkema, H. G., Bell, J. H. J., & Pennings, J. M. (1996). Foreign entry, cultural barriers, and learning. *Strategic Management Journal, 17,* 151–166; Filatotchev, I., Hoskisson, R. E., Buck, T., & Wright, M. (1996). Corporate restructuring in Russian privatizations: Implications for U.S. investors. *California Management Review, 38,* 87–105; Ramamurti, R. (2000). A multilevel model of privatization in emerging economies. *Academy of Management Journal, 25,* 525–550; Pope, K. (1996). A steelmaker built up by buying cheap mills finally meets its match. *The Wall Street Journal,* May 2, A1, A6; www.ispat.com.

50. Steinmetz, G., & Parker-Pope, T. (1996). All over the map: At a time when companies are scrambling to go global, Nestle has long been there. *The Wall Street Journal,* September 26, R4, R6.

51. Clifford, M. L., Harris, N., Roberts, D., & Kripalani, M. (1997). Coke pours into Asia. *Business Week,* October 28, 72–80.

52. Chilton, K. (1995). How American manufacturers are facing the global marketplace. *Business Horizons, 38,* 10–19.

53. Baker, S. (2001). Why Europe keeps gobbling up U.S. companies. *Business Week,* June 18, 56.

54. Garten, J. E. (2001). The wrong time for companies to beat a global retreat. *Business Week,* December 17, 22.

55. Ghemawat, P., & Ghadar, F. (2000). The dubious logic of global megamergers. *Harvard Business Review, 78,* 64–72.

56. Griffin & Pustay, *International business: A managerial perspective.*

57. Blodgett, L. L. (1991). Partner contributions as predictors of equity share in joint ventures. *Journal of International Business Studies, 22,* 63–73.

58. Ghemawat, P., & Ghadar, F. (2000). The dubious logic of global megamergers. *Harvard Business Review, 78,* 64–72; Rose, R. L. (1996). For Whirlpool, Asia is the new frontier. *The Wall Street Journal,* April 25, B1, B4.

59. Phatak, A. V. (1997). *International management: Concepts and cases.* Cincinnati, OH: South-Western.

60. Hill, *International business: Competing in the global marketplace.*

61. Ingrassia, L., Naj, A. K., & Rosett, C. (1995). Overseas, Otis and its parent get in on the ground floor. *The Wall Street Journal,* April 21, A6.

62. Henderson, A. B. (1996). Chrysler and BMW team up to build small engine plant in South America. *The Wall Street Journal,* October 2, A4.

63. Phatak, I*nternational management: Concepts and cases.*

64. Afriyie, K. (1988). Factor choice characteristics and industrial

impact of joint ventures: Lessons from a developing economy. *Columbia Journal of World Business, 23,* 51–62.

65. Geringer, J. M. (1991). Strategic determinants of partner selection criteria in international joint ventures. *Journal of International Business Studies, 22,* 41–62.

66. Weiss, S. E. (1987). Creating the GM-Toyota joint venture: A case in complex negotiations. *Columbia Journal of World Business, 22,* 23–38; Yan, A., & Gray, B. (1994). Bargaining power, management control, and performance in United States-China joint ventures: A comparative case study. *Academy of Management Journal, 37,* 1478–1517.

67. Griffin & Pustay, *International business: A managerial perspective;* Hill, *International business: Competing in the global marketplace.*

68. Phatak, *International management: Concepts and cases.*

69. Newman, W. H. (1992). Launching a viable joint venture. *California Management Review, 35,* 68–80; Osland, G. E., & Cavusgil, S. T. (1996). Performance issues in U.S.-China joint ventures. *California Management Review, 38,* 106–130.

70. Blumenthal, J. (1995). Relationships between organizational control mechanisms and joint-venture success. In *Advances in global high-technology management,* vol. 5, part B, 115–134. Greenwich, CT: JAI Press.

71. ———. (2001). Halfway down a long road. *The Economist,* August 18, 51–53; ———. (2001). Just good friends. *The Economist,* August 18, 53.

72. ———. (2001). Just good friends. *The Economist,* August 18, 53; Gillespie, K., & Teegen, H. J. (1995). Market liberalization and international alliance formation: The Mexican paradigm. *Columbia Journal of World Business, 30,* 59–69; Serapio, M. G., & Cascio, W. F. (1996). End-games in international alliances. *Academy of Management Executive, 10,* 62–73.

73. Hamel, G. (1991). Competition for competence and inter-partner learning within international strategic alliances. *Strategic Management Journal, 12,* 83–103.

74. Kahn, J. (1996). McDonnell Douglas' high hopes for China never really soared. *The Wall Street Journal,* May 22, A1, A10.

75. Baker, S. (1996). The odd couple at Heinz. *Business Week,* November 4, 176–178.

76. Bremner, B., Schiller, Z., Smart, T., & Holstein, W. J. (1996). Keiretsu connections: The bonds between the U.S. and Japan's industry groups. *Business Week,* July 22, 52–54.

77. ———. (2002). Incredible shrinking plants. *The Economist,* February 23, 71–73; ———. (2001). A survey of the near future: Will the corporation survive? *The Economist,* November 3, 14–18; ———. (2001). Downhill racers. *The Economist,* March 31, 60; ———. (2000). The global gambles of General Motors. *The Economist,* June 24, 67–70; Kerwin, K., and Welch, D. (2002), Attack of the killer crossovers. *Business Week,* January 28, 98–100. Ihlwan, M., Armstrong, L., & Kerwin, K. (2001). Hyundai gets hot. *Business Week,* December 17, 84–86; Taylor, A. (2000). Bumpy roads for global automakers. *Fortune,* December 18, 278–292.

Chapter 10

1. This box is based on a number of articles about Exide Corporation. Chief among these was Lublin, J. S. (2001). Place vs. product: It's tough to choose a management model. *The Wall Street Journal,* June 27, A1, A4. Also referred to were Einhorn, C. (1999). Costly deal. *Barron's,* June 7, 14; ———. (1999). The car guy. *Across the Board, 36,* Feb., 29–34; Vasilash, G. S. (2000).

Lutz's laws. *Automotive Manufacturing & Production,* Jan., 34–35.

2. Gomes-Casseres, B. (1993). *Managing international alliances.* Publication No. 793-133. Boston, MA: Harvard Business School Publishing.

3. Kahn, J. (1996). McDonnell Douglas' high hopes for China never really soared. *The Wall Street Journal,* May 22, A1, A10. Reinhardt, A., Browder, S., & Engardio, P. (1996). Booming Boeing. *Business Week,* September 30, 118–125; Reinhardt, A., Browder, S., & Stodghill, R. (1996). Three huge hours in Seattle. *Business Week,* December 30, 39–39.

4. Serapio, M. G., & Cascio, W. F. (1996). End-games in international alliances. *Academy of Management Executive, 10,* 62–73.

5. Hill, C. W. L., Hwang, P., & Kim, W. C. (1990). An eclectic theory of the choice of international entry mode. *Strategic Management Journal, 11,* 117–128; Phatak, A. V. (1997). *International management: Concepts and cases.* Cincinnati, OH: South-Western.

6. Hill, C. W. L. (1994). *International business: Competing in the global marketplace.* Burr Ridge, IL: Irwin.

7. Erramilli, M. K. (1991). The experience factor in foreign market entry behavior in service firms. *Journal of International Business Studies, 22,* 479–501.

8. Phatak, *International management: Concepts and cases.*

9. Roth, K., & Ricks, D. A. (1994). Goal configuration in a global industry context. *Strategic Management Journal, 15,* 103–120.

10. Pan, Y. (1996). Influences on foreign equity ownership level in joint ventures in China. *Journal of International Business Studies, 27,* 1–26.

11. Kogut, B., & Singh, H. (1988). The effect of national culture on the choice of entry mode. *Journal of International Business Studies, 19,* 411–432.

12. Shane, S. (1994). The effect of national culture on the choice between licensing and direct foreign investment. *Strategic Management Journal, 15,* 627–642.

13. Barkema, H. G., Bell, J. H. J., & Pennings, J. M. (1996). Foreign entry, cultural barriers, and learning. *Strategic Management Journal, 17,* 151–166.

14. Contractor, F. J., & Kundu, S. K. (1996). Choosing the best organizational mode: The quest for optimal ownership and control in foreign operations. Paper presented at the meeting of the Academy of Management, Cincinnati, OH.

15. Ghoshal, S., & Nohria, N. (1993). Horses for courses: Organizational forms for multinational corporations. *Sloan Management Review,* Winter, 23–34.

16. Griffin, R. W., & Pustay, M. W. (1996). *International business: A managerial perspective.* Reading, MA: Addison-Wesley; Phatak, A. V. (1995). *International dimensions of management.* (4th Ed.). Cincinnati, OH: South-Western.

17. Hill, *International business: Competing in the global marketplace;* Phatak, *International dimensions of management.*

18. Hill, *International business: Competing in the global marketplace.*

19. Daniels, J. D., & Radebaugh, L. H. (2001). *International business: Environments and operations.* Upper Saddle River, NJ.: Prentice-Hall.

20. Phatak, *International management: Concepts and cases.*

21. Yip, G. S. (1995). *Total global strategy.* Englewood Cliffs, NJ: Prentice-Hall.

22. Hill, *International business: Competing in the global marketplace.*; Phatak, *International dimensions of management.*

23. Moore, What's new and better about ExxonMobil?

24. Lublin, J. S. (2001). Place vs. product: It's tough to choose a management model. *The Wall Street Journal,* June 27, A1,A4.

25. Griffin & Pustay, *International business: A managerial perspective.*; Hill, *International business: Competing in the global marketplace.*

26. Lublin, Place vs. product: It's tough to choose a management model.

27. Hunt, J. W. (1998). Is matrix management a recipe for chaos? *Financial Times,* January 12, 10.

28. Hunt, Is matrix management a recipe for chaos?

29. Latour, A. (1998). Ericsson unveils big overhaul of its structure. *The Wall Street Journal,* October 1, B9; Lelvor, G., & Burt, T. (1998). Ericsson's behavior wins it no friends in the markets. *Financial Times,* October 9, 20.

30. ———. (2001). A great leap, preferably forward. *The Economist,* January 20, 65.

31. Guyon, J. (1996). ABB fuses units with one set of values: Managers get global strategies to work locally. *The Wall Street Journal,* October 2, A9; Reed, S., & Sains, A. (1996). Percy Barnevik passes the baton. *Business Week,* October 28, 66.

32. Woodruff, D. (2001). New ABB Chairman off to running start. *The Wall Street Journal,* January 12, A16; ———. (2001). A great leap, preferably forward.

33. Rhoads, C. (1998). Deutche Bank to give BT no autonomy. *The Wall Street Journal,* December 1, A3, A4, cited in Sanyal, R. N. (2001). *International management: A strategic perspective.* Upper Saddle River, NJ: Prentice-Hall.

34. Ghoshal, S., & Nohria, N. (1993). Horses for courses: Organizational forms for multinational corporations. *Sloan Management Review,* Winter, 23–26.

35. Hill, *International business: Competing in the global marketplace.*

36. Ghoshal, S., Korine, H., & Szulanski, G. (1994). Interunit communication in multinational corporations. *Management Science, 40,* 96–110.

37. Porter, M. E. (2001). Strategy and the internet. *Harvard Business Review,* March, 62–78.

38. Farrell, C. (1992). Industrial policy. *Business Week,* April, 6, 70–75.

39. ———. (2001). Total expenditure on R&D, 1999. From www.imd.ch/wcy/criteria/4301.cfm

40. Kelly, K., Port, O., Treece, J., DeGeorge, G., & Schiller, Z. (1992). Learning from Japan. *Business Week,* January 27, 52–60.

41. Cited on Acer Worldwide, Inc. website: http://global.acer.com/about/news

42. ———. (2001). The internet, untethered: A survey of the mobile internet. *The Economist,* October 13, 7; ———. (2000). Reality bytes. *The Wall Street Journal,* November 13, B14.

43. ———. (2000). A survey of government and the internet: Net neighbourhoods. *The Economist,* June 24, 4.

44. McCartney, S., & Friedland, J. (1997). Computer sales sizzle as developing nations try to shrink PC gap. *The Wall Street Journal,* June 29, A1,A4.

45. Peters, T. J., & Waterman, R. H. (1982). *In search of excellence.* New York: Harper & Row.

46. Mansfield, E. (1981). How economists see R&D. *Harvard Business Review,* Nov.–Dec., 98–106.

47. Glain, S. (1996). Little U.S. firm takes on Japanese giant: Yamaha accused of "patent flooding" to gain advantage. *The Wall Street Journal,* June 5, A10.

Chapter 11

1. Cooley, M. (1997). HR in Russia: Training for long-term success. *HR Magazine,* December, 98–106; Welsh, D. H. B., Luthans, F., & Sommer, S. M. (1993). Managing Russian factory workers: The impact of U.S.-based behavioral and participative techniques. *Academy of Management Journal, 36,* 58–79.

2. Communal, C., & Senior, B. (1999). National culture and management: Messages conveyed by British, French, and German advertisements of managerial appointments. *Leadership and Organizational Development Journal, 20,* 26–35.

3. Granato, J., Inglehart, R., & Leblang, D. (1996). The effect of cultural values on economic development: Theory, hypotheses, and some empirical tests. *American Journal of Political Science, 40,* 607–631.

4. Rodrigues, C. (1990). The situation and national culture as contingencies for leadership behavior: Two conceptual models. In B. Prasad (Ed.), *Advances in international comparative management, 5,* 51–68. Greenwich, CT: JAI Press.

5. Bass, B. M. (1990) *Stogdill's handbook of leadership: A survey of theory and research.* New York: Free Press.

6. Hofstede, G. (1993). Cultural constraints in management theories. *Academy of Management Executive, 7,* 81–94.

7. Lenartowicz, T. & Roth, K. (2001). Does subculture within a country matter? A cross-cultural study of motivational domains and business performance in Brazil. *Journal of International Business Studies, 32,* 305–325; Perlaki, I. (1994). Organizational development in Eastern Europe: Learning to build culture-specific OD theories. *Journal of Applied Behavioral Science, 30,* 297–312.

8. Hofstede, G. (1996). An American in Paris: The influence of nationality on organization theories. *Organizational Studies, 17,* 525–537.

9. Maslow, A. H. (1970). *Motivation and personality* (2nd Ed.). New York: Harper & Row.

10. Greenberg, J., & Baron, R. A. (2001). *Behavior in Organizations* (7th Ed.). Englewood Cliffs, NJ: Prentice-Hall.

11. Bhagat, R.S., & McQuaid, S.J. (1982). Role of subjective culture in organizations: A review and directions for future research. *Journal of Applied Psychology, 67,* 653–685.

12. Shenkar, O., & Von Glinow, M. A. (1994). Paradoxes of organizational theory and research: Using the case of China to illustrate national contingency. *Management Science, 40,* 56–71.

13. Sagie, A., Elizur, D., & Yamauchi, H. (1996). The strength and structure of achievement motivation: A cross-cultural comparison. *Journal of Organizational Behavior, 17,* 431–444.

14. Borg, I., & Braun, M. (1996). Work values in East and West Germany: Different weights, but identical structures. *Journal of Organizational Behavior, 17,* 541–555; Frese, M., Kring, W., Soose, A., & Zempel, J. (1996). Personal initiative at work: Differences between East and West Germany. *Academy of Management Journal, 39,* 37–63.

15. Adler, N. J. (2002). *International dimensions of organizational behavior* (4th Ed.). Cincinnati, OH: South-Western; Ronen, S. & Shenkar, O. (1985). Clustering countries on attitudinal dimensions: A review and synthesis. *Academy of Management Review, 10,* 435–454.

16. Hofstede, G. (1984). *Culture's consequences.* Newbury Park, CA: Sage.

17. Herzberg, F. (1966). *Work and the nature of man.* Cleveland, OH: World.

18. Machungwa, P. D., & Schmitt, N. (1983). Work motivation in a developing country. *Journal of Applied Psychology, 68,* 31–42.

19. Kanungo, R. N., & Wright, R. W. (1983). A cross-cultural comparative study of managerial job attitudes. *Journal of International Business Studies, 14,* 115–129.

20. Hofstede, G. (1984). *Culture's consequences.* Newbury Park, CA: Sage; Hofstede, G. (1993). Cultural constraints in management theories. *Academy of Management Executive, 7,* 81–94.

21. Rehder, R. R. (1992). Building cars as if people mattered: The Japanese lean system vs. Volvo's Uddevalla system. *Columbia Journal of World Business, 27,* 56–70.

22. Mendonca, M., & Kanungo, R. N. (1994). Motivation through participative management. In R. N. Kanungo & M. Mendonca (Eds.), *Work motivation: Models for developing countries,* 184–212. Thousand Oaks, CA: Sage; Robert, C., Probst, T. M., Martocchio, J. J., Drasgow, F., & Lawler, J. J. (2000). Empowerment and continuous improvement in the United States, Mexico, Poland, and India: Predicting fit on the basis of the dimensions of power distance and individualism. *Journal of Applied Psychology, 85,* 643–658.

23. Schaubroeck, J., Lam, S. S. K., & Xie, J. L. (2000). Collective efficacy versus self-efficacy in coping responses to stressors and control: A cross-cultural study. *Journal of Applied Psychology, 85,* 512–525.

24. Mendonca, M., & Kanungo, R. N. (1994). Motivation through effective reward management in developing countries. In Kanungo & Mendonca, *Work motivation: Models for developing countries,* 49–83.

25. ———. (2002). A survey of management: The return of von Clausewitz. *The Economist,* March 9, 18–20; Boyle, M. (2001). Nothing is rotten in Denmark. *Fortune,* February 19, 242.

26. Banerjee, N. (1995). For Mary Kay sales reps in Russia, hottest shade is the color of money. *The Wall Street Journal,* August 30, A8.

27. Adams, J. S. (1965). Inequity in social exchange. In L. Berkowitz (Ed.), *Advances in experimental social psychology,* vol. 2, 267–299. New York: Academic Press.

28. McFarlin, D. B., & Frone, M. R. (1990). Examining a two-tier wage structure in a non-union firm. *Industrial Relations, 29,* 145–157; Sweeney, P. D., & McFarlin, D. B. (2002). *Organizational behavior: Solutions for management.* Burr Ridge, IL: Irwin/McGraw-Hill.

29. Hofstede, *Culture's consequences.*; Hofstede, Cultural constraints in management theories.

30. Bond, M. H. (1991). *Beyond the Chinese face.* Hong Kong: Oxford University Press; Shenkar, O., & Von Glinow, M. A. (1994). Paradoxes of organizational theory and research: Using the case of China to illustrate national contingency. *Management Science, 40,* 56–71.

31. Bond, M. H., Leung, K., & Wan, K. C. (1982). How does cultural collectivism operate? The impact of task and maintenance contribution on reward distribution. *Journal of Cross-Cultural Psychology, 13,* 186–200.

32. Kim, K. L., Park, H. J., & Suzuki, N. (1990). Reward allocations in the U.S., Japan, and Korea: A comparison of individualistic and collectivistic cultures. *Academy of Management Journal, 33,* 188–198.

33. Wonacott, P. (2002). China's secret weapon: Smart, cheap labor for high-tech goods. *The Wall Street Journal,* March 14, A1, A6; Chen, C. C. (1995). New trends in rewards allocation preferences: A sino-U.S. comparison. *Academy of Management Journal, 38,* 408–428.

34. Skinner, B. F. (1969). *Contingencies of reinforcement.* New York: Appleton-Century-Crofts.

35. Sweeney & McFarlin, *Organizational behavior: Solutions for management.*

36. Mangaliso, M. P. (2001). Building competitive advantage from Ubuntu: Management lessons from South Africa. *The Academy of Management Executive, 15,* 23–33; McFarlin, D. B., Coster, E. A., & Mogale-Pretorius, C. (1999). Management development in South Africa: Moving toward an Africanized framework. *Journal of Management Development, 18,* 63–78.

37. Bailey, J. R., & Chen, C. C. (1997). Conceptions of self and performance-related feedback in the U.S., Japan, and China. *Journal of International Business Studies, 28,* 605–625.

38. Podsakoff, P. M., Dorfman, P. W., Howell, J. P., & Tudor, W. D. (1986). Leader reward and punishment behaviors: A preliminary test of a culture-free style of leadership effectiveness. In R. N. Farmer (Ed.), *Advances in international comparative management, 2,* 95–138.

39. Hofstede, *Culture's consequences.*

40. Mendonca & Kanungo, Motivation through effective reward management in developing countries.

41. Locke, E. A. & Latham, G.P. (1990). *A theory of goal-setting and task performance.* Englewood Cliffs, NJ: Prentice-Hall; Sweeney & McFarlin, *Organizational behavior: Solutions for management.*

42. Hofstede, *Culture's consequences.*

43. Hofstede, *Culture's consequences;* Johnson, M. (1993). Doing lee business. *Management Today,* February, 62–66.

44. Jaeger, A. M. (1990). The applicability of Western management techniques to developing countries: A cultural perspective. In A. M. Jaeger & R. N. Kanungo (Eds.), *Management in developing countries,* 131–145. London: Routledge.

45. Porter, L. P., & Lawler, E. E. (1968). *Managerial attitudes and performance.* Homewood, IL: Irwin; Vroom, V. H. (1964). *Work and motivation.* New York: Wiley.

46. Adler, *International dimensions of organizational behavior;* Shenkar, O., & Von Glinow, M. A. (1994). Paradoxes of organizational theory and research: Using the case of China to illustrate national contingency. *Management Science, 40,* 56–71.

47. Pennings, J. M. (1993). Executive reward systems: A cross-national comparison. *Journal of Management Studies, 30,* 261–279.

48. Steinmetz, G. (1995). German banks note the value of bonuses. *The Wall Street Journal,* May 9, A18; Stewart, M. (1996). German management: A challenge to Anglo-American managerial assumptions. *Business Horizons, 39,* 52–54; Walker, M. (2002). Deutsche Bank finds that it has to cut German roots to grow. *The Wall Street Journal,* February 14, A1, A10.

49. Ono, Y. (2001). A restaurant chain in Japan chops up the social contract. *The Wall Street Journal,* January 17, A1, A19.

50. Dubinsky, A. J., Kotabe, M., Lim, C. U., & Michaels, R. E. (1994). Differences in motivational perceptions among U.S., Japanese, and Korean sales personnel. *Journal of Business Research, 30,* 175–185; Ono, Y. (2002). Rethinking how Japanese should think, *The Wall Street Journal,* March 25, A12, A14.

51. Gomez-Mejia, L. & Welbourne, T. (1991). Compensation strategies in a global context. *Human Resource Planning, 14,* 29–41.

52. Dorfman, P. (1996). International and cross-cultural leadership. In B. J. Punnett & O. Shenkar (Eds.), *Handbook for international management research,* 267–350. Cambridge, MA: Blackwell; Yukl, G. (2002). *Leadership in organizations* (5th Ed.). Englewood Cliffs, NJ: Prentice-Hall.

53. Geppert, M. (1996). Paths of managerial learning in the east German context. *Organization Studies, 17,* 249–268; Kostera, M., Proppe, M., & Szatkowski, M. (1995). Staging the new romantic hero in the old cynical theatre: On managers, roles and change in Poland. *Journal of Organizational Behavior, 16,* 631–646.

54. Banai, M., & Teng, B. S. (1996). Comparing job characteristics, leadership style, and alienation in Russian public and private enterprises. *Journal of International Management, 2,* 201–224; Kets De Vries, M. F. R. (2000). A journey into the "Wild East:" Leadership style and organizational practices in Russia. *Organizational Dynamics, 28,* 67–81; Puffer, S. M. (1994).

Understanding the bear: A portrait of Russian business leaders. *Academy of Management Executive, 8,* 41–54; Puffer, S. M., McCarthy, D. J., & Zhuplev, A. V. (1996). Meeting of the mind-sets in a changing Russia. *Business Horizons, 40,* 52–59.

55. Yukl, G. (2002). *Leadership in organizations* (5th Ed.). Englewood Cliffs, NJ: Prentice-Hall.

56. Sinha, J. B. P. (1980). *The nuturant task leader: A model of effective executive.* New Delhi: Concept; Sinha, J.B.P. (1984). A model of effective leadership styles in India. *International Studies of Management and Organization, 14,* 86–98.

57. Dorfman, P. (1996). International and cross-cultural leadership; Misumi, J. (1985). *The behavioral science of leadership: An inter-disciplinary Japanese research program.* Ann Arbor, MI: University of Michigan; Peterson, M.P., Brannen, M.Y., & Smith, P.B. (1994). Japanese and United States leadership: Issues in current research. In S. B. Prasad (Ed.), *Advances in international comparative management,* vol. 9, 57–82. Greenwich, CT: JAI Press.

58. Sinha, J. B. P. (1984). A model of effective leadership styles in India. *International Studies of Management and Organization, 14,* 86–98.

59. Bhagat, R. S., Kedia, B. L., Crawford, S. E., & Kaplan, M. R. (1990). Cross-cultural issues in organizational psychology: Emergent trends and directions for research in the 1990s. In C. L. Cooper & I. T. Robertson (Eds.), *International Review of Industrial and Organizational Psychology, 5,* 59–99.

60. Ayman, R., & Chemers, M. M. (1983). Relationship of supervisory behavior ratings to work group effectiveness and subordinate satisfaction among Iranian managers. *Journal of Applied Psychology, 68,* 338–341.

61. Doktor, R. H. (1990). Asian and American CEOs: A comparative study. *Organizational Dynamics, 18,* 46–57.

62. Smith, P. B., Misumi, J., Tayeb, M., Peterson, M., & Bond, M. (1989). On the generality of leadership style measures across cultures. *Journal of Occupational Psychology, 62,* 97–109.

63. Tolich, M., Kenney, M., & Biggart, N. (1999). Managing the managers: Japanese strategies in the U.S.A. *Journal of Management Studies, 36,* 587–607.

64. Boston, W., & Kempe, F. (2001). Goal is game, set, and match. *The Wall Street Journal,* February 2, B1, B4.

65. Dorfman, P. W., & Howell, J. P. (1988). Dimensions of national culture and effective leadership patterns: Hofstede revisited. In R. N. Farmer & E. G. McGoun (Eds.) *Advances in International Comparative Management, 3,* 127–150.

66. Peterson, M.P., Brannen, M.Y., & Smith, P.B. (1994). Japanese and United States leadership: Issues in current research. In Prasad *Advances in international comparative management,* vol. 9, 57–82.

67. Morris, T., & Pavett, C. M. (1992). Management style and productivity in two cultures. *Journal of International Business Studies,* First Quarter, 169–179.

68. Bass, B. M. (1990). *Stogdill's handbook of leadership: A survey of theory and research.* New York: Free Press; Likert, R. (1967). *The human organization.* New York: McGraw-Hill.

69. Morris & Pavett, Management style and productivity in two cultures.

70. de Forest, M. E. (1994). Thinking of a plant in Mexico? *Academy of Management Executive, 8,* 33–40; .Gowan, M., Ibarreche, S., & Lackey, C. (1996). Doing the right things in Mexico. *Academy of Management Executive, 10,* 74–81; Stephens, G., & Geer, C. R. (1995). Doing business in Mexico: Understanding cultural differences. *Organizational Dynamics, 24,* 39–55.

71. Keys, J. B., Denton, L. T., & Miller, T. R. (1994). The Japanese management theory jungle revisited. *Journal of Management, 20,* 373–402; Maruyama, M. (1992). Changing dimensions in international business. *Academy of Management Executive, 6,* 88–96.

72. Black, J. S., & Porter, L. W. (1990). Managerial behaviors and job performance: A successful manager in Los Angeles may not succeed in Hong Kong. *Journal of International Business Studies,* First Quarter, 99–112.

73. Sweeney & McFarlin, *Organizational behavior: Solutions for management.*

74. Adler, *International dimensions of organizational behavior.*

75. Rahim, M. A., Kim, N.H., & Kim, J.S. (1994). Bases of leader power, subordinate compliance, and satisfaction with supervision: A cross-cultural study of managers in the U.S. and S. Korea. *International Journal of Organizational Analysis, 2,* 136–154.

76. Kipnis, D., & Schmidt, S.M. (1983). An influence perspective on bargaining within organizations. In M. Bazerman & R.J. Lewicki (Eds.), *Negotiating in organizations,* 303–319. Beverly Hills, CA: Sage.

77. Sweeney & McFarlin, *Organizational behavior: Solutions for management;* Yukl, G., & Tracey, J.B. (1992). Consequences of influence tactics used with subordinates, peers, and the boss. *Journal of Applied Psychology, 77,* 525–535.

78. Rao, A., & Hashimoto, K. (1997). Universal and culturally specific aspects of managerial influence: A study of Japanese managers. *Leadership Quarterly, 8,* 295–313.

79. Schmidt, S. M., & Yeh, R. (1992). The structure of leader influence: A cross-national comparison. *Journal of Cross-Cultural Psychology, 23,* 251–264.

80. See Yukl, *Leadership in organizations.*

81. Bass, B. M. (1990). *Stogdill's handbook of leadership: A survey of theory and research.* New York: Free Press; Likert, *The human organization;* Yukl, *Leadership in organizations.*

82. Bass, B. M., & Avolio, B. J. (1992). Developing transformational leadership: 1992 and beyond. *Journal of European Industrial Training, 14,* 21–27.

83. Koh, W. L., Steers, R. M., & Terborg, J.R. (1995). The effects of transformational leadership on teacher attitudes and student performance in Singapore. J*ournal of Organizational Behavior, 16,* 319–333; Popper, M., Landau, O., & Gluskinos, U. (1992). The Israeli Defence Forces: An example of transformational leadership. *Leadership and Organization Development Journal, 31,* 3–8; Singer, M.S. (1985). Transformational versus transactional leadership: A study of New Zealand company managers. *Psychological Reports, 57,* 143–146.

84. Rossant, J. (2002). The fast fall of France's celebrity CEOs, *Business Week,* April 1, 48; Yukl, *Leadership in organizations;* See also Chapter 9 discussion about Carlos Ghosn.

85. House, R. J. (1971). A path-goal theory of leader effectiveness. *Administrative Science Quarterly, 16,* 321–339; House, R. J., & Mitchell, T. R. (1974). Path-goal theory of leadership. *Contemporary Business, 3,* 81–98.

86. Dorfman, International and cross-cultural leadership.

87. Child, J. (1981). Culture, contingency, and capitalism in the cross national study of organizations. In L.L. Cummings & B.M. Staw (Eds.), *Research in organizational behavior,* vol. 3, 303–356. Greenwich, CT: JAI Press; Ronen, *Comparative and multinational management.*

88. Ayman, R., Kreicker, N. A., & Masztal, J. J. (1994). Defining global leadership in business environments. *Consulting Psychology Journal, 46,* 64–73; Tichy, N. M. (1993). Global development. In V. Pucik, N. M. Tichy, & C. K. Barnett (Eds.), *Globalizing management: Creating and leading the competitive*

organization, 206–226. New York: Wiley.

89. Laurent, A. (1983). The cultural diversity of Western conceptions of management. *International Studies of Management and Organization, 13,* 75–96.

90. McFarlin, D.B., Sweeney, P.D., & Cotton, J.C. (1992). Attitudes toward employee participation in decision-making: A comparison of European and American managers in a United States multinational company. *Human Resource Management, 31,* 363–383.

91. Adler, N.J., & Bartholomew, S. (1992). Managing globally competent people. *Academy of Management Executive, 6,* 52–65.

92. Spreitzer, G. M., McCall, M. W., & Mahoney, J. D. (1997). Early identification of international executive potential. *Journal of Applied Psychology, 82,* 6–29.

93. Tichy, N. M., Brimm, M. I., Charan, R., & Takeuchi, H. (1993). Leadership development as a lever for global transformation. In V. Pucik, N. M. Tichy, & C. K. Barnett (Eds.), *Globalizing management: Creating and leading the competitive organization,* 47–60. New York: Wiley.

94. Conner, J. (2000). Developing the global leaders of tomorrow. *Human Resource Management, 39,* 147–157.

95. Cooley, M. (1997). HR in Russia: Training for long-term success. *HR Magazine,* December, 98–106; Welsh, D. H. B., Luthans, F., & Sommer, S. M. (1993). Managing Russian factory workers: The impact of U.S.-based behavioral and participative techniques. *Academy of Management Journal, 36,* 58–79.

Chapter 12

1. Wonacott, P. (2002). China's secret weapon: Smart, cheap labor for high-tech goods. *The Wall Street Journal,* March 14, A1, A6. ———. (2001). Mobility in China: Off to the city. *The Economist,* September 1, 36; ———. (2000). Motorola China adds $1.9 billion investment. Press release, August 21, www.motorola.com/news_center; ———. (2000). Strategic focus: Motorola annual report, www.motorola.com/general/financial/annual_report/2000/focus/index.html; Gross, A., & Dyson, P. (1996). The iron rice bowl cracks. *HR Magazine,* July, 84–88; Hutzler, C., & Leggett, K. (2001). For China's premier Zhu, a critical home stretch. *The Wall Street Journal,* August 29, A6, A10; Nyaw, M.K. (1995). Human resource management in the People's Republic of China. In L.F. Moore & P.D. Jennings (Eds.), *Human resource management on the Pacific rim: Institutions, practices, and attitudes,* 187–216. Berlin: Walter de Gruyter; Schoenberger, K. (1996). Motorola bets big on China. *Fortune.* May 27, 116–124; Shenkar, O., & Nyaw, M. K. (1994). How to run a successful joint venture in China. In S. Stewart & N. Campbell (Eds.), *Advances in Chinese industrial studies: Joint ventures in the People's Republic of China,* 273–284. Greenwich, CT: JAI Press.

2. Miller, E. L., Beechler, S., Bhatt, B., & Nath, R. (1991). The relationship between the global strategic planning process and the human resource management function. In M. Mendenhall & G. Oddou (Eds.), *International human resource management,* 65–82. Boston, MA: PWS-Kent Publishing; Schuler, R.S., Fulkerson, J.R., & Dowling, P.J. (1991). Strategic performance measurement and management in multinational corporations. *Human Resource Management, 30,* 365–392; Truss, C., & Gratton, L. (1994). Strategic human resource management: A conceptual approach. *International Journal of Human Resource Management, 5,* 662–686.

3. Briscoe, D. R. (1995). *International human resource management.*

Englewood Cliffs, NJ: Prentice-Hall; Roberts, K., Kossek, E. E., & Ozeki, C. (1998). Managing the global workforce: Challenges and strategies. *The Academy of Management Executive, 12,* 93–106.

4. Carpenter, M. A., Sanders, W. G., & Gregersen, H. B. (2000). International assignment experience at the top can make a bottom-line difference. *Human Resource Management, 39,* 277–285; Taylor, S., Beechler, S., & Napier, N. (1996). Toward an integrative model of strategic international human resource management. *Academy of Management Review, 21,* 959–985.

5. Sparrow, P., Schuler, R. S., & Jackson, S. E. (1994). Convergence or divergence: Human resource practices and policies for competitive advantage worldwide. *International Journal of Human Resource Management, 5,* 267–299.

6. Odenwald, S. (1993). A guide for global training. *Training and Development,* July, 23–31.

7. Schuler, R. S., & Florkowski, G. W. (1996). International human resources management. In B. J. Punnett & O. Shenkar (Eds.), *Handbook for international management research,* 351–401. Cambridge, MA: Blackwell.

8. Fey, C. F., & Bjorkman, I. (2001). The effect of human resource management practices on MNC subsidiary performance in Russia. *Journal of International Business Studies, 32,* 59–75; Wright, P.M., McMahan, G. C., & McWilliams, A. (1994). Human resources and sustained competitive advantage: A resource-based perspective. *International Journal of Human Resource Management, 5,* 301–326.

9. Briscoe, *International human resource management.*

10. Roth, K., & O'Donnell, S. (1996). Foreign subsidiary compensation strategy: An agency theory perspective. *Academy of Management Journal, 39,* 678–703; Schuler, R. S., & Florkowski, G. W. (1996). International human resources management. In B. J. Punnett & O. Shenkar (Eds.), *Handbook for international management research,* 351–401. Cambridge, MA: Blackwell.

11. Beechler, S., & Yang, J. Z. (1994). The transfer of Japanese-style management to American subsidiaries: Contingencies, constraints, and competencies. *Journal of International Business Studies, 25,* 467–491.

12. Bartlett, C., & Ghoshal, S. (1989). *Managing across borders: The transnational solution.* Boston: Harvard Business School Press; Schuler, R. S., & Florkowski, G. W. (1996). International human resources management. In Punnett & Shenkar (Eds.), *Handbook for international management research,* 351–401; Schuler, R.S., Fulkerson, J.R., & Dowling, P.J. (1991). Strategic performance measurement and management in multinational corporations. *Human Resource Management, 30,* 365–392; Taylor, S., Beechler, S., & Napier, N. (1996). Toward an integrative model of strategic international human resource management. *Academy of Management Review, 21,* 959–985.

13. Bachler, C. J. (1996). Global inpats—don't let them surprise you. *Personnel Journal,* June, 54–64; Greengard, S. (1996). Gain the edge in the knowledge race. *Personnel Journal,* August, 52–56; West, L. A., & Bogumil, W. A. (2000). Foreign knowledge workers as a strategic staffing option. *The Academy of Management Executive, 14,* 71–84.

14. Cascio, W., & Bailey, E. E. (1995). International human resource management: The state of research and practice. In O. Shenkar (Ed.), *Global perspectives of human resource management,* 15–36. Englewood Cliffs, NJ: Prentice-Hall; Dowling, P. J. & Schuler, R. S. (1990). *International dimensions of human resource management.* Boston: PWS-Kent Publishing.

15. Carpenter, M. A., Sanders, W. G., & Gregersen, H. B. (2000). International assignment experience at the top can make a

bottom-line difference. *Human Resource Management, 39,* 277–285.

16. Downes, M., & Thomas, A. S. (2000). Managing overseas assignments to build organizational knowledge. *Human Resource Planning, 20,* 33–48.

17. Hsieh, T.Y., Lavoie, J., & Sarnek, R. A. P. (1999). Are you taking your expatriate talent seriously? *McKinsey Quarterly, 3,* 71–83.

18. Briscoe, *International human resource management;* Phatak, A. V. (1995). *International dimensions of management* (4th Ed.). Cincinnati, OH: South-Western.

19. Lublin, J. S. (1996). Is transfer to native land a passport to trouble? *The Wall Street Journal,* June 3, B1, B5; Millman, J. (2000). Exporting management savvy. *The Wall Street Journal,* October 24, B1, B18; Solomon, C. M. (1994). Global operations demand that HR rethink diversity. *Personnel Journal,* July, 40–50.

20. Phatak, *International dimensions of management.*

21. Latta, G. W. (1998). Global staffing: Are expatriates the only answer? *HR Focus,* July, S1, S2; Woodruff, D. (2000). Distractions make global manager a difficult role. *The Wall Street Journal,* November 21, B1, B18.

22. Adler, N. J. (2002). *International dimensions of organizational behavior* (4th Ed.). Cincinnati, OH: South-Western; Briscoe, *International human resource management;* Schneider, S. C. (1991). National vs. corporate culture: Implications for human resource management. In M. Mendenhall & G. Oddou (Eds.), *International human resource management,* 13–27. Boston: PWS-Kent.

23. Jeanquart-Barone, S., & Peluchette, J. V. (1999). Examining the impact of the cultural dimension of uncertainty avoidance on staffing decisions: A look at U.S. and German firms. *Cross-Cultural Management: An International Journal, 6,* 3–12; Peterson, R. B., Sargent, J., Napier, N. K., & Shim, W. S. (1996). Corporate expatriate HRM policies, internationalization, and performance in the world's largest MNCs. *Management International Review, 36,* 215–230.

24. Boyacigiller, N. (1990). The role of expatriates in the management of interdependence, complexity, and risk in multinational corporations. *Journal of International Business Studies, 21,* 357–381.

25. Dowling & Schuler, *International dimensions of human resource management.*

26. Roberts, K., Kossek, E. E., & Ozeki, C. (1998). Managing the global workforce: Challenges and strategies. *Academy of Management Executive, 12,* 93–106; Solomon, C. M. (1995). Navigating your search for global talent. *Personnel Journal,* May, 94–101; Stanek, M. B. (2000). The need for global managers: A business necessity. *Management Decision, 38,* 232–242.

27. ———. (2000). International assignments: Nasty, brutish and short. *The Economist,* December 16, 70–71; Greising, D. (1994). Globe trotter: If it's 5:30, this must be Tel Aviv. *Business Week,* October 17, 102; Kaufman, J. (1996). Tethered to Pittsburgh for years, an engineer thrives on trips to Asia. *The Wall Street Journal,* November 19, A1, A8; Miller, L. (1996). Pace of business travel abroad is beyond breakneck. *The Wall Street Journal,* May 31, B1, B6; Miller, L. (1996). Why business travel is such hard work. *The Wall Street Journal,* October 30, B1, B2; Silverman, R. E. (2001). Global crossings. *The Wall Street Journal,* January 16, B12; Weber, T. E. (2001). After terror attacks, companies rethink role of face-to-face. *The Wall Street Journal,* September 24, B1.

28. Inkson, K., Arthur, M. B., Pringle, J., & Barry, S. (1997). Expatriate assignment versus overseas experience: Contrasting models of international human resource development. *Journal of World Business, 32,* 351–366; Solomon, C. M. (1995). Navigating

your search for global talent. *Personnel Journal,* May, 94–101; Woodruff, D. (2000). Distractions make global manager a difficult role. *The Wall Street Journal,* November 21, B1, B18.

29. Odenwald, S. (1993). A guide for global training. *Training and Development,* July, 23–31.

30. Peterson, R. B., Napier, N. K., & Shul-Shim, W. (2000). Expatriate management: Comparison of MNCs across four parent countries. *Thunderbird International Business Review, 42,* 145–166.

31. Dimmick, T. G. (1995). Human resource management in a Korean subsidiary in New Jersey. In Shenkar, *Global perspectives of human resource management,* 63–70.

32. Cascio, W., & Bailey, E. E. (1995). International human resource management: The state of research and practice. In Shenkar, *Global perspectives of human resource management,* 15–36.

33. Love, K. G., Bishop, R. C., Heinisch, D. A., & Montei, M. S. (1994). Selection across two cultures: Adapting the selection of American assemblers to meet Japanese job performance demands. *Personnel Psychology, 47,* 837–846.

34. Earley, P. C. (1994). Self or group? Cultural effects of training on self-efficacy and performance. *Administrative Science Quarterly, 39,* 89–117.

35. Feltes, P., Robinson, R. K., & Fink, R. L. (1993). American female expatriates and the Civil Rights Act of 1991: Balancing legal and business interests. *Business Horizons,* March-April, 82–85.

36. Solomon, C. M. (1994). Global operations demand that HR rethink diversity. *Personnel Journal,* July, 40–50.

37. Feltes, P., Robinson, R. K., & Fink, R. L. (1993). American female expatriates and the Civil Rights Act of 1991: Balancing legal and business interests. *Business Horizons,* March-April, 82–85; Scheibal, W. (1995). When cultures clash: Applying Title VII abroad. *Business Horizons,* September-October, 4–8.

38. Erwee, R. (1994). South African women: Changing career patterns. In N. J. Adler & D. N. Izraeli (Eds.), *Competitive frontiers: Women managers in a global economy,* 325–342. Cambridge, MA: Blackwell Publishers; Hollway, W., & Mukurasi, L. (1994). Women managers in the Tanzanian civil service. In Adler & Izraeli, *Competitive frontiers: Women managers in a global economy,* 343–357.

39. Kishkovsky, S., & Williamson, E. (1997). Second-class comrades no more: Women stoke Russia's start-up boom. *The Wall Street Journal,* January 30, A12.

40. Dunung, S. P. (1995). *Doing business in Asia: The complete guide.* New York: Lexington Books.

41. Thomas, P. (1995). United States: Success at a huge personal cost. *The Wall Street Journal,* July 25, B1, B12.

42. Reitman, V. (1995). Japan: She is free, yet she's alone in the world. *The Wall Street Journal,* July 26, B1, B12.

43. Scheibal, W. (1995). When cultures clash: Applying Title VII abroad. *Business Horizons,* September-October, 4–8.

44. Linehan, M. & Walsh, J. S. (2000). Beyond the traditional linear view of international managerial careers: A new model of the senior female career in an international context. *Journal of European Industrial Training, 24,* 178–189.

45. Adler, N. J. (1994). In Adler & Izraeli, *Competitive frontiers: Women managers in a global economy,* 22–42; Adler, N. J. (2002). *International dimensions of organizational behavior* (4th Ed.). Cincinnati, OH: South-Western; Jordan, M. (2001). Have husband, will travel. *The Wall Street Journal,* February 13, B1, B12; Taylor, S., & Napier, N. (1996). Working in Japan: Lessons from women expatriates. *Sloan Management Review,* Spring, 76–84.

46. Linehan & Walsh, Beyond the traditional linear view of international managerial careers: A new model of the senior female

career in an international context.; Taylor, S., & Napier, N. (1996). Working in Japan: Lessons from women expatriates. *Sloan Management Review,* Spring, 76–84.

47. Tung, R. L. (1993). Managing cross-national and intranational diversity. *Human Resource Management, 32,* 461–477.

48. www.colgate.com; Solomon, C. M. (1994). Global operations demand that HR rethink diversity. *Personnel Journal,* July, 40–50.

49. Harvey, M. (1997). Dual-career expatriates: Expectations, adjustment and satisfaction with international relocation. *Journal of International Business Studies, 28,* 627–659; Hsieh, T.Y., Lavoie, J., & Sarnek, R. A. P. (1999). Are you taking your expatriate talent seriously? *McKinsey Quarterly, 3,* 71–83; Harzig, A. (2001). Of bears, bumble-bees, and spiders the role of expatriates in controlling foreign subsidiaries. *Journal of World Business, 36,* 366–379; Shaffer, M. A., & Harrison, D. A. (2001). Forgotten partners of international assignments: Development and test of a model of spouse adjustment. *Journal of Applied Psychology, 86,* 238–254.

50. Carpenter, M. A., Sanders, W. G., & Gregersen, H. B. (2000). International assignment experience at the top can make a bottom-line difference. *Human Resource Management, 39,* 277–285; Harris, N. (2002). Tools to protect traveling employees. *The Wall Street Journal,* March 11, R8.

51. Engen, J. R. (1995). Coming home. *Training.* March, 37–40; Hauser, J. (1999). Managing expatriates' careers. *HR Focus,* February, 11–12; Latta, G. W. (1999). Expatriate policy and practice: A ten-year comparison of trends. *Compensation and Benefits Review, 31,* 35–39; Poe, A. C. (2000). Destination everywhere. *HR Magazine,* October, 67–75; Wederspahn, G. M. (1992). Costing failures in expatriate human resources management. *Human Resource Planning, 15,* 27–35.

52. Black, J. S., Gregersen, H. B., & Mendenhall, M. E. (1992). *Global assignments: Successfully expatriating and repatriating international managers.* San Francisco, CA: Jossey-Bass; Carpenter, S. (2001). Battling the overseas blues. *Monitor on Psychology,* July/August, 48–49; Hsieh, T. Y., Lavoie, J., & Sarnek, R. A. P. (1999). Are you taking your expatriate talent seriously? *McKinsey Quarterly, 3,* 71–83; Klaus, K. J. (1995). How to establish an effective expatriate program: Best practices in international assignment administration. *Employment Relations Today,* Spring, 59–70.

53. Adler, *International dimensions of organizational behavior;* Black, Gregersen, & Mendenhall, *Global assignments: Successfully expatriating and repatriating international managers;* Briscoe, *International human resource management;* Carpenter, S. (2001). Battling the overseas blues. *Monitor on Psychology,* July/August, 48–49; Downes & Thomas, Managing overseas assignments to build organizational knowledge; Garonzik, R., Brockner, J., & Siegel, P. A. (2000). Identifying international assignees at risk for premature departure: The interactive effect of outcome favorability and procedural fairness. *Journal of Applied Psychology, 85,* 13–20; Phatak, *International dimensions of management.*

54. Schneider, S. C., & Asakawa, K. (1995). American and Japanese expatriate adjustment: A psychoanalytic perspective. *Human Relations, 48,* 1109–1127; Ward, C., & Rana-Deuba, A. (2000). Home and host culture influences on sojourner adjustment. *International Journal of Intercultural Relations, 24,* 291–306.

55. Black, Gregersen, & Mendenhall, *Global assignments: Successfully expatriating and repatriating international managers;* Jordan, M. (2001). Have husband, will travel. *The Wall Street Journal,* February 13, B1, B12; Latta, G. W. (1999). Expatriate policy and practice: A ten-year comparison of trends. *Compensation and Benefits Review, 31,* 35–39; Selmer, J. (1999). Corporate expatriate career development. *Journal of International Management, 5,* 55–71; Solomon, C. M. (1996). Expats say: Help make us

mobile. *Personnel Journal,* July, 43–52; Swaak, R. A. (1995). Expatriate management: The search for best practices. *Compensation and Benefits Review, 27,* 21–29; Swaak, R. A. (1995). Today's expatriate family: Dual careers and other obstacles. *Compensation and Benefits Review, 26,* 21–26.

56. Black, Gregersen, & Mendenhall, *Global assignments: Successfully expatriating and repatriating international managers;* Caligiuri, P. (2000). The big five personality characteristics as predictors of expatriate's desire to terminate the assignment and supervisor-rated performance. *Personnel Psychology, 53,* 67–88; Carpenter, Battling the overseas blues.

57. Carpenter, Battling the overseas blues; Phatak, *International dimensions of management;* Sanchez, J. I., Spector, P. E., & Cooper, C. L. (2000). Adapting to a boundaryless world: A developmental expatriate model. *The Academy of Management Executive, 14,* 96–106.

58. Black, Gregersen, & Mendenhall, *Global assignments: Successfully expatriating and repatriating international managers;* Deshpande, S. P., & Viswesvaran, C. (1992). Is cross-cultural training of managers effective: A meta analysis. *International Journal of Intercultural Relations, 16,* 295–310; Fitzgerald-Turner, B. (1997). Myths of expatriate life. HR Magazine, June, 1–7.

59. Black, J. S. (1992). Coming home: The relationship of expatriate expectations with repatriation adjustment and job performance. *Human Relations, 45,* 177–192; Black, Gregersen, & Mendenhall, *Global assignments: Successfully expatriating and repatriating international managers;* Harrison, J. K. (1994). Developing successful expatriate managers: A framework for the structural design and strategic alignment of cross-cultural training programs. *Human Resource Planning, 17,* 17–35.

60. Aryee, S., Chay, Y. W., & Chew, J. (1996). An investigation of the willingness of managerial employees to accept an expatriate assignment. *Journal of Organizational Behavior, 17,* 267–283; Black, Gregersen, & Mendenhall, M. E. *Global assignments: Successfully expatriating and repatriating international managers;* Parker, B., & McEvoy, G. M. (1993). Initial examination of a model of intercultural adjustment. *International Journal of Intercultural Relations, 17,* 355–379; Stroh, L. K., Dennis, L. E., & Cramer, T. C. (1994). Predictors of expatriate adjustment. *International Journal of Organizational Analysis, 2,* 176–192.

61. Reitman, V. (1996). Cramming for the exotic U.S. workplace. *The Wall Street Journal,* July 9, A14.

62. Solomon, C. M. (1996). Expats say: Help make us mobile. *Personnel Journal,* July, 43–52.

63. Hagerty, B. (1993). Trainers help expatriate employees build bridges to different cultures. *The Wall Street Journal,* June 14, B1, B6.

64. Carpenter, Battling the overseas blues.

65. Adler, *International dimensions of organizational behavior;* Arthur, W., & Bennett, W. (1995). The international assignee: The relative importance of factors perceived to contribute to success. *Personnel Psychology, 48,* 99–114; Swaak, R. A. (1995). Today's expatriate family: Dual careers and other obstacles. *Compensation and Benefits Review, 26,* 21–26.

66. Adler, *International dimensions of organizational behavior;* Black, J.S., & Gregersen, H.B. (1991). The other half of the picture: Antecedents of spouse cross-cultural adjustment. *Journal of International Business Studies, 22,* 461–477.

67. Carpenter, Battling the overseas blues.

68. Tu, H., & Sullivan, S.E. (1994). Preparing yourself for an international assignment. *Business Horizons, 37,* January-February, 67–70.

69. Black, Coming home: The relationship of expatriate expectations

with repatriation adjustment and job performance; Black, Gregersen, & Mendenhall, M. E. *Global assignments: Successfully expatriating and repatriating international managers.* Shilling, M. (1993). How to win at repatriation. *Personnel Journal,* September, 40–46.

70. Solomon, C. M. (1995). Repatriation: Up, down, or out? *Personnel Journal,* January, 28–37.

71. Gregersen, H. B., & Black, J. S. (1996). Multiple commitments upon repatriation: The Japanese experience. *Journal of Management, 22,* 209–229.

72. Wonacott, P. (2002). China's secret weapon: Smart, cheap labor for high-tech goods. *The Wall Street Journal,* March 14, A1, A6; ———. (2001). Mobility in China: Off to the city. *The Economist,* September 1, 36; Gross, A., & Dyson, P. (1996). The iron rice bowl cracks. *HR Magazine,* July, 84–88; Hutzler, C., & Leggett, K. (2001). For China's premier Zhu, a critical home stretch. *The Wall Street Journal,* August 29, A6, A10; Nyaw, M.K. (1995). Human resource management in the People's Republic of China. In Moore & Jennings, *Human resource management on the Pacific rim: Institutions, practices, and attitudes,* 187–216; Schoenberger, K. (1996). Motorola bets big on China. *Fortune.* May 27, 116–124; Shenkar, O., & Nyaw, M. K. (1994). How to run a successful joint venture in China. In S. Stewart & N. Campbell (Eds.), *Advances in Chinese industrial studies: Joint ventures in the People's Republic of China,* 273–284. Greenwich, CT: JAI Press.

Chapter 13

1. Oddou, G., & Mendenhall, M. (1991). Expatriate performance appraisal: Problems and solutions. In. M. Mendenhall & G. Oddou (Eds.), *International human resource management,* 364–374. Boston: PWS-Kent.

2. Oddou & Mendenhall, Expatriate performance appraisal: Problems and solutions.

3. Oddou & Mendenhall, Expatriate performance appraisal: Problems and solutions.

4. Cascio, W., & Bailey, E. (1995). International human resource management: The state of research and practice. In O. Shenkar, *Global perspectives of human resource management,* 15–36. Englewood Cliffs, NJ: Prentice-Hall.

5. Dowling, P. J., & Schuler, R. S. (1990). *International dimensions of human resource management.* Boston: PWS-Kent.

6. Garland, J., & Farmer, R. N. (1986). *International dimensions of business policy and strategy.* Boston: PWS-Kent.

7. Dowling & Schuler, *International dimensions of human resource management.*

8. Dowling & Schuler, *International dimensions of human resource management.*

9. Dowling & Schuler, *International dimensions of human resource management;* Garland & Farmer, *International dimensions of business policy and strategy.*

10. Oddou & Mendenhall, Expatriate performance appraisal: Problems and solutions.

11. Oddou & Mendenhall, Expatriate performance appraisal: Problems and solutions.

12. Ali, A. (1988). A cross-national perspective of managerial work value systems. In R. N. Farmer & E. G. McGowen (Eds.), *Advances in international comparative management.* Greenwich, CT: JAI Press.

13. Arvey, R. D., Bhagat, R. S., & Salas, E. (1991). Cross-cultural and cross national issues in personnel and human resources management: Where do we go from here? *Research in Personnel and Human Resources Management, 9,* 367–407; Vance, C. M., Paik, Y., Boje, B. M., & Stage, H. D. (1993). A study of the generalizability of performance appraisal design characteristics across four Southeast Asian countries: Assessing the extent of divergence effect. Paper presented to the International Management Division of the National Academy of Management.

14. Allen, L. A. (1988). Working better with Japanese managers. *Management Review, 77,* November, 55–56.

15. Early, P. C. (1986). Trust, perceived important of praise and criticism and work performance: An examination of feedback in the United States and England. *Journal of Management, 12,* 457–473.

16. See also Morton, C. (1988). Bringing manager and managed together. *Industrial Society,* September, 26–27.

17. Trompenaars, F. (1994). *Riding the waves of culture: Understanding diversity in global business.* New York: Irwin.

18. Vance, C. M., Paik, Y., Boje, B. M., & Stage, H. D. (1993). A study of the generalizability of performance appraisal design characteristics across four Southeast Asian countries. Paper presented to the Natural Academy of Management meetings.

19. Stull, J. S. (1988). Giving feedback to foreign-born employees. *Management Solutions, 33,* July, 42–45.

20. Milkovich, G. T., & Newman, J. M. (1996). *Compensation.* Chicago: Irwin.

21. Kras, E. S. (1989). *Management in two cultures: Bridging the gap between US and Mexican managers.* Yarmouth, ME: Intercultural Press.

22. Milkovich & Newman, *Compensation.*

23. ———. (1994). Mexican labor's hidden costs. *Fortune,* October, 17, 32.

24. Bailey, E. K. (1995). International compensation. In O. Shenkar (Ed.), *Global perspectives of human resource management.* Englewood Cliffs, NJ: Prentice-Hall, 147–164.

25. ———. (2000). Chief executives' pay as a multiple of manufacturing employees' pay. *The Economist,* September 30, 110

26. Parker-Pope, T. (1996). Executive pay: So far away. *The Wall Street Journal,* April R 12.

27. Mesdag, L. M. (1984). Are you underpaid? *Fortune,* March 19, 22–23.

28. Haigh, T. (1995). U.S. multinational compensation strategies for local nationals. *Compensation: Present practices and future concerns: A conference report.* New York: The Conference Board, Report no. 1129-95-CH, 15–18; Helms, M. (1991). International executive compensation practices. In Mendenhall and Oddou, *International human resource management;* Puffer, S. M., & Shekshnia, S. V. (1994). Compensating local employees in post communist Russia: In search of talent of just looking for a bargain? *Compensation and Benefits Review,* Sept.-Oct., 35–43.

29. Townsend, A. M., Scott, K. D., & Markham, S. E. (1990). An examination of country and culture-based differences in compensation practices. *Journal of International Business Studies, 21,* 667–678.

30. Hewitt Associates (1991). *Total compensation management: Reward management strategies for the 1990's.* Cambridge, MA: Basil Blackwell.

31. Flynn, G. (1994). HR in Mexico: What you should know. *Personnel Journal,* August, 34–44.

32. Beatty, J. R., McCune, J. T., & Beatty, R. W. (1988). A policy-capturing approach to the study of United States and Japanese managers' compensation decisions. *Journal of Management, 14,* 465–474.

33. Mroczkowski, T., & Hanaoka, M. (1989). Continuity and change

in Japanese management. *California Management Review,* Winter, 39–52.

34. Taylor, A. (1996). Toyota's boss stands out in a crowd. *Fortune,* November 25, 116–122.

35. Gomez-Mejia, L. R., & Welbourne, T. (1991). Compensation strategies in a global context. *Human Resource Planning, 14,* 29–41.

36. See also Whenmouth, A. (1988). Is Japan's corporate culture changing? *Industry Week, 237*(7), 33–35.

37. Gomez-Mejia, L. R., & Welbourne, T. (1991). Compensation strategies in a global context; Hodgetts, R. M., & Luthans, F. (1993). U.S. multinationals' compensation strategies for local management: Cross-cultural implications. *Compensation and Benefits Review,* 42–48.

38. Fergus, M. (1990). Employees on the move. *HR Magazine, 36,* No. 5, 44–46.

39. Black, J. S. (1991). Returning expatriates feel foreign in their native land. *Personnel, 68,* 17.

40. Reynolds, C. (1994). *Compensation basics for North American expatriates: Developing an effective program for employees working abroad.* Scottsdale, AZ: The American Compensation Association.

41. Reynolds, *Compensation basics for North American expatriates.*

42. Oemig, D. R. A. (1999). When you say, "we'll keep you whole," do you mean it? *Compensation and Benefits Review, 31,* 40–47.

43. Helms, M. (1991). International executive compensation practices; Infante, V. D. (2001). Three ways to design international pay: Headquarters, home country, host country. *Workforce,* January, 22–24

44. ———. (1992). *Guide to major holidays around the globe.* Zurich: Union Bank of Switzerland.

45. U.S. Department of State. (1999). *Indexes of living costs abroad, quarters allowances, and hardship differentials.* Washington, DC: Government Printing Office.

46. Reynolds, *Compensation basics for North American expatriates.*

47. ———. (1997). Market rents. *The Wall Street Journal,* January 24, B8.

48. Anderson, J. B. (1990). Compensating your overseas executives, Part 2: Europe in 1992. *Compensation and Benefits Review, 22,* 25–35; Klein, R. B. (1992). Compensating your overseas executives, Part 3: Exporting U.S. stock option plans to expatriates. *Compensation and Benefits Review, 23,* 27–38.

49. Anderson, Compensating your overseas executives, Part 2: Europe in 1992.

50. Reynolds, *Compensation basics for North American expatriates.*

51. ———. (2001). Cost of living. *The Economist,* January 20, 108; ———. (2001). Where expats spend the most. *Business Week,* June 25, 30.

52. ———. (2001). Big mac currencies. *The Economist,* April 21, 74.

53. Vachris, M. A., & Thomas, J. (1999). International price comparisons based on purchasing power parity. *Monthly Labor Review,* October, 3–12.

54. Logger, E., Vinke, R., & Kluytmans, F. (1995). Compensation and appraisal in an international perspective. In A. Harzing & J. Van Ruysseveldt (Eds.), *International human resource management,* 144–155. London: Sage.

55. Reynolds, *Compensation basics for North American expatriates.*

56. Wilson, L. E. (2000). The balance sheet approach to expatriate compensation: Still with us after all these years. *Relocation Journal and Real Estate News, 14,* 1–9.

57. This piece is based on a Wall Street Journal article and interview with Ms. Lipman: Silverman, R. E. (2000). Pricing zippers, tabasco, prozac in exotic locales. *The Wall Street Journal,* June 13, B1, B14.

58. Bailey, *International compensation.*

59. Dwyer, T. D. (1999). Trends in global compensation. *Compensation and Benefits Review, 31,* 48–53; Milkovich, G. T., & Bloom, M. (1998). Rethinking international compensation. *Compensation and Benefits Review, 30,* 15–23.

60. Reynolds, *Compensation basics for North American expatriates.*

61. Gould, C. (1999). Expat pay plans suffer cutbacks. *Workforce,* September, 40–46; Latta, G. W. (1999). Expatriate policy and practice: A ten-year comparison of trends. *Compensation and Benefits Review, 31,* 35–39.

62. Milkovich & Newman, *Compensation.*

63. Phatak, A. V. (1995). *International dimensions of management.* Cincinnati, OH: South-Western.

64. Harvey, M. (1993). Designing a global compensation system: The logic and a model. *Columbia Journal of World Business,* Winter, 57–72.

65. Anderson, Compensating your overseas executives, Part 2: Europe in 1992.

66. Laabs, J. J. (1993). What is costs to house expatriates worldwide. *Personnel Journal, 16,* 16; Laabs, J. J. (1993). What joint ventures in China are giving employees in pay and benefits. *Personnel Journal, 16,* 16–20.

67. Shenkar, *Global perspectives of human resource management.*

68. Harvey, M. (1993). Empirical evidence of recurring international compensation problems. *Journal of International Business Studies, 24,* 785–799.

Chapter 14

1. Neale, R., & Mindel, B. (1992). Rigging up multi-cultural teamworking. *Personnel Management,* January, 36–39.

2. Triandis, H. C. (1988). Collectivism v. individualism: A reconceptualism of a basic concept in cross-cultural social psychology. In G. K. Verma & C. Bagley (Eds.). *Cross-Cultural Studies of Personality, Attitudes, and Cognition.* New York: St. Martins Press, 60–95.

3. Domino, G. (1992). Cooperation and competition in Chinese and American children. *Journal of Cross-Cultural Psychology, 23,* 456–467.

4. Bond, M. H., & Hwang, K. (1986). The social psychology of the Chinese people. In M. H. Bond (Ed.), *The psychology of the Chinese people,* 213–266. Hong Kong: Oxford University Press.

5. Phalon, R. (1984). Hell camp. *Forbes,* June 18, 56–58.

6. Matsui, T. Kakuyama, T. & Ongltco M. L. U. (1987). Effects of goals and feedback on performance in groups. *Journal of Applied Psychology, 72,* 407–415.

7. Earley, P. C. (1989). Social loafing and collectivism. *Administrative Science Quarterly, 34,* 565–581; Gabrenya, W. K., Latane, B., & Wang, Y. (1985). Social loafing on an optimizing task: Cross-cultural differences among Chinese and Americans. *Journal of Cross-Cultural Psychology, 16,* 223–242.

8. Earley, P. C. (1993). East meets West meets Mideast: Further explorations of collectivistic and individualistic work groups. *Academy of Management Journal, 36,* 319–348.

9. Gabrenya, Latane, & Wang, Social loafing on an optimizing task: Cross-cultural differences among Chinese and Americans.

10. Triandis, H. C. (1988). Collectivism v. individualism: A reconceptualism of a basic concept in cross-cultural social psychology. In G. K. Verma & C. Bagley (Eds.). *Cross-Cultural Studies of Personality, Attitudes, and Cognition.* New York: St. Martins Press, 60–95.

11. Espinoza, J. A., & Garza, R. T. (1985). Social group salience and inter-ethnic cooperation. *Journal of Experimental Social Psychology, 23,* 380–392.

12. Earley, East meets West meets Mideast: Further explorations of collectivistic and individualistic work groups.

13. See also Earley, P. C. (1994). Self or group? Cultural effects of training on self-efficacy and performance. *Administrative Science Quarterly, 39,* 89–117.

14. Earley, East meets West meets Mideast: Further explorations of collectivistic and individualistic work groups.

15. ———. (1992). Work team trivia. *The Competitive Edge.* March/April, 12; Dumaine, B. (1990). Who needs a boss? *Fortune,* May 7, 52–60.

16. Merritt, A. C., & Helmreich, R. L. (1996). Human factors on the flight deck: The influence of national culture. *Journal of Cross-Cultural Psychology, 27,* 5–24.

17. Adler, N. J. (1991). *International dimensions of organizational behavior.* Boston, MA.: PWS-Kent.

18. Adler, *International dimensions of organizational behavior.*

19. Houlder, V. (1996). How to get ideas to hatch. *Financial Times,* September 9, 10.

20. Some of these anecdotal observations have been supported with research findings. See, for example, Salk, J, E., & Brannen, M. Y. (2000). National culture, networks, and individual influence in a multinational management team. *Academy of Management Journal, 43,* 191–202.

21. Browning, E. S. (1994). Computer chip project brings rivals together, but the cultures clash. *The Wall Street Journal,* May 3, A1, A8.

22. Earley, P. C., & Mosakowski, E. (2000). Creating hybrid team cultures: An empirical test of transnational team functioning. *Academy of Management Journal, 43,* 26–49.

23. Jehn, K. A., Chadwick, C., & Thatcher, S. M. B. (1997). To agree or not to agree: The effects of value congruence, individual demographic dissimilarity, and conflict on workgroup outcomes. *International Journal of Conflict Management, 8,* 287–305.

24. Guzzo, R. A., & Shea, G. P. (1992). Group performance and intergroup relations in organizations. In M. D. Dunnette & L. M. Hough (Eds.), *Handbook of industrial and organizational psychology* (2nd Ed.), vol. 3. Palo Alto, CA: Consulting Psychologists Press; Watson, W. E., Kumar, K., & Michaelson, L. K. (1993). Cultural diversity's impact on interaction process and performance: Comparing homogeneous and diverse task groups. *Academy of Management Journal, 36,* 590–602.

25. Elron, E. (1997). Top management teams within multinational corporations: Effects of cultural heterogeneity. *Leadership Quarterly, 8,* 393–412.

26. Earley & Mosakowski, Creating hybrid team cultures: An empirical test of transnational team functioning.

27. Harstone, M., & Augoustinos, M. (1995). The minimal group paradigm: Categorization into two versus three groups. *European Journal of Social Psychology, 25,* 179–193.

28. Lau, D. C., & Murnighan, J. K. (1998). Demographic diversity and faultlines: The compositional dynamics of organizational groups. *Academy of Management Review, 23,* 325–340.

29. Adler, *International dimensions of organizational behavior.*

30. Earley, P. C. (1999). Playing follow the leader: Status-determining traits in relations to collective efficacy across cultures. *Organizational Behavior and Human Decision Processes, 80,* 192–212.

31. Newman, B. (1993). Border dispute: Single-country unions of Europe try to cope with multinationals. *The Wall Street Journal,* November 30, A1 A22; Zachary, G. P. (1993). Like factory workers, professionals face loss of jobs to foreigners. *The Wall Street Journal,* March 17, A1, A9.

32. ———. (1992). Employee dismissals can prove costly for companies in Europe. *HR Focus,* August, p. 18.

33. Toman, B. (1988). Ford, unions agree on contract offer in break-through in 9-day U.K. strike. *The Wall Street Journal,* February 17, 2.

34. Steinmetz, G. (1996). Americans, too, run afoul of rigorous German rules. *The Wall Street Journal,* February 2, A6.

35. Briscoe, *International human resource management.*

36. Hollinshead, G., & Leaf, M. (1995). *Human resource management: An international and comparative perspective.* London: Pitman; Koretz, G. (1990). Why unions thrive abroad, but wither in the U.S. *Business Week,* Sept 10, 26.

37. Gunnigle, P., Brewster, C., & Morley, M. (1994). European industrial relations: Change and continuity. In C. Brewster & A. Hegewisch (Eds.), *The Price-Waterhouse Cranfield Survey,* chapter 9, 139–153. London: Routledge.

38. Ferner, A., & Hyman, R. (1992). *Industrial relations in the new Europe.* Oxford: Blackwell.

39. Gunnigle, Brewster, & Morley, European industrial relations: Change and continuity.

40. Wachter, H. (1997). German co-determination—Quo vadis? A study of the implementation of new management concepts in a German steel company. *Employee Relations, 19,* 27–37.

41. Munchau, W. (1996). Winter of their discontent: Germany's unions are fighting to preserve a social welfare system that employers say is too costly. *Financial Times,* October, 3, 13.

42. Rohwedder, C. (1999). Once the big muscle of German industry, unions see it all sag. *The Wall Street Journal,* November 29, A1.

43. Koretz, G. (2001). Why Americans work so hard. *Business Week,* June 11, p. 34.

44. ———. (2000). Germany: Rebirth of a salesman. *The Economist,* July 8, 22–24

45. Benjamin, D. (1993). Germany is troubled by how little work its workers are doing. *The Wall Street Journal,* May 6, A1, A7; Benjamin, D., & Horwitz, T. (1994). German view: You Americans work too hard—and for what? *The Wall Street Journal,* July 14, B5, B6; Steinmetz, G. (1995). German firms sour on system that keeps peace with workers. *The Wall Street Journal,* October 17, A1, A14.

46. Rhoads, C., & Fuhrmans, V. (2001). Corporate Germany braces for a big shift from postwar stability. *The Wall Street Journal,* June 21, A1, A8.

47. Hollinshead & Leaf, *Human resource management: An international and comparative perspective.*

48. Hollinshead, & Leaf, *Human resource management: An international and comparative perspective.*

49. Hollinshead & Leaf, *Human resource management: An international and comparative perspective.*

50. Brunstein, I. (1995). *Human resource management in Western Europe.* Berlin: Walter de Gruyter.

51. Brunstein, *Human resource management in Western Europe.*

52. Brewster, C., & Hegewisch, A. (1994). *Policy and Practice in European Human Resource Management: The Price Waterhouse Cranfield Survey.* London: Routledge.

53. Reed, S. (1997). Will Stockholm give away the store? *Business Week,* February 10, 54.

54. Taylor, R. (1993). Union membership in Sweden still growing. *Financial Times,* December 21, 14.

55. Hees, M. (1995). Belgium. In I. Brunstein (Ed.), *Human resource management in Western Europe.* Berlin: Walter de Gruyter.

56. Templeman, J., Trinephi, M., & Toy, S. (1996). A continent swarming with temps. *Business Week*, April 8, 54.

57. ———. (2001). Spain cuts a Gordian labor knot. *The Economist*, March 10, 51.

58. Rhoads, C. (2001). With their economy thriving, Swedes curtail the dole. *The Wall Street Journal*, March 28, A18.

59. Inohara, H. (1990). *Human resource development in Japanese companies*. Tokyo: Asian Productivity Organization.

60. Inohara, *Human resource development in Japanese companies*.

61. Nyaw, M. (1995). Human resource management in the Peoples Republic of China. In L. F. Moore & P. D. Jennings (Eds.), *Human Resource Management in the Pacific Rim*. Berlin: Walter de Gruyter & Co. (pp. 187–216).

62. Nyaw, Human resource management in the Peoples Republic of China.

63. Nyaw, Human resource management in the Peoples Republic of China.

64. Barnathan, J., & Forney, M. (1994). Damping labor's fires: Can Beijing calm workers and sustain growth? *Business Week*, August 1, 40–41; Kahn, J. (1994). China orders foreign firms to unionize. *The Wall Street Journal*, June 29, A14.

65. Poon, W. K. (1995). Human resource management in Hong Kong. In L. Moore & P. Jennings (Eds.), *Human resource management on the Pacific Rim*. Berlin: Walter de Gruyter.

66. ———. (2001). Getting organized, with Western help. *The Economist*, December 1, 57–58.

67. Koch, M., Nam, S. H., & Steers, R. M. (1995). Human resource management in South Korea. In L. Moore & P. Jennings (Eds.), *Human resource management on the Pacific Rim*. Berlin: Walter de Gruyter.

68. Brull, S. V., & Lee, C. K. (1997). Why Seoul is seething. *Business Week*, January 27, 44–48; ———. (1997). South Korea: Culture clash. *The Economist*, January 11, 35–36.

69. Solomon, J., & Choi, H. W. (2001). For Korea's Daewoo Motor, a hard sale. *The Wall Street Journal*, May 23, A21.

70. Briscoe, *International Human Resource Management*.

71. Smith, G. (2000). Mexican workers deserve better than this. *Business Week*, September 11, 127.

72. Siddique, S. A. (1989). Industrial relations in a third world setting: A possible model. *The Journal of Industrial Relations, 31,* 385–401.

73. Chege, M. (1988). The state and labor: Industrial relations in independent Kenya. In P. Coughlin & G. Ikiara (Eds.), *Industrialization in Kenya: In search of a strategy*. Nairobi: Heinemann Kenya.

74. Moll, P. G. (1993). Black South African unions: Relative wage effects in international perspective. *Industrial and Labor Relations Review, 46,* 245–261

75. Moll, Black South African unions: Relative wage effects in international perspective.

76. Matthews, R. (1996). Another burden to carry. *Financial Times*, May 21, 15.

77. Newman, B. (1983). Border dispute: Single-country unions of Europe try to cope with multinationals. *The Wall Street Journal*, November 30, 1, 22.

78. Simpson, W. R. (1994). The ILO and tripartism: Some reflections. *Monthly Labor Review*, September, 40–45.

79. Hollinshead & Leaf, *Human resource management: An international and comparative perspective*.

80. Dowling, P. J., & Schuler, R. S. (1990). *International dimensions of human resource management*. Boston: PWS-Kent.

81. Parry, J., & O'Meara, G. (1990). The struggle for European unions. *International Management*, December, 70–75.

82. Martin, D. (1984). A Canadian split on unions. *The New York Times*, March 12, D12.

83. Forman, C. (1993). France is preparing to battle Britain over flight of jobs across the channel. *The Wall Street Journal*, February 3, A11.

84. Borrus, A. (2000). Workers of the world: welcome. *Business Week*, November 20, 129–133.

85. Burkins, G. (2000). Labor reaches out to global economy. *The Wall Street Journal*, April 11, A2.

86. Strauss, 1982

87. But please see de Macedo-Soares, T. D. L., & Lucas, D. C. (1996). Key quality management practices of leading firms in Brazil: findings of a pilot-study. *The TQM Magazine, 8,* 55–70.

88. McFarlin, D., Sweeney, P. D., & Cotton, J. L. (1992). Attitudes toward employee participation in decision-making: A comparison of European and American managers in a US multinational company. *Human Resource Management, 31,* 363–383.

89. McFarlin, Sweeney, & Cotton, Attitudes toward employee participation in decision-making.

90. Sparrow, P., & Hiltrop, J. M. (1994). *European human resource management in transition*. New York: Prentice-Hall.

91. ———. (2000). Labor disputes. *The Economist*, April 22, 96.

92. Sparrow & Hiltrop, *European human resource management in transition*.

93. ———. (2001). Labor disputes. *The Economist*, May 12, 108.

94. Sparrow & Hiltrop, *European human resource management in transition*.

95. Inohara, *Human resource development in Japanese companies*.

96. Browning, E. S. (1986). Japan's firms have a friend: The unions. *The Wall Street Journal*, April 28, sec. 2, 28.

97. Poole, M. (1986). *Industrial relations: Origins and patterns of national diversity*. London: Routledge.

98. Neale & Mindel, Rigging up multicultural teamworking.

Case 1

1. BSA and Software Publishers Association (SPA), *Contribution of the Packaged Software Industry to the Hong Kong Economy*, May 1998.

2. BSA and Software Publishers Association (SPA), *Contribution of the Packaged Software Industry to the Hong Kong Economy*, May 1998.

3. US$1=HK$7.74

4. An illustrative, albeit insubstantive, methodology is provided in both the *1997 Global Software Piracy Report*, and *Contribution of the Packaged Software Industry to the Hong Kong Economy*, both jointly published by the BSA and the Software Publishers Association (SPA).

5. This figure included corporate taxes paid by packaged software publishers, payroll (provident fund) taxes, and value-added taxes on the sale of software.

6. BSA and Software Publishers Association (SPA), *Contribution of the Packaged Software Industry to the Hong Kong Economy*, May 1998.

7. Newell Public Relations, Worsening software piracy important factor in Hong Kong "watchlist" status by U.S. Trade Representative: says BSA, http://www.newell.com/releases/bsa/1997/bsa-r6.phtml, March 1999.

8. A. Lin Neumann, "Information Wants to Be Free—But This Is Ridiculous," *Wired*, October 1995.

9. A. Lin Neumann, "Information Wants to Be Free—But This Is Ridiculous."

10. Sanger D. E., "In Pact with China, a Ghost of Japan," *New York Times,* 27 February, 1995.

11. Kenneth Ho, (1995), "A Study into the Problem of Software Piracy in Hong Kong and China," http://www.houston.com.hk/hkgipd/piracy.html, March 1999.

12. Remark by Kevin Henshaw in an interview, 6 November, 1998. The BSA in Hong Kong is chaired on a rotating basis by members, generally for a period of two years. It is an elected position which is filled on a voluntary basis. The chairs of the BSA in Hong Kong have come from Microsoft (Chris Austin), Lotus (David Lee), Microsoft (Valerie Colbourn) and Adobe (Kevin Henshaw).

13. A. Lin Neumann, "Information Wants to Be Free—But This Is Ridiculous."

14. The full name for the convention is the Berne Convention for the Protection of Literary and Artistic Works (828 U.N.T.S. 221, S. Treaty Doc. No. 99-27).

15. It was later revised at several conferences: Paris, 1896; Berlin, 1908; Berne, 1914; Rome, 1928; Brussels, 1948; Stockholm, 1967; and Paris, 1971.

16. Among the works protected by the Berne Convention are books, pamphlets and other printed materials; dramatic and dramatico-musical works and musical compositions; drawings and paintings; works of architecture, sculpture, engraving and lithography; illustrations and geographic charts, plans and sketches; translations, adaptations, arrangements of music and collections of various works; and cinematographic and photographic works.

17. Initially, the United States lobbied for a different international treaty, the Universal Copyright Convention (UCC) (25 U.S.T. 1341, T.I.A.S. No. 7868), established in 1952 under the auspices of the UN Educational, Scientific and Cultural Organization (UNESCO). The United States became a member of the UCC in 1955. Many countries that already belonged to the Berne Convention—including France, West Germany and Japan—also joined the UCC. The UCC generally operated on the national treatment principle, thus allowing U.S. authors to receive the same copyright protection in a specific country that the country afforded its own authors, and not requiring the United States to reciprocate that treatment for foreign authors.

18. The 1974 Trade Act was amended in 1988 as a part of the Omnibus Trade & Competitiveness Act. BSA, BSA Special 301 Filing Highlights Need for Modernization of Software Management Practices Within Government Agencies Worldwide, http://www.bsa.org/policy/trade/s301_c.html, March 1999.

19. BSA, BSA Special 301 Filing Highlights Need for Modernization of Software Management Practices Within Government Agencies Worldwide, http://www.bsa.org/policy/trade/s301_c.html, March 1999.

20. The interagency Trade Policy Staff Committee advises the USTR on implementation of Special 301, by obtaining information from the private sector, American embassies, the United States' trading partners and the National Trade Estimates report.

21. A Special 301 investigation is similar to an investigation initiated in response to an industry Section 301 petition, except that the maximum time for an investigation under Special 301 is shorter in some circumstances.

22. *The China Business Review,* November-December 1995.

23. *The Economist,* 7 January, 1995.

24. It has also been suggested that the widespread resistance to copyright adherence in Hong Kong and China can be (partly) attributed to historical events and cultural differences. The influence of Confucianism, for example, has strong emphasis on learning by copying, thus "the copying of works of almost any kind has for centuries been regarded as honourable and necessary" (Wingrove, 1995). Perhaps another reason for the non-compliance of the copyright laws lies in the idea that the protection of intellectual property is a pre-dominantly Western concept. As Altback (1988) has noted, Asian nations "traditionally believe that copyright is a Western concept created to maintain a monopoly over the distribution and production of knowledge and knowledge-based products."

25. Newell Public Relations, Worsening software piracy important factor in Hong Kong "watchlist" status by U.S. Trade Representative: says BSA, http://www.newell.com/releases/bsa/1997/bsa-r6.phtml, March 1999.

Case 2

1. Dow Jones Newswires, "IFC Board Approves $200M Loan for Caspian Oil Project," 7/27/98; d'Intignano, A.M "Opening the Caspian Gateway," *Project Finance,* January 2000, p. 19; Dow Jones Energy Service, "IFC, EBRD to Invest $400M in Azerbaijan 'Early Oil' Project," 2/17/99.

2. d'Intignano, "Opening the Caspian Gateway."

3. Pope, H., "Azerbaijan's Top Oil Consortium Pulls In Horns," *The Wall Street Journal,* 2/2/99, p. A16.

4. Croissant, C., *Azerbaijan, Oil and Politics* (Commack, N.Y.: Nova Science Publishers, Inc., 1998), p. 13.

5. "Azerbaijan-Pipeline Knocked Back," *Project Finance International,* 3/24/99, p. 45.

6. Stern, D., "BP-Amoco Alliance Set to Dominate Azerbaijani Oil Industry," Agence France-Presse, 8/14/98.

7. Pope, "Azerbaijan's Top Oil Consortium Pulls in Horns."; "Azerbaijan oil contracts signed," *Financial Times,* 4/28/99, p. 4.

8. Ramco Energy p.l.c. *Prospectus* dated 3/10/97, pp. 41, 47.

9. The $1 billion estimate is from the Ramco Energy p.l.c. *Prospectus* dated 3/10/97, p. 37; the final cost of $1.9 billion is from the EBRD's web site at: http://www.ebrd.com/english/opera/PSD/PSD1998/238chirag.htm.

10. Dorsey, James M. "Pipeline Flap May Clog Expansion in the Caspian Sea," *The Wall Street Journal,* 8/11/99, p. A14.

11. Assumes a $10 billion total cost less $1.9 billion for Early Oil and $3.1 billion for Stage 1. The remaining $5 billion is split proportionally based on projected output—300,000 bpd in Stage 2 and 200,000 in Stage 3—given the similar geology. This reasoning implies Stage 2 will cost 60% of the total $5 billion or $3 billion; Stage 3 will cost 40% of the total or $2 billion.

12. Dow Jones Energy Service, "IFC Board Approves $200M Loan for Caspian Oil Project," 7/27/98.

13. Azerbaijan-Pipeline Knocked Back.

14. Stuart Brown, Director, Citibank Global Project Finance, London, quoted in "For & Against," *Project & Trade Finance,* 2/10/99, p. 48.

15. Azerbaijan-Pipeline Knocked Back; "Turkey gets tough in its push for Ceyhan pipeline project," *The Wall Street Journal,* 11/9/98, p. A18.

16. Azerbaijan-Pipeline Knocked Back; Jessica McCallin, "The Race is On," *Project Finance,* 10/19/98, p.21.

17. Summary of Project Information, International Finance

Corporation (IFC),3/25/98, available at: http://wbln0018.world bank.org/IFCExt/spiwebsite1.nsf/9456cd2430750aa98525688900 61dfd0/854c52d6e0f6d2858525688e0070d9ac?OpenDocument

18. "Azerbaijan Oilfield to Get International Finance," BBC World-wide Monitoring, Interfax News Agency, Moscow, 2/18/99.

19. "Azerbaijan-AIOC To Spend $2 bn," *Project Finance International,* 6/2/99, p. 37.

20. Stuart Brown, Director, Citibank Global Project Finance, quoted in "For & Against," *Project & Trade Finance,* 2/10/99, p. 48.

21. Interfax News Agency," LUKOil Gets $77.2 MLN from EBRD to Finance AIOC Participation, 1/22/99.

22. Assumes EBRD used the same structure that IFC used. The IFC's 10 loans are described in the Summary of Project Information, International Finance Corporation (IFC), 3/25/98, available at:http://wbln0018.world bank.org/IFCExt/spiwebsite1.nsf/ 9456cd2430750aa9852568890061dfd0/854c52d6e0f6d285852568 8e0070d9ac?OpenDocument

23. Cavenagh, A., "Caspian Oil Project Has a Slow Road to Syndication," *Project Finance International,* 2/24/99, pp. 50, 51.

24. "EBRD, The Show Must Go On," *Project & Trade Finance,* Euromoney Publications, 4/10/99, p. 30.

25. Stern, D., "BP-Amoco Alliance Setto Dominate Azerbaijani Oil Industry," Agence France-Presse, 8/14/98; d'Intignano, "Opening the Caspian Gateway," *Project Finance,* January 2000, p. 20.

26. The Economist Intelligence Unit, "Report on Azerbaijan, 1st Quarter 1999," p. 6.

27. Ramco Energy p.l.c. *Prospectus* dated 3/10/97, p. 15.

28. Higgins, A. "Bankruptcy Court Deals BP Amoco Setback in Russia," *The Wall Street Journal,* 3/3/99, p. A15.

29. "EBRD, The Show Must Go On," *Project and Trade Finance,* Euromoney Publications, 4/10/99, p. 30.

30. Cavenagh, A., "Caspian Oil Project Has a Slow Road to Syndication," *Project Finance International,* 2/24/99, p. 50.

31. "Deal Analysis, Leveling the Ground," *Project & Trade Finance,* 5/10/98, p. 8.

32. "Azerbaijan-AIOC Scales Back," *Project Finance International,* 3/10/99, p. 43.

33. "Survey Central Asia," *The Economist,* 2/7/98, p. 8.

34. Pope, H. and Bahree, B., "Turkey Gets Tough in Its Push For Ceyhan Pipeline Project," *The Wall Street Journal,* 11/9/98, p. A18.

35. Pope, Azerbaijan's Top Oil Consortium Pulls In its Horns.

36. Azerbaijan: AIOC Scales Back.

37. Demirmen, F., "Baku-Ceyhan: While the pipeline is far from certain, Turkey should act from a position of strength," Turkish Daily News, 4/4/00.

Case 3

1. Director General Adjunto is the Mexican equivalent of an executive vice president.

2. In late 1996, one Mexican peso was valued at approximately US$0.0128.

Case 4

1. Craig Storti, *Cross Cultural Dialogues: 74 Brief Encounters with Cultural Differences* (Yarmouth, Maine: Intercultural Press, 1994).

2. Roger E. Axtell, *Gestures: The DO's and TABOOs of Body Language Around the World* (New York: John Wiley & Sons, 1991).

Case 8

1. From HP publication "The Test of Time."

2. From HP publication "The Test of Time."

Company and name index

A

A&W, 275
ABB Asea Brown Boveri AG, 82, 305–306
Acer Computers, Inc., 234, 309, 311
Aeroflot, 270
Ages Group, 103
Akio Morita, 163
Akio Tanii, 513
Alibert, John, 363
Ali, Sardar Asif Ahmed, 47
Aliyev, Heydar, 471
American Mall International, 31
Anderson, Amy, 152–153
Anheuser-Busch, 9
Armstrong, Cecil, 489–495
Associates for International Research, 410
AT&T, 98, 309
Au Bon Pain, 275
Avis, 311
Azerbaijani International Oil Consortium
(AIOC), 470–480

B

Banamex, 482
Bankers Trust, 304
Bank of Nova Scotia (BNS), 481–488
Barama Co., 82
Barnevik, Percy, 305
Bauer, Deiter, 490–491
Baum, Herbert M., 76
Baxter International, 64
BellSouth Corporation, 363
Bertelsmann, 85
Bhushan, Jonathan J., 442–443
Big Boy, 275
Birmingham, Todd, 499
Blanchworth China Company, 453–454
BMW, 263, 281, 304
Bo Concepts, 43–44, 71
Boeing, 240, 270, 271, 272, 294
Boonstra, Cor, 508
BP/Amoco, 470–480
Bridgestone Corporation, 174–175, 198
Bridge to Japan, 31
British Petroleum, 417, 451–452
Burger King, 275, 311
Business Software Alliance (BSA), 457–469

C

Canon Corp., 285
Carbanel, Joaquin, 363
Carlsberg, 82

Carrefour, 267
Carrubba, Frank, 507
Carter, Jimmy, 96
Casa del Bolsa, 482
Case, Steven, 316
Caterpillar, 97
Cathay Pacific Airline, 438
Cendant, 358
Chambers, John, 6
Chevron Corp., 82, 275
Chicoine, Susan, 266–267
Chrysler, 87, 255, 270, 273–274, 281
Chubb Insurance, 98
Chubb, Percy, III, 98
Chung Chan Kyu, 181
Ciba-Geigy, 304
Cisco Systems, 6
Citibank, 9
Citigroup, 442–443
Clark, Angie, 434
Coarson, Glenn, 114–115
Coca-Cola, 6, 32, 65, 249, 255, 279, 321
Cohen, Leonard, 163
Coherent, Inc., 378
Colgate-Palmolive, 367, 369, 431
Computer Associates, 396
Corning Glass, 293
Cyberoptics, 315

D

Daewoo, 22, 94, 263, 439
DaimlerChrysler, 13, 262
Danone SA, 361
DataClear, 496–500
Davis, Jim, 3–4, 40–41
Davis, Peter W., 52–53
Dayco International Corporation, 294–295
Dekker, Wisse, 504–505
Dell Computer Corp., 312
Del Monte, 100
Deng Xiaoping, 438
Deutsche Bank, 304, 331
Deutsche Grusskarte Gesellschaft, 489–495
DeWoskin, Kenneth, 64
DICARCO, Ltd., 152
Dimmick, Thomas, 362, 364–366
Dow Jones & Co., 98
Drauschke, Andreas, 434
Dumart, Heinrich, 489

E

Eastman Kodak, 361
Enron Corp., 277
Ericcson, 257

Excell Industries, 309
Exide Corporation, 291–292, 305, 316–317
Exxon Mobil, 22, 302

F

Fast Retailing, 332
Feng, Alvin, 489–495
Fiat, 262–263
Fiorina, Carly, 101
Firestone, Inc., 174–175, 198
Ford Motor Co., 97, 194, 255, 262–263, 280,
287–288
Fox, President (Mexico), 440
Freeport-McMorran, 82
Frito-Lay, 9
Fuentes, Carlos, 163

G

Gabriel, Peter, 88
Galvin, Robert, 77
Gao Feng, 87
Garnica, Eduardo, 317
Gates, Bill, 130, 312
Gateway Computer, 280
Gazprom, 27
GE Canada, 256
GE Capital, 26, 264
General Electric, 30, 33, 239, 247, 269, 280,
337, 502
General Motors, 86, 255, 262–263, 287–288
Gerstner, Louis, 98
Ghosn, Carlos, 284, 342–343
Giga Information, 363
Global Corporate and Investment Banking,
Citigroup, U.K., 442–443
Global Dining, 332
Global Service of Taipei, 489–495
Goodyear, 32
Goodyear Tire & Rubber Co., 98
Goplana, 278
Graeper, Erika, 489–495
Groupe Danone, 249
Grundig, 504
Grupo Industrial Bimbo SA, 12
Guigiaro, Giorgetto, 163

H

Haley, John, 294–295
Hall, Edward, 111–113, 144–146, 149–151
Hardin, Robin, 8–9
Harley-Davidson, 247, 265–266, 300

Subject index